ANATOMY
OF A WAR

PANTHEON BOOKS · NEW YORK

Gabriel Kolko

ANATOMY of a WAR

Vietnam,
the United States,
and the Modern
Historical Experience

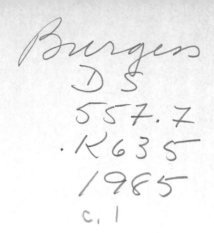
Library of Congress Cataloging in Publication Data

Kolko, Gabriel.
Anatomy of a war.

Includes bibliographical notes and index.
1. Vietnamese Conflict, 1961–1975. I. Title.
DS557.7.K635   1985   959.704'3   85-6299
ISBN 0-394-53874-9

Book design by Joe Marc Freedman

Manufactured in the United States of America

First Edition

*To all those with whom I worked
and shared a common cause, and
who made this book both
possible and necessary*

Contents

Preface

Poetry and fiction have flourished precisely because of the inadequacies of historical narrative in capturing the subtle textures of the human experience —the vast movements of people, their anguish and sufferings, aspirations and joys. But the Vietnam War has so far also evaded poets and novelists, both in Vietnam and in the United States. The sheer scope of this revolutionary struggle and war, the longest in the past two centuries, still surpasses the literary imagination. The reader who personally saw the dust and heat of the war and its terrible destruction will immediately comprehend the limits of mere words. Those among the many millions for whom the war was a part of life, the cause of sorrow, hard choices, and action, will also quickly grasp the difficulties of seeking to capture the elusive sense of reality.

I have attempted in this book to cope with this challenge and to create a justifiable coherence out of four decades of countless events by focusing on those still dimly perceived military, economic, and political institutional forces which operated both in Vietnam and in the United States to shape the structure within which traditional historical narrative is usually written. Such accounts too often concentrate on the now familiar conduct of generals, presidents, and leaders, who frequently do little more than respond to constraints imposed on them from above and below. The reader will find extensive analyses of land problems and peasants, the development of social classes, and urbanization, but also of the predicaments of individuals in a protracted conflict, their changing values, goals, and ways of relating to their community.

I seek to present here a causal explanation of the Vietnam War and to probe its meaning for the modern historical experience. I will examine in considerable depth the Communist Party, the Republic of Vietnam, and the United States. By focusing on how each side was affected by larger military, economic, social, international, and political-ideological structural trends operating simultaneously, I am able to juxtapose forces and factors influencing the outcome of the war and to highlight decisive elements in it. Three perceptions of the same reality, and three interactions with it, demand comparative analyses, of course, and render it possible to grasp the entire panorama of events and historical reality. This approach makes far more comprehensible how one side's human, ideological, and organizational resources led it to victory under conditions of vast material inferiority, and it sheds light on the very nature of change in the contemporary world.

Information on the United States and the Communist Party between 1950 and 1975 is available in abundance; the main task is to weave innumerable threads together and make each side coherent. Not surprisingly, there are few, if any, experts on either of these two adversaries who know much about the other; such compartmentalized understanding has prevented a synthetic treatment of the war as a totality. Those in America who were opposed to the war have still written precious little about it, while those who were in favor of it or pretend neutrality have been productive but have yet to offer new insights, despite their privileged access to sources and funding. They have been obsessed mainly with the traditional issues of why the United States lost or how it might have won the war, and with the lessons to be learned from it. If studies on America have languished analytically, those on the Communist Party have fallen off essentially to a few theses still left in the academic pipeline when the war ended. The single greatest obstacle to our grasping the nature of the war is the amazing ignorance on both sides regarding the Republic of Vietnam and the social system in South Vietnam. Because of the obvious delicacy of an effort to assess a regime the United States was attempting to maintain in power, official American agencies able to sponsor serious research on the RVN during the war did very little, and that almost entirely for internal use. This huge void proved a formidable challenge to me. To comprehend the RVN and the southern social order throughout the vast trauma of war is to understand basic trends and what is truly distinctive to each antagonist. A confronting of the social realities in South Vietnam also requires one to study the people, their strengths as well as their weaknesses. An anatomy of the war demands great sensitivity to how both the masses and impersonal structural forces shape a complex historical experience, as leaders and parties mediate within the boundaries that people and institutions impose on the struggle to guide Vietnam's destiny.

I have attempted to resolve the question of terminology pragmatically, simply accepting each side's designation of itself. Names should not become extraneous distractions or produce barriers to a clear explanation of critical events. The Communist Party is not the pejorative "Viet Cong," nor is the "Republic of Vietnam" (RVN) the "puppets." In general, I have sought to avoid jargon and abstractions, including superfluous academic ones. The Communist Party is also the "Revolution" in my lexicon, a name common among the people and possessing a historical justification that the RVN often sought to preempt. I consider "RVN" a heuristic description, but its effort also to call itself the "Government of Vietnam" had neither a legal nor a historical basis. Who was the government in the south was, after all, what the war was about after 1960. France and the United States sustained the residues of a colonial social system and administrative order in Vietnam south of the seventeenth parallel, one including a certain degree of territorial control, which the Communist Party constantly challenged both politically and physically. Whether these partial attributes of statehood sufficed to create a truly viable nation is one of the key issues examined in this book. I use "South Vietnam" here as a geographic expression only for the sake of convenience, because legally Vietnam south of the seventeenth parallel under the Geneva Accords of 1954 was an integral part of one nation transitionally divided prior to reunification. At first Washington did not use the name, but by the end of the war even the Communists considered it a useful designation.

Much the same pragmatism has guided my use of data on the war. Vietnam was not a laboratory for controlled social science research, and despite a great deal of American, RVN, and Communist data, a large portion of them were hastily compiled and often inaccurate to varying degrees. Ho Chi Minh assessed the Communists' own statistics on one occasion by complaining, "This figure [2,713] seems to be so 'scientific' that we cannot trust it completely. Now, let us 'drop' the odd 713 and say roundly 2,000. . . ."[1] Numbers anywhere are, at best, only approximations of trends. I have not used much of what is available, trying to take into account the time and purpose of the source and its ability to produce measurements, and I have attempted to strike a compromise between my preference for exactitude and my desire to make some reasonably justifiable conclusions about trends which would seem logical in light of the war's effects. I trust data on inflation rates or imports more than those on civilians and soldiers killed and wounded. It would be like proclaiming my belief in virtue to note that I abhor the reduction of such monumental human and social tragedies to computations, yet this was a war the enormity of whose suffering also mocks words. It is best to treat our necessary addiction to numbers as sensibly as possible, if only to keep it to the minimum essential.

The Vietnam War was the most controversial political event during the adult lives of every American over thirty-five years of age. No thinking person could now dare to admit that he or she lived through the event without having a definite opinion on it. In my case, I was from its inception totally opposed to all American involvement in Vietnam. As someone on what one can amorphously call the Left, I have favored autonomous socialist economic development in the Third World, including Vietnam, and I fully welcomed the Vietnamese Communist Party's success over the French and American alternatives to it. In my various books and articles on the United States and foreign relations, I have since 1968 defined a critical, independent position on world affairs, arguing that it was impossible, undesirable, and dangerous for the United States, the USSR, or any state to seek to guide the development of another nation or region.

Socialism in the world since 1917 can no longer be broadly subsumed under the two broad currents of "social democracy" and "Marxism-Leninism." Those labels do not explain the theory and practice of concrete movements, which often have little in common with each other and are not infrequently enemies. In practice, socialism today comprises specific parties emerging out of their unique traditions in response to local realities. They are linked with each other only insofar as they are nominally descended from a political and ideological tradition that Marx originated but that has since evolved in innumerable directions.

I have always felt there is no tension between my partisanship and a commitment to as objective and as informed an assessment of reality as possible. On the contrary, serious Left politics, both in and out of power, can only be based on optimum clarity and realism. There would be no reason for anyone to take this book seriously were it not completely independent and as honestly researched and reasoned as possible. The credibility of radical scholarship in this age of disenchantment and cynicism is precisely in its uncompromising willingness and effort to explain reality in its totality —its complexity included—as truthfully as it can.

Research for this volume began in 1964 with my growing involvement in antiwar activity. From the start there existed an informal network of dozens of American "Movement" researchers who over many years exchanged huge quantities of documents and information, and after 1968 I also maintained invaluable ties with other antiwar experts throughout the world. My book is to some extent based on this prodigious common effort. In addition, I exploited traditional library and other sources in various North American cities, discussing the war with countless Americans who supported it, fought in it, or did both. My sense of U.S. and Vietnamese realities was also colored by direct experience, initially as a graduate student at Harvard, where my foreign policy interests exposed me, if only superficially, to some of the principals mentioned in this volume, and later, in 1967–68, during a year in Washington, where I returned subsequently for brief periods. Some years in Paris and elsewhere in France after 1971 enlarged my knowledge of events. In 1973 I visited the Democratic Republic of Vietnam and a NLF-controlled region in South Vietnam, the first of six visits over the next decade which took me to all corners of the country and made it possible for me to talk to virtually hundreds of people who played every conceivable role in the war. These very extensive discussions with Vietnamese before 1981 were not initially intended to contribute to a book but eventually did so. I was in Hué and Danang during the final days of the war in April 1975, and in Hanoi during most of the remainder of that month.

It goes without saying that I assume sole responsibility for everything contained in this book and that absolutely nothing in it can or should be attributed, even indirectly, to anyone I acknowledge here or have chosen not to thank by name. I state this not merely because it is traditional to do so but also because it is true.

During 1982–84 I was a Killam Research Fellow of The Canada Council, and I am once again deeply grateful to the Killam Program for making available to me the essential time without which this book could not have been written. The Program's absence of constraints and its understanding of what is most essential for creative activity makes it exemplary, and has eased the completion of this book enormously. The Social Sciences and Humanities Research Council of Canada also generously supported research assistance and expenses during 1983–84, thereby greatly facilitating my work, and I am most indebted to it. York University, Toronto, also aided my efforts in many ways I very much appreciate, ranging from material support to toleration of my schedule. A month's residency at the Bellagio Study Center proved invaluable. Obviously, none of these organizations take any responsibility for how I have utilized their important help, and all the views expressed here are, of course, entirely my own.

Many individuals aided my work at various times, and I mention only a few of them here, acutely aware that I shall in no way ever be able to thank adequately all those who shared a common experience and cause, even by dedicating this book to them. Le Anh Tu, Fay Knopp, and the late Stewart Meacham of the American Friends Service Committee, Edward Herman, Stanley Vittoz, Michael Klare, Jim Morrell, and Noam Chomsky in the United States were always generous with materials and ideas. Kenneth McNaught, Robert Jay Lifton, and Jan Pluvier were supportive, and I very much appreciate it. Outside North America, Saburo Kugai, Peter Limqueco, Renato Constantino, the late Peggy Duff, and Jacques Decornoy helped in innumerable ways over long periods of time.

In Vietnam, I wish especially to thank Nguyen Co Thach, as well as Nguyen Van Sao and Linh Qui, Huynh Huu Nghiep, Binh Thanh, Hoang

Tung, Vo Van Sung, Pham Van Ba, Duong Dinh Thao, Phan Thi Minh, Pham Thanh Nam, Phan Tu, Thu Bon, Dinh Duc Thien, Vo Dong Giang, Nguyen Thi Dinh, Vu Van Minh, Hoang Minh Thao, and Tran Van Giau, and also the many people in Quang Tri Province, Song Be, My Tho, Hanoi, and Ho Chi Minh City who generously shared their experiences and thoughts with me.

Ngo Vinh Long and Huynh Kim Khanh each spent a year making accessible to me Vietnamese-language materials found in the Harvard, the Cornell, and various Paris libraries. Khoi Huynh kindly helped me with last-minute additions. The Faculty of Arts Secretarial Service, York University, was incomparably helpful in typing my manuscript, easing the whole task with exemplary grace and efficiency.

Mere words cannot do justice to my appreciation of my wife, Joyce, who shared every day of the two decades of experiences and effort out of which this volume grew. She has added immeasurably to whatever assets and insights it may have, and attempted to impose a sensibility and discipline on this book which comes from both studying and participating in the great events which led to its making. Decorum dictates certain constraints on acknowledgments, but suffice to say that I have been strengthened enormously by her comradeship and our common enthusiasms and commitments.

ANATOMY
OF A WAR

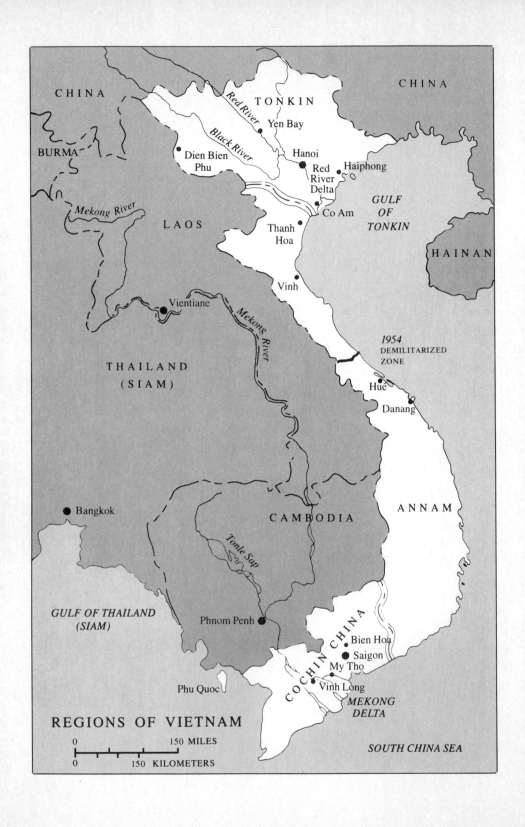

CHINA

TONKIN

Red River

Yen Bay

Black River

Dien Bien
Phu

Hanoi

Haiphong

Red
River
Delta

Co Am

CHINA

GULF
OF
TONKIN

HAINAN

BURMA

Mekong River

LAOS

Thanh
Hoa

Vinh

Vientiane

Mekong River

THAILAND
(SIAM)

1954
DEMILITARIZED
ZONE

Hue

Danang

Bangkok

CAMBODIA

ANNAM

Tonle Sap

GULF OF THAILAND
(SIAM)

Phnom Penh

COCHIN CHINA

Bien Hoa

Saigon

My Tho

Phu Quoc

Vinh Long

MEKONG
DELTA

REGIONS OF VIETNAM

0   150 MILES

0   150 KILOMETERS

SOUTH CHINA SEA

Introduction

The most difficult challenges in comprehending major historical experiences are also the simplest to define. Whether novelists, historians, or social theorists confront them, the main problems of the human condition touch on the same central issues. People have since the beginning of recorded time been fascinated with the meaning of action and the social purpose of their goals and lives. Our desire and growing need to perceive our own society and world, its mechanisms and trends, enabling us to determine our own fates better, obsess us. In various guises, the theme of drift and mastery in the historical process suffuses much of the world's literature and social thought over the past two centuries. Mankind's conceptions of the potential role of conscious and deliberate designs in shaping history, as opposed to the impersonal, the spontaneous, and the mechanistic in a society's development, profoundly affects its incentive to act to control its own future.

Like the entire scope of Vietnamese history since 1940, the Vietnam War is an epic event, the longest, most sustained revolutionary effort in modern history. Constructing an anatomy of the Vietnam War not only allows us to dissect the primary causes and underlying episodes of the main political event in the lives of tens of millions of people; its sheer length and complexity also provide a vast framework for defining the place of freedom and constraint in people's determining their own future. Such a focus primes both the writer and the reader to search for exact causes and explanations of the great events and institutional and human factors which guide Vietnamese history over forty-five years on its uneven yet increasingly irresistible course toward a conclusion which in fact was not always inevitable—and which even today superficially looks implausible precisely because too little is known about the forces, people, and events which shaped this remarkable development in the modern historical experience. Stated plainly, we need to know how and why the Communist Party was victorious in Vietnam and the United States failed. A history of the war, dealing with how various

3

factors in Vietnam, the United States, and the world play variable roles for each side, influencing important forces and institutions, of necessity increasingly touches on the nature of those elements which shape the modern historical experience in Vietnam and, in usually less dramatic but fundamental ways, elsewhere as well.

The very character of Vietnam's history and America's involvement in it force us to confront how and why a handful of young people who set out in 1930 to attain an anticolonial revolution finally succeeded in a process which required them to fight first France and eventually the world's most militarily powerful and richest nation. What were the alternatives before those who sought to define Vietnam's direction after 1940? To what extent and precisely how did impersonal, uncontrollable, and remote events and options impose their will on the adversaries? What were the limits and constraints for each side over time? And did historical forces and the economic and social elements in the protracted war coalesce at some stage to produce new inhibitions, new problems, and challenges for the Communists and those who opposed them?

War profoundly transmutes human and social reality; it is the prism through which one must see the events in Vietnam from 1940 onward. War has determined the parameters of social change in vast areas of the world throughout this century, its effects varying with time and place but inescapably defining the modern historical experience.

War telescopes social time, bringing together new forces and new interactions with traditional institutions, producing predictable as well as original mutations in human experiences and social systems. Changes and transformations in people and societies that take decades or even centuries without war may occur in a few years with it. Colonial systems that required generations to construct quickly crumble at their foundations. The destruction of the old order is not a simple event, for its residues disappear slowly and interact and meld with those of the new, changing and being changed in the process.

Vietnam's development through the longest single war of modern times demands that we not allow chronology, occurrences, and less important issues to occlude the vast context which informs its history at every moment. War is the field in which actors seek to control events, but also become controlled by them. It is the context within which spontaneity, new configurations, new inhibitions, and new choices constantly emerge, determining human consciousness and the nature of social options. All inherited systems, whether ideologically Right or Left, are modified profoundly during wars, whatever the perceptions or desires of those seeking to impose their designs on them. To comprehend the complexity as well as the possibilities of this reality, and both its hopes and its dangers, offers a clarity as a basis of action that is of inestimable value, for it is the only rational way of relating conscious action to the historical process. Knowledge is not necessarily power, but ignorance is surely weakness. The absence of complete choice and freedom in history at crucial moments cannot obscure the fact that as the institutions which make history change, so the role of knowledge and the potential significance of decisions increase.

War is not simply a conflict between armies; more and more it is a struggle between competing social systems, incorporating the political, economic, and cultural institutions of all rivals. The longer the war, the more likely that it will be determined outside the arena of arms and battles. The Vietnam War was no exception to the rule that all wars in this century have increasingly become ideological in both their origins and their consequences. If the social order of a rival possesses internal weaknesses and contradictions unknown to itself at the inception, these will in time inevitably emerge to confront its leaders along with success and failure in combat. To comprehend the mechanisms of war as a social process and ideological conflict is essential to an understanding of the events in Vietnam over four decades.

The manner in which international conflict affects the internal social dynamics of nations varies with time and place, but in Vietnam it profoundly touched all dimensions of the country from the start and also gradually penetrated deep into American life. The social, demographic, and economic consequences of the Second World War, the French return, and the American involvement in Vietnam were monumental. The land system and class structure were traumatized repeatedly over decades, altering both the social condition and the consciousness of an entire nation.

A war's transformation of the existing class structure, in Vietnam as everywhere, leads to a sharp increase in the masses' political awareness and their need for relevant social options. All sides offered them ideologies. But the cultural rationality of the alternatives, their relative effectiveness in mobilizing people and physical resources, and their capacity to analyze social reality and provide men and women a convincing guide to future action, touches the importance of the development of conscious purpose and ideas both as they emerge from and as they influence the stages of institutional change in a society in crisis.

Ideas became critical in determining the outcome of the struggle, both as cause and as effect. In essence, what could each adversary afford, and what did it believe? And how compatible with the tasks before each army was its code of personal conduct and behavior for those in its ranks or for whom it had responsibility? While war has a known material dimension, involving costs and the ability of sides to meet their needs, its inherently more nebulous human dimension is no less vital. Ideology and consciousness subsumed many things during the long war, ranging from the competing concepts of personal behavior and relationship toward community and society to a vision of the importance of technology in the resolution of the war and social crisis. It was both implicit and explicit, articulate and inchoate.

Major historical experiences, obviously, embody many interacting factors and forces of varying significance. As difficult as it is to perceive such multifaceted events, to understand the Vietnam War we need constantly to examine and recall the larger trends and interrelations, treating them all as integral dimensions of a vast but unified panorama. But we must also be aware of the unique character of specific political, military, economic, and ideological developments even as they blend into a single, global phenomenon. However diverse their responses, the Communist Party, their enemies at home, and the United States each responded to many of these complex trends and issues, which affected them all in different ways, and throughout this book I shall juxtapose their reactions to them.

Since Vietnam is a nation of peasants, the starting point for analyzing the influence of the social structure on politics and society is the land and those who till it. The Communists and their opponents constantly attempted to relate to such matters over the decades, as war and upheaval transformed the economic context of land questions. For the Party the complexity of peasant radicalism, at first overwhelmingly concerned with land reform, left it with the especially delicate question of how to reconcile pressures from the masses with a strategy of class alliances around political issues.

The class structure was a basic institutional element in the war, and it altered over time in various ways that were critical for all sides. Every change in the control of the RVN after 1954 carried with it important implications to the distribution of wealth and power. And the expansion of the RVN's military in the south after 1954, and the emergence of new economic activities after the massive American intervention in 1965, made the nature of class and power a fundamental question in the comprehending of Vietnam's subsequent development as trends in the social system were translated into political and social policies and events of crucial importance. So, too, did the growth of a huge urban population and cities, which profoundly challenged all sides politically and posed basic problems of mobilization and social and economic integration. How Vietnamese society changed and how the Communists, the RVN, and Americans understood these trends and dealt with their dimensions are essential factors in the war's outcome.

Protracted war in Vietnam raised enormous economic and social issues.

What could the fabric of Vietnam's society tolerate? What new institutional forms would emerge? How large and what kind of an army could the United States create among its allies in South Vietnam, and how would such a force relate to the population by comparison with the Communists? Could the two enemies transcend their armies to engage in political struggle, and how did each side perceive this aspect of the war and act on it? And what sorts of military strategies did each adopt to absorb the human and economic costs of a war seemingly without end, and what was the relative efficacy of each adversary's military reaction to the other?

The U.S. dilemma after 1949 was how to transform its huge arsenal into an effective means of fighting and winning a local war, especially a war against unconventional revolutionary forces. Could American responses and techniques succeed, and could they be transferred to the RVN's military forces? Could technological advantages and firepower be metamorphosed into victory? As for the Revolution, could it find the means of neutralizing the massive power confronting it and hope eventually to defeat it? And how?

These monumental social trends and challenges to all antagonists were at every stage inextricably linked to the nature of the men and women supporting and resisting the Revolution. Their views of their own and their families' welfare, as opposed to their organization and community, reappear constantly, touching the very ability of armies to fight and survive, economies to work, and people to relate to politics and common social goals. Who would sacrifice the most, and which side could best cope with the fears and needs of its adherents in armies, villages, and cities? What was the basis of personal commitment on all sides, the ideas and institutions which led to successes and failures in protracted war? The war has to be regarded as a struggle not only between armies, competing societies, and visions of change but also between men and women committed to alternative strategies who had profoundly different images of human existence and their roles as actors in history. How important is the issue of morale and motivation, and how did both the Communists and those willing to create a society congenial to the United States cope with it?

The United States' involvement in Vietnam was at first intended quickly to redress many of the postwar global dilemmas and frustrations of its military power, to confirm its symbolic credibility and the technical efficiency of its arms. The goal was to neutralize the rising potential throughout the Third World for revolutionary nationalist regimes. Little did anyone imagine that the Vietnam War would become one of the greatest and longest internal traumas in American history, exceeded in divisiveness and bitterness only by the American Revolution and the Civil War. In certain ways it was more distinctive than any external war the United States has ever fought. In the First and Second World Wars the United States was essentially a secondary causal actor, entering what were European-originated wars to play a determining but surely never the sole role in their conclusions. Both wars were relatively brief, and America emerged from them economically and politically far more powerful than when it had entered. Vietnam began with patriotic gore, but as the frustrations and time mounted so did the bitterness and internal disunity, weakening the economy and the military structure and shattering the foreign policy consensus and domestic tranquillity. What were the economic costs of such a war to America, not only in Vietnam but in its ability to lead the world economy and sustain its military power elsewhere, and what could it afford? The need to confront the total consequences of the war produced distinctive problems for the United States throughout the years, and economic and political events in America had decisive implications for those in Vietnam.

In resolving its symbolic efforts in Vietnam, however, the United States had to face distinctive problems of an excess of arms and munitions, on the one hand, and disagreements among its senior officers as to how, where, and under whom to employ them, on the other. The translation of its unprecedented power into concrete tactics and strategy divided men of power from the inception. Superimposed on these decisions was the American political context, whose significance both in Washington and in the streets of countless cities and towns was to grow each year.

The primary origin of the Vietnam War was the American intervention and effort to establish and sustain an alternative to the Communist Party, and Washington assumed there was a sufficient indigenous basis to give it increasing hope for success. To varying degrees, Vietnam was a microcosm of the many nations throughout the world with comparable social dynamics and dilemmas which the United States has sought since 1946 to keep out of the hands of diverse radical and nationalist movements. A critical problem, equally relevant elsewhere, was how and with what consequences the United States could massively involve itself in the life of a poor nation. On what kind of social system could it build an anticommunist alternative, and was there an economic, human, and political basis for the effort? To a fundamental degree, the entire American undertaking was dependent on the form and nature of the men and social order it was seeking to install and maintain.

Comprehending the nature of this system was to become a major dilemma to Americans during the war. What was the character of rulership and power in the RVN, how durable and resilient was the existing economic elite, and what was the political and economic role of the RVN's military leaders as opposed to their military function? Could an American-defined structure be imposed on the distinctive human, social, and economic conditions both in South Vietnam and in the RVN armies, and could the burden of fighting the war be successfully transferred to it? And what was the basis of the RVN's economy? Could it sustain development as well as cope with the challenge from the Left, and could it ever survive without American aid? Was the RVN, in fact, a viable entity rather than the mere by-product of the French and American money and presence, and did a serious social consensus and institutional foundation for its perpetuation exist? Could the Vietnam War, in essence, become more than a foreign intervention fought for symbolic international reasons, and be transformed into a true internal conflict?

The Communist Party, too, had its special challenges. Hampered by poor communications and an inherently decentralized country, it had to adjust its own structure and policies to the exigencies of war despite its ambition to lead a complex struggle employing Marxist-Leninist concepts of a centralized organization to the maximum extent possible. Adapting to reality was a critical challenge, requiring the Party to balance its desired role as the leader and organizer of the masses against its need repeatedly to respond to the masses' independent pressures and aspirations. To what extent was it compelled to both lead and follow grass-roots movements? This dilemma became a recurrent theme after 1945. And asking its members and followers to make enormous, sustained sacrifices over a period of years was a problem it had to consider systematically, producing a concept of revolutionary conduct, and procedures to communicate and implement it, that was a vital aspect of its war efforts. What was the role of ideas and the function of its followers' material interests in protracted struggle? How could it reconcile the building of socialism in the north after 1954 with the continuing trends and struggles in the south? Responses to questions like these were integral to the Revolution's distinctive war efforts.

The Communist Party had also to deal constantly with its political strategy regarding those outside its own ranks. How could it implement its position on creating a broad united front of many classes, particularly when poorer-peasant militancy persistently undermined its ability to put into practice a political concept that was fundamental to its development? The dilemma of class alliances versus class struggle confronted the Party for decades, emerging as a central theme of its entire history.

The Vietnam War was to involve a vast spectrum of forces and issues. Some are unavoidably complex, entailing the global symbolism of the war and drift and mastery in the direction of modern history. Others are painfully simple, ranging from a soldier's desertion in order to be with his family to the erosion of a peasant's moorings in a world of destruction and lost children. The war encompassed the classic issues of social philosophy, the grandiose problems of world power, the tragedies of countless lives lost and shattered, the shame of corruption and cowardice, the glory of heroism, the consolation of men and women secure in their readiness to make sacrifices —in a word, the entire diversity of human responses and social trends in this century, most of them ageless.

To confront all these dimensions, from the glorious to the absurd, from the simple to the complex, is to comprehend the anatomy of a war which has been the most important event in the lives of countless millions and to perceive the modern historical experience—to hold a mirror up to our past and to ourselves, perhaps to our future, and to the human condition in the last half of the twentieth century.

Part One

THE ORIGINS OF THE WAR TO 1960

DEMILITARIZED ZONE

SOUTH VIETNAM

- Quang Tri
- Khe Sanh
- Hué

Danang

I CORPS
(MR I)

- Chu Lai
- Quang Ngai

THAILAND

LAOS

- Ubon

- Dak To
- Kontum
- Pleiku

Qui Nhon

II CORPS
(MR II)

CAMBODIA

- Ban Me Thuot

Nha Trang
Dalat   Cam Ranh

Cam
Ranh Bay

Phnom Penh

III CORPS
(MR III)

- Tay Ninh
- Cu Chi   Bien Hoa
- Saigon   Long Binh

Phan Thiet

Long Xuyen

My Tho
Ben Tre   Vung Tau

Rach Gia   Vinh Long
Can Tho

Mekong Delta   SOUTH CHINA SEA

IV CORPS
(MR IV)

Soc Trang

Ca Mau

0   150 MILES

0   150 KILOMETERS

Chapter 1

Vietnam's Road to Crisis

Vietnam's history from the mid-nineteenth century until the August 1945 Revolution comprised a series of profoundly traumatic political, economic, and social transformations which non-Communist Vietnamese proved wholly incapable of confronting. They were never independent of foreign domination, which was both a cause and a consequence of the nation's vast, cumulative problems. The basic pattern in modern Vietnamese history was the non-Communists' endemic inability to relate to the dynamics of their own times. Only the Communist Party could fill such a vacuum. Its triumph was due not simply to its own abilities but also to the virtual absence of other serious opposition to French colonialism and to the profound impact of World War Two on that system.

In 1858 the French embarked on their conquest of the moribund Nguyen dynasty, which ended in 1884 with the division of Vietnam into the three administrative units of Tonkin in the north, Cochin China in the south, and Annam in the center. The French replacement of the traditional order accelerated deep ideological and cultural changes already occurring among elite and educated elements of Vietnamese society. The Nguyen dynasty had during the first half of the nineteenth century attempted to Sinicize Vietnam's laws and institutions in order to consolidate its power, widening the gulf between itself and the people. At the same time it was drawn to Western goods and technology even as it resisted the increasingly effective French-backed effort to spread Catholicism. The result was that the royal Confucian ideology was further weakened as a variety of new concepts reached the entire country through the numerous ports along the long coastline. The court's collaboration with the French greatly reduced the legitimacy of conventional wisdom, although some of the displaced scholar-gentry in villages throughout the country articulated militant nationalist variants of Confucianism. Along with large numbers of unemployed and aspiring officials, they produced a real yet quite manageable dissidence and a great amount of nostalgia to leaven the already fragile traditional culture which was reeling under the impact of the predominantly Gallic version of Western culture.

The elite's cooperation with colonialism also predetermined the crucial context for future Vietnamese politics and economic development. One worked with foreigners or opposed them and their local allies, a process of resistance which directly implied rejection of the elite's political and economic foundations. The French by themselves could not have destroyed the traditional Vietnamese order. The opportunism and avarice of the existing and aspiring elites which accomplished this for them created a political vacuum that was to make Vietnam's revolution virtually irresistible.

LAND AND THE RURAL CRISIS

The main economic impact of the French was on the land system, an issue which weaves like a central thread throughout the whole of modern Vietnamese history. Their nonagrarian activities, while important, affected only a small percentage of the work force after 1918. The French greatly intensified and accelerated the land crisis, undermining much of whatever cohesion existed in an agrarian society, and created the objective preconditions for effective radical mobilization.

Land was the most important resource the French had for funding a colonial administration and exploiting the nation, but since the Mekong Delta in Cochin China was underpopulated, consisting of extensive salty swamps in need of large-scale drainage, they first sought to utilize the much more developed and healthier lands of the very populous Red River Delta in Tonkin. Despite local resistance, the French made huge land grants to a few French settlers, and even more to their numerous Vietnamese collaborators: minor bureaucrats, servants, cronies, and those useful to the state apparatus France imposed on the region. Land became capital for France's consolidating of colonial power, and after 1900 the Mekong Delta in Cochin China and, to a smaller extent, in Annam became the source of additional grants. Immense land concessions of mainly empty frontier regions were given to French and Vietnamese who rehabilitated vast tracts and mobilized manpower, either as tenants or as paid labor, to farm it. Although the data are not entirely consistent, they all point to the creation of an extremely unequal landownership throughout Vietnam, the profound transformation of the existing land system, and the replacement of the domestically oriented traditional order with one now subject to rice export and world price fluctuations, the caprices of avaricious nouveau riche landlords, and a variety of grave social and economic problems.

By 1931 Cochin China's population had reached four and one-half million, nearly three times the 1880 figure, with two-thirds the French land concessions located there and nearly another one-fifth in Annam. Notwithstanding the French citizenship of some of the new Vietnamese elite, Vietnamese landowners by 1940 ended up with two-thirds of the concession lands in Cochin China—and with a somewhat smaller portion of those in all of Indochina. In effect, the French created a new and increasingly Gallicized indigenous landowning class, privileged but also wholly dependent on the colonial administrative system.

By the late 1930s, 6,200 landlords with estates of over fifty hectares in Cochin China owned 45 percent of the rice acreage, and that figure remained nearly constant for the next twenty years. About 60,000 owned another 37 percent, and at least three-fifths of the Delta was worked by tenants while nearly three-fifths of the rural population was landless. In land-scarce Tonkin, in the late 1930s 20 percent of the rice land belonged to large estates of fifty hectares and over, with another 20 percent held by those with five to fifty hectares—2 percent of the landowning population. If land was somewhat more equally distributed in the north, there were also many more smallholders whose plots were so little that their lives were generally more precarious than those of peasants in the Mekong.

These figures scarcely do justice to the pervasive misery among peasants throughout Vietnam. The French and their local collaborators traumatized the masses with their commercializing efforts to produce rice for export to a mercurial world market. The mechanisms of exploitation were diverse, but most prominent for the peasants were rent, interest, and taxation.

Depending on time and place, tenants paid landlords 40 to 60 percent of the yield, which in the Mekong was not calculated as a percentage of the actual crop but rather as a fixed amount of a hypothetical yield for a "normal" year. In poor years, therefore, rents could reach 80 percent of real output. In addition, the peasant often had to provide labor services (two days a month was the pre-1945 norm in the Mekong) as well as food and gifts during holidays. But the landlord's main gains were frequently from loans to his tenants, which entangled most of them and the annual interest on which was typically 50 to 70 percent but often much higher. Interest on small loans might be the equivalent of up to 3,600 percent annually. Usury, in its extreme form, hurt all the layers of the economic order, and even landlords who speculated in land or borrowed excessively also fell victim to the system.

No less onerous to the peasantry was the French monetization of the rural economy by means of land taxes and of monopolies on salt and other obligations or necessities, for which peasants had to pay with cash—a burden which further forced them into the hands of the usurers. And since taxes did not fall with prices, the impact on the peasants was often calamitous.

Catastrophe resulted from all these factors when the price of rice in Saigon fell by two-thirds from 1930 to 1933, in the wake of the world depression. From 1920 until the crash, landowners in the Mekong expanded output and invested and speculated heavily. By 1933 a handful of major landowners, with at least one-sixth of the cultivable land, were in serious financial straits. Such trends meant continuous mobility within the landed elite and more suffering for the peasantry.

By the time World War Two began, the agrarian order in Vietnam was in rapid flux, impoverishing the vast bulk of the peasantry and producing profound deprivation and insecurity in their lives. And even a portion of the new upper-class Vietnamese who had gained most from the precarious French system appeared marginal and vulnerable.[1]

THE EMERGENCE OF A SEMI-WORKING CLASS

The marginalization process in the agrarian economy was paralleled from the first French arrival, but especially after 1918, in Vietnam's urban and wage-earning sectors. Agrarian and nonagrarian economic activities in Vietnam were never distinct, especially not in terms of the labor supply and agricultural commodities for export. An immediate consequence of the French impact on the land system in Tonkin was the even greater growth of an excess peasantry available for investment-based development. For the essence of the French economic program was to combine a relatively small amount of capital and technology with a strategic exploitation of the vast surplus, cheap Tonkinese labor supply for the development of labor-intensive export sectors.

The French invested 14.2 billion francs in public funds in Indochina up to 1939, and 11.6 billion in private capital—nearly all of the private capital arriving after 1918. The social impact of this relatively minor industrialization was greater than its economic role, for it radicalized a significant sector of the masses. French investment procedures and practices in Vietnam were unquestionably among the most violent and exploitive known to the twentieth century. Half of its public funds went into railroads, and of the 80,000 laborers hired to build the link from Hanoi to the Chinese border, which opened in 1910, approximately 30 percent died on the job.

The Vietnamese working class was very small, numbering in 1931 only 221,000 in a country of 17 million. Over one-third of these worked on plantations—primarily rubber—as contract labor mobilized, sometimes by force, from mainly northern villages. Nearly all of them endured terrible hardships at work. In addition, 44,000 peasants were recruited to work in

France during 1916–18; on their return, contract labor conditions were improved so that a worker in Cochin China absent without leave from work for more than forty-eight hours then received no more than sixty days' imprisonment! Wages, the ILO reported in 1938, were "abnormally low" throughout the interwar period.[2] In this setting a minute but highly militant working class emerged, and largely spontaneous strikes and workers' actions were increasingly common throughout the postwar decade.

The Tonkin peasants employed on plantations or in mining and factories could not adapt to the onerous regimen. Before the Tet festival many left work permanently, and mines often had to replace most of their labor force after the holiday. The labor turnover was proportionate to the foul working conditions, and this meant that the number of peasants who had once been workers was much larger than the number of those employed at any given time. Yet this mainly transitional, highly fluid working class absorbed something from the cities or mines, including the ideas found there, and peasants who went to France were especially exposed to glimpses of a whole new world and its doctrines. Their knowledge was communicated to the peasantry, above all in Tonkin, from which the vast bulk of the workers came. Capitalism's influence on Vietnam was therefore of great importance, even if difficult to measure in conventional terms, producing a hybrid synthesis of peasant and proletarian which radicalized political perceptions among many of the rural masses.

THE UNDERDEVELOPMENT OF IDEAS AND OPPOSITION

At an intellectual and cultural level, Vietnam had by the turn of the century become a potpourri of many of the world's ideas and philosophies, including those fashionable in China and Japan. The French introduced their conservative wisdom into the country via the primitive school system they began to establish, and a small but significant flow of students from wealthier Vietnamese families to France helped bring more democratic thought back to the colony. The variety of theories among them produced a cacophony of concepts. For the intellectuals the search for ideas was both an impersonal quest for ways to advance Vietnam's interest against the failures of tradition and the challenges of colonialism and a vehicle for promoting their own ambitions. Because the intellectuals were identified with the relatively privileged educated stratum with personal ties to landlords, urban bourgeoisie, and the increasingly large colonial bureaucracy, the interests and possibilities of their class often shaped their opinions. This profoundly limited their mass appeal and led to their making repeated fatal compromises, leaving an increasingly clear field to the Communist Party.

The most bizarre and surely the most successful force which this condition created was the Cao Dai religion. Founded in 1925, Cao Dai merged Christianity, Buddhism, Taoism, Confucianism, spiritualism, fortune-telling, and assorted mysticisms, converting anywhere from a tenth to a fifth of Cochin China's population by 1930. Cao Dai leaders came from the elite of local society. Many held relatively important posts in the French private and colonial bureaucracies or were landlords, and they overlapped the leadership of the Constitutionalist party, a loyally pro-French organization which nonetheless sought greater legal and economic rights for the Vietnamese educated elite. Cao Dai's mass base consisted of poorer peasants living in the regions least affected by the French land system and willing to fall under the Cao Dai leadership's paternalist religious and social mantle. The French, too, tolerated and at times exploited its presence, and for over four decades Cao Dai remained a major but highly localized power broker in Cochin China, turning ideas, politics, mass social needs, business enterprises, and the fortunes of its founders into an original but successful mélange.

None of the other non-Marxist intellectual currents had Cao Dai's impact, if only because they lacked a comparable social basis. The local peasant rebellions which a few scholar-gentry led during the late nineteenth and early twentieth centuries, or even the short-lived February 1930 uprising of the Nationalist party (VNQDD), showed that brave Vietnamese patriotic intellectuals existed. But they lacked a sense of discipline and timing essential both to survival and to success, and in due course their errors enabled the repressive French to remove them as a significant factor.

In the end the hallmark of Vietnam's traditional, inherited ideas—cultural, religious, and intellectual—was their dilution and passivity before the social and political changes to which the nation was exposed. No non-Marxist doctrine emerged capable of overcoming the centrifugal tendencies of Vietnamese thought by a synthesis of traditional and modern concepts relevant to the vast economic and social changes colonialism created.[3]

THE UNDERDEVELOPED
BOURGEOISIE

Alongside an underdeveloped mobile working class, a confused and fragmented intelligentsia, and an increasingly impoverished and displaced peasantry under the yoke of not wholly stable landlords, there emerged an unusually underdeveloped, small, and fragile Vietnamese bourgeoisie. This was because the surest, easiest way for an ambitious Vietnamese to succeed economically was to work politically with the colonial bureaucracy.

The formation of an important national bourgeoisie was blocked in Vietnam, as in all of Southeast Asia, by the dominant role of the Chinese in the economic structure. Legally organized into virtually autonomous, self-governing congregations *(bangs)* on the basis of the five main regions from which the Chinese emigrated, the Chinese by 1930 enjoyed most-favored-nation status and after 1946 practical equality with the French in economic matters. The *bangs* regulated all matters of justice and taxation and were the functional basis of Chinese economic activity within which various Chinese family clans operated. They tended to divide branches of economic activity into monopolies, aiding *bang* members with an informal but highly effective credit system. The *bangs* took over much of the economy through their dominant position as usurers, and they operated in the rural villages in a manner the French bureaucracy never could. Rice milling, opium and pepper growing, the rice, cotton, and sugar trade, export-import, transport, commerce—vast sectors fell into the hands of the Chinese, who by 1954 controlled about three-quarters of all commerce. The French both admired and feared them, but relied heavily on the Chinese for their own needs, farming out a portion of the tax gathering and the fiscal administration to them. For the Chinese mediated between the colonialists and the colonized, and helped the system work far more efficiently both as compradors and as a distinct ethnic bourgeoisie. Vietnamese entrepreneurs and usurers existed in the interstices of the economy, if they were not themselves linked with Chinese interests, and Chettyar usurers from India only reduced the terrain to be exploited.

The Chinese network operated throughout Indochina, but Saigon (with its all-Chinese suburb of Cholon), Phnom Penh, Haiphong, and Hanoi were their main communities. Urban Vietnam was therefore strongly Chinese culturally and largely Chinese economically. The only compromise of the Chinese with the local society was to marry, if necessary, native women, and most retained their legal status as Chinese nationals, even after generations in Vietnam. Because their foreign trade required contact with their homeland and with *bang* and family members in Hong Kong or Singapore, it was essential for them not to dilute their ethnic identity. In fact, Indochina, like all of Southeast Asia, was a vast arena for immigrants from China in search of their fortunes, and most had neither interest nor inclination to assimilate. The Chinese population in Cochin China increased sixfold from 1879 to 1928, when 402,000 Chinese inhabited all of Indochina. With the advent of the depression, however, 76,000 left the colony over the next eight years. The one element which gained most from the existing order was ultimately mobile and unwilling loyally to defend it.

The result was the absence of a unified and indigenous economic elite able or willing to produce its own institutional order and a political structure to reinforce it autonomously of the colonial system. No national bourgeoisie of the kind that led the Indian independence movement could emerge in Vietnam. The large Vietnamese petite bourgeoisie was both marginal and unstable, having no stake in the system and barely more than the resources to educate its children.

The Chinese presence left little space for a strong Vietnamese bourgeoisie. After World War One the influx of French capital opened opportunities for entrepreneurs, and the Chinese could not exclude Vietnamese entirely. But the French guarded the local market for their own profits, reducing the arena of economic activity for the native bourgeoisie. As many of the successful Vietnamese landowners who profited from land speculation and usury moved into towns, they found it difficult to enter the nonagricultural economy. They sent their children off to cities or even to France for their education, and many sought to find their identities as ever-greater consumers of Western goods and as practitioners of its mores. Their fortunes could be made in land, in some services and construction, in the professions, and, above all, in the French colonial bureaucracy, as collaborators. By 1951 the Chinese controlled over half of the enterprises in the region south of the seventeenth parallel and over half of the invested nonagricultural capital, that of the French included. Vietnamese were a majority only in the smallest firms.

The Vietnamese bourgeoisie, in the end, failed to find a clear role or an identity in the colonial system. During the depression the growing marginality of its members condemned most of their economic activities to failure. In this situation the bulk of Vietnamese elite found collaboration, without moral or verbal ambiguity, the surest route to a bigger share of the wealth. A smaller group, however, asked for a larger place in the system. In what was only the most important of many efforts in this direction, the Constitutionalist party throughout the 1920s urged the French to involve the Vietnamese elite in the direction of the bureaucracy and economy. Comprising educated professionals, landlords, well-to-do merchants, and senior civil servants, this ardently pro-French and openly anti-Chinese aspiring bourgeoisie received some solace with nominal posts but never gained access to the important economic opportunities which they demanded. As a result some wandered into the Cao Dai while the party itself became a tiny, consistently collaborationist force throughout the 1930s.

In the end, the Cao Dai, the Constitutionalists, and many similar organizations were mere reflections of the underlying malaise of a relatively small group within the fragile but ambitious Vietnamese elite of landlords, functionaries, professionals, and more prosperous townsmen who had much in common culturally, socially, and politically. Most members of this elite, however, had no inclination for collective agitation, even on their own behalf, since their concerns were limited to making and spending money. Enthralled by French consumer goods and material values, which they transmuted into a deepening identification with Gallic culture, these practical members of the top of the Vietnamese hierarchy were not interested, ultimately, in seriously challenging any authority. Collaboration throughout Vietnamese history was only a symptom of the Vietnamese elite's marginal and unstable economic and social position. Boxed in by colonial masters and Chinese compradors, they never had sufficient power, coherence, or legitimacy to fill the vacuum which the French had created throughout Vietnam. The depression only weakened further their already shaking foundations, as it did those of the entire social order, which World War Two was to destroy entirely.

One crucial distinction between the Chinese and Vietnamese revolutions was that the Chinese Communists confronted a reasonably coherent rival claiming nationalist legitimacy, whereas Vietnam had nothing remotely comparable to the Kuomintang throughout the country. The Vietnamese urban and landowning elite was far less cohesive and developed than that in China, and this difference found expression in the absence of a serious political opposition to the Communist Party for the remainder of the century.

The Vietnamese elite's impasse was only a part of the generalized crisis of the colonial order, which affected the peasantry most gravely but which also hurt the strategically placed working class and highly visible though impotent intellectuals. Given the class and political basis of its malaise, the protracted crisis of the dispossessed set the stage for the emergence of the Communist Party, for it was amid the thousands of hamlets of poor peasants, in mines and rubber plantations among undernourished workers, and among anguished students and intellectuals passionately debating Vietnam's future that the longest epic of human struggle in the twentieth century began.[4]

Chapter 2

The Communist Party until 1945: From Depression to War

Until 1945 the Communist Party had a history of significant failures and too few successes to warrant much optimism among its roughly four thousand members in 1944. The main task facing the Party during its first two decades was to develop a strategy for survival in a repressive context that related to social forces and possibilities. Its ability to persevere while time and circumstances took their toll on its enemies became a recurrent aspect of the Party's theory and practice. Often its role was not to lead events but to respond and adapt and then to guide them, becoming both the leader and the follower in the historical process.

The Vietnamese Communist Party's most original quality was its appreciation of the international framework of its analyses and actions. The Party's power and the fate of its enemies, it believed, would to a critical extent depend on events and forces outside the immediate Vietnamese context, reflecting the internal contradictions in France, and then in the United States, as well as the world balance of forces. The Party's international perspective was the central thread in its learning process.

THE PARTY'S IDEOLOGICAL FOUNDATIONS

The influences on the Party's ideological development were sufficiently diverse to defy a simple weighting. The acute Vietnamese cultural crisis of the interwar period greatly secularized social thought and introduced a vast number of new ideas. Sorting out the exact impact of Marxism-Leninism, Vietnamese social notions embodied in Confucianism and nationalism, or French traditions of rationalism is so difficult because the Party failed to produce a single, overarching theoretician able to integrate precisely quite diverse influences within a unifying system. The Party's genius was in producing brilliant tacticians, above all Ho Chi Minh, reflecting the Party's uniquely cooperative and stable leadership structure, and it created an original and detailed concept of revolutionary action.* The problem of translating theory into practice scarcely existed in Vietnam. The heritage of Vietnamese society and ideas, the depression and then wars, left little time for grand theory building, but it did require acute sensibility to organization and programs. Sectarianism was not to plague the Party after 1941, and the absence of dominant personalities and cults around them helped to prevent the rigidity of doctrines which Stalin and Mao thought essential to their functional control of power. The manner in which the Party was put together, its tactics and strategies, and the peasant and colonial nature of the society all further weakened any tendencies toward doctrinal inflexibility.

Ho Chi Minh best embodied the currents of ideas that were to shape the Party's thought, and his capacity to encourage alternative ideas and strategies created a more permissive absorption of many heritages. Frequent eclecticism among leaders at a tactical level led to an increasingly inclusive mass party of the Left which suffered comparatively few doctrinal schisms. Ho always argued that his role and that of all leaders should be subordinate to that of the Party's, guaranteeing that no less-modest personalities could endanger its autonomous character. Perhaps his ultimate contribution was precisely this ability to see the limits of personalities and egos and to define the Party's decision-making structure among leaders and lower-level members. This self-effacing style made him even more charismatic because it was all too rare and credible at the same time. Indeed, it qualified him as the only important true organizational Leninist to emerge from the international communist movement.

Without underestimating the role of other ideas, the Party's internationalist heritage profoundly influenced the first, critical stage of its development until 1940, when the sheer weight of world events on Vietnam's destiny reinforced this emphasis. Ho left Vietnam in 1911 and for the next three decades related to Vietnam from outside its borders, coming to Marxism-Leninism in France. His interaction with the world, quite different from Stalin's or Mao's provincialism, guaranteed the synthesis of internationalism

---

*To prevent confusion, I use Ho Chi Minh's post-1940 name in place of his earlier identity as Nguyen Ai Quoc and of his other pseudonyms. For the same reason, I call the Communist Party in Vietnam by that name and refer to the "Revolution," regardless of its nominal designation at any given point in its history after 1930.

and patriotism that was to become the Party's hallmark. The collapse of Vietnamese traditional wisdom, so long in process, and the progressive influence of France on many students who went to school there or who read progressive French writers in Vietnam reinforced internationalist influences. Because the first Party youth groups were composed overwhelmingly of intellectuals, theory played a much greater role in gaining adherents initially than it did later, when the Party's concrete demands began to attract the masses.

Throughout its history Ho and other leaders of the Party argued that patriotism was consistent with proletarian internationalism and anticolonialism, which unified the interests of communists in all countries, but that nationalism was potentially reactionary. The Vietnamese Party went to extraordinary lengths to avoid any hint of chauvinism. Marxism, in an overtly relaxed manner, greatly influenced the Party, but precisely because it coexisted with so many influences in the culture, it emerges as a methodology rather than as a precise doctrine on every question. Its greatest influence was among those who were in prison, where studying Marxism became what Ho later called "turning what was a bad thing into a good thing."[1] Since the Party Central Committee in 1960 had spent a combined 222 years in prison and exile, the influence of systematic Marxism may ironically be seen as one of France's contributions to the formation of ideology. Young To Huu, who later became a Politburo member, was taken under the wing of such an ex-prisoner, but when he read *Capital* he complained, "I couldn't understand anything." Having failed, his mentor urged the next best course: "stay close to life—to the laboring masses, the workers, the peasants."[2]

Because it was relatively undogmatic and not exclusive and because the cultural diversity of the existing society was so great, the Party could transcend particularism to mobilize as many elements as possible behind the anticolonialist national-liberation banner and the cause of land revolution. More important, the Party absorbed much from traditional wisdom, even though it also criticized it.

Confucianism was a case in point, and it is futile to try to weight its influence, though it was clearly congenial as well as antithetical to many Party ideas. The matter is largely academic because far less important than the origins of a concept of personal behavior is the question why any large number of people at a given time act according to certain precepts. Every culture has doctrines of individual conduct, many of them theological in origin, and their correlation with socialist morality is not one of causation. Citing what is useful in them becomes a pragmatic rationale for many socialist movements seeking to exploit conventional wisdom for unconventional action, but their catalytic effect on the actions of masses is linked far more directly to their perception of the relationship of their conduct to goals they wish to attain. "Although Confucius was a feudalist and there are many erroneous things in his theory," Ho observed in 1950, "we must learn what is good in it."[3] Emphasis on ceaseless studying and teaching was one of these. A systematic code of personal conduct and morality can, of course, be defined independently of inherited influences and in accordance with universal criteria of individual behavior appropriate to Marxism. Yet only the Vietnamese Party was so deeply and consistently to stress standards of personal behavior—and the responsibility of individuals and Party to each other. And though the Party would in subsequent years work with adherents of far more objectionable theories, ranging from Trotskyists to religious entrepreneurs in the Mekong, its capacity to create as broad a following as possible around a minimal program was from the start a reflection of its nonsectarianism.

The Party's real strength, ultimately, was in its capacity to relate to the class needs of the majority of the nation. And its true originality was to emerge not in the field of abstract Marxist theory but in its development after 1945 of new concepts, and the organizational forms to implement them, of a Marxist-Leninist party as well as in its notions of the relationship of individuals to themselves, the Party, and the larger process of historical change.

Revolutionary ideology and culture in Vietnam embodied many things besides theoretical Marxism-Leninism: poetry, prison experiences, a sense of the land and its nuances, and the continuity of a number of important traditions. Vietnam's Communists avoided chauvinism and thereby early defined the relationship of Vietnam to a world movement and ideas. Ready to protect some aspects of the existing culture, they were also eager to change much of it. At its inception, however, Vietnamese Marxism was the heir to a transitional intellectual heritage that was also managing to produce a still minuscule revolutionary movement. Given the speed with which the society around them was changing economically and socially, it was crucial that the Communists be able to synthesize as many strands of radical and useful older ideas as possible and to relate to the sheer force of these irrepressible developments.

THE 1930S AND THE EMERGENCE OF THE INDOCHINESE COMMUNIST PARTY

Before World War Two the Communists underwent a long, painful period of learning and testing. Ho Chi Minh, in China and the USSR, shared indirectly in the trial, as the failures of others increasingly confirmed his prescience and wisdom while he remained isolated and, for practical purposes, deliberately ignored.

Ho Chi Minh came to Leninism via the colonial question, which Lenin was the first to see as crucial to the world revolution. Ho publicly excoriated the Western European Communist parties for their indifference to this issue, especially to the imperialism of their own nations. And this stress on colonialism meant adapting to the fact that the colonial masses were so overwhelmingly peasant that the Eurocentric Comintern's exclusive emphasis on the critical role of the proletariat was tactically both irrelevant and inappropriate to the future of the Asian Communist movement. Stalin, above all, did not sympathize with Lenin's thesis, and to the extent he could relate to the non-Soviet world he was always to remain essentially European. As Stalin consolidated control over the Comintern, his allies must have seen Ho as a nuisance during his stays in the USSR in 1924 and 1933–38. In the period after 1945 Stalin's suspicion of Ho was certainly open knowledge among leading world Communists.

The colonial and peasant questions were inseparable in reality, and Ho was surely aware of his disagreements with the Comintern in both substance and emphasis by no later than 1931. In a brilliant and original 1927 essay, Ho confronted the basic dilemma of the party of the proletariat in a peasant country—namely, how to fit the peasant into its strategy. It was, he argued, impossible not to do so. Not even the democratic bourgeois revolution could succeed in isolation. The party of the proletariat had to organize the initially spontaneous, isolated, and politically inchoate peasant actions around specific programs and coordinate them with its work in the industrial centers. In the Chinese context, he even argued for focusing on a smaller region which could serve as a base area for fighting in the rest of the country. Ho anticipated all of the crucial future strategic problems of the Vietnamese Revolution, from the political basis of warfare to the linkage of the city to the countryside.

Thanks to his Leninist appreciation of organization, Ho immediately comprehended the vastness and intrinsic decentralization of Vietnam and the need to relate to it with flexibility. Pluralism of tactics was the outcome within the framework of the primarily anticolonial objective. Although it would be a decade before the Party would fully share his views, his independence was clearly visible by the late 1920s. Ho was already becoming one of the most remarkable figures in modern times.

During Ho's 1925–27 stay in China as a Comintern representative, he had managed to create the Thanh Nien (Revolutionary Youth League) among Vietnamese exiles, but in Vietnam itself various essentially autonomous groups calling themselves Communist also existed among a handful of urban students of bourgeois origins, and, like all isolated organizations, they were soon locked in acrimonious disputes over sectarian issues. The Thanh Nien program was devoid of maximalist demands: it wanted a broad anticolonial united front led by workers and peasants, and while it had yet to overcome the ambiguity of the reality of the unimportance and transitional character of the working class, it was already clear in 1927 that Ho's greatest hopes were with the peasantry. But the group was effectively wiped out in China after 1927, and its remnants in Vietnam itself continued operating within the small working class. More important, Ho's personal prestige and charisma did not alter the reality that Moscow's views carried far more weight than his. Some of the former Thanh Nien members who had studied in Moscow, and who were more attuned to the post-1928 Comintern line stressing the need for proletarian purity and defining narrowly the basis for cooperation with other class elements, soon took command.

It was testimony to the nature of the times, the weakness of their potential Vietnamese rivals, and the stupidity of the French that the Communists were able not only to survive the ferocious repression of the 1930s but also to learn much that was essential to their future existence and success. It is too facile to suggest that the 1930s were the decade of crucial schooling and development for the Party, which in 1941 comprised only two or three thousand members, including those in prison; but its tactical and strategic judgments, its organizational structure, its future relations with the Soviet Union, and its sense of its own possibilities and limits were so linked to its profound awareness of its 1930s failures that it was never again to suffer an irreversible defeat. Between 1925 and 1939 there emerged the foundations for a distinctive Vietnamese Communist theory and practice.

Ho Chi Minh organized the founding meeting of the Vietnamese Communist Party in February 1930 in Hong Kong, bringing three disunited factions together and writing its first statement of tactics and its appeal. Making the proletariat the critical class leader, the statement nonetheless unequivocally emphasized the need to rally the peasantry by means of a land revolution coming at the expense of big landlords, feudalists, and imperialists and explicitly exempting rich peasants, middle and small landlords, and that all-encompassing but elusive and poorly defined class—the national bourgeoisie. Contact with such classes in order to neutralize them was crucial to what was to become the Party's most basic, explicit tactic—the creation of united fronts. The national independence and land questions were now linked as means and ends. In essence, the Party's future program was enunciated, but within months the Comintern denounced it as unprincipled, and the following October it was extensively but not completely modified when a Comintern-approved program was imposed along with selected leaders, compelling it to change its name to the Indochinese Communist Party. For at least three more years, Ho was reviled for alleged reformism, passing into almost total obscurity until 1939. Later, Ho and the Party made public many criticisms of the Party's 1931–39 policies.[4]

Uncontrollable events in Vietnam, most of them quite unrelated to the new Party's actions, made 1930–35 a period of immense losses and difficulties. The new ICP had approximately fifteen hundred members, plus many more sympathizers, but in a period of economic crisis and mass discontent it was to win—and lose—many more than this number. Agrarian unrest and workers' strikes reached startling proportions, and the Party's contact with working-class actions was important by virtue of the extensive colonizing of plantations and factories over the preceding years by its largely student membership. In one sense the 1930–31 and later upheavals caught the Party quite unprepared, but they also were partly responsible for them, for Vietnam was such a tinderbox that even a few Party members might have a disproportionately large impact. Events were not going to wait for the Party to get itself in order, but they were to teach it the necessity of being ready for the inevitability of decentralized spontaneous action. To some extent it tried to relate blindly to the most important of these, the famous Nghe Tinh upheavals, which lasted from May 1930 until mid-1931.

Nghe An and Ha Tinh provinces in Annam had an important industrial city, Vinh, which had been greatly affected by the depression. Party activities among workers there had begun only in March 1930, with the arrival of two organizers. They quickly managed to set up a cell, which in turn planned May Day demonstrations. Since many workers were really peasants in transition, their families and friends in the region were soon involved. Calamitous harvests in 1929–30 had made their debts and taxes insupportable. Three May Day marches became mass rallies, and instant French repression left dozens dead. The region was aflame for months, as vast demonstrations led to brutal repression and a further escalation of protests. Tax and administrative offices and their records were destroyed, seas of red flags emerged everywhere around the Party's slogans, and, as the French apparatus retreated from the carnage it had caused, the preponderantly peasant masses, led by the local *lettrés* and students who joined the Party at the time, spontaneously created soviets to administer power. By October, when the French were ready to suppress the revolt in earnest, many cantons and villages were being run by soviets. Between repression and famine the revolutionary power broke down over the following winter and spring, and then came the reckoning. Eventually, at least thirteen hundred people were killed by the French, and many times that number were imprisoned and deported. The last months of the soviets' rule saw the Party's new members and followers turn on each other, and poor peasants began wreaking their own vengeance on richer neighbors, dividing villages that had hitherto been united. Almost nothing, ultimately, was to be left of the Party in the area.

The Party outside the region was caught by surprise, and, though it thought the creation of the soviets premature and unwise, it could not denounce them. Publicly the ICP supported the Nghe Tinh rebels. There is ample evidence that many of the local members as well as the Party's regional committee ignored the central Party's general united-front line regarding rich and medium-peasants and intellectuals—whom the regional committee expelled. More important, there is no indication that direct Central Committee orders ever reached the region before events went beyond the point of no return or that the local rebels obeyed them thereafter.

Without doubt, the Party's Central Committee had lost control of the largest peasant upheaval of the interwar period. In the spring of 1931 the entire committee was arrested, along with nearly all the members of the three regional committees, and many were killed. Ho Chi Minh was picked up in Hong Kong and spent nearly two years in jail. About ten thousand political prisoners were in French jails in 1932. The ICP, with a provisional Central Committee in exile, virtually ceased to exist by 1932. The moral of Nghe Tinh was simple, the subsequent folklore about it notwithstanding. Although Ho later called it a stage of apprenticeship in the August 1945 Revolution, at the time both he and the more sectarian Party leaders thought it hopeless and dangerous to its larger strategy of a united front. In fact, Nghe Tinh showed the inevitability and the immense risks to the Party's future of spontaneous, mass action and made clear the need to guide such events toward some conscious goals, lest events pass the Party by with unpredictable, even fatal consequences.

Until the bitter lessons of the 1930s, including that of the dangers of following the Comintern policies too closely, had been fully felt and absorbed, a process that was to last until the outbreak of World War Two, a coherent organizational system, mobilization strategy, leadership, and even a deeper ideology involving more than slogans were not possible. At a theoretical level, the very process of survival deprived the Party's members of time for basic analyses, and the literalism of Moscow-trained young Vietnamese called in to fill the gaps in the organization was no help. Operating often from safe areas in Thailand and China, the Party's new leaders began to build another legal-front system and illegal structure in Vietnam.

The necessity of superior organization was evident, but even more urgent was a more nuanced balance of the national-independence and antifeudal banners, and the Comintern's stress on antifascist united-front activities after July 1935 attempted to respond to this need, though in fact it had divisive as well as positive consequences. The election, in May 1936, of the Popular Front in France, with its more lenient colonial administrative policies, aided the process and helped the Party grow. Throughout Vietnam the Party set up a large front network but at the same time retained an illegal network of Party cells to counter the repression it correctly believed would follow. It created, as well, working-class and mainly peasant organizations and cells and was able to play an important role in strikes and demonstrations throughout the quasi-legal period from mid-1936 until the outbreak of World War Two, in September 1939. At that time the Party had reconstituted itself and was larger than it had been at its founding. The failures and problems of the 1936–39 period notwithstanding—problems resulting from the eagerness of the Party to temporarily downplay its earlier demands that endangered unity with the national bourgeoisie—it was evolving toward a successful organization and style, particularly regarding front groups. More important, a new and more creative leadership was moving to the fore. In a word, the Party gained a great deal in wisdom, flexibility, and maturity after a long and costly period of youthful errors.[5]

THE PARTY AND WORLD WAR TWO MOBILIZATION

World War Two immediately undermined the French colonial structure in Indochina, and Vichy's collaboration with Germany beginning in June 1940, and with Japan after its consenting in September 1940 to the stationing of Japanese troops, fatally delegitimized the old regime as anticolonialism and antifascism became synonymous. Both before and after Ho Chi Minh's return to Vietnam in February 1941 and the creation of the Viet Minh (Front for the Independence of Vietnam) in May 1941, the basic strategic decision confronting the Party was the relation of the land and peasant question to the issue of the united front, national independence, and the existing class structure, particularly the place of larger landowners and the so-called national bourgeoisie. The Party was intent on avoiding political isolation, and it made a united front at the cost of its social program a paramount goal of its strategy. Its assumption was that the more elements it could recruit into a united front, the fewer potential enemies would remain to challenge it. These issues were to persist in various forms for thirty-five more years.

When the war broke out, the Party instructed its members to go underground in the rural areas, but over two thousand were nonetheless arrested, including many of its key leaders who had been loyal to the Comintern's policies. All of the other small anticolonialist groups disappeared into prisons or exile or turned to collaboration, leaving the Party without rivals. The Party soon began to grow, mobilizing people unencumbered by the doctrinal confusions of the preceding decade. More crucial, its new leaders were politically and personally congenial nonsectarians of Ho's persuasion who saw the primacy of Vietnamese conditions: Truong Chinh, Pham Van Dong, and Vo Nguyen Giap were among them. From this time onward there emerged a collegial, cooperative, yet creative leadership, free of the problems of egoism, that was to provide continuity for the next four decades. Their harmony became a fundamental source of the Party's strength and a basic reason why it avoided the leadership problems which were to plague other Marxist-Leninist parties.

Seeking to define a program and tactics to guide the vast changes racking Vietnam after 1941, the Party embarked on its effort to direct history or, more often, not be swept aside by uncontrollable forces and its own initial weaknesses. Errors, however, continued to cause immense losses, and no other event illustrated this better than the Nam Ky insurrection in the Mekong Delta, which the Party's Cochin Chinese regional committee began to plan in July 1940. Events over the next six months revealed the risks inherent in a situation in which coordination between the Party's higher committees and remote rural areas was intrinsically tenuous, and the Party unable to restrain its local organizations. Both the regional committee and the Central Committee attempted to postpone the revolt, but the former was divided and vacillated, and the uprising began at the end of November and lasted nearly two months in a large area of the Delta. Revolutionary committees took power and in some areas redistributed land. If the genesis of the upheaval was no more spontaneous than Nghe Tinh a decade earlier, what was clear in both cases was that once the process of struggle began, the Party's highest levels could not direct it. Distance and poor communication meant loss of centralized control, especially over the quite independent southern Party. No less clear, as the French proved in arresting nearly six thousand people and killing hundreds, including many of the Party's key leaders, was that the entire Party would pay dearly for actions it thought ill-timed or incorrect. The Cochin Chinese Party, once the strongest in Vietnam, was now shattered, and it would take many years to rebuild it.

The tension between an imposition of its mastery and the autonomous dynamics of change is the greatest challenge confronting a revolutionary party seeking to shape the outcome of historical processes. Under Ho the Party for four more years faced this dilemma by pursuing a cautious strategy to husband its remaining, depleted organization. In a period of immense upheavals and possibilities, the most remarkable aspect of the Viet Minh's tactics was that although they repeatedly failed to preserve the Party in vast areas, particularly cities, in the end the times and international balance of forces favored its basic strategy. It was its acute sense of the implications of the global context and geopolitics to Vietnam, based on an analysis of the meaning of the war to France and the pre-1939 world order, that defined the Party's tactics and overall strategy. The events from the time the harried Party went into hiding in an ethnic minority region along the Chinese border, or operated clandestinely in the populous French and Japanese-occupied areas, to the time it took over Vietnam, in August 1945, were among the most remarkable of the entire Second World War. They revealed both how either inconsequential or decisive the role of self-conscious people and organizations in history might become from one context and time to another.

The Viet Minh program minimized the land question in order to attract as many diverse elements as possible, including landowners, to its front organizations. It proposed to redistribute only the lands of Frenchmen and their Vietnamese collaborators, but the Viet Minh's lack of extensive control in the deltas made even the Party's modest goals difficult to attain. More important, and simpler to implement, was its new stress on rent and interest reduction, crucial issues to the peasants. So while the Party subdued its peasant program on behalf of a patriotic coalition, it by no means abandoned it. Despite its failure in some areas, the Viet Minh became synonymous with the national resistance to a discredited colonial order now allied with Japanese imperialism. Cao Dai and Hoa Hao collaboration with the Japanese and French cost the only other two forces with a peasant base their legitimacy, and the small elitist parties and royal family followed the same route of temporary accommodation with those in power and ultimate self-destruction.

The Party's success at this crucial point in its history was the result of its capacity to survive physically and politically in a political vacuum. Its contacts with diverse social elements gave those among the non-Communists who were patriots a focus for their own defense of the nation. But the Party's attainments were relative, and linked to its ability to understand and respond, if only cautiously, to the vast events around it. Its numbers were still very small, probably two or three thousand by 1944. Its base areas were isolated, and its arms inconsequential. Its urban organization was decimated and haphazard, despite good relations with students and the intelligentsia, and in August 1942 Ho went to China to obtain support from the Allies, was arrested, and after fourteen months in Chinese jails, often under indescribable conditions, and another year under restricted movement, he returned to Vietnam in September 1944. In the meantime the Party's collective strength and sense of its own limits, as well as the propitious times, caused it to survive and grow.

World War Two produced the crisis of French colonialism in Indochina and immense changes in all of Asia, and the Party's successes after 1942 were the effect of that upheaval. Until 1945, when the Party for the first time became a creative factor shaping events, it realistically understood its dependent relationship to the forces of change and its need to be both willing and strong enough to strike when the French were no longer able to rule.

Having created a front and an inclusive patriotic ideology, the Party established links with urban and educated elements not yet willing to join it. Its contacts with the peasantry, despite its subdued land reform program, were much stronger and were to prove far more crucial than it initially appreciated. It did not then believe that the urbanized intelligentsia was too unstable or the working class too transitional to collaborate with it for very long, much less that its most durable support would come from the peasantry.

The Party had a spectrum of issues with which it could relate to the peasantry in the short run, even though the land question's fundamental significance meant that the peasantry's role would inevitably prove crucial to *any* broad or protracted mobilization of the nation. Usury and rent were vital immediate questions, less divisive to its united-front strategy than land redistribution, but tradition and patriotism were others. All soon became synonymous because war and growing French and Japanese demands began gravely to challenge the peasantry's existence far more than the inherited land system did. For despite the traditional order's great internal contradictions and tensions, it still offered more stability than the mounting wartime chaos. Famine and disaster were soon to force a desperate peasantry toward a collective response to its problems. The conditions that French colonialism had created in Vietnam now incubated under the pressure of catastrophic wartime disorder to present the Party with its rare, monumental opportunity to seize power if it could.[6]

European imperialism's fatal decline in Asia, and an essentially fragile Japan's effort to move into the huge void, meant that the Communist Party could hope to win, despite its tiny organization before 1945, because it had no rivals in its challenge to French imperialism. The underdeveloped and venal nature of the other classes and parties made its monopoly over the resistance to France astonishingly easy. Its acquisition of power in August 1945 was to be based not on military might but rather on its organizational and political ability to cope with the terribly destructive impact of the Japanese-French war machine on the Vietnamese economy and society. For the moment, at least, its power was a passive one: it avoided illusions and comprehended the reasons for acting modestly in focusing only on the perfection of an organization capable of making an appropriate decision with some reasonable hope of implementing it. Impersonal wartime processes, at first beyond the Party's control, merged with its conscious efforts to guide changes, interacting as repression and resistance blended and a potential for radical political action was created.

The paradox and dilemma of action is that the operations of war can produce resistance of untold dimensions, and it was Vietnam's destiny to confront the bloodiest and longest of modern history. And the institutional dynamics war unleashes, its consequences for people, classes, and real social forces, changes the framework of revolutionary analysis and action and carries with it structural consequences which persist far beyond the duration of a conflict. The risk of action, and the reward of success, is to have to cope with the new material and social factors that war creates. Clarity of analysis and realism in action become never-ending demands and preconditions of a radical party's survival and triumph.

War is also a critical, frequently exclusive goad to human actions in a political context, imposing at various times both unavoidable restraints and the obligation of action. As actual and potential victims of the conflict, individuals begin to make otherwise unimaginable decisions. Immense personal suffering is possible and often inevitable. The existential problem for the individual in this context has immense social and organizational consequences, and war mobilizes masses, enrolls them, presses them into service, but also leaves few of the apathetic unscathed. If the individual sees his fate outside a social and community context and ignores the relationship of personal actions to a common destiny, then presumably he will find a private solution—even if it leads him in some cases to support the revolution, so long as it is convenient, or the American- or French-backed side when that is safer. If class and community becomes the individual's basis of adjustment, then the revolution is likely to gain an adherent. The tensions of class conflict come to the fore as events dissolve the ties binding an existing society together. That choices between sides must be made is often the inevitable consequence of the war's politicization of society. But the very galvanizing effect of war, its irresistible mobilization of larger and larger numbers and its transformation of rural existence, creates a new context for action.

Chapter 3

Vietnam: From the August 1945 Revolution to Protracted War

THE AUGUST REVOLUTION

The August Revolution set the stage for the Communist Party's coming to power. The Viet Minh in December 1944 created its first armed units mainly for purposes of political agitation, and while it had functional control of six of the more isolated northern border provinces by June 1945 and its armed forces continued to expand, its military power remained negligible. The August Revolution itself was only incidentally the work of armed men. More precisely, it was a Communist-led general uprising of the people throughout the country, in which the masses played the part of a largely unarmed body moving into the political vacuum Japan's defeat created.

Ho discouraged any military actions likely to endanger the organizational work and security of Party members. He and his associates had carefully estimated the world balance of forces and the positions of France and Japan, fully appreciating the tensions between them and the implications for colonialism of an Axis defeat. Too much had been lost at Nghe Tinh and Nam Ky for them to risk premature adventures. By the time the Japanese in March 1945 formally removed the French from nominal control of Indochina—in reality they had been following Japan's bidding since 1940 —more crucial events were defining Vietnam's future.

Mass mobilization is the Marxist's key to power. Because its united-front policy inhibited drastic action on the land issue, the Party hesitated until the colonial administration created the galvanizing issue that would reach the majority of the people. Until then, despite certain relative successes, the Viet

Minh could only consolidate and plan for the power vacuum that would exist at the end of the war. This it did by authorizing local Viet Minh groups to determine how to act at the critical moment, but it did not expect to see millions of people acting with it and virtually guaranteeing its triumph and monopoly of power. Indeed, it even expected an Allied landing to be essential to its strategy, for it did not predict a time for the end of the war or expect the Japanese to transfer power so easily.

The decisive organizing issue was the slogan "Break open the rice stores to avert famine," and while national independence was linked to it, patriotism alone could not mobilize the masses. If anything, for the peasantry independence was mainly an organizational prerequisite for dealing with social problems. And though the Party in 1943 had not predicted the importance of starvation, it alone among all the forces in Vietnam was able to relate to the emergency.

The food crisis was the result of the French agreement to supply Japan with Vietnamese rice and at the same time with agricultural raw materials —cotton, jute, and oil seeds—which required the conversion of rice lands. Tonkin was affected first by these decrees; since it was normally an importer of rice from the Mekong, it was not long before the gravity of the policy was felt. Peasants and landlords who resisted conversion of their lands soon were beaten and arrested, and even killed. Those who could not supply their rice quota had to purchase it on the open market, which meant ruin. In 1943, despite a good harvest in Tonkin, there were still severe shortages; 1944 was a disaster year in Tonkin, and a lack of transport from the south led to the use there of rice and corn as fuel for generators. The first to suffer from famine were the poor peasants, and during 1944 death from hunger spread throughout the north, claiming by March 1945 a minimum of one million and perhaps as many as two million lives—or up to one-fifth of Tonkin's population. A vast flow of starving humanity moved from the countryside to the cities in search of food.

In this context of immense human suffering, the Viet Minh in March 1945 decided to fill the administrative gap the Japanese eviction of the French had created, calling on the masses to seize rice stores. The people responded quickly and decisively. In a moment the Viet Minh united front became the party of action and of the nation. It was clear to most Vietnamese that the movement both for economic reconstruction and even physical survival and for independence would be led by the Viet Minh or by no one. Its rivals were in disorder: compromised, divided, indecisive, or small. During the spring of 1945 the Viet Minh recruited vast numbers of peasants throughout Tonkin and dealt with the famine, all the while preparing its new supporters for the imminent struggle for control of Vietnam the moment the Japanese fell. Even urban elements that had hitherto wavered now saw the Viet Minh as the only force capable of dealing with the country's problems, and the food question moved and unified the nation as nothing earlier had done.

When the Viet Minh declared a general insurrection on August 12, days after the Japanese offer to surrender, the millions of euphoric people who filled the streets of Hanoi, Hué, Saigon, and dozens of other cities also led to Viet Minh takeovers of villages and towns everywhere and transformed a numbed population into a virtually unarmed insurrectionary force. What had initially been a peasant mass movement now merged with the urban population to strike at the crucial organs of the colonial system in the cities, a synthesis that created an indelible model for the Party's future strategy. The enthusiasm and power of the masses had brought to power a party which saw itself as both an agent of history and a creator of historical change. The war's trauma and the Party had converted the people into a conscious force and had led to a transformation of Vietnam's history. The forward momentum of this upheaval was to prove irresistible for decades because although there were accidental dimensions to the vast event, there also remained a vital element of predictability and control. An oft-destroyed Party, numbering merely five thousand in August 1945, had made many errors but had also learned many lessons. It understood the limits of the historical situation so well that it comprehended its possibilities too, for the human experience involves constraints and opportunity at one and the same time. By September 2, 1945, when the Viet Minh declared the Democratic Republic of Vietnam, the Communist Party had already attained a high degree of political, ideological, and organizational maturity. It would need all of these qualities—and more—in abundance as it passed from the stage of clandestine organizing to the beginning of a war that was to become the longest of the twentieth century.[1]

CREATING A NATIONAL COALITION

The next fifteen years were to be a period of critical development and testing of the Party's knowledge, ideas, and administrative talents, but now set on a much larger scale of national power and, increasingly, international forces. By the end of that time, about 1961, the Revolution was to confront the United States in a new context both within the country and in the world.

The essence of revolutionary strategy is mobilization of the masses, whose energies and commitments in a poor nation may be the only durable material and organizational resources for progress in all domains of existence. The August Revolution against foreign control would not have occurred without mass action for mass needs, regardless of the international situation, and any political strategy had, as in the past, to juxtapose external forces and pressures with internal social dynamics. In a basic sense the Party was still balancing its social program, particularly land reforms, against its much stronger desire to sustain a national united front inclusive of all classes as long as the danger of foreign intervention existed. It was to succeed in this intrinsically precarious maneuver until 1953.

The united-front strategy led the Party to declare in November 1945 that it had dissolved itself into a study association, a fiction it discarded in 1950 when it reemerged as the Lao Dong (Workers) Party. The presence of 150,000 Chinese troops north of the sixteenth parallel and the British and French armies south of it unquestionably stimulated this gesture. Given the extreme delicacy of its military position and the imminence of war with France despite the nine months' grace won with the Franco-DRV agreement of March 1946, the Party considered gaining time to consolidate its military and political power the highest priority. Its caution in the past appeared warranted by its success in the present, and its belief that time was always on the side of revolutionaries who knew how to measure their own actions and estimate the weaknesses of their enemy reinforced this irrefutable calculation.

In 1946 a national consensus sustained the Viet Minh, and, as Nguyen Cao Ky recalled thirty years later, "Ho Chi Minh became a national hero."[2] That consensus at this juncture was its most precious asset, and its social program was geared to protecting it. The Viet Minh's most urgent task, therefore, was to cope with the famine and create an effective administrative structure on the basis of the vast mobilization which had swept it to power. For as long as it had the option, the Party successfully worked through the united front, basing its strategy on a class analysis of Vietnamese society and sensing the temporary weakness as well as potential strength of the vast influx of new Party members. It thus made land questions secondary, in the hope of preventing the defection of wealthier elements that supported the Party-controlled provisional government and whose economic resources were still important to the teetering DRV. Time was essential in order to prepare the Viet Minh military forces for conflict with the French and to transform new Party members from simple patriots into Communists ready for the long struggle which the Party saw coming.

The effort to master the famine after August 1945 was accompanied by a vast literacy campaign to transform the peasantry, 95 percent of which was functionally illiterate. Saving lives, making ten million people literate, and linking both endeavors to the anti-French struggle involved a monumental economic and cultural transformation which tangibly and intangibly strengthened the Party's position. The successful campaigns against famine and illiteracy allowed new cooperative organizational and human structures to emerge during the critical months until December 1946, as the French and the Revolution jockeyed for control of administrative organs, symbols of power, and negotiated—all the while preparing to fight if necessary. Mass mobilization by means of fronts and Party recruitment and an elementary cultural revolution became the foundations of the Party's first strategy while in power. By December 1946, after the French bombarding of Haiphong on November 23 and the departure of the new government to the carefully prepared guerilla zones, the Party had irrevocably consolidated its power.

The DRV's 1946 constitution guaranteed the right to private property, and private enterprises existed parallel with the state sector in the liberated zones after the war with the French began in December 1946. The Party had constantly to meet, avoid, or resolve a myriad of domestic challenges, potential pitfalls, and complex problems. The first challenge came from the Cao Dai, which had during 1945–46 switched from supporting the Japanese to backing the Viet Minh, but as French military power grew it put its militia on the French payroll from 1947 onward, despite wavering and minority opposition, giving the colonial power effective control within the Cao Dai's suzerainty. Another dilemma was posed by the small Chinese-backed parties that wished to fight the French immediately, thereby protracting the Chinese military occupation. The Party also had to create an army and define a military strategy, a matter of primordial importance. Any diversion from the resolution of these difficulties entailed serious risks. The thorniest issue to contend with was the class struggle over land.

Despite growing problems, the Party's efforts until 1950 to mobilize the population and neutralize opposition by a united front marked a period of immense finesse. "The Communists are playing a winning game" in their internal strategy, the CIA reported in September 1949. The "vast majority" of the people, including a majority of the generally anti-Communist Catholics, supported Ho Chi Minh in the fight against the French.[3]

THE PARTY AND THE DILEMMA OF
LAND REFORM

The Party tried to postpone the land problem as long as it felt insecure militarily and was free to do so. But its ultimate social base was the peasantry, particularly once the French controlled all cities after 1947. Sooner or later the ramifications of the land and peasant question had to touch fundamental political, military, and economic policies, and this was surely one of the most delicate issues the Party confronted for eight years. Stated simply, the question was whether the Revolution could fight a protracted war by motivating the masses with predominantly patriotic as opposed to class appeals.

The new DRV government in November 1945 called for a 25 percent reduction in land rents and for a redistribution of the lands of the French and of those landlords who had collaborated with them or abandoned their land. These decrees were applied unevenly, or not at all in many regions, and during 1946 the Party in Cochin China had to discourage poor peasants seeking to redivide lands belonging to apolitical landlords. Throughout 1946 and 1947 the Party opposed any land policy likely to drive landlords into the French camp, making it clear there was no place for "leftist" experiments. The August Revolution was a national democratic revolution, Truong Chinh, the Party's secretary-general, announced, and did not endorse an "agrarian revolution."[4] Landlords after August 1945 began to take over many local village administrations; some even joined the Party and played an appreciable role in enforcing policies involving their own material interests. In January 1948 the Party was forced to deal with the issue as modestly as possible, demanding an application of the 1945 law on rent reduction and a temporary repartitioning of mainly communal lands (of consequence only in Tonkin and Annam) on behalf of poor peasants as well as of those in the army. Priority was given to those who fought, and land was beginning to be used in a relatively small way as an incentive to those ready to make sacrifices in combat. At the same time, wages to farm labor, now in short supply and able to extract better terms, were to be controlled so that the landlords did not lose too much. Until July 1949 the Party's strategy was, in effect, to try to cajole peasants and landlords into doing their utmost within an inclusive united front.

The inadequacy of this approach emerged during 1948 when the French began to reoccupy rural sectors of Tonkin and when many landlords, including some who had supported the Revolution, became collaborators. Apathy and alienation increasingly threatened the taxes on land which sustained the Revolutionary treasury. More important, the peasants needed a greater motivation for the risks they were now called upon to take.

The opportunism of the Cao Dai in the south and the landlords in the north revealed that the Party could not take for granted durable support for the Viet Minh and that it could not separate the economics and politics of mass mobilization. No less crucial was the emergence of *attentisme*, the readiness of many people to float with the political and military tides in order to make certain that they were always on the winning side. It became a serious obstacle—and indeed remained one until 1975—to the attempt to estimate the true support the Party had and to determine whom it could rely on. The worst of all possible worlds would be a policy of conciliation that failed to gain the enthusiastic support of a major class.

Studying the situation closely, the Party found that over two-thirds of the landlords were not respecting the reform laws. In July 1949 the Party took a firmer line on behalf of its earlier decrees, giving poor peasants and tenants first priority to lands put up for temporary redistribution. Within these two categories, however, those who worked for the Revolution or fought for it, or their families if they were dead, received preference. The following May it attacked usurious interest and wiped out all debts predating August 1945. Although lands of landlords supporting the Revolution or neutral were not touched, the rise of collaboration made more land available even as the French presence rendered its allocation more difficult. Fearing the destruction of the united front, the Party still hesitated to employ land as its primary mobilization weapon. But it now began exploiting the land issue, in addition to making more abstract patriotic appeals, and understood far better its importance and potential.

Available statistics leave much to be desired, but it appears that 254,000 hectares belonging to the French and collaborators were redistributed during 1949–51 to about half a million peasants. Most of this land was in Cochin China. In Tonkin very little noncommunal land was distributed before July 1949, but between 1949 and 1953 some private land was taken, even though landlords and rich peasants in 1953 still possessed 59 percent of their original holdings.

The evolution of the Party's land position reflected, in the last analysis, the weakness of its assumptions regarding the united front and the well-to-do classes' motives. Even when it was unable to tolerate the serious liabilities of a front strategy, it backed away from it only temporarily, returning to it later. The tension between the class struggle and the united front remained a constant dilemma for the Party, one which the masses themselves created.

In mid-1948 Truong Chinh was arguing that French aggression had produced "many revolutionary classes" in Vietnam, even though the working class was the most revolutionary. By 1951 he was less emphatic, since a significant number of the united front's non-Communist members had turned to collaboration or had withdrawn from politics. The national bourgeoisie was essentially nationalist and democratic; though it had equivocal sectors and was a "conditional" ally, "the national bourgeois in general sympathize with the resistance." The petite bourgeoisie of small traders, craftsmen, and intelligentsia in its own way was the least recalcitrant element of the front, and a "reliable" ally. In fact the opportunism of its former allies was acknowledged but never explored analytically, for in a nation with no important industrialization, and in which precious little large-scale non-agricultural economic activity was in non-Chinese hands, the very concept of a national bourgeoisie was an ideological legacy from the Party's 1920–40 period that would later reemerge repeatedly to influence and confound its strategy. Tactically, however, in a period of mass mobilization for armed struggle in which illusions could prove costly, the Party put emphasis on the peasantry, the working class's "most loyal and most powerful ally," for "without the participation of the peasantry, the Vietnamese revolution certainly cannot succeed." Among these, the poor and the landless peasants were most crucial. Although the small proletariat, a mere 4 percent of the population, was the only class capable of leading the revolution and the united front, the ties with the land of even its members left it "not yet purely proletarian."[5]

TOWARD A REVOLUTIONARY
MILITARY STRATEGY

At the same time when the land weapon was being sharpened and the perplexing vestiges of the united-front strategy resolved, the Party also had to construct a military structure and theory. In the most fundamental sense, however, the questions of mass mobilization and military mobilization were one and the same. Equally crucial was the creation of the military arm during the period after September 1945, when the Party was transformed from a small elite into a mass organization.

The theory and practice of the Party's military force are well known. The first armed units which Vo Nguyen Giap led in 1944 were political organizing groups, numbering five thousand partially armed men by spring 1945, and the military's cardinal rules were determined at its inception, to some extent because of Ho's insistence that it avoid premature combat. Simply stated, the Party's military theory was to rely on the masses for manpower and support and to fight only when there was a reasonable chance to attain its objectives. The military techniques that such a highly politicized premise involved were to develop and vary over the decades with the Party's changing resources and aims, but the alterations were quantitative only. The political cadre from the start became decisive to the operations, goals, and very essence of the military. More important, the most critical role that military power played from 1945 to 1975 was to create a security screen to protect the political and nonmilitary activities of Party members. In the 1946–48 period this was especially important. But the military's ultimate strength was the support and sacrifices of the people among whom it moved, and without whom it would have lacked men, matériel, cover, and intelligence. In this human context no army which was not suffused with politics —indeed, was not political first and military second—could hope to achieve its objectives. And against the enemies it confronted, such a political people's war was the only kind with any hope of victory.

If the Party's caution and use of force for political goals was the keystone of its grand strategy, its highly developed sense of the balance of forces militarily and politically guided its shorter-range decisions. This acute perception always informed its view of itself, the world, and history. But the unsuccessful mass uprisings in 1930–31 and 1940 profoundly influenced it, for the consequences of defeat had been seared into the lives and minds of virtually every Party member of importance. Its politics and diplomacy in 1946 was influenced by this obsession not to fight prematurely, and thereafter only at a time and place of its own choosing.

The totally political basis of the creation of the People's Liberation Army (PLA) and the impact of the Party's great failures before 1945 were critical, but so was the fact that its greatest triumph was a result of its successes in the cities in August 1945, when the Party's strategically decisive role far outweighed its numbers. For the Party's enemies were located in the cities. The doctrine of a general uprising involving cities, and the proletariat's role in it, later reemerged to define its actions. Although the Revolution during 1946 created a regular army of about eighty thousand and a vast irregular force and after December 1946 took virtually all of its urban-based members into rural areas, the Party always saw the urban and rural fronts as linked in a comprehensive fashion, if only because cities and towns had been areas crucial to the creation of the Party and because most of its senior leaders came from them. And given its class character, and the role of the militant proletariat in it and united-front strategy based on it, the mass struggle in cities remained important in the Party's general strategy even when it was a dormant aspect of its military theory. This belief in the rough equivalence of urban and rural fronts created only one of several fundamental distinctions between Vietnamese and Chinese Communist military doctrines.

The Party needed time, of course, to create and arm a coherent military, but its political analysis of its enemies and their position in the world and internal contradictions determined its definition of its tactics. To allow the balance of forces to weigh France down, Truong Chinh explained in the spring of 1947, "to achieve all these results, the war must be prolonged, and we must have time. Time is on our side—time will be our best strategist, if we are determined to pursue our resistance to the end." Premature battles with excessively large forces would be heroic but suicidal. Positional warfare would lead to doom if it became an end in itself, and in the meantime guerilla and mobile war—based on surprise and quick dispersal, ambush and harassment, and sabotage—would receive the main emphasis. With more arms positional warfare might prove a useful secondary form, "according to the concrete objective and subjective conditions at each particular time and place," but only with guerilla warfare could the people's decisive role come into play. "The people are the eyes and the ears of the army, they feed and keep our soldiers. It is they who help the army in sabotage and in battle.

The people are the water and our army the fish. The people constitute an inexhaustible source of strength for the army."[6]

Such a war without fronts would wear out and disperse the enemy, exposing him to attack. It would go through three stages, the first being a defensive stage in which Truong Chinh speculated there would be highly mobile warfare in both rural and urban areas in which the PLA would fight flexibly, only at the time and place of its choosing, and attempt to conserve its forces. Eventually, the war would pass into a stage of equilibrium, in which the PLA would take the offensive with many small attacks and guerilla warfare, wearing the enemy out and attacking him piecemeal. Ambushes would be important, and regular, militia, and guerilla forces would be coordinated. This key stage was to see the Revolution's forces increase their mobility and prepare for the final stage of the general counteroffensive. At this point the political and economic contradictions in France would prove critical. Tactically, many guerilla units would resort to coordinated mobile combat, and eventually mobile warfare would turn into positional warfare for key points, including cities. This stage, the shortest, would lead to the breakdown of the enemy army, which would become demoralized. Final victory would occur on the battlefield.

The essence of the Revolutionary military doctrine was always a theory of an army as a political organization and of its relations to the masses. This concept was inviolable. Ho Chi Minh enunciated it in April 1948, shortly after the Revolution had taken the initiative, in his "Twelve Recommendations" to soldiers and all those in contact with the masses. Local customs were to be respected faithfully, and the people were also to be helped in their daily work. Nothing could be done to hurt their property, nor could they be forced to part with their goods by any means. The masses had to be respected and helped, for victory was "built with the people as foundation."[7]

French strategy caused many variations in the PLA's timing of its military doctrine, but they were always differences of degree rather than of kind. The doctrine's essential principles, modified by vast experience, were greatly to influence the Party's war with the United States as well. What remained constant was people's war, fought ultimately for political purposes and in a political context. By the time, in February 1950, seven months before the French lost the vast area north of the Red River, the Party announced it was going over to the third stage of the general counteroffensive, it had managed to build a coherent military organization out of the ragtag structure existing in 1946, and its access to Chinese Communist arms after 1950 was vital to its planning and possibilities. It had also created a Party that was capable of giving political direction to vast military, administrative, and economic undertakings.

Chapter 4

The Internal World of Vietnamese Communism: Theory and Practice

The Communist Party's ability to confront all of the monumental challenges of the war with the United States was to a critical degree the result of its development of an organization and a method of analysis during its first decade in power. Comprehending its theory and practice during this period is indispensable to understanding the reasons for its toughness, durability, and success after 1960.

THE DEVELOPMENT OF THE COMMUNIST PARTY

The five thousand Party members at the time of the August Revolution were profoundly political people whose knowledge, character, and continuity were to remain a crucial asset to the Party. Revolutionary politics, in its purest form, is a question of constant personal choices regarding one's life and commitments. Only those who forgo personal comfort, repeatedly risk imprisonment and even death, and accept the certainty of ceaseless toil and deprivations can develop a special élan and a mutual confidence in each other's motives. Until August 1945 the Party's members were persons of this special, rare breed of true revolutionaries. They were few in number because in no country, in any age, are there many people ready to devote their lives to causes offering so little chance of success and so great a certainty of sacrifices in every aspect of their existence. Many were from relatively well-off families and could easily have chosen less trying paths in their lives.

A significant proportion of them were highly educated and all were devoted Marxists, since years in jail had given them ample time to refine their own life commitments and to study and discuss. All understood the importance of the international context in which Vietnam's future would be shaped.

Similar personal qualities emerged among many who joined the Party after August 1945. The majority were from petit bourgeois families; to cope with the dilemma of the Party's self-assigned role as the proletariat leading all other classes in a nation with only a tiny one, it was said as late as 1961 that anyone who joined the party "joined the ranks of the working class."[1] But there was no hiding the fact that the Party now had a degree of power and the potential of gaining it totally, and for a significant minority joining it was a means of advancing themselves, ultimately, in a manner that would otherwise have been impossible. And no matter how diverse the motives of the new Party adherents, all also assumed great administrative or military responsibilities. They had little time to study what the Party's leaders had painfully assimilated over a much longer period. The Leninist role and conception of the Party, in effect, had changed dramatically, its elite quality being endangered for the sake of mass mobilization and the creation of a state apparatus.

The Party membership grew from 5,000 in August 1945 to 20,000 at the end of 1946, 50,000 at the end of 1947, and 180,000 at the end of 1948—66,000 of the latter being in the south. At the end of 1949 the Party had 700,000 members. The class origins of recruits were largely ignored, their education was neglected, and the pressure to enlist members—especially in the south and in major cities—was far greater than the desire to maintain high standards.

The Party's leadership immediately perceived the dangers in its growing mass of functionaries, and by October 1945 Ho was castigating some members of the people's committees, including those in the Party, for abuse of power, favoritism, and corruption. Too many, Truong Chinh complained in September 1946, had been taken from former employees of the old regime. In 1948 Ho publicly admitted that many cadres had been recruited too quickly and were not well trained, a problem he was to return to often. But in 1951, as soon as the Party felt secure, it used the occasion of its fiscal crisis to begin firing at least one-third of the members of the state's nonmilitary administration over a two-year period. By 1960 the Party's membership also had been reduced by about the same proportion.[2]

It was in this context that the Party's leadership was compelled to define the very nature and meaning of the Party. From 1946 through the next decade and a half, the Party systematically and publicly constructed its own, unique theoretical system. Mainly a response to the problems of membership growth, the war with France also influenced the form and content of its concepts. In effect, the Party's Leninist ideological heritage had to be merged with the exigencies of the long struggle for power, the responsibilities of directing it, and the knowledge gained from experience. This synthesis was explained to its many members, patiently and repeatedly, in the hope they could grasp and apply Marxist analytic tools specific to Vietnam's conditions and lead lives capable of producing a revolutionary culture and socialist men and women. By 1960, when their fundamental contours were fully outlined, these values and ideas were central to the Revolution's strategy and tactics in its monumental war with the United States.

The Party's views on the nature of its leadership, decision making, and bureaucracy, the relationship of the Party to the masses, the role of cadres and personalities, the values and motives of Party members, and the self-critical and adaptive function of discussion were all interrelated components of its general theory even when it treated them as separate topics.

The Party's various ideas were subsumed to a great measure under the abstract concept of historical materialism, which the leaders invariably applied concretely whenever they could, so that while in inspiration and broad methodology its theory was Marxist, in application it was an attempt to cope with Vietnam's distinctive conditions. The question of the relationship of economic development and the historical process to conscious action and the human will suffused the Party's thought and action for thirty years. Its mode of reasoning and perception was persuasive so long as it appealed to rationality rather than to blind faith in the Party's mass of new members, without whom the struggle would quickly have ceased, and possessed the inherent validity and capacity to evoke realistic, successful actions capable of giving form to alternatives in history and society.

To make choices and decisions relevant to reality, the Party believed that its study of an exceedingly complex past had to be combined with a grasp of the nature of critical forces, and particularly of the balance between them, in the present. Social phenomena, Le Duan argued in 1966, have too many complicated and interacting causes to allow for simplifications. Without such comprehension, which took both time and subtlety, the Party could not "find out the rules governing the dialectical development of things, and, of course, [could not] manipulate this development."[3] "The revolutionary leader," Vo Nguyen Giap recollected about the period after 1945, "must find out the general and particular laws of events in a maze of phenomena in which the false is hardly distinguishable from the true. . . . The accurate, scientific forecast of trends . . . is of the utmost importance in revolutionary work. . . . a true forecast is the work of geniuses."[4]

To study history and understand it was to gain a necessary but hardly sufficient condition for changing it. The Party's leaders were not merely military and political administrators but also intellectuals with an exceptionally nuanced curiosity about many topics. They never tired of reading and discussing, and their essential conclusions and methodology were invariably published, especially after 1954. As Marxists they understood that time and history, as an abstraction, favored the revolutionary cause. As men who had spent years in prison, they knew that a naive reliance on destiny without a concrete sense of timing and its relation to action would produce the Party's inevitable destruction, since historical materialism without a decisive role for human consciousness and action was just a frivolous café topic. Structural developments and objective laws largely beyond the Party's control created potentially prerevolutionary situations with which the Party's clarity and consciousness, leading to correct ideas and decisions, had to interact dialectically to create qualitatively new circumstances from which revolutionary possibilities might emerge. To aspire to change history, according to this view, one had also to be aware of how and why the task was difficult and slow; in effect, an understanding of one's own limitations was essential to one's abilities. Tactics had to reflect this knowledge in order for these limitations to be overcome. It was better not to act than to act hastily and foolishly. History was not a blank check onto which the Party could inscribe its desires. But neither was it an impersonal process to which political people abandoned themselves. First, social forces had to be identified and mobilized, and the Party's vanguard role was linked to its knowing whom and what to lead. This also required learning from the masses, which meant, inevitably, a symbiosis which at times required it to follow social forces in order to later direct them. At every step there were choices to be carefully made and connected to a longer, ongoing historical process; once made, however, such choices meant that political people and historical forces are to some degree shaped by each other. The Party respected the limits of power imposed upon it, but it also saw as deeply as it could the constraints on its adversaries and their specific vulnerability, and it always weighed the two together. Neither France nor the United States nor those they supported in Vietnam had a concept of historical trends, the balance of forces operating over time, or of the primacy of a larger social context over immediate events.

This concept of the relationship of the past to the future made dealing with the present far easier, since it gave a realistic, nuanced, and materialist meaning and justification to actions which might otherwise seem purposeless, and it evoked commitment and patience from many of those often undergoing unbelievable human hardships. It is reassuring that the side one is on will eventually win, and behavior and motivation will be profoundly affected by any other belief. No matter what the strategy or the weapons, Truong Chinh pointed out in February 1951, "in the end, *the basic factor deciding victory remains the human factor.*"[5] The Party's notion of revolutionary optimism and morality tried to cope with the morale problem.

Pessimism among the new Party members became a challenge during 1946 because of a lack of political training, and in the hectic months after the Revolution optimism was justified as much as possible in terms of realistic assessments of the balance of forces. The Party quite accurately defined in advance the reasons why the Revolution eventually defeated France. Elaborate lists of unfavorable and favorable factors were drawn up for the Party membership, and overoptimism was considered just as corrosive to the maintenance of high morale as pessimism. This mode of realistic, pragmatic analysis became integral to the Party's thinking and was a quite functional application of materialistic reasoning essential for policy-making. The world balance of forces after 1951 began to receive greater emphasis, though always with the caveat that self-reliance was ultimately essential.

Revolutionary optimism was not a myth or a self-fulfilling prophecy but a means of summing up the logic of Marxist historical method and the dialectics of human action and social forces. It was never presented as an act of faith but rather as a rational argument—which later proved repeatedly valid. To be with the Revolution, in effect, was to be on the side that inevitably would win. So long as it sufficed, it greatly helped to produce highly motivated Party members and soldiers. This line of reasoning was not, at bottom, subtle, nor did it evolve out of residues of a Confucian wisdom comprehensible to only a small number of intellectuals. When loss of morale occurred because of errors in Party policy having nothing to do with a vision of the future, the land question being one of the most obvious, the Party either changed its policy or suffered for it. In the long run, optimism and the reinforcing of Marxist premises underlying it, as well as a very realistic sense of the balance of forces, also required a consensus on a vast number of immediate economic and social issues, along with a Party organization able to relate to the daily experiences of the nation. It ultimately managed to produce a psychology of determination resulting in an astonishingly long period of high morale among a large enough mass of people to create a precondition for the defeat of two countries and for a decisive shift in the course of Vietnam's history.

THE NOTION OF REVOLUTIONARY MORALITY

More ambitious was Ho Chi Minh's campaign for revolutionary morality: "to make the revolution," Ho affirmed, "one must first and foremost remould oneself."[6] Strict personal behavior and discipline on behalf of a belief is a standard component of many cultures at various stages in their history. The existence of Confucian precepts on many such questions was a correlation but hardly a cause, though Ho exploited the legacy of Confucian doctrine still lingering among intellectuals to sanction his ideas.

Personal morality for a Party cadre was not incidental to the performance of his functions but a precondition for success, and he could scarcely be effective in inspiring others to take risks and make sacrifices unless ready to lead by example. The Party's work, after all, was based on personal privations, not occasionally but constantly, and on a readiness to put "the Party's interests above everything else."[7] Apart from frequent perils to life, there were long separations from families and a lack of funds and materials with which to work. Revolutionary optimism without revolutionary morality would quickly lead to passivity and fatigue unless the Party argued that it was impossible for optimism to be warranted without personal sacrifices. Such values were essential to mobilize the masses; but even among state administrators of a very poor country, existing until 1954 with an immense deficit in its fiscal system, a sense of thrift and modesty was the absolute prerequisite of organizational survival. A Party in a revolutionary struggle involving life-and-death issues could hardly afford many frivolous people, an elemental fact which led to the campaign for revolutionary morality.

Ho's concern for personal behavior antedated the Revolution, but the pre-1946 Party members were of the same mettle as Ho, and with power came the possibility of abusing it, which risked alienating the masses. More important, after December 1946 the underground government's personnel forced into the forests and mountains were generally of urban origins. "Before you worked at fixed hours," Ho reasoned. "Your life was quiet and relatively comfortable." Now it was one of constant moving and privations; as entertainment they had only "the songs of birds, cries of apes, dense forests."[8] To urge them not to oversleep or overeat, and to study whenever possible, was scarcely ideological puritanism but a necessity. A disciplined Marxist party's strength was in its organized collective response to class problems, but its members had to be prepared as individuals to shape their lives to the Party's general goals even when, as often occurred, they had to work in isolation and exert initiative without allowing a bureaucratic mentality to inhibit them.

The questions of morality were intimately linked with the bureaucratic vices which the Party made prime villains from 1945 onward. "The two main enemies are egoism and bureaucracy," To Huu was to write many years later. "Industry, thrift, integrity and uprightness" were major pillars in the creation of a socialist personality and culture.[9] It had to begin in the Party and state apparatus and then be combined with the antibureaucratic struggle, and it was this campaign for personal morality that became a permanent component of the Party's style and education. Careerism, ambition, egoism, waste, and laziness among Party members were all deplored, far more than the cultural, religious, and political ideological residues still very much present throughout Vietnam among the non-Party masses. Under conditions of scarcity and deprivation, revolutionary ethics offered the only effective way of coming to grips with such timeless human problems. It was less consequential that an unknown but significant number of Party members failed to attain such standards than that they existed as a set of values and goals to which a sufficient number were to conform to compensate for countless difficulties facing the Revolution over many decades.

CREATING AN ORGANIZATION

The Party's conception of its methods and organization evolved and shifted over the fifteen years after 1945, sometimes even reversing itself, flexible and adaptive to the larger needs of its struggles with the French and, later, the Americans. These external imperatives, as much as desire, merged with the knowledge gained after 1945 to produce a Party that by 1961 was capable of adjusting to yet far greater challenges.

The Communist Party's responsiveness to reality, its desire to gain mass support, and its own definition of bolshevism forced it to cope with distinctive organizational problems. It had to find a way past the dangers of bureaucratic centralism and local initiative while retaining the assets of both; it had to stake out a creative role for the people even while perfecting the Party; it sought criticism and self-criticism within the Party and from the masses, but in proportions and intensity it could not precisely define in advance. In the long run, it succeeded sufficiently in balancing the tensions inherent in its goals, and though it continued after 1960 to fine-tune them, it was by that time highly familiar with the means for doing so.

The Party maintained that the discipline it demanded of its members was intended not to inhibit their freedom but to mobilize it for a class, or even for the nation, and that political reality demanded collective action as a precondition for social, and individual, progress and freedom. But the Party's real problem after 1945 was not to defend the legitimacy of serious politics in a serious world but rather to confront the fact that mere organization and discipline by themselves are quite insufficient. Essential, too, was creative innovation and initiative without transcending the Party's policies, since creativity in local and specific situations was essential to effective action—and was occurring in any event. The resolution of these tensions functionally was the Party's most important organizational success; ultimately, it was vital to the attainment of all of its political and economic goals.

The Party was guided by a Bolshevik theory of organization and could be monolithic from the top downward, but once the Politburo defined its general policies and goals it was in due course often responsive to adaptations and changes the masses desired, and comprehending their feelings was a major concern to its leaders. In a basic sense a party, any party, guides historical developments in certain ways but follows them in others, and its ability to lead is conditional on its keen understanding of its own capacities and of the basic sources of its strength. A party aware of its own power and limits, in brief, is far better able to cope with experience. This perception suffused the Party leadership's view of itself and made it acutely concerned with the moods of the masses—moods it knew the Party's members might not reflect adequately and which could thereby elude the leaders' knowledge.

The key to this delicate task of transcending its organizational constraints was the constant effort to improve the Party's members, and particularly the cadres. The cadre was the Party's crucial link to the masses, the majority of the Party's members, the soldiers, and the state administration. Whatever the strength or weakness of the Party's membership, the cadres —who composed a mere one-tenth to one-fifth of it—had to be outstanding, for they were the Party's elite and had formal responsibilities to it. They in turn consisted of a small minority of high-level cadres and a minority of middle-level cadres. Most cadres were also assigned organizational or professional roles, but the higher their level, the more likely they were to be generalists able to assume many duties.

The cadre was supposed to embody the qualities of revolutionary morality, optimism, and heroism. In 1957 General Nguyen Chi Thanh conceded that Party members and cadres should not feel they had no right to have some "small concern for their private affairs," including their families, and it was this absence of sufficient family life that was to prove a weakness of the cadre system.[10] The cadres made the Revolution run, but, ideally, the main factors making them behave correctly were the masses and, more regularly, self-criticism.

The campaign for self-criticism began shortly after the August Revolution, essentially in response to the open admission of Party members. Too many cadres had been given responsibility too quickly, Ho complained in April 1948, and political cadres in the army were exhorted to accomplish exceptional tasks, not the least of which was to be "as just as a brother and as intimate as a friend" to soldiers.[11] Such admonitions were to continue more or less regularly as part of the constant process to improve the cadres and the Party through self-criticism and an attack on bureaucracy.

Self-criticism always was one aspect of the Party's overarching personal style of constant communication and human interaction at all levels, and the ability to function well in this time-consuming role and also to get some work done and to study was the characteristic of the good cadre. A conception of the Party as a human community was fundamental to its success and integration, and its attainment sustained individual morale through some of the most difficult and trying periods. The Party, from the three-man cell upward, became each member's surrogate family and alter ego. "Now I am the child of a thousand families," To Huu wrote in 1938 about joining the Party, "younger brother of a thousand thousand humiliated lives. . . ."[12] It would be difficult to exaggerate the importance of such shared community and values.

Communication between all levels of the Party, and between the Party and the masses, was vital to the Party's role as both an informed leader and a reflector of the masses' desires and feelings. Self-criticism and criticism were intended to keep this process of communication going, and thereby also to mitigate the dangers of "commandism," corruption, waste, arrogance, and bureaucratic vices of every sort. The cadres' responsibility was to "keep in close touch with the people and learn from them."[13] Regular sessions, diaries which then became topics of analysis, small-group talks—everything was proposed both to improve the work and the exchanges between Party members and cadres at all levels and to educate and win the confidence of the masses and obtain their opinions and public criticisms of cadres.

At no time did the Party consider self-criticism a sufficiently developed or successful practice, and improving it became a standard theme in Party exhortations to cadres and members. Cadres' errors, like those of other people, were "very understandable and even natural," for there were no supermen. What was crucial in acknowledging the normal limits of humanity was the ability to admit a fault in order better to overcome it. "Generally speaking," the Party's leaders felt in 1957, "our cadres are good," and excessive attacks on them risked humiliating those who were straining to their limits to accomplish their tasks.[14] Yet "a workers' party," Le Duc Tho wrote in 1961, "regarding criticism and self-criticism as its law of development, uses them to detect and correct the shortcomings and mistakes of the party. . . ."[15] But this system posed extremely human problems—which was one of the reasons for its quite limited success. The capacity to accept and give disinterested criticism in front of others tests the individual in ways that risk touching the most diverse aspects of humankind: ego and pride, self-esteem, ulterior motives, ambition, as well as positive social commitments.

With this persistent, restless dissatisfaction with itself, nebulous at times, the Party sought a solution to compensate for the shortcomings of people and institutions which are an inevitable concomitant of the human condition. Whatever its theory and organizational practice at any time, the Party made the antibureaucratic campaign its overriding obsession. It worried about how the size and quality of its membership produced bureaucratic manifestations and their economic and political costs, and it continually tried to overcome the limits of formal structures in order to incorporate the initiative and dynamism of creative innovation. Criticism among Party members and cadres was directly linked to the problem. As Ho complained in 1951, "Inner Party democracy has not been broadly practiced."[16] To overcome these constraints, General Nguyen Chi Thanh admonished in 1957, "When the Party makes a mistake it bears responsibility and the Party accepts critical suggestions."[17]

The problem of bureaucracy is universal, of course, predating the Bolshevik Revolution. Its danger to socialist parties is all the greater because their social goals are large, and it is a trap into which countless social democratic and Leninist states have fallen. But given the more cohesive and centralized nature of Leninist parties, which they have argued is essentially a necessary precondition to the involvement in crisis politics and the avoidance of destruction, the risks of bureaucracy are greater if there is no mechanism to cope with it. A sclerotic Party in a protracted struggle was sure to lose, and its leaders acknowledged this fact by making antibureaucracy a repetitive theme. For revolutionaries in isolation the capacity to work on their own initiative is crucial to their survival, and this fact had been obvious since 1945. Their values and motives must then be autonomous and internalized, based on a sense of revolutionary morality. Discipline was like iron, but it was also "self-imposed." "Self-reliance" was the internal and external hallmark of the long resistance, Ho Chi Minh observed in July 1952.[18]

In a sense the Party's leaders had to deal with the classic tension between discipline and creativity, and it managed to find a tentative solution by accepting both, to varying degrees, according to the time and the place. So long as it was a revolutionary Party in a fluid situation, it had to accept, in order to struggle, "the regionalism and dispersion inherent in the resistance," and the antibureaucratic ethic was essentially characteristic of the armed resistance and vast distances and poor communications between central organs and the local Parties.[19] The Party's leaders were never quite to balance their fear of "bureaucratic centralism" and their desire to provide guidance. The resistance and underground had their own styles of operation by necessity, since bureaucrats were both useless and dangerous in a world where creative adaptation and quick response were preconditions of success. But bureaucracy certainly became a problem in the vast liberated zones of Vietnam before 1954, and then in the DRV thereafter, and the Party freely admitted it. Its dilemma was that many bureaucrats neither would or could acknowledge that they played that role in the pejorative sense. Self-criticism was designed to correct this problem, but, as Ho ruefully observed in 1958, many members were ready to criticize others but did "not like being criticized."[20] In the end the Party did not solve the problem of bureaucracy but acknowledged it as a never-ending challenge to its revolutionary ethics and to its organizational interests. Although it began expelling members after 1950, it remained dependent on the process of criticism and mass opinion, along with appeals for revolutionary morality, to keep bureaucracy under control. In the final analysis it was the Party members' consciousness which was seen as the key not just to bureaucracy but to the very goals of the Revolution.

THE ROLE OF THE POLITBURO

The Party's pluralism in its practice, its theoretical and organizational flexibility, and its creativity in the face of new difficulties were to a very great degree due to the fact that its leadership system was totally different from both the Soviet and the Chinese. More important, it was a relatively cohesive and effective leadership that was keenly attuned to the myriad external challenges the Party was facing.

The absence of turbulence even when there was significant disagreement among senior Party leaders was Ho's ultimate contribution. Compared with the other major Marxist-Leninist leaders of the world after Lenin, he was exceptional in all regards, not only in his lack of egoism but also in his remarkable practical capacity to define problems and the solutions to them. The Soviets irrevocably condemned the cult of personality in 1956, and Ho strongly endorsed the decision to demythologize Stalin, attacking any symptoms of the practice in Vietnam. In May 1967, during the peak of the Mao craze and the Cultural Revolution, the Party used the occasion of Ho's seventy-seventh birthday to distance itself from the Chinese events and to define the role of "Leaders and the Masses," and of Ho in particular, in a manner that also reflected Ho's own views. History was made by the masses, and the Party practiced collective leadership and self-criticism precisely because of its respect for Marxist laws of history and its need to act, like Ho, as "a servant of the people."[21] To do anything else would ruin the Party's credibility among the masses.

This rationalism was an integral part of the Party leadership's habitual style of working. Many of the senior Party leaders had spent years in prison, and all had been in forests and confronted danger together. The distinctive, collegial nature of the Politburo notwithstanding, two important aspects of its method of work quickly emerged. The most significant was that all understood, in varying degrees, the delicate relationship of the Party leaders to the desires and needs of the masses and to autonomous structural developments at home and abroad, and when necessary they accommodated to both. To the extent that a Party both leads and follows history, as it never tired of pointing out, its leaders were often very aware of the limits of their power and of their need to bide their time. The constraints on Ho applied to them also. With a few exceptions, they were extremely modest men, many were proud of their anonymity, and none ever took the personal privileges commonly taken by their peers in the USSR and China. Their second dominant characteristic was a strong tendency after 1941 to compromise their differences as long as possible for the sake of policies that often were eclectic and at times at odds with each other.

The Party's leaders moved slowly, constantly studying, discussing, and analyzing problems, learning in the process but tending to avoid decisive measures. They could spend a vast amount of time and effort assessing basic issues, as in the case of the southern situation after 1955. They would often test credible options and experiment, the results often proving decisive to a debate, and they tried to avoid closing doors behind themselves. At the highest levels they very rarely engaged in public self-criticism. But their private discussions were as tough-minded as communications between serious people must be. On major policy questions they interacted with lower levels of the Party, including ordinary Party members. Discussion of such issues often appeared in the Party journals, and the news that they were under consideration invariably led to inputs from diverse Party elements.

This essentially cautious leadership structure reflected not just the personalities involved but also the basic ideological definitions of the Party and its minimization, ultimately, of individuals. The Politburo's goal was also to preserve its own corporate identity and cohesion. A more brilliant and decisive procedure would have endangered the genuinely pluralist quality of leadership, and it might have produced irrevocable errors. Such a system was unified and relatively slow. Protected against the foibles of any one man, stable, and highly rational in institutional terms, it proved remarkably resilient and successful over the following decades.

THE SEARCH FOR A VIETNAMESE SYSTEM

By the late 1950s the Party was beginning to form a more comprehensive approach to the critical problems of mobilizing a society and the Revolution's means for dealing with countless organizational and human difficulties. There was so much to accomplish at the level of internal economic and political development, and there were so many external challenges, that a synthesis was all the more urgent. Criticism, improved Party membership, collective leadership, antibureaucracy, and personal transformation of values were all merely parts of the common effort.

The need to resolve material constraints meant that practical organizational problems and the tasks at hand turned theory into scarcely more than a generalizing on practice and experience. In 1950 Ho thought that teaching Marxist-Leninist theory to peasants was a "real waste of labour and money." But seven years later, when the Party opened a course on theory at its central school, Ho felt that the Party's successes had been based on many virtues but that there was still a "low level of its ideological understanding" in dealing with new and future tasks. Ho acknowledged the need for theory, though one always integrated with practice and informed by reality. He knew, of course, that the paucity of Vietnamese theoretical writings would force a dependence on those of other countries, the USSR and China in particular, and theory not linked to Vietnamese conditions might be not only useless but damaging. Ready to pay his due respects to his major allies publicly, Ho at this point was eager to see a specifically Vietnamese conceptualization. "We do not carry on studies to learn by heart every sentence and every word and apply the experience of brother countries in a mechanical way." Marxism-Leninism could be applied only to the "circumstances of the given time and of the given place." Yet, he went on uncomfortably, to argue for Vietnamese exceptionalism was to court revisionist errors, and by Vietnamese specificity Ho reiterated the internationalist orientation of the Party's intellectual origins. "Although we have the rich experiences of brother countries, we cannot apply them mechanically because our country has its own peculiarities. Disregard for the peculiarities of one's nation while learning from the experiences of the brother countries is a serious mistake, is dogmatism."[22] In searching for their own distinctive synthesis, the Vietnamese were consciously building their own model.

THE PARTY AND THE DILEMMA OF MASS MOBILIZATION

The mobilization of the masses was crucial to the Party's definition of the potential sources of its own moral and ideological strength. The front groups and mass-interest associations therefore had a dual relationship: the Party led them, but they reciprocated by giving it insight and legitimacy. In addition, though, to the basic organizations among youth, women, workers, peasants, and such, which existed since 1930 and were far larger than the Party, there were the various local people's committees created to help run the state after the August Revolution. In a nation more than 3,000 kilometers long with poor, or often no, system of rapid communications and contact, the existence of effective, adaptive local organs of authority and power became crucial to the Revolution's ongoing efforts over many years.

While it was the function of such parallel structures to "uphold the leadership of the party," administrative constraints often made this impractical and hypothetical.[23] For the Party itself had become a mass organization of very unequal membership, in certain ways more difficult for the older Party veterans to deal with because of its relatively privileged political status, and it could not merely dominate the masses in some authoritarian fashion, lest it lose their devotion and energy—and their willingness to take risks for the Revolution. To work out an equilibrium between the needs and desires of the Party and masses satisfactory to the ongoing struggle along socialist lines, to determine, in effect, who leads and who follows whom, was a formidable task and took fifteen years to master. In a fundamental sense it was the most important challenge confronting the Party, but by 1960— after trial and error and much upheaval—the Revolution's total organizational system was in place, operating with reasonabe effectiveness. When the war with the United States began, a mobilized nation of sixteen million was prepared for every contingency.

The Party's leaders understood that an organization alone, however structured, could not succeed without the masses and that all its military, economic, and political needs depended on them. They never stopped exhorting members and soldiers to "keep in close touch with the people and learn from them."[24] Mobilizing the masses into networks was a crucial part of that process, of course, but so, equally, was learning from, listening to, and even, if necessary, following them. During the weeks and months after the August Revolution, millions of people became involved in the immense upheaval and were the real force behind its success at the crucial moments. Over the following period the new government organized people's councils. These councils were direct representative bodies based on universal suffrage and a means of obtaining the participation of the host of people on the scene and of channeling them. The councils also elected administrative committees, which were really executive organs representing the masses, the Party, and the government; resolving the function and role of this structure— which sometimes became inefficient or pro forma, or had to be modified during the war with France—and its relation to the Party was a focus of attention for the next fifteen years. Still, as a means of transcending the limits of relying exclusively on the Party, the assets of the council system far outweighed its liabilities. The Party dominated its key positions but brought the people closer to real power and gave them a means by which to influence it. More important, the Party's members increasingly were locals whose strength was their relationship with the persons who, especially after 1954, more and more determined who was nominated for Party membership.

The real problem confronting the Party's mass line during the early 1950s was far less the imperfections in its organizational forms than the contradictions in its united-front strategy. The united front was intended to neutralize the Party's potential enemies, but this was done to a significant extent by a dilution of its own, distinctive class program and by major concessions on social policy, particularly land reform. The masses were not, ultimately, some abstract and undifferentiated entity but comprised mainly poor and marginal peasants. Their devotion and needs were in the end synonymous, and there were growing limits on ideological appeals to them as the rewards of struggle failed to match the ever-greater sacrifices demanded. The risks of playing loosely with their dedication were apparent to many of the Party's leaders, for Vietnam's history since the French colonization was studded with local peasant rebellions, and after the Nghe Tinh and Nam Ky uprisings the Party was acutely aware of the dangers to itself from spontaneous peasant action it could not control. To avert such predictable risks and mobilize the masses for the sacrifices which war against France demanded, the Party was by 1952 compelled to choose between purely patriotic appeals and class struggle. Whether it led or followed the masses was less critical than success against the French.

Not for the first or the last time, the Party rediscovered that the ultimate reservoir of incentive for mass struggle was the land question. In a peasant country, as a motor of mass mobilization and social change, land reform emerged as the clearest and most persistent of the Revolution's many appeals. The poor peasants—who together with lower-middle peasants composed about 60 percent of the north Vietnam rural population—were always ready to act in their own interests. A process of revolutionary change inevitably involves the question of who wins and who loses from it. Until 1953 the united front had succeeded quite admirably in co-opting or isolating the potential class opposition, and even over the next several years the Party always planned to return to it, but the military struggle against the French between 1950 and 1952 proved more difficult than had been anticipated, even though the Revolution's military power grew rapidly. To end the protracted war and resolve its growing organizational and economic problems, the Party leaders decided in late 1952, after experimenting in trial villages, to mobilize the poor peasants for greatly intensified combat—and sacrifices. The reward would be land for them or, if they were wounded or killed, for their families, and the means would be, to a remarkable degree, class struggle not merely against the French and their collaborators but also against a portion of the Party and people's councils and their administrative committees. The Party's leaders resolved to deal with all of the weaknesses in the Party and state mechanism as well as with the implementation of land-reform laws, at one and the same time, for they were all interrelated.

Many of those who joined the Party and dominated the local administrative committees were from landlord or rich peasant families, and while the poor peasant in the village was materially better off than before, he was far from being their equal. Existing land reform legislation had often been implemented or circumvented in many places in favor of the families of wealthier Party members, causing resentment among the poor. "Since the August Revolution of 1945," Truong Chinh revealed in November 1953, "the landlords have seized the leadership in our rural organizations in many places."[25] The changes that were to occur throughout most of 1953 were based largely on the 1949 reform legislation, greatly elaborated in a new law in December 1953, but the truly radical innovation was its thorough implementation. The problem, as Truong Chinh admitted in 1953, was that the Party had underestimated the peasant's role in the resistance, which led to a lapse in administering the reform and to an exaggeration of the importance of the need for a united front to the exclusion of all other considerations—an error he attributed to a mechanical imitation of the Chinese Communist model. To accomplish needed changes, the Party Central Committee sent outside cadres, most of whom were themselves from a poor-peasant background, into villages. They were directly responsible to the Central Committee and not to local and district Party organizations. Their assignment was to mobilize the poorest and landless peasants into Peasant Associations, which then were to take direct action to confront landlords and implement the law.

By any criterion, the 1953 land reform initiated far-reaching changes both in the existing agrarian structure and in the Party. Its major implementation was scheduled for 1954. The risks were immense. Not just apolitical landlords but also those who had been loyal to the Viet Minh, or had perhaps even belonged to the Party, were fined, lost land, and were occasionally imprisoned or, less often, killed. The Party's leaders attempted to define constraints on action and preserve a semblance of its combined-front policy, but in many places it failed as poor peasants joined with often overaggressive cadres to act in their own economic interests. Although the Party's leaders increasingly lost control over local actions, the deliberate unleashing of poor-peasant enthusiasm nonetheless produced the desired recruits and élan for the next and winning phase of the military struggle. Victory at Dien Bien Phu, Giap made it clear in his stirring March 1954 appeal to his forces there, will "help to insure that the land reform achieves success."[26] The destruction of France in Indochina that occurred at Dien Bien Phu in May 1954, based as it was on over 200,000 peasants who carried supplies or attacked the French positions, was a direct consequence of the changes and even the chaos in villages throughout Vietnam which began in 1953 and were to continue for over two years. The peasantry would carry the Revolution to its triumph.

Mobilizing the masses for land reform was the key to military victory, Ho Chi Minh, Truong Chinh, and other leaders repeatedly argued. "Land reform is an immense, complex and hard class struggle. It is all the more complex and all the harder because we are conducting a war of resistance. But it is precisely because we want to push the resistance forward to victory that we must be determined to make land reform a success."[27] Assorted measures to protect "upper" peasants and sympathetic landlords were enacted, but often to no effect.

The reform movement's risks were not just to a successful united-front policy but also to current food output and, above all, in the future problems the land reform might present. For though land reform was a reliable means of mobilization and a route to power, the Party's leaders had no illusions about the small peasant's mentality and his possible role later as an obstacle to socialist agriculture. These very problems were to emerge immediately after the 1954 victory over the French and then again after the 1975 triumph in the south. The Party's land reform strategy in 1953 was a response to urgent military tasks, but not its preferred solution to the land problem.

The Party's leaders understood the social forces now loose in Vietnam. And while they saw the balance decisively shifted in their favor, they knew, too, that they could squander their advantage if they took excessive risks. By unleashing the masses' desire for reform and their power for war, the Party had created a major dilemma for itself. Its problem was who was leading whom, at what cost, and for how long.

The mass mobilization of the peasantry saw the Party through Dien Bien Phu and its remarkable triumph over France after one decade. The thousands of peasants who died there were patriots, but they were also often first and foremost fighting for a revolution in land relations. That incentive would later succeed again and again, and it would also evoke spontaneous, dynamic mass action and devotion to the cause. The peasant would fight for land, with or without the Party, and that passion could overshadow ideology and discipline. If this commitment was to guarantee the Party's future successes throughout Vietnam, it also left the Party with a fundamental crisis in the northern part of the nation and within a few years would confront it with its gravest challenge in the south.

The Vietnamese countryside in the north before the May 1954 Geneva Conference was in disorder, in some regions approaching chaos, because of the way land reform was implemented. Many local Party organizations, in the process, were badly mauled, and much had to be done to repair them. Mass mobilization and action proved a decisive weapon, but its price to the Party's cohesion was enormous. This elemental reality was one of the critical factors influencing the outcome of the Geneva Conference as the Party was forced to consider all the effects and costs of its triumphant strategy.

Chapter 5

The Communist Party's Consolidation of Power

THE GENEVA CONFERENCE
AND THE VICTORY OVER FRANCE

War for the Revolution was not a simple military exercise but an integral dimension of politics and its relationship to the people. Military strategy always reflected this primary assumption. The ability of the Party to play its leading role over the long run was therefore contingent on its tactical capacity to follow the masses at certain points and to acknowledge realistically the material restraints on itself and the balance of forces at each phase of a protracted struggle. After 1953 the initiative on the land issue was left increasingly to the poorer peasants, the Party stimulating a policy that a large portion of them had always favored but that had unpredictably great consequences. The Party's leaders were in a passive position, and their disagreements were so large that their resultant inability to reach a consensus inhibited any decisive action.

In 1954 there began a transition, lasting until about 1959, in Party policy and leadership as economic necessities forced it to make diplomatic and political accommodations and as desires gave way to the pressure of reality. Policies were rarely, if ever, categorical; rather, they became even more nuanced and sometimes experimental as the Party left itself options to correct any possible errors. In a sense, 1954–59 saw the maturation of Vietnamese Communism's theory and practice and of its methodology of overcoming limits and exploiting possibilities.

In addition to the political, organizational, and social consequences of the land reform, the DRV had to resolve the accumulated problems of the wartime economy it had created in its growing liberated zones. From 1946 to the end of 1951, it had funded three-quarters of its mounting expenses merely by printing money, producing a vertiginous inflation in its zone that in the long run could threaten the nation's very survival. In 1951 it began to try to balance its budget, with the result that 1953 became the first year the Revolution was not in the red. But the Revolution needed time to consolidate and resolve its many internal problems, after a decade of exhausting struggle, and then confront the remaining tasks. It was in this context of material pressures that it went to the Geneva Conference.

China went to Geneva with comparable internal dilemmas, torn between national priorities and the more disinterested internationalist ones Marxists claim to follow. And just as both China and the DRV were under similar constraints, national interests in the last analysis determined the goals of each. It was simply that the consequences of such self-serving policies on the part of China had far greater implications for its neighbors and the region.

The tragic history of Chinese-Vietnamese relations after 1975 cannot obscure the fact that although China's policy always evolved with its needs and power, the relations between the two nations throughout the decade were extremely cordial. While the Party's ideological debt to China was large, the Vietnamese were nonetheless building their own, distinctive theory despite some overlapping experiences and practices unavoidable in two predominantly peasant countries. On a material and diplomatic level, their ties were very close. China began giving the DRV arms early in 1950, as soon as it was in a position to deliver them; in 1953, when it doubled arms aid over the preceding year, it began supplying heavier equipment. Most of the munitions used at Dien Bien Phu, not to mention training in their use, came from China. At the same time, it never supplied enough aid before 1954 to threaten France's forces with a defeat sufficient to bring America into the war, and the May 1954 victory at Dien Bien Phu was, ultimately, the consequence of French stupidity and the DRV's mass mobilization. China's policy was largely the result of its experience in the Korean War, in which it lost about half a million men. Its primary goals were to promote peace in the region, so that it could devote more attention to internal economic development, and, above all, to avert a possible U.S. intervention in the Indochina War. In the summer of 1953, after the Korean armistice, China had endorsed the Soviet position that the Korean settlement should become the model for Indochina. The DRV rejected this stance, which implied a partition and revealed that its two major allies would be quite ready to push it toward a political solution before the Party thought the military situation ripe for one. By the time the May 1954 military balance in Vietnam had altered, the Party was also weaker domestically, having almost no economic and military reserves and being unable to resist the pressures its allies exerted.

The Geneva Conference was Vietnamese Communism's first major lesson on the nature and limits of proletarian internationalism, and its impact profoundly affected its conception of the world. While the Soviets gave the Vietnamese no more comfort than the Chinese did and informed the French that they opposed a unified Vietnam, lest it lead to an extension of Chinese influence in the region, they were more concerned with using Indochina as a means of keeping France out of the European Defense Community. But since the USSR acceded at Geneva to China's mastery over purely regional issues, China's leverage made it the principal power broker in the negotiations. Once the Chinese realized there was slight risk of an American intervention, they sought through direct talks with the French to exchange constraints on the DRV for greater diplomatic recognition and prestige and commercial openings to the West for themselves. As all the prospects of its advantageous position emerged, China even held out the possibility of protecting the French position in the Red River Delta, a neutralization of the region, a partitioned Vietnam for an indefinite period and a consequent Balkanization of the region that would legitimize many anti-Communist regimes, and much else. Partition, in particular, which the Russians had first broached to the United States the preceding March and which, they explained on the very first day at Geneva, would offer China a buffer to its south, was the most fateful of the concessions raised. The heady regional power broker's role soon revealed China's willingness to engage in classic big-nation diplomacy at the expense of Marxist internationalism, and in the end both it and the USSR, in their different ways and for their very diverse and mutually antagonistic reasons, prodded the DRV into accepting the Geneva Accords, particularly the "temporary" division along the seventeenth parallel. The Chinese and the Russians were much closer to each other in their interests and actions than they were to the Vietnamese Communists. The French, whose diplomatic prowess far exceeded their military talents, appreciated the gap between the DRV and its Chinese ally and sought through direct contacts to extract as much as they could from the Chinese.

Later revelations of the tawdry details of the role of China and the USSR have not much altered the contemporary accounts of the split between the DRV and its allies. Pham Van Dong, leader of the DRV delegation, did not conceal his profound displeasure with both the Chinese and the Soviets, whose cynical appeals on behalf of the DRV's "international responsibilities" were blended with promises of future economic aid. It was this intense pressure from its allies, who from beginning to end had dunned the DRV with the dangers of U.S. intervention to force them to make concessions and avoid allegedly risking the peace of the world, reinforced by its own, painful awareness of the urgency of its internal problems, that led the DRV to forgo exploiting its favorable military position against the French at a time, we now know, when the United States almost certainly would not intervene. But the DRV's public anger soon disappeared as the facade of friendship returned, to last for nearly two more decades. In fact, the fateful events at Geneva made an indelible impression and influenced the DRV's conception of its international strategy from this time onward.

The DRV's speedy reconciliation with China was simply one phase of its general effort to consolidate its power north of the seventeenth parallel before coping with the problems of national unification. For it was not, ultimately, the Chinese or Soviets who forced the terms at Geneva on the Party but its estimate of its own limitations, its most immediate needs, and its prospects and potential resources in the future. Had the DRV felt stronger, it could have withstood Chinese and Soviet insistence. The success of its allies was not the cause of its weaknesses but reflected them. Facing myriad land, administrative, and economic difficulties, the Party's leaders concluded that a consolidation of power in the north was essential and that their prudence and time would shift the balance of forces in the Party's favor. They assumed that it would later be able to confront the question of the south from a much stronger position—an assumption that eventually proved correct. The Geneva Accords' promised July 1956 election to reunify Vietnam peaceably seemed to them a possible, but by no means certain, antidote to partition. But the election itself had value only because of an expected vacuum of power in the south, and the absence of a serious challenge to the Party there. All of the components of its optimism had a rational basis, but the analysis turned out to be incorrect.[1]

LAND REFORM AFTER 1954

Land reform had mobilized the poorer peasants into a victorious military force, and by the end of 1954 it had helped significantly to increase agricultural output and efficiency. By 1957 the land system north of the seventeenth parallel was essentially equitable, and the landless and poor peasants had improved their position radically while even the middle peasantry was able to enlarge its land ownership. Yet the social, political, and human problems that the Party's leaders confronted mounted as the reform traumatized the countryside, the Party, and state structures and profoundly constrained the Party's options and priorities.

The 1954–57 land reform experience was perhaps as difficult a challenge as the Party was ever to confront, and the transformation of the inherited order exacted a great price, even as it paid still larger dividends. The Party was never again to be quite so buffeted by forces beyond its control as during this period, when it strove mainly to master the spontaneous dynamics its policies had unleashed. Until March 1955 it continued the land reform strategy it had initiated in 1953, but it also appealed for a more discriminating policy toward landlords in the hope of retaining the commitment of a portion of them—and especially of their families—to the united front. But the next year of the reform effort was even more turbulent, as exhausted, reluctant cadres taken from wartime posts were sent to the solitary and exacting work of organizing the poor in the villages. Many of the reform's subsequent difficulties can be attributed to these demoralized cadres. The much greater reliance on People's Special Agricultural Reform Tribunals, the major source of abuse, was a direct outcome of the cadres' haste to complete their tasks. Until late 1956 the land reform organizational structure was functioning not only independently of the Party but often against it, basing its power on the poor peasantry.

By early 1955 it was apparent that the struggle for unification would take much more time and that the United States might indeed delay the Geneva settlement's implementation, and so in March the Party decision to consolidate the Revolution in the north, even to the neglect of the united front, was reaffirmed. Landowners who supported the Revolution, or whose children did, had been partially insulated from earlier reforms, but it was not long before poorer peasants began to assail them as well. For the fact was that the sheer scarcity of land in the north required all available ground to be reallocated, or else the reform's impact on the poor would be minimal. As the peasants in denunciation sessions and court trials developed both class consciousness and self-confidence, they began to exploit the Party leaders' leftist stand to move into direct confrontation with all landowners. While it is true that the Party's leadership, working directly through selected cadres rather than through the normal Party organization, had initiated the poor peasantry's mass action, the peasants needed very little prompting to act in their own interests, ignoring the Party's restraining efforts throughout 1955. In reality, both wanted and obtained something from the other, and it was never quite clear who was leading and who was following. In any event, the Party Central Committee's decision the following August to intensify the reform campaign led also to a purge of many of those Party members who were large landowners and whose positions or connections had prevented the implementation of land reform legislation in the distant and recent past. During this period, which lasted until mid-1956, the toll on wealthy landowners and on many Party members alike was very high economically and psychologically, and it was substantial in terms of people executed and imprisoned—including many old Party members. Anywhere from five thousand to fifteen thousand landowners were killed by local peasant courts, probably closer to the latter figure, and nearly twenty thousand persons were imprisoned, the majority of whom were released by the end of 1956 and most of the remainder during the first half of 1957.[2]

This phase of the land reform became the most divisive issue within the Party's leadership between 1940 and 1975. During late spring and summer 1956, it began demanding an end to excesses, particularly against middle and rich peasants. After Ho in mid-August apologized to the nation for the land reform errors, the Party's Central Committee went into a forty-day session to resolve the impasse. At the end of October, Ho replaced Truong Chinh as the Party's secretary-general, and those in charge of land and organizational reform were removed from all posts of responsibility. Politburo members then engaged in a period of public self-criticism. The Party praised the reforms, which had finally solved the land problem and even expanded production, but it embarked on a campaign to "rectify errors."

The Party now sought to reunite itself, to reassert the primacy of the united front over the class struggle, and to end the internecine struggle in its own ranks, but in certain ways the next year was as difficult as the preceding period, though it was different from it. Some reinstated Party members who had been landlords began demanding their land back, and poor peasants and cadres were now put on the defensive. Although the final land distribution was still highly equitable, in innumerable villages there were confrontations over land, housing, and power, and disunity continued in an atmosphere of tension and revenge, rumors of an imminent return to the status quo, and incipient class struggle. The net effect was to demoralize a large number of Party members and cadres, who tried to avoid responsibilities and turned to personal affairs, and to depoliticize and render passive the poor peasants.

As a synthesis of military and economic needs, the land reform movement was a historic success, but its implications for the Party's essentially pragmatic strategy were far greater than its leaders could have imagined. By 1957, signs of a traditional individualist peasant mentality and economy reappeared in the form of usury, land transfers, and all the symptoms of the old order. Only sharp increases in output and efficiency dulled the edge of incipient problems, but there was little stability and control in such a system, and its equity was already being challenged. In a nation of peasants a rational and predictable agricultural system is an absolute precondition to attaining the basic goals of modernization and unification. And the cohesion within the villages, whose traditional communities had always been under the more decisive strain of an exploitive land system and class conflicts, had to be greatly strengthened to promote the sense of solidarity that any struggle for unification would inevitably demand.

To a critical extent the Party's problem stemmed from the fact that land reform and socialism were very different goals, and by mobilizing the peasantry around its desire for more land, the Party had created its own dilemma. The Party well understood the peasantry's potential smallholder

acquisitive habits and never trusted its impulses to become relatively inefficient owners. Its satisfaction of the peasantry's most elemental desire for
land threatened it with rural chaos after 1954, and in South Vietnam after
1966 the NLF's reform success helped make possible the lessened radicalism
of a section of the peasantry. To some extent the Party in a peasant society
was a captive of the constraints the masses imposed upon it, and it was quite
aware of the fact. On the other hand, it could not afford, after the chaos of
1954–57, to do otherwise than move from the stage of land equalization to
that of social cooperation, and it had to gamble that a desire for stability,
security, and community integration among a sufficient number of peasants
would allow it to move from land reform to socialism.

Beginning in 1958 the Party introduced its cooperativization plan in a
manner intended to resolve the many problems which had appeared over the
preceding years. It differed radically from Soviet and Chinese collectivization efforts in its deliberately slow, voluntary, and at first relatively unambitious character. Essentially mutual aid in its first and most common form,
the plan allowed land and tools to remain privately owned, but it integrated
their use, along with all the factors of production, in a fashion that rewarded
peasants for their labor or material contributions while assuring them of a
minimum income and a common solution to common problems. Fully
socialist co-ops were also created, but these were of slight consequence
during the critical 1958–60 period.

For poor peasants the co-op system represented a much desired form of
insurance and stability, and they were the first to join, confirming that,
whatever the earlier instincts of peasants, many preferred security with
cooperation to the precarious alternatives of the old order. Of far greater
consequence, it also offered a structured system of poor- and middle- peasant
control and participation in village government at a time when many Party
members and cadres were demoralized and the danger that landlordism
would return seemed all too great. Neither landlords nor Party were required routinely to make the system work, for the Party no longer wished
to recruit en masse, and it strongly preferred maintaining its latent rather
than dominant role in the villages. Most Party members lived in cities, and
many resisted being sent to villages. All that was necessary was to guarantee
the poor peasantry two-thirds of the co-op administrative committees, and
direction would rest with a class rather than the Party.

The Party sought, above all, to avoid errors which might renew the corrosive class divisions that had marked its earlier, hasty reform efforts. The
voluntary nature of the program was reflected in the fact that only 4 percent of
the peasant families joined the co-ops in 1958, a figure that rose to 45 percent
the following year. The attraction of the system enabled it to grow to embrace
86 percent of the peasant families in 1960, and more economically integrated

socialist co-ops with some common land and tool ownership began to emerge. On the basis of voluntary membership, mutual aid, and democratic discussion, the new agricultural system stabilized the land system and wiped away the legacies of the old order and the preceding decade of discord. In the rural areas a new social unity emerged, far more durable than any that had existed before the French colonial impact, and the Party's direct role was reduced. The system, for all its problems, possessed a cohesion and resiliency that exceeded anyone's expectations and made land reform synonymous with development. Food production grew throughout the next decade and created a powerful foundation for both socialist industrialization and protracted war. The Party had finally moved the land question beyond necessity and constraint to the realm of desire and power. It had relied on the peasantry's land hunger to mobilize the masses, but the dynamics of mobilization could clearly cause the Party to lose its mastery unless the land issue was definitively resolved. Had its agricultural policy failed, the events of the next fifteen years would not have been possible.[3]

ECONOMIC DEVELOPMENT IN THE DRV

The DRV's success with agricultural organization was reinforced by its primary strategy of economic development. Industry in the DRV was heavily oriented toward creating an infrastructure for agricultural modernization and growth. More important, the costs of such industrialization were not borne by the bulk of the population out of current consumption, as had occurred in the USSR; rather, they were covered by growth itself, foreign aid, and the productivity the land equalization process unleashed. Whatever the formidable problems that had to be overcome, the large majority of the population after 1957 experienced both security and higher living standards. Agricultural cooperation became the basis of industrialization and its major beneficiary. The Vietnamese saw in this interaction an original method of proceeding directly to socialism.

For several years after the Geneva Conference, the Party had to confront the difficult responsibility of absorbing the urban economy. The first problem was the speculation and inflation sparked by the scarcities from which the small merchants and traders were always ready to profit. Getting the formerly French-owned industries, especially coal, cement, and textiles, back into operation was a major task, because Vietnamese technicians were not numerous and nearly all the French personnel left the DRV. But the absence of any important Vietnamese-owned large industry simplified nationalization.

Until 1957 the DRV dealt on an ad hoc basis with the three thousand small firms composing the private sector, a third of which were actually industrial. The main objective during this period was reconstruction and the utilization of existing capacity, but even though industry's output from 1954 to 1957 increased over four times, the artisanal workshops were still twice as important. To go beyond reconstruction to development required training peasants and soldiers to become workers and technicians. From 1957 through 1960 a mixed sector was created from the innumerable private firms, the state sharing the capital and giving direction. But by 1960 the private sector, employing small numbers, had virtually disappeared. The state sector, based on the former French investments, now embraced slightly more than the majority of industry, and artisans in co-ops or working alone made up the bulk of the remainder. Aid from the Soviet bloc and, primarily, China was important for both reconstruction and development during 1955–57 but was of secondary significance by 1960.

By that year the DRV economy was growing quickly and had created a foundation for expansion. The government more than doubled the transportation system's capacity between 1958 and 1960. It gave special priority to the training of technical personnel and skilled workers, and the number of industrial workers more than doubled in this period, rising to 43,000, while that of technically trained managers went up about fivefold, beginning the vast increase in trained, technically qualified personnel that became the hallmark of the DRV's economy. Growth in industry was uneven but, on the whole, statistically very high, increasing by nearly half in each of the three years after 1957 and 1960. The share of industry and handicraft in the national product rose from 31 percent in 1957 to 42 percent in 1960, and though it was still relatively small and primitive, its growth had also solved some crucial problems.

Whatever its substantial deficiencies, the DRV's industrial growth during the eight years after 1957 was the highest in South and Southeast Asia. Planning problems arose and were adjusted, and after 1960 agriculture's share of national investment climbed substantially. National income grew significantly, and the socialist sector of industry was now dominant. Not the quantity of economic change, however, was critical but rather its nature relative to future tasks. First, the chief organizational challenges had been essentially overcome in the agricultural and nonagricultural sectors, and while both faced major difficulties, the era of crises and traumas was past. Next, the vast educational system was producing growing numbers of technically skilled personnel loyal to the DRV and increasingly unencumbered by ties to the ways of the old order. Then too, a significant transportation infrastructure was installed, and its utility in war was to prove enormous. Equally important, at the end of 1958 the state decided to expand regional industries capable of meeting local needs for consumer goods, less complex agricultural and production equipment, and construction materials. They accounted for only 12 percent of the industrial and artisanal output in 1960, but four times that share in 1964. The adaptability and resiliency in the DRV's economy was thereby increased immeasurably.[4]

The period after the Geneva Conference had been a time of consolidation on the organizational level as well as on the economic, but it was success in the latter domain that was most striking and, at least for the time being, most crucial. The Party had survived organizational crises before, and it had gone on to define appropriate political responses to overcome them. As a military force it had found creative solutions to seemingly overwhelming challenges, but again and again its fate both organizationally and militarily had been linked to the overriding economic issues that were vital to the masses.

Had the Party failed to cope with the consequences of the 1945–54 period and to accept the responsibility of administering the economy after 1954, it would have been unprepared for the events after 1960. Its success made it all the more formidable as a foe, because by adding its increasingly significant administrative knowledge to its ideological, political, and military perceptions and experience, the Party overcame the last major challenge on its march toward its primary goal of removing foreign domination over its country.

Chapter 6

America's Confrontation with the Limits of World Power, 1946-1960

The Vietnam War was the United States' longest and most divisive war of the post-1945 epoch, and in many regards its most important conflict in the twentieth century. Obviously, the Vietnamese Communist Party's resiliency made Vietnam distinctive after 1946, but that the United States should have become embroiled with such formidable adversaries was a natural outcome of the logic and objectives of its role in the modern era. In retrospect, it is apparent that there existed two immovable forces, one of which had no conceivable option but to pursue the policy it had embarked on, and that it was far more likely for America to follow in the footsteps of the French than to learn something from their defeat. How and why it made that momentous decision and what it perceived itself to be doing reveals much about our times and the social and political framework in which contemporary history is made. For Vietnam was ultimately the major episode in a larger process of intervention which preceded and transcended it. All of the frustrations and dilemmas which emerged in Vietnam existed for Washington before 1960, and they persist to this day. The only thing that made the Vietnam War unique for the United States was that it lost completely.

The hallmark of American foreign policy after 1945 was the universality of its intense commitment to create an integrated, essentially capitalist world framework out of the chaos of World War Two and the remnants of the colonial systems. The United States was the major inheritor of the mantle of imperialism in modern history, acting not out of a desire to defend the nation against some tangible threat to its physical welfare but because it sought to create a controllable, responsive order elsewhere, one that would

permit the political destinies of distant places to evolve in a manner beneficial to American goals and interests far surpassing the immediate needs of
its domestic society. The regulation of the world was at once the luxury and
the necessity it believed its power afforded, and even if its might both
produced and promised far greater prosperity if successful, its inevitable
costs were justified, as all earlier imperialist powers had also done, as a
fulfillment of an international responsibility and mission.

This task in fact far transcended that of dealing with the USSR, which
had not produced the world upheaval but was itself an outcome of the first
stage of the protracted crisis of the European and colonial system that had
begun in 1914, even though the United States always held Moscow culpable
to a critical extent for the many obstacles it was to confront. The history
of the postwar era is essentially one of the monumental American attempts
—and failures—to weave together such a global order and of the essentially
vast autonomous social forces and destabilizing dynamics emerging
throughout the world to confound its ambitions.

Such ambitions immediately brought the United States face to face with
what to this day remains its primary problem: the conflict between its
inordinate desires and its finite resources, and the definition of realistic
priorities. Although it took years for the limits on American power to
become clear to its leaders, most of whom only partly perceived it, it has
been this problem of coherent priorities, and of the means to implement
them, rather than the ultimate abstract goals themselves that have divided
America's leaders and set the context for debates over policy. What was
most important for much of the post-1945 era was the overweening belief on
the part of American leaders that regulating all the world's political and
economic problems was not only desirable but also possible, given skill and
power. They would not and could not concede that the economic, political,
and social dynamics of a great part of the world exceeded the capacities of
any one or even a group of nations to control. At stake were the large and
growing strategic and economic interests in those unstable nations ex-
periencing the greatest changes.

The interaction between a complex world, the constraints on U.S. power,
and Washington's perceptions, including its illusions and ignorance, is the
subject matter for most of the history of contemporary American foreign
policy. The "accidental" nature of that policy after 1946 was a consequence
of the intrinsic dilemmas of this ambition rather than its cause. To articulate
its priorities was quite simple. Europe was, and still is, at the top of the list
of America's formally defined economic, strategic, and political interests.
The dilemma of priorities was that none precluded others wholly, so that
America's leaders never excluded intervention in any major part of the
world. In the last analysis, it was the sheer extent of its objectives, and the

inevitable crises and issues which emerged when the process of intervention began, that imposed on the United States the loss of mastery over its own priorities and actions.

By the late 1940s the United States had begun to confront the basic dilemmas it was to encounter for the remainder of the century. The formulation of priorities was an integral part of its reasoning, and so was resistance to communism in whatever form it might appear anywhere in the world. Its own interests had been fully articulated, and these found expression in statements of objectives as well as in the creation of international political, military, and economic organizations and alliances the United States effectively dominated, with American-led "internationalism" becoming one of the hallmarks of its postwar efforts.

Describing the various U.S. decision makers' motives and goals is a necessary but inherently frustrating effort because American capitalism's relative ideological underdevelopment produces nuances and contradictions among men of power which often become translated into the tensions and even ambivalences of American diplomacy. But the complex problem of explaining the causes of U.S. foreign policy can never obviate a description of the real forces and considerations which lead to certain actions and to an optimizing of specific, tangible interests rather than of others. Complexity in serious causal explanations has existed since time immemorial and is intrinsic to the analytic process, yet the importance many care to assign to caprice and accident itself looks frivolous on closer examination of the historical facts and political options. There are, ultimately, main trends and forces, and these must be respected regardless of coincidental related factors.

Prevention of the expansion of communism, the "containment" doctrine, became formally enshrined no later than 1947, and in 1950 the "rollback" of communism was secretly adhered to in the famous National Security Council 68 policy. In 1947 the so-called domino theory first emerged in the form of the Truman Doctrine on Greece. Were Greece to fall, Secretary of State George C. Marshall argued in February of that year, Turkey might follow and "Soviet domination might thus extend over the entire Middle East and Asia."[1] Later that year the same logic required the reconstruction of West Germany, lest its weakness create a vacuum of power into which communism could enter and thereby spread throughout Europe. An area was, by this calculation, no stronger than its weakest link, and the domino mode of analysis, involving interconnections and linkages in estimating the effects of major political upheavals, well before Indochina was becoming the first and probably the most durable of conventional U.S. doctrines on the process of change and power in the modern world.

Such perceptions led irresistibly to the official decision in mid-1949, when the Communists triumphed in China, to draw a line against any new communist states in Asia, even though Washington was then preoccupied with European problems. But in Indochina the interaction of European with Asian affairs was always important to American leaders, for France's growing absorption with Indochina was causing it to veto West German rearmament, and the more quickly France won and brought its troops back home to balance projected German power, the sooner it could be brought into existence. No less crucial was the future position of Japan in Asia and in the world economy should it lose access to Southeast Asian raw materials and markets.

In a word, intervening in Vietnam never generated original international political dilemmas and issues for the United States. America's leaders clarified their ideas about dominoes, the credibility of their power, or the raw-materials system in the world long before their action on Indochina had more than a routine significance. It was precisely because of the repeated definitions of containment, dominoes, intervention, and linkages of seemingly discrete foreign policy questions elsewhere in the world that the United States made the irreversible decision to see the war in Vietnam through to the end. Even many of the purely military dilemmas that were to emerge in Vietnam had been raised earlier in Korea. Until well into the 1960s Vietnam was but one of many nations the United States was both involved in and committed to retaining in friendly hands, and from 1953 through 1962 it provided more military and economic aid to Turkey, South Korea, and Taiwan, about as much to Pakistan, and only somewhat less to Greece and Spain. Given its resources and goals, America was deeply involved throughout the world as a matter of routine. This fact encouraged a new intervention to the extent that it succeeded in maintaining client regimes but could also be a restraint once the demands of one nation became so great as to threaten the United States' position elsewhere.

SOUTHEAST ASIA AND THE DOMINOES

The domino theory was to be evoked initially more than any other justification in the Southeast Asian context, and the concept embodied both strategic and economic components which American leaders never separated. "The fall of Indochina would undoubtedly lead to the fall of the other mainland states of Southeast Asia," the Joint Chiefs of Staff argued in April 1950, and with it Russia would control "Asia's war potential . . . affecting the balance of power." Not only "major sources of certain strategic materials" would be lost, but also communications routes.[2] The State Department maintained a similar line at this time, writing off Thailand and Burma should Indochina fall. Well before the Korean conflict this became the United States' official doctrine, and the war there strengthened this commitment.

The loss of Indochina, Washington formally articulated in June 1952, "would have critical psychological, political and economic consequences. . . . the loss of any single country would probably lead to relatively swift submission to or an alignment with communism by the remaining countries of this group. Furthermore, an alignment with communism of the rest of Southeast Asia and India, and in the longer term, of the Middle East (with the probable exceptions of at least Pakistan and Turkey) would in all probability progressively follow. Such widespread alignment would endanger the stability and security of Europe." It would "render the U.S. position in the Pacific offshore island chain precarious and would seriously jeopardize fundamental U.S. security interests in the Far East." The "principal world source of natural rubber and tin, and a producer of petroleum and other strategically important commodities" would be lost in Malaya and Indonesia. The rice exports of Burma and Thailand would be taken from Malaya, Ceylon, Japan, and India. Eventually, there would be "such economic and political pressures in Japan as to make it extremely difficult to prevent Japan's eventual accommodation to communism."[3] This was the perfect integration of all the elements of the domino theory, involving raw materials, military bases, and the commitment of the United States to protect its many spheres of influence. In principle, even while helping the French to fight for the larger cause which America saw as its own, Washington's leaders prepared for greater intervention when it became necessary to prop up the leading domino—Indochina.

There were neither private nor public illusions regarding the stakes and goals for American power. Early in 1953 the National Security Council reiterated, "The Western countries and Japan need increased supplies of raw materials and foodstuffs and growing markets for their industrial production. Their balance of payments difficulties are in considerable part the result of the failure of production of raw materials and foodstuffs in non-dollar areas to increase as rapidly as industrial production."[4] "Why is the United States spending hundreds of millions of dollars supporting the forces of the French Union in the fight against communism?" Vice-President Richard Nixon explained publicly in December 1953. "If Indo-china falls, Thailand is put in an almost impossible position. The same is true of Malaya with its rubber and tin. The same is true of Indonesia. If this whole part of Southeast Asia goes under Communist domination or Communist influence, Japan, who trades and must trade with this area in order to exist, must inevitably be oriented towards the Communist regime."[5] Both naturally and logically, references to tin, rubber, rice, copra, iron ore, tungsten, and oil were integral to American policy considerations from the inception. As long as he was

President, Eisenhower never forgot his country's dependence on the importation of raw materials and the need to control their sources. When he first made public the "falling domino" analogy, in April 1954, he also discussed the dangers of losing the region's tin, tungsten, and rubber and the risk of Japan's being forced into dependence on communist nations for its industrial life—with all that implied. Always implicit in the doctrine was the assumption that the economic riches of the neighbors of the first domino, whether Greece or Indochina, were essential, and when the United States first intervened in those hapless and relatively poor nations, it kept the surrounding region foremost in its calculations. This willingness to accept the immense overhead charges of regional domination was constantly in the minds of the men who made the decisions to intervene.[6]

The problem with the domino theory was, of course, its intrinsic conflict with the desire to impose priorities on U.S. commitments, resources, and actions. If a chain is no stronger than its weakest link, then that link has to be protected even though its very fragility might make the undertaking that much more difficult. But so long as the United States had no realistic sense of the constraints on its power, it was ready to take greater risks. The complex interaction of the America's vast goals, its perception of the nature of its power, the domino vision of challenges, and the more modest notions implicit in the concept of priorities began in 1953 to merge in what became the start of the permanent debate and crisis in American strategic and diplomatic doctrine.

THE SEARCH FOR A COHERENT STRATEGY

Washington had by 1947 become wholly convinced that the Soviet Union was in some crucial manner guiding many of the political and social upheavals in the world that were in fact the outcome of poverty, colonialism, and oligarchies, and that it was, thereby, seriously subverting the United States' attainment of its political and economic objectives of a reformed, American-led capitalist world order. Toward the end of the Korean War, the incipient conflicts built into such a definition of the world were paralleled and aggravated by a crisis in U.S. military technology and doctrine. These two threads inevitably intertwined late in 1953 in the "New Look" debate and in the beginnings of a perpetual search for a global strategy that could everywhere synthesize America's objectives and resources.

The Korean War tested the U.S. military's overwhelming superiority of firepower and technology, along with its capacity to sustain the economic and political costs of protracted war. Given the inconclusive end of the war along the thirty-eighth parallel after three years of combat, and given the total failure of Washington's September 1950 goal of reuniting the country by force of arms, the war had fully revealed the limits of American power. The domestic political controversy it created was less decisive, but it, too, disclosed the formidable political liabilities that such dismal struggles brought to the party in power. And in fiscal 1953, with military spending at 13.8 percent of the gross national product—three times the 1950 proportion —inflation and budget deficits exposed the constraints on American economic resources. In a word, the United States had undertaken a massive effort and achieved only inconclusive results; this reality raised the issue of the credibility of its power. No less important was the fact that it had become bogged down in Asia at the very moment its main priorities and attention were focused on Europe and the Middle East. To resolve these dilemmas became an obsession in Washington, one that affected every area of the world and influenced the U.S. strategy debate for the remainder of the century.

The effort to define a "New Look" for American foreign policy, culminating in Dulles's famous January 12, 1954, speech, was stillborn, for the Soviet test of a hydrogen bomb in August 1953 decisively broke the U.S. monopoly of strategic nuclear weapons. Land war, Dulles declared, could be fought with the forces of America's allies but the United States itself would rely on its "massive retaliatory power . . . by means and at places of our choosing." It was the only "modern way of getting maximum protection at bearable cost," for limited conventional war in Korea had involved potentially unlimited costs.[7] The dark intimation that America might destroy Peking or Moscow because of events in some distant place was the beginning of a search for a new strategy, but the internal contradictions of that view were immediately criticized in Washington. That quest did not preclude relatively minimal responses to what seemed to be small challenges, and even as the weight of military spending on the national economy was reduced substantially over the remainder of the decade and as strategic weapons became more prominent, the White House increased its reliance on covert warfare waged by the CIA—the success of which in Iran and Guatemala greatly encouraged this relatively low-cost, often inconspicuous form of intervention. For whatever the theory, in practice the United States continued to be deeply involved in very different political contexts in every corner of the globe. Throughout the 1950s Washington never husbanded finite resources rationally to attain its primary goals, because, while it could reduce the role of military spending in the economy, it was unwilling and unable to scale down its far more decisive political definitions of the scope and location of American interests in the world.

To a remarkable extent, America's leaders perceived the nature of the contradiction but never ceased to believe that they could find a solution. The intense defense debates of the middle and late 1950s, which made the reputations of numerous articulate and immensely self-confident military intellectuals like Henry Kissinger, Maxwell Taylor, and W. W. Rostow, inconclusively contradicted and neutralized each other. But what was constant in all such theories was the need to be active rather than passive in responding to new problems and challenges, for American power both to appear and to be credible, and to seek to control and direct, rather than be subject to the dictates of, highly fluid outside forces and events. To develop a sense of mastery was the objective, but the fact that the technologies and strategies for attaining it were constantly being debated produced a perpetual dilemma.

It was in this larger context of a search for a decisive global strategy and doctrine throughout the 1950s that the emerging Vietnam issue was linked to so many other international questions. Washington always saw the challenge of Indochina as just one part of a much greater problem it confronted throughout the world: the efficacy of limited war, the danger of dominoes, the credibility of American power, the role of France in Europe, and much else. Vietnam became the conjunction of the postwar crisis of U.S. imperialism at a crucial stage of America's much greater effort to resolve its own doubts about its capacity to protect the larger international socioeconomic environment in which its interests could survive and prosper. By 1960 every preceding event required that the credibility of U.S. power be tested soon, lest all of the failures and dilemmas since 1946 undermine the very foundations of the system it was seeking to construct throughout the world. It was mainly chance that designated Vietnam as the primary arena of trial, but it was virtually preordained that America would try somewhere to attain successes—not simply one but many—to reverse the deepening pattern of postwar history.

Chapter 7

South Vietnam to 1959: Origins of the Conflict

U.S. POLICY: FROM BAO DAI TO THE GENEVA CONFERENCE

From the end of the Second World War until the Geneva Conference, the basic U.S. position on Vietnam was to give critical support to France's effort to retain control over its colony. Washington always looked at the European implications of its policy with an eye both to Vietnam's role in influencing French internal politics and to the overall relation of France to European issues. As its containment policy became more prominent, particularly after the collapse of the Kuomintang in China during 1949, the question of preventing the emergence of another Communist state in Asia began to weigh more heavily. Both considerations led to support for French attempts to wipe out the Revolution, and at the end of 1949 Washington anticipated a crisis in Indochina.

The United States always urged the French to create an anti-Communist nationalist alternative and to move toward the formation of an autonomous Vietnamese state, a position the French thought a pretense for Washington's desire to expand its influence in the region. Their selection of Emperor Bao Dai in June 1948 to head a "State of Vietnam" without any powers struck the Americans as a step in the right direction, but one unlikely to create an alternative appealing to the people. Bao Dai's record as a collaborator with France since 1932, then with Japan and even with the Viet Minh very briefly, was well known, as were his weaknesses of the flesh and the mind. And while these made the French concessions appear a travesty to most of the world, John Foster Dulles summed up the American position late in 1950 when he called "it necessary as a practical matter to choose the lesser of two evils because the theoretically ideal solution is not possible for many reasons—

the French policy being only one."[1] American backing for the French was, in practice, unequivocal. Early in 1950 Washington recognized the nominally independent states in Vietnam, Laos, and Cambodia that France had created on paper and began direct economic aid to the "Associated States" even as it prepared to greatly increase support for France. The United States favored more, but not too much, reform, lest France lose the incentive to fight, but its unanticipated preoccupation with Korea, and France's greater leverage because of the growing American concern for winning its support in European rearmament, left France an essentially free hand on political matters. During 1950–54 France received $3.6 billion in military aid, much of which went to Indochina, and the majority of the war's expense was thereby covered. But whatever the French thought they were doing on their own behalf, they were in fact increasingly becoming a pawn in American global strategy. To play this role adequately, France had to win a military victory. But failing this, Washington still opposed a negotiated end to the war.

When the Geneva Conference opened on May 8, 1954, the public position of the United States appeared very belligerent, but the Eisenhower administration was improvising until it clarified its policy. The "New Look" debate, with its ominous warnings of possible U.S. reliance on atomic arms long before the battle of Dien Bien Phu began, was designed to make Washington look ferocious. Beneath the rhetoric, though, there existed a profound uncertainty. Its hostility toward any negotiations with China and the DRV at a time when they were inevitable reflected Washington's inability to control the important diplomatic initiatives of its British and French allies, a challenge to its hegemony which transcended the question of Indochina. It was thus foreordained that an increasingly divided American government would consider the options before acceding to the fated negotiated end of the war, and it was this very process of studying alternatives that made its subsequent support for the Geneva agreement unavoidable.

Since possible U.S. military intervention in the war was always conditional on British acquiescence and major French concessions on Vietnam's political affairs, and since neither would be forthcoming, all Washington was eventually to receive as a face-saving measure was the agreement to create SEATO (Southeast Asia Treaty Organization) to cope with eventual future crises in the region. The deliberately cultivated rumors early in April 1954 that the United States might use its air power to save Dien Bien Phu seemed plausible for a moment only because of Dulles's ambiguous public ruminations in the preceding months, but neither Dulles nor Eisenhower ever supported the use of American air or sea power, much less that of atomic weapons. What they did explicitly favor was the raising of doubts and fears about a possible U.S. adventure, for even if it found itself militarily and politically incapable of acting, the administration could still serve its goals if it looked as dangerous as possible. Admiral Arthur Radford, chairman of the Joint Chiefs of Staff, suggested various options, including the use of atomic bombs near Dien Bien Phu, but the President, Dulles, and the other members of the JCS rejected all such proposals. In fact the United States favored neither war nor peace, as it was compelled reluctantly to confront the political and military limits of its "New Look" strategic doctrine in the context of the Vietnam War. It was this painful realization, as much as the events in Vietnam itself, which explains the administration's behavior in the spring of 1954.

Apart from its political isolation and its own divisions, Washington's opposition to the Geneva Conference began melting in private as it learned more about the conference's potential for gaining at the negotiating table what could not be won on the battlefield. The French had assiduously studied the divisions between the Vietnamese Communists, China, and the USSR, and its feelers to China and particularly to the Soviet Union had encouraged it with the prospect of exploiting their mutual fears and ambitions. If the United States was made well aware of these prospects before Geneva, its comprehension of their importance became far greater after the conference opened. Washington decided, therefore, to sulk and act threatening publicly, knowing it would deepen the divisions between China, Russia, and the Vietnamese and increase Sino-Soviet pressures on the DRV to make concessions. The British and French were soon to encourage the assuming of this posture.

The United States refused to vote for the conference resolution on July 21 and declared itself not bound by its decisions, but privately it was convinced that it had obtained a precious respite and the best settlement possible, given the political and military realities and the Vietnamese side's "relatively moderate [demands] in terms of their actual capabilities." The primary question for Dulles was "whether we could salvage what the Communists had ostensibly left out of their grasp in Indochina."[2]

America's salvaging operation immediately had to confront a number of problems. The most urgent was to strengthen the anti-Communists in Vietnam, which the United States considered synonymous with removing French influence. Next was the problem of transforming the temporary division of Vietnam along the seventeenth parallel into a permanent partition by frustrating the accords' proviso for a mid-1956 election to reunite the country, for in mid-May Dulles had stated publicly that he would oppose any elections in the indefinite future. Even before the accords were signed, the United States had managed to take a major step in this direction when it persuaded the French to allow Bao Dai to appoint Ngo Dinh Diem as his prime minister and to get the emperor to agree to stay in Europe's spas while Diem returned to Saigon to run the south. By July 7, 1954, Diem had a fully organized cabinet in place.

NGO DINH DIEM, THE UNITED STATES, AND THE BEGINNING OF THE NEW ORDER

Ngo Dinh Diem had worked in the French bureaucracy for a decade until 1933, when he became Bao Dai's minister of interior. He retired from politics after a bitter dispute with the French over his powers, and during the war he established relations with the Japanese and came under their protection. In March 1945 he negotiated with them to become prime minister, but they could not reach terms in time. Diem was by 1954 one of the very few unequivocally anti-French and anti-Communist politicians of any note to whom the United States could turn.

Diem had established ties with prominent figures in America during his two-year stay there in 1951–53. Although his contacts eased his way, these were mainly with liberal Democrats, who alone would not have gotten him very far in a Republican government. No one had to lobby the Eisenhower administration to support a rearguard Indochina strategy. Bao Dai himself knew that the French could not fund a future anti-Communist government, and he was as ready to swing to the Americans as he had been to the Japanese. Diem was also Bao Dai's man, and had been since 1953, but the French did not oppose his nomination, also because they were and felt beaten and could offer Bao Dai little more, but partly because Dulles himself had convinced the sybaritic emperor this was the wisest policy. In view of what they were hoping to accomplish, the Americans were unable to find anybody as promising as Diem.

Little did the United States realize in 1954 how momentous a decision it had made when it chose to back Ngo Dinh Diem. That it would usher in a major phase of American history, shaped to a crucial extent by the strengths, desires, and weaknesses of one man, seemed unimaginable. And that the United States' advancement of its own objectives and interests would depend on this exotic figure revealed, not for the first or the last time, the extent of caprice in the conduct of its foreign policy.

Diem had spent a good part of his adult life as a reclusive, solitary bachelor, especially renowned for his celibacy, and during these long periods he turned to philosophy, producing a syncretic version of personalism into which he threw his Catholic faith, assorted Confucian and Indian ideas, various personalist notions once fashionable in Paris, and much else besides. The result was an incomprehensible hodgepodge which could be dismissed immediately as someone's private confusion were it not for the fact that Diem had power and that his philosophy was the official ideology of a government with U.S. support. The only interest his ideas have is their influence on his relations with people, on political trends, and on the Americans who were backing him.

Diem's ideological pretensions immediately became dysfunctional even in a region which always had a ready market for philosophical mumbo jumbo, and his exotic ideas made him appear all the more remote and obscure to the people. But because he had power, Diem also amassed adherents. Personalism was quickly translated into an ideology of the private use of power by Diem's family and cronies in a circle around a ruler who allegedly personified the national interest as well as rational community and individual values. And along with its corporatist and authoritarian idealization of the state over private and class interests came an antitechnological bias which had implications for social policy. While it took several years for the Americans on the scene to come to grips with the problems Diem's philosophizing might produce, they could not avoid them in the end.

Meanwhile, U.S. officials had to exploit the respite which the Geneva conditions on temporary partition and elections gave them, as well as expunge the remaining French control over Vietnam's political and economic life, which during August 1954 Washington in vain asked the French to terminate. The probability confronting the United States, the CIA concluded one month after the Geneva Conference, was the following: "If the scheduled national elections are held in July 1956, and if the Viet Minh does not prejudice its political prospects, the Viet Minh will almost certainly win."[3] Communism would thus try to take power in the south by peaceful, legal means, and it would find that the chronic political disunity in the south would facilitate its already easy task. The Americans and Diem therefore immediately formulated and exploited for several more years various pretexts for refusing to hold elections. Nevertheless, throughout 1954 the American experts on the area saw nothing but failure ahead.

Diem had returned to a cacophony of political opposition and intrigues, overt French opposition, and the possibility of a French-backed army coup. Not the least was the problem of Bao Dai, who in the same month he had appointed Diem prime minister had also sold to the Binh Xuyen crime syndicate the post of Saigon police chief for over $1 million and who soon regretted his decision to appoint Diem. Then there were the predominantly Catholic refugees from the north, eventually numbering around 850,000, who were beginning to move south under the terms of the Geneva Accords.

Although almost unanimously pessimistic reports arrived in Washington, Diem's prospects were no worse than those of other dictators the United States was sponsoring elsewhere. In November, General J. Lawton Collins was appointed ambassador to Saigon to review the situation and recommend future policy. Despite doubts about Diem's ability to obtain popular support, and even his acrimonious arguments with Diem about how to organize his army and deal with the land problem, Collins nevertheless finally proposed aiding him. Given the enormous problems confronting Diem, the U.S. endorsement was all that saved him from disaster. In the year after the Geneva Conference, Diem's regime received $322 million in aid from Washington, and yet more later. Diem could now proceed to consolidate his power.

The initial relationship between Diem and his sponsor was turbulent, and during April 1955 Washington nearly replaced him. The frequent and often stormy complaints of the Americans notwithstanding, Diem soon learned he could count on them, and this only increased his freedom of action. Basically, the United States supported Diem, whom it acknowledged to be independent and whose exotic ideas they ignored as much as possible, because he also served its overall purposes far better than anyone else available. He was just as eager as the United States to thwart the Geneva Accords, and quite as ready to expunge Communists and eradicate the French legacy. To the Americans, Diem seemed a major step in the nation-building process and in the creation of political legitimacy as well as the extension of their sphere of influence. For Diem was the toughest player in the rough arena of Saigon politics, and his single-mindedness and gall gained him the begrudging admiration of even those Americans who criticized his politics.

The pro-French and French-backed Vietnamese posed a greater immediate threat to the consolidation of Diem's power than the Communists. His ability to purge French influence was directly related to the amount of economic and military aid the United States provided. During mid-1955 his forces managed to attack and rein in the Binh Xuyen, Cao Dai, and Hoa Hao private armies, all of whom France had funded until early that year. In October he had Bao Dai dethroned; at the end of the year he broke off economic relations with France and left the French Union, proclaiming the creation of the "Republic of Vietnam." The formal vestiges of the French colonial order were now gone, along with hopes for implementing the Geneva Accords. If Diem never played the role of a wholly reliant comprador, the tensions with the United States were largely overlooked after 1955, as their mutual goals coincided and he became indispensable to Washington's general purposes.[4]

DIEM CONSOLIDATES POWER

With Washington's backing assured and growing firmer, Diem proceeded to consolidate a political order in his own image. His first move after coming to power in July 1954 had been to make his family the core of the political structure. Of the nine cabinet ministries in his first government, Diem held the three most important, the father-in-law of his brother, Ngo Dinh Nhu, held another, and Nhu's wife's uncle was foreign minister. Another relative was minister of education. Diem's brother, Ngo Dinh Can, ran the northern provinces around Hué without any nominal post whatsoever, and another brother, Bishop Ngo Dinh Thuc, ran the Catholic Church in Vietnam. Ngo Dinh Nhu and his wife, who headed the Women's Movement, were from the inception the regime's famous éminences grises, with enormous influence over Diem. Diem's concentration of key decisions in his family's hands led immediately to grave administrative inefficiency. His relatives were also all thoroughly corrupt and soon began amassing funds in foreign banks.

After the family at the center of power, the next layer of authority for the most sensitive and important posts was Diem's loyal supporters from the central region around Hué. These were mainly ambitious landlords and members of the social elite. Regionalism was reinforced by Catholicism, which was an important entrée into politics and power for the refugees from the DRV, who gave the regime its sole semblance of mass support in a territory that was 90 percent non-Catholic. The last layer, and the one intended to give an organizational basis to the regime, was the Can Lao party (Personalist Labor Revolutionary party), which was not created until 1956 and was the only legal party.

The Can Lao party comprised roughly sixteen thousand secret members in 1959, directed, ultimately, by Diem and Nhu. Nominally personalist in ideology, the Can Lao was a combination of private political machine and mafia, and membership in it was a prerequisite to advancement to higher posts in the government and military. By controlling recruitment, Diem and his family could guarantee the loyalty of key persons in both the state and the army and purge them of all those left over by the French as well as of any other opposition. Can Lao members of the army were at times able to give orders to their nominal superiors, and under Nhu the Can Lao took over much of the south's crime in order to build the party's funds. The Can Lao also served as a secret police, modeled after the system the Japanese used in Vietnam during World War Two—which Diem had studied in detail.

The creation of the Can Lao compelled the United States to agree to give Diem an essentially free hand to run South Vietnam as he thought best, and not until 1963 did it revoke that mandate. The party's establishment, coming on top of the existing nepotism and informal empire, meant that political legitimacy and the succession would also be Diem's prerogative, and could only lead to instability. Colonel Edward Lansdale, who had been one of Diem's firmest supporters among the officials working on Vietnam, vainly tried to mobilize American opposition to his policies, predicting that the emerging police state would produce political fluctuations and crises and drive all other political parties into underground opposition. But apart from the Communists, the CIA argued, Diem's potential political rivals were "primarily power seeking opportunists."[5] Many, too, were pro-French.

The United States was scarcely interested in opposing Diem's repression so long as Diem blocked the implementation of the elections agreed on in Geneva, and this both Saigon and Washington did by stating that neither had signed the accords. The United States' first goal was to help Diem build his army and police, the administration made public in June 1956, and this, too, was done in a fashion that violated the terms of the accords. American opponents to a reunification election in any form included the *New York Times,* Senator John F. Kennedy, and many others, and neither Diem nor the United States ever consented to repeated requests by the DRV and Geneva Conference cochairmen to meet to discuss modalities of an election. The administration, convinced the Communists would win it, simply endorsed Diem's obduracy, and meanwhile Diem consolidated power.[6]

DIEM'S ELIMINATION OF POSSIBLE CHALLENGERS

The most urgent task facing Diem was to consolidate his power over the 200,000 or more Vietnamese collaborators the French had after 1950 formed into an army to fight the Viet Minh. For in a one-party regime the military was the only non-Communist group with the potential to challenge his dictatorship. The highly personalized nature of the state, without a class or institutional basis, made the coup d'état the only method of succession, and in the first year of his regime the undisguised French desire to get Diem removed from office meant that he had to strike first at the only force the French could rely on for quick results. In the course of accomplishing his mission, Diem totally dismantled the century-old French institutional and bureaucratic system and replaced it with his overtly totalitarian political machine.

The United States and France in June 1954 agreed that the Americans would assume a responsibility for training and supplying Bao Dai's army. Although the first American thought was to prepare Diem for coping with insurgency, he easily shifted its primary commitment to creating a conventional army capable of blocking an invasion from the north. In fact, Diem's main objective was to create an army whose real purpose was to protect his political machine against rival anti-Communists and which was incapable of turning on him. While many other factors also explain the ARVN's weaknesses, its intrinsically political nature meant that the army would ultimately be incapable of ever successfully fighting either an unconventional or a regular war.

Diem's first step in 1955 after smashing the independent sect armies was to fire without compensation over six thousand battle-experienced noncommissioned officers to add to the growing constituency of sulking former French loyalists. To weed out those officers beholden to the French and not ready to transfer their loyalties unequivocally, Diem created new officer schools which were primarily political indoctrination centers, and from them came the large majority of the RVN's senior officers. Those whom the Diem circle trusted were enrolled in the Can Lao party until the higher officer corps was fully organized. The importance of membership to advancement made ambitious men ready to join it. But even more crucial was the Diem clique's personal evaluation of the loyalty of all key command appointments, for this group alone controlled senior promotions.

Those officers whose loyalty appeared beyond reproach soon supplied Diem with his most important civil administrators. In 1956 the police was taken over by military officers, and by 1962 all but a small number of his province chiefs were military men; this led to the militarization of the civil order. Meantime, in the army he set up a convoluted and overlapping command structure whose only purpose was explicitly to prevent any group of officers from obtaining sufficient control to challenge his authority. The United States could never, try though it might, end this parallel system, which persisted in various forms until 1975. Innumerable conflicting military jurisdictions as well as compartmentalized military regions and branches unable to cooperate or even communicate with each other directly meant that power ultimately rested only with the man at the top. This was the object of the whole Byzantine structure, and Diem exercised his power constantly. For all these political reasons, the ARVN never operated as a coordinated, integrated military arm in large operations.[7]

Having begun to consolidate his control over the sects and the army, Diem decided in 1956 to confront the Chinese community's colonial-based privileges. By the early 1950s the Chinese composed about one-tenth of South Vietnam's population but held well over one-half of the public capital invested in commerce, industry, and artisan shops, plus nearly all of the larger hidden capital. They controlled over four-fifths of the retail trade and dominated textiles, import-export, transport, metalworking, and much else.

The fact that they were legally subject only to their *bangs* was not merely an issue of nationalist pride for Diem. It was also a question of control over taxation and the economy. In August 1956 he granted Vietnamese nationality to all Chinese born in Vietnam and required them to Vietnamize their names. The *bangs* themselves were dissolved and much of their property confiscated. Then, to compel their cooperation, the following month he banned foreign nationals from eleven categories of economic activity which were the basis of Chinese domination of the economy. They were given up to a year to liquidate their businesses or turn them over to Vietnamese, which for most meant simply taking Vietnamese nationality.

The impact on the otherwise passive Chinese community was electric, creating a panic and a sense of insecurity which were to politicize it in a way that would otherwise have been impossible. The Chinese refused almost en masse to take out Vietnamese nationality cards, and the Chiang Kai-shek government in Taiwan immediately entered the picture on their behalf, for in 1948 it had been given the right to help select *bang* leaders. Creating diverse fronts to hold on to their interests, the Chinese decided to confront Diem by attacking the piaster and closing the export market for rice. They also ceased lending money to farmers and stopped water transport in the Delta. Their resistance was quite effective, but Diem remained adamant, and while the Chinese managed to run the economy as before by using various facades, they were unwilling to invest more than necessary. Although even Diem's family was compelled to make alliances with various Chinese to carry on their enterprises, the Chinese never recovered confidence in Diem. He had managed only to mobilize a critical social force against himself. The Chinese quietly waited.[8]

Once his system of power was consolidated into a comprehensive personal political machine, Diem moved to exercise it thoroughly in all domains of society. Urban repression was the easiest to implement. Though exact numbers are unknown, a conservative estimate is 40,000 political prisoners in jails by the end of 1958 and 12,000 killed during 1955–57. Newspapers were closed routinely. A patina of legality for repression was provided in August 1956 in Ordinance 47, strengthened in Law 10/59 in May 1959, which made being a "communist" or working with one a capital offense. Both were administered by military tribunals with no appeal, and their existence was a stark warning to the population that the regime would brook no rivals.

With growing power came more arrests, and estimates of approximately 150,000 political prisoners by the end of 1961 appear reasonable, although DRV figures were far higher yet. The RVN admitted to nearly 50,000 arrested by 1960. Diem rounded up opponents without concern for ideology, and pro-French Vietnamese were especially vulnerable. In November 1960 eighteen of the most important collaborators with France, the so-called

Caravelle Group, issued a manifesto against Diem's repression and politics: "Continuous arrests fill the jails and prisons to the rafters . . . public opinion and the press are reduced to silence."[9] Most of them were thrown into prison.

The emergence of Diem's totalitarian, personalized regime caused increasing ambivalence among American officials, especially after it became starkly clear that his army's ultimate function was not to fight either conventional or guerilla war but to maintain Diem in power. Diem was "pro-American," however, even when he refused to accept its advice. Were he to leave office, Washington believed, South Vietnam probably would not survive. The United States freely acknowledged the authoritarian nature of the regime, but in 1959 it was still considered stable, and reports on Diem in the U.S. media remained highly favorable. Since 85 percent of the RVN's military budget and two-thirds of its combined 1955–58 civil-military budget was supplied by the United States, Diem's mandate from Washington was virtually total. It was to remain that way until 1963, notwithstanding the head of the U.S. Military Assistance Advisory Group's warning at the end of 1960 that Diem would confront mounting political, and therefore military, problems.

While Diem controlled every aspect of the RVN army touching politics, he nonetheless was willing to accede to America's desire to organize and train it. The entire military budget of the RVN was prepared under the guidance of the Pentagon, which decided what sort of equipment it would receive as well as the capability of the military. A compromise on the military's size had been reached only after hard bargaining. But Diem refused to allow the Americans to do anything more for the economy than give essentially unrestricted aid. In varying ways, in the first five years after the Geneva settlement, the essential precedents and procedures of military and economic aid to Saigon were fixed for the next two decades.

Diem's economic ideas embodied an exotic mélange of mandarin anti-capitalism and Catholic feudalist ideas and a keen desire for personal power and profit. Diem refused to allow American economists to advise him and embarked on economic policies the United States regarded with alarm. In addition to attacking the Chinese, he reduced French economic power in the south. He agreed to fully protect American investment, but there was none. Diem soon decided to build a state economic sector which was eventually to produce a number of national firms in sugar refining, paper, cement, textiles, and much else, rejecting a cardinal American principle regarding the role of private investment in development. And he quickly learned how to manipulate the import program and currency exchange rates in a manner American officials were to condemn but tolerate for two decades. Diem did this so well that by 1961 his foreign-exchange holdings were the size of

England's and gave the piaster one of the highest gold and hard-currency backings in the world. With a flood of luxury goods beginning to enter the static economy to create what one U.S. official in 1961 thought was an extreme inequality between cities and countryside which was one of the "major causes of dissatisfaction which contributes to the present insurgency," the RVN had virtually no taxes.[10] Paying for what every U.S. official thought was a policy both wasteful for America and fraught with dangers for Saigon, the political compulsions to continue subsidizing the RVN nonetheless kept mounting. The result was a totally dependent and poorly balanced economy from the inception of Washington's sponsorship of the RVN's existence.

DIEM AND THE CREATION OF A VACUUM OF POWER

Diem's regime managed to alienate every traditional, conservative stratum of an otherwise deeply divided nation in the course of replacing the colonial order which the French had built up over a century. The family system he put in place combined elements of feudalism and gangsterism but provided no orderly method of sharing benefits. The ambitious young officers whom Diem advanced over those the French had favored were the only group among the non-Communist forces capable of implementing swift changes, but only at Diem's expense and by installing some type of structure of military politics. It was perfectly clear by November 1960, when officers once close to Diem mounted an abortive coup, that elements in the military would inevitably attempt to create such a mechanism of succession.

There was neither a class nor a coherent ideological base for the Diemist regime, but only functionaries related to a political machine whose very private family nature made it incapable of institutionalization or respectable intellectual justification. Since the raison d'être for Diem and any possible successors was power, those working for Diem could gain from change if they were a part of it. Most of the Chinese compradors who might have played a greater role in support of Diem if allowed to do so were alienated by his assaults on their national identity. Ultimately, there was not a state but scarcely more than a foreign-backed family.

In its own way, Diem's destruction of the position of those who had been shaped by the French colonial order guaranteed the instability in South Vietnam's urban society that led to his overthrow in 1963 and much of the subsequent turbulence in the south. The French colonial experience was not a casual affair for a large part of the urbanized, educated Vietnamese. French education and values profoundly affected the south's pre-1954 urban social order, and Diem's opaque alternative had absolutely no influence on it. The existing social hierarchy incorporated many more than just those receiving direct economic benefits from the French presence. Together with those who had been in the French bureaucracy—some of whom, of course, were willing to serve Diem loyally but were relegated mainly to lesser posts—these groups, as shallow, diverse, and dependent as their class base was, constituted the only large, natural element with even a remote chance of creating a substantial anti-Communist coalition. The moment Diem sought to erase the French colonial residue entirely and superimpose a nouveau riche class of younger officers over them, he guaranteed that many of these normally intensely divided groups would be ready to unite around one issue—opposition to Diem and to the military machine and military politics he was to leave as an enduring legacy. This residual Francophile element would later constitute an important part of all urban opposition to the military regime.

Diem, in a word, could attack the French heritage, but he could not put a durable alternative in its place. He could produce only instability and a vacuum in political and social power—and crisis. He also guaranteed that many southerners hostile to Diem would have to oppose America, the only solid pillar on which his regime stood, for a new U.S. intervention had replaced French domination. In what was only very superficially a civil war, behind the fragile veneer of one side stood a foreign nation whose support alone made Diem's very existence and repression possible.

DIEM AND RURAL COUNTERREVOLUTION, 1954–1960

The control of land and the condition of the peasantry remained the most socially volatile issues in the south after 1954. Neutralizing land's mass appeal became the crucial political challenge confronting the Diem regime, which had little inkling how its land policies would create the very menace they were intended to prevent.

The Communists controlled 60 to 90 percent of the territory in the south prior to the Geneva Accords. From 1941 onward the Viet Minh land policies in the south had managed to sharply reduce the number of poor peasants in some areas, driving many of their landlords into the cities. The peasants of the Mekong were, if anything, more militant than those in the north, in part because so many were only laborers. The Revolution redistributed over 600,000 hectares of land, under a third of that available, to landless peasants and those who had supported the resistance. Since much of this land was transferred at the expense of French and some of the largest Vietnamese landowners, it did not affect its united front with rich peasants and the majority of landlords. Squatters, in addition, simply occupied abandoned land.

The sheer size of the landless peasantry, which exceeded that with land, made the land question far more complicated than one of simple land distribution. At the time of the Geneva Accords, the richest tenth of the landholders held, at least on paper, 65 percent of the land. The rent question was a more urgent and universal issue and less threatening to the Party's political coalition. Rents were lowered to 25 percent maximum, and the worst abuses of usury were outlawed and pre-1945 debts abolished. In some regions absentee landlords ceased collecting rents altogether. Also important was the question of the fate of sons and the various armies, for in the life of a peasant the son is the ultimate form of security in a world full of risks and disasters, and integral to the peasantry's basic economic unit. The French puppet army had by April 1953 mobilized 112,000 Vietnamese soldiers in Cochin China, whereas the Communists had only 45,000. But families of those serving the French received nothing but social ostracism, while those with sons in the Revolution were given preference in land redistribution to compensate for their sacrifices. All of these factors played a role in the land question, so that by 1954 the Communists had been instrumental in beginning a major transformation of the southern land system that was still under way at the time of the accords and had already affected about four-fifths of the population in some manner.

Diem's so-called land reform which began in early 1955 and was consolidated in October 1956 was an extremely complex effort to reestablish political control in the Viet Minh regions in the Delta only, where it was applied most rigorously. Precisely because it was a major part of a larger effort at political consolidation, it touched different landlords in diverse ways, hurting a substantial group of them too. But since driving the French out totally gave Diem a quarter of a million hectares to confiscate, he was able to establish his pretension as a reformer. For the substantial portion of the peasantry that had benefited from the Viet Minh's reforms, Diem's measures represented a counterrevolution, and its fear of losing valuable gains and returning to the traditional peasant-landlord structure created a crisis in the rural areas. For it was Diem's land program, not the Party, which led inevitably to renewed conflict in South Vietnam. The moment he abolished the legal standing of the Viet Minh's land reforms, he unleashed social discontent and created actual and potential enemies. This was particularly true where the Revolution's reforms had gone the furthest.

Diem fixed the maximum rents at 25 percent and confiscated French-held lands while limiting Vietnamese-held land to 115 hectares. Apart from many peasants now being compelled again to pay rent, if not back rentals, on land the Viet Minh had made theirs, rents everywhere were in practice often as high as 40 percent. And while 115 hectares is a very large amount, landlords were allowed to keep the best land and sell the surplus mainly for bonds, though the RVN's practice of pricing it at about half its real value alienated many. Those eager to retain their land could distribute it to their families, or influence the responsible officials. Every account has treated the administration of this land program as corrupt.

By 1961, when his program had come to a virtual halt, Diem had collected 422,000 hectares plus the French-owned lands, or about 650,000 hectares. Of these only 244,000 were redistributed after late 1958, mainly to Catholic refugees or former soldiers and newcomers who created social tension with their arrival. French land, which was the richest, remained in RVN hands, undistributed. Only 12 percent of the tenants were to receive any new land, which they had to purchase—the Viet Minh's policy had been free distribution—and one-tenth of the landholders in 1966 still owned 55 percent of the rice land, compared with 65 percent at the reform's inception. Far more peasants lost land under RVN laws than were to gain anything from them. Not only were the Viet Minh rental and usury reforms undone, but the RVN emerged as the nation's largest landlord. As a U.S. consultant later reported, "Provincial and local officials were allowed to retain and rent out the best of the acquired land."[11]

Before 1955 the landlord had been the primary object of the peasants' bitterness; now it included Diem's offensive officials. Indeed, where landlords could not return to reimpose their control over villages still operating under the Viet Minh land reform, they often hired local civil and military authorities to do so, generally paying 30 percent of the proceeds for the service. Along with the widespread belief that Diem's family had made a fortune off the land reform transfers, Diem's functionaries and army became ever present and thoroughly hated.

The main change in the ageless landlord-tenant relationship was less in the restoration of the pre–Viet Minh order than in the dominating state bureaucracy which Diem created. But the alteration in the relationship of the landlord to the state was greater, even if the political consequences of this change were not so far-reaching. For while most landlords desired a return to the pre–Viet Minh land system, they did not welcome Diem's alternative. The only exceptions were absentee landlords who were happy to find a market for much of their land and retire to the relatively safe cities with a more diversified investment. The majority were unhappy with their low compensation, with having to deal with chiseling officials, and, perhaps most of all, with the end to their political power in the villages.

The French at the turn of the century had created councils in every village to serve as the self-administering local authority of the colonial order, collecting taxes, performing civil functions, and mediating between the state and the masses. Only local landowners, officers, and mandarins obtained these posts, and soon they ran villages to enrich themselves in the name of France. Indeed, much of the local elite's land had come from the French or by an abuse of this political authority. These councils were corrupt tools of political and economic oppression, and the Viet Minh abolished them in 1945. The French and Bao Dai had attempted to restore them. For Diem, however, the village councils were not merely the hated French legacy but also a grass-roots challenge to his political power. In June 1956, much to the chagrin of the Americans, who were neither told nor asked, Diem abolished the councils and had his district and province chiefs, who were his direct appointees, designate officials to replace them. These were mostly Catholics and/or Diem cronies from the Hué region, and all were out to make money. As outsiders, they and their police personified the RVN's daily oppression and corruption over the peasantry as contrasted to the somewhat mellower style of the local rich. For their part, the landlords were no less unhappy. Even the Party, keenly aware of the landlords' growing alienation as well as that of the entire pro-French middle class, sought with little success to reach out to them, even moderating its land strategy somewhat in the process.[12]

Diem's rural curbs came in two phases. First, he rounded up and eliminated the opposition, including the village councils. In 1955, wholesale arrests and intimidation began, directed primarily against the religious sects the first year. Local village meetings were called everywhere to publicly denounce "Communists." Forty thousand persons were accused in a five-week stretch in just one province in the southern Delta. Looking back at this period, a senior ARVN officer writing for the U.S. Army noted, "President Diem's campaign against the VCI was effective but indiscriminate. By authorizing province chiefs to execute suspects without a hearing or even a police record, he in effect encouraged abuses. There is little doubt that many political enemies—who were not actually VC—disappeared as a result of the anti-VCI campaign."[13] A few years later, another ARVN general recalled, Diem's brother, Ngo Dinh Can, created a special police in his central Vietnam fiefdom, and the "task force members indiscriminately slaughtered every VCI member they hunted down."[14]

Physical control of the population followed the RVN's terror. Diem moved to experiment with major population transfers, a program which the United States funded and which it continued long after he was shot. Ultimately, Diem subordinated all issues, land included, to his desire for military security. Given the large number of Catholic refugees from the DRV, it was possible to find people for new settlements, and this was done routinely after 1956. The placing of local peasants who were or might become anti-RVN where they could be neutralized was far different and implied varying degrees of coercion, and small efforts along this line were attempted in early 1959, culminating in the *agroville* program of July 1959. Had the half a million or more peasants assigned to move cooperated, a series of strategically placed farm communities organized on military lines would have extended from the north to Saigon, but peasants refused to build these *agrovilles,* and the program instead became the focus of peasant resistance. In the meantime the Diem regime lost money and time, and the program petered out by the end of 1960, creating countless hostile peasants. By the time "strategic hamlets" came into existence in 1962, the events in the countryside following the Geneva Accords—the land tenure changes, the new administrative system, mass arrests and murders, and, finally, population transfers—had greatly angered the peasantry. The southern peasantry had never been docile, and it had no reason to become passive after 1954. Diem's policies began setting an ever-growing section of simple peasants over the vast flat stretches of the Mekong Delta into almost unstoppable motion.

Surveying the situation in the south in May 1959, the State Department reported, "There is no evidence of any widespread restiveness among the population at large," nor any "grass-roots support" for Diem either.[15] Within a year the future looked far less tranquil, but not alarming. America paid the bills, and a series of relatively minor officials worked with Diem's system, aware that without him the state Washington created from potential disaster at Geneva would finally fall.

At the core of the problem was a mutual dependency. It was clear both that Diem could not exist without U.S. backing and that U.S. goals in the region could not be served without Diem. It was this dilemma that permitted Diem to pursue his policies without serious inhibition. Americans on the spot recognized the constraints on their freedom to push in other directions despite mounting reservations about Diem's policies. In reality, the United States had only minor criticism to make of Diem's programs, for it was deeply involved in land reform matters and in building the police and various bureaucracies. Diem did no more than other dictators Washington funded at the same time, and less than some. All that was unpredictable in the situation was the response of Diem's potential enemies to the conditions emerging in the south.

Chapter 8

The Communist Party's Dilemma in the South, 1954-1959

From its inception, the Party and the Viet Minh in Cochin China reflected those distinctive characteristics which vast distances and poor communications among the three main regional committees made inevitable. During the 1930s the southern Party had often mobilized greater mass support than its northern counterpart, but the ruthless French and British reoccupation of Vietnam south of the sixteenth parallel immediately after August 1945 made political conditions there far more restrictive, and the Party's role was quite different. The southern Party had many more rivals for power, though they were highly fractured and localized, than existed in the north.

The Party in the south evolved, therefore, in its own fashion, the Party Central Committee being in charge of its overall policies but physically unable continuously to guide it. The southern leadership was never independent, but in the absence of direction it did at times define its own lines, and these often had to be corrected. In 1946 Tran Van Giau, the south's brilliant, charismatic leader, was removed because of his failure to apply the united-front strategy successfully and enlarge the Party organization. Notwithstanding the Viet Minh's success with its land policy, the Party itself in early 1948 had only 9,000 members in Cochin China. Aggressive recruiting enlarged it to 23,000 later the same year. Regardless of the Party's relatively small size, by national standards, its mass following was still enormous.

In 1951 the Central Committee set up a special directorate for the south, but Party leaders knew they had lost a certain control over the events there. Despite dark days for the Party in the Mekong Delta until 1952, its land program and French preoccupation with the north caused a great resurgence in its fortunes in the two years before the Geneva Accords, by which time it controlled most of the rural areas and population. In June 1954 the French confided to the Americans that if the war continued and if they lost the Tonkin Delta, which was probable, there would be no southern Vietnamese ready to fight against the Revolution.

The DRV delegation at Geneva had linked a temporary partition line to French political assurances in the accords that there would be elections in the south, but the French quickly reneged on them, and the United States and Diem were allowed to take over the south. Meanwhile, over 130,000 Revolutionary regroupees from the south went north fully anticipating to return home within two years, when the reunification elections were held.

The DRV's dilemma was to emerge quickly enough. It expected to win any Geneva election and reunite the country, a view which the U.S. senior experts shared, and throughout 1955 and 1956 the DRV combined its constant appeals for them with a willingness to have them under international supervision as provided for in the accords. As Diem and the United States ignored the accords' provisions and refused to meet, the Party had to confront basic policy issues. Some senior leaders argued that the DRV's preoccupation with socialist development would prevent it from dealing with reunification. Furthermore, it could not ignore the plight of the southern regroupees who were beginning to confront the likelihood of a much longer separation from their homes and families. No later than March 1955 the Party's basic policy was that the consolidation of the north served the interests of those in the south, a position it was to hold for over three years. By mid-1956 Ho was encouraging the demoralized regroupees that "to work here [was] the same as struggling in the South."[1]

This greater stress on developing the DRV was disputed, and, as in all such disagreements among themselves, the Party's leaders guarded an option on the minority policy. Le Duan went to the south for over a year to study the situation, taking with him a slightly more flexible set of tactics. But the strategy of emphasizing the north was not altered. Reiterating that the approved activity was "political struggle and not armed struggle," the Party permitted self-defense and the protection of its few bases.[2] A broad united front to create a political coalition in the south, however, was the Party's basic objective. But until the Party lost all hope for the application of the Geneva Accords, it refused to risk premature violence. Moreover, though it knew that the accords might not be fulfilled, it still believed that Diem would not solidify power so thoroughly and that his policies would soon create a far more promising situation.

Given its economic difficulties and the accumulated dislocations of the first Indochina War against France, the Party's decision to consolidate the north as a foundation for reunification was consistent with its leadership's mode of work—which was to hedge on its options while striving for the most attainable objective. Its economic program indicated a clear desire to use its time and resources to gain absolutely vital goals, and not to be paralyzed by indecision, but there can be no question that both in fact and in its own view the Party now faced an enormous and growing dilemma. Events were not standing still, the success of the DRV's reconstruction program notwithstanding.

THE PARTY'S POSITION IN THE SOUTH AFTER THE GENEVA ACCORDS

Whatever the Party's expectations for the period after July 1954, there is no indication it fully anticipated the events that were to traumatize the south. It envisaged France's refusal to apply the Geneva Accords and the U.S.-backed effort to wipe out the Viet Minh and the Party as a possibility but not a probability. But it did not foresee Diem's land and political policies, which created such mass discontent and a largely spontaneous prerevolutionary environment for armed struggle and Party growth. As the Party's misjudgments in one domain were offset by Diem's in the other, the stresses and strains on the Party in the south and the leaders in the north compelled it to consider its moves in a context and manner unlike any in its entire history.

Most of those who repatriated to the DRV were military personnel, and only a maximum of 15,000 active Party and Viet Minh political elements were left in the south by 1957. Of the much larger number who had been Viet Minh, a significant proportion dropped out of politics, hoping to care for their personal affairs. A still active minority were told to focus on mobilizing the masses to demand the fulfillment of the Geneva Accords. The Party's overwhelming emphasis was on political struggle. As the Diem regime consolidated control over the countryside, the vast majority of the activists were arrested or killed—in some places the proportion reached 90 percent and more. It was the overriding fact of terror that quickly defined the actions and fate of those who remained in the south, forcing many ex–Viet Minh who had hoped to pursue quiet lives to return to the struggle.[3]

Political activity for the remaining activists had become virtually impossible, and those who were not immediately caught or who refused to defect either hid in cities or escaped to a few existing secret base areas in the jungles and marshes or created their own. Several thousand chose the latter course. Others resorted to self-defense, including assassinations, refusing to move. The Party asked some to infiltrate the RVN bureaucracies, a tactic that was to prove the most humanly exhausting for all those who attempted it but one of the most dangerous to Diem and subsequent regimes. Far more clandestine Party cells attempted to continue political organization in the villages, and most of these were caught.

The southern Party's relationship to the Diemist terror had both a controlled aspect, reflecting its carefully considered policies and coordinated efforts, and a spontaneous, local dimension in which remnants acted according to their own judgment of the Party's likely policy and in response to immediate circumstances. These survivors were joined by many whom the repression was politicizing. Most of its predetermined efforts quickly proved dangerous in light of the terror, but the improvised adaptations prevented the total destruction of the existing Party. Despite incredible difficulties and perils, the southern Party maintained a skeleton organization, which could quickly be built upon, as well as sufficient discipline, despite much disagreement with the Party strategy, to sustain minimum cohesion. Those who constantly risked their lives for the Party were loyal but also extremely strong individuals, and telling the Party what they wished it to do was essential to preserving their devotion to it under such conditions. Informal and effective, self-confident in their own sacrifices, capable of functioning autonomously and often doing so, they were radicals and leftists on most policy questions. It was their commitment and ingenuity, which often involved no more than one person acting alone for long periods to reestablish contacts, that produced an amazingly resilient hard core of people with a dedication equal to that of the Party's pre–August 1945 members. The 1954–59 period was terribly destructive and incredibly tempering at the same time.

When Le Duan arrived in the southern Mekong Delta in spring 1956 he found an unhappy set of local Party leaders. In large part his work consisted of sustaining the Party's policy (even as he gathered impressions that were later to help him change it) and, above all, of keeping a cohesive Party in the south. The main tasks, he argued, were to rebuild the Party, engage in political action, and agitate for the Geneva elections. Limited violence and military force were to serve only as a shield for political work. So long as elections were possible, arms were to be minimized. "To combat the idea of violent, reckless, and dangerous armed struggle" was declared an aspect of building the Party.[4] On returning north in mid-1957, Le Duan was ready to endorse some of the southern membership's position. He was now convinced not only that the conditions were riper for action but also that without it the southern Party might be destroyed. These questions were not reduced to bald options but were nuanced, involving degrees of emphasis rather than radical changes. The southern Party's local leaders, reinforced by the senior southerners among the regroupees in the DRV who lobbied for more use of force, still chafed at the restrictions. In November 1957 the Party had Tran Van Giau broadcast a message to the south urging avoidance of a premature uprising. About this time members in a number of areas began taking armed actions on their own initiative. Others bluntly asked the Party to reverse its policy, most favoring much greater emphasis on armed struggle. Still, the Party's line in the south from late 1957 through 1958 was to stress political work among the people and to shun violence as much as possible. Although data are only approximate, the Party probably lost at least two-thirds of its southern members to arrests and death during that period, and more in 1959. Its leaders remained unwilling to take decisive action but were instead pushed to it by Diem's policies and mass responses to them.[5]

As difficult as the conditions were, the social and political terrain on which the Party worked made it possible to replace losses quite quickly. Those who fled to secure areas could relate to the tiny military organization left in the south against the contingency which arose—the failure of the Geneva Accords. The Party's military arm was intended only to exist, not to fight, until such time as it was unnecessary or the line changed. This group itself at first had no real potential save insofar as the returning Viet Minh provided manpower; they had equipment for about 6,000 men and cooperated with the remnants of the religious sects' armies that Diem had attempted to wipe out in 1955.

The Cao Dai and Hoa Hao sects, which were always something of a polyglot, offered Party military personnel the best cover for their work. In 1955 they were told to utilize their local groups while avoiding their top leaders. The sects had collaborated with everybody by 1954, primarily with the French, in order to guard their autonomous regions. The Cao Dai had 25,000 troops in 1954, paid by the French, and Diem destroyed most of their power. Remnants existed in the region northwest of Saigon, and Hoa Hao and Binh Xuyen groups operated elsewhere. A faction of the Cao Dai had worked with the Viet Minh after 1946, something the poor-peasant composition of its following made inevitable. In late 1955 the Party began to cooperate formally with roughly 2,000 of these elements as part of a united front, some of whom were to join the National Liberation Front later. Together they managed to assassinate some of the worst local Diemist officers after 1957, which made them popular with most peasants, but they generally avoided large operations. While the Party increasingly led the sect forces in the Delta, in the Central Highlands its members who fled there linked up with rebellious ethnic tribes who in 1957 had initiated armed resistance to Diem's authorities. Diem dubbed this Delta coalition the "Viet Cong," and the CIA estimated that it had only about 1,700 fighters in early 1958 and slightly more one year later.[6]

Despite minor adaptations, the basic situation in the south was for the

Party a massive contradiction, which began seriously to demoralize its remaining members. Everything Diem did made the Saigon government unpopular, and the masses looked to the former Viet Minh with ever-growing sympathy. Repression had forced many Viet Minh followers back into the maquis, and Diem's universal military draft of May 1957 was producing many evaders who refused to serve him and were ready to engage in illegal acts. In the summer of 1958 the Party responded hesitantly to this dire crisis and agreed to set up base areas, mainly in the remote Central Highlands. These were intended primarily for survival. The problem of spontaneous actions and efforts remained within the far more critical populated regions.

Above all, the peasants wanted their land back. Without cohesion and direction, the southern Party was struggling defensively for its survival, and many members were working either alone or in small groups. As an organization, it was deeply unhappy with the Hanoi-based Party's position on the role of the Party in the south. The Party's argument that the Diem regime's terror reflected its political weakness ignored how the terror endangered the very existence of a large part of the southern Party. Loyalty, discipline, and Diem kept many in the struggle despite the enormous personal risks, but this cohesion could not last forever. To survive, the Party had to exploit the objective social conditions and build its power, and to do so required far greater reliance on arms.

THE DRV AND THE DILEMMA OF THE SOUTH

The change in the Party's policy in the south came in installments. In effect, the DRV tried to pursue several courses at one time, balancing multiple, often contradictory factors and attempting to do justice to each.

First was the need to relate to the desires of the masses in the south, lest they lose rapport with the Party. Diem's land and other policies had brought this crisis to a head much sooner than had been expected. While the Party had anticipated that the Geneva Accords would not be implemented, it had not imagined that a ruthless, catalytic power would emerge in the south to accelerate the resistance that inevitably accompanies repression. Second, the southern Party wanted a much more militant line, and to preserve its ranks physically and politically as well as to forestall more radical local initiatives, it was essential to make concessions. The Party's overwhelming desire to stress consolidation of the north had also begun to bear fruit, and it was far stronger in 1959 than it had been in 1954 or even in 1945. In brief, a variety of spontaneous and potentially dangerous factors were to merge with deliberative considerations to bring about a step-by-step change of policy. To lead people, the Party now had no option but to follow their desires.

Le Duan returned to Hanoi in late 1958 from another trip to the south, and during January 1959 the Central Committee defined a new policy. Repression in the south was reaching a peak intensity, and the destruction of the remaining Party political activists, who unanimously demanded armed resistance, appeared imminent. His desire for a shift in policy was reinforced by strong pressure from a large number of senior southern leaders among the regroupees in Hanoi. These exiles were openly declaring the situation in the south ripe for action, and they actively campaigned for it. Less prominent regroupees were no less eager to return and take up the fight. In January 1959 the Central Committee revised its policy, which was dubbed Resolution 15, giving its approval to more armed struggle, mainly to defend political efforts. At the same time, it reiterated the need to consolidate power in the DRV. The preeminent importance of political activity was strongly emphasized. That it was a relatively ambiguous effort to synthesize very different strategies among the leaders was reflected in the fact that Resolution 15 was not disseminated in the Delta and the zone east of Saigon until December. The Politburo was aware that it had procrastinated in the south and now had to show leadership, lest it lose control of events there, but at the same time it sought to continue developing the north. This tension was to persist for four more years.

Not until the Party approved armed action in the south were there large-scale upheavals, though a growing number of symptomatic unauthorized peasant conflicts had occurred earlier and local Party elements had initiated combat without the knowledge of superior echelons. As the local southern leaders saw the new policy, "The higher levels had followed exactly the aspirations of the lower levels. . . ."[7] But it was less the Party's decision that moved so many to action over the subsequent months than the Diem regime's repression, and the Party did not so much lead as provide its organizational skills to a mass movement whose sheer force soon created anxieties in the Party.

The Party's military units now emerged from the sects' armies, possessing few arms and compelled therefore to "stay close to the masses," who would provide numbers and protection. The DRV's only significant aid was to allow about 4,500 regroupees to return south by the end of 1960. By the end of 1959, Party members and followers had begun to take over many villages, wrecking the detested *agrovilles* and establishing its presence in large areas. Its major mobilization technique was simple: land for the peasants. The famous Ben Tre uprising in January 1960 was considered an experiment to decide whether other uprisings should be authorized. Virtually unarmed masses briefly took over much of the province; land was distributed during the uprising itself. The formula worked virtually everywhere and soon gave the Party a vast presence and power despite the ARVN's ability to quickly retake public buildings. Within months a major shift in power had occurred in South Vietnam.

For all the initial emphasis in Resolution 15 on political work, events had created a new situation for the Politburo's priorities and the leadership of the Party in the south. In February 1960, apparently surprised by the scope of events in the south as well as by their potential serious risks, the Party's journal of theory stated plainly that neither guerilla war nor protracted fighting to create a liberated zone was possible at the time. But long preparation for a general uprising was necessary, and before that event occurred there were other options. One, though small, was a "peaceful" solution. Another, "very limited at present," was direct U.S. intervention.[8] A third was a long-term armed struggle without adequate political support from workers and urban elements and other classes. Such a struggle was foredoomed to failure. The Party's alternative to these risky policies was essentially to confine armed struggle to self-defense for a broadly based political mobilization, to fight only if there was no other choice. It had always intended this emphasis. Having looked into the abyss, the Party's leaders now pulled back, unquestionably fearing to lose control over events in the south.

Reiterating this concern, the southern regional Party at the end of March addressed a solemn letter to all members, briefly surveying their recent successes but focusing on their "errors," including some "very serious" ones. First, they had with "rash impatience" attacked many of the RVN's administrative functions, which endangered the "legal standing of the masses" and their ability to infiltrate and utilize the RVN's institutional order. They had interfered too much with the normal workings of the economy and not discriminated between landlords who were reactionary and those who were not. The creation of armed units had been overemphasized compared with political mobilization . . . the litany of errors went on. While weak, it argued, the Diem regime was still not on the verge of collapse, and the balance of forces made a general uprising at that point foolhardy. What was essential was a political-struggle movement, to which armed activity would be auxiliary. Members had to work more carefully, capture the enemy's administrative structure, and bring the people into mass organizations for an ongoing effort. Self-defense units had to conform to this essentially political line, avoiding useless violence and terrorism. Once this political foundation had been laid, the Party-led "national democratic movement" could think about eventually taking power.[9]

Despite its initial effort to contain what looked like a radical poor-peasant movement, the Party no longer had that option, and there was sufficient division within its leadership to compel it to accept the inevitable. The whole social structure in many provinces was changing, and land and economic issues were now very prominent. After its initial repossession of the symbols of government, the Diem administrative system continued to decline, and the Party's social and political base was growing. It could now operate far more openly in a large and expanding area. By the end of 1960, when it announced the creation of its directly controlled Liberation Army to replace the fragile, encumbering military front with the sects, it had a main force of 5,500 and about 30,000 guerillas, compared with only about 2,000 two years earlier. A "significant part" of the population, Lieutenant General Lionel C. McGarr, head of the U.S. military advisory team, reported during November, supported the Communists.[10] The events of late 1959 and early 1960 were irreversible and had only exposed the basic weaknesses of the U.S.-backed order. If two years later the Party admitted that it had overestimated the enemy at this time, it nonetheless had correctly defined the dangers it might also face.

Notwithstanding its success, the Party moved to hedge against the political fragility of a spontaneous peasant movement. It sought to do this, above all, by making the united front against Diem and U.S. domination the more prominent basis for long-term struggle for a national democratic revolution, minimizing social issues likely to divide it. Since the Party's national congress, the third in its entire history, opened in September 1960 to outline future national objectives, it sought greater control over the southern developments, lest events there greatly alter the Party's priorities. Its desire for greater industrialization, even at the expense of defense's share of the national budget, was contingent on limiting the potential drain of the conflict in the south on its finite resources.

The Party made the National Liberation Front of South Vietnam, publicly announced the following December, the vehicle for realizing its southern strategy. It was totally candid about its purposes, and since it never sought to conceal the relationship of the Party to the NLF, the question is why it created the often costly and complex parallel structure. Every peasant in the south supporting the Revolution identified the NLF with the Party and a movement dating back to the early 1940s that was legally and historically part of one country, which the U.S. sabotage of the Geneva Accords had temporarily divided. By the same token, every group the Party might ally with in the south knew that the Viet Minh and its successors had not lasted beyond 1953 in terms of sharing real power in the DRV.

The fractured class structure of the south was also far more promising to a front strategy in 1960 than it had been when the Viet Minh was created nationally. The power of its possible rivals, particularly the sects, was greater than that of any comparable group ever found in the north. But Diem had in fact forced most of the country into opposition or neutrality. There was so much anti-Diem potential that the Party had to attempt to channel it, lest another force or coalition preempt it.

Apart from this quite persuasive consideration was the problem of the southern Party and peasantry. Both conditions and popular attitudes and actions presented the Party with immense opportunities, but the southern Party's organization and mass groups were still far less formidable than they could be. It was also under the influence of the poorer peasantry. The unstructured uprisings had shown the peasants to be concerned with their own immediate needs and the southern Party with the peasants. The NLF offered the Party's leaders a solution to the political underdevelopment of the peasants and a superior arrangement for mass mobilization. The Party also wished to educate and reorganize its southern section and did not want later to confront the potential risks of indiscriminately signing up a large membership, as it had after 1945. The front was a logical context for the Party. It served to inhibit any impulses to take power in the Party's name alone—impulses that had existed earlier, and that its successes with the poor peasantry again made plausible, but that the Party's leaders deemed sectarian. The southern Party at this time passed from the control of a regional committee, which had been more removed from Hanoi, to a special branch of the national Central Committee itself, bringing it under tighter supervision. While the Party controlled the NLF, the NLF reduced the number of Party responsibilities by creating a much more efficient organization than the Viet Minh. The NLF was a more flexible and comprehensive structure, capable of serving as a shadow government. Such a policy in the south was paralleled in the DRV by greater reliance on mass organizations than on the local Parties.

The NLF also offered the logical means of absorbing the vast number of new peasant and political activists into a political framework, and it was the best place to install potential but untested Party members. It was in this sense an antidote to the existing and potential radicalism of the southern Party and masses, which in its own way manifested the same uncontrollable energy as had plagued the north's land reform after 1954. Furthermore, it was a way of taming and controlling such energy under the umbrella of a projected alliance among different class and religious elements in the south.

Given all of these factors, the Party's leaders persuaded themselves of the NLF's efficacy. Time and events were not to diminish the arguments for this belief.[11]

THE RESUMPTION OF THE
STRUGGLE: PARTY AND MASSES

In one sense the conflict which began about 1961 may be designated the second Indochina War. Contemplating the social, political, and economic nature of that violent interregnum between the French departure and the massive American entry reveals a great deal not merely about the origins of the war but America's eventual defeat. For it is the continuity between the two periods that explains the insoluble dilemmas the United States was to confront when dealing with a fragile political facade imposed on the vacuum the collapse of French colonialism left behind. It was this dynamic social process inherited from the old order—above all, the land revolution and the absence of even a basis for a ruling class—that set the context for the most important developments affecting the entire Vietnamese experience in modern times. Neither the French nor the Americans could stem the social forces that the war and the Revolution had deeply rooted throughout the south by 1954. Unless there was an international intervention, the Revolution would quickly attain total victory. The history of Vietnam after 1954 was only incidentally that of a civil war, for the artificiality and fragility of the anti-Communist social order precluded a serious conflict between the Revolution and its opponents. The process of conflict after 1954 was essentially a struggle between a radicalized Vietnamese patriotism, embodied in the Communist Party, and the United States and its wholly dependent local allies.

The Vietnamese Revolution which had begun in 1945 had been both a vast political movement against foreign domination and a social movement. Its social dimension made the Geneva Accords ephemeral. The Communists had been able to create their political force by organizing the masses largely around social issues; once the people acted, however, the Party never fully controlled them. On the contrary, the masses had irresistibly defined parameters of action for the Party and had at critical points threatened it with a loss of control if it ignored their desires. The Party fully appreciated this relationship and saw it as the source of its ultimate strength. For armies and police could wreak havoc on the Party and its organized political and military branches, but its connections to the people gave it remarkable powers of regeneration. The August Revolution and then the final assault against the French during 1953–54 bore testimony to the potential strength of a mobilized social cause. The Geneva Accords could not wipe that force away, and after they were signed the south was not going to remain quiescent. Least of all would it conform to anyone's timetable or priorities. The Party could not, ultimately, control the peasantry but only relate to it. Diem could do neither, and of all his self-destructive acts, his land policy was his most important. The traumatized peasantry that emerged from French colonialism's land policy had after 1945 begun to recast the social order in the south, and this transformation was, by 1955, too firmly rooted to be reversed.

The DRV had confronted its own poor-peasant movement, which created the most important internal challenge that the Party was ever to encounter. Ironically, an important reason for the DRV's desire to prevent the southern question from dominating its agenda after 1954 was precisely its own necessity to fully integrate the northern peasantry and create an economy capable of satisfying their desires. Residues of this tension between the needs of the northern economy and society and the obligations the southern war imposed were to face the Party for the remainder of the war.

Most of the Party's leaders had hoped that the southern movement, which required them to authorize some armed activity after over four years of Politburo opposition to it, would restrict itself primarily to political efforts. They lost control over this policy not only because of the radical goals of the southern masses but also because of the responses of Diem and the United States to the crisis in South Vietnam in the post-Geneva period. The Party, to a significant extent, was having its freedom of choice on vital tactical issues increasingly circumscribed from without, and the role inherent in its very identity and purposes confined its options. It could not turn back, because even that would not have forestalled the crisis in the fragile political order the United States had created and in the society Diem ruled. The crucial determination for war or peace, in brief, was no longer really under the Party's control. Washington would make that decision.

Part Two

THE CRISIS IN SOUTH VIETNAM AND AMERICAN INTERVENTION, 1961-1965

Chapter 9

The U.S. Involvement in Vietnam: From Sponsorship to Air War

It was for the United States in 1961 to resolve whether there would be war or peace in Vietnam. It alone could aspire to reverse the social and political forces irresistibly making the southern half of the country again an integral part of one Vietnam. Washington's definition of its national interests would determine its responses to the political imbroglios of the RVN and South Vietnam's social dynamics. Arms and war would serve, as always, as a final means of attaining what politics and the remnants of a colonial order could not.

WASHINGTON DEFINES THE STAKES IN VIETNAM

The credibility of American power since 1945 touches the overarching issue of the relationship of America's resources to its problems, interests, and goals. Above all, it raises the question of its confidence in itself and its capacity to attain its ends. The goals and interests of U.S. foreign policy are sometimes defined in connection with the problem of credibility but often also quite autonomously of it. Precisely because objectives often transcend the instruments for achieving them and because they are ultimately the result of interests, the gap between desire and reality creates an impasse in Washington's policies. The American obsession with the successful application of power—"credibility"—is the inevitable overhead charge of its foreign policy after 1945 with its ambition to integrate a U.S.-led international political and economic order.

By 1960 the issue of U.S. potency possessed Washington. Each new challenge or sense of failure, whether the space race or a local upheaval, intensified its frustration. The fluidity of the world order, with its constant and diverse changes, guaranteed a steady succession of trials. And with each new advance in U.S. instruments for imposing its military or organizational hegemony, there was a desire to prove their efficacy in reality. It was this autonomous logic of arms and power that always threatened to transcend the narrower economic and geopolitical aims of imperialism.

Because they assumed that the employment of power was a matter less of principle than of tactics and priorities, even when they disagreed about the choice of Vietnam as a testing ground for the United States' counterrevolutionary role, key figures in American foreign relations never doubted that the global goals of the foreign policy were attainable with proper management of resources and that the means were both appropriate and sufficient. This deep consensus on the utilization of American power was the legacy of the entire post-1945 U.S. ambition and interaction with an unsettled, changing world. Because of it, American power and prestige were deeply invested in Vietnam before anyone raised pragmatic doubts about this application of its strength.

Vietnam was a conjunction not merely because the domino theory made every nation the key to a region, which in turn had varying but always significant implications for the U.S. position in the entire world, or even because by 1960 the debate over local and strategic war had reached a shrill pitch, which colored the 1960 presidential campaign. The domino and credibility theories began to merge into a unified conception, credibility growing weightier over time. More crucial in 1960–62 was the specific impact of the Cuban revolution on Washington's self-confidence. The failure of the Bay of Pigs invasion in April 1961 was a humiliating reverse for the counterinsurgency and local-war concepts just then coming into great vogue. The Berlin confrontation of the spring of 1961 also goaded the United States to seek to exhibit its power elsewhere.

The year 1961 was thus one in which the accumulated postwar frustrations in regulating the affairs of so many little states outside Vietnam galvanized America's leaders to take yet stronger action in Indochina. Laos was an especially pernicious problem; it consumed a vast amount of the Kennedy administration's time during its first several months in office. The United States' ability to keep the Pathet Lao out of power became a test of U.S. influence, motivated by fear of the domino effect of a Laotian coalition government on the stability of the RVN. The Kennedy administration saw

Laos as "a symbolic test of strengths between the major powers of the West and the Communist bloc" and perceived U.S. weakness there as requiring stronger policies in South Vietnam to counterbalance its impact on the region and the world.[1] The day after the Bay of Pigs, it created a special task force on Vietnam with the mandate "to grasp the new concepts, the new tools" of counterinsurgency, that might defeat "subversion" everywhere in the world.[2] Vietnam was becoming a test case in counterinsurgency, and with an eye to Laos, Cuba, and the entire world, the administration was to begin a long series of escalations, each raising the ante to establish credibility.

This perception of Vietnam from 1961 onward gave it a symbolic global significance that far outweighed the specific U.S. interests there, but behind this notion there nonetheless existed more tangible goals, which varied somewhat in importance but always remained a part of a justification of the effort. Raw materials, though less publicly cited than earlier, were still prominent in the decision makers' vision. This included the preservation of existing markets. The retention of South Vietnam was invariably linked to U.S. relations with other nations in the region, particularly with Indonesia, where Washington considered Sukarno the most important threat to its interests.

Credibility rose in importance with the successive failures of each escalation of advisers and resources in Vietnam, reaching 11,000 by the end of 1962 and 23,000 two years later. The domino and the global contexts were incorporated into all justifications of the war. The concepts finally merged late in 1964, when General Maxwell Taylor, a leading limited-war theorist and the ambassador to Saigon, argued typically, "If we leave Vietnam with our tail between our legs, the consequences of this defeat in the rest of Asia, Africa, and Latin America would be disastrous."[3]

As Washington's commitment grew, both the credibility and the domino concepts became more refined and comprehensive. Washington generally regarded the open Sino-Soviet split after 1962 as a direct threat, seeing a seemingly unrestrained China as much more hostile and in favor of wars of national liberation against the American "paper tiger" throughout the world. By 1963 the Kennedy administration had come increasingly to believe that resisting the Revolution in South Vietnam was also a matter of U.S.-Chinese relations. As John T. McNaughton stated the dominant idea in March 1965, the United States' war aims were "70%—To avoid a humiliating US defeat (to our reputation as a guarantor)" and "20%—To keep SVN (and then adjacent) territory from Chinese hands."[4] The containment of China, presumably now the dominant influence in the villages in the south, was treated in a comprehensive March 1964 National Security Council articulation of war aims, which linked the domino theory with credibility to define the war in the south "as a test case of U.S. capacity to help a nation to meet the Communist 'war of liberation.' "[5]

By increasingly making credibility the overarching consideration in the escalation of the war, America's leaders positioned Vietnam in the world power balance and postwar history, touching the efficacy of its traditional counterrevolutionary policies, and in this manner its symbolic role enormously enlarged the stakes involved there. All the important leaders supported this logic until its deficiencies appeared after the damage had been done. In a certain way this definition was rational. The loss of U.S. mastery in the Third World was a reality, but the changes occurring in the world were not the consequences of U.S. passivity. Rather, they resulted from the normal transformations of all societies, a fact that brings the Left to the fore repeatedly as an integral element of modern history. Weapons might in some places abort this process temporarily; the cost to America was variable. Essential to the counterrevolutionary role is the selection of a war at the right time and at the right place. The dilemma of credibility is that even the slightest error in the application of power must lead to the utilization of yet more force, or else the price to America's reputation mounts. As a basis of foreign policy, it is the highest-risk game any nation can play. If there is no valid sense of the constraints of social reality, then credibility leads to escalation, humiliation, or both. For while the United States could measure its resources and interests clearly, it could not fathom their relevance to the more crucial social, human, and military conditions which existed. Colossal self-confidence made it appear virtually certain that its power could compensate for any surprises.

Given the dilemmas of the United States since 1949, with its growing sense of impotence and frustrations over the course of events in the world, it was not in the least accidental that a foreign policy based both on symbolism and on interest merged at some point to plague the nation. The challenges in Vietnam at the start were no more problematical than those in many other nations, and American interventions elsewhere had often succeeded. The process of reasoning during 1961–64 was not, therefore, unique to Vietnam but merely a legacy of post-1945 U.S. foreign policy. Had the United States avoided Indochina entirely, it would eventually have become involved elsewhere in much the same way, for two decades later it was to confront its Central American problems with virtually identical reasoning and responses.

WASHINGTON AND THE ENIGMA OF
NGO DINH DIEM

The six-year-long U.S. undertaking in Vietnam after the Geneva Accords was to a great extent due to its good fortune in finding Ngo Dinh Diem, and its reverses after 1960 were also largely the consequence of this choice. Diem was a rare leader whose sheer violence, organization, and ruthless determination had retarded the military, political, and social momentum behind the Revolution's successes and France's failures. The possible dangers to Diem came from three directions: first, from the NLF, whose emergence out of the Revolution's battered forces in the south made it the sole national opposition to Diem to a crucial degree because his repression made it both necessary and possible for the Party to resume its historic struggle; second, from elements of the machine Diem himself was building, above all from the growing military establishment; and third, from the United States, which had increasing reason not to endorse Diem's self-destructive policies.

The Revolution was the key factor keeping the Americans behind Diem until as late as mid-1963. By the early 1960s the United States could not ignore the growing threat that Diem's blatant corruption and repression posed to its project to make South Vietnam a symbolic test of its will and arms. As Secretary of State Dean Rusk accurately stated the dilemma the week after Kennedy took office, the United States was "caught between pressing Diem to do things he did not wish to do and the need to convey to him American support."[6] "Diem is all we have, and there just aren't any alternatives" was the universally accepted definition of American policy.[7] By 1961 Diem fully appreciated the Kennedy administration's dependence on his regime. The details of this increasingly troubled U.S.-Diem relationship have been well charted elsewhere; suffice it to say here that Diem largely ignored America's modest proposals, at best agreeing to study them, while accumulating vast funds against any eventual reductions in aid. The United States saw its economic and growing military presence as a precondition, if not a guarantee, of eventual reforms. Apart from trusting most of Diem's information on the progress of the war until the end of 1962, Washington believed that his acceptance of more of its advisers and equipment would counterbalance his failures.

These failures could not be disregarded indefinitely. As the United States more aggressively tried to streamline the RVN's military establishment, its efforts brought it into more intimate contact with the only potential alternative to Diem and the NLF.

The military posed challenges and promises to the Americans as well as to Diem. Whereas Diem saw this from the beginning, the United States was slower to recognize the centrality of the officers to its position. Given Diem's destruction of the inherited elite-class stratum and the arrest of thousands of civilian non-NLF critics, his only potential anti-Communist rivals were of his own creation—the senior military officers. Since Diem could not abolish the military, his only option was to control it as thoroughly as possible. But the dilemma for the United States was that Diem was ready to sacrifice military efficiency for political reliability, which in turn required a greater U.S. presence to prevent an NLF victory.

Although the United States saw the dangers of Diem's political isolation, until 1963 this concern was not so urgent as to require action. Even several weeks before Diem's overthrow, official Washington persisted in believing, in McNamara's and Taylor's words, that the "military campaign has made great progress and continues to progress."[8] It was in the command and the coordination of the military establishment that Diem proved wholly unwilling to respond to suggested U.S. changes, which began in 1960. Apart from screening military officers and commands as carefully as possible, Diem prevented any coordination or control other than his own over military or counterinsurgency efforts, agreeing only to a Joint General Staff, in turn headed by his appointees, which never had any real powers. All province chiefs and regional and field commanders reported directly to him—and they could not cooperate with each other. If this left Diem power over all military and paramilitary forces, it also meant a greatly reduced effectiveness against the NLF. The system, in short, was designed to prevent a coup. During the abortive November 1960 coup against Diem, the CIA was in touch with the plotters, even though it did not aid them. Diem was unquestionably aware of this fact, and he appreciated the military's potential role for the United States should it choose to overthrow him. In May 1961, when Vice-President Lyndon Johnson visited Saigon and communicated an official decision to make reform of this command structure a precondition for continued military aid, Diem agreed but then changed nothing. The structure was never to alter substantially until Diem's overthrow, and General Nguyen Van Thieu later reinstalled a variation of it. What this meant, in effect, was that the expanding RVN military was ultimately prepared to fight neither a conventional nor a guerilla war but rather was designed to reinforce the existing political structure. A disunited military is, of course, a guarantee of instability, and in the end this politicized army proved wholly unable to fulfill Washington's demands in any domain.

To the United States the ineffective RVN military was potentially fatal, and throughout the period of growing American commitment to making South Vietnam a test case, the increasing political isolation and corruption of the Diem family, and particularly the paranoid antics of Nhu, affected

American thinking about their allies. During 1962, after studying the question, the administration concluded there was then no possible alternative to Diem, but the matter was one of timing rather than principle. By early 1963, however, W. W. Rostow had initiated discussions among Washington planners of the military's role in the Third World, bringing the then fashionable military "modernization theory" to the executive's attention. In effect, he argued, the reliance on civil authorities in the Third World after 1945 had been an error. The military establishments were far better transmitters of Western values and the most promising modernizers of the traditional orders. And because the United States controlled aid to them as well as direct training, Rostow urged much greater exploitation of these levers to advance U.S. interests. Its "benevolent authoritarianism" would both create national unity and hold power in trust for the less competent civilians.[9] Getting to know the military was essential. In Indonesia or Vietnam there were few options to a reliance on the military; the idea was then, as it is today, quite respectable among decision makers.

When troops killed nine Buddhists at the May 8, 1963, anti-Diem demonstration in Hué, the United States immediately concurred in the demands of the leaders of the largest religion in the country. By mid-June it was threatening a break with Diem over the issue of the repression of Buddhists, and it was then that Nhu secretly used the French to contact the DRV to discuss the reestablishing of trade and postal relations between the two zones. Whatever reticence existed in Washington melted, and the oft-told story of Diem's overthrow began.

While Diem had control over most of his officers, he really had to dominate all of them, and that was impossible. As a social stratum the military officers were very much in transition and were to remain that way for the remainder of the RVN's existence. The military's function as the administrator of political power at numerous levels and its access to resources made it the only quick avenue of social mobility for Vietnam's educated elite, and many ambitious men who joined the Can Lao party were never satisfied with their subordinate roles. For those who aspired to control of real power in their own right, the coup was the only route available, and there were careerists everywhere—a reality that did not end with Diem's assassination. Moreover, many who were nominally senior officers were entrusted with mere titles rather than with true authority, and as General Tran Van Don, then acting chief of the JGS later commented, "one of . . . Diem's greatest errors was to give some of his most efficient and highly regarded generals meaningless jobs." Sitting around idle, "[n]ot only did they become bitter, but they used their time to think, make plans, and perfect strategies."[10]

It was this group, whose ambitions were their politics, with whom the

Americans worked after they decided in Washington on August 24 to get rid of the Nhus and to change the government, with or without Diem. Most U.S. advisers believed that the Diem regime was rapidly losing the war, and they were disappointed when the first discussion of a coup led to no action. But the plotters' indecision was partly due to America's waffling on cutting aid to Diem. Coup planning resumed in early October with the CIA's knowledge. All the generals asked for was continued aid if they were successful, and while their American liaison gave unequivocal assurances of U.S. support, he also admonished them to act with "a high prospect of success" or not at all, indecisiveness being worse than no action.[11] The CIA also promised funding for the coup leaders' expenses. Since Diem had carefully screened his officers, there was no doubt that he retained the capacity successfully to challenge a coup effort *if* he had the time. This was perfectly obvious, as was the fact that the whole regime was embodied in one man and his family. The only sure way to prevent Diem's mobilization of resistance was to assassinate him, or at least his brother Nhu. The CIA knew this and said so to Washington at the beginning of October when the planners of the coup presented the assassination of Diem's brothers, Nhu and Can, as the way to avert "a protracted struggle."[12]

Washington actively supported a successful, decisive coup. It said nothing to dissuade anyone from attempting to assassinate Nhu and Can, and knew full well that the coup plotters did not feel strong enough to win without eliminating Nhu. Nhu had from the inception been the arch-villain in Washington, and so the CIA headquarters informed its Saigon office that while it "would not favor assassination of Diem," it also opposed "engaging ourselves by taking position on this matter"; the "best approach is hands off."[13] A few hours after the coup began on November 1, the CIA supplied it with the cash needed to pay the troops involved, and it was only the assassinations of Nhu and Diem the following morning that brought the precarious effort to a successful and swift conclusion. So ended the relationship that had evolved over years to make Vietnam the front line to establish the United States' credibility in the face of revolutionary insurgencies.

THE MILITARY TO POWER

America's goals in South Vietnam reflected its traditional definition of its interests in the world, interests that transcended the specific political structure of any nation it chose as an instrument by which to establish its credibility. The protracted Saigon political crisis gave the United States all the more cause to persist, and it changed the form but not the content of American behavior as Washington was forced to acknowledge that it could not rely upon the ARVN to fulfill America's objectives. But the policy which preceded its new confrontation with reality also prejudged the actions that would be taken to implement it. The administration, in a word, escalated primarily to save not the succession of regimes in Saigon but its own credibility.

The context in which the United States dealt with the generals was very much like that under Diem, and reflected the underdeveloped and ultimately highly artificial class basis of its allies. Diem had managed with U.S. encouragement to uproot the narrow class foundation the French colonial regime had established, leaving a void in its place. Anti-Diemism and anti-Communism were hardly sufficient underpinnings for a stable government. Diem's greatest mistake was to allow a few ambitious officers to become autonomous, but the military's great weakness was that its purely self-serving basis left it necessarily divided. No one could ultimately trust anyone else. Despite all the efforts to control it, Washington never overcame this fatal flaw in the RVN military machine.

The eight power plays and coups that produced changes in governments and the two coups that failed between Diem's overthrow and the accession of General Nguyen Van Thieu and Air Marshal Nguyen Cao Ky, on June 19, 1965, left the Johnson administration exposed and unable to rely on the RVNAF to establish the credibility of U.S. power. The moment the first coup's leaders took over, their main concern was that there was insufficient boodle for them all. Serious politics in the RVN would henceforth consist of competing military fiefdoms struggling for power and privilege. All the divided military did was further militarize the state machinery by appointing officers to those few remaining important posts that Diem had allocated to civilians. The four corps commanders became virtual warlords, designating the heads of the provinces in their respective domains from among the ranks of their loyal officers. Local political parties and many of the quasi-political religious bodies were made appendages of these regional suzerainties. As American officials could easily see, it was a situation ripe for perpetual instability.

Washington gave solid support to General Nguyen Khanh's bloodless coup at the end of January 1964, allegedly to head off pro-French neutralist officers ready to take power. The creation of a military council caused it to hope that there might be stability. Diem's former protégé disappointed this wish. For the next year the United States lived with the "appalling impression," as Rusk put it, of conspiracies, plots, and intrigues of every nature.[14] News of these imbroglios filled the dispatches back to Washington, along with reports that the ever-growing ARVN was increasingly demoralized and ceasing to fight and that in many regions "live and let live" arrangements were being reached with the NLF.[15] What disturbed the United States most about the RVN's generals was the existence of a pro-French and neutralist group among them, an anxiety which General de Gaulle's frequent proposals for the neutrality of Vietnam fueled. The August Tonkin Gulf affair to some extent was designed both to exhibit the potential of U.S. power and to begin the long process of ending the war in the south by penalizing the DRV for moving into the vacuum America's allies were creating. It was also a gesture to buoy up the sinking morale of the Khanh junta. Khanh, indeed, exploited the opportunity only to create a short-lived near dictatorship for himself; after rioting throughout the country, he resurrected his more benign junta.

Following the RVN's Byzantine politics and power struggles, the CIA gave Washington an accurate picture of chaos. In September 1964 it warned that the odds were "against the emergence of a stable government capable of effectively prosecuting the war."[16] The entire panoply of groups, factions, miniparties, and aspirants to power was lobbying the military establishment, which was the real arena of politics. The civilians, which the CIA thought "more concerned with personal power and prestige" than with anything else, were all split. The only united force in South Vietnam was the NLF.[17] War weariness and neutralism were the outcomes. When Khanh reacted to growing U.S. disillusion with him and secretly contacted the NLF to explore the possibility of a neutralist solution to the war, momentarily raising the Party's hopes for a quick end to the war, Washington abandoned the increasingly anti-American leader.

In the successive Saigon cabinet changes after August 1964, a coalition of "Young Turks," from which Nguyen Cao Ky and Nguyen Van Thieu were eventually to emerge as the most important individuals, began building its position as power broker until some of its members formally assumed strategic posts the following June. While the politics of these men was identical to that of all the other contestants, their careers and social standing gave this caucus somewhat more coherence than the older officers, whose backgrounds were rooted primarily in France and then in intimate collaboration with Diem. After months of immersion in the surrealist world of Saigon politics and of helplessly watching street demonstrations and the disintegration of the regime, the Americans consented to the accession of this group to power not so much because they saw it as a superior alternative but because Washington's former allies had enervated it. In fact the United States was now relying on its own resources by necessity; it could no longer expect the ARVN to attain America's goals at a relatively low human and financial cost. Its objectives along with its perceptions of the growing magnitude of the military tasks required far greater U.S. commitments of men and money. As for the tottering cabinets and coalitions in Saigon, the United States treated them with benign neglect, expecting little that was useful for the moment. It hoped the RVN's politics would improve after American forces reversed the balance of power in the war.

It was obvious soon after Diem's death that the problem the United States faced with its wholly dependent proxy in South Vietnam involved a bevy of interrelated issues: the RVN's politics, the military implications of a highly politicized army in a war without fronts, and many connected economic and social questions. To establish America's credibility, most of its leaders failed to appreciate, would require a simultaneous, effective answer to the extremely diverse and quite insoluble institutional difficulties inherent in the artificial RVN system that the United States was sponsoring.

STEPS IN AMERICAN POLICY

The problem confronting the administration until well into 1964 was how to communicate persuasively with the public and Congress as it became clear that Vietnam would take more time and effort than they had originally anticipated. Apart from the later, intense disputes over the value of the Vietnam effort, there was scarcely any before or afterward regarding the *process* of international relations, the overall objectives of foreign policy, and the role of violence, including implied threats conveyed to adversaries by exhibits or warnings of force. In one sense, the academic analyses of the levels of military power and international relations which flourished in the major universities after 1955 made the calculations that went into the first years of the Vietnam War appear as if the United States was embarking on a war whose rationale and logic had been conjured up in Cambridge, where ideas were considered valid merely because peers confirmed them with the smooth self-assurance characteristic of the Harvard-MIT community. But the small foreign affairs establishment which shared ideas as well as power lacked an effective method to communicate even to its domestic friends. While it thought much about the process, procedures, and levels of violence, war, and the international system, it had yet to learn how to avoid the potentially perilous shoals of the American political process and to understand the real constraints of the domestic social and economic order. It was this fact that defined the style of the first major stages of the escalations in Vietnam. The administration's desire and growing need to mobilize domestic constituencies and opinion behind itself guided so many of its actions, justifications, and stilted definitions of reality that it was always unclear, often even to itself, whether it was responding to problems at home, to those in Vietnam, or to both.

The bipartisan consensus on foreign policy which had existed since 1950 had been the single greatest accomplishment of the Truman administration, permitting continuity in the application of U.S. power in the world. It had been dearly bought not merely with doctrines of every conceivable nature but also with a greatly enlarged defense budget, which built a pork barrel, and an ideological constituency, for expansionism and military spending. Despite nuanced differences over defense matters and diplomacy, that unity among executive, Congress, and public was the greatest precondition for the continuity of postwar foreign policy. To maintain it was the most critical task of U.S. imperialism, but this in turn required that an important foreign policy should not seriously damage the interests of a powerful economic constituency whose support was essential to the consensus.

CREATING A CAUSE: THE TONKIN GULF RESOLUTION

The core of Washington's eventual political problem was the contempt of the decision makers for the Congress, press, and public—a manipulative relationship that was to produce a deepening mistrust that was to culminate in Watergate and the collapse of congressional-executive unity. McGeorge Bundy, former Harvard dean and Kennedy's national security assistant, sought from the inception to run foreign policy with a minimum of publicity, and the President encouraged him in this. The consummate self-confidence and profound disdain for the general public intrinsic to Kennedy's Cambridge circle, which itself had only the vaguest notion of the immense complexities it was so blithely preparing to confront, was a combination virtually certain to undermine public and congressional confidence in the executive. The 1961 debacle in Cuba, successive failures in Vietnam, and the expansion of covert war required a thicker veil over the conduct of American foreign policy. But each failure in Vietnam eroded the premises of past U.S. optimism and necessitated an increased commitment. Diem's death and the chronic instability that followed stimulated a still small but persistent, and eventually growing, public doubt about the Vietnam undertaking. The executive's major effort to cope with the potential domestic hostility to a Vietnam policy in the process of escalation was the series of events culminating in Congress's Tonkin Gulf Resolution of August 7, 1964.

Until the collapse of the Diem regime, the administration had finessed its policy with silence or relatively rare extensive statements regarding the DRV's relationship to the southern war. Its own data on the movement of manpower and arms merely confirmed the reverse of its thesis that the DRV was imposing the war on the south. Apart from substantiating the claim that southern regroupees were trickling back to their native regions, it could show only that the flow of arms moving southward was trivial and that the

NLF was winning the war largely by its own wits and efforts. When Senator Mike Mansfield returned from a tour of Vietnam for the President at the end of 1962, his public disproof of the administration's explanation of the nature and causes of the insurgency was just an indication of the problem a more forceful policy might confront even in Washington.

Whatever the disagreement on the specifics of a greater U.S. involvement in Vietnam, virtually all of Johnson's advisers—the uninfluential George Ball was among those holding out—favored some degree of escalation, and the unraveling of the Khanh regime only increased the need to act to stem its demise. The first measure, designated OPLAN 34A, was begun in the form of diversionary raids on the DRV in February 1964 by the Studies and Observation Group (SOG), an ultrasecret "unconventional war task force" composed of Special Forces and CIA personnel who hired Vietnamese mercenaries. All SOG operations, which continued through most of the war, required the approval of the Secretaries of Defense and State as well as the White House. OPLAN 34A, which mainly failed in its first effort, was paralleled by what General Westmoreland later described as "a related program," the Navy's "DESOTO" patrols, which ran electronic intelligence missions in the Tonkin Gulf as close as four miles offshore.[18] OPLAN 34A also utilized these data.

While such small nuisance measures rested in abeyance, the desire in Washington for important new escalations culminated in the National Security Council's March commitment to make Vietnam a test case of U.S. credibility. In March, too, William Bundy, assistant secretary of state and McGeorge's brother, argued that serious punitive measures against the DRV for the NLF's action in the south would require congressional approval, and a resolution was drawn up modeled after the Offshore Islands Resolution of January 1955, sanctioning the defense of Formosa. Comparable Cuban and Middle Eastern resolutions also existed for "continuing crises."

The President's advisers debated the exact pressures that would cause the DRV to cease its support of the NLF, fully conscious that they might not work. As William Bundy conceded, "the Viet Cong *do* have a lot of appeal in South Vietnam and *do* rely heavily on captured US weapons," though he nonetheless considered the DRV's role crucial.[19] In any case, McNamara and others could argue, action against the DRV would be good for the otherwise sagging morale and fortunes of the fast-sinking Khanh regime. At a conference in Honolulu during the first days of June, the key advisers approved a variety of contingency plans for air strikes against the DRV, including preparation to continue them on a sustained basis, and various options for an increased buildup of U.S. troops and equipment for the beginning of what was clearly going to be a larger, longer war.

Johnson had been essentially passive on Vietnam issues since coming to office as a confused, insecure figure, and because he was in the midst of his campaign for reelection and the civil rights bill was then before Congress, he postponed major policy innovations. Meanwhile, his aides planned the systematic education of the public to eliminate "the basic doubts" hindering a greater commitment, even requiring, as William Bundy was to put it, "a degree of overemphasis" of the facts.[20] The Bundy brothers prepared multiple drafts of a congressional resolution, hoping it would enlist the cautiously pro-administration elements, such as Senator Mansfield, but they worried that with "no drastic change in the situation to point to" the Senate might resist such an effort. Without a congressional resolution the administration's "freedom of action" would be excessively limited, and they targeted its passage for early July through September, or November at the latest, whenever the opportune occasion presented itself. It would be necessary, too, if and only if it was decided "that a substantial increase in national attention and international tension is a necessary part of the defense of Southeast Asia in the coming summer."[21] During this same time the United States had Canada send a specially briefed diplomat to Hanoi to warn that Washington saw the war in the south as a test case for the resisting of insurgency throughout the world and that it would bomb the DRV extensively if it did not call off the war against the Saigon government. The Party replied with an offer to create a neutral coalition government in the south, but it also prepared for escalation.

In the meantime, while the various options were being considered and Johnson was on the more urgent campaign trail, the Khanh government began pressing the United States to help it march to the north and thereby allegedly solve its burgeoning problems at home and lift morale in the south. By the last weeks of July, a veritable eagerness to invade the DRV was manifest in Saigon circles, and the DRV was fully aware of it. It was throughout this June–July period that the United States resumed its OPLAN 34A operations in the coastal DRV areas, utilizing, as the Pentagon Papers later described it, "South Vietnamese or hired personnel and supported by U.S. training and logistical efforts."[22] OPLAN 34A was in fact always an American project and was active in the DRV coastal region around the nineteenth parallel when the USS *Maddox* on July 31 was sent on a DESOTO patrol, with a special electronic-intelligence crew aboard, planning to electronically simulate an air attack and gather information not closer than four miles off the DRV coast. There is no question it was ordered to draw DRV boats away from 34A operations. It was this combination which caused the forewarned DRV authorities correctly to conclude that the OPLAN 34A and DESOTO boats were collaborating and to attack the *Maddox,* leading to the so-called Tonkin Gulf incident on August 2. George

Ball later accurately described the DESOTO missions as serving "primarily for provocation."[23] The U.S. air attack on the patrol boat sites and oil storage facilities was the beginning of the air war against the north, and the passage of the long-prepared Tonkin Gulf Resolution on August 7, with virtually no dissent, authorized the President "to take all necessary steps, including the use of armed force," to aid any Southeast Asian state.[24]

House and Senate members voted for the Tonkin mandate with very different conceptions of what they were endorsing. Some saw it as a response to a single event, others as a virtual mandate for war. The resolution was in fact a blank check, the amount of which the administration itself had yet to determine. Congress would regret its actions only when it revised its opinions or after the administration's promises of action tempered with restraint had long since been broken. Most of its members eventually renounced the resolution's mandate because the policy had failed and because they could no longer ignore larger questions of national priorities and interests. But to some extent they could conveniently claim a largely unjustified innocence, for the administration had indeed lied to Congress regarding the details of the Tonkin affair, obscuring the political fact that the policy had been drawn up much earlier, and had predetermined its responses. Above all, the White House claimed that it had been provoked when in reality it was the provoker.

What was crucial about the Tonkin affair was the precedent of manipulation that it created for future administration relations with Congress and the public. It was this effort that gradually undermined the domestic basis of the foreign policy consensus that had existed for nearly two decades and that was, ultimately, U.S. foreign policy's greatest strength. White House decisions, meanwhile, could now increasingly reflect external considerations rather than internal needs and constituencies, and for three years it could ignore the Congress's and the public's potentially decisive roles in vetoing the thrust of the executive's foreign policy—a role that was much more a part of the American foreign policy tradition before 1950 than of the essentially exceptional interlude after the Korean War. The Tonkin affair, in all of its dimensions, later proved to be a major administration error in the conduct of the war.

Chapter 10

The War and Rural Vietnam

LAND AND THE CONTEXT OF STRUGGLE

While the turmoil in Saigon among Diem and his successors only improved the NLF's prospects, it was the Revolution's ability to exploit political paralysis to build its own strength which proved most critical. The Revolution's development in the south after 1960 cannot be separated from its experiences in the 1950s, above all, the relationship of the united front to the class struggle over land. Moreover, the specific conditions of the south, particularly the problems of decentralization and coordination, were just as real after 1960 as before, and continued to express themselves in the problem of local initiatives and tensions with central Party policy.

Divorced from the specific economic and social issues, an analysis of the southern Revolution's evolving organization is meaningless. As the war proceeded, American experts attached great significance to the NLF structure without, in the main, ever comprehending that it was the Party's relationship to real problems and immense organizational flexibility that made it indestructible. The relative importance of these problems cannot be fixed in some statistical fashion. Land and security—economic, personal, and community—were fundamental, the struggle for land being the single most important issue not only of the war in the south after 1960 but in the entire history of the Revolution. Political questions, including the desire for peace and national independence, were most meaningful to the masses when linked to material factors.

The Party Central Committee's southern branch, the Central Office for South Vietnam (COSVN), was in command of the entire struggle in the south. It, in turn, directed the interprovincial, provincial, district, and, finally, village branches of the southern Party, called the People's Revolutionary Party (PRP) after January 1962. It played the dominating role in the NLF's Liberation Committees, which nonetheless had a non-Party majority, and in the mass Liberation Associations, composed of such groups as peasants, students, and women. All of these organizations existed parallel to but autonomously of each other, acting as reinforcement in case one was destroyed. This interlocking system made the Party's network extremely difficult to uproot. Cadres were, as always, the indispensable motivators and problem solvers wherever and whenever required.

As a highly adaptive organization in constant danger, the Party did not adhere to protocol and rules of a literal sort, and its early advocacy of the need for self-motivating and antibureaucratic Party members made pragmatic effectiveness as well as security and survival much more important. This flexibility was a vital source of strength, and it had in 1959 forced the Politburo to respond to the southern Party's initiative. Highly motivated and disciplined in the ultimate sense of being committed to a revolutionary cause and the Party, the men and women who composed the southern movement were not mindless organizational people, because in order to make immense sacrifices they also had to have confidence in themselves.

The Party always understood the crucial role of local initiative and mass participation, particularly as the increasing demands of security reduced the higher level's quick access to grass-roots organizations, and adaptively strove to overcome any elitist, passive tendencies which existed, all the while defining a broad, common framework for action. The Peasants Liberation Association was the largest of the NLF mass groups, and in many older revolutionary areas it was the real local administration. By mid-1965, according to the CIA, the various liberation associations had roughly half a million members. Other U.S. estimates for a later period showed that anywhere from one-half to three-quarters of the rural society in the NLF-controlled regions participated in the many facets of the local administrations' work—compared with one-fifth in "contested" areas and with less in solid RVN regions. The local Party branches, too, were instructed to assume as many key responsibilities as possible and to operate autonomously of the higher Party on local administrative questions. This made local Revolutionary government far more responsive to the masses than was the typically bureaucratic RVN system, as well as capable of surviving on local resources for military and for other functions.

This dependency on the masses in a local context created much more integrated communities in regions of the spacious, frontier south where few had ever existed. The cohesion the NLF imposed made life in the villages less precarious in general because of its land-related policies. It also sought to eliminate gambling and social vices, including usury, efforts a few deplored

but many benefited from. Moreover, NLF activists used their family relationships with apolitical or even hostile villagers to integrate them. For
many, family ties were the most vulnerable political consideration. Ever
present was the cadre, sharing the daily lives of the people and meeting with
them constantly, keeping the Party in contact with the masses' concerns and
problems. The Americans who studied the cadres' role in the villages found
them popular and respected both as leaders and as human beings. The
flexibility and autonomy of the system meant that the local Revolutionary
administration was remarkably sensitive to village needs, and its policies
reflected this. Although taxes in solidly controlled liberated zones were by
1963 supposed to be 6 to 10 percent of the rice harvest, the individual rates
were to "be made in accordance with their own will and should not be forced
to follow above figures."[1] In contested regions rates were lower. By early
1967 only 18 percent of the NLF's income came from taxes on agricultural
production, which the United States correctly viewed as part of a long-term
NLF effort to avoid placing any burden on the poorer peasantry. Political
mobilization was always the prime consideration.

The NLF's popularity rested on its social policies, on which its organizational efforts capitalized. Indeed, its organizational policies followed from
the logic of its political ideology and were the only successfully adaptive
strategy for a vast, often isolated rural society. What is crucial, of course,
is that the poorer peasants supported the NLF's program because they
benefited from it. At the same time, its military recruitment was far less
burdensome than the RVN's. To a peasant, the loss of a son was not only
an emotional sacrifice but also a tax on his resources and a family-based
economy. In 1960 the RVN's regular military numbered 146,000, a figure
that nearly doubled over the next four years, while the NLF forces at the
end of 1962 had 23,000 to 34,000 men, according to varying American
estimates. The RVN's compulsory draft risked sending young men to distant
areas, for which they would receive nothing. Many preferred joining local
NLF guerilla forces—a choice that helped their standing in the community
as well as their chances of obtaining land. Land was the NLF's key to
recruitment, and it successfully focused a great deal of effort on mobilizing
the children of landless and poor peasants, who had the most to gain from
the struggle. It was, ultimately, their revolution.

The NLF's grass-roots effectiveness exposed it to the constant threat of
attack. Taking advantage of its local autonomy, it was at times ready to
violate Party policy in order to defend itself. On no issue was this more of
a problem than on that of the assassination of its enemies. The context of
the use of "terrorism," as the Americans called it, was not complex. The
control of areas was often changing, and anyone who was with the Revolution had to worry about eventually being denounced—with prison or even

death as a consequence. Moreover, local RVN officials and landlords tended to be corrupt and hated, and popular enmity toward them was normal. The Party held that terror was, in Douglas Pike's accurate phrase, "the weapon of the weak."[2] It was discouraged because it alienated some people, though most of those killed were widely hated locally. For this reason the Party established very explicit procedures to prevent arbitrary punishment of real or alleged enemies, and only the provincial-level Party could authorize executions. In practice, however, much of the local organization's work was autonomous of the often distant provincial officials, who were loath to allow excessive use of the punishment anyway. At least two-thirds and possibly four-fifths of the executions were never sanctioned, as local village organizations meted out their own justice. The Party often complained about this, but in fact the local NLF organizations' settling of accounts with unpopular RVN officials generally made them all the more welcome to the masses.

This local autonomy and power allowed the NLF to reconstitute itself again and again, leaving the United States with the frustrating reality that, no matter how successful the RVN was, it could never destroy the grass-roots NLF. The paradox for the Party leadership was that the southern movement was by its very flexibility, autonomy, and community basis often quite ready to take care of its own problems in its own ways, the punishment of enemies being just one example. Another, and more important, was the southern Party's substantially greater emphasis on land reform, as opposed to a united front against the RVN, than Party leaders in Hanoi deemed wise.

Since the August Revolution the Communists had favored a broad class alliance, and during the early 1960s the Party's journals repeatedly analyzed what it considered to be land reform excesses and their threat to the united front in South Vietnam. The NLF, however, was struggling for its very existence. The peasants, too, were being called on to make sacrifices in a life-and-death struggle. Events themselves were the context of all policies; abstract formulas were less impressive than what appeared to most to be obvious necessities. This is not to say that actions were not carefully considered, but the NLF's land policy generally was determined locally and could not be modeled on a priori plans. The Revolution's power was with the majority of the people, and their desires determined many decisions, which thereby penetrated more deeply into the fabric of society. The result was that the Party's united-front policy suffered.

By 1961 the RVN's land reform program had ceased operation, leaving over two-fifths of its expropriated land undistributed and the Saigon authorities as the largest landowners in the country. Legal limits on rent were ignored, and Diemist officials, who were among the major beneficiaries of the distributed lands, were now collecting rent for their own accounts as well as for the RVN's. All that Diem's land reform had managed to accomplish was to make opposition to the RVN a precondition of justice on land distribution.

The NLF land reform policy was both aggressively pursued and perfectly adapted to this situation administratively. It left to every village the cumbersome distribution problem, and it used no paperwork in regard to titles. The reform was contingent on the NLF's obtaining and retaining power, which gave those receiving land the incentive to continue to sustain it. Land presented the NLF with a powerful weapon for mobilizing support as needed, and preference went to those who aided the Revolution.

The land the Diemist reform failed to touch as well as the RVN-owned land posed no distribution problems. By fixing a limit of 5 hectares on ownership as compared with the RVN's 115, the NLF made available most of the landowners' holdings. This immediately had a far-reaching impact on landholding patterns in the Delta. Five hectares was a highly popular figure, the amount held by middle peasants, and with it the NLF consolidated its political monopoly as the advocate of just land reform. The RVN later had little to give away in vast areas. The NLF's problem was that in some areas successive land distributions, dating back to World War Two, and population pressures had eliminated large landlords and that in a substantial number of cases only the land of middle peasants remained available for redistribution. Because the Party's hamlet and village units retained control over land distribution, and because the poorer peasants were increasingly the backbone of the struggle, reform was often relentlessly implemented in their favor. By 1965, however, the Party perceived the dangers of what it termed the "poor-peasant line" to its united-front policy and belatedly sought to end the divisive conflicts which accompanied the actual process of redistribution. An almost classic dilemma for the Party had reappeared.

Difficulties notwithstanding, the NLF's land policy was on the whole immensely successful. It mobilized a large part of the peasants to participate directly in the process of distribution, giving them a permanent vested interest in the Revolution's success. This process was essentially political, and violence was incidental to it, for it evoked a consensus and developed an interest which would protect the NLF throughout all sorts of trials. It was a fundamental factor in the recruiting of soldiers, whose morale and tenacity under the most difficult conditions were never surpassed. It made thousands of villages bases for the NLF and satisfied the most cherished of all peasant goals—land ownership. But even where it was unable to redistribute land or where it chose not to, the whole tenancy system was affected by the mere threat or presence of the NLF. Where RVN control was really "secure," and the NLF not a real challenge, tenants were paying as high as double the legal maximum rent, but elsewhere they never paid in excess of it. The message was clear to every land tenant and unquestionably affected the political loyalties of the masses and their willingness to support the NLF. In this way the Revolution from the start grasped the initiative in the war.[3]

THE UNITED STATES AND THE DILEMMA OF PACIFICATION

Throughout its involvement in Vietnam the United States never seriously defined "pacification" of the insurgency in social or economic terms, minimizing explanations that linked the Revolution's power to the desires and needs of the masses. Whether the ARVN was to fight a conventional or a guerilla war was a more momentous issue to American advisers than the much more important questions why there was a war in the first place, the population's true loyalties and desires and the consequences of its violence to their political commitments. In essence, the counterinsurgency and pacification efforts became interchangeable conceptions, centering on the military and technical means for physically controlling the population.

The logic of this emphasis was to pit the United States and the RVN against the population and in the long run profoundly to alter the basic demography and social order of the nation. And as this transformation emerged out of explicit policy decisions and the relentless, terrible structural consequences of both conventional and antiguerilla warfare, it became perhaps the most important factor determining how the war was fought as well as its outcome. Although the population's first response to repression had strengthened the Revolution, the immense social, demographic, and human upheaval that war engendered ultimately created quite different but potentially fatal challenges to both the United States and the Party.

Diem had from the inception sought to keep Americans away from land and rural social problems, preferring to centralize his control over the countryside with the United States' money but without its advice. His disastrous *agroville* program during 1959–60, which mobilized peasants for the NLF more effectively than anything else did, had received American backing, but the administration was not interested in the rural areas save insofar as counterinsurgency issues were involved. In 1962 it transferred its economic assistance programs to civilian agencies for the duration of the war. From 1960 to 1965 no U.S. financial or advisory assistance on land reform was given to the RVN, and only in 1966 were the first studies of the question initiated. "The basic reason land reform was not pursued," one of the first American experts to examine the question concluded in 1968, "was that U.S. officials did not believe that land-based grievances were important."[4] What was crucial for the United States and

Saigon was physical control of the population, whose desires and needs were for practical purposes minimized. Whatever the differences between the United States and successive RVN regimes or among Americans on the organization of pacification, ARVN military doctrine, or U.S. counterinsurgency efforts, this consensus on population control made such debates secondary. It was demographic change and social transformation, not military action, that would set the critical context for the outcome of the war.

As in everything involving Diem, however, the United States found it difficult to work with him on pacification efforts. By late 1961 the U.S. MAAG was convinced that the time had come for Diem to accept new counterinsurgency techniques which overwhelmingly stressed reliance on new weapons and military strategies and required a reorganization of the ARVN command structure. While the U.S. plan proposed some population transfers and anticipated the later search-and-destroy doctrine, Diem believed that it also threatened his control over the army and therefore his political machine. His response was to define his own counterinsurgency alternative, bringing in Robert G. K. Thompson, the prestigious British expert, to help formulate a plan which emphasized static defense and, above all, RVN control over the population. As it emerged, the Diem-Thompson plan for "strategic hamlets" left Diem firmly in command of the military and governmental apparatus, and Thompson managed to persuade the civilians in Washington enthusiastically to fund it rather than the U.S. military's somewhat different option.

Beginning in spring 1962 the program stressed the placing of fortifications around a majority of South Vietnam's 11,300 hamlets and the concentrating of people into them. The police, self-defense units, as well as a secret RVN apparatus in each hamlet was strictly to control population movement and destroy the NLF infrastructure, attempting first to create wholly secure clusters of hamlets from which to expand to others. The plan possessed military and administrative dimensions to control and to convert the population, but no one ever claimed it was intended to deal with land and social issues. For Diem it was primarily a means of sidetracking potential threats to his power from within his military.

In its own way, the MAAG option to the strategic-hamlet program placed greater importance on the regular army and firepower, and its plan for population displacement was far more drastic. It involved shifting those in border areas much longer distances than the strategic hamlets required, effectively taking them away from "dead zones" open to what would later be called "free fire."[5] What they had in common was an emphasis on physically controlling people in the expectation that the NLF's influence among them could thereby be neutralized. To the extent that it was not, it would still give the RVN ready access to the bulk of the population, depriving the NLF of its mass base.

Diem wanted quick results and mobilized his entire army to create the strategic hamlets by force. In September 1962 Diem could claim that one-quarter of all hamlets were in the program, and one year later about three-quarters were strategic hamlets. Despite warnings from some officials, the United States' leaders generally accepted most of Diem's claims at face value, and this colored their growing optimism on the war in 1963, at least regarding its nonpolitical aspects. For Diem the strategic hamlet was "a state of mind," and most American officials were eager to share it.[6]

The sheer brutality of the program, as the Party admitted in 1969, for a time "reduced significantly regions of importance to us. They caused us many difficulties."[7] A senior ARVN strategist later described the strategic hamlet as "a concentration camp of sorts."[8] Peasants were ordered to abandon their homes and lands for new sites in defensible, often quite distant locations. The cash and building materials they were allocated were inadequate, and they were compelled to give much of their labor to build stockades and defense installations. The RVN officials governing them were, as the Marine pacification expert Lieutenant Colonel William R. Corson described most of the pacification efforts of that period, there "to loot, collect back taxes, reinstall landlords, and conduct reprisals against the people."[9] When the people refused to move into strategic hamlets, the ARVN used artillery and aircraft to compel them to seek refuge in them.

The results were predictable, ranging from military-age men in many places slipping into the country to join the NLF forces to an immense upsurge in popular grievances, which now went beyond land issues to include the entire peasantry's right to its possessions and the perpetuation of a rural society. At the beginning of 1963 the NLF gave the highest priority to the destruction of the strategic-hamlet program. Since its infrastructure among the people in the hamlets was intact and growing, the effort was crowned with quick success. By September 1963 it had dismantled 2,500 hamlets, the entire populations of which were now outlaws in the eyes of Diem's government, badly damaged another 1,000, and planted its influence more deeply in many of the remaining 2,500. Diem, on the other hand, shortly before his murder, claimed that 8,500 hamlets were under his firm control, and despite a certain growing skepticism in Washington—sufficient to add one more reason for getting rid of Diem—the official American data still maintained that the NLF in April 1963 dominated only 14 percent of the rural population.

With Diem's death the hamlet program fell into abeyance, despite several successor projects, and until February 1966 comparable efforts to control the rural population ceased to interest either the United States or any of the Saigon juntas. As the successive RVN regimes' compounded failures in all domains confronted Washington with defeat, it turned to reliance on its own, massive military power.

While the strategic-hamlet program was from its inception a total failure politically, ample data on its success existed to bewilder American officials, almost none of whom comprehended the politics of the upheaval they were attempting to suppress. By March 1963, one set of data argued, over 6,000 of nearly 11,000 targeted hamlets had been integrated. By mid-August the number had climbed to 7,600, and Diem added 1,000 to that figure the following month. When the Diem regime's collapse required revision of the data, the U.S. Operations Mission reduced the number of strategic hamlets to about 4,000 in June 1964. Another official U.S. estimate put it at 6,500 at the same time, and finally at 3,800 at the end of 1965. Data notwithstanding, all those whose opinions mattered knew that, as General William C. Westmoreland, the new commander of the MACV, put it in November 1964, pacification was "not going well."[10] Using real control as a criterion, the RVN in 1964 estimated that it did not have more than 1,200 hamlets, with the remaining 90 percent indefensible or NLF penetrated. Preparing to argue for greater commitment to the war, Secretary of Defense Robert McNamara drafted a memo for the President on March 13, 1964, attributing to the NLF domination of about 30 percent of South Vietnam's territory, but a final version three days later increased it to 40 percent. From the start the statistical hamlet-evaluation systems on the control of people and villages, which were to play such an important part in assessing the war's progress, were subjected to the greatest distortions and doubts, not merely for bureaucratic reasons but also out of genuine ignorance. In policy analyses data immediately became a means both of comprehension and of obfuscation.

UPROOTING A RURAL SOCIETY

Poor peasants initially saw the conflict in terms of land distribution and rent, but by 1963–64 a large and growing portion of all peasants also experienced it in terms of security and their very social existence. The peasant wanted land and peace, but staying on the land was far more important to many peasants regardless of whether they desired more to till. Distinctions between poor and middle peasants were eroding. This primal attitude, which was, not surprisingly, one of the major findings of a combined U.S.-RVN study in 1967, when the refusal to move was even more dangerous than in 1964, transcended all other aspirations among the rural population. It was worth fighting in order to own or hold land, and the United States and its dependents directly flouted this deep-seated goal. The effort to put the peasants in strategic hamlets threatened this even when increasing ARVN and American use of firepower did not, and became a challenge of immense magnitude. The NLF did not yet have heavy artillery, much less air power. Even pro-RVN peasants were now suffering from both the military and the population-control dimensions of pacification. To add to their woes, the ARVN continued taking far larger numbers of their sons.

Everything that peasants, whatever their class, held precious was now being threatened, including the very existence of the family system and the traditional culture. The NLF menaced large landowners, but the sheer magnitude of the assault on a peasant society from the United States and the RVN was much more fundamental. Patriotism and hatred of the foreign invader and all he stood for thus increasingly merged with class issues; as a result the NLF tried to push its united-front position more prominently, after championing the poor peasants' interests between 1960 and 1964. The violence enlarged the peasantry's mutual needs and interdependence and created a collective basis of social life as well as, for some, responses to new common challenges.

Only a part of this growing alienation from the RVN was reflected in the size of the NLF military forces, which, including guerillas, went from 34,000 in 1962, according to one set of U.S. data, to 51,000 in 1964. And though the RVN had 250,000 men in its regular military by 1964, their effectiveness had dropped enormously, and the military balance, in conjunction with political instability, had swung decisively against them. Such mass alienation also possessed more intangible aspects and created a bloc of shifting opinion among the rural population which became increasingly important. For if in reality the war's traumatizing effects, with the extremely hard choices they presented to or imposed on every individual caught up in them, evoked radicalization and commitment from some and prudent, self-oriented caution as well as exhaustion from others, this was no more or no less true in Vietnam than in occupied Europe throughout the Second World War—or in all other times and places. Most of those who are disinclined to become either heroes or unconscionable opportunists are often not free to make a choice. In the ambiguous stages of history when there are no clear losers or winners to whom such survival-oriented people relate, their role is not crucial, for war and peace, victory and defeat, may often be determined by social processes as well as the by weight of the opinion and actions of those prepared to take the risks of leading in the belief that they can create the context in which the lives of others will be defined. For while the war's growing horrors produced those who attempted to withdraw, it also created those ready to join the resistance, and these were the people who counted most. Suffice it to say, the absence of any American equivalent to the NLF meant that whatever consolation some experts were obtaining from their specious assertions about the existence of a floating population, let alone one that supported the RVN, it was not to get help where and when it really counted. Only the NLF, whose members were ready to take personal risks for a common cause, was able to address the complex human as well as material conditions emerging in the Vietnamese countryside. For it was a characteristic of many of those who became *attentistes* that they were neither politically neutral nor apathetic but, essentially, more concerned with their personal survival and unwilling to take chances—and therefore often passive. Some were simply exhausted, if only temporarily. However troublesome they were to prove to the NLF, for the United States and the RVN their existence was far more menacing—indeed, potentially fatal—since the Revolution could continue, albeit less effectively, among them.

The need for the majority of peasants to decide whom to support presented itself less often than the daily need to choose ways of surviving, which had their own logic and led to the apolitical pursuit of private interests. The NLF had responded to the class interests of the majority of the rural inhabitants, and they had fought all foreign invaders for decades. Now the immensely larger U.S. and RVN firepower presented them with much greater risks. Caught between life and death, many peasants were willing passively to maintain a private life in RVN-controlled zones if they had that option, but they could have no illusions after the first decade of U.S.-sponsored dependency about who stood for their very existence on the land and who threatened it. Nor were U.S. experts ever in doubt about the core of the peasants' real aspirations and values. "The Vietnamese peasant has a strong desire to survive," Lieutenant Colonel Corson ruefully observed about his experience, "and more often than not hopes the Vietcong will win because he imagines a Vietcong victory will eradicate the conditions he currently faces. Our experience showed that the Vietnamese peasant will help the Vietcong when there is not too much risk in doing so and that in the great majority of cases the peasant considers it unthinkable to betray the Vietcong to the enemy."[11] Most peasants had by 1965 experienced the RVN's pacification efforts, some as many as three times, and their land outside the RVN-created villages to some extent was theirs only because of the Revolution's land reform and rent control programs. Even those whose true loyalties did not lie with the Revolution nonetheless were often ready to cooperate with and support it. Family pressures also often required them to do so. These questions of identity and mobilization in rural South Vietnam were to become the most enduring ones confronting the United States and the RVN.

Beginning in 1962 the strategic-hamlet program claimed to have moved 8.2 million people, or a majority of the nation, by the time Diem fell. A number of them, however, had been uprooted by earlier programs as well. For some it involved moving a short distance, indeed often nothing substantial. For others it meant important changes in a stable, traditional order, and no figures on proportions have any meaning. Suffice it to say that it was a major disturbance in the lives of the peasantry, full of personal anguish and disorientation. But this was only the beginning. None of these people were considered refugees, about whom we have more information.

As pacification failed in its nonmilitary aspects and as the programs that Diem sponsored capsized, the United States increasingly returned to its initial desire to rely primarily on firepower to fill a growing political, social, and ideological vacuum. In 1971 the best-informed American expert on refugees, Ambassador William E. Colby, then head of pacification and later director of the CIA, estimated that 25 to 30 percent of the south's entire population had been refugees sometimes during the preceding seven years, not to mention since 1954. This profound displacement of the population, due mainly to firepower, created about 720,000 refugees in 1964 and about 2.4 million during 1964–66.[12]

Ultimately, the question was whether arms and foreign intervention could compensate for the RVN's fundamental weaknesses or only further aggravate them.

Chapter 11

The Challenge of Defining Military Strategies

THE NLF AND THE DILEMMAS OF POLITICAL STRUGGLE

The basic dilemma confronting the Revolution in South Vietnam after 1961 was the degree to which it could stress political over armed struggle. While the DRV was not yet in a position to arm the NLF or reinforce its manpower significantly, even more constraining was its traditional vision of the phases of revolutionary struggle, which emphasized political work among the masses as a precondition of either armed or unarmed efforts. Without them warfare was impossible for long periods and would lead only to premature destruction. This overriding principle guided the Party until the pacification and counterinsurgency programs of Diem and the Americans forced it to adapt the new realities to its long-term perspective.

The Party's view in early 1960 was that peaceful unification of the nation by means of the Geneva Accords was improbable, a conclusion which a good section of its leaders had been slow to accept. Ultimately, it was Diem and his backers who decided whether there would be war. Even without direct U.S. combat intervention, the Party's leaders felt that the Americans' testing of their counterinsurgency capabilities in South Vietnam meant that the Revolution's victories would come in stages, and only after many trials. If America was to intervene directly there would be "a difficult and long struggle," but victory would come nonetheless if the political and military efforts were treated integrally. The length of the war would in all cases be influenced by the contradictions within each enemy camp, by "objective realities."[1] If the masses were mobilized and supportive, the Revolution would possess the greatest number of options in its military and political responses to the enemy's efforts. Spread throughout the country, the people gave the NLF both military and political flexibility and a depth denied its enemies, including the possibility of protracted struggle. The military principle was to remain close to the people and to win their allegiance, and that made politics paramount.

The southern Party's need and desire to take up arms caused the Politburo to stress as strongly as possible that military action should be defensive and secondary. It denounced any underestimation of the strength of the United States and the Diem regime as a "very dangerous" illusion.[2] Armed struggle at this point was distinctly *not* guerilla warfare or the creation of an official liberated zone, for the Party's theory of a general uprising as the road to power, a concept which reflected its own experience with the August Revolution, focused also on its obtaining political mastery, especially in the cities. Developments could emerge out of this process in phases but would not transcend those political efforts essential to their progress.

In reality, the Politburo was defining a position which took account of its own political theory, the pressures coming from the southern Party, its real resources and priorities, and, above all, the intentions and actions of its enemies. Strong insofar as its following among the southern people was concerned, it remained materially far inferior to Diem's army. While it was, so to speak, strategically on the offensive in terms of its prospects for winning a protracted war, tactically it was still on the defensive. Its stress on political struggle was in keeping with its traditional theory and with the real balance of forces. The Party's leaders sought, above all, to study and test the situation in the south before making irrevocable decisions, a process that conformed both to their long-established, cautious, but reliable way of confronting issues and of meanwhile setting other priorities, particularly in the DRV, and to their need to build a stronger consensus among themselves for greater commitments.

The NLF's political consolidation after December 1960, the fivefold increase in its main-force army, the grave decline in Diem's political power, and the strategic hamlets' radicalization of the people caused the Party to believe by the end of 1961 that both the military and the political preconditions of successful struggle were being attained in the process of the mass mobilization of the southern population. In October 1961 the COSVN informed the Party's senior members that "the period of continuous crisis and continuous decline has begun" for the Diem regime and its U.S. backers.[3] While armed struggle then became equal to political, under no circumstances could the former take primacy over the latter. All of the principles of warfare enunciated in the war against France were still the basis of the Party's military strategy and tactics. "We maintain that the *morale factor*

*is the decisive factor in war, more than weapons, tactics and technique.
. . . * Politics forms the actual strength of the Revolution: Politics is the root
and *War is the continuation of Politics.* "[4]

The nation was now divided into three rough areas, each with its own
balance between political and military work. The mountains were capable
of being held militarily, giving the NLF access to the ranges running from
the seventeenth parallel southward through the least-populated two-thirds
of South Vietnam. Larger and more mobile military action was possible
there. The Delta was still disputed territory, but the NLF's strength was
growing quickly; it was a region from which manpower and supplies could
be drawn and where clandestine political and military struggles were to be
about equal. Combat would be carefully planned and based on surprise if
possible, with small units using their advantage to move in and out of
combat quickly—the efforts having some political purpose at all times. In
the cities Diem's control made political struggle essential. Unlike the Chinese Communists, though, the Vietnamese never thought in terms of a
rural-urban dichotomy but saw the two areas as complementary, as the
August Revolution had shown, both for political reasons and because urban
activity pinned down much of the enemy's forces. Political efforts in cities
would take innumerable forms, from the converting of students or the
building of sympathetic groups within legal mass organizations to the formation of underground cells. The masses would in the rural areas be primarily the poor peasants and in the cities laborers and poorer elements, as well
as the petite bourgeoisie and students. The NLF also welcomed middle
peasants opposed to Diem and after 1964 attempted to reduce its emphasis
on the poor peasant. The cadres were instructed to apply and frequently
adjust this overall strategy not only to prevent overemphasis on either
military or political struggle but also to help forestall the growing danger
of direct U.S. intervention. For whether the struggle would be brief or
indefinitely long would now, in the Party's view, depend on the actions of
the Americans.

Until Diem's fall this was the Party's basic strategy on military affairs;
the struggle was to be won "mainly through the efforts of the South Vietnamese people," with only some assistance from the DRV.[5] The DRV's
material commitment to the southern resistance, which the southern leaders
welcomed, was far from total. The Party always stressed self-sufficiency in
arms, to be achieved mainly by capturing them. In 1961 no Soviet or Chinese
arms were taken from the NLF, and in 1963 the United States claimed that
8 percent of the NLF arms were Sino-Soviet, the remainder being American,
French, or homemade. And though the Front was ready to move toward
larger-unit warfare, neither its resources nor its policy allowed it to do so
before 1964.

The Party's political struggle impinged dangerously on successive U.S.-backed regimes, not merely because it persuaded large numbers to support the NLF but also because the Party always set a high priority on infiltrating and on capturing as much of the RVN civil and military apparatus as it could. This involved sending highly disciplined people into the RVN's organizations as well as proselytizing those already there for their own reasons. Indeed, urban activities often took mainly such forms since more-overt efforts were much more likely to get the NLF's followers thrown into prison. At the same time, contacts between NLF members and their families in the RVN zones offered a large audience of potential converts, and RVN personnel sometimes cooperated with the NLF for quite personal reasons. Moreover, whenever the NLF appeared to be winning, there were always many more people in the RVN ready to help in diverse ways, hoping that this would give them insurance against being on the losing side. It was this opportunistic calculus that won over many, if not most, lukewarm collaborators or caused various RVN military units to reach private accommodations with the local Revolutionary forces.

Party members sent into the RVN apparatus, especially into the military and police, were carefully compartmentalized from each other, and their highest-priority task was to reduce bloodshed by whatever means possible. When Diem was killed, the new deputy director of the National Police released all NLF prisoners, destroyed documents, and planted as many NLF supporters as he could in high offices, and the CIA concluded he was probably a Party agent. Indeed, such disciplined infiltrators played vital roles throughout the war, particularly in providing intelligence and logistics. It was also common procedure for some NLF to join local RVN militia to steal their arms or to open their installations at crucial times.

Whether based on disciplined persons, opportunists, or simple businessmen, this symbiosis between the NLF and the RVN became an absolutely vital logistical factor in the war and the Front's policy of optimum self-sufficiency. Until the mid-1960s the majority of its arms and of all its other needs came from the nominally RVN-controlled regions. Even after Soviet and Chinese weapons became standard, the NLF and DRV units kept meeting some of their munitions requirements with the stocks captured from U.S. and ARVN forces and those under the control of cooperative ARVN soldiers. "As of April 1967," a Pentagon-sponsored report concluded, "U.S. intelligence personnel were of the opinion that the Viet Cong could purchase almost anything they wanted in Saigon by using various fronts and agents."[6] By 1968 the NLF was acquiring the bulk of its essentials other than arms in this fashion, and it raised the funds it required in the south.

Spread out among the people and dependent on them, far more political than military in nature, immensely flexible, self-sufficient, and elusive in its movements, this was the enemy the United States first confronted in its effort to establish its credibility.

AMERICA'S SEARCH FOR EFFECTIVE WEAPONS AND ORGANIZATION

Just as the NLF thought that military action without a strong political base was premature, the United States and Diem had to rely increasingly on military means precisely to compensate for their already profound and growing political weaknesses. For this reason it ultimately made little difference which strategy guided the use of the ARVN's rapidly expanding army, because the approaches of both the United States and Diem were predicated on indifference toward the population's desires, an attitude which turned to hostility once it was clear that only the NLF had a mass following. Their contempt appeared in all of their programs for forced resettlements of the people, and created cycles of failure, escalations to compensate for them, and yet more failures.

From 1961 to Diem's fall, the United States searched for arms and doctrine, an effort that often divided its leaders even when they agreed on the political objectives of their growing intervention. To some extent the debate over how to organize the RVN military reflected the United States' own later dilemmas. South Vietnam, from the inception, also served as a laboratory in which to test new American ideas, strategies, and equipment relevant to counterinsurgency warfare everywhere. They used ARVN partly to try out these weapons and concepts in the context of immediate military problems. But just as the administration could experiment, so the NLF could begin to learn how to cope with comparable, if more intense, problems in the hands of U.S. soldiers.

Although Diem never relinquished his absolute control over the army's chain of command, he was willing to allow the United States to incorporate many of its new concepts and weapons into ARVN. His main desire was to increase the size of his army. Senior American advisers disagreed throughout this period on whether ARVN should be prepared to fight a guerilla or a conventional war. Its structure was modified during 1960–61 to allow it to fight either, but it did neither effectively. While the United States clearly saw Diem's constraints on the ARVN's operations, it never doubted that they could defeat insurgency if technical and organizational changes were made according to the opinion of this or that expert. The American myopia regarding the politics of destroying the Revolution was from the beginning acute, and many who wanted the ARVN revamped to conform to the latest counterinsurgency tactics and weapons also strongly endorsed the strategic-hamlet program as integral to the overall counterinsurgency approach. The RVN regular forces and local militia were increasingly committed to establishing static positions. The holding of populated territory was to become and remain an obsession with both the United States and Diem—one which required the introduction of yet more technology and mechanized mobility as a compensation. For without political appeal for the masses all that the successive RVN regimes could do was control the population physically, at a cost fatal to their military capabilities.

The U.S. experiments with weapons and organizational concepts, at a time when events in the countryside forced the ARVN to confront greater challenges, produced several years of intense American analyses and efforts, from which emerged the central pillars of the future war: mobility and firepower. The U.S. satisfaction with alleged ARVN military progress during this period produced a guarded optimism among even those who were opposed to further escalations after 1964. It was in this context that the ARVN was locked into its dependency on airmobility and on firepower, including its own tactical aviation. The Pentagon concluded late in 1961 that helicopters were crucial to extricating the ARVN from static defense roles better handled by local and irregular militias. The ARVN would then be able to mass its men and greatly increased firepower whenever the enemy appeared. The immediate effect of this change, which Taylor and Rostow recommended, permanently addicted RVN logistics to what its chief logistics expert later described simply as "American doctrine, American equipment and American money."[7] It also required American advisers, whose numbers quintupled between the end of 1961 and the end of 1963, to run the system.

During this gestation period the United States decided to create a command structure for its own forces in or near Vietnam, one which was to last until 1973. Whatever else the U.S. Air Force, Navy, and Army have in common, the sharing of power and money has always proved a source of disunity among them, a fact that has profoundly influenced the strategies and even the conflicts they advocate. Every modern war has seen this problem arise, and it became a major frustration because in 1962 Washington did not believe that its involvement in Vietnam was a large affair or one likely to last long. In what initially was a minor bureaucratic arrangement, the Pentagon in February 1962 placed the newly created and Army-dominated Military Assistance Command, Vietnam (MACV) in Saigon under the jurisdiction of the Commander in Chief, Pacific (CINCPAC) in Hawaii, rather than directly under the Joint Chiefs of Staff in Washington. The CINCPAC controlled all forces in the Pacific and was therefore run by the Navy, which ended up having less to do in Vietnam than either of the other services. The arrangement ended only in the loss of much time and the use of much paper for the entire war effort because the Navy refused to relinquish its nominal participation in all Pacific-related issues. The command problem later grew even more complicated because helicopters proved central to the war and because global responsibility for "airmobility," as it was called, was assigned to the Army. The Air Force strenuously objected to this arrangement until April 1966, when it traded away its claims. This recipe for confusion was compounded by the Air Force's further division from the start into three commands, and it also left helicopters, Marine Corps aviation, and Navy aviation under entirely separate control. In a word, with each new escalation of the war, these jurisdictional issues were to increase until they finally became the source of raging, bitter disputes, the importance of which would grow with time.

This organizational context existed in spite of the 1958 Defense Department reorganization which intended to make U.S. military power more credible by the elimination of public divisions between the three services. When McNamara took over the department, he brought with him a core of civilians, mainly from universities and the Rand Corporation, who believed that foreign policy, military strategy, budgets, weapons, and forces were all related problems and could be analyzed rationally and quantified. Once this was done, objectives could be attained efficiently. These empiricists put the naturally divided officer corps on the defensive, and their exterior self-confidence unnerved numerous senior officials. It was not their specific formulas which seemed impressive but their capacity to give crisp answers as if there were no basic obstacles inherent in their goals in the first place. Academics like McGeorge Bundy and W. W. Rostow reinforced this stress on form without real content. Together with McNamara's coterie they managed to preempt decisions and disarm objections. Vietnam was the first test of this new technocratic political mind, which greatly influenced the milieu in Washington under Kennedy in all thinking about national security problems—for it strongly appealed to the President—and it intimidated Johnson during his first, relatively passive year in office.

It was in the context of this arrogance and supreme confidence that new weapons systems were tested in Vietnam. Herbicides were the first to be employed experimentally, beginning in August 1961. The debate over the use of defoliants immediately led, in the words of the Air Force's later study, to fear of "charges of barbarism for waging a form of chemical warfare."[8] But arguments by civilians in the Pentagon convinced the President, and in November 1961 the program began on what was at first a strictly controlled basis, including attacks on food crops. For public relations reasons, it was intended to be confidential. Whatever the initial anxieties, the program was effectively ignored in the United States until late 1965. Meanwhile, the program went from 6,000 acres treated in 1962 to a peak of 1.7 million acres in 1967; over a nine-year period 20 percent of South Vietnam's jungles and 36 percent of its mangrove forests were sprayed, with 42 percent of the 1965 spraying being allocated to food crops. In 1963 the United States began to study the dioxin in Agent Orange, the major defoliant being used, suspecting it might cause cancer, birth defects, and other grave problems—a fear that was confirmed by 1967 but that never affected policy in any way.

In addition to destroying ground cover and food crops, the defoliation program was intended to move civilian populations into RVN-controlled regions. But it soon became apparent that it was alienating a very large number of peasants, and in the Montagnard regions the program involving the CIA, Special Forces, and RVN irregular militia collapsed partly because of massive crop destruction in the course of the spraying of forests. General corruption in the small program to compensate peasants for lost crops added fuel to the population's dislike of the United States and the RVN, and a confidential Rand study for the Pentagon in 1967 cautiously concluded that crop destruction was counterproductive, politically and militarily. The Nixon administration finally ended the program not because of public outcries or moral afterthoughts but because the spraying in Vietnam left insufficient herbicides for U.S. domestic users and because Thieu in 1968 decided that the political impact on Vietnam's peasants and on the world had been too negative.[9]

Bizarre and comic as well as tragic proposals were also studied to find a shortcut to success, and some involving urbanization or the use of religious sects were later important. Vast amounts of social science research were financed on the assumption that the comprehension of societies and culture might also lead to a more effective counterinsurgency strategy. But the only immediate effect was to create a well-funded, prestigious academic constituency which legitimized the war in the minds of those in Washington and held out hope of America's winning it. Meanwhile, the United States relied on its helicopters, napalm, and firepower—which, as General Paul D. Harkins, then head of the MACV, put it in 1962, "really puts the fear of God into the Viet Cong."[10]

The helicopter was initially the key to giving the ARVN freedom from static defense and a capacity to employ their overwhelmingly superior firepower, and the United States also relied on it very heavily. The eleven thousand U.S. advisers in South Vietnam in 1962 were more concerned with training the ARVN to use the helicopter than with any other task, and in 1962 the NLF's People's Liberation Armed Forces (PLAF) began to study helicopters very carefully after its first frightening and costly encounters with them. Indeed, the PLAF systematically examined every new weapon or arms system introduced in the war. It was the first army ever to have to fight an airmobile enemy. During 1962 it found the way to shoot at helicopters and predict their landing zones, exposing the machines to preregistered mortars, upright bamboo poles, and punji stakes. The element of surprise was lost with helicopters, though American advisers tried to find answers to PLAF methods, the most effective—and costly—being to escort transport helicopters with armed helicopters. But the helicopter's problems were both expensive and complex, involving the need for huge fuel supplies and extensive maintenance as well as constantly rising protection against ground fire. Moreover, enormous numbers were required to carry both troops and logistics. Without friendly forces on the ground, the United States was eventually to conclude, they were vulnerable.

In January 1963 the PLAF in the region of the central Mekong Delta decided to test the ARVN and militia units and the helicopter system by massing and fighting in one place, which it had avoided until then, selecting the village of Ap Bac. Exposing one hundred men to sight, it soon attracted a heliborne force of over three infantry battalions. In a quick engagement five helicopters were destroyed and nine damaged while about four hundred were killed and wounded. Only nine PLAF soldiers were confirmed killed.

Notwithstanding this key lesson regarding the capabilities of the respective armies and their weapons, the majority of the U.S. advisers believed that the military balance of forces in South Vietnam favored them until late 1963, when political and military events became inextricably tangled. And they never lost confidence in the weapons and technology then being developed. Such self-assurance led irresistibly to the conclusion that the same weapons in the hands of Americans, if not in those of the ARVN, along with the other means of destruction available, could save the credibility of U.S. power.[11]

THE REVOLUTION'S MILITARY IN TRANSITION, 1963–1964

By 1963–64 the leaders of the Party had amassed a wealth of experience in what they termed the military art, which was really their conviction that the successful combination of the material and human factors in war required subtlety and a sense of the appropriate strategy for a given context. This strategy was, in essence, a thorough but also intelligent application of materialist conceptions of the relationship of strategy to tactics and of the character of the enemy and the entire physical and political environment in which warfare takes place. Compared with analyses then operational in Washington, it was far more advanced not only because of its concern with the totality of the war but also because Party leaders knew vastly more than their enemies about their nation's terrain and resources.

The core of the Revolution's military art was politics and people, who were both means and ends—means insofar as support for all phases of warfare was concerned, and ends insofar as the Revolution's goals were designed to meet their needs. Tactics and strategy might be flexible, but this central premise was inviolable. To treat war as a continuation of politics in 1963 was not, by itself, an approach requiring great insight, for it was perfectly clear that political struggle had to precede warfare in the context of ever-greater opposition to Diem and of the RVN's crisis. Diem's demise confirmed the Party's emphasis on political work in all save the mountainous regions, which served as base areas, giving it an option on expanded military effort should it prove necessary.

Although the Revolution understood how to fight the ARVN, during 1963–64 it, too, was at a critical transitional stage, both politically and militarily. Without the Americans, the RVN would quickly collapse. But were the United States to make greater commitments to the regime in power, providing its own troops as the principal force, the war would be very different and might last a long time. By December 1963 the Party saw this as a very real possibility. Clearly, at this point the initiative rested with the Americans.

The Party first responded to the military problems it confronted in 1963–64 with study and analysis. It sought to turn the Revolution's weaknesses into assets and the enemy's assets into weaknesses. The helicopter was singled out for examination, as was armored transport. Discussions and experiments took place throughout the country, and in due course the helicopter's main vulnerabilities were made known to all units. The battle at Ap Bac had been an important stage in this learning process. Armored troop carriers, mainly M-113s, took longer to master, and in 1964 the DRV asked both China and the USSR for arms to deal with them. At the same time, the techniques of employing sappers and mortars against aircraft on the ground were refined into a major weapon, the consequences of which would prove enormous throughout the war, just as they had against the French. Constraints in U.S. technology and tactics were minutely studied and exploited for the remainder of the war.

At the end of 1963 the Politburo had to consider the military problems of the war if, as seemed more and more likely, the United States decided to increase its manpower beyond the 16,300 men already there in 1963. Although the guerilla and the local NLF forces had been successful until then, it was now critical to determine whether they alone had the technical and the human resources to cope with American power. While it now made political and armed struggle equal in principle, military efforts would now play the direct, decisive role, and this would require the use of DRV regular forces, the People's Army of Vietnam (PAVN), and the sending of more advanced arms and logistics to supplement the sources and expertise already available to the NLF. To help define the new policy's requirements, the Politburo sent General Chu Huy Man south for four months, particularly to study the situation of the Ho Chi Minh Trail, which was then only a meter wide and the main link from the north to the south. Those living near it generally opposed its expansion, fearing that a wider road would be exposed to air attack, but the decision was taken to enlarge it into a truck route and to send antiaircraft batteries and engineers to maintain it. The trail was never intended to be used for ordinary needs, which could be supplied mainly from the NLF's existing locally based logistics system, but primarily for the movement of advanced arms and men. In October 1964 the first PAVN tactical unit left the north, and in that year only a tiny fraction of the NLF military—probably less than 5 percent—was born in the north. The Revolution, in effect, prepared its option, but it was for the United States to determine how it would employ it.

Had the Party had its way, political struggle would have continued to receive the priority assigned to it at the end of 1961, especially after the failure of the strategic-hamlet program and then the paralysis in Saigon following Diem's death. The great surge in desertions among ARVN units and the senior officers' preoccupation with political cabals opened up endless military as well as political options. The ARVN failed to find military tactics appropriate to the PLAF's flexibility, which used large forces whenever the ARVN broke into smaller units and reversed itself to take over undefended hamlets whenever the ARVN attempted big-unit tactics. Unable to correct the dilemma with its arms and advisers, as perpetual chaos in Saigon continued, the United States' opinion shifted from McNamara's and Taylor's optimism of October 1963 to a deepening conviction that both militarily and politically the RVN was on the verge of losing the war.

Meanwhile, the basic principles of the Revolution's tactics and strategy were further indoctrinated into all of its forces, southern and northern alike. Combat was to occur at the time and place of the Revolutionary army's choosing. Surprise and maintenance of the initiative were considered crucial, especially since the enemy had mobility, an advantage it was essential to take from him. To fight at night was an obvious solution, and to exploit the rainy season was another. The PLAF perfected camouflage and the use of tunnels. To force the enemy to spread out as much as possible was no less critical, and people's war by guerilla and local forces compelled him to do that. The dependence on local logistics and the preparation of forces for maximum self-reliance were also vital to the overall need to keep the enemy dispersed and local forces fighting with as little aid as possible from other PLAF units. The PLAF raised the tactic of ambush to a fine art, since it allowed the Revolution to employ small forces against large ones to the maximum extent, as did all sapper attacks and sporadic attacks against bases and installations which put the enemy on the defensive. Ingenuity in finding the enemy's weak points and in utilizing the Revolution's assets was crucial, and imagination and limitless innovation emerged. Above all, the Revolution had to fight the war in a manner that could protract it as long as necessary, for time was the ultimate ally of the Revolution and the people.[12]

THE U.S. DECISION TO ESCALATE

The events leading to the Tonkin Gulf affair had left the United States with no doubt that its alternative to defeat was a much heavier use of military power, and the Tonkin Gulf Resolution had cleared the way for a sustained escalation of the war. The abysmal state of strategic hamlets and the RVN's military capabilities, the ceaseless wrangling among Saigon generals for power, and a growing awareness that the NLF was a tough foe forced the administration back to the basic question of what interests were involved. The maintenance of a pro-American government in Saigon was only a means to its goals; it was not in itself a primary objective. In the end, the problem was America's credibility and its power in the whole region.

Once the decision to bomb the DRV had been made, the whole paralytic, dangerous logic of credibility extended to it as well. Once initiated, the escalatory process cannot be terminated until it delivers success, lest it, too, appear an implausible and ineffective instrument—thereby depriving military power of its ultimate menace and role as a deterrent. The Tonkin Resolution was in fact the critical threshold regarding the use of U.S. military resources. All that the irresistible disintegration of the RVN did was guarantee its continued application, because the notion of the ARVN as a surrogate for direct American force was now increasingly chimerical. However much key advisers sought to link escalation to RVN progress, as Maxwell Taylor did in September 1964, they always came back to the reality that if the United States was forced out of South Vietnam, the implications for its global position would be "disastrous," as Taylor himself phrased it.[13] The administration's formal decision to bomb the DRV repeatedly, especially in response to predictable attacks in the south, was made on September 9, 1964, primarily because of the credibility-domino synthesis and of U.S. global interests allegedly arising from it, and exactly that argument would repeatedly sustain yet greater commitments, regardless of the consistently depressing vagaries of Saigon politics.

During the summer of 1964 the presidential election was a temporary inhibition to further action. When a combined sapper-mortar attack on November 1 against the Bien Hoa air base north of Saigon destroyed five B-57s and damaged fifteen others, a loss equivalent to some of the worst of the Second World War, it was still inconvenient to retaliate. Later that fall the United States tied escalation of the air war to RVN cooperation, but it was never forthcoming, and the United States proceeded in its own way for its own reasons. It was aware that even if the DRV sent nothing more south, the war would still continue because, as the the CIA admitted, "the basic elements of Communist strength in the South remain indigenous."[14] By that time, too, the administration shared the Party's belief that the war would soon end unless the Americans entered it with their own troops. The air war against the DRV would not alone suffice.

At the beginning of December the administration reaffirmed its September decision to bomb the DRV in retaliation for any major NLF action. The possibility of a further escalation, including even a naval blockade of the DRV, was approved contingent on improvements in the RVN. But political erosion in Saigon and ceaseless imbroglios, which led to Khanh's return to power on January 27, 1965, and to the menacing prospects of a neutralist political solution, meant that the United States could either accept a virtually total defeat diplomatically or calculate the chances of military victory. Given the over 23,000 highly equipped American military personnel in South Vietnam at the end of 1964 and their increasing military functions, attacks on their bases were both inevitable and foreseeable. It was also clear by then that if the war was to continue, the United States would have to send its own men into direct combat. The first expression of this compelling logic came in late January, when, without waiting for an ostensible provocation, the White House decided to allow American jets to attack NLF forces.

Given its established policy, the administration's reaction to an NLF sapper-mortar attack against a U.S. advisers compound in Pleiku City on February 7 was wholly predictable. McGeorge Bundy was in Saigon with Westmoreland, who later recalled that Bundy acted "intense, abrupt, at moments a bit arrogant" when news of Pleiku arrived and that "he developed a field marshal psychosis."[15] Telephoning the White House, Bundy urged the President to approve reprisals against the DRV, which he did immediately.

No one of importance in Washington favored the withdrawing of advisers, much less the cutting of aid. They did not consider how American military success would make the RVN more durable or change its basically artificial nature. No one raised the fundamental dilemma as to the inherent viability of Americans being in South Vietnam in such a predicament, because that was an illegitimate question which men at the highest level of state could not contemplate. Indeed, it was also quite incidental that the United States had already received careful estimates on the limits of air war against the DRV and the capacity of the NLF to fight on without help. Military decisions are made for political reasons, which the military must then implement, and in late 1964 the United States was certain that the technical resources available to it would suffice. For if the United States did not have the power to win over ill-equipped forces in an incredibly poor country, then of what use was its power elsewhere? This challenge was only a variation on the theme of the credibility of U.S. power that had constantly faced it since the end of 1945, but it was nonetheless now deemed unavoidable in Washington. Few doubted that success could be obtained, for such skepticism could lead only to a profound crisis in American global perceptions and objectives. The question by early 1965 was merely how much effort and time would be required.

Chapter 12

The United States, the Revolution, and the Components of Struggle

COMPONENTS OF STRUGGLE AND CHANGE: POLITICAL

Each side's decisions in the Vietnam War reflected its ideology as well as its material abilities, and since the war was now between one of the poorest nations of the world and the richest in all history, the contest involved, among other things, the relevance of competing political theories to the history of mankind and the possibility of human mastery over social forces.

Events after mid-1964 caused the guarded American military optimism of 1963 to turn into a deepening pessimism, culminating in McGeorge Bundy's and McNamara's belief early in 1965 that "our current policy can lead only to disastrous defeat."[1] The larger political and economic context of the struggle, however, was, at best, a matter of secondary importance. Reliance on arms seemed natural in light of the fact that their utility against insurgencies everywhere was a major point in question. Moreover, their potential political allies evoked little American enthusiasm. The United States could not confront the basic political issues of fighting the war. "We are trying to fit our familiar tools and way of doing things to a problem we have never really bothered to analyze," the uninfluential Michael Forrestal warned in May 1964.[2]

The question why there was a war in the first place was considered irrelevant at this time, compared with the seemingly more manageable question of the tactics of war—whether mobile, conventional, or by whatever military approach seemed workable. The nature of the United States' system defined its goals and also its perceptions of reality, which in turn circumscribed its possible actions. Its consciousness was a function of needs and interests rather than of a desire to perceive facts by some objective, scientific criterion, for the concern of the system was not truth but rather power, and this was partly the cause of its contradictions and failures.

The Revolution was left, therefore, with a virtual monopoly on politics and the insightful assessment of social factors. Because it had so little military power and economic resources, its assets had to be its consciousness and the accuracy of its reasoning and analysis as the basis of its conduct, or it was certain to fall victim to the impersonal balance of forces which always strikes the weak ruthlessly when their actions are not suffused with correct and ample wisdom. Never was the relevance of social analysis and reason to the mastery of events and historical forces quite so starkly presented for the judgment of mankind. For apart from Vietnam's distinctive military and physical dimensions were the intellectual and political resources of America's enemy, all the more dangerous because the Revolution's creative methodology could be applied not just in Vietnam but everywhere. The United States chose the wrong country in which to test its credibility.

By 1959 Diem's policies in the south had compelled the Politburo to follow the initiatives of the southern peasants and Party remnants, and Diem's actions repeatedly forced the Party's hand until its best guarantee against major, if not fatal, errors in tactics was to make certain that its ties with the masses left it with the strategic initiative regardless of what happened. A major lesson of the Party's entire history was that once the masses began to act they could be led but not stopped, which meant that during crucial periods the Party followed them in order to be in the vanguard. When the masses again became passive, the Party returned to goading and educating them.

When the United States began to increase its role in South Vietnam in 1961, the Party's leaders could see only the broadest options in the coming struggle and prepare for them, and they did not think it likely America would use its own troops. Indeed, since the United States' increasing involvement until 1964 was minimal compared with its later actions, the Party's stress on political efforts seemed rational. Politics was seen as the basis of protracted war, the most effective counterbalance it had, should the United States escalate militarily. Time was the one decisive resource the Revolution possessed in coping with both the United States and the RVN. By instinct the Party disliked risky ventures, and its very slow approval of the resumption of resistance in the south was just a reflection of its ingrained caution. By 1963 the Party felt that the NLF could win the war against Diem without any major commitments of resources from the DRV, if only because its land policy gave it a virtual monopoly over the peasantry's allegiance, and the former Viet Minh southern regroupees were its main material commitment to the NLF until then. But every time its assumptions failed, it minutely reassessed the causes of the failure and tried to plan its moves to avoid repeating the errors. In 1964, however, its earlier optimism regarding U.S. action found it physically unprepared for sudden escalation, so that until it could implement its military contingency plans its emphasis on political mobilization was all the more imperative.

In the very process of assessing the United States' goals and potential roles as an imperialist state and trends in the world balance of forces, the Party's bias became guardedly optimistic regarding possible enemy action precisely because it always placed American objectives in the same international context that Washington's decision makers thought so important. It appeared unlikely to the Party's analysts that the United States would invest so much of its power in Vietnam at the expense of its other global interests. Nonetheless, the Party also prepared for the worst. But its reasoning was not so much incorrect as too rational, and therefore premature.

THE MILITARY COMPONENTS OF STRUGGLE

America's entire postwar foreign policy has relied repeatedly on the use of arms to compensate for the failure of its political strategy and that of its allies. It became increasingly dependent on these allies to sustain its efforts to achieve global hegemony, and South Vietnam was neither the first nor the last case of this inherently precarious mutual dependency. By its very nature the politics of this relationship produces weak, unstable regimes, and America's armed intervention is its inevitable consequence.

By 1964 and early 1965 the war was almost lost. The PLAF held the initiative. Had the United States escalated the war sharply with air power, Westmoreland later recalled, it would have risked provoking a significant increase in NLF action, which would have swept it into power. This alone meant that the first escalation had to be gradual. The Revolution in 1964 was not yet prepared, however, for large commitments of U.S. troops, which would require soldiers from the DRV, the creation of a superior logistics system, and the upgrading of its military equipment. Nor was it able to introduce a sufficient number of main forces able to snatch the victory nearly within its grasp. The question of time for both sides now became critical.[3]

By 1964 the Vietnamese struggle was over twenty years old, and its leadership understood the liabilities and rewards of patience; they could wait another twenty years if necessary. The Party's leaders, especially in the military, immediately began debating various strategies to exploit the initiative they held by 1965. In the end, however, they reiterated the need always to be able to rely on traditional principles of dispersion, surprise, and flexibility, whatever the tactics of the moment. In fact, although the Party's leaders were prepared to undergo protracted war, they certainly never wished to, and they consciously combined the doctrine with a readiness to win victory in a short time if it were possible. Prolonged war was an ultimate weapon and under certain circumstances could be a realistic utilization of limited means as well as an exploitation of the constraints on the resources of the United States and the contradictions of its system. And while it was far more realistic in its assumptions than the Americans in their definitions of their options, the Party also hesitated before the prospect of abandoning the peaceful development of the nation.

The United States appreciated the Party's desire to preserve and expand its hard-won economic gains in the north. On this basis most in Washington thought that graduated air war would extract critical concessions and allow the RVN to avoid defeat. What they failed to see was that the very rationality the United States correctly imputed to the Party's leaders would cause them to rely on the peasant nature of the DRV's economy, which ultimately made time unlimited, as the final guarantor of victory. The Party's leaders understood the restriction of time on America better than the administration. In an industrial society time is money, and the United States in 1964 could not imagine that a protracted war of a decade or two would be either necessary or possible. Neither its society nor its cultural rhythm could absorb the concept. Its military doctrine was alien to passive, if successful, tactics. The U.S. Army's principles of strategy required that a commander "will never permit him[self] to have circumstances dictate his actions, but that he will rather determine the circumstances himself," taking the offensive and keeping the initiative.[4]

Whether the administration could accomplish this depended not merely on Vietnamese strategy, which could ultimately be infinitely varied, but also on testing its own weapons systems and new methods of counterinsurgency warfare. For arms had to fill the political void. Improved napalm, chittering lice geared to electronic sensors, defoliants, and the ever-growing family of American science's imaginative weapons were still being tested. The results in 1965 were inconclusive. The air power the United States was ready to apply was already awesomely formidable, but the November 1964 attack by a few men on the Bien Hoa air base was, as a historian of the Air Force later recounted, "without an Air Force precedent." In developing air power for counterinsurgency since 1961, the Air Force "did not actively consider the impact of insurgency warfare on air base defense," an oversight of no small importance![5] Learning and adapting with the money and time available to it was an integral part of the new stage of the war emerging as the United States prepared to shift from a reliance on the ARVN to the use of its own forces, and the Revolutionary soldiers had to find methods of neutralizing as many American advances as possible. To do so quickly was critical to each side, above all for the administration, whose political liabilities both in the United States and in Vietnam made time of the essence.

The true balance of military forces was unclear to Washington in 1965 precisely because it could not assess the eventual importance of organizational, economic, and political factors in Vietnam and, later, at home. But it had ample self-confidence and believed its vast reservoir of mobile-fire-power force could fill the void its earlier failures and those of RVN regimes had created. The classic postwar American dilemma of bringing arms and military doctrines together to cope with the elusive political realities of foreign nations was emerging once again.

THE EQUALIZATION OF ARMS

However intense its confidence in the masses' ultimate role in the war, the Party had no illusions about the time and the human and economic costs involved, which it wished to minimize as much as possible. It also desired to counterbalance U.S. power with relatively small but qualitatively decisive amounts of advanced arms and military technology, arms that would offer it far greater flexibility in its military tactics. This need compelled it to turn to the infinitely complex, subtle problem of its relations with the Soviet Union and China and to master the intricacies of socialist diplomacy. Whether it succeeded or failed would be of inestimable significance to the military struggle and the war's duration.

The Geneva Conference of 1954 illustrated how its allies could damage its interests and consequently its need for an independent foreign policy to protect its own welfare. In late 1957 both China and the USSR encouraged the DRV to avoid upsetting the de facto partition on the seventeenth parallel. The DRV in 1956 saw the Sino-Soviet split emerging to divide the world Communist movement, and by 1959 the problem was so grave that the Party's leaders decided that they could not postpone an autonomous foreign policy. Still, both nations were giving it economic aid, and neutrality between them was essential until 1960, when Khrushchev's peaceful-coexistence line and the USSR's failure to endorse the NLF's struggle led the Party to tilt toward China. The Party also managed to straddle both the Chinese and the Soviet positions by favoring coexistence and national-liberation struggles at one and the same time, but its criticism of Yugoslav revisionism and opposition to Soviet demands for unity on all key issues publicly made it appear increasingly friendly to China until 1963. In reality, however, the DRV had serious complaints about Chinese actions as opposed to Peking's posturing with heroic anti-coexistence statements. Its arms aid to the NLF and the DRV was limited to light weapons so that it could conform to the dominant Chinese theory of small-unit guerilla warfare as the sole mode of national-liberation struggle. The Party thought this inflexible and a guarantee of a protracted war it was both prepared to fight and eager to avoid. Then, in the 1962 Laos agreements, China abandoned its verbal commitment to armed struggle in Laos in order to obtain a peaceful border for itself. It also publicly advocated negotiations for a similar plan for South Vietnam. The Chinese sought to prevent a possible U.S. escalation, revealing in the process China's exclusive emphasis on its own national interests. China was now urging national-liberation struggles only where its own security was not endangered.

The Party never trusted China thereafter, but cool relations with the USSR over policy issues foreclosed a shift in its public posture. In 1963 the Chinese unsuccessfully tried to enlist the DRV in a new "international" aligned against the Soviet-led bloc. The Party's stand against revisionism and coexistence, but in favor of international unity, left it in an ambiguous though independent position, for its politics reflected its unique definition of the world. In effect, as Le Duan made clear at the end of 1963, the Party would base its line on the specific conditions in Vietnam. Revolution could be neither imported nor exported. When the Party made its December 1963 decision to prepare for much greater aid to the NLF if the United States escalated, relations with China quickly changed. American experts followed every nuance of this shift, carefully estimating the risks in escalation, and were reassured as the Chinese throughout 1964 progressively reduced the deterrent of its implicit threats to send troops to help the DRV.

Meanwhile, in February 1964 both Le Duan and Le Duc Tho went to Moscow and unsuccessfully sought more aid. While the Chinese helped the DRV with air defenses after the August 1964 Tonkin Gulf affair, they privately told the United States that despite public declarations they would not go beyond the provision of material aid—which was still limited in nature—short of a full-scale invasion of the DRV threatening China's borders. Throughout 1964 the administration could move without fear of serious Chinese involvement, an anxiety that might have constrained it. Both the USSR and China publicly distanced themselves from the Vietnam crisis immediately before and after the Tonkin Gulf events and took an optimistic view of U.S. intentions that greatly disturbed the DRV and left it relatively isolated.[6] The aid it needed most still eluded it.

The Party's rude education forced on it the realization that Sino-Soviet disunity could become one of the Revolution's main assets. Neither country could simply abandon the DRV and the NLF without irreparable damage to its international standing. This control over the symbolism of international proletarian legitimacy was to become a crucial factor in the Party's dealing with both nations. When Khrushchev was removed from power, in October 1964, the DRV succeeded in obtaining greater Soviet aid and tested its capacity to play on the split to get as much support as possible from both sides. Moreover, the new Soviet leaders probably saw the advantage of keeping an independent DRV from falling into excessive dependence on Chinese aid, which might increase China's influence in the Southeast Asian region. And they could not be oblivious of their own immense advantage should the United States turn away from European questions and sink into the South Vietnamese abyss.

It was in this context that Premier Aleksei Kosygin was in Hanoi on February 7, 1965, to conclude an aid agreement when the United States attacked the DRV again and began what all knew would be a continuing air war and a probable troop buildup. Washington had carefully analyzed the tension between the DRV and its allies, and it also recognized the DRV's increasingly subtle utilization of bitter Sino-Soviet differences to gain military and economic aid. It was aware, too, that the USSR was more and more committing its international prestige and would not be able to extricate itself easily. In effect, the DRV's diplomacy had finally managed, at the critical moment in the war, to obtain the minimum aid essential to its introducing a qualitatively vital, though not decisive, technological factor of its own against the imminent American influx. It could now fight the war in many ways, ranging from the most elementary types of people's war with simple arms to advanced weapons capable of producing endless military combinations against the United States and the ARVN and increasing their costs in the war immensely. Although the United States was fully aware of the DRV's success materially and diplomatically, but barely mindful of the enormous amounts of supplies it might eventually obtain, this development did not inhibit U.S. decisions significantly.[7]

THE PROBLEM OF EQUATIONS OF POWER

Politics had been the key to the Vietnam War since 1941, and social and economic issues were the ultimate basis of the Communist Party's successful struggle until 1965. On this level the war was unequal during the early 1960s, and from the inception the military balance between the United States and the Revolution was far less favorable to America than it appreciated. Indeed, given the addition of a small but qualitatively important amount of arms to the PLAF as well as manpower from the DRV, the United States had an enemy far stronger than it ever imagined.

But one factor by the end of 1964 was beginning to alter radically the Revolution's power and introducing a new social dynamic for both sides to confront. War in the modern era is shaped not only by decisions and their immediate effects on the balance of forces but also by the emerging structural consequences of the process of conflict itself. By 1964 the war in South Vietnam was becoming a monumental struggle and reaching a level of ferocity which was starting profoundly to affect society at all levels, altering the distribution of the population with astonishing rapidity. This uprooting of people, the repeated breaking of their cords with the past, and this increasingly traumatic alteration of the very fabric of a whole nation opened the door to innumerable problems for both of the adversaries. It is not possible with mere words to capture the true meaning of this experience to each individual involved, the incessant personal dilemmas and choices for them and their families, or the pressures of existence and survival. Protracted war meant that an entire nation would pay a growing social price, one that would reveal the latent weaknesses of each side as well as its sources of strength, and the way this vast human drama's consequences might translate into political and military forms could be critical, perhaps even decisive.

The Revolution saw this immediately, realizing that though time worked for it militarily, the war's impact on the social order was growing and would pose ever-larger problems with each year. It sought to stay close to the masses, but many peasants were now being driven off the land, either because of their elemental instinct to survive the rising level of combat or at the point of U.S. and RVN guns. This transition of the peasant from the land to the cities posed untold problems and dilemmas, touching the Revolution's social base and raising inevitably the significance of the urban question in its strategy, particularly after the peasants underwent the distinctive drama of the city's brutal uprooting of a cultural, political, and, ultimately, human core formed in a rural society.

The RVN and the United States would also have to face the problems of a traumatized, rapidly urbanizing nation. Their short- and long-term political and economic implications at first appeared manageable and favorable to the anti-Communist cause, if only because they were ultimately seen as an aspect of the military struggle and one more indicator of success in combat. This, too, was to prove a fatal error, for the RVN could not simply survive militarily. It also had to find a way of molding the social forces of the south into a nation willing to give it legitimacy and support.

In brief, both the Revolution and the United States and its dependent in 1964–65 were entering a critical transition period. While both perceived the same trends very differently, neither yet fully grasped their enormous importance to the very outcome of the war and the country's future.

Part Three

TOTAL WAR, 1965-1967, AND THE TRANSFORMATION OF SOUTH VIETNAM

Chapter 13

Escalation and the Frustration of American Politics

The Johnson administration's foreign policy at the beginning of 1965 was the product of two decades of fixed goals tempered by postwar frustrations which did much to define its thoughts and actions throughout the following three crucial years. Beginning with a sense of immense power and freedom, the bitter phases of the war and the failure of its efforts successively closed off its options until, by the beginning of 1968, it was compelled to accept the irreversible military, economic, and political constraints that the protracted war imposed, at the same time remaining oblivious to the gravity of yet others. Military events, the rural balance of power in South Vietnam, the transformation of the very fabric of the society, and the costs of the war all merged to alter the context of the war's future and the choices before America's leaders.

Until they finally acknowledged those forces and dilemmas, ranging from the war's financial burdens and an increasingly hostile American public to its allies in Saigon and enemies everywhere in Vietnam, U.S. decision makers acted entirely within the inherited framework of postwar objectives and assumptions, yet also with an astonishing degree of self-confidence which minimized the bitter lessons of earlier fruitless efforts. In one sense, their perceptions of previous failures, from the risk of land war to the stalemate of nuclear strategy, made the conjunctural role of Vietnam in postwar American foreign policy all the more important, goading leaders to take action rather than making them more prudent. Their anticommunist instincts, their fear of uncontrolled Third World upheavals, and their desire to prove the relevance of weaponry to the politics of insurgency greatly enlarged Vietnam's significance to men of power in Washington. The increasingly obsessive hold of such justifications over the minds of those who mattered made them virtually sanctified doctrine, around which all other considerations orbited until the very health of the United States' economic, social, and political institutions was at last seen to be at stake during the early months of 1968. Not until then was the nature of the limitations on decisions and power in American society fully revealed, for social reality is best perceived not when a system operates relatively normally but when it falls into crisis.

In February 1965 the administration approached what McGeorge Bundy considered "a major watershed decision" on the basis of a whole series of earlier explicit commitments and definitions of economic and political interests. Credibility was the hypnotic justification which unified virtually all those who shaped fundamental policy.[1] As an emotional belief, credibility was immensely effective, especially for President Johnson, who equated it with the twentieth century's experience with appeasement and the faith American allies everywhere would have in their many security treaties with Washington.

Credibility as a theme pervaded the memos of John McNaughton, former Harvard law professor and assistant secretary of defense, who considered it a matter of "reputation." "The integrity of the U.S. commitment is the principal pillar of peace throughout the world," Rusk advised the President in July 1965, adding, "If that commitment becomes unreliable, the communist world would draw conclusions that would lead to our ruin and almost certainly to a catastrophic war." "Humiliation" was for McNaughton synonymous with the loss of credibility.[2] Both publicly and privately, the doctrine was accepted in its many forms by almost all administration members, including their most influential outside consultants, whether they were raw politicians, academic sophisticates, or macho generals. And even if they debated the extent of the actions required to save credibility, they did not disagree on the basic need for resolute efforts to justify the essential assumption it embodied.

DECISIONS FOR WAR

The Johnson administration made its crucial decisions to increase U.S. forces and activity in South Vietnam between August 1964 and February 1965. A number of small but important supplements to these policies during the spring of 1965 created an irreversible situation before July 1965—when Johnson made the commitment to increase American troops to 175,000. In one sense, it was this early series of relatively obscure, unpublicized decisions that revealed the administration's preferred style—to act privately and shun publicity—to minimize the political liabilities of every choice. For Johnson this meant avoiding the role of the war President and assuming that of the domestic reformer, an ambiguity in his mind that shaped the form but not the content of irresistible escalations. Instead, of course, the public and Congress became increasingly aware of a mounting deception over the deepening United States involvement in Vietnam. It was this guile, as much as the escalation itself, that was to alienate many Americans.

Ultimately, however, the full significance of the administration's key decisions on the war depended on the Communists' response to the growing American presence, particularly to its air power. Its September and December 1964 policy of escalating the air war against the DRV, for example, was designed to give the United States a direct carrot-and-stick negotiating lever, boost the RVN's morale, and reinforce U.S. prestige. The February 13, 1965, initiation of what soon became the "Rolling Thunder" air campaign against the DRV, ostensibly for eight weeks, but lasting until November 1968, almost immediately created a profound challenge to U.S. military power. For it was one thing for the successive RVN juntas to face defeat at the NLF's hands but quite another for the United States to do so—and this quickly became the major issue. Although from the end of 1964 onward the U.S. military and its defenders complained that it had been unable to employ as much air power as victory required, the fact remains that during late 1964 and early 1965 it found it difficult to use what it had available. The most urgent problem was not how to turn the tide of the war but rather how to defend the planes while they were on the ground. It seemed obvious that the NLF's response to air power would be to attack planes at their bases, but no one in the Pentagon actively considered this probability—with entirely predictable consequences.

The February 7 attack on Pleiku revealed that America's bases and hundreds of new planes were increasingly vulnerable. Since the RVN was failing to defend these bases, the MACV requested in late February that Marines be sent to Danang to defend its giant air complex. It was, as the Pentagon Papers noted, "a major decision made without much fanfare—and without much planning."[3] The air war and pacification had both been exhaustively assessed, but troop commitments were an afterthought, largely because they were a logical outgrowth of an offensive air war.

Two Marine battalions landed on March 8, followed by an unpublicized authorization from the President three weeks later that they could fight as far as eighty-five kilometers from the installation. An Army brigade arrived at the giant Bien Hoa base at the beginning of May for the same purpose. Base defense became the primary rationale for troop deployments because

Washington realized there could be no air war without ground war. About half of the ground forces at the beginning of 1966 were assigned to protect base areas, and 40 percent at the end of that year—as the number of American military personnel reached 485,000! The United States never solved this dilemma.

While several senior advisers, like Maxwell Taylor, expressed skepticism about phases of this air-ground program, all save George Ball thought persistence essential to the maintaining of credibility. All who counted, their differences notwithstanding, favored some degree of escalation. It is important to stress that there was a continuity in the many steps after summer 1964, some of them quite obscure, leading to the maximum U.S. war effort. No one decision or discussion was a critical turning point, just as the events of 1964 have their antecedents in more fundamental strategic and political commitments. On March 1, 1965, for example, McNamara discussed aid to the RVN—whether it should be in the form of goods or of U.S. forces—and informed his service secretaries, "I want it clearly understood that there is an unlimited appropriation available for the financing of aid to Vietnam," a "blank check," as the Army's chief financial manager later described it, "which military leaders normally expected to receive when preparing for a war."[4] In early April and again in mid-June, troop authorizations increased, and between the end of March and the end of June the actual number of American military personnel in Vietnam doubled to 60,000, with over 10,000 more authorized to go.

By April 1965 both McNamara and the JCS were committed to major escalations of both ground and air war. W. W. Rostow at the end of May argued that total victory was now possible—indeed, that it was nearer than anyone could imagine. McNamara thought 200,000 or so men would be the maximum needed to reverse the tide of the war before reducing U.S. forces. By June, Taylor's earlier reticence melted before the desire of the JCS and McNamara to assign 175,000 men to the war immediately, a commitment later climbing to forty-four American battalions. It could keep the NLF from winning, they claimed, and shift the balance of power by the end of the year. McNamara and Westmoreland argued that with yet more troops in 1966 and 1967 the United States could take the initiative—the higher the number of troops, the sooner success. The President prudently decided to pause at thirty-four battalions and 175,000 men for the time being, shrewdly refusing the Pentagon's request to take the politically unpopular step of calling up the Reserves. Nonetheless, convinced that the NLF was winning, the President became increasingly eager to send a massive U.S. force to turn the tide of the war, allowing him to return to his domestic program without being accused of having caused the nation's failure overseas and of having undermined its credibility. By the end of the year, there were 184,000 American military personnel in South Vietnam, and the logic of the vast escalation of American involvement in the war between the summer of 1964 and one year later had yet to reach its climax.[5]

THE EMERGING DILEMMAS OF POLICY-MAKING

To comprehend the freedom and constraints on Washington's policy choices, one must also compare the events and decisions of the 1964–67 period with those after 1968. Until 1968 the war consisted for America of responding to a series of challenges, above all to the imminent victory of the NLF, and the administration had few institutional or ideological inhibitions on it. After Tet 1968 the very economic and political health of the United States was involved, starkly revealing the ultimate institutional parameters of the system as it approached its economic and social limits. During the three years of escalation, the weaknesses of American foreign policy emerged, proving that however unifying the broad consensus among deci- sion makers on goals and general methods, specific realities eventually could —with growing failure—produce important differences on concrete tactics and unavoidable choices of priorities which acknowledged the limits of power. In this confrontation with a materially far weaker Revolutionary movement, directed by men with a relatively high degree of unity and analytic realism to guide their actions, the importance of the leadership equation on both adversaries in the war began to mount. The degree of combined cohesion and clarity on each side of the war was a possibly decisive factor, if only because the structural limit of the American system was also translated eventually into a prolonged crisis of leadership in which a materially great but increasingly confused and disunited United States found itself outmaneuvered by the physically much poorer Communists.

Precisely because conventional wisdom on the war has stressed the im- portance of differences among decision makers, it is worth focusing on the nature of leadership in foreign policy, the consensual values shaping it, and the context in which to place normal differences within American foreign policy circles. Whatever the convoluted way command decisions were made after 1946, or the personal chemistry of each set of men of power, in the end the consistency of responses far outweighed any rare deviations from it, and Vietnam was no exception.

The foreign policy consensus does not make the actual process of im- plementation immune to lesser, normal human considerations, especially as the policy to achieve the ends begins to fail and as some leaders gradually question the very viability of the goals. The human element exists in every time and place thoughout history, of course, and only the importance of an event leads to the dissection of its components. If personalities, egos, and individual factors were the dominant building blocks of crucial historical decisions, there would hardly be more than chaos to cope with, and social processes, forms, and patterns would be buried under a mass of idiosyncratic behavior. Vietnam's place in postwar American foreign policy can be traced very clearly and explained as part of a coherent strategy as well as a continuous dilemma. It is one that we still live with today in Latin America and elsewhere.

President Johnson's often bizarre personal conduct is not unimportant, but the case that his boorish manners were crucial to policy has yet to be made. A shrewd politician who could see the weaknesses of his sycophantic advisers very clearly, a consummate, instinctive fixer, he self-confidently played off people and problems to attain his elusive goals. His commitment to his domestic program was no more his obsession than it had been for other Presidents; the tension between foreign and domestic priorities has repeatedly broken up reform efforts. Whatever the technical differences among key presidential advisers, as a group during 1965–66 they minimized the extent to which earlier dilemmas of the limits of American power and weapons were reappearing. When they acknowledged them, it was only to reinforce the need to redeem prior failures in a new context, with new resources. Few attempted to predict the losses that might arise from the intervention in Vietnam, and they responded to such economic and political costs quite differently until 1968, when external forces and raw facts constrained their choices immeasurably. In this relatively narrow interregnum of 1965–67, the foreign policy consensus did not eliminate real tactical differences. But far more important than the essentially minor eddy of colorful anecdotes and rumor of the sort that makes good journalistic copy, let alone the personal frustrations of those like McNamara who were to lose confidence in themselves or be outmaneuvered by rivals, was the central reality of another massive failure of an essentially consensual system. The drama of this failure, ultimately, was institutional rather than individual, infringing on the very rationality of American imperialism, its postwar foreign policy, its perceptions of the world, itself, and the disparity between its desires and interests on the one hand and the limits of its power on the other.

A consensus on the role and goals of U.S. power and on the nature of the world is a precondition for being a part of the decision-making process, and when the specific policy dimensions of this worldview prove dysfunctional to the larger interests of the system, there will usually be a crisis of policy, priorities, and personnel. This consensus has never kept people and organizations from differing on means, for various arbitrary reasons ranging from bureaucratic interests to personal ambition, but the very nature of the selection process of such individuals prevents radical departures from the scale of options conventional wisdom imposes. Once the pursuit of purely personal interest threatens the overall needs of American capitalism internally and externally in some visible fashion, the political players are replaced by others—as occurred at several crucial times after Tet 1968.

Ambition not only serves to create organizational disputes or rivalries at the level of lesser matters of decisions and their implementation; it also is the way of socializing aspiring political players to the overall norms and premises of the system. For in order to rise, the ambitious must also conform, and accepting the system's premises is a precondition of survival for bright and able men, regardless of their innermost personal doubts about the wisdom of policies. This socialization process begins at an early age, and unconventional types simply do not rise within the system. Tested from university days for a decade or two thereafter, the "best and brightest" are ultimately team players. Their political premises are inherited, and their internal differences are no greater than those one finds in business. Options offered must be relevant to the defined goals and needs of the system, and these are not decided capriciously. But apart from the fact of the interlocked and interchangeable power structure of corporations, finance, big law, universities, and politics, which creates a closed and very finite circuit of ideas, people, and socialized norms and behavior, the real world of U.S. foreign policy decision making allows scope for personal differences and ambition within the framework of a consensus. Certainly, Lyndon Johnson's own aspirations for his domestic program and reelection profoundly affected the form, though not the content, of Vietnam policy until the policy itself had failed. Because of his stress on European priorities, George Ball argued against Vietnam plans within the administration, but at the same time unequivocally defended its policies in public—ostensibly to maintain his own influence.

Just as it does grievous violence to an understanding of the war to make too much of the idiosyncrasies of the men who decided on it, so it also obfuscates issues to attribute the failure of a program to its implementation, and even more to ignore the reasons for a course by focusing on the details of its administration.

By early 1965, as Washington leaders weighed the imminent defeat of their Saigon dependency, they responded to their dilemma essentially as they had to earlier challenges. They chose massive force in this case but preserved the basic principle of the need to intervene wherever the responsibilities of America's self-appointed, unlimited destiny took it. But if Vietnam was originally consistent with the basic methods and goals of postwar American foreign policy, that it was the right war, at the right time, in the wrong place scarcely made it an accident, a quagmire, or any of the other shibboleths that have been brought out to explain it.

America's problem emerged because of collective ignorance both of the forces it was confronting and of itself, two forms of blindness which produced consensually supported actions. The immense hubris of academics with clever, facile answers was the effect, not the cause, of the American dilemma—for they were scarcely alone in promising "quick fixes" to accumulated problems. For in various ways the limits of its power had already been revealed in other contexts, those of Korea and Cuba among others, and it was precisely to compensate for past failures that success in Vietnam became all the more important.

Given every encouragement, officially sponsored analysts poured out a Niagara of studies and recommendations along with weapons and organizational strategies to accompany them. "Reality" for such people consisted of the prejudged world as they collectively defined it; action academics, researchers, and experts reinforced each other's perceptions of it. Here self-confidence was an occupational badge, the basis of personal advancement, and an anodyne for those who listened. Immune to critical analyses out of choice, and ignoring those few skeptical studies it inadvertently sponsored, official Washington's assessments of the military, social, and global aspects of the war left it reliant on sheer physical power—arms, money, and men —with very little comprehension of the larger meaning of Vietnam to the future of American power and interests. Making decisions was all the more difficult for the United States because plausible ignorance buttressed increasingly dysfunctional goals, making inherited conventional wisdom look feasible. Yet their hegemonic objectives were inevitable and identical to those motivating every postwar administration. And it was the persistent failure of American efforts which made decision making so difficult and the choices all the more perplexing.

THE EROSION OF CONSENSUS

The foreign policy consensus between Washington, key power constituencies, and the public which existed after 1950 was crucial to America's pursuit of a protracted war, and it is here rather than in the tortuous debates within the executive and the military that the United States was to quickly fall into a defensive position while fighting an aggressive war. Although the dilemma was largely one which the Revolution's staying power created, it was also to some degree one of the White House's making. In the end, the internal conflicts and style in the Johnson administration proved far less decisive than its growing clash with a crucial portion of the public by 1968, a development which set the stage for the later shift of Congress to the opposition.

The Tonkin Gulf Resolution reinforced the administration's inherited disdain for the public's sagacity and encouraged its natural impulse to continue to manipulate public and congressional opinion while escalating the war. It could mask its preconceived strategy as a response to provocations, or feign surprise and innocence while embarking on new military efforts, only if its more optimistic military assumptions succeeded. If they failed, the magnitude of the conscious deception required to sustain opinion behind the war would have to increase with each new military effort to compensate for past shortcomings. Since each failure in escalation produced surprises for the administration, it soon found itself locked into a cycle of deceit as it desperately sought to redeem its policies, a style which profoundly affected their form rather than their content. The "credibility gap" between its actions and statements soon guaranteed that deliberate lack of candor would provoke a crucial challenge.

The White House knew that a war fever would derail the Great Society economic program and politically permit the Republicans to exploit jingoism. With increasing difficulty, Johnson's public relations experts contrived to keep the war out of sight. Occasional administration efforts to issue supporting documents for its policy, such as the August 1965 "White Paper," failed because, in the later words of one of its authors, "[i]t was impossible to provide sufficient documentary evidence" for its case.[6] Worse yet, an initially small but crucial and growing sector of the public recognized the guile and began to erode the national consensus on foreign policy.

A minor Washington press officer early in June revealed the use of Marines in combat roles after March 1965 only because their losses could no longer be concealed. Press revelations over subsequent years compelled the administration publicly to admit the truth often long after it was common knowledge. Even in November 1967 the administration's Senior Advisory Group, the so-called Wise Men from corporate law, finance, and industry with long experience in Washington, endorsed the dominant executive view, as one of them recalled, that the "major problem . . . was how to educate American opinion."[7]

More remarkable than its conscious desire to manipulate the public, was the degree to which the administration deluded itself with its confidence in its own ability to exploit militarily the time and patience it was wheedling from the public to reverse the losing tide of the war. Its faith in the surgical use of firepower and its own programs, at a cost of manpower and money consistent with its other domestic and foreign priorities, meant that the administration was deceiving itself gravely about the war's very viability. This self-confidence, along with his keen political sense, caused the President to resist mobilization of Reserve military manpower or the economy before 1968, for he believed that time was on his side. This ironic confusion at the highest level produced a major failure in the American war effort.

The administration's policies and its "credibility gap" eventually profoundly affected the American political universe in ways that will continue to influence its international role for decades. Growing domestic economic and political constraints on foreign policy began to evolve dramatically after 1964, and by 1968 mass opinion was spontaneously moving away from the imperialist consensus in complex but fundamental ways. The trends begun in 1964–67 eventually shattered the post-1950 foreign policy unanimity and reestablished Congress's role in the determination of foreign policy, a role which had traditionally inhibited and destabilized the smooth application of executive authority during the half-century after 1900.

This transformation proceeded in several parallel ways, as unorganized growing public hostility toward the war emerging after 1964 on immediate war-related questions, but also as an increasing conscious alienation of people toward the government in general. While their alternatives to the impasse differed greatly, endorsement of the war declined. By the end of 1967, more Americans opposed the decision to send troops to Vietnam than supported it, a trend that continued until the U.S. troop withdrawal in January 1973, at which time they opposed the war by two to one. Rather consistently, the older population was most strongly against the war, the highest support coming from those aged twenty to twenty-nine. The correlation between class and education was also close, those with the least education being the most critical of the war. The older blue-collar workers were most hostile, and they were the audience the organized antiwar movement ignored. It was the blue-collar class and lower-income groups which from 1964 to 1970 exhibited the greatest alienation from the political system, including their feelings about its main economic and foreign policy decisions. At first the elite which had both knowledge and interest in foreign policy issues supported the war, and included, naturally, those who were benefiting from it with contracts, ideological solace, or the like. The three-quarters of the nation that Washington politicians considered uninformed or marginally concerned about the war did not have strategic leverage against the articulate elite minority, and in a crucial sense they never developed it—save in spontaneous forms if they were inducted into the military. But ordinary Americans whose sons were drafted or killed, or who were impatient with the extended chaos the war began imposing or with war-related inflation, in due course began developing an inchoate, prepolitical hostility toward the system largely along class lines.[8]

The war proved that profound disunity in American society would accompany protracted war, and by 1968 neither the White House nor Congress could afford to ignore this fact. The administration's indifference to the public's growing skepticism and its concealment of unpalatable facts did not endear it to anyone, and this set the framework for its confrontation with a historically unprecedented, critical antiwar elite that emerged to far exceed in size, and certainly in activism, the articulate minority that supported the war. By definition, those opposed to a policy have to work harder and become more visible to be effective. Since organized foreign policy constituencies have always been a minority in American society, the real debate over the war took place between elites. The largely youthful, educated antiwar constituency failed to link up with the blue-collar masses increasingly sharing its position, save partly through the leadership of the black community and, later, a small portion of antiwar GIs of working-class origins, and thereby deprived itself of a mass base. But given the nature of the organized antiwar movement this, too, was inevitable. Not only did relatively affluent activists have much more time to agitate and no understanding of the working class, but the masses had no tradition of organized protest in the form of congenial unions or parties through which to express themselves.

If the administration could not anticipate the loss of popular support for the war between 1964 and 1968, still less could it imagine that an articulate, visible, antiwar movement, concentrated in elite universities, would emerge to confront it. The significance of the antiwar movement's role is more difficult to assess than that of the alienated majority, which was an important influence on Congress but whose lack of cohesion and explicit political ideas and alternatives largely condemned it to passivity. That the antiwar minority did not seriously organize a broader constituency was the result of its own immaturity and the history of the American Left. But, suffice it to say, the antiwar movement still had a profound impact.

In 1964 radical political culture and groups were virtually nonexistent in the United States, having disappeared after 1949, and the small religious pacifist organizations were largely unable to communicate with nonbelievers. The tiny residues of such movements—if only in the form of their children—consisted of a small minority of the intelligentsia, mainly students at better universities, who were attracted to both the anti–nuclear bomb and civil rights causes. The absence of any umbrella organization for radical action, let alone a reasonably serious, cohesive party, left the antiwar movement open to an apparent cacophony of ideas, groups, and individuals. While a party is a channel for the averting of chaos, its absence means that every style of opposition can express itself. The antiwar movement accurately reflected the organizational, political, and intellectual disorder of American society at mid-century by creating a politicized form of inchoate but nonetheless real opposition. That the mass media could play a role by selecting people out of this mélange and forging leadership images for them, often moving unstable, unprepared, or simply ambitious people to the fore, was less the cause of the antiwar movement's dilemmas than a reflection of its original underlying weakness. Without ideas symbiotic with real forces and analyses, with a still immature and mercurial constituency of privileged and potentially mobile young people, the politically radical antiwar elements soon turned inward with their own illusions and underdevelopment to exhaust their role as a force in the antiwar movement.

By the late 1960s the antiwar movement's very pluralism was, ironically, an asset as well as a liability. No unified force could have emerged from the instantaneous mass momentum which it incarnated; even if a real comprehensive, organized effort had been possible, it might have made serious errors, because it would more than likely have at that point been seduced by, rather than have rejected, the illusions of American political life. Since the vast majority of antiwar activists would still have been unprepared for a movement capable of functioning as a cohesive party with a common program and plan of action, the sheer diversity of groups and modes of activity absorbed many more than might otherwise have been possible. The consequent outpouring, including its highly visible proportion of egoist politics, existential intellectual posturing, and sectarianism among religious bodies, bourgeois leftists, or simply people with growing anxieties, nonetheless created a large critical mass which produced one decisive effect: social disorder. No one of the antiwar efforts was important, but combined they became very significant. Active students and academics could immediately hobble the institutional role of the university in the war system, temporarily affecting the recruitment and training of essential ROTC officers as well university-based military research. The movement also mobilized information, developing a core of expertise which in due course proved increasingly important with Congress and, to a lesser extent, the media. Above all, however, its sheer visibility and activism, which in every way, shape, and form bordered on pandemonium, disturbed elements of the conservative elite from which many of the antiwar youth were drawn and which preferred stability at home to victory in Vietnam. At a minimum, it fixed to the war an unprecedented social price for the status quo after a sustained postwar era of apathy.

In the long run, the antiwar constituency barred a return to the pre-1964 era of social passivity and naïveté, spilling over into all areas of American foreign policy opposition and creating a much larger base of committed and relatively experienced activists. In effect, the antiwar movement became a prepolitical force transforming attitudes and laying the foundation for a critical and cumulative political consciousness that in the 1960s was only in its earliest stage of development. While most activists dropped out during the evolution of the movement, the emergence of many people who took the personal risks intrinsic to serious radical politics was a new phenomenon in the post-1945 American political experience and rare enough before it. The political environment the war produced also created an imperative for a philosophy of action, imposing choices between collaboration and resistance to the war for many which evoked responses ranging from the holding of candles at vigils to sabotage. Without clear options, this amorphous, unprecedented movement existed because of the growing alienation of a significant sector of the public from the political goals of American imperialism and because of its unwillingness to accept the claims of successive administrations.

Chapter 14

The Continuing Search for Effective Military Strategies

THE UNITED STATES AND THE DILEMMAS OF WARFARE

The Vietnam War was the most challenging military experience in U.S. history, a synthesis of politics, technology, the residues of past wars, convoluted logic, and symbolism—all merged with enormous firepower and a surrealistic mixture of illusion and clarity on the part of American leaders. It cannot be simplified in terms of strategy and tactics, goals, or conventional categories of explanation. At the start, the United States fought the war for three years without hope or without serious concern for the constraints and consequences of its various military programs and strategies. There are many lessons to be gained from the military outcome of the war, but the ability of a determined, able revolutionary force to defeat immensely richer Americans was the lesson most crucial to the future of the modern historical experience.

In dissecting the evolution of American military goals and strategy in Vietnam, one must separate the generals from each other as well as from the civilians above them who defined the war's aims. The generals did their job as they knew how, each parochially thinking in terms of success in his own small domain for the one year most of them spent there. They largely evaded the complexities embedded in Washington's motives and policies as they applied the incredibly destructive tools of their trade. As a group they were optimists and naive technocrats. Later many of them were to claim they could have won the war if permitted to do so, but nothing in the vast efforts they undertook indicates that this might have happened or that serious inhibitions put on them applied in South Vietnam, where the war was lost. But to caricature the military simply as mindless technocrats, careerists, or incompetents tripping over each other is to bypass the formulation of overall objectives for which they were not responsible. It also ignores the capacity of the Revolution persistently to best the United States both on the battlefields and in the larger arena of political struggle everywhere in Vietnam. In the end, the U.S. military strategy combined many elements: the tragic, the absurd, the dangerous—all mixed into a formula for disaster for America and the relentless, unconscionable attack on the bodies and minds of virtually the entire people of Vietnam.

The United States always fought the Vietnam War on the strategic defensive, for its military mission was to attain essentially nonmilitary ends which frequently became obscure in the minds of most politicians and generals. The war was waged to gain time for the RVN to become a viable political and military entity, to convince the Communists that they could not win, and, above all, to show the United States' determination and credibility in defense of its global ambitions. But the administration believed that a clear-cut military victory was elusive during 1965–67, and the Joint Chiefs of Staff generally shared this view. The Revolution could retain the strategic initiative, freely shifting its tactics as necessary, because its political goal was victory, and its military efforts were tailored to help the attainment of its political ends by whatever means were necessary. For the United States this admixture of war and politics produced constant dilemmas, and as it increasingly focused on the problems of arms, it lost sight of political objectives.

One can comprehend the military events of 1965–67 only in this political context of deep American pessimism, for in isolation the debates over enclaves, search-and-destroy missions, air war, and attrition lack relevance. The American troop escalations of early 1965 and attacks against the DRV were to stave off the RVN's collapse and win time for it to assume the burden of what was seen as a protracted war, a factor that wove in and out of U.S. thinking until it culminated in the doctrine of "Vietnamization" under Nixon. In this sense, to "win," as John McNaughton put it, was "demonstrating to the VC that they cannot win."[1] The bombing of the DRV would force it to stop aiding the NLF, those who advocated it initially believed, causing the only sustained U.S. offensive action to take on a symbolic life of its own long after official studies informed all important decision makers that it was not affecting significantly the flow of aid south. For political reasons, therefore, the air war against the DRV soon became irreversible— serving the immediate function of preserving a degree of U.S. credibility and also playing the potential role, Washington believed, of a blue chip in eventual negotiations.

The United States never thought that there was a serious prospect for negotiations during this period. For the same reason, it deemed its intervention essential since the RVN was too weak to survive any form of political coalition or rivalry with the NLF. Subjected to endless official and private efforts to end the war through diplomacy, the United States regarded them as a matter of public relations, and "many of Washington's plans for a 'political solution' involved," according to Chester L. Cooper, then a senior official, "for all practical purposes, a negotiated surrender by the North Vietnamese."[2] Both sides, in any case, believed that serious talks would come only after a period of warfare to determine the balance of forces.

As the years of experience weighed on hawks like McNamara and the JCS, they acknowledged privately what they refused to admit publicly: quick military success was increasingly unlikely, and this fact justified a greater emphasis on other strategies. For McNamara, by October 1966, this meant improving the RVN politically and militarily, a conclusion the Joint Chiefs shared in part because the NLF's tactical shifts required a "long-term, sustained military effort."[3] A "long and costly" war was the CIA's prediction at the turn of 1967. By then even the most congenital optimists conceded that America's military goals were more elusive than ever.[4] "By themselves," Robert Komer, the head of pacification, argued in February 1967, "none of our Vietnam programs offer high confidence of a successful outcome." Added together, all of these individually insufficient efforts were "grinding the enemy down by sheer weight and mass." Westmoreland in March 1967 sanctioned this emphasis on multiple efforts on many fronts to gain time for the RVN to grow stronger: "Military success alone will not achieve the US objectives in Vietnam."[5] To some extent a military, bureaucratic machine was in motion, and barring a serious military, political, or economic rout, it was likely to persist. The United States had many ways to enter a war but no way to get out—short of a defeat in symbolic terms that it was unwilling to accept.

America embarked on its imprecise military mission to fight a war quite unprecedented in history. The sheer bulk of its equipment acquired an impetus of its own: it had to be used and protected, and its relationship to a coherent strategy often became secondary. The very cacophony of arms and military bureaucracies produced a momentum that demanded a very costly eclecticism in American military strategy. And since the strategic initiative on the battlefield always rested with the Revolution, the American military to some extent always had to respond to its challenges.

Whatever the public and private debates over the creation of enclaves, the undertaking of mobile warfare, or the attrition of the enemy, the United States in reality pursued all of these approaches simultaneously. There were at the outset certain preconditions constraining any of these strategies.

Given the inability of the United States ever to obtain the ten men Washington thought desirable to fight every one guerilla, it had to employ firepower and mobility as a substitute for manpower. The vast amount of equipment and logistics necessary for such a war meant there would always be large enclaves to pin down American forces. By mid-1967 American military personnel in Southeast Asia exceeded half a million, equivalent to 1 percent of its civilian male labor force, while the DRV forces in the south were less than 2 percent of their male labor force. The administration knew from such data that the Revolution could easily match its troop increases or neutralize its successes.

After 1965, American officials debated whether to concentrate on creating coastal enclaves or on sending men out on "search-and-destroy" missions to sweep enemy base areas, nominally deciding on the latter. But by mid-1966 base defense absorbed nearly a third of the new American arrivals and their allied South Korean forces, and fewer than half of the U.S. troops were ever available for offensive operations. As more equipment was brought in, the demands of base defenses increased, and the Air Force considered the withdrawal of any defending soldiers as a calculated risk exposing them to great danger from sappers and the ever-more efficient NLF rockets and mortars. But Westmoreland soon obtained forces for "attriting" his foes, culminating for three months in early 1967 in the largest single offensive of the war, "Junction City." The 35,000 American and ARVN soldiers involved along the Cambodia border northwest of Saigon, one official account later concluded, "had little to show for their effort."[6] In one critical sense, the main function of troops patrolling throughout the country was to locate targets for the massive firepower poised in enclaves. "You don't fight this fellow rifle to rifle," one Army general observed. "You locate him and back away. Blow the hell out of him and then police up."[7] The primary goal of attrition was to destroy the enemy's manpower and equipment at least as fast as he could replace them and to build U.S. and, above all, ARVN strength at the same time. Whatever the theory, in reality the U.S. strategy employed passive and aggressive tactics simultaneously, combining mobility and firepower.

At the beginning, Westmoreland thought the holding of static positions would allow the PLAF to attack at will elsewhere, but by mid-1966, as DRV regular forces began to enter the south in greater numbers, the U.S. Marines were becoming pinned down in the I Corps, responding to the PAVN's effort to draw Americans to the remote north so that the NLF could focus on the populous areas. Quite aware of the risks, the United States increasingly bit the bait where it was thrown out, in the hope that the casualties it could inflict on enemy forces would compensate for the American loss of the strategic initiative and give the ARVN time to consolidate its hold over the populated regions. Westmoreland and the Joint Chiefs defended the efficacy of such attrition publicly because they had to justify the previous years of escalation as well as their request for more troops and money, yet by early 1967 everyone important in Washington knew from CIA and Pentagon reports that the strategy was failing. Indeed, the Americans won large numbers of battles, and the PLAF and the PAVN lost enormous numbers of men, but the Revolution throughout this period dominated the overall military situation.

The combined U.S.-ARVN manpower superiority over the Revolution's forces grew consistently after 1965, reaching by 1967 a ratio of 4.7 to 1. In the same year, though, they so pinned down the United States and its allies in static positions that the Revolution surpassed them in numbers of combat troops available for offensive operations. However the United States defined its strategy, the Revolution's much smaller forces retained the tactical as well as strategic initiative. By mid-1967 nearly four-fifths of the contacts between U.S. and Revolutionary forces were at a time or a place of the Communists' choosing, a pattern that persisted for the remainder of the war. This meant that the Revolution could also always control its losses at a level it thought it could absorb, and until the end of 1968 it defined U.S. and RVN casualties levels. From the inception the U.S. war of attrition failed because firepower and mobility were not decisive in military, much less political, terms.

ONE WAR—THREE AMERICAN SERVICES

To some extent the very nature of the American military establishment made the war extremely expensive and wasteful and its politically unattainable goals even more elusive. For rather than performing as a totally integrated, efficient organization, the three branches of the U.S. military spent a great amount of time and money in tawdry disputes with each other over jurisdictions and power.

The American command structure in Vietnam was astonishingly complex. There were the growing rivalries between the Army, Air Force, Navy, and Marines, because of overlapping air technologies and a historic struggle for a larger share of the military budget. Exploiting this division, the White House preferred the status quo to a strong war commander presiding over a unified military, not simply to avoid arbitrating bitter service disputes but also to preclude a possible political challenge from one general—as had occurred during the Korean War. The command chain ran, as I explained earlier, from the White House to the Joint Chiefs of Staff, to the CINCPAC in Hawaii, and then to multiple commands in and around Indochina.

The biggest source of intramilitary wrangling was the Marines, who saw Vietnam as a chance to save their antiquated amphibious functions, boost their reputation among congressmen, and even obtain money to add another division to their forces. The Marines agreed to fight as a unit in the I Corps, but they had their own logistics system and tactical aviation, which they used as a costly substitute for heavy artillery. They refused to relinquish any control over it until early 1968, when after extremely time-consuming and emotional wrangles, they made some moderate concessions. In effect, two separate tactical air forces operated in one theater, at great cost and with much confusion. Simultaneously, the Army and the Air Force were at loggerheads over the Army's fixed-wing aircraft (over five thousand in 1960) and its helicopters. The Air Force wanted control of both throughout the world. In April 1966 the services resolved the often bitter dispute, the Army keeping its helicopters but abandoning its future claims to new types of fixed-wing aircraft. The entire Air Force based in South Vietnam was under MACV control, but over the DRV both the Navy and the Air Force fought for autonomy. Eventually the DRV was divided into exclusive target areas for each service, the Navy operating directly under the Pacific Fleet and the Air Force under the Pacific Air Force. B-52s over the DRV were controlled by the Strategic Air Command until the last weeks of 1972. In Laos the Air Force, the CIA, and the embassy were all entangled and often at serious odds.[8]

With this array of fiefdoms the various service bureaucracies remained happy, and the White House had little to worry about from ambitious generals. Indeed, the prestige of any commander over a truly unified effort might easily have weakened Washington's constraints regarding adventurous military operations—particularly those risking conflict with China. In the end, McNamara's effort to overcome service interests on behalf of a more disinterested set of priorities failed. Divided, the three services offered the administration no coherent strategic alternative, largely because none existed. In addition, no service would relinquish its conflicting claims on the issue of how arms produce victory in the modern era. The most important effect of this confusion, from the U.S. viewpoint, is that it made the war even more expensive at a time when costs could have a crucial influence on the war's duration and intensity.

THE REVOLUTION'S MILITARY DOCTRINE

The Party's leaders painstakingly analyzed all of the dilemmas emerging from the United States' military experiences after 1964, their strengths as well as weaknesses, and then exploited them. The Americans, too, spent an immense amount of time studying the Revolution's military strategy, and by 1967 the two sides had attained a truly impressive comprehension of each other. But whereas the Revolution's senior leaders systematically examined their own strategic doctrine and tactics as well as those of the enemy, American efforts were undertaken by lower-level officers and sponsored specialists who tended by sheer dint of effort to find differences among Revolutionary leaders who basically shared a large consensus on the nature of military struggle. Key Party strategists, therefore, understood both their enemy and themselves thoroughly while American leaders never grasped the central military factors in a comparable manner.

The Revolution's need to reassess its military doctrines in light of the massive influx of U.S. men and equipment came at a point when it was on the strategic offensive and on the verge of victory. By mid-1965 its basic military position was firmly set, and only its tactics were to alter over the next decade. Predictably, at its core this line remained political. The combining of armed and political struggle was not merely a cliché, for it required a subtle understanding of the political consequences of the Revolution's military action on the masses, the socioeconomic effects of American-style warfare on the Vietnamese people and culture, as well as the world context in which the United States fought the war. If the sheer analytic challenge of such a definition of the war's total context appears enormous, it was nonetheless linked with the effort to develop such a global Marxist perspective, focused on the overall balance of forces, that the Party determined highest military policy. For the Revolution was led by intellectuals with two decades of thought, experience, and success behind them.

Its past triumphs notwithstanding, the Revolution found the vast American armada arriving in the south a monumental challenge. In the broadest sense, 1965–67 was a learning and testing period for both sides, each assessing the other's tactics and capabilities in specific situations—and, for the Revolution, adjusting accordingly. There were serious debates within the Party over strategy and tactics, but they were marked by pragmatism and considerable shifting of positions by many key generals and were nuanced rather than doctrinal in form. Whatever the differences, which were sharpest in 1965–66 over the use of the battalion and larger-size operations which had nearly produced victory in 1965 but which were now vulnerable targets for the U.S. forces, it was not long before a typical, eclectic consensus emerged. The Party's leaders always agreed that the U.S. military was strategically passive and incapable, for geopolitical and domestic reasons, of fighting a protracted war. Given the PLAF's mastery of the tactics, location, and scale of the war, they were convinced that they could retain control of the overall strategic initiative. Crucial to their doing so were creative tactics which preserved the element of surprise while optimizing the Party's resources and political objectives.

The definition of the terms of battle, flexibility, and deep respect for U.S. firepower became integral aspects of Communist strategy. In 1966 the PAVN/PLAF ranks grew by 60,000 to compensate for the 400,000 new Americans who had arrived since mid-1965. After much discussion it sharply reduced its large-unit operations, switching instead to small-size attacks and harassment spread quite evenly throughout the country. From 1965 through 1972 over 95 percent of its assaults were conducted by units smaller than a 300-to-600-man battalion, forces which stressed high mobility and surprise, thereby depriving U.S. and ARVN firepower of prime targets. From the beginning the U.S. war of attrition failed, and in January 1967 the CIA concluded that the Communists could sustain their main forces at the size they desired and keep them adequately supplied. The Party believed that the United States was unable to adopt a definite strategy, much less an attainable set of war aims, and it is not surprising that all of its discussions of the American military were suffused with a consummate confidence in eventual victory. It regarded the air war against the DRV as confirmation of American strategic confusion and passivity, contemptuously noting the folly of the United States' embarking on a course of isolating itself throughout the world while illogically attacking the north to compensate for its failures in the south.[9] "In some respects," the PAVN/PLAF commander, General Nguyen Chi Thanh, observed in a secret speech in mid-1966, "the war is more arduous and fierce than we expected; in other respects, it is easier to win than we had contemplated."[10]

To a critical extent the Revolution's key to maintaining the strategic initiative was its ability to keep U.S. and ARVN forces dispersed through the vast country, a factor that was to prove crucial until 1975. Ironically, it publicized its intentions repeatedly, even printing them in English, and many U.S. analysts understood that the Communist strategy was to seek in this way to wear out American forces. But the simple measures the Revolution took were like bait to those few in Saigon and Washington who controlled the firepower, making America's leading generals appear to be amateurs. The Party carefully synchronized the three branches of its army. The main forces largely remained along the borders from the seventeenth parallel through the Central Highlands and south to Cambodia, close to supplies and refuge, and baited the United States to fight them in their own, carefully prepared terrain—a challenge Westmoreland quickly accepted. Meanwhile, in the populated coastal provinces and in the Mekong Delta, the regional militia and guerillas operated among the people, far better equipped to mass their forces, attack, and disperse when they chose to do so. The United States, by contrast, preoccupied with servicing its needs, protecting its bases and cities, and patrolling in largely empty zones, lost its capacity to be militarily decisive anywhere, even with masses of its own men and helicopters. For this reason the Revolution's troops available for combat about equalled the combined U.S./ARVN combat force from 1967 to 1972, although their total army was generally less than a quarter of the enemy's. Sacrificing its mobility, the Americans and ARVN remained permanently wedded to a defensive, costly strategy. By 1967, soldiers from the DRV outnumbered those from the south in Communist main-force units, but the key to their role and the future of both military strategy and political struggle was the local guerillas, who immobilized the growing ARVN forces seeking to hold the populated regions and "pacify" them and who were far better able to engage in the critical political tasks.

Its relative success in implementing this strategy justified the Party's belief that, if necessary, the Revolution could drag out the war and exhaust the Americans, and that time was on its side. Meanwhile, the NLF initially expected the effects of the long war to further radicalize the population. That it might also lead to demographic and physical changes capable of socially transforming the nation, and the Revolution's political universe thereby, was not yet a serious Party concern. The Party's major argument against the extension of the war was its impact on the DRV's economic development. For this reason, among others, the Party always regarded protracted war as a strategy of last resort, to be averted if possible. It understood full well that the longer the war lasted, the greater the war's dependence on DRV main forces.

The most critical military goal for the Revolution, after the containment of the U.S. forces, was to attack the ARVN, the only threat once the Americans departed—as inevitably they would. Even as the Americans were pouring into the south in March 1966, Le Duan stressed that though they had to fight the foreigners, "the most important thing" was that they "must continue to basically annihilate the puppet army" in order to expose the fragility of Washington's political objectives.[11] At the end of 1967 this was still the Party's main target.

The imperative need to spread a far larger enemy force thinly over a vast terrain required maximum creativity and intelligence. Without it, the people's war—and its main forces—would fail. The Revolution demonstrated an astonishing surge of ingenuity in coping both with weapons and with new organizational challenges. It was primarily the capacity of the Party's leaders to adopt organizational and political forms able to harness the devotion and resources of the masses in all corners of the nation that was to produce victory.

Local efforts against the United States and the ARVN were ultimately linked to the NLF's political and social program, but once this is said, it is still crucial to comprehend the major steps it had to take to stymie and then defeat a vastly better equipped enemy. The basic principle of the people's war was to inspire as much originality and responsibility as possible among the guerillas and local forces. During the first two years of the American troop influx, the Party's directives and journals called on the local NLF to invent and create in every manner possible, and they responded in countless ways. Coping with awesome realities, they would find methods to deal with enemy weapons and tactics, and methods developed in one place would be sent to central authorities who would then filter the information back to other local branches. When confronted by immense challenges, people managed, under pressure of necessity, to find solutions beyond anything they might have once imagined possible. This exhilarating creative interaction was in certain ways the Party's greatest triumph after 1964, yet one it did not mystify into revolutionary élan divorced from its politics.

Almost every conceivable technique was employed. The night virtually became the NLF's property, since it deprived the enemy of freedom to use most of his firepower. The exploitation of the rainy season was another method. The alteration and improvisation of tunnels and mines became a fine art. Fighting at very close quarters was a further means of depriving the enemy of firepower. High mobility and ambushes, and avoidance of routines which the enemy could anticipate, were other ways. The role of women increased greatly, especially in towns and strong enemy areas. Inventiveness helped retain the initiative against stronger forces, as did timely retreats to avoid losses—and withdrawal became a standard procedure, particularly for main forces.

Both the geography and the nature of the enemy's armies demanded a high degree of decentralization and important modifications in the Party's organization. The classic tension between Bolshevik discipline and local initiative and autonomy was quickly resolved in favor of an acceptance of unavoidable realities. Any other approach would have been virtually suicidal, especially since the Party thought that cadres had to be close to the masses at any cost. In this way the best of all worlds emerged: quick, effective local initiative and adaptions, but the maintenance of the Party's general authority and hegemony over the long run. The Party's antibureaucratic ideology made this much simpler, yet it had no other option, and by gracefully accepting this fact, it not only avoided a repetition of the 1956–59 period of strained relations with the southern Party but its overall southern strategy succeeded at the crucial grass-roots level.

The four Revolutionary zones in South Vietnam began with a very comprehensive organizational system linked with Hanoi to ensure discipline and coordination, but it soon began eroding under the pressure of U.S. attacks. Although it survived in various forms for the main forces, the crucial local and regional operations were often cut off for long periods. By August 1966 from 60 to 70 percent of the Party's southern members were acting independently of their cells. While the need for members to be able to function alone was always a tenet of Party doctrine, it posed serious risks in terms of coordinated action and morale. When the hierarchial system failed to work, local commanders were authorized to make decisions as they were needed—and later to answer for them. By late 1966, Party organizations in the south were operating flexibly on a largely autonomous basis, guided by broad COSVN policies which they applied as best they could.

In order to protect the senior Party structure, this decentralization of power to various localities was imperative, the outcome of decisions and circumstances alike. Security for high-level cadres was extremely time-consuming, and many stayed in remote areas. The COSVN itself was spread out over a vast terrain—it required four days on foot to travel from one end to the other—and this was true of other major regional centers as well. Security's price was a loss of communication, and at enormous personal risk many lower-level and relatively inexperienced cadres soon assumed many of the responsibilities of senior officials. Autonomy at the intervillage level was therefore high by 1967, and it grew thereafter, making the Party structure increasingly vulnerable to destruction at the critical lower levels. While this gap between the lower and higher Party organizations solved many real immediate political and military problems, it also became a growing threat to the Revolution—one that was partially realized after 1968.[12]

THE REVOLUTION'S SYMBIOSIS WITH ITS ENEMIES

The sheer size of the Revolution's military and political structure in the south required maximum local ingenuity logistically, and the fighting capacity of all the main forces would have been far weaker had local cadres and the NLF organization not mastered basic economic problems. Although figures on the size of all of the Communist forces were hotly contested in American official circles throughout the war, by 1967 there were from 221,000 to 281,000 full-time PAVN/PLAF members in South Vietnam, about a third of whom were guerillas. In addition, about 120,000 irregular forces existed, and there were 75,000 to 90,000 political cadres. The Revolution's order of battle remained in this range until 1972.

Feeding and equipping this force was a major, crucial task, which could be carried out only because of the Party's effort after 1955 to penetrate the RVN, create legal fronts, and symbiotically obtain all the economic and military aid that it could from the system it was seeking to overthrow. The structure it had put together between 1955 and 1964 was quickly expanded to counteract the American bombing of the routes from the DRV. Its tax gathering was perfected, and it fell most heavily on businessmen. Main-force units routinely grew food where possible. Guerillas staying in villages were required to help peasants with their crops, and often lived with them. They captured arms and munitions. But trade with RVN-controlled regions became increasingly important. The NLF tried to prevent the movement of rice and buffaloes out of its territory, and it unsuccessfully restricted certain imports into its zones. Whatever its limits, the economic symbiosis of the NLF with merchants, and even with the families of key ARVN officers, eager to do business, worked very well.

In 1967, in addition to its local purchases, the United States imported an average of 21,000 tons of general supplies and munitions daily for its own needs. The daily PLAF/PAVN consumption of all supplies in 1967 was estimated by the CIA to be about 215 tons, rising to 250 tons in 1968. Food was the main item. In 1968 only 24 percent of its food was imported, mostly from Cambodia. Indeed, only 30 percent of its weapons and nonfood supplies were imported in 1968, and it even supplied 16 percent of its munitions from sources in the south. Its imports in 1968 were 80 tons daily, a mere third of its wants in terms of weight. All together, the Pentagon estimated, the Revolution obtained in South Vietnam about 70 percent of the supplies its armies needed, a figure that was probably too low.

The Revolution also utilized its symbiotic relationship with the RVN for intelligence. Apart from a large number of opportunists or dual agents, which the CIA in 1970 put at about thirty thousand in the ARVN and RVN agencies, were genuine agents, which the leading CIA expert on the topic thought to be about three thousand persons, a figure reasonably close to reality. From them the NLF obtained extremely valuable warning of many ARVN and U.S. operations—including the catastrophic ARVN invasion of Laos in February 1971. And it was also able to reach accommodations with the ARVN in a number of areas—arrangements of convenience, but also occasionally due to NLF agents or collaborators in key places. Its symbiosis with the RVN in every domain became a critical means of protracting the war and maintaining the initiative.[13]

Chapter 15

The Dilemma of the American Way of War

THE STRATEGY OF TECHNOLOGY AND FIREPOWER

The crisis in American strategic doctrine after Korea was crucial to the nature, form, and outcome of the Vietnam War. Motivated by a desire to surmount the dilemmas of limited war which obsessed its strategy debates after 1953, Washington turned Vietnam into a testing ground for its doctrines and weapons. But the premises of U.S. action reflected a global context, and its major weapons systems were designed primarily for use in urbanized, technologically advanced nations and only incidentally in Third World interventions. As its experiences in Vietnam strained its available resources, America's strategic frustration intensified, goading it further into irrevocable commitments to sustain not merely its credibility in terms of its will to act but its very material capacity to succeed anywhere in the world once it plunged into a struggle. Vietnam almost immediately exposed the technological foundation of U.S. power in the world, including its profound limits, verifying its weaknesses not simply politically or morally but militarily as well. Instead of solving its postwar crisis of strategic doctrine, Vietnam only deepened it.

U.S. military strategy after 1945 was inflexibly wedded to high technology and unable to respond to the specifics of local war. Washington reacted militarily in Vietnam essentially in the way it would have reacted to any conventional war in the world. Whether it would prove sufficient hinged not only on the outcome of battles but also on cumulative political, economic, and moral factors. The Revolution's decisive strength in this context rested on its ability to counter U.S. military efforts and protract the struggle in order to allow all the forces at play to bear upon the war. Weapons, and the doctrines based on them, therefore had to be not only efficient but rapid as well, for time unleashed economic and political constraints capable of turning the most technologically advanced military machine into an immensely inefficient and irrational burden. Technology's real costs can be seen only in this total framework.

A useful measure of this growing reliance on high technology and massive firepower was the quantity of munitions for each man-year of exposure to combat. Between the Second World War and the Korean War, the tons of munitions per man increased eight times, but during the Vietnam War it was twenty-six times greater than in 1941–45. This trend can also be defined in other ways. Throughout World War Two, the United States used a total of seven million tons of munitions; during 1964–72, nearly fifteen million tons. During that period the Air Force and Navy became more important; the proportion of combat manpower in the Army dropped from 36 percent to 22 percent. Tactical aircraft alone by the end of the Vietnam War absorbed nearly a quarter of the total military budget, not to mention strategic air power and artillery. In Vietnam the combat soldier was primarily a bait for the technological colossus behind him. "It was our policy," General William W. Momyer, the head of the Air Force in Vietnam during the peak of the war, later wrote, "that after contact with the enemy was established, our ground forces would pull back a sufficient distance to allow artillery and airpower to be used without restraint. Then the Army would follow up these attacks. . . ."[1] Air power alone, then, absorbed almost a third of the war's cost. "The unparalleled, lavish use of firepower as a substitute for manpower is an outstanding characteristic of U.S. military tactics in the Vietnam war," another Air Force analyst stated.[2] By 1964 it was the only kind of war the Pentagon was capable of fighting, and that situation has remained to this day.

On trial in Vietnam was the military basis of U.S. hegemony and the efficacy of its vast trove of technology. The realization that these were the stakes mobilized the military solidly behind the war and the reliance on firepower long after even its own evidence proved it would fail. For as long as it could find a receptive audience, the Joint Chiefs of Staff argued that at some point the sheer quantity of firepower would be transformed into quality and reverse the tide, making tactics a strategy. While even the military originally saw air power against the DRV as leverage in persuading the north to abandon the NLF or to negotiate, or even to sustain the RVN's morale, they used it in the south as a weapon which they believed could reverse the military situation on the ground. Even when political pressure required various administrations to suspend bombing over portions of the DRV, the planes merely shifted to bombing Laos, and the quantity of air power engaged in the overall Indochina theater was never reduced. Laos and the DRV received half the total sorties.

Air power delivered half the munitions the United States used in the war, and B-52 strategic bombers were added to tactical aircraft in June 1965, when it became clear that they could not saturate many areas quickly enough to keep the NLF from dispersing. Indeed, tactical aviation immediately proved "relatively ineffective," to cite Westmoreland, against well-dug-in forces.[3] The B-52s, on the other hand, dropped their crushing, twenty-seven-ton loads from thirty thousand feet, in half the cases on targets where the NLF was later found not to have been. In brief, they were very inaccurate terror weapons, destroying many civilians and their property.

According to excessively conservative official Pentagon figures, the United States lost 3,689 fixed-wing aircraft by the end of 1972, plus 4,857 helicopters—valued at over $10 billion. But the cost of its standard tactical planes was now five to seven times the average during the Korean War. Much more sophisticated equipment was performing the foot soldiers' role, but not effectively enough to warrant the immense difference in costs. The sheer quantity of bombs reflected their inaccuracy. The cost of the air war was enormous in terms of destruction of lives of civilians and combatants alike. While it could affect the relatively few larger battles of the war, it could not basically influence the strategic balance, and its costs began immediately to erode the U.S. economic capacity to fight a protracted war. Later it also provoked massive political opposition.

The air war against the DRV was a failure from the inception, and 80 percent of the casualties there were civilians. Even if the United States had used more air power against the north, it could only have been at the expense of the air war in the south—or at a far higher price than the U.S. economy could afford to pay. In fact, the ultimate constraint on air power was the NLF's logistical autonomy, which in addition to providing the bulk of its own needs could adjust its combat and activities to the resources available without losing the strategic initiative. While the Revolution in the south benefited greatly from the aid from the DRV, in the final analysis by 1965 it did not wholly depend on it.

Nor could the United States manage to stop the logistical flow coming down the Ho Chi Minh Trail. The trail was an astonishing product of human ingenuity, persistence, and ceaseless sacrifice. Everything from hand labor and buffalo to bulldozers kept it open against bombs, mines, and every conceivable device. The PAVN's ability to speedily repair the road outstripped the Air Force's capacity to attack it effectively; the repairs were aided, ironically, by the intensive bombing's creation of immense amounts of gravel. By 1966 the antiaircraft system along its Laos portion was so effective that it had destroyed a quarter of the highly vulnerable U.S. gunships, the best weapon against trucks, and their use over Laos was suspended from mid-1966 to early 1969, and partially again after 1971. Traffic over the trail rose two-thirds in 1967 over 1966, but the number of trucks destroyed remained the same. America's experts never doubted the DRV's capacity to move as much tonnage as it needed. Although the PAVN lost, consumed, or stored two-thirds of the supplies it sent into southern Laos, Soviet-bloc and Chinese aid to the DRV was twenty times the amount it attempted to send down the trail.[4]

Over the most developed part of the DRV, a very modern and skillfully operated air defense system also inhibited U.S. escalation. A dense radar net, SAM missiles combined with antiaircraft guns, and fighters created ever-greater problems for the invaders. Feinting attacks to compel the U.S. planes to jettison their bombs, the DRV air force did not aggressively confront the much more advanced and costly intruders until it was adequately trained. Despite heavier DRV losses earlier, by the summer of 1972 the United States was losing two F-4s for every three MIGs it shot down.

Air war against the DRV could not have succeeded militarily even if the United States had had the aircraft and logistics to use it unsparingly early in the war. But it did not, and after authorizing numerous studies, the highest circles were virtually unanimous in thinking almost from the inception that air war against the north could not significantly alter the southern military balance. Maxwell Taylor, who saw bombing simply as a means of inflicting pain and establishing credibility, regarded air war alone as a chimera. The CIA in February 1965 warned that the DRV would create a sophisticated antiaircraft system, and for the next four years it documented the point that air power was never decisive. As for the diversion of DRV manpower to repair roads and damage, estimated to be absorbing 500,000 to 800,000 people in 1968, Pentagon experts at the end of 1967 concluded that nine-tenths of this number would come from normal population growth. Aid to the DRV from its allies outweighed the damage the United States had inflicted, a Pentagon report argued, and bombing had unified and motivated the people as never before. As for the losses of planes over the north, in June 1971 the Pentagon's research director admitted, "it is very clear that we lost far more to their antiaircraft and surface-to-air missiles than those systems cost them."[5]

In the south the Communists partially neutralized air power by sappers, by careful use of tunnels and the night, and by compelling the enemy to devote a significant number of aircraft to base defenses. This was especially true after February 1967, when the NLF used the extended-range 140-mm rocket for the first time against the Danang base, destroying and damaging eleven planes, revealing its capacity to target any base in the south. By the summer of 1967, at the latest, the NLF possessed a fairly effective warning system for impending B-52 attacks, probably by tapping U.S. communications and possibly also with Soviet aid.

Of all the new weapons systems and innovations the United States sought to apply in Vietnam, the helicopter proved to be the most important, and to a critical extent the military became dependent on it. Westmoreland claimed that without it a million more men would have been required to accomplish the same tasks, which was primarily to transport infantry into remote places to locate the NLF in order to unleash American firepower.

The helicopter was developed in response to the Korean War experience, and after that conflict the industry kept pushing new designs on the Pentagon, which showed no great interest in the airmobility concept. It was McNamara who enthusiastically regarded the helicopter as the single most important key to counterinsurgency, embodying mobile men and firepower in a way he found irresistible. Despite initial advice to the contrary and some Army reticence, by mid-1968 there were 3,500 helicopters in South Vietnam —substantially fewer than the number that the Communists eventually destroyed by the time the United States withdrew its forces.

As American critics of the choppers predicted, they were extremely vulnerable to ambush; and though they provided mobility, they also revealed troop numbers and location. Like tactical aircraft, they eliminated the element of surprise. With exposed gas tanks and pilots, the early UH-1s could carry only eight to ten combat soldiers, and therefore the Army required them in ever-growing numbers. While their losses were very high, their routine cost was even more of a burden. Each hour in the air required ten hours of maintenance, and the choppers' fuel consumption was enormous. By the late 1960s the Army had slashed its future commitments to helicopters to a fifth of its peak Vietnam War purchases and publicly acknowledged the grave faults of its technology and its tactical premises.

Artillery was a more conventional weapon than the helicopter, and it consumed half the munitions tonnage. Almost from the start of the war, the United States used vast artillery firepower for every conceivable situation, and except for the period of the 1968 Tet offensive, the Pentagon estimated that about 70 percent of all American artillery rounds were fired "in situations of light or inactive combat intensity."[6] Yet artillery was very destructive. The costs of "harassing and interdiction" random firing where U.S. officers thought there might be enemy forces were enormous in terms of civilian casualties and American expenses, and militarily, as a deputy comander of the U.S. Army in Vietnam admitted later, it did "practically no damage to the enemy."[7] The rules of engaging possible NLF forces were so flexible that each commander could judge what was to be done, invariably opting for high firepower.

Artillery was never of decisive military value. It, too, gave warning of impending ground attack, eliminating surprise. Tunnel defenses against it were highly developed, and unexploded shells provided abundant supplies for booby traps, the building of which all NLF forces quickly mastered. Revolutionary forces responded to artillery, ultimately, by targeting U.S. permanent and field bases, and after 1967 they greatly expanded and improved their sapper units. The insatiable Pentagon data machine found that by early 1969 there were an average of five sapper attacks a month on U.S. bases, each causing at least $1 million damage. Most important, fear of sappers forced the Americans to reallocate a vast amount of time and resources to base defenses.

Ironically, the U.S. attempt to go on the strategic offensive with firepower demanded an increasingly defensive, passive posture as the effort's necessary logistics and manpower immobilized ever-larger portions of its forces in static positions. The Revolution perceived this dilemma and adapted in sufficient time to each weapon. Along with using simple, low-cost means of dispersion and defenses, the seasons, night, and a tremendous innovative imagination, the Revolution had an access to small quantities of advanced weapons and air defense systems that cost the United States much of its freedom to employ the firepower it possessed. Virtually all major U.S. weapons concepts quickly became partially neutralized. Late in 1966 a Pentagon journalist close to the military could conclude that the huge array of new American gadgets and weapons was not adequate: "U.S. brain power has been baffled by the wily and resourceful Viet Cong who is fighting his war on the cheap."[8] The Americans were now committed to a destructive war in which victory was elusive, but whose costs were potentially unlimited in terms of money, national priorities, and manpower.

TECHNOLOGY AND DATA: REALITY, ILLUSIONS, AND COSTS

Between 1965 and 1967 the United States was drawn into a highly complex dilemma, one ultimately involving the nature and future of its military and political power in the world. The trap was of its own making: the inexorable logic of credibility and symbolic acts, on the one hand, concrete ambitions and interest in the Pacific, on the other, as well as the tortured, mechanistic, and increasingly futile search for an effective military means by which to assert American might throughout the globe. There was a cynical, dangerous irony in its aggression in Vietnam from the inception. With certain reservations and lapses, the men who guided U.S. policy never believed they could win an outright military victory. Yet they fought the war as if they did, inflicting incredible destruction and death on the Vietnamese people, their land, and their culture.

The administration's objective on the battlefield was to gain time for the RVN to grow strong enough to partition the country, or perhaps use the war to gain leverage in negotiations. Yet the highest level was thoroughly informed with facts which would have shattered even these hopes for such limited goals. The problem, ultimately, was their endemic inability before 1968 to accept accurate information as a basis for policy. The reasons for this are of fundamental importance to understanding the nature of the postwar dilemmas of American imperialism. But the core problem then, as before and after, was that despite a great deal of analytically and factually correct information, there were no decisive rational restraints from within the social order on American power and its vain ambitions.

The Vietnam War involved a tremendous intelligence effort, the analysis of which required a much higher order of perception than was needed in any previous conflict because this was a war without traditional fronts. Admittedly, the sheer volume and diversity of information was indigestibly enormous, and a certain portion of it was inaccurate either for reasons of policy, personal interest, or simple ignorance. As many as thirteen intelligence organizations duplicated efforts and competed with each other in parts of Vietnam, and captured documents in less than one year during 1966–67 amounted to over three million pages, a tenth of which, or a thousand pages daily, were translated or summarized. By early 1967 the Army alone in Vietnam was producing fourteen hundred pounds of reports daily. And though the sheer mass of information buried the effort to exploit timely data on NLF activities in a mass of dross, making most of it useless for purposes of combat, the information available to key officials in Washington, for all of its limits, was certainly accurate enough to allow them to base policy decisions on facts—if they were able to do so.

The CIA's reports were often highly informative. Most key decision makers read them, at least in part. The Rand Corporation studies of the war were generally highly pessimistic about the United States' prospects for victory, even though their influence was quite limited. Perhaps the most interesting overall assessment was the *Southeast Asia Analysis Report,* which the Pentagon's Systems Analysis Office issued about every six weeks beginning in January 1967. Some 350 classified copies went to key officials in every war-involved agency. Attempting statistically to quantify and assess military, political, and economic trends, it soon became a source of dour pessimism, and the JCS several times tried to prevent its circulation. Whenever elements within the administration challenged basic military assumptions of the war, whether the efficacy of search-and-destroy missions, the bombing of the DRV, or even the reliability of statistics, the Systems Analysis Office was, in the words of the Pentagon Papers, the "vanguard of the reaction."[9]

So many studies and numbers could be found that soon all lacked credibility because ardent hawks, of whom Walt W. Rostow was the best known, possessed those figures necessary to reinforce their preconceived conclusions. While bad or useless data were far more numerous than the good, advisers at the highest levels saw much more of the accurate information than its share of the total output. The core of the problem was that truth never influenced policy sufficiently to change it, and the major obstacle was that rationality was buried by inherited geopolitical frustrations and conventional class wisdom. To do less than pursue futile goals with unsuccessful military means would have been to acknowledge that U.S. power to police the world was now smaller than at any time in the postwar era—and in 1967, facts notwithstanding, Washington was unable to admit it.

When facts cannot shape action, then sooner or later the chief decision makers will be compelled to respond, however intense their devotion to conventional wisdom, consensus, and their own careers. For most, this confrontation was imposed by the 1968 Tet offensive. McGeorge Bundy quietly resigned in March 1966, and McNamara left, or was pushed out, in November 1967—the two men who did most to involve the United States in Vietnam for futile ideological and technocratic reasons. Those who remained saw more and more that the United States was not succeeding, but no one of importance resigned in public protest against policies that were consummately dangerous to the world and, increasingly, to America. Their future careers could not have survived such assertions. Above all, the enigmatic, symbolic nature of the Vietnam War as the culmination of the compulsive, irreversible global crisis of U.S. military and geopolitical power was one which they all understood and with which they truly sympathized. And that dilemma was the primary origin of their universal inability to accept and to act on realities.

Meanwhile, the generals who led the war in Vietnam produced their own data for their own purposes. The war's "credibility gap" grew as Saigon-based press officers insisted that a war that was being lost was increasingly successful. In order to tell the whole truth publicly the military would have had not only to comprehend the war's subtle, complex nature but also to preempt policy, and the generals merely followed their orders. Meanwhile, most generals remained in South Vietnam just one year; each had his career to tend to, and careerism produced what a later Army study called "statistics for promotion and decorations."[10] Numbers became vital for ambitious officers, and if the data were inaccurate or irrelevant to an overall assessment of the war, it was ultimately not their problem. Bodies counted, structures destroyed, and shells exploded became a dehumanized rationale as higher officers pressured those beneath them to produce results impressive in Washington. In the end this vast orgy of violence was the product not of ambitious officers and their numbed, harried subordinates but of the capital-intensive premises of U.S. reliance on firepower. Officers fought the only war possible, and the Vietnamese people paid a monumental price not because of individual caprices but because the United States' entire military system performed exactly as it was intended to do. The results, of course, were false data almost routinely, with "VC" combat deaths often being reported at twenty-five to seventy for each American. The daily announcements of body counts personified the extent to which sanctioned slaughter would go, but as most knew then, and openly admitted later, this emphasis on inflated numbers bore no relationship to who was winning the war. The Pentagon's Systems Analysis experts routinely discounted such figures. Meanwhile, they simply horrified ever-larger sectors of American and world opinion.

"The Vietnam conflict is testing . . . almost all of the tactical (and some of the strategic) military equipment and concepts developed in the last 20 years of R.&D.," the Pentagon's director of research told Congress in March 1967.[11] The military employed exotic, futuristic technology at immense costs, ranging from people sniffers linked to computers to the ultrasophisticated F-III aircraft costing over $15 million each. Since 1946 the United States has increasingly prepared for wars employing complex technology geared to delivering high firepower; this surreal dimension in Vietnam assured costs and complexities in addition to those the Revolutionary forces in villages and forests would present to them. America's high technology and firepower was a promise, but it could also prove a trap, a source of useless frivolities and dangerous illusions about wars against peasants in modern times.

THE COSTS OF PROTRACTED WAR

The Vietnam War became a nightmare for the supremely self-assured managers of the Pentagon who were now locked into a situation in which victory was impossible and defeat increasingly likely. The precocious program and budget experts who accompanied McNamara to the Pentagon with their maze of presumably neutral techniques for quantifying choices were soon mired in the irrational contradictions of imperialism as a system with its own logic and imperatives. In this collapse of the pretensions of science before politics and ideology, McNamara himself was to prove the greatest sinner of all.

McNamara's March 1, 1965, decision to unlock unlimited funds for the war in Vietnam came before the Pentagon had established any logistical structure to spend the blank check rationally. Available firepower was constrained over the next two years less for political reasons than by the physical resources available. The buildup that was to occur was unprecedented in the history of American warfare, and the Pentagon ordered everything it needed on a crash basis. As a later official review of the experience put it, "The zeal and energy and money that went into the effort to equip and supply U.S. forces in Vietnam generated mountainous new procurements, choked supply pipelines, overburdened transportation systems, and for a time caused complete loss of control at depots in Vietnam."[12]

The Pentagon ordered boats to deliver goods even though ports were still under construction (eight were created where before there had been only one), liberally sprinkled bases and airfields throughout the country, built vast storage installations, and created an immense transport and communications system as part of a $4 billion program. Goods piled up, documents and the cargo to go with them were lost and more ordered to replace them, items deteriorated or were pilfered. Thirty-nine different-size paper cups and 337 varieties of screwdrivers were ordered, and davenports and liquor glasses were assigned the same priority as bombs and shells, and in one place twelve thousand tons of toilet paper was lost in the books. The Army required two to three years to untangle this logistical maze. But the decision to proceed in this fashion was deliberate and based on the awareness that acting efficiently would take longer. This dilemma was insoluble for the United States, time appearing more precious than money. The result was what the official wartime review of logistics described as "great cost and great waste."[13]

Part of the rationale for this vast extravaganza was the need to make firepower quickly available. The celebrated luxuries of air conditioners, steaks, miniature golf courses, and PXs stocked with Chanel No. 5 and everything imaginable were there for morale; they were also related to an unsuccessful effort to keep Americans away from towns, where their money and lifestyles were beginning to profoundly distort the economy and social system. What was purposeful in the over eighteen million tons of dry cargo shipped into South Vietnam during 1965–69 was the desire to have unlimited firepower and to use it.

Having fixed the means and ends, the United States had to calculate the costs, and McNamara's blank check soon became far too expensive. The war had cost $5.8 billion in fiscal 1966, but in 1967 the Pentagon had planned on 5.5 tons of logistics per man-year in Vietnam, and the Army reported that logistics and combat doctrine required 9.0 tons. McNamara then fixed the limits at 7.8 tons per man-year, and the blank check was withdrawn, but not before the war's costs had shot up to $20.1 billion in fiscal 1967 and the defense and entire federal budget plunged into a wholly unexpected deficit, requiring the administration to go back and ask Congress for a $12.3 billion supplemental for 1967. This error was of far-reaching importance, making the war enormously complex at home as well as in Vietnam.[14]

Capital-intensive limited war was much more costly, difficult, and less efficient in Vietnam than anyone in the American Establishment could predict. This weakness was to weigh heavily against its success. Protracted war was the least expensive for the Vietnamese and the most arduous for the Americans. But to fight a poor man's war over a long period would have been to reject the very logic and premises of U.S. strategic doctrine since World War Two, and it was impossible to imagine Americans remaining at low cost in the tropical Vietnamese countryside without their amenities. Time for the Revolution was a necessity, and patience its great asset. For the Americans time became not just a growing forfeiture of money but also an increasingly formidable loss of political and psychological control of themselves. Their own methods and goals had now created a trap from which they had to extricate themselves. By late 1967 this, too, was clear to the leaders in Hanoi.

Chapter 16

War and the Transformation of South Vietnamese Society

The war's economic and social impact on South Vietnam between 1965 and 1970 was decisive to its eventual military conclusion. The accumulated effects of war produce their own internal dilemmas and contradictions as well as unintended consequences which may prove far more consequential to a war's outcome than anyone's conscious desires, thereby fixing the boundaries of historical possibilities. The U.S. intervention in Vietnam produced such ironies from the inception, but by the late 1960s their impact was decisive and irreversible.

These economic and social trends appeared less than critical to American leaders, and measured in the form of numbers—the only index available to men whose values preclude empathy—they were quite elusive. Even today, information on South Vietnam's demography, the class structure, or the economy is poor and masks unconscionably the enormous human drama and suffering of fully one-half of a nation. It offends the sense of real human experiences to attempt to reduce such events to aggregate, measurable proportions, but to fathom their meaning and importance is to understand, as fully as frail human capacities allow, controlling factors in war and history, the forces which decide the outcome of the more easily described, much more closely studied world of battles or of decision making.

The nature of South Vietnamese society was not incidental to the U.S. effort, but a critical factor, by itself sufficient to determine whether Washington's fate would be victory or defeat. It explains not only the sources of the Revolution's initial efforts in the south but also the subsequent directions imposed upon it, the nature of its triumph, and the peace that followed. The strength, fragility, and evolution of the U.S. dependent determined the very viability of its undertaking and the extent of the obligation the Americans assumed in their naive optimism.

THE DEMOGRAPHY OF WAR

Firepower shaped the demography of South Vietnam after 1964, reducing the issue for a substantial portion of the peasantry to one of physical survival. At the core of the vast panorama of events emerging from this protracted conflict were men and women whose commitments and lives were ceaselessly affected by innumerable challenges and travails. Their responses ranged across the whole spectrum of possible individual reactions, from heroism and conscious efforts to resolve their problem through collective action against foreign invaders to an elemental decision to survive physically as a person by whatever means necessary. To comprehend that process of constant choice for most of the adults is quite impossible, because the destruction, grief, and physical anguish around them, the extremes of human bravery and human degradation, defy description.

The United States in Vietnam unleashed the greatest flood of firepower against a nation known to history. The human suffering was monumental. The figures on all aspects of this enormous trauma are inadequate, and between 1968 and 1970 the refugee reporting system alone underwent three major revisions. The Pentagon's final estimate of killed and wounded civilians in South Vietnam between 1965 and 1972 ran from 700,000 to 1,225,000, while Senate numbers for the same period were 1,350,000. Deaths in these two assessments ranged from 195,000 to 415,000; "enemy" killed were 850,000 minimum, and a substantial part of these were civilians. The Revolution's figures are much higher. In a nation of about 18 million people in 1970, the war exacted an immensely high toll in killed and wounded.

Munitions was the primary cause of casualties, and the vast bulk of it was employed by the United States and the ARVN, which accounted for nearly all the artillery and 100 percent of that delivered by air. In 1969, internal U.S. discussions admitted, "the information available . . . on the overall scale and incidence of damage to civilians by air and artillery . . . is less than adequate."[1] They did know, however, that in the single month of January 1969 over four million people, nearly a quarter of the population, had one or more air strikes within three kilometers of their hamlet. The U.S. and RVN pacification programs sought to empty the NLF-dominated regions of their population, not merely by firepower but also by defoliation, forced removals into strategic hamlets, and other means of separating the peasants from their land. While the reasons for this vast population displacement were both political and military, American officials also considered it "desirable" in making available the huge labor pool they required for their own bases and logistics.[2] And once displaced, the peasants had to be kept, the Americans believed, from returning home. For all these reasons, Komer said in April 1967, the United States should "[s]tep up refugee programs deliberately aimed at depriving the VC of a recruiting base."[3]

In essence, a substantial part of the peasantry was consciously forced off the land against its will, permanently transforming the nature of South Vietnamese society. The most conservative estimates are that at least half of the peasants were pushed into refugee camps or urban settings one or more times, many repeatedly. The statistics are, again, far from precise, not least because the United States was hardly inclined to expend the effort to document accurately the brutal consequences of its policies. Senate figures for 1964–72 give only 5.8 million persons as refugees, but additional data show that provinces under the NLF, primarily north of Saigon, and in the Mekong as well, generated the largest proportion of refugees. The correlation between firepower and population displacement is very close. RVN numbers on refugees or war victims during 1965–72 are substantially higher than U.S. figures, about 7 million people, or about one-third of the population or well over half the peasantry. Once in refugee camps, the peasants saw their standard of living drop by about two-thirds, and their psychic loss was incalculable. The result was the urbanization of a rural society in a manner unique in this century, for it was far more brutal and disorienting to the population than any that a large Third World nation has ever experienced.

Urban Vietnam before 1960 had been remarkably comfortable, its cities scarcely more than colonial enclaves. The French had controlled them until 1954, of course, but the Chinese also were always vital economically and physically. Even in 1966 one-fifth of South Vietnam's urban population, comprising about a million persons, was Chinese. The virtual Chinese monopoly over important economic activities left little space for newcomers, whose commerce was really marginal subsistence. A portion of them made up the most dynamic, entrepreneurial sector, and were in the best position to amass the benefits of the new foreign presence. Into this turbulent world came millions of peasants after 1964.

In 1960, 20 percent of South Vietnam's population lived in urban areas. The proportion had reached 26 percent by 1964, 36 percent by 1968, and 43 percent by 1971—a growth rate of five times that of all less developed nations during the same decade. Saigon's expansion, though great in the surrounding suburbs, was astonishingly small in the metropolitan area, and far less than that of such provincial towns as Can Tho, Danang, Bien Hoa, Hué, and cities closer to actual combat. Danang and Nha Trang grew fourfold between 1960 and 1971, mainly after 1964, while Can Tho's population tripled. The suburbs surrounding Saigon absorbed most of its inhabitants from the nearby military regions, the vast bulk of whom were escaping the war. Indeed, Saigon's share of South Vietnam's urban population declined by more than half between 1960 and 1971, and greater Saigon's share also declined, by not quite half. Urban life in South Vietnam until 1960 had been virtually synonymous with greater Saigon. By 1971 its share of the urban population had fallen to 43 percent; without its suburbs the city proper was now slightly more than a fifth of the urban population. With this partial exception of Saigon, the south's urban growth was the product of physical necessity, security from combat being the most important reason urban dwellers in 1972 gave for being there—far greater than economic opportunity, which ranked a distant second as a reason. By 1971 three-quarters of the urban residents were not native to their city.[4]

This urban explosion created a much greater bifurcation between rural and urban South Vietnam in terms of social and human life patterns—with a vast number of political, economic, and human implications. Within this urban sector there was a dual culture; the majority were peasants who had moved to the interminably boring, packed refugee camps and who now, perhaps after many efforts to return to the country, were compelled to adjust to the city. Cities, in turn, can be further divided into those that can be said to have been truly urban centers before the massive American intervention and those that were essentially frontier conglomerations the war had created in the dusty lots encircling older provincial towns. Outside this urban frontier, with its total disorder, was old Saigon, the city which the Americans knew best, strangely insulated from the national urban experience as well as from the beleaguered peasantry, a city of privilege, power, and luxury.

THE URBAN FRONTIER

Peasants in their village, all their differences notwithstanding, had a deep linkage to their community and people in it, many of whom accompanied them through their entire life experience. The family, above all, was the basic unit of economic activity, and the patterned, predictable relationship of people to one another was often the basis of collective survival in a precarious world.

The city profoundly challenged the peasant's individual role and family cohesion, especially the connection to a community. The city, with its cacophony of sounds, congestion, and challenges, was a traumatic encounter. Urban in name only, the new city quarters were generally just haphazardly placed shantytowns with little or no sanitation and few, if any, physical services. Surrounded by people, from officious bureaucrats manipulating his existence to other former peasants also competing to survive, the peasant displayed several basic patterns of responses, ranging from extreme human disorientation to some type of functional means of personal survival within the radically modified but still intact family unit.

In its most benign form, the urbanization experience consisted of peasants making a neighborhood their own community. Such communities were usually fragile, temporary, and vulnerable to external pressures. But it was precisely the anonymity and alienation of urban life, the endless distractions of existence, that made the family persist for many peasants as both an economic and a social entity. The family was a traumatized population's last anchor of stability and security.

The immediate problem confronting the newly arrived peasant in the city was to survive economically, a time-consuming necessity which often ruptured contact with his immediate community and family and made an anonymous existence a reality for many—thereby also making anonymous politics possible in a way unimaginable in rural areas. But the first ask was to get food and shelter. There are no plausible data suggesting how this was obtained, only impressions and a few facts for various towns. Atypical Saigon, of course, was comparatively well studied. One-fifth of those arriving immediately became street merchants, living off the sidewalk economy by selling food, shining shoes, peddling, and the like. Temporary or permanent unemployment was the lot of over one-third of those arriving in Saigon. By 1974 the sidewalk economy was the largest single source of nonfarm civilian employment in South Vietnam.

Nationally, construction and services grew dramatically. The Americans employed 160,000 workers directly in 1969, mainly to tend to the needs of their soldiers and build their bases. Prostitution in its various forms involved at least 200,000 women. Membership in the RVNAF and police eventually totaled 1.2 million. The typical family survived as a unit with a combined income, or it soon did very poorly, save for some prostitutes. The children cadged on the street, and the mother peddled on the sidewalk or worked as a maid for U.S. soldiers. The father, assuming he was not in the army, might be fortunate to work as unskilled labor or in transport. More likely, however, he was often unemployed or also living off the street economy. This very marginality and precariousness drove some peasants back to their rural homes, perhaps several times, as they attempted to preserve the unity of the family.

Per capita consumption during 1960–70 increased very slightly. The AID in Saigon acknowledged that the deluge of consumer durables imported into South Vietnam had "given the illusion" that per capita consumption had risen by "staggering" amounts even as it admitted that the standards of living of some had fallen. Had there been no war, it felt, Vietnamese standards of living would have been higher.[5] Only after 1972 did the drastic decline in urban standards of living reopen the possibility of the Party's influencing the urban masses in regard to economic issues. By 1971 urban per capita income had begun to decline sharply, but subsidized U.S. rice imports kept food consumption from falling, and in the early 1970s South Vietnam had the highest per capita caloric consumption in Southeast Asia.

Overall, the per capita gross domestic product between 1965 and 1973 remained constant, which meant that only an increasingly unequal income distribution made high consumption for some possible. U.S. economists in Saigon concluded that those working in the public sector did poorly but that merchants were prospering, while the marginalized recent families could, by pooling incomes, obtain some of the consumer goods beginning to deluge the cities. Ownership of consumer goods bounded upward, largely because of two factors. First, the United States used consumer goods to counteract the inflationary pressures which the American military's enormous presence created. Second, Washington's explicit policy was to make free and cheap radios and TV available so that it could wage extensive psychological warfare. Moreover, as early as 1964, senior American economic planners thought it especially important to satisfy the needs of the urban masses, lest they "constitute fertile ground for VC blandishments" and create a two-front insurgency almost certain to defeat the RVN.[6] South Vietnam was therefore the easiest place in the world to acquire some external attributes of prosperity, and the most difficult place to enjoy them.

The reality behind this facade was quite different. Forced urbanization not only produced a wholly untenable RVN economy but also created a profoundly disturbed human order, fraught with immense political implications. Looked at objectively, the United States in less than a decade did more damage to an entire society than other colonial nations or the urbanization process elsewhere accomplished over generations. No one, the Revolution included, at first fully perceived the magnitude of this cultural assault, which touched the basic question of the nature of politics and individual commitments in a social context of personal and family crisis. By necessity, this experience can affect people in various ways, one of which is egoism, personalism, and *attentisme* or apathy toward politics. The adult peasantry forced into cities became profoundly alienated from a culture and society succumbing to Americans who devoured their sons and daughters, patronized successive juntas, and wreaked havoc on Vietnamese lands and traditions. One split in urban society which emerged was between those who had absorbed the officially sanctioned urban mores and those who remained rural and traditional in either their economic lives or their values. More dangerous, the newly arrived city dwellers were alienated from their children.

Curiously, the studies of U.S. experts in Saigon confirmed the underlying malaise of the urban masses. Theft, housing, garbage, and comparable problems bothered many, and by 1971 the vast majority of urban dwellers thought the RVN's handling of economic problems was poor. In 1969 at least two-thirds of the adult refugees preferred returning home, if possible, to remaining in the city, and only a small minority of those in Saigon in 1972, by far the most prosperous city, believed they were better off than they had been in the countryside.

The former peasantry's greatest loss was their children. The young lacked their parents' political experiences and values; being exceedingly vulnerable to the American presence, many thrived on the sidewalk culture of incessant noise, congestion, and human interaction which throbbed amid the dust of the cities. Many fell victim to all of the possible problems that must arise in such a disintegrative human and social context: crime and corruption, drug addiction, prostitution, promiscuity, and unrelieved egoism. Families became split by age differences, and this not only immobilized parents politically but also made it increasingly difficult for them to return to villages the children scarcely remembered. As a transitional youth culture cut through a class culture, the children of the urban poor to a great extent broke the solidarity of the masses with the Revolution.

These children spent much of their lives in the streets and were poorly educated. Some were orphans, and those who were not were frequently badly neglected. They had few opportunities for regular jobs, and those under twenty composed 60 percent of the southern population in 1972, compared with 38 percent in the United States. The GIs corrupted a significant fraction of the women and hypnotized the men with clothes, motorcycles, and their musical styles. The Revolution simply could not reach this lumpen constituency, and it never claimed to have succeeded in doing so. Such street people increasingly gave the RVN military its manpower base, and by early 1968 a growing majority of the ARVN volunteers and draftees was drawn from them. Their officers were almost entirely of urban origins, which further reinforced the urban character of the RVN's army and strategy.

A critical problem for the NLF was whether the former peasantry's involuntary rupture with its rural origins and the Revolution was irreversible, but the decisive question for the United States and the RVN was whether it would ever leave its cocoon of private concerns to sustain the RVN in some effective fashion. For while the Revolution had other means of struggling, without a measure of support from the urban population the RVN would remain politically unstable and the cities only a fatal economic burden.

The social order that urbanization created was ultimately the functional outcome of many policies, and though the new society was largely incremental and ad hoc in nature, aspects of it were certainly planned. Urbanization was the unavoidable logic of the high-firepower war, and its cultural form was strongly influenced by the over two million GIs who passed through the country. Many in America and Saigon regarded population reconcentration as both an opportunity and a hidden blessing. That Washington did not understand the critical economic and political implications of the war's demography until it was too late was one of its great miscalculations in the war.

Thousands of Americans were involved in "nation building" projects, including social scientists eager to test their wares in practice. These ranged from the surrounding of air bases with civilians they attempted to make happy with subsidies of every kind so that they would not aid the NLF (a policy that failed dismally) to an effort to write a Vietnamese equivalent of the song "God Bless America" to win over the masses. The radio propaganda that incessantly swept the nation had very little impact, even in the opinion of the RVN's experts, and the most powerful tool that both the United States and the RVN had to consolidate their influence among the masses was the dollar—a weapon which worked best among the youth on the streets but proved also to be finite both in quantity and in effectiveness.

The dollar's assault on the culture, whether traditional or Revolutionary, profoundly alienated a significant element of the older urban dwellers, particularly the students and intelligentsia who had the leisure to observe and think about it. Secondary school and university enrollment increased over ten times between 1954 and 1970, when the RVN claimed there were about 680,000 in the two categories. The children of the petite bourgeoisie, merchants, and even civil servants and RVN functionaries, many transcended their class position and related to their own peer culture in much the same way the children of uprooted peasants did.

The intellectuals, too, were as fragile in South Vietnam as they are anywhere, full of moods, variations, and typical equivocations, but many became increasingly sympathetic to the NLF as they observed what the United States was doing to the nation and its culture, though a significant portion always did what those in power demanded. Many among them, particularly teachers, were poorly paid. The students, especially, reacted to the nightmare of human degradation around them, and some preserved their capacity for action, even as many retreated into their privileged private worlds. Among people in these social categories, the NLF certainly increased its influence as a by-product of the American cultural offensive, and a significant portion of this crucial social stratum was always alienated from the RVN and the United States.[7]

The final test was less the alienated urban intelligentsia's relationship to the Revolution than its willingness to make those commitments and sacrifices necessary to maintain the existing order in power, and the effects of urbanization prevented this from occurring. As a physical solution to the problem of cooperation between the Revolution and peasantry, the urbanization of the south appeared sensible to the United States. Despite its immediate advantages, however, it was by the late 1960s increasingly alienating the expanding urban population, leaving a growing political, economic, and psychological void. France's struggle against the Communists had not altered the rural society's structure, character, and values in any basic way. Even during its entire colonial reign, only a small minority of the people had been affected ideologically. But the American style of war was far more damaging to the population's identity and existence. The reconciliation of the economic and political contradictions in its policies was almost immediately beyond Washington's abilities. Ultimately, the cumulative effects of urbanization on the RVN's economic, political, and military system immeasurably aided its total collapse.

Chapter 17

Nguyen Van Thieu and the RVN Power Structure

MILITARY AND CLASS IN THE RVN

The Communist Party's virtual monopoly on the opposition to French and American imperialism reflected the impact of colonialism on the Vietnamese class structure and its evolution. All of its potential challengers were too divided, too sectarian, or too ambitious to fill the void in the political system, and religious differences, especially in the south, gravely weakened the non-Marxist opposition. Chinese domination of the economy meant that the stratum with the most to gain from the status quo was unable directly to relate politically to the rest of the system and was mobile, should need arise, and no other potential class-based leadership existed. This vacuum in power and politics was institutionalized for most of the RVN's brief life in the hands of two men, producing hybrid ruling elites without an autonomous class constituency and dependent ultimately on foreign support. Diem's nearly decade-long rulership at the inception of the RVN's twenty-two-year existence, with his systematic attacks on the fragile French bureaucratic legacy and class-based elites, the Chinese particularly, further narrowed the social basis of rulership, reducing it essentially to his clique and the military —the only large institutional force he could not abolish or decrease in functional power. Put simply, the military was the only non-Communist stratum able to succeed Diem and to aspire to power.

The RVN was very much in the same position as many non-Asian Third World states dependent on foreign aid or created in a vacuum to perform a comprador role for a foreign imperialism, and the military in this context traditionally serves as the political arena and instrument of political succession, even though the sponsoring state—the United States in this case—hopes also to utilize it primarily as a way of transferring the techniques of violence and administration necessary to maintain foreign influence. Should the army's political function become its dominant preoccupation, then its tools of violence will ultimately be crucial only within the military establishment's political process, for arms will become the only real or potential means of political change—making its concern for external threats to the state quite secondary. And where the militarized political structure defines the nature and boundaries of economic development and accumulation to a critical extent, corruption drastically erodes its fighting capacities. In brief, politics neutralizes military capabilities decisively by making all purely military considerations subordinate to the control of political and economic power. The state, the economy, and military and political power all become integrated. The overcoming of this contradiction is the United States' main dilemma every time it creates a dependency on which it in turn becomes dependent to attain its own national objectives.

Such a context makes the social nature and function of the officers a fundamental issue, their class origins and linkages being facts of potentially great significance to their definition of their social and economic role as well as their personal aspirations. This is especially true when the military in underdeveloped nations with a vacuum in institutional power is the dominant mechanism within which rulership is determined. The marginality or stability of a class society at its various levels is critical where a cohesive opposition exists, and it becomes a crucial factor in determining how wars are concluded.

The officers in the RVN's armed forces, some 25,000 by 1967, as well as the tiny elite of senior officers at the rank of major or higher, were homogenous to an astonishing degree. The junior officers, composing 95 percent of the total number of officers, were very young. Since they had to have at least a high school diploma, they were overwhelmingly urbanized and born into families that could afford to educate their children. Soldiers could not rise through the ranks to become officers. A quarter were born in the north, and the percentage of Catholics was double South Vietnam's average, which meant that the military was an important avenue of social mobility for displaced refugees coming from the DRV after 1954. Economically, though, the profession was poorly paid, second lieutenants earning but $55 monthly in 1967 and enjoying few legal perquisites. For the majority who were married and had families, this fact became critical to their real functions. At least one major distinction between officers was their training academy and their year of graduation. Without a definable class or ideological differentiation among the officers, the "school tie" became inordinately important. The National Military Academy at Dalat produced 13 percent of the officers in the military in 1967, but 30 percent of the general-ranking officers graduated from it, while Thu Duc academy graduated two-thirds of the officers and a mere 5 percent of the generals and 30 percent of the field-grade officers. Catholics accounted for a third of the generals.

Of a sample of sixty generals in 1972, one-third were the sons of landowners, another quarter of government officials, and over a quarter of officers and urban professionals and middle- and upper-class elements. They were upwardly mobile; their families were not yet important but at a point where they might aspire to be, and this profoundly affected their use of power. Thieu, for example, was the son of a small landlord, and he graduated from Dalat. A scant majority were graduates of Dalat academy, 14 percent of Thu Duc. Nearly all had begun their careers under the French. The military, given the role of war in the French and the RVN's priorities, was the chief channel of social and economic mobility for an important sector of the marginalized middle classes ready to work for the dominant colonial power.[1]

The motive of the senior officers after Diem's death was simple: power in the form of careers and money. This was just as true of the congeries of civilian miniparties, factions, or religious sects who were always moving in and out of various coalitions or plotting on the sidelines. Where neither coherent class interest nor ideology exists, there is no basis of collective action and responsibility, and personal welfare becomes the motive of politics, resulting in individual corruption as an institutionalized dimension of society.

The Americans always watched this charade with the utmost cynicism. Perhaps the most dangerous aspect of this period was the effort of civilians to link up with military factions and encourage them, which was a guarantee of continuous turmoil and, by mid-1966, of various degrees of warlordism in the four military regions into which the RVN was divided, particularly MR I in the north. Indeed, as the successive military juntas passed through Saigon, mutual suspicions justifiably became axiomatic among those in the perpetual imbroglio the United States was sustaining. As they conspired and as membership in the ruling juntas changed, the system was made ripe for a superior political fixer, and in Nguyen Van Thieu the senior officers met their master.

THE EMERGENCE OF NGUYEN VAN THIEU

Thieu was surely the ablest politician to emerge in the RVN's history, and his conversion from Buddhism to Catholicism to advance his career proved he was supremely flexible. He was a member in the June 1965 junta representing the "Young Turks" with no close past ties to the French and Diem. From there he moved unobtrusively to find ways of maneuvering around potential opponents and, above all, to try to find the price or weakness of any who might resist him. Unlike Diem, he had no serious ideological pretensions, and the initial key to his success was his readiness co-optively to share the spoils. Thieu was much more interested in obtaining stable control over power rather than a monopoly of it, and not until 1973 was he to seek total authority in his own hands.

In the wake of Diem's death, one of the most important factors in his rise to power was the aid he obtained from the Chinese business elite. Thieu's sister-in-law married Ly Luong Than, who was already one of the richest Chinese in Saigon, held a U.S. passport in his traditionally abundant collection, and was a key figure in the Fukienese *bang*. Than brought Thieu together with Francis Koo, first secretary of the Taiwanese embassy in Saigon and a senior figure in SEATO intelligence circles. Koo decided Thieu would serve the embattled Chinese community well and provided him funds and contacts to advance his career. When Nguyen Cao Ky, his main rival, in early 1966 excoriated speculators and had one Chinese publicly executed as a warning to the others, the still nervous Chinese elite gave Thieu massive financial backing and intervened on his behalf with U.S. officials. Thieu was a shrewd operator in his own right, but his access to funds also smoothed his way. He had far more tact and cash to employ than Ky did. The United States' obsessive desire to see military unity was the single most important element in bringing Thieu to power, but his Chinese connection undoubtedly shaped the regime's distribution of economic benefits.[2]

Thieu in 1967 was the sole general with sufficient talent to survive the chaos of Saigon politics and create a powerful political machine. In June 1967 he had the junta nominate him for the new presidency, after he promised to abide by the will of a collective leadership. Even when he was most powerful, Thieu neutralized, co-opted, and pressured many of his military and civilian elite rivals far more gently than Diem did, trying to divide the rewards of office widely to gain time to enjoy the prerogatives of power and, above all, to prevent any threats to his increasingly durable machine from the other senior military commanders. As for the Chinese, one of his first acts in 1967 was to allow them to reestablish their *bangs* and to return their associations' confiscated property.

THIEU CREATES A MACHINE

The moment he came to office, in September 1967, Thieu embarked on building a largely private power machine which integrated the military, the political structure, and the economy in numerous formal and informal ways.

Complex in certain aspects and baldly simple in others, his system assured that the RVN's destiny after 1968 would become synonymous with Thieu's ambitions, his power, and, ultimately, his weaknesses.

In an underdeveloped class structure traumatized by the effects of Diem's own power machine, the demography of the war, a subsidized war economy, and an enormous American presence, Thieu temporarily and partially remolded the elastic class system to suit his interests. He unified ambitious, essentially marginal class elements and the rich Chinese around only one common denominator: money and access to privilege. As a Rand Corporation summation of the views of twenty-seven high RVN officers and officials after the war said, "A central feature of the South Vietnamese regime . . . was corruption."[3] His integrative effort encompassed a variety of approaches, ranging from a vast number of people brought into the RVN's employment to a higher elite which was incorporated into the war economy formally and informally, together sharing the main prerogatives of power. The fluid RVN power structure possessed intersecting economic, political, and military components in varying degrees, according to the people and elements involved, but it was never fully formalized before it collapsed both from its own contradictions and from the pressures the Revolution as well as the United States imposed on it.

The analysis of transitional and dependent social orders is potentially misleading if one attributes excess coherence and form to constantly evolving relationships. The task in Vietnam is made all the more difficult because the senior officers, Chinese capitalists, and civilian Vietnamese politicians were each internally divided, and only from 1969 to 1973 (but not later) did Nguyen Van Thieu sufficiently control power to make the structure susceptible to some generalizations. Thieu used his family as much as possible, of course, but his real strength was his ability to find and reward generals ready to cooperate with him loyally in running both the military and the civil administrations. Such a co-optive strategy was successful so long as there was enough to share. It was the sheer enormity of the American economic impact which defined the parameters of the RVN's class development and the political life intimately linked with it.

Both the Revolution and the U.S. government had a handful of analysts who tried to assess the structure of power within the RVN. Their work, as well as that of former RVN officials who have written postmortems, was remarkably parallel in both methods and conclusion. All assigned special significance to the Chinese capitalists in the running of the RVN system.[4] Yet one cannot attribute causal power to them, because it was the French and later the Americans who ultimately controlled the collaborationist system. Without them, Thieu could not have undertaken so much, so well and

so quickly. But while it is true that the Chinese by the 1960s were a traditional elite and the generals a distinctly new one, the political leverage the
generals possessed made the Chinese highly dependent on their favors. A
huge amount of money could be made in the economy and in the state's
operations, and the Chinese obtained the major share in the former and a
significant proportion of the latter. Opportunities for corruption available
from direct control of state positions were vast, and officers and key bureaucrats dominated them.

Thieu was ultimately the functional master of the whole order during
four years. His access to money was crucial to political cohesion in the
military elite, and it kept most senior civil servants docile until 1973. The
hybrid power structure which emerged was really a very personalized synthesis of Thieu and his coalition of loyal generals as well as a Chinese elite,
and it is futile to try to determine their relative importance since each
without the other was inconceivable. Getting rich was the common consensus which united them, and as Thieu manipulated their avarice, his machine
possessed all of the subjective, arbitrary qualities one associates with the
accumulation of capital by political means and corruption during a war
which was sponsored entirely by a foreign power. Ultimately, the RVN's
existence was improvised in an environment of chicanery, desperation, and
tragedy which made absurdity and audacity common coin, with marginalized gangsters the mainstay of the social order the United States was attempting to keep in place.

THE COMPONENTS OF THIEU'S SYSTEM

A crucial aspect of America's funding for Thieu's system was mass employment and the perquisites that went with it. When Diem was overthrown,
there were 121,000 civilian employees working for the RVN; by 1965 the
number had grown to 179,000, increasing very slowly until 1968 (when Thieu
took full command of the state administrative apparatus). From 208,000
government employees in 1968, the bureaucracy bounded to 337,000 in 1972
(the police composed 38 percent of this number), its share of the labor force
having more than doubled since the early 1960s. The civil service had been
fickle and inept in the stormy sea of post-Diemist politics, and Thieu sought
to make it a reliable instrument of his power. Although their nominal
salaries were low and kept falling, he allocated to them a whole panoply of
corrupt practices to deepen his hold on their loyalties. The most common
were bribes to obtain essential papers, ranging from normal legal transac-

tions or identification documents to draft deferments, plus numerous petty
forms of boodle. Corruption suffused and financially lubricated the state
bureaucratic system at all levels.[5]

The junior officer corps also became a major source of support for Thieu,
for he satisfied their ambitions far more than any of his predecessors did.
The regular military grew rapidly from 1961 to 1965, but the junior officer
appointments failed to keep pace with it. When Thieu took power, he
increased the number of first lieutenants from 8,764 in 1968 to 17,353 two
years later and that of captains from 4,793 to 10,654, at a time when the
regular military grew by less than a fifth. They too, of course, were allocated
a share of condoned corruption as a supplement to their low salaries, and
they often received their appointments because they were beholden to some
senior officer for critical recommendations or, more simply, because they
bought his favor. Their rackets were generally petty, ranging from the
collecting of rice rations and salaries for dead or deserted soldiers to the
funneling of military gasoline and supplies into the local markets, some of
which the NLF purchased. Along with political officials, some participated
in local usury, which during the Thieu period was 50 to 90 percent monthly.
Together they could enforce their claims if necessary.

Higher-level officers were far more important, and their appointments
were treated more seriously, since they alone could challenge Thieu's growing hegemony. Success in combat or purely military competence was increasingly ignored in senior appointments; political tendencies and personal
ambition were far more critical. This made staff rather than combat officers
ever-more preponderant at the upper ranks. Friends and relatives were very
important. All appointments at the level of major or above had to be carefully approved by one of Thieu's closest allies in Saigon. He alone chose
every general officer. There were only 40 generals in 1967, and 82 colonels,
and it was to these men that Thieu turned his attention as he consolidated
power. Shunting some of them off to powerless positions and avoiding any
challenges to powerful generals' corruption, Thieu increased his control over
the military apparatus by enlarging the number of generals to 73 and that
of colonels to 200 in 1972, but the senior officer corps, in various degrees,
remained seriously underbilleted after 1967, as Thieu cautiously filled the
higher positions primarily with political appointees and assigned the lower
officers duties which far exceeded both their rank and their abilities. Such
a bottom-heavy officer corps was designed essentially to prevent a coup
d'état. Those at the top were repaid for their devotion with a significant
share of the state's diverse economic resources, ranging from normal commerce to sanctioned corruption of every variety, from larceny and graft to
import licenses. "We would be left with practically no one to fight the war,"
Thieu's vice-president, Tan Van Huong, admitted, "if all corrupt command-

ers were to be prosecuted and relieved."[6] Thieu's genius was to deflect the ambitions of his select group of senior officers from a desire for real political power and to make them, as two former generals recalled, "motivated by money."[7] By the most cautious estimates, fully two-thirds of all generals and colonels were corrupt.

The RVN's administrative system moved from being in near chaos preceding Thieu's accession to having virtual dictatorial powers by the end of the war, and the military and political organizations overlapped in ways which were informal and rarely clear to outsiders. Precisely because military loyalty was purchased with economic favors, the whole power apparatus intertwined. The most crucial issue for Thieu was to obtain control over the generals he found in place during his ascent to power, his appointments and demotions revealing his immense agility.

During the post-Diem period the commanders of the four military regions began choosing their province chiefs, creating a de facto warlordism, especially in the northern I Corps. Within a year of taking office, after having checkmated Ky's allies, Thieu regained a virtual monopoly over the military and the police and made certain his potential enemies stayed divided. One of the four corps commanders had been his ally and remained in power, but the others were carefully picked men who allowed him to select the forty-three province chiefs and even district chiefs, half of whom he had replaced by spring 1970. The generals commanding the three divisions in the Saigon area were chosen with particular care.

The four corps commanders were charged with military responsibilities, and they reported directly to Thieu, from whom they received personal orders. They could coordinate the military activities of the provincial chiefs in their own regions if necessary, but they were absolutely forbidden to collaborate directly with each other on any question without first going through Thieu's office. This prohibition applied until the war ended. Thieu chose the commanders primarily on the basis of their loyalty to him; their military talents were wholly secondary. For only cooperation among corps commanders could mobilize sufficient force to threaten Thieu, and this became exceedingly difficult without his becoming aware of it.

The province chiefs were also directly accountable to Thieu. Being both military commanders and civil administrators, they were rarely controlled by Saigon ministries. They could, however, profit handsomely, selling lucrative posts and privileges in the provincial bureaucracy, helping family and friends, and even, occasionally, maintaining their own businesses. Since the office was their one great opportunity to grow rich before being transferred back to their original military units, few chose not to exploit it.

Parallel to the entire military structure, there also existed the Joint

General Staff (JGS), headed by General Cao Van Vien, an exceedingly docile, unusually naive, and wholly unambitious vegetarian who had passively worked for Diem. He was said to be highly corrupt by way of his wife. Ostensibly charged with strategic-planning functions, Thieu kept Vien in office precisely because he was safe. The JGS also became a repository of potentially untrustworthy officers without commands. Thieu utilized his National Security Council, which he created in July 1970, according to his mood, and often bypassed it and the minister of defense on major questions. He usually consulted his assistant for security, Lieutenant General Dang Van Quang, a major arbiter of patronage, whom Thieu trusted entirely. By the war's end, however, Thieu was in the habit of asking for reports from his corps commanders and an informal group including Quang. He never requested policy opinions but absorbed information, making all the key decisions entirely by himself.

The RVN's military and political machinery increasingly merged in Thieu's hands and could not operate without him, and this fact was far more important to its eventual destiny than the issue whether it was trained to fight conventional or guerilla warfare. The military establishment's primary function was to maintain Thieu's power, and the United States' ability to fight a counterrevolutionary war depended on the durability of a regime which was, in the words of one of Thieu's generals after the war, "intrigue-ridden, dictatorial, and repressive."[8] American officials knew by 1971 what was not fully revealed until spring 1975—that Thieu's talent as a military leader was mediocre at best. His role was political, and Washington supported him for this reason.

Thieu understood that by permitting corruption, indeed even encouraging it, he could win loyalty: "The best way of avoiding coups d'etat . . . ," as one of his aides quoted him.[9] But the fundamental dilemma of such an order for America's anti-Communist crusade remained. The various constituencies Thieu drew into his expanding system were usually linked to him informally rather than institutionally, a fact which somewhat disturbed U.S. officials, although not enough to alter their overwhelming wish to see stability maintained. Elections were, as Nguyen Cao Ky aptly phrased it from his own experience as the victorious vice-president in 1967, "a loss of time and money. They were a joke. They have served to install a regime that has nothing in common with the people—a useless, corrupt regime."[10] The National Assembly, which Diem himself created, had no significant powers, and Thieu ignored it. Even the most sympathetic American analysts thought that at least one-third of its members were fortune seekers—and Thieu let them enjoy this search often.

FORMS OF ELITE POWER

The Thieu machine's power gave it access to two levels of economic activity. First, daily administrative power meant endless opportunities for everything from petty graft to substantial but generally less-public corruption, the magnitude of the operations increasing with the importance of the official. Such exploitation was the most visible to the masses and the Americans, and therefore of greater political importance. Fewer people but much larger amounts were involved in the RVN ministries' control over licenses for imports, monetary operations of every sort, or taxes. The RVN military purchased everything from food to barbed wire; other agencies could distribute contracts for everything from fertilizers to construction. This immensely lucrative world of Saigon-centered state prerogatives involved innumerable nonmilitary constituencies, the most important being the Chinese. Overseeing the linkage between large transactions and elites outside the military were power blocs to whom Thieu allocated areas of responsibility.

The various constituencies Thieu drew into his machine were informal, and they played many roles; love of lucre was the one thing they had in common. Thieu attempted to use as many of his relatives as he could, but they alone were insufficient. His wife and her extended family managed his money, and even if Thieu and his wife's brother-in-law were not, as was commonly claimed, the two richest men in South Vietnam, they were surely not far behind. His inner core of allies included Pham Kim Ngoc, who was minister of economics longer than anyone else; apart from being a critical link with Chinese businessmen, Ngoc was also a favorite of the AID and the owner of the building in which it was housed. His account in Chase Manhattan's Taiwan branch alone amounted to $8 million in 1974.

Efforts to identify the other critical sections of Thieu's machine are largely derived from overschematized studies of power coalitions and particularly of the opium trade, a lucrative economic activity which implicated Thieu, his allies, and such rivals as Nguyen Cao Ky. Yet it was not nearly as important as many less colorful economic activities. The problem with such analyses was that alliances often changed and that the Byzantine world of Saigon politics could not sustain stable blocs, if only because many of Thieu's initial supporters were ready to break with him after 1973, when the economic depression shattered his coterie and Thieu was compelled to replace waverers. Moreover, his alliances were not exclusively economic but often had vital military and political functions, and these also shifted. Thieu's most important lieutenant, Dang Van Quang, loyally administered many of Thieu's affairs and was highly devoted to him until the end. Quang's major participation in the opium trade made him dependent on Thieu.

Quang's specialty was keeping track of province chiefs and crucial generals, making certain they were both happy and loyal to Thieu.

Thieu maintained control over the National Assembly through Nguyen Van Ngan, who was later to be pushed aside by Thieu's ambitious cousin Hoang Duc Nha as well as by Quang when Ngan became too assertive. Until 1972 he knew the price of the majority of the assembly. Thieu's most powerful ally, and the only one able to threaten him, was General Tran Thien Khiem, a favorite of many American generals, who became prime minister. Khiem was in charge of the defense department and made fortunes from military contracting, customs evasion, and provincial graft. His brother-in-law was mayor of Saigon, and his family connections made his power with the police and customs enormous. Although he was also a major factor in the heroin trade, his economic power was far greater. Thieu was afraid of him and, at best, only chipped around the edges of his power. The main restraint on Khiem was the Americans and his recognition that Thieu could not be eliminated without a mutually destructive battle.[11]

The politically favored generals who made money did not have sufficient time, much less ability, to manage all of the entrepreneurial aspects of their peculations, though they spent enough at the task to seriously undermine their military talents. Most were from moderately comfortable and ambitious families, above all the Catholics, whom the French had cultivated and the Americans later utilized. As businessmen, many needed help. Their power was in their official prerogatives, which gave them access to the immense largesse Washington was making available to fight a war. In this context, the United States was not merely transferring military techniques and equipment; rather, it was much more significantly constructing the context of class mobility and power in all its social dimensions, a structure which eventually had a negative influence on the military balance of forces and the outcome of the war itself.

The general dilemma confronting the United States' efforts to expand the military's power and role in numerous underdeveloped nations since 1950 has been the senior officer class' utilization of American support to assume far greater political power. And given the weak economic elite in most nations, the military's political role quickly dominates and exploits the nation's economic development, which ultimately produces instability and crisis politics and thwarts genuine development. In the end, the militarization of the RVN not only monopolized politics but also catalyzed social and human transformations which gravely eroded the coherence and future of the non-Revolutionary ideologies and followers. Those strata of South Vietnamese society without political links could scarcely compete for a large share of the new riches, even though a small number of individuals, mainly Chinese, managed to succeed in the highly fluid context in one way or another. The urban masses lived on the narrowest margins, and even some brothels and bars belonged to the elite that was forming from officers, key bureaucrats, and the Vietnamese and Chinese elements directly allied to them.

American officials always saw clearly the role of the new RVN elite in making vast private gains from political power. They were often informed by various senior generals currying U.S. favor that "corruption exists everywhere, the rich get richer while the mass of the poor Vietnamese see little hope of improvement"—as Marshall Ky told American leaders in July 1965, while jockeying for a greater share of it himself.[12] Far worse than corruption, in American eyes, was tension among the generals and political instability. This consideration caused Washington increasingly to support Thieu, until the officer corps rightly came to believe that he was their surest, perhaps only, link to the Yankee cornucopia. "Patterns of existent political alignments are greatly affected by corruption because of its endemic character in GVN and RVNAF functioning," the national Security Council's early 1969 review of the war concluded.[13] Since reformers could only upset Thieu's cohesive and firmly managed dictatorship, American interest in reform never went beyond occasional subtle changes palatable to Thieu in the aid program.

In this sense, the Americans knew they were ultimately responsible for the Thieu regime, for without their money the RVN would not be able to buy allies who assured stability. The economic basis of its very existence would vanish. "Moreover," the NSC acknowledged in early 1969, "it is natural that many Vietnamese will hold the United States responsible for not controlling its aid so that corruption will not flourish."[14] This relationship was the critical linkage in the social and class structure in the south after 1965, and all else would ultimately prove secondary. Conversely, since the United States now correctly saw that its entire mission was contingent on the RVN's stability, which only Thieu was able to provide, it in turn was wholly dependent on Thieu's remaining in power, a fact he perceived and exploited ruthlessly. Ironically, who was master and who was puppet was increasingly blurred with time.

THE RVN ELITE'S STRUCTURE

Analyzed structurally, the apex of the Thieu system was a narrow clique of officers and key civilian officials, not more than several thousand. Immediately below them was a far more numerous set of lower-ranking officials and officers. Directly allied with this elite were various merchants, entrepreneurs in service industries, and businessmen, including a small group of landlords, who collectively channeled money to and from the higher levels via con-

tracts, kickbacks, licenses for imports, and the like. While they never estimated its size, the AID's experts on the upper echelons of this system
concluded, "Many of the larger industries in South Vietnam are currently
controlled by a small number of coalitions of Chinese businessmen who are
allied with strategic Vietnamese government personnel."[15] The Fukienese,
according to American officials, were by far the most powerful, Ly Luong
Than was their most important leader, and they controlled or had major
shares in textiles, scrap metal, construction, banking, insurance, food proc-
essing, and imports. Chinese from Swatow were congregated in banking,
insurance, diverse manufacturing, and textiles.

All of the analyses of the dominating persons in this system number in
the hundreds the officers and senior politicians and officials involved, and
their capitalist allies—the large majority being Chinese—could not have
been more than one or two thousand. This tiny but critical element accounted for the bulk of the accumulated capital and capital flight. Most of
the capitalists had been wealthy before the war, but not on a remotely
comparable scale. Directly beneath them was an altogether new group of
largely politically based rich whose primary power lay in access to the state's
largesse, and these were paralleled by entrepreneurs, mainly Chinese, but
with a growing number of Vietnamese, who simply made money in conventional ways inevitable with the boom the American forces brought.

This larger new element beneath the men at the top spent its capital on
diversification, conspicuous consumption, and expansion along with a prudent export of funds, and comprised approximately 35,000 to 70,000. Petty
grafters in the civil and military systems account for roughly a quarter of
a million. Taking the 80,000 firms in manufacturing, commerce, construction, transport, and services in 1968 as a baseline, employing about 750,000
persons, an additional 200,000 to 500,000 civilians could have thought they
directly benefited from the Thieu machine's bounty. Estimates of a million
persons who perceived they had benefited from Thieu's system would be
very high. The total number both within and outside the state apparatus who
in fact directly gained more than small sums could not have exceeded
100,000 and was possibly much lower. Catholics made up one-tenth of
the south's population, a section of whom were particularly ideologically
motivated, and many at first provided Thieu with significant backing. Combined, Thieu's supporters per se, as opposed to his other anti-Communist
rivals, could scarcely have been more than one-eighth of South Vietnam's
population.

The problem in assessing the class structure during the decade after 1964,
apart from its fluidity and overlap with state mechanisms, was the role of
Vietnamese, as opposed to Chinese, entrepreneurs in the wartime boom. The
AID's analyses concluded that the Chinese managed to dominate the new

economic opportunities because their informal modes of business organization, based on *bang* and clan solidarity, allowed them to raise capital and act speedily, while Vietnamese businessmen had no comparable system and were both undercapitalized and cautious. On the other hand, the Vietnamese often had superior political contacts, which gave them access to new ventures. And the sheer growth of the economy and innovations led to more economic possibilities than the Chinese could handle. Apart from this, the Chinese who had dominated the rural economy now began to seek bigger opportunities, to some extent because the rice exports which had been the foundation of many fortunes now ceased, and their movement into urban activities left a rural opening that local Vietnamese could enter. Former landlords particularly favored taking over local commerce and credit as well as the market for agricultural machinery and supplies which was emerging. Although they also shared in the incredible profits in "services" and construction in the cities, the Vietnamese played the role of junior partner to the Chinese in the urban economy but to a considerable extent replaced their traditional domination of the rural sector. Had there been more time, a true Vietnamese bourgeoisie with a real interest in the system might have emerged. But since this would have required a continued American troop presence as the major market, the nouveaux riches prospering on the fringe of the system never acquired the attributes or psychology of a class ready to assert itself or confident in its own future. Thieu relied on the Chinese because they were best able to take on the immediate tasks, thereby strengthening the group least loyal to his system and denying himself the opportunity to build a truly formidable indigenous class basis for his effort.[16]

Thieu, of course, never attempted seriously to create a broad class foundation for his regime, but the cumulative effect of Thieu's system was to create a congenial if fickle constituency out of those who were the direct or indirect beneficiaries of the American-funded society. There was never a class base for the Thieu regime in the true sense of class as an institutionally stable and broad element of society. The disintegration of the French legacy and the marginalization of the educated elements who had earlier been ideologically or economically predisposed to anti-Communist politics continued, inevitably conditioning a substantial portion of them for anti-Thieu coalition politics with virtually anyone, including the NLF. The shallow privileged class residues inherited from the French era continued to narrow, especially as inflation after 1965 began to whittle away at the economic resources of all except the Chinese.

The very context in which Thieu's regime developed convinced most of its new elite that it could not endure, and this especially affected its Chinese members, who had traditionally been mobile, prone to keeping wealth highly liquid, and often linked to families and interests elsewhere in Southeast Asia. Between the Chinese and the officers, the basic paradox of the Thieu regime was the opportunism of its most powerful and favored supporters, which took the form of a vast flight of capital, an exodus of children, and a reluctance to invest in long-term economic development. The Chinese capitalists were by definition the weakest class on which the military elite could rely. And precisely because they knew that the generals were vulnerable and transitional, they tried to make certain that their options outside the country were always ready. The Chinese, American officials in Saigon accurately concluded in 1972, for the most part "do not consider themselves a part of the nation in which they live. For the large entrepreneurs, the business decision to invest here or transfer funds abroad is made on business calculations and not on any consideration of national need—exactly, in fact, like any foreign investor does."[17]

The fragile class structure that the French had created and Diem eroded now became even weaker in the flotsam and jetsam of demography, social disintegration, and changes far too rapid to be absorbed coherently. The new lumpen element of war profiteers destroyed the final vestiges of the national and the petite bourgeoisies, plunging them into economic and moral crises which compromised some and radicalized others. And being wholly dependent on American money and support for the very existence of the RVN, the new profiteers had no nationalist or cultural legitimacy for their politics, a fact they could not alter. The underdevelopment of a possible conservative class characterized the pre-Revolutionary order until its end. Both the French and the American colonial legacies made this ephemeral, fluid class development inevitable by their reliance on the Chinese and on dependent, obsequious arriviste generals whose only loyalty in serving comprador roles was ultimately to their own, personal welfare.

Chapter 18

The Dilemma of Economic Dependency and the RVN

THE ECONOMICS OF DEPENDENCY

Though South Vietnam's economy under Diem was wholly dependent on American aid, after 1964 it was far more fragile. The intensified war and the exponential growth of American GIs posed potentially catastrophic economic challenges to the United States' ambition. For agriculture was being uprooted and the population displaced into cities wholly unable to absorb them with local resources.

The purpose of American economic policy was to stanch the immense economic wounds the war was inflicting long enough to allow its vague military objectives to be attained at a time, as the Agency for International Development later ruefully admitted, when "no one thought the war would last ten years, let alone that we would lose it."[1] The cost to the United States could, if its military assumptions were valid, remain tolerable only for a short period. But to cut its losses was tantamount to military surrender, which was unthinkable. Meanwhile, Washington's temporary economic solutions produced fabulous opportunities for growing corruption, becoming the key to Thieu's political consolidation and, to a lesser degree, the maintenance of more social stability among the masses than would otherwise have been possible. In effect, the RVN's very existence was linked to sufficient economic and military aid, surpassing in importance the outcome of battles or diplomacy, for the very artificiality of the economy and the war's impact left it vulnerable to countless potentially fatal problems.

In retrospect, the AID accurately concluded in 1975, the "period 1965–67 in Viet Nam was unlike anything ever experienced by an underdeveloped country."[2] While the various mechanisms the United States employed may seem complicated to nonspecialists, in essence they were merely manifestations of a simple policy. An escalating war was destroying the existing economy, and Washington made the decision that it was vital to prevent inflation, which could only further radicalize the people and make defeat more certain. The Korean War, which was much smaller in terms both of troops and of areas affected at any one time, had created a runaway inflation, the memory of which was still fresh in Washington in 1964. To combat inflation, the United States decided to maximize imports, neutralizing the vast inflow of dollars accompanying its half a million soldiers, the American expansion of bases and military construction, and the ruination of South Vietnam's traditional productive economic sector. The RVN's seeming prosperity, so illusory for the majority of the nation, was based wholly on this strategy.

Agricultural production by 1968 was a quarter below the already low 1961–65 average. Not until 1970 did it finally surpass it, although per capita output never equaled it. Industrial production, mainly to service U.S. troop demands and provide supplies for construction, rose during 1964–67, dropping sharply in 1968. In 1964–67 imports increased over 100 percent, and imports during 1969–71 exceeded exports by a factor of over fifty-five. By 1967 about 40 percent of the RVN's gross national product was composed of imports entirely dependent on U.S. aid, and by 1970 nearly 50 percent was. Proportionately, the share of gross domestic product devoted to manufacturing dropped dramatically throughout this period—making South Vietnam the only major nation of Asia to experience this form of deindustrialization and leaving it with the lowest proportion in manufacturing of any of them. The South Vietnamese economy was sharply diverted from the production of goods, the only basis of real economic development, into the provision of services, making it structurally very weak and vulnerable to an economic crisis the moment the Americans started to withdraw.

In terms of the larger pattern of the RVN's economy, the government sector of the net domestic product grew from 15 percent in 1960, when it was already heavily dependent on aid, to 21 percent in 1964 and 34 percent in 1972. Most of the rapidly expanding service sector was also a result of the U.S. aid and presence; together with the government's share of the domestic product, it grew from 56 percent in 1960 to 78 percent in 1972. Prices between 1964 and 1972 rose about tenfold, and inflation remained a serious economic and social problem even with the enormous American largesse. What the minimum of $5 billion in U.S. economic aid from 1964 to 1975 (it was actually much higher) did was merely postpone the inevitable reckoning.

Although the data were much debated, the RVN budget was from 1966 onward usually at least 85 percent aid funded, since most of its internally generated revenues were mainly due to U.S.-financed imports. When aid was insufficient, the RVN relied mainly on the printing of money, which in 1965 accounted for almost a quarter of its budget. A majority of the RVN's budget went to the military, reaching two-thirds of it in 1970, but there was *never* adequate internal funding to pay for the war. The successive regimes in Saigon flaunted their indifference toward their own costs in the face of American economic advisers, who unanimously agreed that "the Republic of Vietnam does not have an effective tax system" and that its large staff of tax gatherers cost more than they collected in revenue.[3]

The RVN's economic functions opened numerous channels to wealth for those with connections, but none involved so much money as its import program and the legal (as opposed to black-market) rate of the piaster, the RVN's currency. Given the role of imports in the overall U.S. economic strategy, this was inevitable. While over the years both the Commercial Import Program (CIP) and the artificial piaster rate were controversial in Washington as hidden subsidies, in the end successive administrations supported them.

The CIP began in 1950 but under Diem soon assumed enormous value as an instrument of patronage and corruption. The system was quite simple. An importer obtained a CIP import license, and AID dollars paid the supplier, for which the importer paid the RVN at a certain exchange rate with piasters. The piasters nominally gave the RVN a means of taxation and a way of gathering counterpart funds for its own needs, which in fact occurred when the importer was charged more than the official exchange rate. But as he was also charged less than the black-market rate, he immediately made an exchange profit before selling a single commodity. Between 1966 and 1968, for example, the difference between the CIP and the black-market rates permitted importers immediately to earn 39 to 56 percent on the exchange alone, which allowed them to sell goods very cheaply. Between October 1967 and 1972, despite chronic inflation, the piaster was not devalued. The potential profits were enormous, and suppliers colluded with importers to overbill, which was probably the chief method of allowing importers and their political patrons to create their foreign-currency nest eggs abroad. The flight of capital was to remain a hemorrhage in the RVN economy; while estimates of its volume were huge, no one will ever know the exact amount. A majority of the AID's aid was given via the CIP, amounting to over $4 billion, and the system was from the start marked by kickbacks and scandal. Trying to estimate the number of importers who controlled the vast CIP, the AID confidentially concluded that about one hundred importers in 1969–70 accounted for well over two-thirds of the trade and exercised a virtual monopoly on what was probably the single greatest source of gain in the vast range of corrupt practices. The large majority were Chinese and the same individuals who dominated all other major economic activities.[4]

The CIP tied its funds to imports from the United States to keep various American export interests happy, and it also had special subsidy arrangements for specific commodities, fertilizers being the most important, to implement American economic policies. But since consumer goods were the best means of soaking up piasters and dampening inflation, and since Japanese and Asian-made products were better and cheaper, the RVN also had its own import-licensing program, which was even larger than the CIP.

The single most important means of financing RVN-licensed imports was the Pentagon's purchase of piasters directly from the RVN, which was amassing piasters in exchange for CIP and other approved imports, for the use of its troops and expenses in Vietnam at far above the black-market rate. In 1971, for example, the Defense Department paid Saigon $271 million for piasters which bought goods and services costing $116 million at the open-market rate. In 1969–71 alone this indirect subsidy was officially estimated at around half a billion dollars, and America's purchase of $2.6 billion in piasters from the RVN during the war was largely a gift added to the AID's $7.5 billion in aid.

The RVN import program was more overtly corrupt than CIP imports, since importers and suppliers were mainly Chinese with direct links to key RVN bureaucrats and far better able to manipulate documents. AID officials thought not only that "licensing officials were granting GVN import licenses to their friends" but also that they were "hindering import activities of those importers who refused to cooperate with them."[5] Sparks flew when CIP-funded imports from the United States ceased to be competitive, and the import question troubled American officials to the bitter end.

Food-for-Peace (PL-480) amounted to $1.3 billion in American farm surpluses during 1958–75, half of which arrived in the form of rice, with cotton, wheat, tobacco, and milk composing the bulk of the remainder. Rice had been the south's major export prior to the war, but by 1965 it had become a net importer, and it remained one until the war was over, requiring nearly 700,000 tons in 1967. Cheap rice was the RVN's sole subsidized commodity, and since it was aware of the political risks of rice shortages, the RVN imported the rice itself and, despite inevitable corruption, made an effort to keep prices low. While this generally benefited urban elements, it reduced the peasantry's incentive to expand rice production, contributing to the RVN's long-term dependency on the United States and leaving postwar Vietnam with major food problems. The remaining PL-480 items were imported by private interests and complemented the CIP role in the RVN's budget and economy.

The magnitude of the profits from windfall gains to the small group of

privileged importers who had access to all of the programs involving the
RVN was something the AID approached very circumspectly, for fear of
discrediting its efforts. The one study it authorized went through successive
drafts, admitted the data were poor, and was never released. It naively
assumed that importers did not buy the piasters they needed to obtain AID
dollars for imports at the black-market rate. Even so, it conceded that by
late 1969, when the study ended, importers could make 40 to 50 percent
windfall gains on the exchange differences, and that from 1964 through 1969
at least $264 million in windfall profits were made. In fact the largest sums
could be made after 1969, when the gap between the import rate and the
black-market rate of the dollar grew with inflation. A very conservative
estimate of windfall gains to the small elite of importers and their allies for
the entire wartime period ending in 1975 would be not less than $1.5 billion
on total imports funded with U.S. aid, and twice that sum was much more
likely, excluding the RVN's own licensing. Fortunes made from them both
were certainly sufficient to fill the coffers of the top echelons of the RVN
power structure and Thieu's most devoted followers.[6]

The RVN economy was in grave difficulties throughout its history and
would have been so even without a huge drainage in the form of corruption.
All factors combined, there were not sufficient funds for this unique economy, and there never could be. Both American and RVN economic planners
were aware of this reality and directly confronted it by making a basic
decision, the significance of which was enormous, to save costs in the one
area that lacked the power to resist—namely, the salaries paid to the military
personnel and civil servants. U.S. economists in Saigon knew that civil
servants' real income in the three years ending January 1, 1968, fell from 40
to 50 percent, depending on rank, and later continued to fall even more
sharply. They also knew that this was a critical stimulus to corruption.
Military pay was held down as a matter of economic policy. By August 1969
the real income of ARVN personnel was less than a third of its 1963 level.
Had it kept up with inflation, the military budget's share of the gross
domestic product in 1969 would have been over 22 percent, as opposed to
about 16 percent, and the RVN's visible deficit would have been far larger.
"Another way of expressing the same point," the Harvard professor Arthur
Smithies, the leading consultant on the RVN economy, dryly noted in
August 1970, "is to say that the war is being financed in Viet-Nam partly
by the levy of a heavy implicit tax on the public sector, civilian as well as
military."[7] Since there was no tax system and revenue to provide the army
and civil servants a minimal living, as another American analyst expressed
it, "the soldiers and police can easily end up financing themselves."[8]

Looting and corruption therefore became a routinized part of the system,
a hidden tax on the population, lest the RVN administration disintegrate.

As inflation drove real income down, this accepted corruption in the civil service grew, reducing the RVN's internal tax revenues and increasing its dependency on U.S. aid. The entire tax and customs system functioned in this manner, and senior officials sold all potentially lucrative posts and left it to their subordinates to raise the price. "With attempts to counteract corruption by frequent changes of personnel," one AID official said of the situation, "required payoffs increase dramatically, since officials have a shorter period of time to recoup the amount paid to secure the position in the first place and put something away for the future."[9] One typical example was the most junior post in customs in Saigon's airport. To obtain it cost about $2,000, with daily kickbacks to superior officials of $20 daily, though the salary was $35 a month. Should anyone wish to complain about corruption in the routine workings of the RVN society, he or she could go to the Censorate, created to investigate such charges and chaired by Thieu's uncle.

CORRUPTION AND THE DILEMMA OF AN ARTIFICIAL ECONOMY

From the inception of the war, all senior American officials knew that, as McNamara phrased it in October 1966, there was "corruption high and low."[10] It upset many initially, but they quickly became inured, and it did not take long before some began appreciating its political and even economic assets. "It is generally acknowledged that Vietnam is corrupt," Arthur Smithies noted in one of his 1970 economic analyses for Washington. "But there is no evidence that it is more corrupt than its South-East Asian neighbors. If it is, the reason may be that the war and wartime policies provided many opportunities for corruption." But the issue of corruption could not be divorced from the "political significance" of those gaining from it, from its role as a political "lubricant," as Smithies felicitously termed it, and from its usefulness in providing cohesion and stability.[11] American officials made no secret of their preference for Thieu, and this foreclosed any stopping of the corruption.

When the war ended, however, the AID's final internal report on its experience in Vietnam was unequivocal: "Corruption was pervasive throughout the period of U.S. involvement at all levels." The AID's international operations exposed it to all degrees of the world's corruption, but with the RVN, they concluded, "there was an inordinate amount of corruption —by any standard." It was "far beyond" lower-level affairs "greasing-the-wheels" of the state, "often involving fantastically large amounts of money —among top officials and generals."[12]

Coping with the economic problems of its dependency in this environment profoundly frustrated the Americans responsible for the task. In early 1970, as Ambassador Ellsworth Bunker recalled the following year, the embassy thought that economic "problems were becoming more serious than the military threat and if left unsolved might undo everything that had been achieved."[13] The Vietnamization of the war contained a military plan to replace the U.S. presence, but the equally crucial goal of making the RVN economically self-supporting was a far more complex challenge, which declining American troop levels and spending only aggravated. It was all the more difficult because of the "temporary" U.S. effort to gear an entire economy, and the political machine running it, to imports. This had gone so far as consciously to reduce agriculture's role in the overall economy, although it had been the most productive in the past, and to addict what was left of it to a higher utilization of imported fertilizers than prevailed in any nation in South and Southeast Asia. The United States' subsidized imports throughout the RVN's life had, as the AID later admitted, "aborted development in many areas of both industry and agriculture."[14] But the contradiction the United States confronted after 1970 was that a failure to develop the economy would make the RVN dependent on aid indefinitely, a situation that could eventually undo the Vietnamization of the military aspects of the war. Consequently, the best guess among those American advisers most familiar with the problem was that the RVN would require high levels of aid from public donors, half a billion dollars annually being a common figure, for at least a decade or two.

The most influential U.S. experts thought it unlikely that the RVN could overcome its economic problems. They all assumed that combat would require military mobilization indefinitely, and Smithies did not feel that the RVN could expect forever its $700 million economic aid annually from the United States or any other country. By the fall of 1971, as the Senate Committee on Foreign Relations unsuccessfully cut aid to Indochina drastically as the first sign of serious discontent in Congress, the urgency of the need to find alternative sources seemed clear. While American advisers thought the RVN should integrate itself into the world capitalist economy in a classic fashion, avoiding excessive protection of domestic industry or hostility to foreign investment, Smithies warned that foreign capital was not going to invest where there was military insecurity. Virtually two years after the start of their analyses and planning, key U.S. experts were complaining that Thieu had shown almost no interest in the problem of his regime's economic survival and created no competent governmental staff to deal with what, in effect, was a crucial phase of Vietnamization. Thieu, for practical purposes, was counting on receiving U.S. and foreign monies forever!

In this context a handful of Americans confronted this monumental challenge. At the end of 1970 they had the RVN promulgate a petroleum law designed by Walter Levy, the American petroleum industry's leading adviser, and they initiated a new investment law to encourage foreign investments. The pessimism of its ablest economists notwithstanding, both the U.S. embassy and the AID in Saigon embarked on a campaign to obtain private investment to fill in the aid gap certain to emerge. In May 1971 the AID director in Saigon estimated that in four to five years foreign investment and multilateral economic aid would be able to make up the decline in American economic assistance. Implicitly, the failure to develop these two options would create serious, even grave, problems for Thieu's economy.

Oil as the savior of the RVN economy became a wistful hope beginning in late 1970, lasting until the final months of the Thieu regime. Given the absence of anything serious to invest in, especially in a war-torn nation, foreigners would invest in offshore oil or nothing. In late 1968 the U.S. sponsored offshore surveys, and several American firms followed with their own, so that by mid-1970 oil industry journals showed a mild case of Vietnam oil fever. Not only was the promise far greater than the facts to support it, but by early 1971 highly publicized pressures from antiwar groups and members of Congress had put most oil firms on the defensive, though from mid-1973 onward some made relatively small investments in leases and exploration, never striking any bonanzas which might indeed have earned the RVN large royalties. Although oil failed to reach its goals, it hypnotized Saigon until the end and was surely just one of the many factors reinforcing its passivity in the face of its impending economic crisis.

Multilateral and international aid to the RVN was even more chimerical. By 1970 Smithies and other experts were irate that Japan was profiting enormously from the RVN's imports, which the United States was making possible with its piaster purchases, while doing nothing to help save its market from extinction. The World Bank was already involved in Mekong Delta studies, and Washington considered desirable an aid consortium of the World Bank, the Asian Development Bank, and the IMF. But in the fall of 1971, when State Department consultants analyzed this approach more carefully, they concluded that the official assumption that the ARVN would remain large and that the war would continue made multilateralization of aid to the RVN a far more difficult alternative. There were never any unqualified illusions about this substitute for American aid as a means of sustaining the RVN's economy—and the war.[15]

The creation of a viable economic basis for its surrogate in South Vietnam was essential to the success of the American war effort, but the very social, political, and economic distortions involved in the entire process of the war and the need to keep Thieu in power made the goal that much more elusive. With time, the decisive significance of this critical challenge would become increasingly obvious.

Chapter 19

The Building of the RVN's Army and the Struggle for Rural South Vietnam

THE UNITED STATES AND THE RVN AS A MILITARY PROBLEM

The United States' deepening frustration with the RVN's military role in the war was as old as the conflict itself, and touches the central predicament of the entire, ill-starred effort. The core of Washington's dilemma with the RVN's senior officers until 1975 was that their political origins and roles were in constant tension with their military missions, producing a tangle of conflicting functions and objectives that the United States could not reconcile. To a critical extent America's epic effort to assert its own military power in South Vietnam was tied to the essentially uncontrollable actions and destiny of its successive dependents in Saigon.

The RVN's senior officer corps constituted Saigon's real political arena after 1963, and its factions ceaselessly vied with one another for power and lucre until 1968. For the military to have withdrawn from politics would have removed the political underpinnings of the American venture, since the United States wanted stability and continuity above all and only the military could promise it. Any serious civilian challenge to it could merely lead to a renewal of the chaos which had existed for almost two years after Diem's death. As a result, the Americans begrudgingly accepted the increasingly systematic corruption essential to the RVN's stability.

The United States after 1965 was trapped in a grave dilemma. Its leaders always saw its massive intervention as an effort to gain time for the RVN to consolidate its total power over South Vietnam. Everyone in Washington understood that failure to do so would determine the extent and duration of the American presence. Even if Saigon's generals stubbornly refused to give up their preoccupation with politics, it was still essential for the United States to have the RVNAF perform significant military tasks and to improve its forces. In this overall context of the RVNAF's conflicting functions, the administration obsessively sought to define a military role for its dependents. Ironically, the sheer mass of U.S. manpower and arms after mid-1965 also permitted the RVN the luxury of internecine politics. Only Thieu's later consolidation of power and virtually total politicization of the senior officer corps finally allowed a somewhat greater ARVN military mission to evolve. Throughout this period its military activities developed in the context of an American presence which Washington never intended to be permanent, gearing the ARVN to fighting a war dependent on U.S. high technology and firepower.

From the very beginning the United States was uncertain of the ARVN's strategic doctrine and missions. Apart from aspiring to hold the maximum territory possible, the RVN had no strategies of its own other than those the Americans assigned and equipped it for. By mid-1965 the ARVN was on the verge of defeat, tied down in static positions against an enemy one-third its size. As U.S. forces poured into the country and set up bases, it was expected that the ARVN would also defend them, but it did this very badly from the inception. The expanded American role further immobilized the ARVN both in terms of its formal missions and psychologically.

By mutual consent with the United States, after 1965 the RVNAF assumed three military functions. Its primary role was to provide territorial security in the form of the static defense of bases, cities, and such. Its combat activity was less important at first but remained a major task despite the American responsibility for most offensive operations. Pacification of the villages also became a critical assignment. This division of labor remained to trouble the United States for three years.

Every factor in South Vietnam from 1964 onward reinforced the ARVN's development as a static, defensive army incapable of taking the initiative. Its senior officers stayed preoccupied with politics and the accumulating of wealth, and the increasing need of its soldiers to live off the land further immobilized it. The U.S. advisers first trained the ARVN to fight a conventional war, but ultimately it was unprepared to fight any kind. The American forces' functions relegated the ARVN to defensive roles, as did pacification of the villages, but its need to control the population was primordial, since the NLF was certain to fill any vacuum. In a larger sense every policy decision and objective influence in Vietnam after 1964 reinforced the development of the entire RVN military system's defensive strategy, for the moment it gave up holding populated territory, it was doomed to failure politically. A mobile reserve of significance was never created, for both physical and political reasons, and whatever tactical mobility the ARVN possessed was dependent to a great degree on U.S.-supplied helicopters and logistics. The Revolution's high proportion of mobile forces and its ability to retain the strategic initiative were realities that the Americans could not overcome.

The American effort to rectify the ARVN's deficiencies was a long sequence of frustrations. Training in 1966 was regarded as virtually nonexistent, and the ARVN's capacity for small-unit, night, or ambush operations was considered poor and no better at the end of 1968 than at the beginning of the U.S. troop influx. Its usual, mid-afternoon siesta infuriated American officers. As late as 1969, when ARVN controlled far more of its own artillery and helicopters, the average maneuver battalion spent only three hours a week receiving mainly mediocre training. Its usual approach during its increasingly less frequent large-scale operations was to avoid contact with enemy forces, a fact which filled U.S. officers with contempt. Throughout 1966 and 1967 most U.S. officials were convinced, for good reason, that the very presence of the vast American army was causing the ARVN, not to mention the 300,000 men in the Regional and Popular Forces (RF/PF), to fight even less.[1] As U.S. manpower spent more and more time filling in the void the ARVN created, Washington eagerly searched for ways, as the President put it, of "getting value received from the South Vietnamese troops."[2] The most important obstacle to its doing so, in American opinion, was the quality of the senior officers. This was one reason Washington reinforced Thieu's dictatorship over the next years, since it saw political stability as an absolute precondition of any progress in strengthening the ARVN. Precisely because of this leverage, it would ultimately be Thieu, not the Americans, who decided how the RVN's military structure would be employed.

America's attempt to define a military role for the RVN's armed forces was always suffused with contempt and pessimism. Although the administration was intent on gaining time for its surrogates, it was unable to implement policies capable of transferring the burden of combat to its shoulders. To confess privately, let alone publicly, to the hopelessness of the task was as good as declaring that the United States would remain in Vietnam indefinitely or be forced to leave in total defeat. In 1965–67 no one was ready to admit that the administration's ability to attain its geopolitical goals and strategy to win local wars was ultimately dependent on a chaotically led and tawdry army.

Even ignoring its senior officers' preoccupations, the ARVN had problems that ranged from the petty to the structural, and all merged to doom American efforts. In May 1964 the U.S. military was quite uncertain whether important sectors of the RF and the PF were "loyal to RVN or VC," an apprehension that delayed the distribution of arms to all of them until 1969.[3] And while GIs avoided teaming with ARVN soldiers as much as possible, their constant complaints were also paralleled by poor cooperation at senior levels. The PLAF attack against the Bien Hoa base on November 1, 1964, was one that U.S. officers believed could have been avoided had the local ARVN commander passed along his intelligence and not withdrawn troops the night of the attack. Tense relations with RVN officers led to frequent harassment of American base defenses, even to the extent of occasional firing at U.S. soldiers. The entire RF and PF structure, so crucial to the protection of the bases, was mired in red tape in order to prevent any senior commander from being able to mobilize it for a coup attempt, Brigadier General Edward Lansdale complained in October 1966, a condition the MACV only partially modified in mid-1967.

Given such difficulties, American advisers chose to make up with quantity what the RVNAF lacked in quality. The RVN armed forces increased by 129,000 men between 1964 and 1967, and over the next year they grew another 177,000, to reach 820,000—peaking at 1,048,000 in 1972. "The great challenge . . . ," Westmoreland wrote in 1968, "was to alter the image of a defeated, demoralized army."[4] The sheer size of such an army, which grew from being 5 percent of South Vietnam's male population in 1956 to 7 percent in 1964 and 11 percent in 1972, left the RVN social order with monumental challenges even as it gave the Americans the cannon fodder they thought essential.

Both by example and by training, the United States from the start taught the ARVN to rely on firepower. Firepower, of course, depended on technology, money, and a competent logistics system. As a senior ARVN general later described it, the logistical system was "founded on American doctrine, American equipment and American money."[5] "Basic to U.S. combat doctrine, which we successfully imparted to the South Vietnamese," the State Department summarized at the end of 1974, "is the concept of achieving maximum effect with minimum loss of personnel. This requires high equipment utilization and expenditure of ordnance. . . . The South Vietnamese (and American) way of waging war costs more money. . . ."[6] After 1964 the ARVN was simply integrated into the U.S. war machine as a poorer dependent, and it imitated failing American tactics.

ARVN soldiers increasingly expected to advance with the aid of air and artillery cover and never learned to fight without it. To the extent that artillery remained immobile, so too did ARVN troops hesitate to advance aggressively. They did not concern themselves overly much with the accuracy of their fire, often regarding it as an invitation to Revolutionary forces to withdraw if they chose to, and from 1965 to 1969 American analysts in the south saw no basic improvement in the ARVN's use of artillery and aviation. Ammunition was largely wasted, and it was much more casual than U.S. forces in employing ground and air power against villagers, politically alienating the masses in a fashion many advisers thought foolhardy. Yet complicated new weapons of mass destruction, such as fixed-wing flying gunships, with their electronic sensors and battery of machine guns, were transferred to the ARVN from 1965 onward despite an American consensus that they were not able to operate effectively with or without them.

The ARVN made the worst of all this complexity and expense, being burdened by technology's decisive liabilities and unable to exploit its potential assets. By the time the Americans left, it was therefore extremely vulnerable. It could not coordinate its large-scale offensives or provide intelligence security for them, and during its ill-fated invasion of southern Laos in February 1971, the U.S. Army still was in charge of its logistics. Geared to high technology, its logistical system was a powerful reinforcement of its de facto strategy of holding static positions and avoiding mobile operations if possible. Even when everything necessary was available—munitions, spare parts, and ample funding—the RVNAF found it too challenging to digest and employ them, logistics remaining an insoluble difficulty until the end. More crucial, however, was that the RVN never developed a strategic doctrine or plan of its own. It did not even have coherent doctrines for major forms of firepower, such as artillery. From 1964 to 1972 it naturally assumed that, should a serious military threat arise, the Americans would save them and that the future would resemble the past. A variation of this belief persisted until the final debacle in 1975.

The RVN's senior generals were excellent political infighters or businessmen but very inferior military leaders, and this fact was basic to the nature of the RVN as a social system. The challenge facing the United States was therefore all the greater: the need to gain time for the RVN to consolidate politically still left it with the dilemma of who would fight the war—and for how long. Indeed, the RVN's attainment after 1968 of an increasingly stable political structure based on a military dictatorship merely intensified the political character of its military system, making combat a quite secondary function. It was this, far more than its dependence on technology, that rendered the RVNAF so fragile. Meanwhile, however, its military needs and failures became a sponge absorbing American money, forces, and time. By the end of 1967 it was unclear how much of these the Johnson administration could afford.

THE AMERICAN AND RVN
PACIFICATION AND RURAL
STRATEGY

In this military context the United States and the NLF struggled for mastery of the countryside, the task of "pacification" being assigned largely to the various components of the RVNAF. The chaotic succession of efforts under the Diem regime to herd the rural population into assigned areas had raised the basic dilemma for the Americans of whether pacification was to remain simply a matter of physical control over population and counterinsurgency, as under Diem, or whether it meant ideological-social changes capable of neutralizing the Revolution. To gain time for Diem's successors to resolve these questions in their turn was, ultimately, a strategic mission of the U.S. armed forces.

It was essential for the war's planners to separate the Revolution from the rural masses. By 1965 they were committed to relying primarily on firepower to do this, although they freely acknowledged the need for "nation building" and for nebulous changes in the status quo they could only vaguely define. The American military was impatient with such notions and preferred to see other agencies and the RVN assume responsibility for what it nonetheless admitted to be activities essential for "pacifying" the population. For the United States, therefore, the Vietnam War and the pacification program always embodied the same addicting mixture of tough-minded massive force and the amorphous liberal rhetoric which has been the peculiar hallmark of American imperialism since the end of the nineteenth century.

The problem, of course, was that pacification programs until 1964 had only further radicalized the peasantry. Whatever its ultimate objectives, the administration after 1965 always felt unsure of its policies, fearing any premature actions which might weaken the successive Saigon juntas. Since these regimes never shared even the modest, if erratic, U.S. commitment to such projects, Washington always had to consider the extent to which it could pressure and alienate its allies. Pacification, functionally, became overwhelmingly a military program, almost synonymous with the entire war effort, yet American civilian leaders knew it must become something more than that if they were to defeat the NLF.

In 1965 neither the RVN nor the United States had an organization to cope with pacification. They were still recovering from the shambles Diem's strategic-hamlet program had bequeathed them. The consensus among Americans at this point was that pacification would reflect the military balance of power. Primarily at Westmoreland's initiative, Washington from the inception defined its role as preventing the military defeat of the RVN by going on offensive operations while the RVNAF allocated a significant part of its resources to local security and, presumably, pacification. This conception of the relation of war to politics was never reversed. Nevertheless, the Americans in 1965 began a large number of programs, dubbed "civic action." These absorbed some U.S. forces and also required an ironing out of bureaucratic problems involving the relationship of various American agencies to each other, but above all to the RVN, and consumed much time and attention. By the end of 1965, as U.S. forces stalled the PLAF's march to victory, pressure came from Washington, and particularly from the President, to modify its pacification program.

In early 1966 the American nonmilitary program was mired in confusion and bureaucratic log jams. Johnson, on the other hand, was still convinced that his reputation as a reformer, begun with the "War on Poverty" at home, would be his claim to greatness. Reform in South Vietnam might give the war a legitimacy it badly needed for his increasingly uncomfortable public and Congress. During 1966, beginning with the impulsively convened Honolulu conference in early February and ending with the Manila conference of October 24–25, he met with Thieu and Ky and each time left believing that their joint communiqués, stressing rural democracy and construction, including a promised electrification and agricultural program laden with New Deal rhetoric, made the war seem merely a necessary, if unpleasant, means of creating a liberal order in Southeast Asia. Ky, in particular, understood the President's mood and cynically played up to it, agreeing to go out to the villages and shake hands in the best Texas tradition —a pledge he ignored, preferring to remain in Saigon and cabal against his enemies there. After the Honolulu meeting the various U.S. pacification programs were better coordinated. They were ultimately unified in March 1967 in Saigon as the Civil Operations and Revolutionary Development Support (CORDS) under Robert Komer, the President's much-favored, ebullient advocate of a far greater pacification effort. Komer, despite his brashness, in his private reports accurately assessed the political, economic, and organizational constraints operating to keep his programs from succeeding. Until his removal in November 1968, his private realism simply encouraged a natural tendency for the rest of Washington and the generals to rely on firepower. By early 1970 he publicly acknowledged that the "sloppy and inefficient" effort had been begun too late and that, despite its successes, its results remained fragile.[7]

Arranging a division of labor with the RVNAF was crucial to the U.S. pacification scheme. By the end of 1966 the program's failures had begun to discourage McNamara and the civilians in the Pentagon, who thought that

American forces would inevitably be called upon to remain much longer. During this period the United States pressed the ARVN to commit half of its forces—in addition to the RF/PF—to offensive operations and support for what was now dubbed Revolutionary Development (RD), in the naive hope it might grasp the legitimacy of the revolutionary banner from the Communist movement. By early 1967 the ARVN was pledged to do so.

The contradictions in the pacification program condemned it to failure in ways that were quite clear in 1966–67. Most obvious was U.S. support for the Thieu-Ky regime, which was providing growing political stability based increasingly on corruption, including that in the pacification program. When compelled to choose between stability or efficiency, the administration opted for stability every time. Much more crucial was the impact of U.S. military operations on the rural structure and the irreconcilable conflict between its policies of construction and those of destruction.

THE CONTRADICTIONS BETWEEN WARFARE AND THE STABILIZING OF A RURAL SOCIETY

By 1965 a decade of sustained upheaval had physically uprooted rural South Vietnam, radicalizing the peasantry or dissolving its community structure. Any attempt at rural reconstruction would require ending the massive fire-power which constantly threatened the peasantry's existence and produced the vast flow of refugees. At no time did Washington ever consider abandoning its overwhelming emphasis on arms. Even in the many places where the NLF was ready to work semilegally, the United States and the RVN had no political and social option for the masses, much less an organizational structure capable of co-opting the Revolution's reform program. Their alternative to the Revolution was population displacement, which generated a vast number of new problems for the NLF but even more for the United States and the RVN. Pacification in this context remained a chimera until late 1968, by which time the war's military, political, and economic consequences had destroyed whatever lingering hopes had existed for such puny efforts.

The refugee problem almost immediately absorbed most of the American and the RVN resources for rural development, minus, of course, the enormous corruption which taxed all programs. Washington concluded that it was far easier and less dangerous to move the population of NLF regions to RVN-controlled areas than to enter them and laboriously attempt to pacify and convert the people. The use of herbicides against food crops, which the State Department and the Pentagon repeatedly endorsed, was merely one aspect of this policy. "After crops had died in target areas," as the official Air Force history describes the JCS position at the end of 1967, "groups of civilians had moved to areas under government control, further aggravating the guerrilla's manpower problems."[8] All decision-making agencies in Washington and Saigon were wholly aware that the combat and firepower were causing suffering to the people and huge population movements, amounting to three million refugees by the end of 1967, a fact that had political liabilities for one form of pacification but that also gave the United States physical possession of its real or potential enemies, the peasants. "Although the policy to create refugees for military purposes does not, in so many words, appear in any MACV document," the JCS's counterinsurgency head observed in December 1967, in the course of advocating the production of two million more, "the necessity is openly recognized as a realistic requirement. . . ."[9] First in a more candid memo to the State Department in December 1967 and then in a widely noticed article in the Establishment's *Foreign Affairs* in mid-1968, Harvard's Samuel Huntington correctly asserted that urbanization more than any factor explained the rising RVN control over the population. "The depopulation of the countryside struck directly at the strength and political appeal of the Viet Cong. . . . The Maoist-inspired rural revolution is undercut by the American-sponsored urban revolution."[10]

Pacification, at least insofar as it was supposed to combine politics and war, was therefore the victim of the United States' local-war strategy. Its essentially paramilitary nature continued throughout the 1960s. For the United States winning meant doing as much as possible to master physically the NLF while blowing up millions of tons of munitions and supporting an increasingly corrupt but presumably stable RVN. But it never explicitly chose between pacification in place and population displacement or between terror and material blandishments. Rather, in typical American fashion, it sought to apply many diverse programs in tandem. Ideologically incapable of defining a theory that condoned its consistent practice, it preferred justifying its enormous terror from the skies and its uprooting of a rural nation with liberal jargon or, as in the case of an ideologically conservative Huntington, with the social science rhetoric of "modernization." And while the problem of the enormous gap between practice and theory was a lesser cause of America's failure, it does explain how it suffused and obscured its own decision makers' actions and goals and led them to make repeated errors at great cost in time and money. In brief, American-style liberalism encumbered itself again with the dilemmas of being an international policeman, of subsidizing repressive and hated Third World societies, yet of being unwilling because of the ideological legacies of past centuries to perceive itself candidly in terms of its real functions and roles. This intense, even pathological, desire to appear unsoiled to itself and to have those under its yoke esteem it continued throughout the Vietnam War and was a peculiar attribute of the United States' sustenance of police states everywhere.

Meanwhile, in the midst of the smoke and carnage, the pacification program swung into action. The Americans defined and paid for it, restructuring various activities they thought especially important—ranging from the increasing in late 1967 of the Phoenix program to round up and "neutralize" the NLF political infrastructure to the setting up of health dispensaries in various villages. The effort to measure the extent of its success soon became an obsession to Washington, and the Hamlet Evaluation System (HES) became probably its most important index of the direction of the war.

Begun in 1963, the HES was an audacious attempt to assess a complex political and military event statistically with a synthesis of indicators on who controlled a hamlet at the time a monthly report was filed. It was a sign of its accuracy that in the spring of 1965, as Washington committed vast numbers of new troops to prevent a presumed imminent NLF victory, the HES reported that the Revolution controlled only 24 percent of the population. The reporting system was modified at the end of 1966 and again in 1970, when it was admitted that "subjective, spotty reporting" had consistently characterized the HES.[11] From the inception a small part of the American confusion regarding a war they were losing was due to the influence of the HES. Successive administrations consistently used it publicly to defend, sometimes without guile, the efficacy of their war policies, for most key Americans did not understand the nature of revolutionary warfare, much less the NLF's policy of hiding in and remaining symbiotic with the existing RVN structures. It nonetheless consciously misled the public by including marginal hamlets rated "C" as RVN-controlled, thereby being able at the end of 1967 to more than double the pacification successes it claimed while privately acknowledging a "minimal government presence" in "C" hamlets.[12]

As a general rule, however, the vast movement of refugees to cities meant that especially the NLF's strongest regions lost population. The Pentagon's confidential analyses showed that the population drop in NLF hamlets from June 1965 to June 1967 was twice as fast as the decline in the number of hamlets they controlled. But this movement did not mean that the NLF ceased to have access to the masses. By the end of 1968, when the HES indicated that 73 percent of the population was living in relatively secure areas and another 13 percent in contested areas, both the CIA and the State Department privately estimated that the NLF still significantly affected at least two-thirds of the rural population. Even at the end of 1972, when the HES claimed that over 90 percent of the people were under RVN control, Pentagon analysts believed that the NLF infrastructure existed in or close to 71 percent of the population. The RVN itself knew full well that the population, as Major General Tran Dinh Tho, the ARVN's former pacification chief, expressed it after the war, "had to maintain a fence-sitting stance in order to survive irrespective of which side should eventually prevail." Survival, more than any single other factor, meant avoiding U.S. or ARVN firepower, and all villagers told HES officials anything necessary to avoid subsequent attacks. The NLF's logistical system required it to be planted in villages and areas with access to essential commerce, which meant places that the RVN claimed to control. "There were also," General Tho later recalled, "double-agent village cadres who worked for the GVN during the day and reported to . . . the Communist village commissar at night."[13]

The HES system was misleading because of errors of both omission and commission. Guilty of errors of omission were ambitious RVN or U.S. pacification officers who knew that poor data on control would reflect on their unit's accomplishments and automatically lead to a loss of development funds. Most of the American data gatherers spoke little or no Vietnamese, and the compiling of such monthly data on an average of thirty-seven hamlets for each of them was only one of their many tasks. It was common for them to take the word of their RVN associates, who as often as not were pocketing aid funds, and to fill out the forms without visiting the hamlets—sometimes for as long as a year. It was a procedure which Congress exposed repeatedly during the late 1960s. A village was considered "secure" if it had an RVN office. If the office was in a PF outpost and was used by someone who left after dark, the village was still considered secure by one critical measure. If RVN-controlled hamlets bordered NLF hamlets, the NLF was considered not to have a significant presence save in their own territory. In one location a U.S. expert found that hamlets the HES ranked as most secure were the strongest NLF areas, apparently so much so that, rather than visit them, RVN officials filled out the questionnaires themselves from a safe distance. Pro-NLF villagers lying to data gatherers caused errors of commission, knowing this would insulate their work from attacks. It was always in the NLF's interests to deceive the HES analysts, and the HES always pretended to measure not political attitudes but only physical control. "As for gaining the allegiance of the people," the National Security Council admitted early in 1969, "this is almost impossible to measure."[14]

Pacification could not become a matter of statistical measurement, numbers of leaflets dropped, or any of the techniques which so appealed to Washington and which were imposed on its dependents in Saigon. The war was a monumental human, political, and social event whose complex effects required nuanced analysis. Yet it was in this context that responsibility for winning a political and ideological struggle was passed on primarily to the RVN to meet.

THE IMPACT OF THE RVN'S
PACIFICATION

Successive Saigon governments responded to the relentless American pressures on behalf of pacification activities, so that by 1967 they had assigned half of the efforts of the ARVN, and even more of the RF/PF, to the program. But as a former RVN head of pacification euphemistically summed up later, "at the field levels, corps and division, staff officers did not always possess a thorough understanding of the pacification concept and its programs."[15] The RVN's leaders passively acceded to U.S. plans in order to avoid useless arguments and be free to struggle with each other for political control. Programs the Americans thought appropriate were imposed on bewildered or uninterested Saigon officers, and when these invariably failed to implement them quickly, minor U.S. officials took over their supervision.

The most important of these sponsored efforts was the Revolutionary Development (RD) program, which originated with a CIA project created from remnants of Diem's rural cadres. The RD forces eventually peaked at sixty thousand men in 1968, but they were less than half that in 1972, broken down to fifty-nine-man teams dressed in black peasant pajamas and originally supposed to build schools, medical stations, and the like. The ARVN had not been trained to work as a military shield for such units, and there were constant jurisdictional disputes between it and the highly politicized military services, province chiefs, and others. More important, the RD cadres failed to get along with the PF troops who were most directly responsible for their protection. In many cases, PF forces sat by as the beleaguered RD personnel in the same village were attacked. The RD's major preoccupation soon became armed self-defense, and rather than live among the peasants, as had originally been intended, many spent their nights in safe places. By the end of 1967, American experts believed that the RVN had failed to integrate its forces to support pacification, and the RD teams, according to Komer's deputy, were taking a "beating."[16]

The RD program's problem was not merely the coordination of military and nonmilitary action but also the nature of the RD personnel, who created a good part of their own difficulties wherever they went, alienating the local troops who were supposed to defend them and the villagers whom they were to ideologically transform by their deeds and example. The RD cadres' role was merely a reflection of the overall nature of the total RVN governmental system when it attempted to work among peasants: the cadres were mainly urban, educated, and petit bourgeois. The RD program's leaders, according to a former RVN pacification chief, "came mostly from wealthy and influential families, including those seeking refuge from mandatory military service." The cadres arrived in villages and challenged existing RVN political machines with their own bureaucratic systems. They had the city dwellers' contempt for the peasants, and "the abuse of power for personal benefit and the pursuit of worldly pleasures were widespread." "Hard-pressed by soaring prices and meager salaries, they were usually compelled to make ends meet through petty corruption or moonlighting."[17]

The RD program's goal after 1967 to build self-governing village units also failed. As had been true since 1955, few candidates for village office born in the village ever stood for election. Most were "sponsored and introduced by province and district governments" or by local religious groups, according to General Cao Van Vien. "When elected . . . they behaved like henchmen of the district or province chief and local religious leaders."[18] And all those elected had to go for special indoctrination before taking office!

Since the RD program was a failure from the start, its alienation of the peasantry neutralized any possible RVN gains from American military successes. Added to the peasantry's suffering from munitions and the induction of its sons, the pacification program proved to be a political liability for the United States and the RVN even when it impressed many peasants with the futility of further resistance against the massive juggernaut intruding into every aspect of their existence. Such personal resignation before seemingly overwhelming force was a subjective withdrawal not from politics or class issues but only from positive activity. Less personally dangerous support for the NLF was the general outcome. There was growing apathy, U.S. opinion experts warned Washington as early as 1965, but "a somewhat pro–Viet Cong apathy."[19] Most of those who became circumspect and neutral as a consequence of this pressure nonetheless retained, Rand analysts told Washington in 1969, a basic hostility toward the RVN, its actions, and its aims. Their negative feelings, more in "sorrow rather than in anger," toward the NLF were often due to the fact that their presence brought bombings and that they were still too weak to win.[20] In reality, the peasantry was increasingly struggling to survive the vast, fiery assault the United States was mounting—the bombs, the search-and-destroy missions, the loss of sons and daughters to the RVNAF and to brothels, and the very disintegration of a whole social system around them. The need to cope with daily pressures and existence now began to create a cleavage between the peasant and the NLF, to an extent which greatly encouraged America to continue these relentless pressures, but its terror did not strengthen its political alternative. On the contrary, such violence began to alienate and depoliticize, for practical purposes, an increasingly important sector of the south's population— and to create an insoluble political crisis for its RVN dependents from which only the NLF could eventually benefit.

Whatever defeats had been inflicted on the NLF militarily, McNamara by the end of 1966, and the CIA in the course of 1967, concluded that the RD and pacification program, and the "apathetic, inefficient, and corrupt" officials who ran it, created a stalemated situation in which the United States could not win the war.[21] From this point on, the bulk of American decision-makers and even some RVN leaders thought war weariness and apathy were the main peasant responses to their efforts. None deluded themselves that they had won their allegiance. "Efforts to achieve political cohesion and enlist popular support were unsuccessful," General Tho later admitted, in reference to the whole course of the war.[22]

The most important cause of the failure of America's pacification efforts was its mode of warfare and its terrible human impact. Its support for the RVN's political structure was also crucial. These two factors created insurmountable obstacles to success.

THE CHANGING RURAL ECONOMY

Land reform was the central issue of peasant politics during the early 1960s. By the February 1966 meeting with Thieu and Ky, some key Americans thought they had won public support for more rapid land reform. Washington, however, had appropriated no funds for it during 1961–65, $84,000 in 1966, and less than a million dollars the following year—all of it to pay American experts. Komer at first insisted that land reform move forward, even though landlord resistance to it stymied it shortly after the Honolulu conference. The RVN remained opposed to raising the issue. Although the October 1966 Manila declaration promised, "Land reform and tenure provisions will be granted top priority," Komer and most U.S. pacification officials began to waver. In early 1967 Komer no longer considered it important. While most senior American advisers favored land reform throughout this period, in practice the majority opposed any action because of the need to keep the many landlords in the RVN hierarchies from feeling "alarmed and attacked."[23] The pressing of reform, some of them argued, would only intensify the class struggle, and it was more than likely to be maladroitly implemented, and so the United States in practice counseled inaction. Although they complained that the ARVN's pacification successes often led to its collecting back and current rents for well-placed landlords, they were unwilling to strike at the roots of the system. While the RVN's resistance to land reform was undoubtedly the major inhibition, the embassy also believed that reform might topple the RVN regime then in power. A minority of American land reform experts on the scene were horrified by this position. Early in 1967 its opponents produced an astonishingly inaccurate statistical analysis by someone who had never been to Vietnam who argued that land inequality was not a cause of peasant radicalism. Reinforced by the contention that the NLF was merely an organizationally coherent machine whose land reform program had nothing to do with its power, this analysis unquestionably reassured many Americans that the Revolution had no permanent claim to the loyalty of the peasants. Stymied politically by the pretense of scholarship, the advocates of land reform could do no better than commission a massive study of the problem which buried the issue until mid-1969.

Ironically, the enormous structural impact on the rural economy of the war and of U.S. pacification and aid policies began profoundly to alter the land situation before the United States and the RVN chose to reconsider the land issue. Largely unconsciously, such changes created a carrot-and-stick situation for the peasantry, but it was not one which altered its political responses in some measurable way or its basically adversary relationship with the RVN. It did, however, create important new realities to confront both the RVN and the NLF.

The vast flow of refugees to the cities greatly reduced the rural population in large parts of the country, as did the war's deaths and injuries. The expansion of the RVNAF by half a million men between 1964 and 1970, plus a much smaller fraction of that to the PLAF, sharply reduced the most active rural male work force. Older men, women, and children attempted to fill the gaps but never fully replaced the lost males. The result was a shortage of farm labor in the Mekong Delta for the remainder of the war and a sharp increase in their wages.

Despite difficulties with the data, the AID assumed that about 900,000 hectares went out of production from 1964 to 1966. As late as 1973 it estimated that about 560,000 hectares of abandoned farm land still existed. From being a rice-exporting nation in 1964, South Vietnam became an importer of 700,000 tons in 1967. And for most of the war, U.S. rice was sold to the RVN at below world prices in order to prevent a food crisis in the cities. The peasantry, then, had slight incentive to return to rice production, even though American experts knew that the long-term consequences of this trend would be extremely harmful. In effect, after 1966 South Vietnam had both an unprecedented land surplus and an acute shortage of rural labor.

To grow rice was also dangerous, since it exposed peasants to combat. The market for secondary crops—vegetables and fruits—in the cities and in U.S. bases grew enormously, and they fetched far higher prices. Both the Americans and the RVN encouraged secondary crops, providing supplies at low prices, and, given the inflationary economy, the peasants responded to the incentives. Such crops were labor-intensive in small plots near the peasants' houses, minimizing peasant exposure to attack, and now the landlord had less rice on which to levy traditional rents. Because land was plentiful, landlords often were unable to find tenants; they lowered rents and increasingly could not collect them all. By 1966, landlords were redirecting as much of their capital as possible into the urban land and building booms and into service industries catering to Americans. From a purely economic viewpoint, there had been a dramatic shift in favor of the peasant, and he no longer needed land reform. Indeed, reform might even benefit the landlords more than the peasants.

Eager to avoid the complexity and dangers of basic land issues, the AID's advisers tried to improve the unusually backward rural sector in uncontroversial ways. Productivity innovations, involving breeding and new seeds, along with their improved market leverage, had the greatest impact on the peasantry, which needed all the help it could get after the loss of so many of its sons. Pumps and better pigs had a significant effect, but in terms of tractor horsepower South Vietnam lagged even further behind the rest of Southeast Asia than it had before the United States initiated its aid to farm output. Vietnam consumed a great deal of cheap, subsidized American fertilizer, but by regional standards its irrigation system remained very underdeveloped and its use of high-yield rice was only average.

Largely because of high-yield rice, production began climbing after 1968, though never enough to end dependency on cheap American imports. The peasant in this overall context was able to maintain his real income. Some did better and created an illusion of prosperity, which was in reality quite limited to the most successful commercially oriented peasants with access to credit and labor or tractors. But the peasantry was less and less land poor, as landlords now became rent poor. The peasant's most desperate need was for security and survival. At the same time, his economic world was being rapidly transformed in ways that made political tasks far more complex for both the United States and the Revolution. The combination of war, relentless personal tragedies, and technical innovation—the rupture between the past, however troubled, and the rapidly changing present—confronted the peasantry with myriad challenges and confusions.[24]

THE REVOLUTION'S RESPONSE TO PACIFICATION

By 1967 massive American firepower and persistent RVN depredations were imposing almost superhuman pressures on the NLF. Each family in the Revolution's areas had a story of traumas and individual tragedies, and the flight to refugee camps and cities was the single most important consequence of this extraordinary assault. The NLF's response to the great upheaval of a rural society explains to a high degree its capacity to continue in the countryside despite astonishing difficulties.

The altered economic environment of rural South Vietnam was one to which the NLF reacted immediately, since it had as early as 1960 urged peasants to obtain higher wages where there were labor shortages and, of course, to pay lower rents. Notwithstanding the constraints of its formal united-front policy, the NLF after 1965 explicitly became even more of a poor-peasant movement advocating land reform in a setting of growing peasant economic leverage. The middle peasants made up about 30 percent of the rural farm population, the NLF calculated, but the landless and poor peasants were twice that proportion. To the extent the RVN acted as a protector of the larger landlords, the Front's position was inviolable. Despite those rural economic gains after 1966 which reduced the importance of land distribution, the Revolution's prestige among the rural masses remained powerful.

The Front also became a major channel for rural social and economic mobility. As older cadres and key activists were killed or captured, local organizations absorbed outstanding youths, especially from poor families, "in search of personal dignity," as Rand experts informed the Pentagon.[25] Many of their families had received land from the NLF, and the vast web of family and economic common interests between the NLF's local cadres and the people meant that peasants maintained sympathy for the Front even if its organization was driven from the villages. Rand Corporation analyses of the village NLF structure stressed the hopelessness of efforts to uproot it. Despite the immense firepower and hardships the NLF faced, the CIA and the Army from 1967 onward reported that in the populous I and IV Corps regions the local guerillas and the NLF maintained high morale and were immune to all of the many psychological-warfare efforts that were by 1969 having some success among main PLAF and PAVN forces a long way from their homes.

Many of the weaker and potentially most hostile rural elements abandoned their villages early in the war, leaving the remaining population closer to the NLF. But even if U.S. and RVN officials could later admit that "the enemy's capability to recruit and replace surpassed everything we usually attributed to him," the Party itself regarded its situation in the south as much more complex.[26] Its first response to the more physically difficult situation it confronted was to strengthen the cadre system and discipline among its military forces in contact with the villagers. The cadres were exhorted to study harder and maintain higher revolutionary morality. Local cadres assumed ever-greater responsibilities as communications with senior echelons became increasingly difficult after 1966. Given the constant difficulties and dangers they were enduring, the cadres behaved as much like revolutionary idealists and heroes as any people have ever been known to do, becoming the vital core of the political struggle and success in the south until the war ended.

American specialists believed the Party was coping successfully with its problems and capable of persisting indefinitely, but the Party better understood the difficulties of the changes in the rural south, the pressures on peasants, and its own dependency on them. Pacification was one of the few aspects of the war which it rarely analyzed in depth publicly, but at the end of 1967 Tran Van Giau, the Party's most influential southern intellectual, assessed it comprehensively. Fully conscious of the contradictions between the RVN's corruption, U.S. firepower, and a successful pacification program, he nonetheless was deeply concerned about the sheer pressure on the masses both from the destruction and from the efforts to buy them off. Pessimistic about the political fate of the peasants should they abandon their villages for the cities, Giau argued that it was crucial to resist forced evacuation. To this end the cadres had to remain close to the people under all circumstances, and especially to attempt to influence them ideologically and politically. An appeal to their national and local traditions was a critical part of this struggle, for the "traditions represent a force."[27] In fact, Giau and many others saw the political implications of economic and agricultural innovations for the peasants. Peasants welcomed many of the changes in the agricultural economy, and the Party was still not certain how far this process of accommodation or desertion of the land would reach. Eventually, it went further than the Party feared but less far than the U.S. and the RVN needed.

What Giau was considering for the first time was that the Party in the south at its core was now a rural movement and that the urban struggle might not prove decisive in determining the war's outcome. More than that, he believed, the land issue's significance might also be declining, and the Party would gain more by merging energetically patriotic appeals and a defense of the traditionalist rural culture with the Revolution's earlier programs, attempting to stem the disintegration of the social fabric the United States was both consciously and objectively affecting. Even though Giau was expressing his own opinions, they were based on the impressions and experiences of many who had been in the south. In fact, Giau was groping with perhaps the single most important question of the war: the future relationship of the Communists to the masses after almost a decade of a terrible, bloody war that was changing the entire social fabric of South Vietnam.

The relation of the Party to the peasantry by the end of the 1960s was complex and difficult, but no more so than throughout its entire history, for it had been both leader of the rural masses and led by them. Ideally, of course, it sought to fulfill the role of leader as much as possible, but objective conditions often made that dangerous and premature. The Party's power was based on its ability to play the passive as well as the active role, and it repeatedly acknowledged its need to accept guidance from the masses. Throughout the history of the Party, the peasants had frequently initiated action of their own volition, and all the Party could do was to provide a structure to their impulses and desires and, if possible, a direction. Yet the major problem confronting the Revolution after 1968 was less the exploiting of diminishing possibilities than the guarding of what had been gained in the past and surviving the massive assault on the very existence of a rural society. Its role at this stage was not unlike that during numerous earlier periods of crisis, and what the Party provided was *continuity* as much as leadership. Throughout its history its most critical leadership role came not when the peasantry was willing or able to act, when indeed the Party often trailed behind it and attempted to restrain it, but rather when the people were relatively quiescent. Ironically, maintaining its existence in a period when it often was doing scarcely more than remaining in hiding was the time of its greatest leadership as well as difficulty, for by the very act of survival it retained the ability to relate to future historical possibilities. For a revolutionary party to lead when events are favorable for it is far less of a challenge than when defeat and destruction appear imminent, and it is at this point that its finely honed elite qualities prove most crucial.

The rural society the United States hoped to pacify had become far more complicated by the late 1960s than it had been after the Geneva Accords. The Revolution had gained its momentum after 1956 from the land question, an issue that embodied not just the distribution of land but also rents, taxes, and the role of the peasantry in their own villages and society. Combined with the preceding, often less intense Viet Minh experience, the Revolution had over two decades profoundly affected the peasantry's culture, values, and consciousness—so much so, in fact, that both the Americans and the RVN often tried to apply the label "revolution" to their own programs. The network of its personal and family ties was now very large and deep, and it was no longer devastating when RVN or U.S. forces pushed the NLF activists out of a village, for only an elimination of the people would remove the Revolution's influence. The Party had succeeded as a land movement based on one set of social conditions, exposing the peasantry to a radical culture and community. When the conditions which had given rise to it changed, the roots of this political culture remained in a new context. On this foundation it left residues of values and goals far larger than its own organization. Although many of its former supporters became distracted or exhausted by the overwhelming pressures imposed on them, remaining passive for long periods, it was this legacy which made it possible for the Revolution to reconstitute itself repeatedly from 1945 until the war ended. Even as the war and U.S. money undercut the NLF's leadership over the whole spectrum of economic issues and reforms, the peasantry's emerging attitudes toward the Americans and the RVN, its actions and politics, broadened its political consciousness so that the NLF could still lead it even if its appeals changed.

The peasant's somewhat improved economic prospects were meaningless without peace, and this produced an enigma for both the United States and the NLF. The peasantry did not require a sophisticated understanding of the world to see who was using the most munitions to endanger its existence, drafting the most sons, and profoundly undermining a traditional rural order with its enormous challenges and intrusions. The minimum consequence of this widespread attitude was a hatred of Americans and of those who acted on their behalf, and this primal opinion precluded success for the U.S./RVN pacification and political program. While this profound alienation gave the NLF a potential appeal to a new constituency, population losses and class and more complex personal issues nonetheless reduced the NLF's active following by the late 1960s to a smaller group whose exact size varied from region to region but which was never less than approximately one-third of the remaining peasantry. This element provided the NLF's main support until the end of the war, and though it had been much larger at the beginning of the decade, those who remained were also much more committed and more willing to take risks, thereby making the critical difference in the war's outcome.

Next to this group, and never less than a third of the peasantry, was a body of floaters and *attentistes* of the type who become classic survivors in wartime everywhere, as well as those whom the war's toll had exhausted. Their peace was made at once in a typically individual fashion by a growing number of people who believed they were better able to avoid getting hurt if they remained cautious and silent. Given the enormous personal tragedies of so many Vietnamese, the behavior of this element was predictable. Its consistent characteristic, however, was that while "many naturally remained uncommitted to the GVN cause," as General Tran Dinh Tho confessed, very few would do anything to hurt the NLF, but they were often willing to side with it when they thought it was to their advantage.[28] A portion shared with it a consensus on peace, and some had family active with the Revolution. Many also wished to preserve the land reforms the NLF had achieved. The winning over of this group became the NLF's key political objective, if only to keep it from growing larger, but despite the Front's successes and failures with it, at the very least the group's passivity assured the RVN's isolation.

To relate to the rural masses meant creating a local Party structure that would survive all U.S. efforts to root it out, decentralizing and popularizing it at the same time. Decentralization had been a consistent trend since the early 1960s and now reached its final development after 1966, as the liaison of the higher Party organization with the villages was increasingly interrupted. This autonomy and self-sufficiency required the senior levels to urge greater ideological development among cadres. They had no option but to accept the loss of control over the grass-roots organization on a growing number of matters. Marxism-Leninism in this context was for the Party in the south far less an organizational theory and practice than an ideological and political frame of reference—above all, a belief in the autonomous individual's commitment to politics and a radical political vision of one's relationship to immediate realities and a larger movement.

The local Party groups were free to run affairs in a manner best suited to local needs. This led to a high degree of local initiative and democracy, which conformed to the united-front policy the Party increasingly took as its guideline, especially after 1967, when the NLF's strategy was to create a broader coalition than it had yet managed to establish. To some extent this occurred in those places where it took over nominally RVN-controlled village governments and used them as a cover or created a parallel structure. Retaining a clandestine structure, save in wholly NLF villages, was often essential, and this made the policy of building "a democratic regime in a war situation" difficult.[29] The giving of power to the people led to the deaths of more hated local RVN leaders than the Party thought desirable, but it was a price for democracy as well. In strong NLF regions tacit agreements with local RVN administrations were often established, especially, the CIA complained in April 1967, in "many parts" of the southern Mekong Delta.[30]

The NLF made special efforts in the Delta to collaborate with the religious sects. But the general trend was to encourage as much democracy and decentralization as the circumstances allowed. Local NLF organizations were required to respect the physical possessions of all those who were not overtly hostile to the Revolution, preserving the basis of a united front. This meant that the committed and apolitical masses could coexist.

Whatever the problems of the new system, which increasingly exposed low-level cadres to capture, the NLF working among the villagers were by 1969 at least double the size of the RVN personnel assigned to tasks the United States roughly designated as "pacification." At a national level, the NSC ruefully observed in 1969, the RVN infrastructure was thirty times larger, which meant it was clustered almost entirely in safe cities. By June 1971, long after the Phoenix program to destroy the infrastructure was under way, the Pentagon believed that the NLF was still operating among two-thirds of the entire population in one manner or another. Whatever the successes and failures of the two sides, on balance the NLF had found a way to remain deeply rooted among a friendly or neutral population and to foil the U.S. plan to pacify South Vietnam.[31]

Chapter 20

The Character and Consequences of the Two Vietnamese Armies

In a revolutionary and counterrevolutionary war, the nature of the armies is decisive. Such a war is ultimately for the loyalty of the masses, who are influenced profoundly by the rival military systems. An army's political and economic role may be more important over time than its military one. In addition, each side's economic viability is more significant than the outcome of battles.

An army's internal world reflects the social and class system from which it emerges. The functions, actions, and values of officers and soldiers are the inevitable consequences of the kinds of societies they are seeking to create or to defend. This social context defines the character of the officer corps and the soldier, their relationship to each other, and their human, social, and economic impact on the population. Strategy mirrors this reality and in turn weighs strongly on the balance of forces. This framework exerts an overriding influence on soldiers' motivation in battle and an army's ability to endure protracted war. In this vital regard the Vietnam War was from its inception a very unequal battle between radically different kinds of armies.

THE NATURE OF TWO ARMIES:
OFFICERS AND CADRES

After 1963 the RVN's political universe was the officer corps, and politics preoccupied the large majority of senior officers. To become an officer meant one might aspire to social, political, and economic mobility. Being drawn largely from the urbanized, privileged elements, and the relatively well educated, the officer corps was the place for ambitious men. Power, posts, and careers obsessed most of them, and Americans in Saigon often complained about their preoccupations, and especially that able soldiers from poorer social and educational classes were barred from rising to positions of military responsibility.

The junior and middle-ranking officers had numerous economic paths open to them. After the war General Cao Van Vien listed twenty-one common forms of corruption in the RVNAF. They ranged from the misappropriation of funds, the cheating of soldiers of pay or food, kickbacks from contractors, the sale of promotions or safe posts, and the diverting of gasoline or medicine to the private market to the charging of other military units for the provision of transport and even artillery support during combat. The entire ARVN system was corrupt on a daily basis down to the smallest unit. The most widespread sources of gain were the so-called ghost soldiers, who may have accounted for as much as one-quarter—and never less than one-tenth—of its rolls at various times. Ghost soldiers were dead men, deserters, or soldiers who held civilian jobs and whose superiors pocketed their pay and allowance. Thieu himself was a recipient of a share of the vast proceeds from this racket.[1] To a large extent, the relationship of the RVNAF's officers to its soldiers reflected this system of shakedowns, which in turn defined the rapport between the soldiers and the population. Important, too, was the urban or urbanized nature of the ARVN officer corps and the largely rural origins of the soldiers, at least until about 1968, and the enormous gap this created in behavior, attitudes, and communications between them.

The Revolutionary army leadership was, of course, wholly different, being under the tight direction of the political cadres. The Pentagon analyzed the cadre system minutely, and those at the Rand Corporation responsible for the effort quickly developed an awe and admiration for the cadres. The cadres existed at many levels, but the Rand assessments focused on those lower cadres who were captured or deserted, dealing with their work among the rank-and-file combatants.

The political cadres serving in the main forces performed the roles of fathers, brothers, and friends to the soldiers. Their primary task was communication between the various ranks and the soldiers. Their constant discussion, encouragement, and evocation of feelings and fears kept morale high during very difficult hardships. Increasingly drawn from poor-peasant stock in the south, and overwhelmingly rural in origin, the cadres never suffered from the urban-rural dichotomy which divided the ARVN's officers and soldiers. Still, despite their relationship to the troops, they possessed the power to control military decisions at the highest levels if necessary. This prevented officers from losing sight of the political implications of their actions or the needs of their troops. The Party sought to create an army based on "democratic principles," and not merely a pro forma one in which superiors met with their juniors and then went about their business as if nothing had happened. Party military directives made it clear that communication was essential, and while officers had to enforce discipline, they were strictly to avoid "militarist and paternalistic" control.[2] Cadres, ultimately, were in charge of the entire army.

This did not mean that without cadres a human or social barrier would have existed between the soldiers and officers, even though officers were distracted by duties that consumed a great deal of their time. During working hours officers' ranks were strictly adhered to, but after hours all addressed them as elder and younger "brothers" and mingled informally.[3] Nearly all had rural origins, and their pay and style of living naturally precluded the material differences which existed in the ARVN.

The cadres were, of course, ideologically more advanced than the soldiers and were constantly being exhorted to improve themselves, but as the war progressed and cadres came up from the ranks, their personal leadership in combat situations was given somewhat more emphasis. A cadre, above all, was required to be an exemplary individual whom soldiers could respect and follow, but one also able to confess publicly to error so that others would correct their own. The cadre's code of behavior required infinite patience and leadership in cultivating close mutual "love and care" among soldiers as a brother or uncle.[4] It also required that he relinquish "his private life" and traditional family ties and adopt his comrades as family in the interest of the Revolution—the most difficult demand, ultimately, for some cadres to accept for so many years, though the vast majority did so.[5]

Once their personal integrity was confirmed in the eyes of soldiers, cadres worked best by gentle contacts, and even though their capacity to issue orders and require discipline was unquestioned, they were considered failures if they resorted to it. Whether dealing with individuals or small and large groups, the cadre understood that the soldier's fears, anxieties, loneliness, and deprivations were intensely real, and he was to relieve these concerns as much as possible, partly by his own efforts but also by building real solidarity among those who would have to fight together. "The VC army," Rand's experts reported to the Pentagon after interviewing hundreds of former combatants and cadres, "seems strikingly undisciplined, with persuasion rather than order, forebearance rather than punishment, the generally applied rule."[6]

The Party repeatedly stated that motivation and morale was "always the decisive factor" in combat, and strengthening it became the objective of the Party's entire military organization.[7] The Party's military line was extremely clear: "It is most important to ensure the practice of military democracy and political mobilization before and after each battle. . . . If it is carried out well, it can develop the collective combat strength, and heighten the troops' sense of being masters, friendship, unity, sense of discipline and mutual trust. If it is carried out in a superficial manner or not carried out, victory will be greatly hampered."[8] Some units had military councils with representatives of cadres, officers, and soldiers to methodically discuss operations, and in all units the cadres were required to maintain the interaction between all levels before and after combat. Rather than endanger morale, cadres occasionally canceled some actions when the majority of soldiers objected. The communications built into the system assured that the maximum number possible would feel a sense of responsibility for military operations.[9]

THE RANK-AND-FILE SOLDIER

The recruits in both the ARVN and the PLAF and PAVN were fairly homogeneous at the beginning of the war, but the ARVN's soldiers were increasingly drawn from the ranks of urban poor. Its officers were largely urban in origin. Apart from the urbanized army's uncanny inability to fight at night or to communicate effectively with peasants, there was the ARVN's typically urban dependence on motor travel. The ARVN's main problem, however, was that its draft, at least in the American view, was scandalously unfair. As the army grew larger, it scoured the nation, particularly the cities, for those too weak to escape it. The impressed soldiers brought with them the habits and values of an urban system in the process of decomposing, including street mores and a knack for surviving as an individual. The ARVN recruits from rural backgrounds were soon exposed both to the urban habits of their fellow soldiers and to the cities.

The PLAF was a far smaller army, and much more select. Even the Rand studies indicated that its members joined the struggle "in order of importance [because of] personal socio-economic frustration; GVN oppression; VC recruiting devices; issues of social justice; pressure of family and friends; miscellaneous reasons."[10] They also tended to be better educated and of higher intelligence, and they had the most to gain from the NLF's winning. It was a powerful basis for an army. The Revolution and the RVN created forces very different from each other.

The social nature of the ARVN made it unique, for it was really a quasi-civilian structure made up of impressed soldiers increasingly compelled to survive by their wits. Even as the RVN's leaders and officers were exploiting the system, they also managed partly to transform the regular army into a social instrument with calamitous military and sociopolitical implications.

The ARVN, unlike the Revolution's soldiers, usually did not live and fight as a social unit. By 1968, 23 percent of the ARVN was earning additional income outside the army. Others were also ghost soldiers. In brief, they were not full-time soldiers. All ARVN members had to stay in the army until the age of forty-five; consequently, 46 percent had their families living with or near their units. The ARVN kept most soldiers in the general region in which they were recruited for these reasons, and this helped deprive the army of a strategic reserve and mobility. In 1968, 74 percent of its personnel were married. These married soldiers each had an average of 3.9 children. Put another way, in 1968 the wives and children of the RVNAF amounted to about three million persons, or 17 percent of the entire southern population! The number living with or near their husbands or fathers was well over a million and possibly as high as 1.8 million, which meant that in addition to their static strategy the RVNAF was always weighed down in or near its bases by a number of relatives considerably larger than the army itself. And this sad mass of poor people was to grow both absolutely and relatively after 1968.

Married personnel from the rank of sergeant up could live outside the base. While this solved certain morale problems, it created others. Many ARVN soldiers did not eat together, and cooking took an inordinate amount of their attention. In 1968, 42 percent of all ARVN units did not have a cooking service of any kind, and soldiers had often to pool their money to prepare their own food. Much of the army's time was spent in coping with such difficulties.[11]

For the Revolution, the maintenance of morale under conditions of awesome challenges and deprivations was critical to survival, becoming a major factor in shaping the life of the army. To a remarkable degree, soldiers related to each other and created a surrogate family, "just like brothers in a family," as the captured diary of one of them put it.[12] The cadres tried to help the soldiers overcome their individual, self-contained fears and anxieties and to give them a sense of collective strength and wisdom to meet challenges. "Self-consciousness" not for egotistical purposes but to comprehend their relationship to political and ideological realities was the basis of discipline and motivation.

Self-criticism sessions were encouraged, despite their problems. They often became very personal and embarrassed and alienated a small group on most occasions. Nevertheless, the barriers to communication eroded, and soldiers increasingly identified with each other's needs and aspirations. Such public self-criticism and criticism was often substituted for punishment of serious military offenses, including desertion and a refusal to fight. The Party believed that in acknowledging individuals' weaknesses openly it could also maximize their collective strength.

Soldiers entered the army in the south under varying conditions. If they were northerners, they often underwent great hardships traveling south.

Malaria was widespread. Adjusting to the climate was also a problem. Making efforts to "welcome recruits in such a way that they have the impression that they are members of this family" was a recurrent theme.[13] Veterans and new soldiers were combined into three-man cells which lived together as a nuclear social unit and whose members aided each other in every way. This basic unit of the entire army was highly successful in providing continuity and in sustaining morale. Although the RVNAF attempted to imitate it, it failed completely.

The lives of the Revolution's soldiers intertwined constantly, and as a total experience the army involved as many of their needs as was possible under difficult conditions. Cooking was a special concern, and there was a great deal of discussion of the need for troops to eat well. Among the captured or deserting Revolutionary soldiers, praise for the cooking was always high. Preparation of especially delicious meals before offensives was common, and even during combat good food was frequently available. Needless to say, the army ate together whenever possible. When there was little to eat, the troops shared what there was.

The PAVN and PLAF military leadership sought to protect soldiers from excess risks precisely so that their confidence would not be sapped for protracted war. Revolutionary forces fought relatively seldom. Battalions fought only two to three times a year on the average, generally for a short period, and usually only after a careful study of each action and even a partial rehearsal of it. Small-unit operations were more frequent, but their dominating the initiative in combat and the exposure to risks allowed the soldiers to analyze and correct their errors after each battle and, if necessary, to rebuild their morale. Several weeks after a losing engagement the spirits of units were generally as high as ever. Warned of difficulties before they went south, soldiers from the DRV particularly needed to be introduced to the realities of war in a controlled manner. Those from the south comprehended local conditions better and were the more highly motivated.

The Revolutionary army sought to engage the total consciousness of each soldier. The army advocated revolutionary ethics and morality, of course, but also made explicit the most sensitive of all questions to each man, the meaning of life and death. "A communist is a revolutionary combatant who loves life very much," a senior officer explained in 1967. "Yet, when need be, he is willing to and dares make sacrifices, because he clearly understands the reasons for life and death."[14] Social solidarity, ultimately, required such a commitment, and the hardships of the present were essential for happiness in the future. It was crucial for soldiers to believe that they were fighting for a just cause. Many poor peasants knew that success would provide material security and justice for their families and villages. The

Party sought constantly to internalize such values among as many soldiers as possible, repeatedly acknowledging that the most powerful army was a politically conscious one.

The Revolutionary army also encouraged each individual to find personal expression and consolation in ways that ultimately transcended even his comrades and the cadres. Part of the Revolutionary army's soldiers grew up during the anti-illiteracy drive following the August Revolution. A great number kept intimate personal diaries, which the Americans often found on dead or captured soldiers. Many soldiers hoped to preserve the memory of the experience as a form, even, of immortality, and in them soldiers talked to themselves, reflecting on events and preserving confidence as a way of confronting dangers. Some also wrote poems, and these diaries revealed an aesthetic sensibility in the face of war for which there are few, if any, parallels.

The PAVN's and the PLAF's officers understood the importance of this mode of expression to combatants. Not only did some soldiers write their own poems, but many larger units had writers attached to them who were expected, even required, to produce poems. Once written, their verse was commonly criticized and revised by the soldiers, and this created a dialogue of immeasurable value to them. Dramatic and theatrical groups also visited troops, and soldiers gave their own artistic performances. ARVN units had no comparable collective experiences; fewer than a fifth ever had organized recreation in any form. The Party maintained and deepened a community culture and poetry that was already embedded in rural Vietnamese society, but it also respected the boundaries of privacy beyond which each person had to make his own commitments and define his own values. Such experiences and relations cannot be assigned any specific importance, but they existed to reinforce morale.

Vital, too, was the Revolutionary soldier's sense of the balance of forces and of his cause's chances of winning. His perception was the object of extensive, systematic political education, which consumed at least two nights a week for ordinary soldiers and as much as a third of the officers' time. Informal discussion made it even more extensive. But the average soldier knew a great deal about realistically assessing the importance of various factors that would shape the outcome of the war, including the assets and limitations of the enemy's vast firepower. Politics became the average soldier's link with understanding his own future, and there is little doubt that such education fostered higher commitment and motivation. American interrogators were dismayed to learn that two-thirds of their prisoners still believed the NLF would win the war.

The Revolutionary army's approach was, on the whole, very successful. The Americans who confronted it directly understood its effects but never its causes, and this was best summed up by a Special Forces major who, under siege in October 1965, described his attackers as "the finest soldiers I have ever seen in the world except Americans." He added, "I wish I knew what they were drugging them with to make them fight like that. They are highly motivated and highly dedicated."[15]

Soldiers on both sides deserted. While the Revolution spent a minor amount of time encouraging RVNAF desertions, the U.S. Army and the RVN allocated significant resources to their Chieu Hoi (Open Arms) program, which promised NLF and DRV defectors a pardon, training, and even jobs. Apart from believing in the political value of the program, the United States calculated that in 1969 it was spending $60,000 to kill each main-force enemy soldier, but only $350 on each defector. Communist defectors numbered 108,000 persons between 1965 and 1971, fewer than 200 of whom were high-level officers and fewer than 1,000 middle-level personnel. Less than a fifth of the Revolutionary defectors were regular forces. The average deserter was an ordinary local guerilla with a grievance or, more likely, unable to endure separation from his family or the hardships of war. If he chose to return to the Revolutionary army after an interval, he often could do so, and apparently a significant number did. The RVN failed to keep most of its promises, and former NLF soldiers usually found life in the RVN zones difficult. Given the vastly greater physical dangers and daily rigors confronting the Revolution's soldiers, its relatively minor desertion problems testify to the effectiveness of its organization and purpose and its ability to guard its men from the strains of prolonged conflict. Beginning in 1967 the Revolution assigned some men to "rally" and then join local PF units or to take up posts in cities. By late 1970 the United States considered such false "converts" a growing menace.

Desertion was always a far more serious problem for the RVN than for the Revolution, if only because most of its deserters remained on the payrolls and their officers collected their pay. It was often impossible to know the strength of units being sent on military operations. The ARVN's desertion rates were far higher than those of the PF or RF, who were close to their homes and better able to cope with both their economic and their personal problems. The RVN's proportionate loss of its main-force combat units was much greater than the Revolution's, and it posed a grave military threat to it. ARVN soldiers left for economic and family reasons, seldom political, and almost never went over to the Revolution. And they tended to desert before the combat season, when they were needed most. To some extent, the vast size of the RVNAF was due to desertions, which numbered 113,000 men in 1965 and 132,000 in 1972 alone—and nearly one million men over that entire period. About 150,000 draft-age men each year replaced them and some military losses, but the turnover was a constant source of difficulty. In an average year the ARVN lost 30 percent of its combat strength through desertions. Poorly led and trained, ARVN battalions throughout the war usually went into combat with at least 25 percent fewer men than they were entitled to. Desertions and soldiers killed in combat were extensively under-reported. As the war progressed, the deserter problem grew, and the combat efficiency of the ARVN declined with it. Relative to size, the desertion rate of the entire RVNAF was always two to three times that of all the Revolution's military forces. Among crucial regular combat units, it was at least twenty times greater, sometimes even twice that.[16]

THE CONSEQUENCES OF TWO ARMIES: SOLDIERS AND SOCIETY

The social system and function of each army determined the manner in which it related to the population, and the extent to which each could mobilize it for the larger political cause. The Revolutionary army confronted the tension between the individual soldier, discipline, and his family by explaining that "personal and family interests are closely associated and jibe with the national and class interests."[17] Success for the cause would bring personal happiness; the Party never confined this position to rhetoric but always shaped its land policy to reinforce it. Soldiers' families received first priority for land distribution, an extremely powerful incentive. In the case of soldiers from the south, the large portion from poor-peasant backgrounds revealed the importance of this factor in the mobilizing of fighters. But in addition to this basic reward, which was effective mainly with southern soldiers, families of those from the DRV were formally insulated from numerous problems—and to a much smaller extent this was true of PLAF soldiers as well. PAVN soldiers' families, dependent parents, and children were paid fixed sums monthly. If a soldier was killed or wounded, his family was protected and his children were given preference for education and jobs. In the south the NLF attempted under far more difficult conditions to aid the families of killed and wounded soldiers.

The RVNAF soldier was in an entirely different position, not least because some of the worst corruption known to the RVN debilitated the organizations administering benefits to military families. Both the military and the economic implications of this situation were obvious, although it was not until April 1972 that the first major panic and rout as a result of soldiers' families fleeing combat in the I Corps occurred. Meanwhile, every married RVNAF soldier had to cope with his family responsibilities, and this increasingly consumed his time. Family allowance and housing pro-grams disappeared with inflation and senior-level corruption, and the giant

RVN military force was left increasingly with the problem of providing for itself as well as its families.

The sheer size and economic implications of the RVN's military system, with the vast social and human problems it created, can hardly be overemphasized, since in a protracted war the socioeconomic viability of an army is ultimately much more decisive than its capacity to win or lose battles. The RVNAF soldier, whatever his fighting quality, was consciously subjected to intolerable and ultimately decisive pressures. He was deliberately allowed to slide down the economic ladder in order to keep him from draining the RVN budget. By 1969, as I noted earlier, the average soldier's real income was less than a third of its 1963 level, and his purchasing power continued to decline until 1975. Had military salaries kept up with inflation, between 1963 and 1969 the share of the gross domestic product going to the military budget would have been at least 50 percent higher, according to American experts dealing with the problem, and it was already 16 percent and far higher than the economy could tolerate. The war, again to cite Arthur Smithies's analysis of it in 1970, was "being financed in Viet-Nam partly by the levy of a heavy implicit tax on the public sector, civilian as well as military."[18] The importance of this arid proposition was monumental; apart from the suffering it meant for those being "taxed," it was one of the most critical factors leading to the Revolution's victory.

How would the civilians and soldiers and their families pay? It was scarcely a clinical, impersonal experience, for the economic compulsions of an increasingly moribund society broke down the human solidarity and individual dignity of each soldier, subjecting him to degradation and deprivation on a daily basis. Soldiers were always short of money. In 1968 two-thirds exhausted their pay before the twentieth of every month, and less than a fifth made it through the month. Over a third were in debt. When they went out on operations, an average of 38 percent reported, they experienced food shortages. Most could not support their families, and, as several RVN generals later observed, many had to live with the fact of "wives turning into bar girls, and daughters into prostitutes."[19] Nearly a quarter were by 1968 working part-time outside the army. Some ghost soldiers simply made deals with their commanders to keep their salaries and showed up only during unit strength audits or inspections. Family obligations and loyalties, above all, became a constant source of demoralization and corruption.

The relationship of each army to the people was based both on ideology and on necessity. The Revolutionary armies were highly indoctrinated in how to deal with the civilian population, and every squad leader carried a guide on the matter, with its famous "12 points of discipline," which was continually being read aloud and memorized. Bathing, sleeping, religious mores—nothing escaped notice. Food was never taken or bought if the peasant refused to give it, and soldiers were often to work in exchange for it. This aspect of the Revolution's discipline exceeded all others, and infractions were most likely of all to lead to serious penalties. The soldiers were told that the peasants were suffering in the same struggle and yet were giving unhesitatingly for its success.

On an operational level, the RVNAF neither could nor would concern itself with the position of the peasants or people. In the RVNAF, as one of its own analysts later admitted, "little thought was given to the political results or side-effects of any operation."[20] The ARVN's reliance on firepower hit the civilian population hardest, and the ARVN's generals knew this. Confirmed reports of its use of torture of civilians began to appear no later than 1961, and ARVN officers conceded afterward that the PF was notoriously trigger-happy. Defoliation operations especially alienated the peasants, but the cordoning and searching of villages was standard procedure and, naturally, was resented just as much. Key American leaders were worried by 1967 that the RVNAF was victimizing the people, but the war was being fought on their model and under the economic constraints that their economic planners and the RVN's corrupt leaders imposed on the lowly soldiers.

Under the French the collaborationist soldiers had become habituated to what an ARVN general later described as "looting, arson, rape," and this image of the RVNAF persisted in the minds of the people because it never changed its ways.[21] The soldier collected his "tax" from the people throughout the war, and looting persisted as a pervasive, systematic aspect of all RVNAF activities. "The problem of petty pillaging among combat soldiers defied solution," two ARVN officers later commented.[22] Petty larceny, threats, extortion, and shakedowns were regular occurrences. "Low-level looting," the National Security Council concluded in early 1969, "has long appeared to be endemic among RVN units throughout the country." It was not, they added, penalized in any way, and it was obvious to the Americans that it had "undermined the confidence of the people."[23] Arbitrary beatings, too, were common.

The RVNAF was composed of poor men who had been mainly impressed into becoming impoverished mercenaries. They and their families, 22 percent of the entire South Vietnamese population by 1968, were among the most highly oppressed, disoriented, and marginal people in the war. The Revolution sought to appeal to them on the basis of their class position but rarely succeeded, for U.S. policy and their superiors' corruption were making them survivors in a relentless war. Like all such marginalized, lumpen elements everywhere, they wrested as much as they could from other poor people. The army's scavenging and robbery imposed an enormous economic tax on the peasants, not merely because of incessant looting but also because they could see that their own sons and daughters were at once victims and victimizers. This condition exacted an immense economic toll and altered a traditional way of life very quickly. By the late 1960s a growing number of peasants who had been pro-NLF were emotionally and physically exhausted by the war and awed and cowed by the ferocious U.S. and RVN military machines, and this significantly increased passivity and circumspection among many of them. As a group they did not transfer their loyalties to the RVN, much less aid it, for its corruption and alienation were wholly foreign to a way of life suffused with either traditional or radical values—and both influenced the peasants. The catalytic impact of the U.S.-sponsored "modernization," with its economic tax and social values, built a huge reservoir of hostility which wholly neutralized all pacification efforts. It also continued to goad a significant number of young people to join the Revolution both for traditional reasons and out of a desire to maintain their personal humanity and values.

The military in the Third World is never a neutral institution either politically or socially. Its very nature, size, and human role carry immense implications for any dependent nation. Seen as a simple instrument of combat, in which weapons, men, and their use are measured, it appeals even today to its American sponsors whose conventional comprehension of war as an integrated political, social, and human process is extremely limited. Yet when the RVN's forces grew, the capacity of the social structure to digest them declined; as it became stronger in material terms, it thus became less capable of defeating a lean, effective, and integrated Revolutionary opponent. By the late 1960s the social forms and consequences of the total system that the United States and the RVN had created were beginning to corrode the foundation of their entire effort.

Chapter 21

The Communist Party's Responses to Total War

The Communist Party in Vietnam existed both as a state north of the seventeenth parallel and as a resistance movement south of it, and its ability to fight the war reflected the strength and weaknesses in the south as well as the power of the northern-based Party which guided it. This indissoluble linkage of the Party in two geographic sectors, dating back to 1930, was much more important than the real differences in style and objective circumstances in the regions. The north, as it never ceased to proclaim, was the great rear base of the war in the south, and as the ranks of the NLF thinned, the DRV committed all the men and resources necessary to continue a common struggle. But the essential distinction between the regional parties was that the north was a state in power, with the myriad opportunities and problems that such power imposed, whereas the southern Party was a highly adaptive entity always responding to the conditions in which it operated. It was at one and the same time a clandestine organization, an autonomous administrative entity, and symbiotic with the enemy—anything but a formal bureaucratic system in a reasonably stable context.

The DRV had, of course, evolved through the same phases until 1954. Its resistance ethic was solidly implanted among men who had led the Party since the precarious years before the Geneva Accords. These leaders were concerned that power, and the officials who accompanied it, would blunt the Party's successful revolutionary élan. It had defeated the French because of its capacity to identify and use social and political issues to mobilize the masses under the Party's leadership. But in the process of doing so, the Party had at critical times responded to pressures from below, and this often produced dilemmas it later had to resolve. The most important of these had been land reform; another had been its determination to create a mass party of the proletariat in a nation without a working class and despite a Leninist organizational theory which had originally been formulated for a very small party and which, from its genesis, had stressed that every member should attain elite standards.

Certain problems the Party faced in the early 1960s were not qualitatively different from those of the preceding decade. It had to mobilize the maximum possible from a very poor agrarian economy to develop the nation for peace as well as war, and the only way it could overcome the constraints poverty imposed was to harness the masses' energy and commitments to larger social goals. This interaction of the Party with the people, both explicitly leading and in reality also following them, had been the motor of the Revolution until the massive American invasion of the south, and it would remain its formula for success for the remainder of the war.

THE DRV: ECONOMIC AND ORGANIZATIONAL POLICIES

To confront the struggle for land was the single most important challenge as well as opportunity for the Party throughout the 1950s, and if it had not resolved the problem in the DRV by the early 1960s, its ability to respond to the upheavals in the south would have been far more limited. The concerns that this had not yet been accomplished sufficiently had caused a section of the Party's leadership to oppose too large a commitment to the southern Party's struggle, but it was eventually swept along by mass action and the force of circumstances in the south. The DRV's cooperative movement had managed to create social unity and consensus within the once bitterly divided northern peasantry while avoiding a return to inefficient, parcelized agriculture.

At the beginning of the 1960s, the DRV had committed itself to industrialization, with emphasis on heavy industry, but it always recognized that simultaneous agricultural development was necessary to achieve it. By 1965, however, the war, particularly the prospect of American bombing, had changed its priorities to an emphasis on food production essential to the DRV's continuing the struggle. In 1965, 90 percent of the peasants were in co-ops, the majority of which were now organized on socialist lines. Agricultural production grew moderately during 1961–63, but the war threatened to undermine the rural sector unless steps were taken to compensate for the loss of men to the army.

The DRV solved its dilemma by mobilizing women much more extensively, so that in 1967 they composed 70 percent of the rural work force. More important for the long run, it undertook to expand greatly the irrigation system in the north and the use of pumps. Between 1965 and 1972 mechanization, new rice strains, and fertilizers increased rice output per hectare even as the land under cultivation declined slightly. Despite all the economic traumas of the war, DRV agricultural production from 1965 to 1971 remained stable and began to grow substantially thereafter. Thanks to this supply, supplemented with food aid from China and the USSR, per capita food consumption in the DRV rose significantly from 1965 to 1972.

The existence of co-ops and modernization, which greatly increased the state's role in overall planning, allowed it to give major responsibilities to local village party groups as well as to non-Party government organs. The leadership encouraged such local initiative, especially urging grass-roots participation. Peasant income grew, and some co-ops chose to make as much as they could, while a private market, which fluctuated in size with the state's policies toward it, always persisted. What was most significant was that the DRV's food system worked adequately and that the most dangerous problems of a peasant society had been resolved in a socially responsive and productive fashion.[1]

Agriculture, by definition, was a decentralized sector, but the DRV's industrial economy was further regionalized throughout the period after 1964, when already nearly half of the industrial and artisanal output was accounted for regionally. The Party correctly believed that local state industries were primitive technically and relatively inefficient in peacetime. Given the inherited underdevelopment and wartime realities, though, they were extremely valuable. They were managed provincially and locally after 1965, they used mainly their own raw materials, and their output required little transport. Above all, they were difficult for the Americans to bomb. Often involving little more than a small forge or a few machine tools in a hut or cave, this largely artisanal system produced everything from agricultural tools to pottery and electric motors, and from 1964 to 1973 its output grew by nearly two-thirds, as the centralized state sector's production fell sharply because of massive bombing. While total production in the north recovered after 1968, the wartime improvisation sacrificed the dynamism and balance which had marked the DRV's industrial growth between 1956 and 1964.

It was in the area of transport that the DRV's war economy accomplished most, allowing the north to supply the south as well as allocate its own resources rationally. It was also the achievement which most disturbed the United States, which committed vast resources to destroying it. From 1964 to 1968 the DRV's road system more than tripled and continued to grow until the war ended, and despite the destruction of virtually every bridge in the DRV at least once and the constant air attacks on the railroads, the tonnage the entire transport system carried from 1964 to 1972 dipped only slightly during 1967–68 and then returned to the prebombing level. Also important was the DRV's creation of technically competent personnel to help guide its responses to wartime challenges. Between 1960 and 1969 it trained nearly 400,000 people, ranging from skilled workers to higher scientific and technical experts. Since this sector was recruited from the peasantry, it was an occupationally mobile element deeply committed to the society that had provided it with such opportunities. At the same time, expansion of the entire education system continued, particularly at the higher levels.

Whatever the limits of the DRV economy, the most remarkable thing about it is that it survived. Motivated, creative, yet highly autonomous, the people of the DRV responded successfully to the needs of the nation in wartime. Given the integral connection between the success in the north and the war in the south, the Party's ability to cope with the enormous legacies of underdevelopment and of the destruction of its still fragile modern industrial economy was a critical factor in determining the war's outcome. The secret of its success was mass mobilization.[2]

THE DRV AND MASS MOBILIZATION

One of the most important differences between the war with France and the war with the United States was that while the same men led the Party, its members in the north and south were becoming increasingly distinctive in terms of their local Party's internal life and styles of existence. The southern Party was clandestine, and the risks there demanded immeasurably greater personal commitments. Older Party members in the north had shared the dangers of political activism in the past, of course, and many went to the south to resume it; yet in the north their daily experiences were incomparably different. Southern Revolutionaries were highly motivated and devoted, informal, and forced to make correct decisions quickly on matters which frequently involved their lives and those of their comrades. As the war proceeded, local Party leaders in the south assumed ever-greater responsibilities in their regions and were daily in much closer contact with the masses than was the southern senior Party hierarchy, whose need for security greatly constrained them.

To be a Party member in the north was a social asset and a potential source of authority, and the Party's leaders were quite aware that its huge size—over 500,000 members in 1960—offered ambitious people the possibility of abusing power. The criteria for Party membership in the north were less high, new members' motives and commitments more opaque, the tests required after 1948 far lower than they were in the south. Despite the expulsion of many members over the following decade, the Party's leaders remained very concerned about improving the quality of the rank and file. Aware that the ingenuity, energy, and commitment of the people alone could win the war, it had by 1965 no tool comparable to land reform in the 1953–54 period to galvanize them to undertake greater efforts. The Party embarked on an ambitious effort, without acknowledging it in so many words, to transcend the constraints of a Bolshevik elitist organizational structure and theory through what it called the "mass line."

The Party had always advocated staying close to the masses and seeking their opinion, but the intensity of the position generally fluctuated with what the Party needed from the people and with the problems it was anxious to resolve. Party membership after 1960 was to triple to nearly 1.6 million over the next decade and a half, and it was important to select the new members from among the best candidates. The mass line also implicitly subsumed the creation of a mass party, a policy which greatly diluted the Party's exclusiveness. After 1965 the "mass line" was a question of urgently decentralizing operational power and responsibility so that the war effort could be more effective. The facts that the army was draining off many of the traditional local leaders and that women were taking up tasks without the same degree of self-confidence required a much greater assertiveness on the part of the new local activists. The DRV's problems were especially serious in villages, where Party membership was traditionally sparse and a revitalizing of the village people's councils and entire state managerial system was essential.

After mid-1966 the Party's leaders sought, in repetitive, detailed public statements, to mobilize the masses for war and purify the burgeoning Party at the same time. The revolution was not, To Huu argued, the monopoly of the Party, but "primarily a matter concerning the laboring masses." The Party was the general staff of the struggle, but its success "depends on whether or not the basic organizations of the Party can mobilize, gather, and organize the masses to be active with them."[3] Party members therefore had to know how to listen to the people, stress the masses' mastery of their situation, aid them, and rely on the progressive elements among them. Socialist democracy, *Nhan Dan,* the Party daily, declared in April 1967, was dictatorial only in relation to recalcitrant members of the old ruling class or to those opposed to socialism, but the rights and benefits of the people were inviolate, and the Party was their servant. The streamlining of socialism and resistance to the United States required the democratic enthusiasm of the entire population.[4]

MAINTAINING PARTY PURITY

The Party's policy toward the masses was the key to two crucial dimensions of the war. First, and foremost in terms of its implications, was its role in motivating people to devote their time and, if necessary, their lives to the defense of the country. The Party knew that without the people's working long hours under primitive conditions, after work standing guard against aircraft, joining the army—that without such sacrifices the war would be lost. Next, the rapidly expanding Party could not master alone the new administrative responsibilities of the total struggle. And the masses were best able to keep a rein on the Party's raw new recruits.

While the Party's highest leaders always stated that the Party should have absolute control, their justification for their establishment of the dictatorship of the proletariat was not its ability to impose its will on the people but rather the people's support for the Party's leadership standards and its closeness to the masses. As Le Duc Tho put it, "The biggest danger every ruling proletarian party must try to avoid is this bureaucratic and order-giving evil and being separated from the masses."[5]

These themes were almost identical to those of the decade after the August Revolution, and the Party reprinted some of Ho Chi Minh's statements from that period. The "mass line" included the people's right to attack the bureaucratic practices of Party members, to resist having certain candidates imposed on them from on high during elections, and the obligation of cadres to create a real dialogue. By working with the masses, the lower-level Party members could learn from them as well as teach them, and while it was the base-level Party organization which was most often admonished, the higher Party organs were also warned of their responsibility should the relation between the base Party and the people become bureaucratic. Meanwhile, though the Party members were instructed to mind their manners while talking to people and "resolutely oppose bureaucracy and authoritarianism," they could not neglect the work that had to be done.[6] The Party had to strike a balance between its ultimate hegemony and the people's rights, between efficiency and consensus, and while the Party was fully aware of this tension in its position, it also knew that only by striving for and attaining a workable equilibrium could it hope for success.

The leadership considered criticism from the masses and Party members' self-criticism before them an essential means of preventing authoritarianism in the DRV, and by the mid-1960s it was a standard aspect of the Party doctrine. While the Party's press periodically urged more self-criticism, it was, at best, only very partially successful in the north. Like people everywhere, many disliked criticism, particularly in public, and those who needed self-criticism least practiced it most. The major targets of criticism were the base-level cadres, most of whom in the late 1960s were relatively new members, and they were most often encouraged to engage in self-criticism. The dual practice, however debatable its fulfillment, was the most important means of ideological enforcement the Party had.

The poverty of the DRV notwithstanding, its mass line and mobilization proved to be a highly effective way to make the society relevant and efficient, and had it been anything less, its very survival might have been endangered —at the least it could not have sustained the war in the south. Theory and practice therefore produced a fresh synthesis, and whatever else the Party accomplished, its efforts helped minimize the bureaucratic excesses which marked all other Marxist-Leninist parties in power, and it was rational by any criterion. The Party, then, coped, adapted, cajoled, and admonished the people and its own ranks to find the means by which to organize and mobilize the masses for a popular struggle. However variable the system that emerged, and whatever its deficiencies and contradictions, the DRV was by 1968 a highly integrated society based on mass consensus.

Cadres and Party members in the south were scarcely in need of reminders on how to relate to the masses, and the southern Party's problems were very different. Its civilian activists were remarkably committed, tough people, and their personal and political lives were largely inseparable. The masses, rather than other Party cadres, often provided the only human contact they had, and rapport with them was essential to their survival. As the war became longer, their connections with higher Party levels were greatly reduced and their responsibilities and scope for initiative grew. Party civilian cadres often did not know each other, for security reasons, and at meetings they sometimes masked their faces. Living in three or four different houses to avoid detection, rarely able to see their families, they made the struggle their very life. Most attained the Vietnamese Party's ideal of being revolutionary individuals able to continue working on their own momentum. Their loyalty and persistence during periods when the masses were relatively inactive and the war most dangerous, particularly 1969–72, was a remarkable feat of human commitment, critical to the Revolution's success and the outcome of the war.

The Party leadership's goal in the DRV was to cultivate new cadres comparable to the astonishing people who had developed in the south and to keep those who had performed equivalent deeds before 1955 from losing these precious traits. Raising their quality and knowledge was essential, given the basically elite standards the Party's leaders prescribed for them. Members were expected to spend a great deal of time obtaining ideological training, especially if they were cadres. Party leaders asked them to develop a wide variety of practical skills, while striving to work as generalists. The ideal Party member was constantly studying. No matter how good a member or cadre, he was expected always to attempt to overcome shortcomings. Most important was the development of members ready to put the interests of the Revolution before their private desires. "In a rather large number of cases," To Huu noted in 1971, this was a real problem.[7]

The Party's members were initially drawn from the petite bourgeoisie, the intelligentsia, and, increasingly, the peasants—most of whom were fairly well off by Vietnamese standards. Residues of these classes' individualism persisted, and while the Party thought that class background did not predetermine a person's destiny neither could the Party dismiss it casually. Regardless of the recruits' class background, the Party's leaders knew they would always have ambitious people to cope with. Criticism and self-criticism or education was intended to solve most of such problems, but the Party admitted that its task would be easier if it could find good people who had been tested by experience. Here it came back to the masses' opinion, since it was at the lower levels that positive human qualities and talents were most likely to be discovered. While there were other ways to recruit members, the Party considered the proposals and evaluations of the masses as important as any other method to neutralize the preponderance of those from educated and more affluent families. By the late 1960s the Party was also aware that its failure to recruit more women had been a serious error at a time when they played an increasing role in the civilian labor force.

In practice the Party never managed to solve all its problems, but it freely acknowledged them as real and sought to meet them as best it could. That was to prove sufficient. In trying to reconcile the demands of discipline and criticism, the Party sought to guard the assets of both, its stress on the right to criticize being much greater than the extent to which criticism actually changed policy. The Party justified unity and discipline on the explicit assumption that leaders made the correct decisions, and in order to do so they had to receive criticism. Leadership had to crystallize collective intelligence, and its capacity to do this was held to be the ultimate legitimation of its authority and right to demand compliance.

In fact, however, since the Politburo's members often had fundamental disagreements on policy, its insistence on consensus within its own ranks required it to adopt eclectic policies so frequently that the lower Party ranks were often free to interpret the meaning of central directives quite differently —an ambiguity that was to prove particularly troublesome on economic issues. Party unity was preserved in this fashion, but policies were sometimes less than successful. The Party nonetheless thrived on such contradictions, which absorbed many points of view and possessed a certain solid common sense in the way in which policy eclecticism reduced internal tensions.[8]

REVOLUTIONARY VALUES,
CONDUCT, AND SOCIAL CHANGE

For the Revolution's leaders the ultimate key to the Party's success and the attainment of socialism was its ability to create new socialist men and women who were highly motivated, conscious of the role they were to play, and ready to lead others by both personal example and knowledge. While the Party had its own structure and life as an organization, unless it was dominated by such revolutionary individuals, it would not succeed. It therefore constantly raised the themes, especially after 1965, of what may be termed revolutionary morality, heroism, and optimism, often inserting them into discussions of Party matters, particularly into those involving criticism and bureaucracy. Long before Mao Tse-tung's Cultural Revolution, the Vietnamese Party had begun to develop an increasingly nuanced and unique vision of a humanistic Marxism-Leninism which involved not only values and ideology but also science, one in which the Party was defined both as an organization and, ideally, as an embodiment of certain kinds of persons.

Revolutionary morality and ethics involved, ultimately, the readiness to make sacrifices, ranging from the type of daily life a Party member chose for himself to the ultimate willingness to die for the cause. Such a total demand required some basic definitions of the meaning and purpose of life, since it was clear that without conviction Party members would avoid not merely heroism but many other forms of selflessness as well. Functionally, the leadership stressed not ultimate sacrifices but a simple existence which shunned anything, ranging from vanity to too much luxury, which could cause the masses to become cynical. Since self-indulgence was not a major problem for the Party, a readiness to move where the Party needed its members was perhaps the most common difficult demand it could impose, because it touched the delicate issue of the role of family in a member's life. Clean living was a cardinal tenet, and the model for it was, of course, Ho Chi Minh, who was virtually the only Party leader whose personal lifestyle was discussed publicly. Ho himself declared, "Nobody can say he is perfect; however, being determined to correct oneself helps to make one a good person."[9]

Party theorists categorically differentiated socialist morality from the remnants of Confucianism, which they denounced as reactionary. Some acknowledged a traditional Vietnamese heritage, yet they saw its influence in the form of a national psychology, one which for social, economic, and historical reasons produced good and bad customs and habits, the most beneficial being a "realistic and flexible way" of thinking.[10] Precisely because of this, however, the official Party position described nationalism as reactionary. From its inception it had declared itself a "patriotic" movement that was part of an international proletarian revolution from which it was inseparable, and at no time did it ever evoke chauvinist, antiforeign slogans to mobilize the population.

Looking at the situation practically, the Party acknowledged that it had inherited a large cultural and ideological legacy from the presocialist period and that peasants and workers were often addicted to old beliefs and customs. In order to neutralize these residues inside and outside the Party, it was important to explain socialist values and conduct. In 1966 the Party defined the socialist revolution as one based on three organically related elements: a change in the relations of production, an ideological and cultural revolution, and a technological and scientific revolution. Unlike the Chinese, whose Cultural Revolution was ideological in emphasis, the Vietnamese believed the technological revolution was the most important one to stress. This doctrine was Le Duan's main theoretical contribution, and the official Party position, even though Le Duc Tho publicly said he feared technocrats whose indifference to ideological leadership was also producing indifferent economic results.[11]

This three-phased revolutionary process required a change in ideological and cultural thought, but ideas alone would not eliminate the negative features of inherited concepts. It was essential to introduce science and technology into society and into its way of thinking, so that by changing the society and economy it could alter the context in which the traditional legacy had flourished and in which ideological change could occur. Le Duan's triple-revolution doctrine soon allowed the Party's theorists to focus clearly on fundamental questions of the relationship of ideas and will to the historical process and their capacity to affect the course of events. The Party found itself in a delicate position in this discussion. On the one hand it knew that morale and personal sacrifices required individuals to believe that their actions and attitudes could make a crucial difference. Indeed, the "spirit of revolutionary optimism" was hardly a myth, since in combat it repeatedly became a self-fulfilling prophecy.[12] Nor was motivation secondary in military and in political struggles, particularly in the south, since its capacity to protract the war against a materially far stronger enemy itself became a material factor as time brought out both the United States' and the RVN's crucial contradictions. At times the Party's press carried simplified statements that spirit and the very will to win, evoking a readiness to sacrifice, were emerging as a great material force.

On the other hand, China's Cultural Revolution was just then stressing the primacy of the will over the material, and the majority of the Party's leaders not only rejected the idealism in it but even found it corrosive to its desires to use technology to transform the framework in which ideologies emerged and existed. Although the Party never abandoned the centrality of revolutionary morality and optimism, in due course it modified the concepts to conform to what the Party thought a more defensible intellectual position. In military affairs, it declared man "the basic factor in winning victory in war."[13] Conscious action was crucial, however, if it proceeded according to objective laws of social development, and "man cannot make history according to his will."[14] He had to define actions according to reality and the nature of historical development and then act within the constraints and possibilities of his theoretical comprehension. Historical determinism and free will were not contradictory, for the Party linked them by mobilizing purposive mass action to unify freedom and necessity, exploiting to the maximum the objective possibilities for change, to attain the Revolution's ultimate goals. Action could not simply be mindless heroism and sacrifice; rather, it had to be focused, deliberate, and geared to material elements both within Vietnam and throughout the world, for the Revolution had to comprehend as well as to relate to global forces which operated, often with their own logic and momentum. Revolutionary processes everywhere, not just in Vietnam, were the product of coordinating "a series of essential objective and subjective factors."[15]

Fully aware that its justification of individual action was a fundamental asset that its enemies could not duplicate, but also eager to sustain the primacy of reason and organization, the Party attempted to create a synthesis which gave it a maximum advantage. When, in its effort to develop a resilient pluralist theory, the Party proclaimed, "we should never regard ideology as the only factor and use only ideological study sessions . . . to resolve every problem," it made plain its materialist appreciation of the constraints affecting its control of the future.[16] Economics and material forces shaped societies, and ideology could stimulate but not eliminate this process. "Determination and enthusiasm are extremely important factors, but not every activity will be successful just because we have a revolutionary will, and not everything will be victorious just because we have the determination to win. . . ."[17]

DEFINING AN INDEPENDENT VIETNAMESE REVOLUTIONARY THEORY

The need for the Vietnamese Party to formulate its theory of history and its own role independently of the USSR and China converged in Le Duc Tho's authoritative February 1968 essay entitled "Developing the New Type of Marxist-Leninist Party." Dismissing those who wanted to follow the

Soviet or Chinese line, he asserted, "To be a Marxist-Leninist means to know how to combine the universal truths of Marxism-Leninism with the reality at home and to know how to adapt the successful and unsuccessful experience of fraternal parties in a critical and creative manner. . . . we must firmly maintain independence and autonomy in the matter of devising our political line and method of revolutionary struggle; we cannot imitate and copy other people."[18] The Revolution's creative power, its major theoretical journal wrote the following June, "originates directly from our party's absorption of the principles of Marxism-Leninism, its maintenance of an independent and free spirit, and its concern about synthesizing the experiences of the Vietnamese Revolution and studying selectively the experiences of world revolution."[19] Well before the diplomacy of the war had begun to corrode the Party's relationship to its allies, it was clearly staking out its own, distinctive methodology, with Party schools stressing the differences between the historical conditions in Vietnam and those in the rest of the world. By 1972, of course, the Party was stating that its Marxism-Leninism was based on "ideological independence," making it "highly creative."[20]

Apart from its articulated dissimilarities with the other Communist Parties, there was the more important fact that the Vietnamese Party was the only one to come to power that did not subsequently proclaim many radically different and contradictory policies which caused it to lose confidence in its major leaders and discredit them. Although the Party deepened its theory after 1964, the continuity of its leaders and ideas since 1940 had given it the internal strength and self-confidence which fostered candor regarding its problems and a real dialogue concerning its policies. Its unity and the absence of an exclusive, dominant leader allowed it to encourage a rationalist view of the world and itself in a way unknown in other Marxist-Leninist states, avoiding the obscurantism and internal contradictions which had befallen them. The Vietnamese Party had abandoned "mechanical and inflexible reasoning," as Le Duan described it, better to grasp revolutionary realities.[21] "We do not create a theory to do what we want just because we want to do something. . . . our thoughts and actions must have a scientific basis."[22]

By the mid-1960s the Party had successfully fathomed the critical problems confronting it economically, militarily, and ideologically, developing a policy which integrated all three elements. The least well known of these, then as now, was its mode of reasoning and assessing itself as well as its enemy. It had synthesized a set of beliefs for its members and the people that produced a balance between optimism and realism, one that led them both to action and to sacrifices in a socially cohesive and rational fashion. But rather than being a self-fulfilling prophecy, the Party's definitions of personal values and conduct for the masses and its members were linked to highly materialistic social analyses. On the whole, such perceptions provided a coherent doctrine and set of objectives which further altered the nature of historical possibilities in the most decisive manner possible—producing victory rather than defeat.

This molding of events and control of history through organizational and individual actions, decisions, and commitments, as well as through a comprehension of their relevance to reality, was something the Vietnamese Party sustained long enough to survive the mounting violence it confronted after 1964. The ultimate wisdom of its leaders was to see their own limits as well as those of their enemy, always avoiding a high-risk policy if possible. But their sense of their adversary's constraints at that time gave them cause for both optimism and prudence. In the end, the basic Party mode of analysis was to estimate the balance of forces, which included a weighing of the contradictions in the enemy camp, in order to examine its own and America's weaknesses and the international context of American as well as its own actions. Such assessments gave a persuasive basis for revolutionary optimism, which was then translated into action which would only further affect the balance in the future.

The Party's appraisal of the causes and consequences of events, trends, actions, and decisions was linked not to some abstract theoretical model of reality intended either for intellectuals or for keepers of pure doctrinal faith but rather to a multifaceted yet unified concept of objective and subjective forces in historical change and of the nature of the contemporary historical experience. It was a concept that could not be reduced to a simple formula, because, though the methodology of analysis was historical materialism, its application was by definition nuanced and always being revised and recast in the light of changing events and of the parameters of action—since the Party did not separate theory and praxis. And precisely because the final goal of the exercise was not merely to describe history but to change it, the burden of the theory required constant thought and redefinitions within the framework of both fixed methods of reasoning and a constant objective. Its theory of revolution bore no relationship to academic notions of them, because it operated at a higher level, concerned with the practice rather than the description of revolution, and its own success or failure was proof of its validity.

Explanations of the Vietnamese revolutionary movement, not merely of the initial growing out of the forces which gave birth to it but of the stages by which it consolidated and sought to implement its goals, must comprehend a far greater range of historical factors and be more nuanced. Those autopsies of the classic revolutions which today prevail among those who study revolutions and history do not help describe the Vietnamese case. For they focus on the revolutionary experiences of France, Russia, and China, whose revolutions were much more the outcome of vast, autonomous structural dynamics in history as well as, generally, the result of short-lived periods of transition in which the revolutionary parties' actions were not by themselves decisive, and indeed were sometimes quite tangential. For protracted periods of upheaval it is not merely the impersonally created forces which produce successful revolutions but also the ability of a party adequately to comprehend and interrelate with them, at least to a minimally essential degree, thereby itself becoming a dynamic causal element in the entire historical process and helping decisively to define its outcome. The dependence of a revolutionary party on chance, such as external wars which open vast new opportunities, is less important than its need to be sufficiently correct over a period of decades about itself and the many contexts it operates in. In protracted revolutionary processes, of which the Vietnamese was the longest of modern history, time favors the wise rather than the merely fortunate. For this reason, Vietnam was to offer the most important illustration in the modern historical experience of the degree to which consciousness profoundly affects a revolutionary process.

THE REVOLUTION'S RESPONSE TO URBAN SOUTH VIETNAM

For the Revolution the comprehension of the complex transformation of South Vietnamese society and politics which occurred after 1964 was a paramount task which deeply influenced its actions. The Party saw that the urban regions constituted "the important rear of the enemy, the places where the enemy's nerve center and command organs are concentrated."[23] But as the Revolution coped with the reality that its enemy's strength was in the cities, its commitment to political struggle there, through legal and illegal means, including the use of fronts and infiltration into the enemy's organizations and army, remained complementary to its various levels of armed struggle elsewhere. The enemy's urban foundation was also the logistics base for the Revolution's armed forces. In the Party's vision, it was crucial, both politically and militarily, to prevent the creation of areas isolated from it.

The Party had evolved in a peasant society in which in fact and in Party theory the peasantry constituted "the greatest force of the revolution," but only because it was led by the Party of the working class, though not the working class itself, in what was a worker-peasant alliance.[24] The proletariat was too small and too weak to play that role directly rather than symbolically, by means of the largely nonproletarian elements that made up the bulk of the Party's membership. Yet, to the extent a working class existed, the

Party thought it inevitable and natural for this class to support the Revolution, and it viewed urbanization as a precondition for the emergence of class consciousness. In this sense, the United States' displacement of former peasants supposedly carried with it the seeds of its own defeat. The impact of chaos on urban dwellers was by 1966 clearly designated in Party assessments as a justification for its devoting more effort to the entire urban population, public employees and RVN troops included. Students, as always, were a key element in that amalgam of city forces. Implicit in the Party's assessment was the belief that urbanization was compatible with the emergence of a sense of community and class among those in common economic and social straits, and that united action was therefore possible.

The notion of a national democratic revolution like the August Revolution also assigned a role to the other class strata. Although the concept of the national bourgeoisie was the Party's analytic inheritance from its early Comintern period, by the 1950s it had few illusions about its importance or its political constancy. Still, the exact nature of both the national bourgeoisie and the urbanized working class remained a nagging analytic and tactical question by the mid-1960s, and the very ambiguity of these classes was to prove of major significance to the Party's actions. It did not want to make any errors, for these elements—or something akin to them—had indeed been vital to the August Revolution's victory and, even more important, to its subsequent consolidation. The NLF's program reflected this doubt about the nature of class formations and political dynamics, and in 1966 Le Duan could still state, "The revolution in South Vietnam has to pass through several transitional phases prior to advancing toward national reunification and socialism."[25] In a word, the Party typically defined its class analysis and political strategy in such a way as to permit itself maximum future flexibility. The need to maintain as broad a united front as possible to weaken the enemy's potential power was still considered the August Revolution's most important lesson.

In a sense, the very nature of political and class realities in the RVN's urban areas demanded equivocation, not least because the urban elements were themselves obviously divided, confused, unstable, and subject to numerous pressures and influences. The Party studied and defined the RVN itself in order to find its weaknesses, and by the late 1960s the Party had constructed a model of the RVN's nature and role in the war. It was a central question and vital to its strategy.

The facts themselves required the Party to focus on the "scramble for power among the puppet rulers," until Thieu consolidated control after 1968.[26] Until then, the regime's social base was accurately described as very narrow, its main source of support coming from compradors and corrupt officers struggling with each other for dominance. Neither the intelligentsia nor the workers were rallying to the tottering Thieu-Ky regime and the Revolution dismissed the civilian politicians as opportunists divided by region, religion, and personal interest in much the same terms used by both Washington and a number of RVN generals. Until Thieu's consolidation of power, the chaos in the ranks of RVN's upper strata shaped the Party's definition of the relation of its actions to reality.

By early 1966, when a quarter of a million American troops were already in the south, senior Party leaders were convinced that the United States' political and military dependency on the RVN was the weakest link in the imperialist effort and that the smashing of this military and administrative phase of the war would convince the Americans they could not win. This assumption was increasingly influential in the analyses of the Party leadership, reflecting a realistic assessment of political facts, and it was its main premise for future action by the latter part of 1967 and again during 1971–72.[27]

THE PARTY'S CONCEPT OF THE GENERAL UPRISING

In approaching the urban question, the Party's leaders based their conclusions not simply on a quite rational assessment of the class nature and problems of the urban sector or on the vulnerability of the RVN in the American strategy but also on their own experiences with the August 1945 Revolution and Vietnam's cities in the decade following it. Unlike the Chinese Communists, the Vietnamese Party came to power quickly precisely because urban and rural resistance had been combined in an objectively favorable situation. Cities were crucial as centers of political power, and though the Party's potential in Hanoi early in 1945 had improved, it was not qualitatively better than it was in Saigon in 1967. Indeed, after the Viet Minh departed for the rural areas late in 1946, the Party's position in Hanoi declined dramatically and was in many ways weaker there than in Saigon in 1966–67. Even Hanoi's population growth paralleled that of Saigon, exposing both to comparable developments. Radical fluctuations in the Party's urban position were scarcely deemed decisive if all the other factors favored it. The Party during 1965–67 persisted in seeing the urban role as both crucial and promising.

In warfare, the Party believed, the "highest form of combination is that of general offensive with general insurrection [uprising]," one linking urban and rural areas and combining military and political warfare.[28] Varying modes of PLAF warfare by 1967 had dispersed the United States and the ARVN throughout the country, exposing them to a massive attack at the place and time of the Revolution's choosing, including urban areas. Given the military equilibrium and political context, the combination of general uprising and general offensive was by 1966 the Party's ultimate (but not exclusive) means of relating to the urbanized nature of the RVN—the weakest link in the American effort. The uprising and the offensive were to interact and overlap, building their own momentum, and take advantage of the enemy's dispersion.

The general offensive and uprising might be simultaneous or successive. They might not necessarily produce a final victory but would at least strike at the American "will" and seriously damage the ARVN, setting the stage for its "inevitable collapse."[29] Ultimately, the Party considered the concept a quite flexible formula, to be applied creatively according to circumstances, and left open the possibility that it might stimulate spontaneous events. Its premises were that there was ultimately no rural-urban dichotomy, that the cities in the late 1960s were basically like those of the mid-1940s, and that their social and economic crises would radicalize those affected and produce appropriate forms of resistance. What these might be depended on the actual experiences the NLF had in the cities, but only by daring to apply the strategy could the Party realize its promise and uncover its enemy's weaknesses.

The situation in the southern cities in the mid-1960s was quite different, however, from that in the famine-ridden north of 1944–45, where the Party itself had provided the framework for solving the food crisis. But there were certain similarities as well. During 1963 and 1966, urban political crises had aided NLF offensives by compelling the RVN to spread its troops thinly. But such coordination usually occurred more by accident than by design. In mid-1967 Le Duan criticized the NLF for its inability to create urban united fronts in Danang and Hué and to help lead those forces that were creating powerful contradictions within the RVN. Urban struggles, in brief, were scarcely exotic events; the Party saw them as crucial to its efforts.

The Party concluded, "We must conduct investigations of the urban situation."[30] The facts regarding poverty and displaced peasants were undeniable, but it soon became apparent that the poorest, most oppressed, and largest class—the former peasantry—was preoccupied with daily existence. The NLF understood clearly the impact of a "luxurious and dissolute life" not just on ex-peasants but even on their own people. The enemy's "sugar-coated bullet" was often described as being at least as fatal as a real one, easily capable of wrecking the political roles of the masses or anyone who was not wary.[31] In the short run, this was a liability for the Revolution and an asset for the RVN, but in the end the egoism of the urban masses proved to be one of the RVN's fatal weaknesses. Those youths who were fortunate enough to obtain stable jobs as part of the urban working class as well as some children of former resistance members were the exception, but the large majority of young people were immune to the NLF's appeals, unless they were students. And since most students were also the children of elite elements, the Party thought they could play a disproportionately large role and remain relatively safe from repression. Intellectuals, too, responded to the NLF, and though the existing society alienated them profoundly and though they were usually poor, many were also hedging bets, and their position reflected the fortunes of the Revolution. The same was true of members of the RVN administration, thousands of whom were in Saigon itself (though fewer than the fifteen thousand the Americans suspected existed), and while some had been won over to cooperation by family contacts, most were really neutrals whose *attentisme* was quite obvious. Still, among intellectuals, the *attentistes* and the real NLF supporters were probably a majority, one which grew with every NLF success. Among workers, religious groups, and mass organizations, however, the NLF's strength remained relatively quite limited.

The Party's Saigon operations were directed from within the city until Tet 1968. The local leadership was clandestine and inhibited, preoccupied with survival as well as mobilization. Given the political chaos among the RVN's parties and organizations, the NLF could freely infiltrate them, but it could not so easily overcome their fractious ineffectuality. Many such efforts proved to be a waste, but given the large student-intellectual constituency, which optimized talk and debate, it was the overhead charge that the most receptive elements imposed on the NLF's efforts. The Party and the larger NLF organization in the cities were most successful among the least disciplined social strata. Increasingly, women began assuming ever-larger roles in the urban structure, since in sensitive locations they were less suspect and far more mobile.

By 1967 it was clear that the Party's urban work was not going well. It regarded the effort to proselytize the enemy as inadequate and the urban Party as insufficiently organized. The RVN's base, however narrow, was urban, and it was crucial for the party to relate to it. Objectively, the cities were ripe for change, and the Party wished to lead it. A general uprising could bring out all of the RVN's latent contradictions, destroying its strength in the cities and removing the crucial prop on which the entire U.S. effort rested.

No one fully grasped all the implications of urbanization for the outcome of the war. Early in 1967 the Party began to prepare for the Tet offensive of 1968, aware that only such a test of the role of the cities could determine their critical importance for the war's outcome. The dilemma facing the Party was to measure the assets and liabilities of both sides in their attempts to relate to the urban masses. Its own problems were the demoralization and

apathy of the larger part of the poor masses—people who in the country had
sustained the Revolution. It was not yet clear just how much they had been
disoriented and politically neutralized. Also inhibiting its progress was the
widespread *attentisme* of many of its contacts, a posture that only the
necessity of choice would shatter. Given the fluidity and tensions of the
entire urban class structure, the political possibilities that could emerge from
such elements seemed endless.

Despite its own real weaknesses, the Party could see the problems of its
enemies even more clearly. The "cynicism and scorn" of the established
urban population toward the RVN, as the State Department phrased it early
in 1967, were obvious to all.[32] In any case, the Party's unwavering commitment to politics in wartime required it to relate to the urban communities
in transition. The extent to which it would be forced to collaborate politically with other anti-Thieu forces, which it assumed would be necessary, its
notion of the transition to reunification—all these issues could be resolved
only by shaking the RVN's foundations and the urban apathy in which it
flourished.

The complexity of the urban experience and the war's demography
both defied the Revolution and worked for it. In the end the RVN required enormous sums for its very existence and stability, and without it
the United States had only an intolerably distorted socio-economic structure on its hands. If the NLF was stymied, at least it had alternatives and
could survive indefinitely. America created an urbanized South Vietnam as
a challenge to the Revolution, but it might also prove the RVN's downfall.
The real issue was not whether the NLF could come to power in the cities
but how long the RVN could survive in them, given the political and
economic burdens it was carrying. Military events could therefore affect
the speed with which both Washington and Saigon had to confront such
problems and contradictions.

Chapter 22

The Economic Impact of the War on the United States

Imperialism in modern world history has never been an exclusively economic phenomenon, and that reality has been the main source of its demise. Although the economic rationale was crucial at its inception, the justification for imperialism transcended strictly materialist factors to take on geopolitical, cultural, and military dimensions and to form a character and motive too complex and convoluted for simplification. The importance of each element varied among key decision makers. Militarily and politically, Vietnam and, above all, Southeast Asia formed a crucial test for the United States as an imperialist power seeking militarily to impose its geopolitical as well as economic hegemony over major political, economic, and social developments throughout the Third World. By 1965, however, the economic basis for American imperialism in Southeast Asia had created its own fatal contradictions, and these proved to be crucial in inflicting defeat even when, militarily, the United States still appeared capable of success.

Economic factors of imperialism cannot be divorced from the political context in which they operate, and immediate economic consequences may quickly subvert the long-range economic rationality of an action. Economic costs of war always interact with other contemporaneous problems and may undermine a coherent ultimate objective, such as U.S. integration of Third World economies into the world capitalist system. The total, long-run historical process profoundly reflects a sequence of short-run phases, and while they may share identical elements, each stage may nevertheless possess a uniqueness which sets it apart, threatening to transform the success of one epoch into the challenge of another. Out of these differences and specific characteristics there emerge the contradictions and tensions of the imperialist system. To understand them is also to grasp why imperialism as a way in which great nations relate to the world is at once a dying and a terribly destructive aspect of the modern historical experience, producing war as well as the decline of great powers.

The United States' escalation in Vietnam came at a critical juncture not only in its definition of its military and global political strategy but also in the domestic and international economy, creating a basic tension for the Johnson administration from the start of its intervention. American involvement in four earlier wars since 1898 had begun at times when the economy was in a recession or emerging from a period of idle productive capacity; in addition to attaining the nation's military or political goals, these wars also created higher prosperity and few, if any, structural challenges to the economy. Such timing reinforced the momentum behind its global role, so that the pattern of U.S. imperialism was established with a minimum of internal political opposition from crucial factions in the economic elite or in society, nearly all of whom gained. Given the infinitely more complex global context and power balance that was emerging, by the early 1960s this firmly entrenched legacy of elite and public perceptions and responses toward war, with its endorsement of America's aspiration to be the world's directing power, no longer had relevance to the United States' economic position.

The massive 1965 intervention in Vietnam began well into the longest sustained period of expansion in the postwar American economy. Starting in 1961, long before outlays for Southeast Asia further stimulated it, it lasted until 1969. The growth of the military budget in this context could only increase inflation. Rather than creating prosperity, it jeopardized it. Internationally, the United States was highly vulnerable. It attempted to play the role of stabilizer of the world economic structure, which was geared to the strength of the dollar, while it simultaneously exported investment funds and goods on the one hand and made costly political and military commitments which undermined its economic role in the world on the other.

By the late 1950s the dollar was still the basic unit of international trade. Dollars and gold backed most of the currencies of the capitalist world, even as foreign economies grew immeasurably and began to capture ever-larger shares of world trade and industrial production. The dollar's position was stabilizing so long as the American economy itself was prudently managed, and this required a great many things, from the avoidance of inflation and budget deficits to a favorable balance of payments. In a sense, the very success of the United States in integrating the postwar world economy around the Bretton Woods system and the dollar gave the major capitalist nations a potential role in defining and constraining the economic consequences of Washington's political and military policy. For implicitly transferred to them was a measure of control over the full range of America's policies in the world—a reality of which the administration was still unaware as it embarked on its Vietnam escalations. It introduced an important though initially very subtle division in the higher circles of American capitalism between those who saw the imperatives of the dollar's role in the world, and its implications for military and political policy, and those who were either oblivious or indifferent to such issues. It would grossly oversimplify this division to say that the Treasury Department and those concerned with financial affairs, including many important world-oriented bankers, stood against the Departments of State and Defense and their outside political-military allies. However, in reality such a dichotomy at crucial times played a major role in influencing and constraining the options of various decision makers.

During the late 1950s these problems had arisen with increasing frequency as the United States had short bouts of inflation and large federal and balance-of-payments deficits which greatly disturbed powerful fiscal conservatives. Joseph M. Dodge, banker, former Budget Bureau director, and one of the most influential figures on the political and economic scene in the postwar era, in 1959 examined the stresses on the country from its desire to meet domestic economic needs and pay for the cold war while regulating the world economy. He concluded that it was simply a matter of time before the dollar's stability would be seriously undermined: "The real question is—How long . . .?"[1] Other foreign currencies were becoming both stronger and convertible, and after 1957 the major capitalist nations began quietly and slowly to hedge against the dollar by redeeming it for gold. From nearly $23 billion in gold stocks in 1957, the U.S. holdings dropped to $16 billion at the end of 1962 and then leveled off as the American economy experienced high growth with very low inflation. No less important was the concerted American effort to collaborate with Europe's central bankers to protect the nation's gold reserves and, thereby, the dollar. So long as Treasury and economic officials in Washington were ready to pledge fiscally conservative policies, the Europeans felt that it was to their own advantage to preserve the dollar's privileged position.

By the early 1960s the Western capitalist world's potential control over the economic consequences of America's economic and military policies represented an important shift in the world's balance of power. The decline in the United States' share of world trade, from 48 percent in 1948 to 25 percent in 1964 and 10 percent by 1969, made the dollar's hegemony an anomaly left over from the wartime conditions. Dominant initially because World War Two had so destroyed its capitalist rivals as to allow it the freedom to regulate the world financial system, the United States in the early

1960s could scarcely afford a war which might at least partially turn the tables. Even if those who made the decisions to escalate ignored such considerations, they could not avoid the eventual consequences of their actions. George Ball, the sole "dove" among them, was also the only one seriously concerned with the international economic consequences of the war.

THE WAR'S COST AND THE
DILEMMA OF THE DOMESTIC ECONOMY

The United States' failure to recognize the limits of its economic power and its relation to its military and diplomatic policy was surely not unique in the mid-1960s and remains today a fundamental issue troubling American imperialism. Recognition of one's weaknesses is more difficult for a nation than for an individual, since states have conflicting interests and ample means of procrastinating. In 1965 the United States chose to do so, falling into an economic imbroglio through both naïveté and ignorance, becoming entangled in self-deception and cynical political maneuvering, and eventually reaching a predictable economic impasse, one which only a quick victory could keep from evolving into a prolonged military and political struggle whose economic costs would greatly accelerate America's defeat.

However Washington administered its war effort, its military strategy in limited war by the mid-1960s was certain to be expensive. Nearly half the war's cost arose from its reliance on air activities, not to mention the immense cost of high firepower. Still, the United States took the most expensive way out when McNamara gave a virtual blank check to the generals in March 1965. By early 1968 about 700,000 tons of building supplies were stockpiled in South Vietnam, "all literally deteriorating in place," as the general in charge observed at the time.[2] The blank check included numerous other outlays which the Pentagon charged to the Vietnam War with the aim of getting more money from Congress.

Most important in making the war budget a source of potential economic mishaps was McNamara's explicit premise in the annual Pentagon requests to Congress that the Revolution's level of military activity would not increase and that the war would be over by the end of June of each fiscal year! Since this meant too little money—which was politically more palatable—after 1966 the Pentagon returned to Congress annually for special supplementals for the war, discomfiting Congress politically by forcing it to take public responsibility for the war's continuation. Its ability to administer the war in this fashion allowed the Pentagon to lose control of the war's costs, the exact figures being to this day a mystery save in one regard: the war was far too expensive for the domestic and international condition of the U.S.

economy. While various leaders in Washington sought for political reasons to deceive the Congress and the public concerning real costs, the fact remains that they often first deluded themselves. They had lost command of the money, thereby threatening to wreck the administration's economic program. This was to prove a more unpardonable sin in a capitalist society than the uses to which they put its expensive firepower.

Very complicated debates over vast sums, sometimes exceeding $10 billion, arose throughout the war to plague those seeking to comprehend its costs. Military procurement and contracts about doubled between 1965 and 1967, and official budgeted war costs (which were as good as such estimates are ever likely to be) rose from $5.8 billion in fiscal 1966 to $20.1 the following year and $26.5 billion in 1968.

The administration's ignorance of its Vietnam outlays first became serious in 1965. At stake was the President's domestic Great Society program. When the question how to fund the war first arose in mid-1965, McGeorge Bundy mixed his desires and genuine beliefs to argue that inflation was not a problem. Johnson should not ask Congress for special war funds, lest his opponents use the request to cut spending on domestic reform. By the end of 1965 Johnson was ignoring warnings from his Council of Economic Advisers that the war's cost would require a tax increase if a vast budget deficit was to be averted, but even then no one in Washington was fully aware of how high the costs might be. For political reasons the President chose to press for domestic reforms as well as for war and a postponement of new taxes until after the November 1966 elections. The administration fell back on fiscal and monetary measures, and as it deluded itself its various branches consciously deceived the public and Congress, lowering its domestic credibility as it attempted to raise its international credibility by its intervention in Southeast Asia. Its experts confidentially concluded that the war's cost would be higher than the public projections, and by the end of 1966, when Johnson realized that McNamara had underestimated it by $11 billion, the President had lost confidence in his defense secretary and was stuck with a major economic problem. When in the following January the executive asked Congress for a $12 billion supplemental for which it had no funding mechanism, it was clear that it had lost control of the war's costs and of the internal economy at one and the same time. In the process it had also deliberately misled Congress for the sake of its own political advantage. Unwilling at first to ask Congress for a tax hike, and unable from 1967 to mid-1968 to get the increasingly alienated Congress to pass a tax bill, the White House was forced to eliminate $2.5 billion from earlier congressional authorizations for social welfare in fiscal 1967. The Great Society program was badly hurt, success in Vietnam was as remote as ever, and the economy entered into the most complex phase of its history since before World War Two.

First came the budget deficits: $3.8 billion in fiscal 1966, $8.7 the following year, and an astonishing $25.2 billion in 1968, far greater than that for any year since 1945 and 3.0 percent of the entire gross national product. From 1965 onward, the capacity utilization of the American manufacturing industry reached the highest point in the postwar era, industrial output leaping virtually to its physical limits, rising 23 percent between 1964 and 1967. The Pentagon's share of government outlays rose sharply, all because of Vietnam. The inevitable result was inflation. Given the long period of full employment and production that began in 1961, it was unavoidable that the higher interest rates the government paid to finance its deficits and the supercharged economy would drive up prices. These peaked at a 6.1 percent rise in 1969 to begin the permanent inflationary pressure that has marked the U.S. economy since then. Only 1.3 percent in 1960–65, annual price rises averaged 4.5 percent the next five years. And because of inflation and a high demand for labor, women poured into the work force. The demand for consumer goods grew. The efficiency of U.S. manufacturing fell dramatically after 1965. Growth in output per man-hour became the lowest of the major industrial capitalist nations. Despite rising unit labor costs, the real income of workers rose until 1969 and then, for the first time in postwar history, began fluctuating sharply, eventually declining in a manner unprecedented in this century.

The sheer diversity of America's structural economic problems by 1968 was awesome. And the cause was clear to all able to analyze the problem. "Our involvement on the Asian mainland," Allan Sproul, the powerful former president of the New York Federal Reserve Bank, confided to a friend in February 1968, "[is] . . . at the core of much of our domestic and international political, social, and economic difficulties."[3]

THE INTERNATIONAL ECONOMIC CONSEQUENCES OF THE WAR

The political and economic impact of the war on the domestic economy could be postponed temporarily because of the administration's manipulation of information and because of continued strong congressional support for its war aims, but no such latitude existed in the world economy. The dollar, though weaker structurally, remained the overvalued basis of world trade and finance. Overvaluation accelerated America's direct investment abroad as its multinationals bought vast sections of Europe's and the world's productive resources. From $33 billion in 1960, U.S. direct investments rose $22 billion over the next six years, reaching $78 billion in 1970. At the same time, American exports were overpriced, and undervalued foreign imports into the United States more than doubled between 1960 and 1969, wiping out the huge postwar favorable balance of trade and creating a serious balance-of-payments problem.

While the extent of this deficit is a complex technical question, its implications to politics are not. Even the most favorable official data show the U.S. current-account balance dropping sharply after 1965. From 1968 to 1972 there occurred the longest and largest postwar deficit. Influential private estimates showed that the investment outflow and the shifting trade balance along with the war increased the $3.3 billion balance-of-payments deficit in 1964 to $9.4 billion in 1968, sums far greater than Washington was reporting. Whatever the exact data, it was certain that foreign holdings of dollars grew enormously, giving European nations a mounting vested interest in the stability of the dollar.

In August 1965 the French treasury informed U.S. Treasury Secretary Henry Fowler, George Ball, and others that American deficits were hurting Europe's now powerful and largely balanced economies. The French specifically identified the war as the cause of the deficit, and they were assured it would not be allowed to become an economic problem. Meanwhile, leading American bankers on the government's international monetary advisory committee began in October 1965 to warn that failure to maintain economic discipline would seriously jeopardize the dollar's role as the world's reserve and trading currency. Foreign central banks might simply begin to demand gold for dollars. In fact, during 1965 they again quietly began to do so, reducing the U.S. gold stock by $1.7 billion.[4]

By fall 1966 the war's role in creating three-fourths of the net overseas military deficits was very much on the minds of Douglas Dillon, David Rockefeller, and the banking community's leading advisers to Washington on world monetary issues. They did not question the political justification for the war, but they insisted it should not further upset the nation's balance-of-payments issues. The problem was that there was no way both to fight the war and to prevent its economic consequences. While such bankers had access to most of the major administration agencies, they managed to persuade only the Treasury to consider finance seriously along with political and military factors.

Although the key European bankers granted Washington time during 1966 to straighten out its affairs, by mid-1967 it was perfectly clear what inflation and deficits were beginning to do to the value of their dollar holdings. But because they, too, had a vested interest in protecting the dollar until they could create a better medium of trade and finance, they had since 1965 cooperated with a gold pool of eight nations and various collective arrangements to protect the link between the price of gold and the value of the dollar. Washington's failure to cure its malaise kept the future of the pool and gold in limbo until July 1967, when the French withdrew from the arrangement. The basic problem by then was that the dollar was weakening but was still legally backed by gold, which central banks could claim. They could force the United States to cease its gold backing or raise the price of gold, a step fraught with risks. For the moment, America's allies were unwilling to take such chances. Meanwhile, deficits caused dollars to flow out of the United States as inflation seriously diluted their purchasing power, and it was clear that the entire dollar-based world financial system was becoming increasingly vulnerable to a run on gold.

On November 17, 1967, the British devalued the pound after months of difficulties, and what had been a matter of concern only to a specialized sector of the official U.S. banking system now began quietly to draw the entire administration into a complex matter crucial to the American economy but comprehensible to a mere handful of experts. The British devaluation triggered a run on the pool's gold and by mid-December, when the panic abated, $1.5 billion had been withdrawn. Sixty percent of it came out of American gold reserves, which dropped another $1.2 billion in 1967. U.S. gold reserves were now almost depleted for purposes of the pool, whose members were also privy to confidential data on the serious deterioration in the U.S. balance-of-payments position during the last quarter of 1967. By mid-December its six allies in the pool were ready to abolish it and leave the United States to its own devices. In response the White House had finally to confront in public the politically inflammable issue of the economics of the Vietnam War.

Its first step was to announce that it would control the outflow of capital and ask Congress for new income taxes to finance the war. The administration also requested that Congress lift the gold-reserve coverage of the dollar from its 25 percent minimum in order to free gold to defend the dollar. The Europeans now agreed to continue the gold pool. On the surface, the gold crisis appeared to have passed, yet small nations secretly began to redeem dollars for gold so that nearly a quarter of a billion dollars left the pool during January and February 1968. Charles A. Coombs, the American most involved in the problem, later described the first two months of 1968 as ones in which "market psychology remained highly inflammable."[5] On January 24 the chairman of his Council of Economic Advisers warned the President of "a possible spiraling world depression" if the gold and dollar issue and the basic economic causes behind it were not resolved soon.[6]

THE ECONOMIC DILEMMA OF
PROTRACTED WAR

Like almost all of America's postwar strategic and military theories, its limited-war doctrine ignored the price tag that every strategy carries. While at various times a capitalist economy has structural imperatives for expansion, under different conditions the structural constraints may be at least as powerful. The period after 1960 saw an interconnected crisis not just in the application of America's military power in the world but also in the economics of U.S. imperialism.

Ironically, the war soon exposed the inherent inefficiency of arms when confronted by an enemy capable of eluding them and protracting a conflict indefinitely. In this technologically sophisticated and expensive war, the weapons had to prove decisive quickly or else they would become transformed into a liability to U.S. power. The basic American dilemma from the Vietnam War onward was that it was unable to fight a cheap war or to afford a long, expensive one. By unleashing economic dynamics, the costly war produced critical political reactions, gradually reducing the administration's freedom from pressures at home. Important sectors of the financial and business community, normally in favor of or, at most, indifferent toward expansion, were compelled to see the conflict of economic priorities the war was now generating, and pragmatically began to oppose such a high-cost, protracted contest. More crucial was that the very success of the United States in integrating the postwar world economy now gave European nations both the incentive and the ability to inhibit seriously those American political and economic policies which impinged on their own economic interests. This, too, was an unprecedented situation confronting American foreign policy.

Long wars inevitably create their internal contradictions, which in due course can produce challenges which may prove decisive. The high-cost technological solutions of counterinsurgency warfare produced a serious economic impasse before it inevitably precipitated major political and social challenges. By late 1967 the United States could not afford a war that had become a military stalemate and, more important, an economic impossibility. Had the economic context been different then, it might have gained more time, but the Revolution's ability to protract the conflict would sooner or later have repeated the scenario which was ineluctably emerging in late 1967. Many of the contradictions in the American economy which the war deepened were inherited from its earlier dilemmas, including its expansive global military and economic policies and its addiction to capital-intensive warfare. As a result, just as it was the Communists' misfortune to confront a nation seeking to redress its political and military failures elsewhere, so it was to their advantage to deal with one that had inherited economic difficulties which the war would bring to fruition.

When a war for the United States can become a great commitment, its ultimate ramifications will always be unclear to it at first. The linkage of politics and economics with military decisions and expensive strategies soon transforms the nature of the undertaking, the outcome of which will invariably mean defeat if its enemy comprehends the complex, total nature of the war and responds appropriately. Time, above all, is America's most dangerous nemesis, for it will provoke countless difficulties which can only intersect and compound each other.

At the beginning of 1968 the Johnson administration had yet to learn this lesson.

Chapter 23

The Balance of Forces in the War at the End of 1967

The outcome of war depends on imperceptible as well as visible factors, and the ability of each side to assess its enemy as accurately as possible and to relate to reality in a manner that acknowledges both its own weaknesses and its power can decisively affect the conclusion. Though it is easy to exaggerate the importance of reason and clarity in the interaction between people and history, it is even worse to minimize the importance of their blindness to facts in influencing great events and the historical process.

The Vietnam War was no different from any other insofar as its subtle social, economic, and human consequences grew more important with time. Though it had never been primarily a military conflict, its institutional consequences increased qualitatively with its intensity and duration. To the extent the Communist Party comprehended the relevance of its actions in such a context, both to the conventional military balance and, above all, to the myriad other factors which decide the outcome of war rather than battles, it also possessed the ability to know *how* to act successfully.

THE REVOLUTION AND THE BALANCE OF FORCES

In 1967 it became increasingly obvious that the Revolution's ability to adapt to each U.S. escalation had created a military stalemate. The Revolution always understood that military activity was only ancillary to political struggle, and it constantly assessed the whole range of problems it faced. In this way it had been able to compensate for its vast material inferiority by optimizing its human resources until 1967. By that time it was evident that the war was creating new challenges which demanded important adjustments. Automatically, the Party's leaders evaluated the war's changing balance of forces, their own weaknesses and strength as well as those of the United States and the RVN, and the outcome of the Politburo's analyses was eventually translated into policies and actions intended to retain the Revolution's political, as well as military, strategic initiative.

Despite important disagreements among Party leaders concerning the facts and the conclusions to be drawn from them, they could readily identify the basic difficulties they confronted. The demographic transformation of the nation and the relative successes of the U.S.-RVN pacification program were among the most critical. Population movement to urban areas had seriously weakened the Party and NLF village structure despite the cadres' many successful adaptations. They considered it important, and some leaders thought it decisive, to stop this rural erosion and attempt to shift the trends in control of the countryside back to the Revolution. Not only was the declining access to the material factors of the war—people and resources —at stake, but the NLF also had to arrest the growth of peasant *attentisme*.

Just as the war's upheavals had deeply corroded the rural areas, so too had it created even more imposing urban challenges for the Revolution. A priori the Party had assumed that the majority of the poor urban masses were pro-NLF, but reality was proving much more troublesome. Ironically, it was precisely those who could afford to think about the larger issues of the Vietnam calvary—students, intellectuals, some petit bourgeois elements —who now appeared most receptive to the NLF's program or ready on behalf of peace to make common cause with it.

Still, the Party's urban strategy and concept of the simultaneous rural and urban general uprising was as much a part of its heritage as was its class analysis, for its stunning successes in the cities in 1945 had helped bring it to power. It had desired to respond creatively to the urban challenge after 1965, but its organization in the cities in late 1967 was still weak. The Party leaders believed that they had to test the existing urban potential in order to mobilize it. Not to do so, they felt, was to allow the urban structure to become increasingly the RVN's strength while the NLF remained essentially passive.

While the urban areas largely eluded the NLF, they marked, more significantly, a fundamental weakness of the U.S. effort. Indeed, for the very reasons so many people in the RVN-controlled regions were not working with the NLF, they also failed to support the RVN, which evoked little political allegiance from the people. This absence of a social base for the RVN impressed the Party greatly. But from 1966 onward the Party had focused on the destruction of the RVN and its military and administrative apparatus, calculating that its demise would remove the raison d'être of the Americans' presence and compel them to acknowledge that there was no institutional foundation for their attempt to control the south's future. In this sense, both the Revolutionary and the U.S. strategies concentrated on the fate of the American surrogate installed primarily in cities. Even if the NLF could not mobilize the cities as part of a general uprising, at the very least it had to challenge the RVN's hegemony in the urban areas.

The Party always felt it had retained the strategic initiative in the military phases of the war by virtue both of links with guerillas and local forces and of its sustained ability to fight in its own way at the time and place of its own choosing. Events after 1965 had left the Party confident of its resources. Despite the debates among its generals on tactics, their differences were in the end settled pragmatically, on the basis of experience. "Let us fight both the US and puppet troops," General Nguyen Chi Thanh summed up the logic of this approach, "and we will find the guide line. . . . This is real Marxism and realistic."[1] Testing the enemy's capabilities became a way of relating to his weaknesses and heightening them as well as honing the Revolution's power.

The Party's military successes by 1967 had begun greatly to outdistance the political benefits that came from them, in part because of the decentralization of its main forces and its adoption of a strategy and tactics which exploited the weaknesses of American high technology. It also reflected the military's desire to reduce its casualties to an acceptable limit, so that by 1967 those most in danger in the south were cadres and guerillas whose political work began to suffer seriously. And having learned how to fight the Americans successfully and organize the DRV into a functional economic and manpower base for the war in the south, the Party's leaders waited for their opportunity. While in theory and practice ready to fight a protracted war if necessary, the Party no later than March 1966 was committed to attaining, if possible, "victory within a relatively short period of time."[2] Although the American leaders thought the DRV weak and growing even weaker, in fact the Party considered itself materially more fit than ever for a major military action at the right moment. To attempt one, it reasoned, was "not in itself hazardous," because even if it failed, the Party's material strength in both the north and the south was now highly developed. Repeating its commitment the following January 1967, it began preparations for the Tet offensive several months later.[3]

The Party always publicly and privately perceived the United States' problems in a context involving its global strength and dilemmas as well as its internal social dynamics. By the spring of 1967 it understood clearly America's growing difficulties with Western European and Japanese economic interests, and the impact of the war on the distribution of power in the world capitalist system. It considered itself in a position of strength if it could exploit all these factors. To expose America's weaknesses by a strategic offensive would test the accuracy of the Party's conception of its adversaries' power and of its own. Compelling the Americans to become realistic concerning the true balance of forces both in Vietnam and in the world was of prime importance if the Party was to reduce its own, growing difficulties and to shift the balance decisively in its own favor.[4]

THE UNITED STATES AND THE BALANCE OF FORCES, EARLY 1968

By the end of 1967 the Johnson administration's war effort had ceased to gain any significant assets, but it was confronting a number of increasingly serious liabilities. Foremost among these, if only because it appeared irreversible, was the problem of the RVN.

The United States had intervened in part to create an alternative to the NLF, and by 1967 it had failed to do so. Except for a few individuals, senior officials in Washington throughout 1966 and 1967 were pessimistic about the pacification program, which was the key to retaining control of the rural areas. This was largely due to the endemic weakness of the RVN's armies, which the administration also acknowledged. Despite his public optimism, the President at the end of 1967 was more anxious than ever that the leaders of RVN "take increasing responsibility for their future" by whatever means possible.[5] For if they could not do so the Americans would have to remain in vast numbers indefinitely or find another solution.

The American dilemma, basically, was that the RVN was not capable of creating an alternative to the NLF and that its leadership was just a reflection of the crisis of Vietnamese society in this century and of the absence of a stable foundation for an indigenous ruling class. Dependent wholly on U.S. money and troops, it was now locked into a social transformation of a nation for which the only solution was a continuation of vast American subsidies and the American military presence. Its army was a political machine based on institutionalized corruption at the higher levels, and underfed, poorly led, and demoralized at the bottom—and the military system and the state bureaucratic apparatus were becoming virtually synonymous. Most members of the administration were fully aware of this reality.

The time the United States was gaining for the RVN at growing cost to itself was being squandered, and problems were multiplying as the original justification for U.S. military actions became ever-more irrelevant. The urbanization of the nation, which American firepower and policy were accelerating, left an artificial economy that was more and more precarious and a population that was uninterested in supporting the RVN—which relied on the army for its legitimacy. The United States did not consider seriously who would pay for the RVN in the years to come, because virtually all of its analyses focused only on its surrogate's immediate needs. As a political and economic system, the RVN had become hopelessly dependent on American subsidies, but the dilemma was that it failed to operate as an effective army despite its huge size and growing reliance on technology that it was never able to master. Having opted for political stability, the administration went along with the conditions the Saigon generals imposed on it for fear of restoring the chaos that the elimination of Diem had brought. The attainment of its goals therefore became completely dependent on the fate of a mélange of corrupt generals. From any viewpoint, the United States was beset by hopeless contradictions in its relationship to the RVN.

Militarily, the United States was reaching an impasse in the war. From its inception serious contradictions plagued the American mobile-war strategy, which required vast base areas and enclaves and enormous quantities of technology and logistics. Bogged down to a large extent with static defense and vast expenses, the U.S. generals failed to gain the initiative and exploit their immense firepower superiority. Able to define and implement successful tactics, they could not develop a winning strategy. The result was that they lost control of both time and costs—a control that in the American political environment was the essence of the war's viability.

America's military leaders never fully perceived these contextual political and economic realities either at home or in Vietnam, much less globally, where they were increasingly neglecting their other interests. Empiricist and technocratic, relying on arms without a coherent and relevant basis for employing them, America's limited-war doctrine and capabilities, it was clear by 1967, were being checkmated in the vast reaches of Vietnam's jungles and mountains, where the main forces of the Revolution were drawing off ever-larger numbers of GIs in a game of cat and mouse. At the same time, its massive air arm was relentlessly pounding the DRV and the Ho Chi Minh Trail, proving that the impact of air war was ultimately as ephemeral as that of high troop mobility in determining the outcome of a limited war. Rather than solving the dilemma of its limited-war strategy, one of the crucial elements which had prompted U.S. intervention from the inception, Vietnam was increasingly exposing its failures.

Westmoreland notwithstanding, the Joint Chiefs of Staff had by 1966 never seen the possibility of a quick end to the war, and by the end of 1967 the deepening pessimism in the Pentagon and CIA that the war was and would remain stalemated was beginning to affect a growing majority of senior officials. But no conclusions regarding alternative policies emerged.

Publicly optimistic, the administration by the end of 1967 still had failed to articulate realistic war aims, even confidentially, yet it also refused to establish a limit on the time and effort the war required. What began as a limited war with partially symbolic objectives—credibility and dominoes being the most commonly cited—now impinged on the United States' strategic and economic priorities elsewhere in the world, particularly in Europe. In effect, the war had long ceased to be limited for purposes of U.S. power worldwide and had begun seriously to erode its economic, military, and political foundations. Militarily inconclusive, the war became extremely expensive to the even more chimerical, but still widely held, American desire since 1945 to maintain a guiding control over the broad direction of international affairs. Most important, the war's effects helped erode the essential prerequisite of the United States' role in the world order: the internal political consensus for American globalism.

Because of the failure to define a set of coherent objectives and the means to attain them consistent with the United States' other international and domestic interests, an uneasiness and a mounting skepticism began to penetrate to all levels of its social and political order, ranging from the powerful to the powerless, whose passive acquiescence was still essential to the health of the system. This malaise was far larger in extent than the antiwar movement but remained relatively inarticulate. The administration had gained its patience with assertions and promises which enlarged its credibility gap. Only success could reverse such unprecedented and growing incredulity toward the executive's reasoning, and any serious failure could create an opposition of critical magnitude.

The administration's perception of the nature and state of its enemy was equally inconclusive, in part because its information on it was both massive and contradictory and because the sheer abundance of it allowed the optimists and pessimists to find the information they desired. The denying and the ignoring of reality had been major elements in the formulation of Vietnam policy from the inception, but by 1967 time had made this exercise more costly. While some saw the Revolution as simply an organizational system for which they could substitute another, other official experts were telling all who would listen that it was deeply rooted among the people for serious social reasons. The impact of bombing on the war effort was equally disputed, as was the ability of the Revolution's army to deal with the American challenge by fighting a protracted war.

The problem of how to confront reality had by 1967 become the major challenge emerging from postwar U.S. foreign policy, because reality now involved not just the domestic and international limits of its power on all levels but the very health of the system. Meanwhile, ideology and culture caused American leaders either to deny what was occurring or, increasingly, simply to refuse to draw obvious conclusions and act on them. This war, instead of being rational and finite, calculated in the most careful manner geopoliticians and strategists could contemplate, was becoming increasingly surreal and destructive—a war not like those analyzed in a Harvard or West Point seminar but like those in Tolstoy's or Hasek's novels. The demolition of the ideological wall that kept Washington's evasive, inconclusive vision of its freedom and policy shut off from reality would require a tremendous shock.

Part Four

THE TET OFFENSIVE AND THE EVENTS OF 1968

Chapter 24

The Tet Offensive

The 1968 Tet offensive was the most important and most complicated event of the Vietnam War. The reverberations of Tet reveal the rich texture of the forces which determine the outcome of war in the modern historical experience. Its political, military, and psychological dimensions were so far-reaching and interrelated that any simple explanations do injustice to the larger context of warfare between imperialism and revolutionary movements in recent history.

When the Party's Central Committee in January 1967 resolved to embark on Tet 1968, it prepared both for a "a decisive victory in a relatively short period of time" and for a continuing protracted war or, at worst, an American escalation.[1] It hoped to shorten the war greatly but was also aware that no matter how far it fell from its optimum goals, the war would not be as long. Its main concern was with the impact of military action on the political context of the war, both in South Vietnam and in the United States. That political framework, the Party's leaders correctly understood, would prove crucial, and an offensive was an essential catalyst in the process of change. It would shock the United States out of its complacency. The Party considered this the key to the future of the entire conflict, for without an unlimited American commitment, the Party could expect victory in the not-too-distant future.

From mid-1967 onward the Party contacted various intellectuals in the major cities and exiles in Paris and began negotiating a broad united political front. Some sort of coalition was therefore on the agenda as an integral aspect of the Tet effort. At the least, it would incorporate symbolically important urban elements into a Party-led opposition, and its role in a future diplomatic-political solution might also prove invaluable. Still, in the largest sense, the primary objective of the offensive was to influence the United States. Although the Politburo regarded a coordinated military offensive and general uprising leading to a final victory as possible, its dominant opinion in December 1967 was that the enemy would continue to fight the war, though from a decisively less favorable military, political, and psychological position. The Party believed that it could compensate for its military losses quite quickly. The objective conditions for a final victory would probably not emerge during a brief campaign of three months, but they would nonetheless be the eventual assured outcome of the imminent massive effort.[2]

Smashing the United States' illusions at this time was all the more crucial because of the dollar crisis, which the Party's press analyzed in great detail throughout January 1968. The Party also openly assessed the limits of American military strategy, its doctrinal confusion, and the overextension of its forces. In fact, it felt that it now understood its adversaries far better than they understood themselves and that the Party could create the context which would compel them to confront the limits of their situation and power.

During the last half of 1967, the Party began to explain the offensive to senior officials in the field. The vast increase in logistical preparation throughout 1967 alone revealed to most of them that a relatively massive campaign was planned for the near future. For purposes of morale, the forthcoming general offensive and uprising was described as decisive—the critical tilting of the balance of forces in favor of the Revolution's eventual victory. The extent of success would depend on how well the Revolutionary forces fought, how badly the ARVN was defeated in the cities and countryside, and what the impact of these events was on Washington. To forestall demoralization in the wake of the offensive, throughout January both the Party and the PAVN dailies published numerous assessments of the war, the overall balance of forces, and the meaning of victory. No one who read them carefully could be under any illusion that the imminent offensive meant the final victory. There would be victories "greater" than earlier ones, but there would be more struggles later, leading to a final victory "gradually." While the Party saw this as a process of educating the Americans, it was fully aware that its own assumptions, strength, and weaknesses would be identified in the course of the combat, compelling it to reassess fundamentally the balance of forces as well.[3] Yet, on this occasion, to make Tet the turning point of the war and a crucial precondition for eventual total victory, those about to go into battle were called on to make the maximum sacrifices and to do everything to create as great a victory as possible. Only action and commitment could affect history, yet it was with this knowledge of certain success that people were being asked to act with confidence.

THE AMERICANS PREPARE FOR AN OFFENSIVE

Tet was an operation so vast and important that though the Revolution took precautions to conceal its exact plans, it made no attempt to avoid an overall public appraisal of the conditions and assumptions underlying the imminent effort. Anyone who followed their publications, and Washington spent large sums doing so, could tell that an exceptional effort was in the offing. By September 1967 the Central Committee was dispatching orders to all major sections in the south, and American intelligence immediately began to pick up information on a forthcoming offensive. By early December all of official Washington was fully aware of an impending "all-out attack" which was to be the war's turning point, including assaults on many urban areas.[4] The scope of the effort was described in a press release which the U.S. mission in Saigon issued on January 5, 1968, and which predicted an attack on Saigon but not the time of its occurrence.

The U.S. military saw the offensive as coming in three phases: first, U.S. troops would be enticed away from population centers into the mountain and border areas; next, attacks throughout the country would attempt to wrest control from those segments of the RVNAF left to guard the populated regions; and, finally, these two phases would be followed by a major ground battle in a northern province, as the Communists would possibly attempt to capture one or two provinces. The CIA, too, influenced by this reasoning, predicted an attack against Hué, Pleiku, and perhaps Saigon, but it could not decide on the exact time. The notion of a "general uprising" perplexed the CIA because it believed that the Revolution did not have the capacity to mount one and that it would not risk staking its military resources and future on such a seemingly ambiguous objective. Throughout January, Westmoreland and his officers gathered irrefutable news of an approaching attack, differing only on its imminency, and shifted large numbers of troops into the Saigon region and away from the borders.

Meanwhile, a massive buildup of forces by both sides around the remote Khe Sanh base, near the seventeenth parallel, locked U.S. and PAVN soldiers into the most intense battle of the war. Imposing a siege on Khe Sanh from January 21 to early April, the PAVN saw it as a diversion intended to draw American forces to a remote area along with their covering air power. This obvious role was widely discussed among Western military analysts at the time. Westmoreland, however, thirsting for a classic military battle despite the better judgment of many U.S. officers, in his turn sought to engage up to twenty thousand PAVN soldiers with his own six thousand men, using nearly 100,000 tons of munitions against them. The events at Khe

Sanh also convinced Westmoreland that an offensive would be launched in the northern provinces. By the end of February, with half of the American maneuver battalions concentrated in the I Corps, Westmoreland had fallen into the obvious trap.

While the administration expected an offensive, it nonetheless came as a shock. The President, fully informed of the imminent attack, later morosely summed up the astonishment: "it was more massive than we had anticipated. . . . we did not expect them to attack as many [cities] as they did. . . . we did not believe they would be able to carry out the level of coordination they demonstrated. . . . it [the attack force] was larger than we had estimated."[5] The choice of Tet, curiously, caught everyone unawares. "The enemy's TET offensive," the authors of the Pentagon Papers wrote shortly after the event, "although it had been predicted, took the U.S. command and the U.S. public by surprise, and its strength, length, and intensity prolonged this shock."[6] The Americans now revealed that they had not understood either their enemy's strategy and capabilities or themselves. Tet introduced Washington to the central fact that the United States lacked a basic grasp of the nature of the war to which it had already committed over half a million men.

This lapse was all the more surprising because by the end of 1967, as evidence for an imminent offensive became irrefutable, most of the agencies in Washington reviewing the war's development and prospects were describing it as stalemated. McNamara was now convinced the war might drag on indefinitely, and the CIA argued that the Revolution could protract the war beyond 1968. The Joint Chiefs of Staff concluded that unless it were permitted to escalate the war sharply "progress would continue to be slow," with no end of the war in sight in the near future.[7] But the President himself ruled out escalation. Westmoreland at the end of November returned to Washington and gave a much-publicized speech extolling the progress that had been made in the war, but when skeptical journalists pressed him to predict when American forces might be withdrawn, he could only lamely foresee token withdrawals by the end of 1969, depending on the speed with which the ARVN could take over responsibility. A distinctly sodden, if not pessimistic, mood was settling over a fatigued capital.

The basic American problem was not intelligence but perception and a traditional analytic framework rooted in a class and national myopia. Still, the United States' intelligence at this time was in especially poor condition. The sheer amount of it, burying essential information in mounds of chaff and false reports, and the general inability to use it accurately allowed various sectors of the executive to utilize whatever data reinforced their preconceptions or bureaucratic interests. This occurred most spectacularly during the last half of 1967 with official estimates of the size and nature of the Revolutionary forces—the so-called order of battle.

The problem of estimating the Revolution's fighting forces was very complex, and an increasingly acrimonious debate over it began in May 1967. The CIA argued for about 200,000 more people than the Pentagon until September, when the CIA retreated from what was now a purely bureaucratic struggle with the JCS. Whatever the merits of the lower numbers, they were accepted as valid for the media mainly because the military in Saigon thought they were more flattering to past American successes and future prospects. Nonetheless, the Systems Analysis Office of the Pentagon circumvented the argument at the end of 1967 and distributed to key officials all the estimates being offered, so that they could make their own judgments. Optimists like Walt Rostow, the President's national security assistant, naturally fed their data preference to Johnson. It was not long before the CIA was again using its own numbers, and the episode is useful only as a lesson on the limits of intelligence in an overcharged political and bureaucratic context. The highest levels of decision makers, in any case, by late 1967 knew fully how fallible their own intelligence was, and most of them increasingly trusted only their own direct knowledge and intuition.[8]

Insulated from reality by walls of paper and layers of officials, the United States' leaders simply could not absorb the fact that they were in a strategically defensive position. Often mesmerized by figures, even those who knew that the data were tailored to needs and biases and who advocated the extricating of Americans from the morass could not grasp the magnitude of their nation's military and political weaknesses in Vietnam. Few responsible for combat contemplated the war's full implications for the domestic political structure. Parcelized in various offices, those who saw problems in one area failed to see them elsewhere. No synthesis of the overall failures and challenges existed at the highest levels of power. The United States had become fatally ensnared in its own illusions and desires.

Equally dangerous, America's leaders not only did not comprehend their own weaknesses but could not understand the Revolution at all strategically —its way of thinking, potential resources, sense of politics, and objectives. To have been able to do so would merely have driven them to lose confidence in their own strength to relate not merely to Vietnam but to revolutionary movements elsewhere. Their illusions involved not questions of intellect or malevolence but profound culturally and class-sanctioned assumptions about the nature of social reality and power in the modern historical epoch and about the relationship of American arms to America's global interests and goals. Understanding implied defeat for their cause, and such a profound level of insight required a great, profound trauma.

THE OFFENSIVE BEGINS

The wall between American perceptions and realities crumbled on January 31 when sapper units and local forces began a largely synchronized attack on all the major cities, 36 of the 44 provincial capitals, and 64 of the 242 district towns. Smashing into the U.S. embassy grounds in Saigon, the Revolution's exhibition of its power electrified and traumatized an incredulous Washington and America. "The enemy struck hard and with superb attention to organization, supply and secrecy," the State Department's Philip Habib reported.[9]

Although the Revolution's forces attacked in the I and II Military Regions twenty-four hours before the offensive in the south, and although American units had already been put on maximum alert and all ARVN leaves canceled, the shock was overwhelming because no one had imagined the scope of the attack and, more crucial, as the CIA concluded, the United States "had degraded our image of the enemy."[10] What Westmoreland estimated as anywhere from 67,000 to 84,000 forces, or only about a quarter of the Communists' available troops, now dominated the entire urban portion of the nation. More important, Saigon, with its mass of journalists and TV photographers, was the scene of a battle being watched by the entire world. Virtually unlimited American and ARVN firepower accompanied the struggle to regain physical control over the cities against a relatively small number of attackers. The Revolution's plan, with the exception of Hué, had been to assault the cities with local forces and sappers for up to five days while regular troops waited nearby. If there had been popular uprisings or a total collapse of the ARVN, then the main forces would have entered the cities and the fighting would have been far greater in scope. In the Saigon region, however, the last-minute U.S. redeployment around the city blocked the Revolution's hope of moving most of the main forces positioned in the region. The uprisings did not occur even though most of the ARVN remained on leave or deserted. The Revolution's immediate decision, therefore, was to restrict its losses unless the offensive's impact warranted greater risks and to assess the results of the first attacks.

The successes of such small numbers of largely NLF and some PAVN fighters was surely one of the hardest lessons of the combat for the United States. A mere one thousand armed personnel in Saigon, with the aid of local political units, managed for three weeks to hold off over eleven thousand U.S. and ARVN troops and police. In Hué one thousand PAVN regulars captured the Citadel despite accurate intelligence reports a week earlier that an attack was imminent—information that failed to reach Hué—and held it until February 24 while American firepower reduced 80 percent of the city to rubble. Artillery and air strikes leveled half of My Tho, a city of 80,000, and the provincial capital of Ben Tre, with 140,000 inhabitants, was decimated with the justification, as an American colonel put it in one of the most quoted statements of the war, "We had to destroy the town to save it."[11] During the month of February the Revolution's offensive ebbed and flowed throughout the south, switching after the first week to a greater reliance on mortars and small attacks, abating in most locations after the twenty-first. Around Khe Sanh, under siege since January 21, it initiated a major conventional ground battle designed to absorb American firepower and attention. For one month the waves of war touched every corner of the country, entered the lives of every person, and created about a million temporary refugees.

In the context of ferocious combat and uninhibited use of firepower, there was nothing remotely like an urban uprising. The overwhelming majority of the terrified urban dwellers remained passive to both the NLF and the RVN. The Party had expected difficulties and harbored no illusions about its weaknesses in the cities. It knew there was a good chance that the United States and the RVN would maintain control of much of the cities' key administrative and military strongholds, but it had also anticipated that Party and NLF members who surfaced in or entered cities would be able to mobilize a substantially greater number of people than actually responded. In fact, the visibility of the cadres' efforts, which compelled them to act as if the battle were indeed the decisive one, led to the death or arrest of a large proportion of the urban infrastructure almost from the inception, hobbling the entire effort in a manner that surprised the Party's leadership, and it hesitated to plunge more forces into the fray than absolutely necessary. The CIA on February 10 estimated that the Communists had already accomplished their main psychological, political, and military objectives, gaining control over vast new rural areas, smashing the RVN's military, economic, and political system, and at least relating to the urban sector in a more direct, influential fashion.

On February 4 *Quan Doi Nhan Dan*, the military daily, reflecting the realism which the first days of the offensive imposed on the Party leadership, celebrated the great achievements of Tet but added some significant warnings. "The enemy has been badly beaten," but "he still remains very stubborn" and "the struggle is still very difficult and ardent." Victories and attacks would now help advance the cause to "final" and "total" victory, but there was no precise indication when it might come.[12] The Party was clearly asking for an optimum effort from those now committed to the battle, and to have equivocated would have deprived it of the very great measure of success it was in the process of obtaining. But even as the battle had begun to rage, the Party had reverted to the contingencies in its earlier discussions of the stages of struggle leading to ultimate triumph.

The Revolution's offensive succeeded to a critical extent in all of its initial major objectives save the urban uprising. The latter failed not merely because of the towering firepower being thrown at anyone resisting the United States and the RVN but also because the political preconditions for it simply did not exist and marginal sympathizers—and there were many—would not risk their lives. Had a significant number of city dwellers joined the fray, the RVN might have capsized entirely, but instead the NLF lost most of its already fragile urban infrastructure. While the Party's desire to impose the necessity of immediate choice and action on the urbanites was unsuccessful, it did impress on them that the war would inevitably affect them directly and that ending it was profoundly relevant to their personal futures. Tet goaded many educated urban elements eventually to engage in activity, persuading a significant proportion of them that the NLF could not be excluded from the future direction of South Vietnam. The Party's other calculations, however, quickly proved valid, and apart from the event's profound impact on the United States, its effects on the RVN military, rural, and political position only confirmed the Party's initial optimism.

As the ARVN and U.S. forces were withdrawn from the rural areas to defend the cities, the pacification program was dealt what General Earle Wheeler, head of the JCS, described as "a severe set back."[13] It was no easier to calculate this in terms of percentages than the earlier claims on RVN control had been, but there was a consensus both in Washington and in Saigon that though the NLF failed in the cities, it made great advances in the countryside, from which it could now replenish its manpower losses.

The ARVN's defeats at this time were more important for Washington than the Party's successes. The ARVN desertion rate reached an all-time high; 1968 as a whole was its worst year of the entire war until 1975. ARVN infantry battalions during the first two weeks of February were at half strength, the elite Ranger forces even lower. Four of its nine airborne battalions were ineffective for combat. American officials greatly resented its lack of discipline and its looting throughout this period. But what disturbed Washington officials most was that as the NLF moved to within a short distance of complete success, the politicians in Saigon remained self-serving and corrupt, scarcely noticing the crisis at hand. "The national government appeared at first to be in a state of shock," Westmoreland publicly complained later that year.[14] The politicized basis of the entire ARVN command structure made it glaringly unwieldy for combat coordination. Thieu himself had been off on holiday celebrations when the offensive began, despite warnings of an imminent attack and his own promise to Westmoreland to limit the ARVN's Tet leaves. For two weeks Thieu appeared to absent himself from his duties. This convinced Ky and his other rivals that he was cowardly and incapable of leading and that they could exploit the situation to their own advantage. But Thieu was easily able to outmaneuver Ky, and he began irrevocably to consolidate his power, quite oblivious of the fact not only that his machinations profoundly alienated the population in areas he still controlled but also that the American leaders were reassessing the war and their nation's role. "The Viet Cong received virtually no popular support," the CIA noted at the end of February, "but neither was there a rallying to the government side. . . . further military defeats could cause a sudden swing away from the government. . . . its ability to provide energetic leadership throughout the country and all levels is in serious doubt."[15] There was a consensus in Washington at the beginning of March that the RVN might collapse within a few months should any more serious challenges to it arise.

Chapter 25

The Tet Offensive's Impact on Washington

WASHINGTON BEGINS TO CONFRONT ITS LIMITS

The Tet offensive revealed the structural constraints on policy and decision making in contemporary America and compelled the Johnson administration and Congress to acknowledge, to an extent none of their predecessors ever had, the limits that economic, military, and political realities inexorably imposed on them. The sense of crisis that emerged was justified primarily because America's leaders, not only in Washington but in all the major sectors of social power and influence, had to confront candidly the meaning of Vietnam, its symbolism to the region and the world, and its role as a test of national strategy and might. Until 1968 the costs of illusions and errors were not so apparent, and support for a large war existed among the country's leaders.

Only during crises does the real locus of power and interest expose the decisive constraints on political decision makers. To the extent that a society then defines its core needs and goals, the state's alleged autonomy and discretion in the balance of forces and power within a society tend to disappear. The presidency itself is brought to heel before what may roughly be designated as the larger interests of the American system and of those who have the capacity to define it. To the degree that those interests can be clearly and factually articulated, either by those at home or by those foreign nations linked into the U.S.-led world economic, political, and military order, the executive's options are circumscribed. Men whose ideas had earlier led the nation in different directions, as was true of the President's key advisers from 1963 until early 1968, now cease to prove influential. Their myopia, ambitions, or individual styles of work no longer have anything more than incidental interest. Should the institutional order at this point make basic errors of policy, it would be due to broader social illusions and an unrealistic consensus rather than to the caprice of this or that faction or person. In brief, bureaucratic forces are no longer decisive in a framework where choices are visibly not discretionary and the irrationality of conventional wisdom is not yet blind to the dangers of self-destruction. Decisions at this late stage reflect the interests and imperatives of a system. The Tet offensive's most decisive effect was to articulate clearly the fact that the United States was now confronting a potentially grave crisis. The first three months of 1968 were therefore the most important in the history of the entire American aggression in Vietnam.

Just as one must see America's intervention in Vietnam as contextually motivated—with its desire for credibility, regional domination, the propping up of dominoes, and the devising of a successful local-war strategy all evoking greater involvement—so one must comprehend the global events which compelled the infinitely slow process of American disengagement and defeat in the Vietnam War. Even before Tet, increasing institutional and political constraints began casting their shadows on American efforts in Vietnam. The war itself dramatically exacerbated older economic difficulties, but there were yet other dilemmas confronting the administration. These ranged from such intractable problems as the mounting racial tension in American cities and the war's debilitating impact on U.S. military power to the decline of its strategic manpower reserves for other world or even domestic crises. The significance of this erosion was dramatically illustrated in early 1968 when North Korea seized the USS *Pueblo* and its eighty-three crew members on January 23, an act which humiliated the administration and made it appear helpless. Tensions along the thirty-eighth parallel also led the South Koreans at the end of January to consider an immediate withdrawal of their 49,000 men from South Vietnam, and Washington was confronted with the possibility of having to replace them at the very moment of the Tet offensive. The danger of war along Korea's thirty-eighth parallel momentarily appeared real.

Yet it was the gold and dollar crisis that created the most sustained and irresistible pressures on Washington. Although the administration's promises to lower its deficits had managed to keep the gold pool with Europe alive after December, steady gold purchases showed that Europe's bankers remained extremely nervous. They were especially concerned because Congress refused to act on the President's tax surcharge proposal to reduce the deficits. It was in this context that the President's advisers considered their responses to a possible imminent defeat, and McNamara's parting advice to the President was not to allow another troop escalation in Vietnam to ruin the dollar abroad and the economy at home.

The gold and dollar crisis colored all of Washington's thoughts on responses to the precarious military situation in South Vietnam. At the end of February Senator Jacob Javits of New York called for an end to the gold pool, triggering a panic, and $118 million was withdrawn from the pool in only two days. For two weeks, as the United States reached an impasse in the war in Vietnam, the highly complex and technical dollar-gold problem traumatized Washington and the Western capitals, consuming vast amounts of the time of the President and his advisers. "The specter of 1929 haunted him daily," Doris Kearns reports of her intimate later interviews with him; "he worried that if the economy collapsed, history would subject Lyndon Johnson to endless abuse."[1]

On March 4, Treasury Secretary Fowler warned the President that the gold rush and the flight from the dollar were serious and could worsen rapidly, with a gold embargo leading to "exchange rate wars and trading blocs with harmful political as well as economic effects." At the same time other key advisers were carefully and pessimistically assessing the consequences of any additional troop buildup to European bankers' confidence in the dollar. While Europe's gold-pool members had agreed in early March to sustain the dollar, on March 11 banks rushed the pool, which lost nearly a billion dollars in gold before it suspended operations four days later. "We can't go on as is," Rostow warned the President on March 14, and on the same day several European nations began to redeem dollars for U.S. Treasury gold to recoup the bullion they had lost in support of the dollar.[2] That afternoon, having lost $372 million that day, and fearing a loss of a billion dollars the following day, the Treasury arranged immediately to close the gold market. With memos and meetings constantly before him and with his chief economic adviser's late January warning of a possible world depression still fresh in his mind, Johnson on March 15 wrote to the European prime ministers that "these financial disorders—if not promptly and firmly overcome—can profoundly damage the political relations between Europe and America and set in motion forces like those which disintegrated the Western world between 1929 and 1933."[3]

At first the White House wanted its allies to accept unlimited amounts of dollars without gold backing, but Fowler and Martin opposed this as both unrealistic and a license to continue fiscal irresponsibility. Instead, European central bankers were called to Washington for an emergency meeting on March 16. As antiwar pickets paraded outside their secret sessions, reminding them that the war was the origin of the dollar crisis, the key decisions over the future of the dollar were being made by Europeans. Abolishing the pool altogether, Europe's bankers refused to use their gold to save the dollar. They categorically rejected an American request that they forgo their right to claim gold for dollars from the U.S. Treasury. They offered restraint only if the administration acted more responsibly in managing its economy. In effect, if it refused to place the defense of the dollar above all other considerations, then they reserved the power to demand a reckoning that could profoundly upset America's position in the world economy, with all that this implied for its political leadership.

After Tet the administration finally acknowledged that any increase of troops to Vietnam threatened not just the country's economy but all of its domestic and international priorities. Those in Washington who had for some time opposed the war's overshadowing of other military and regional commitments now became more outspoken. Although they were especially strong among civilians in the Pentagon, there was a near consensus in the government that the war should not cause the nation to sacrifice its other responsibilities, especially to NATO. With America stretched thin globally and with a crisis brewing in Korea, the Joint Chiefs of Staff immediately revived its earlier request for a call-up of reserves—a politically unpopular move for the President—and its chairman, General Wheeler, spent the rest of February conniving to get more men for the military services. In a virtuoso performance he flew to Saigon and after four days was back in Washington on February 27 with an extremely pessimistic report and a demand, allegedly from Westmoreland himself, for 206,000 men. Vietnam had greatly weakened the strategic manpower reserves for crises elsewhere in the world, and Wheeler gambled that he could rebuild them by claiming that the 206,000 were essential to reverse the tide of the war. To deny him the full request, Wheeler argued, was to jeopardize the position of the commander in Vietnam, if not to imperil his forces. One hundred thousand of the new men, however, he planned to send elsewhere than to Vietnam.

The guileless Westmoreland later sharply rebuked Wheeler for pretending that he was the author of the famous 206,000 request, but Wheeler was in fact dissembling largely out of concern for the mounting pressure in Washington over the weakening of the U.S. military elsewhere. Indeed, the President himself was worried that there would be insufficient regular forces to cope with the anticipated summer turmoil in American cities—an anxiety that was justified when huge riots broke out in Washington and in over fifty cities after the Reverend Martin Luther King was assassinated the following April 4. The most immediate result of the request for 206,000 more men, however, was that the President on February 28 asked Clark Clifford, his new Secretary of Defense, to create a committee to study it—and it was this committee's effort to turn its attention to a full-scale review of the war that became the main focus of opposition to further escalation among key Washington decision makers.[4]

THE ADMINISTRATION DEFINES
A LIMIT

When men who have heretofore perceived no limits to their power confront reality, there will always be drama and tension. There were, of course, very dramatic moments during February and March 1968; remorse and doubt led to a debilitating loss of self-confidence unknown among American leaders for decades. But from the inception of Tet to Johnson's epoch-making speech of March 31, there was an inexorability to Washington's command decisions.

The American military's first response was a paralyzing incredulity at their gross underestimation of their enemy's resources and their failure after nearly three years of massive efforts to blunt the Revolution's growing offensive capabilities. Even while Wheeler was actively cajoling Westmoreland to call for reinforcements, the JCS itself on February 12 recommended deferring a decision to send them. By the time Wheeler had mobilized the Joint Chiefs behind him, he confronted other opposition from all sides. While the civilians in the Pentagon were the most aggressive, they had the backing of most of the CIA and the State Department for their immediate contention that sending more troops to South Vietnam would be futile. Not only would more troops encourage the already inefficient ARVN to fight even less well, the opponents of Wheeler's request pointed out, but the critical battles then taking place would be decided long before new soldiers could reach Vietnam. It was also in response to these conflicting views that the President had created the Clifford committee to help him reach his decision.

The Clifford committee began by gathering the basic facts. Initially, it did not intend to question the efficacy of the war. The departing McNamara had warned the President that 400,000 men and $10 billion would be required if he approved the commitment of a large new offensive force. The JCS contended that the 108,000 men definitely intended for South Vietnam out of the 206,000 requested, would tip the scale in the otherwise stalemated war. But even Rostow, who had earlier endorsed the new escalation, now had to admit that the DRV would meet any American buildup. Also crucial in the committee's discussion was the argument that the war was causing the United States to sacrifice its many interests elsewhere in the world, impairing its overall international objectives. Piece by piece, the case for continuing the war by escalating was destroyed. The CIA, especially, argued that the war was stalemated and that the Communists retained the strategic initiative. By the time the Clifford committee's intense discussions and analyses were completed on March 3, Clifford had changed his position and no one favored the 206,000 plan save Wheeler and the JCS. "1968 will be the pivotal year" of the war, Wheeler had correctly argued.[5]

The result was a nominal stalemate among the President's key advisers, which meant a continuation of the status quo, though in fact opinions were changing subtly with the burden of reality. While the possibility of committing 206,000 men was left open on a "week by week" basis, only 22,000 men already authorized were to go immediately as "all we can give at the moment," as the President put it. Johnson later asserted he had rejected the 206,000-man request by early March, but in fact he remained quite ambivalent and unwilling to accept the growing constraints on his freedom of action. Even after the *New York Times* on March 10 revealed the secret debates, he hesitated, although the publicity hurt the advocates of escalation. What the Clifford committee proposed was that the administration do nothing decisive until it could complete a basic reassessment of "political and strategic guidance" of the war.[6] But for two weeks, apart from a desultory consensus that much more had to be done to get the ARVN to assume a far greater role in the war, nothing new was decided on Vietnam, and the President was under the greatest pressure of his life as every conceivable problem weighed on him.

"I felt," he later confided, "that I was being chased on all sides by a giant stampede coming at me from all directions." There was Vietnam, but also the economy. Blacks were rioting, students protesting, and hysterical reporters pressing. "And then the final straw. The thing I feared from the first day of my Presidency was actually coming true. Robert Kennedy had openly announced his intention to reclaim the throne. . . ."[7] The strain on Johnson made his behavior erratic; rumors of his overwrought emotional state and exotic religious experiences abounded—and later enough of them were confirmed to reveal that the President had indeed lost touch. Antiwar Senator Eugene McCarthy's 42 percent vote in the New Hampshire primary on March 12 reinforced the President's desperation.

Politics and economics now merged to affect the future of the war. Clifford, perhaps the shrewdest adviser to Presidents in the post-1945 era, was a critical link in this synthesis. As he was to recount later that month to Rusk and Rostow, "I make it a practice to keep in touch with friends in business and the law across the land. I ask them their views about various matters. Until a few months ago, they were generally supportive of the war. They were a little disturbed about the overheating of the economy and the flight of gold, but they assumed that these things would be brought under control; and in any event, they thought it was important to stop the Communists in Vietnam. Now all that has changed. . . . these men now feel we are in a hopeless bog. The idea of going deeper into the bog strikes them as mad. . . . It would be very difficult—I believe it would be impossible—for the

President to maintain public support for the war without the support of these men."[8] In fact, two days after the McCarthy victory, Kennedy approached Clifford and proposed not to run for the presidency if Johnson would create a commission to study and change Vietnam policy. Clifford presented the offer to Johnson, who rejected it brusquely, only to see Kennedy announce his candidacy.

Clifford, meanwhile, was not happy with the President's paralysis and incapacity to reverse the disastrous course toward escalation. The opinions of his corporate friends reinforced his own real but habitually cautious desires to redefine the nation's Vietnam strategy. "I was more conscious each day of domestic unrest in our own country," he wrote the following year. "Just as disturbing to me were the economic implications of a struggle to be indefinitely continued at ever-increasing cost."[9] On March 19 he proposed to Johnson that he call another session of the Senior Advisory Group of the State Department—the so-called Wise Men who the preceding fall had strongly supported the President's war policy. Dean Acheson, its chairman, had since late February, at the President's request, been informally reviewing the war and its conflict with American interests elsewhere in the world, and he had become highly critical of the unlimited commitment. On March 15 he had informed Johnson that the JCS was giving him very poor advice and that it was time to disengage from the unpopular war. Clifford knew he had a powerful friend in the former secretary of state, whose prestige with Johnson was enormous, and he also sensed what his group would advise. Johnson consented to the project probably aware of its likely position, and the Wise Men picked up the debate the Clifford committee had left hanging.

The role of the Wise Men was illustrative of the parameters of power and ideas in the United States in moments of crisis. The basic military, economic, and political facts which so profoundly influenced the Wise Men had already reached most of the President's key advisers and the President himself. Even arch-hawks like Rostow admitted that though putting the country on a war footing in February had been possible, "the changing political environment at home and the international financial crisis of March reduced that possibility."[10] Nothing could change those realities, and in a certain sense the ideas of the Wise Men were anticlimatic, reflecting the tide of events rather than shaping them.

The world of big industry and finance, so amorphous to those outside it but so real to those in it, had been for the war because its members believed in the objectives of American foreign policy which had led to the intervention. Yet key individuals were often called on, both formally and informally, to comment on economic affairs that the war strongly affected, such as budget deficits and inflation. While they had never assumed a critical position on the war before 1968, they consistently favored efforts to eliminate these economic challenges. Such expediency meant that should the nation's financial difficulties become sufficiently serious, they would oppose escalation and might even favor a reduction of the war to economically manageable proportions. Such a stance was strictly pragmatic and graphically revealed the contradictions which led to American involvement in the first place, for its ideal would have been for the United States to have won the war both quickly and cheaply. The Wise Men—who included men with close links to the world of finance, corporate law, and big business like George Ball, Douglas Dillon, Cyrus Vance, John J. McCloy, McGeorge Bundy, Arthur Dean, Robert Murphy, and Henry Cabot Lodge—understood such nuances. It was virtually certain that impersonal calculations of this kind would influence their recommendations. As men used to confronting facts and their implications, they were better able to internalize the larger material balance of forces in the war than most, particularly because it was not their personal reputations that were at stake but their class interests.

Also important during this decisive month was the state of public opinion and that of politicians who instinctively thrive on relating to it, quite unconcerned with their own past inconsistencies on the war. The entry of McCarthy and Kennedy in the race for the Democratic nomination would not have been such a formidable challenge to the President had the polls on March 16 not shown him to be at the lowest point of popularity since he came to office. The public's feelings about the war had become consistently more critical since 1966; by the end of 1967 they were evenly divided. The Tet offensive caused opposition to rise sharply. By the summer of 1968 those Americans who thought the sending of troops to Vietnam was a mistake far outnumbered those in favor of it. This trend profoundly affected many officials, who felt that growing public impatience was imposing a real limit on how long politicians could continue to sustain the war. And the emergence of a larger and more militant antiwar movement on campuses, especially among the children of the elite, struck key defenders of the war personally. By the end of March 1968, it was quite clear that even ignoring the military and economic constraints, the administration was confronting an unprecedented postwar situation in the virtually total collapse of the crucial foreign policy consensus between the executive, the traditional establishment, and the public.

However belligerent or aggressive the President appeared to his advisers or the press at this time, it was clear that he was now implementing the Clifford committee's cautious policy of no further escalation. However, the committee failed to alter the President's basic commitment to an ongoing war. On March 22 the final allotment of new men to South Vietnam was reconfirmed at 24,000 more, nearly half of whom were already there, and the request for 206,000 men was shelved permanently. As with all his fateful March decisions, Johnson later offered the explanation that his freezing the commitment to the war at existing levels after six years of steady escalation was due to a variety of factors, foremost of which was the expectation that there would be no additional NLF offensives and the belief that the ARVN was now fighting harder. But, in fact, both premises proved incorrect, and Johnson still did not escalate when the second Tet wave came, because his other concerns were quite decisive. These included "especially our financial problems," with the gold crisis and budget deficit still hanging over the economy, as well as public opinion.[11] And for a consummate parliamentarian like Johnson, the conviction during March that Congress would no longer support escalation undoubtedly also weighed heavily in his calculations. Whatever his bluster and style, the facts had sunk into the President's consciousness. U.S. policy would get neither worse—nor better.

The famous, often detailed meetings of the Wise Men on March 25–26 only confirmed this reality. Acheson was firmly in command of its proceedings and so preconceived in his judgments that he brooked little opposition from a minority which preferred not to offend the President's martial instincts. The war was stalemated, and the nation could not afford to commit more resources without sacrificing its economy and other global interests in an effort to win it. The public, too, both in South Vietnam and in the United States, was now deeply opposed to the effort. Most of the Senior Advisory Group favored the ending of escalation and the taking of steps toward disengagement—ranging from less bombing of the DRV to a reduction of American forces and the transfer of greater responsibility for the war to RVN.[12]

LYNDON JOHNSON'S MARCH 31 SPEECH

For the President, emotionally overwrought during these weeks and merging the greatest personal crisis of his lifetime with the most important failure of American military and foreign policy in this century, the last days of March were excruciating. The shrewdest politician Texas ever produced was for the first time wholly isolated and compelled to assume the burden not simply of his own political errors in Vietnam but also of the failure of an entire class in pursuing the war and the hegemonic goals of American foreign policy, a class that was now abandoning escalation and the President's commitment to it. Carrying the weight of failure, Johnson hesitated and considered persisting with the war without any inhibitions. After terrible days of intense emotional strain, he also decided to withdraw from the race for the 1968 presidential nomination and to retreat to the tranquillity of his Texas ranch.

The President's March 31 speech touched on everything from a bombing halt to negotiations, but the most important and tangible part of it was the announcement of his decision to retire from politics. His erstwhile concessions of a bombing halt in all but vague areas north of the seventeenth parallel in return for reciprocal DRV actions was within only a day to embarrass the administration when planes attacked sites nearly five hundred kilometers north of that line. Rather than extricating himself from the war in a forthright manner, Johnson quickly raised basic doubts about his intentions and further alienated domestic and world opinion. By April and May, bombing attacks against the DRV were far greater than in February or March. From this time until October 31, when Johnson called a total bombing halt over the DRV in a last-ditch effort to win votes for Hubert Humphrey's faltering campaign for the presidency, it was obvious that bombing would both become a tool of public relations and politics for himself and set a precedent for his successor. For while the March 31 speech was an explicit pledge not to escalate the war, the President remained very much committed to sustaining the struggle until he left office, and Rusk and Rostow reinforced his devotion to bombing. Clifford and those who wanted to redefine national policy and scale down the war knew that the President would never agree with them, whatever they said, and all they could do for the remainder of 1968 was try to keep Johnson tied to what they regarded as a schizoid policy and prevent it from becoming something even worse. It was not, in their opinion, to get better.

Johnson's open offer for negotiations was soon mired when the United States retracted its proposal to meet the Communists anywhere, embarrassing the administration even before the long, futile Paris talks were to begin the following May. Conceding that he would not raise troop levels by more than 24,000 or escalate the war, the President asked for Congress's help in solving the budget deficit, the gold and dollar crisis, and the other economic problems that his past escalations had unleashed. The most prominent new proposal in the President's message, which became the basis of Nixon's subsequent Vietnamization policy, was an expanding of the RVN's military forces to take a progressively larger share of combat and, implicitly, lay the basis for a reduced dependency on American troops. It was only here that the advice of the Wise Men may actually have moved the President.

The American presence in Vietnam was directly related to the RVN's chronic military and political weaknesses, and interpreting its performance during the weeks after Tet was central to Washington's definitions of its own role and alternatives. The first, careful reports were highly pessimistic, and the persistent internecine political struggles between Thieu and Ky in the midst of a life-and-death struggle particularly discouraged officials. The CIA believed that the political dimension was critical, but it also confessed that if there was no chance of reform, a U.S. role, regardless of its size, would prove hopeless. The State Department called the RVN's collapse "a strong present possibility over the next few months." By the end of March, however, General Creighton Abrams, who had already been designated quietly to replace Westmoreland, was arguing that the ARVN suddenly had far better morale than earlier.[13] With the bulk of military opinion on the RVN highly skeptical, and the legacy of experience even more negative, the Wise Men focused on the linkage of reconstituting the ARVN and American disengagement, fully aware that it was unlikely to succeed. Yet the notion of a decent interval to conceal the failure of American forces was clearly articulated. Publicly committed to the myth of the RVN's growing successes and strength, the administration saw the claim as the pretense which would justify eventual troop reductions. Even if there was no clear timetable, the unspoken assumption in Washington's plans was that victory was unobtainable and that "Vietnamizing" the war would buy time for whatever diplomatic or political alternatives might arise—or at least postpone the need to confront the very real defeat until after the election.

Given the absence in Johnson's speech of any references to credibility, dominoes, and the like, the implicit shift of emphasis in his statement was crucial. American war aims were neither victory nor some other abstraction but providing the RVN a "shield" behind which it could grow. On the efforts of the RVN's people "the outcome will ultimately depend."[14] This redefinition of basic national objectives conformed both to military, political, and economic necessity and to the overwhelming opinion of leading advisers and decision makers. It was this new American readiness to limit its commitments and later partially to disengage, however amorphously stated and defined at this time, that was the major outcome of the Tet offensive.

WASHINGTON AND THE NEW BALANCE OF FORCES

Vietnam became America's first foreign war since 1812 to produce a profound domestic social crisis and political polarization. During the First and Second World Wars, political leadership in Washington made key decisions gradually and deliberately as changes occurred in the global balance of forces. Not so with Vietnam. Unlike all earlier wars, it aggravated many of the problems of American capitalism rather than relieving them. Amid a protracted trauma in race relations, the war increasingly became the focus of protest and dissent for millions of people who knew what the President was privately being told: so long as the war absorbed so much money, it was impossible to deal with internal social needs.

The vast bulk of Americans who opposed the war had no basis for analyzing it coherently, and the efforts of the Left within the antiwar movement to explain it failed. While they were incapable of truly perceiving its horror for the average Vietnamese, the gore of television coverage notwithstanding, a sense of this terrible experience nonetheless penetrated their consciousness. The issue of war crimes entered the debates over the war, and the enormity of the damage the United States was inflicting profoundly disquieted the consciences of a small minority. However inchoate opinion and attitudes were, there was a growing appreciation of the vast, ever-larger gap between conventional wisdom and reality, filling some Americans with a deepening sense of outrage and many more with a growing skepticism and sense of alienation. If, in the end, analytic conceptions never caught up with the sheer magnitude of the events, they nonetheless broke the apathy and consensus which had given the successive administrations the freedom from political pressure to test their strategies in Southeast Asia. This growth of skepticism and radicalization accelerated after 1967 to become a serious variable in the politics of the war. Even if protest waned with events and no one group could unify it, the accumulated opposition to the war now became a permanent reality which would emerge periodically to challenge the government in multiple and often exotic and complex ways, ranging from extremely polite middle-class constituents entreating their congressmen to forms of direct action. While no single effort made a difference, collectively all such activity indicated that for the first time in modern American history the national consensus or apathy on foreign policy was irretrievably broken, thereby creating the mass basis for opposition. The politics of opposition evolved not deductively or ideologically but as a part of a cumulative set of choices the state presented to people whose responses were based on an enormous variety of motives. Time and events were shaping consciousness, and thereby action, especially among those who had the most to lose from the war. Vast numbers were being politicized, and Tet was a powerful catalyst in this process. A new reality was being created in the American political universe.

Confronting unprecedented opposition from traditional elites as well as from the public, the White House chose a way out of the impasse that was extremely tortuous but whose direction was clear. It was on the defensive even though no one in government dared to admit total defeat. Only days after Johnson made his March 31 speech, black rioting erupted and for weeks took up much of the administration's attention. In part because the May 1968 riots in France subdued the French ardor for making gold central to the world exchange system, the United States was able to breathe more freely on that question for the remainder of the year, though the precariousness of the dollar remained an inhibition to any costly new adventures. Yet although its military, economic, and political options had been drastically reduced, the administration made the fateful decision to struggle in a losing context to save its "credibility" by relying on two major, interrelated efforts to gain time during 1968 for alternatives it could only vaguely envision—a policy which was guaranteed to lose the election for virtually any Democrat who chose to run.

The first was merely to continue the war at the same high level of combat and firepower which American forces permitted, with a full awareness of their inability to alter the military equation and shorten the war. This desperate dependence on firepower was symbolic, concealing failure with brutal revenge, as well as a means of obtaining time for the second approach —namely, to begin to transfer the war to the various RVN armies. For Johnson this meant essentially continuing the war within those constraints he abhorred and turning it over to his successor with the strongest military position possible.

American leaders knew that more firepower would not change the position of the Revolution militarily or reduce its ability to mobilize recruits. Still, when the President promised a pause in the bombing of the DRV to encourage negotiated solutions to the war and reciprocity, the Air Force immediately increased its fighter-bomber sorties over the DRV, setting a wartime record during July. The DRV's skepticism toward American initiatives naturally rose with them. The tonnage of bombs dropped on the DRV during 1968 nearly equaled that of 1967, but bombing greatly increased in the south, where a growing part of "the countryside," one American general reported in 1969, "looked like the Verdun battlefields."[15] This emphasis on firepower meant, of course, that the administration would fight what it increasingly knew to be a futile war in ways which could only further wreck South Vietnam's human, social, and economic fabric. As the American generals continued the habitual search-and-destroy tactics throughout 1968, some reported their "coldly realistic, if not pessimistic" conclusions back to Washington that the strategy was still ineffectual.[16]

The successive waves of combat which began on Tet created nearly one million refugees, and over $200 million in capital goods were destroyed during Tet alone. Agricultural output and private-sector output dropped sharply in 1968, as did the revenues of the RVN, which was now more dependent on aid than ever and less able to take over the military responsibilities the Americans proposed to transfer to it. Linked to this mounting economic burden was the accelerating transformation and urbanization of the society. The Americans were impressed that the urban population had shown a distinct apathy toward the RVN's ordeal, even, in some places, engaging in low-level cooperation with the NLF. "The ineffective GVN political response may still further improve the VC cause in the cities, as well as in the countryside," the Clifford committee had presciently warned.[17] In effect, the war created structural forces, such as urbanization, that might define the context of the RVN's politics, so that even if an articulate portion of the urban population did not rally openly to the NLF, the RVN, with its sordid struggles between Thieu and Ky, might nonetheless further alienate them.

The administration's decision to concentrate on strengthening the RVN's various armed forces was crucial both politically and structurally. To the extent that the administration planned to transform the nature of the war from a conflict between Americans and the Revolution to one between the RVN and the Revolution, it was making a fateful choice, since scarcely anyone knowledgeable believed that the RVN had the ability to win such a conflict. The Party had calculated this very question before Tet, and forcing such clarity on the United States was a prime objective of the effort. The new strategy was an excuse for leaving some Americans in South Vietnam at a time when pressure at home was mounting for their removal. While this was a consideration for the White House, many in Washington really saw Vietnamization as a face-saving formula for acknowledging their own failures.

Ironically, the creation of a larger RVN military machine was to become another vehicle for guaranteeing the defeat of its cause. For the RVNAF's growing role goaded the peasantry and urban masses, including many elements indifferent or even hostile to the NLF, to oppose the RVN's war policies. In the spring of 1968 the RVN declared a general mobilization of eighteen- and nineteen-year-olds. All men between eighteen and thirty-eight were now subject to induction and required to stay in a branch of the full-time military until forty-five, while sixteen- and seventeen-year-olds and thirty-nine- to fifty-year-olds were subject to incorporation into the largely unarmed, part-time People's Self-Defense Forces. By 1969, 150,000 new men had been added to the ARVN and 250,000 to the RF/PF. The mass levee at a time of growing RVN economic difficulties further profoundly distorted the wholly artificial nature of the RVN social system, imposing a vast new tax on it.

The forced recruitment of the nation's sons alienated the people in multiple ways. The most obvious was their personal and economic losses, so that such families more and more perceived the RVN as the main burden on their lives. For the rest of the nation, the ARVN was a growing tax as looting, which had reached new levels during Tet, increased with the mounting economic problems confronting soldiers. "Looting and other misconduct by Republic of Vietnam Armed troops toward the civilian populace have undermined the confidence of the people in RVNAF," the NSC's early 1969 assessment concluded, and they saw no way of reversing it.[18] The ARVN became less cohesive, despite it new arms. The rate of desertions rose substantially, especially among new recruits, and the so-called ghost soldiers became even more common. Their officers were equally unprepared for their tasks, which contributed to growing demoralization. "All agencies agree that the RVNAF could not," the NSC stated early in 1969, "either now or even when fully modernized, handle both the VC and a sizable level of NVA forces without U.S. combat support in the form of air, helicopters, artillery, logistics and some ground forces."[19] Increasing the size of the RVN's army only weakened it as a fighting organization, further undermining the entire social order and leaving its economy more dependent and vulnerable. Unwilling and unable to confront these dilemmas, the Johnson administration preferred to bequeath them all to its successor.

Chapter 26

Assessing the Tet Offensive

THE REVOLUTION'S POSITION AFTER FEBRUARY 1968

Assessing the results of the first wave of the Tet offensive was an urgent problem for the Party. Although its human losses were nowhere near the figures the U.S. military claimed, they were nonetheless higher than many senior Party leaders thought tolerable. This was especially true among southerners and those who had spent years working with the PLAF, who believed that had the offensive's tactics been more realistic, the victory would have been greater with fewer casualties. And while this was a difference of degree, the fact remained that although the Revolution could replace its lost numbers, there was no question that it could not, and did not, compensate for its qualitative sacrifices. For its greatest toll of dead was among its most experienced southern political and military cadres, both urban and rural.

Ironically, while the first American analyses appreciated the Communist military successes, the Party leadership's initial estimates focused on its failures. Only later did it make more accurate, balanced judgments. Poor coordination and pessimistic local reports reaching higher echelons pushed the leaders from their pre-attack optimism to greater caution as they sought to tailor the later phases of the Tet offensive to preserve as much of their forces as possible. They comprehended their achievements in damaging the basic RVN military system and administrative structure, but they treated the general uprising as a failure and thought their plans for rural activities were still too vague and naive. Some also believed that the Revolution's guiding role had lagged badly at a critical moment. The next phase of the offensive was to take both the promise and the problems into account.

The leadership, however, immediately made less critical public assessments for the Party's activists, but they were more explicitly nuanced than those in January. During March the Party's major journals for higher cadres reviewed the progress of the first Tet wave, stressing its success in smashing the RVN military and political structure and thereby undercutting the long-term basis of the American effort. The Johnson administration was now on the defensive both at home and in Vietnam. While the Revolution had attained a strategic triumph, laying the foundation for a final victory, and while Tet had indeed been a turning point insofar as the United States and the ARVN were concerned, the war would nevertheless require more time.

The next stage of the offensive was much more cautious. Soldiers and cadres from the DRV now replaced the many dead southerners, whose numbers were far smaller than the Americans asserted but larger than the Party dared confess. Their main focus was still the RVN military and political system, but the attacks which began May 4 were better organized, involved only small groups with flexible objectives, and were more dependent on the use of mortars and rockets. Altogether, they hit 119 towns, cities, bases, and targets the night of May 4, but advance warning of an attack on Saigon seriously blunted the Revolution's main focus on the capital. The Party vainly hoped for a spectacular success there. Still, units penetrated Saigon, and a week of street fighting was followed by weeks of intermittent rocket attacks. During this phase of the offensive, the Communists did not attack American installations, proving that the RVN itself, and its very capital, remained the most fragile part of the United States' war effort. Even though the masses had not joined the deadly fray, the Revolution had still attained its most important objective. Assessing the results of the second wave of the Tet offensive, the Party concluded they duplicated those of the first attacks. The Revolution did poorly in mobilizing both the urban population and the ARVN troops, and it exhibited military inadequacies, but politically this phase, too, was a major accomplishment.

The Tet offensive's third and last phase began on August 17 and lasted for six weeks. It differed from the first two in that it also attacked U.S. installations and did not attempt to mobilize mass uprisings. Largely dependent on mortars and rockets, it again used local forces and minimized the loss of manpower by relying on small units. It sought to keep the RVN off balance and to remind the Americans that they, too, were vulnerable, a point that was politically relevant to the presidential campaign then in process. The Revolution could mass forces and attack cities or break down into small-unit warfare and draw enemy forces out into the countryside—or do both simultaneously. The enemy, Pentagon analysts stressed at the end of March, "can limit his casualties to a rate that he is able to bear indefinitely."[1]

Although the Revolution's ability to control U.S. and ARVN casualties declined after mid-1968, to a vital extent it never lost its own power to husband its manpower. The Communists' capacity to pursue protracted war and a flexible strategy left them with the strategic initiative.

The leaders of the United States and of the Party were both acutely conscious of their own shortcomings. American generals in the field found their enemy's usual ability to avoid contact frustrating and discouraging; others saw even the Communists' tactics before Tet as a "significant victory."[2] Such reports only reinforced the view in Washington after Tet that the Revolution retained its capacity for protracted war regardless of its momentary losses. The Politburo, however, while impressed by its great successes, was very deeply conscious that it "still did not meet the basic requirements that had been set forth," causing it to embark on the military policy of rebuilding its forces and reemphasizing small-unit and guerilla warfare with minimum risks.[3]

The Politburo had not expected an urban uprising to prove decisive, but neither had it foreseen such great losses among its urban infrastructure and those units sent to aid it. Sustained urban combat caused it to concentrate more on the cities than it had planned, leading to what it perceived as a serious weakening of its rural position. By making an exceptional effort to establish its power in the cities, the Party failed in both the urban and the rural areas to emerge organizationally stronger than it had been prior to Tet. The Party's criterion of urban mobilization, however, was quite narrow, gravely minimizing the differences between the current urban situation and that of 1945, when the Japanese had been defeated and infinitely less well armed and fewer in number than the Americans and their dependents. As in Europe during World War Two, cities revolt when victory is imminent or when literally no other options for survival exist. The failure of the general uprising did not exhaust the political role of the cities, but it redefined the modalities of opposition to something much more complex and subtle.

The Americans read the same facts to reach quite opposite conclusions. During the first phase of Tet, the Clifford committee decided that the urban attacks were really a successful diversion for what was intended as a Communist "takeover of the countryside."[4] At the end of 1967, it estimated, the RVN really controlled only 30 percent of the rural population. Even Westmoreland publicly conceded later that year that the urban attacks had drawn RVNAF forces protecting villages into the cities, which "dealt our pacification program a substantial setback."[5] At the beginning of 1969 the most authoritative American estimate was that the NLF village infrastructure extended to up to three-quarters of the rural population, and that the RVN's local organizations had grown weaker throughout 1968. American experts on specific provinces were confident that the NLF's political apparatus had not been weakened throughout 1968. Hypnotized by their own data, they thought that the NLF infrastructure at the end of December 1968 was as large as it had been a year earlier, with its liberation committees more numerous than the RVN's organizations, and that the "Phoenix" program set up in 1967 to locate and destroy the NLF's civilian infrastructure had been spectacularly unsuccessful.

The Revolution, however, knew that its political infrastructure was being badly hurt in the rural regions and decimated in the cities, and this pattern of losses was to continue for several more years. It was looking at reality while the American experts had devised an abstract notion of the Party and NLF's organization which seriously misled them. The Party appreciated that the formal, hierarchial structure it had designed had become largely irrelevant before Tet and that it had for some time been essentially replaced by an informal yet working alternative. The NLF's structure had been decentralized since its creation—inevitable given the problems of communication and wartime disruptions—and while this had been a source of creative local adaptions, it also made the village organizations increasingly vulnerable. The CIA disdained to regard rank-and-file NLF members, sympathizers, occasional workers, or tax collectors as real infrastructure and therefore thought its Phoenix program was failing even as it rounded up and killed so many—over thirteen thousand in 1968. It sought, above all, high-level cadres because it was convinced the infrastructure was dependent on a formal operating command system, when in fact it had become largely self-motivating, explicitly encouraged to operate autonomously, and reliant on thousands of such low-level, obscure people. In reality, however, the Revolution could continue if only senior people were captured, but it was incapable of persevering without its grass-roots workers, many of whom had no official positions. The role of such people was based on years of experience and personal, often familial contact between cadres and Revolutionary workers, on the one hand, and the villages and people with whom they lived, on the other. Inestimable in importance, they provided the cohesion from which all else emerged, making them central to all dimensions of the struggle. In addition to those the Americans could count as "eliminated," an untold number of cadres and infrastructure members were killed and wounded throughout 1968 of whom the United States knew nothing. Others were forced to leave their villages because they could now be identified.

Yet the Americans comprehended one subtlety that more than offset their myopia, ultimately giving them reason for their pessimism and making that of the Revolution excessive. They were far better informed about the weaknesses of the rural administration of the RVN than the NLF was, and they were acutely aware that the Revolution's ultimate power was its enemy's incapacity to satisfy the peasants or gain their positive commitment. American experts were quite conscious that even where the NLF failed to recover organizationally from Tet, it retained a crucial residue of sympathy, making the nature of politics less one of formal organizations than one of broader contexts, including local grievances and social issues. So long as their sons were drafted and their property looted and destroyed, or as corrupt officials exploited them, most peasants would not support the American-sponsored side, and for the United States that was tantamount to losing. Others, of course, were convinced that *any* commitment would only hurt their already precarious lives. It was not that the NLF had left the countryside or been destroyed but that the RVN had also been eliminated and could not fill the vacuum.[6]

THE PARTY'S UNITED-FRONT POLITICS

In a basic political sense the Revolution's losses in 1968 were relative. As many of those who had not rallied to the Revolution remained hostile to the RVN, the Party stressed a united-front strategy far more than it had since 1960. The need to do so to some extent reflected the failure of the NLF's tactics during Tet as well as the ambiguous and diverse nature of the opposition to the Thieu-Ky regime.

The Tet offensive was also intended to lead to proselytizing among the RVN's troops and all sectors of its system, yet little had been accomplished during February. The Party judged that effort unsuccessful as well. In the shift toward the united front, religions were considered especially important, and in villages it began to create "People's Liberation Councils" to broaden its basis of support and attract new supporters. At the end of April 1968, it also organized the Alliance of National, Democratic, and Peace Forces for urban elements that had been ready to cooperate with the NLF in the cities but that were unwilling to join it directly. These new fronts were an acknowledgment of the NLF's past failures to absorb much of the urban opposition, and the two new organizations complemented each other and overlapped with the NLF.

Tet compelled the Party to revise its work and goals in the cities. The senior leaders of the Saigon Party moved to the security of the tunnel complex of Cu Chi, forty kilometers away. Saigon was still a crucial focus of activity because of its symbolic and functional role, but the new Party structure there and in other cities was painfully and slowly rebuilt with optimum stress on security, secrecy, and autonomy among Party and NLF branches. City cadres usually wore masks in each other's presence during larger meetings, and the precinct Party committees within Saigon, Hué, and Danang had no direct contact with each other. The new system successfully protected the basic NLF and Party organization, and the Phoenix program failed totally in the cities, but the NLF could not grow in size or function. Yet the urban political context made the remaining NLF urban structure inadequate, and the Party's emphasis throughout the south after mid-1968 was on building its military apparatus outside the cities—a task which absorbed most of its able people and caused its political work to slip appreciably. In part because of their feeling after Tet that they had overemphasized their urban effort and managed it quite haphazardly, the Revolution's distinctive theory of interrelated rural and urban struggle now was partially modified to minimize further losses.

The Party's renewed emphasis on a united-front strategy was both the product of its objective reading of realities and a reflection of its own weaknesses and incapacity to operate alone. To an extent unknown since 1963, the NLF became relatively passive in the cities, transferring to others the major responsibility for urban political opposition. The complexity of the urban political scene notwithstanding, the Party realized that the sheer size of the cities and the RVN's entire dependency on them made them crucial in the short run. The *attentisme* and circumspection of many urban elements, particularly among the intelligentsia, increased for several years, but in the long run only those who gained from the RVN's corruption were to prove immune to the desire for peace and stability—which was what the RVN could not provide. The Tet offensive had shown that the NLF could define the extent to which peace was possible, yet the RVN was responsible for creating a workable social and economic system during the turbulent interim between war and peace, and its intrinsic inability to do so meant that it would produce opposition elements in due course, some of which might be willing to work with the NLF when they saw that peace and the social and economic reconstruction of a profoundly war-torn nation were indivisible.

The diversity and complexity of the urban condition was now starkly evident to the Party. The huge lumpen, apathetic, disoriented sector had not responded to its appeals during Tet, despite that group's miserable economic position and marginality. Time was taking a toll on the poor that no one had quite predicted. Coping with it was a major challenge to the Communists, so that while the Americans perceived the importance of such apathy to the very survival of their surrogates, the Party, too, had to reassess its theory of the road to power, including a possible transitional sharing of it with others as a "national democratic" phase prior to later reunification. It was in this context that the Party throughout 1968 began to move toward a much more comprehensive united-front line based on the emergence of a "Third

Force," an immensely inclusive category which was to incorporate an end-less variety of groups and tendencies in a nation whose political fractiousness remained deeply rooted.

THE PARTY'S ASSESSMENT OF TET

The Party's assessment of Tet's overall impact influenced its subsequent military and political strategy, for the offensive allowed it to appraise realistically the balance of forces. Yet, of the three alternatives it outlined before February, ranging from quick and total victory to an escalation of the war, the one which emerged was also the most expected—namely, that the Americans would suffer major defeats yet keep fighting. But the new balance would give rise to later victories. Its contemporary evaluation of the military equation was very much like the one it holds today. The United States had to be convinced that the Communists possessed the ability to strike simultaneously throughout the country, and that it would be compelled to spread out its forces to protect the cities, putting it in a position of strategic passivity. The Americans now knew that the Communists could protract the war indefinitely, that they could not rely on the RVNAF, and that all of the strategies it had or could attempt were failing. The defeatism which was to emerge from this clarity was to compel Washington to withdraw over time, perhaps agreeing first to useful negotiations.

The Party had expected some success in demoralizing Washington, but it was not wholly prepared for the magnitude of Tet's impact in influencing domestic American politics, damaging its economic position at home and abroad, and weakening its status as a world power. Virtually euphoric at the results in this domain, the Party leaders immediately realized that they had been lucky in choosing the exact conjunction with the dollar crisis. When all of these factors were combined with the RVN's military defeats, the Johnson administration lost its will, and in warfare that was, as the Revolution saw it, decisive.[7]

The Revolution's own losses, however, were very significant, and they knocked the breath out of the Communist military and political organization, a fact which only greater American and RVN failures obscured. The Party's journals immediately added opaque contingencies to its definition of the general uprising as a single stage leading to eventual victory, to its possible role as merely one in a series of successive insurrections, and indeed to the meaning of victory itself. For those relatively few who had time to study its exegeses, these nuances were both perfectly coherent and consistent with its earlier theses. But in its desire to evoke a maximum exertion, the Party in practice minimized those subtleties which risked inhibiting its members' actions. In reality it asked the vast bulk of those who were to act to take unlimited risks to produce a victory of the proportions the Politburo thought possible but unlikely. Both then and much later, senior Party leaders thought, as General Tran Van Tra wrote in 1982, "if we had weighed and considered things meticulously, taken into consideration the balance of forces of the two sides, and set forth correct requirements, our victory would have been even greater, less blood would have been spilled by the cadres, enlisted men, and people. . . ."[8] While the casualties were not insurmountable, they were nonetheless very great. During 1969 the Revolution lost, by far, the largest number of deserters of the entire war, mainly in the Mekong Delta. Never again was the Tet 1968 strategy repeated, and conserving its forces became critical to the next phase of the Revolution's political and military efforts.

THE TET OFFENSIVE'S SIGNIFICANCE

The Party has ever since 1968 regarded the Tet offensive as the turning point in the war and as a decisive triumph, the consequences of which would eventually mature in final victory. By 1968 the Vietnam War had become much more difficult to analyze, for the very process of protracted conflict had made it not only a military struggle but one in which the political, economic, and ideological and human domains became increasingly crucial. Of all the factors, none alone was decisive, but their growing interactions were the raw materials that would shape the final outcome of the war.

For the United States, Tet was a long-postponed confrontation with reality; it had been hypnotized until then by its own illusions, desires, and needs. The belated realization that it had military tactics and technology but no viable military strategy consistent with its domestic and international priorities made Tet the turning point in the administration's calculations. Those who had earlier favored the war finally made a much more objective assessment of the balance of forces. To attribute Washington's new perceptions to falsehood on the Communists' part or to naïveté by the American media, as Johnson and various generals were later to do, is to beg the central question of the impact of the military events which imposed a sense of reality on the administration's leading advisers and authorities. For despite the shift in public opinion as a consequence of Tet, it was still not yet so great as to make the difference to those called on to evaluate policy. It was true, of course, that Tet caused the media to become more skeptical of official reports on the war, but they were never to become critical of the imperialist politics that had led to the intervention in the first place. Another reason for their new disbelief, apart from the Revolution's attaining successes the

Pentagon had alleged were impossible, was that those U.S. spokesmen who dealt with the media were frequently ignorant of the nature of the war themselves. Having also been treated with condescension and a great deal of intentional distortion, the media's readiness to break with official illusions was quite predictable, not least because many in the administration themselves no longer shared these misconceptions.

Decision making on Vietnam had until 1968 been subject to optional policies because the consequences of those choices had not yet reached insupportable levels, and the magnitude of the costs of errors to the overall stability and interests of the system was still obscure, while the advantages of victory to the assertion of American power geopolitically and militarily were quite clear. The weight of opinion was therefore for war to the extent needed to attain quite rational objectives: the hegemony of American power over social trends in the Third World. By 1968 the costs of the war to the system were measurable, and, whatever their earlier impulses, the small circle of critical advisers reached a basic consensus on the interests of the system. Most of the bureaucrats gave in to the weight of opinion in 1968 for the same reason they had gone along with the dominant conventional wisdom earlier—their own futures depended on operating within a consensus. The dissenters who wanted more war were now just as rare as those who favored less war had been two years earlier.

After Tet it was not the ever-present differences between various groups and personalities which shaped Washington's command decisions but rather the political order's relationship and interaction with all of the powerful economic, political, and social institutions and people which exist in an informal but real fashion to constitute power in the American social system. The chemistry of human and institutional interaction, from ambition to weakness, will always be extremely diverse within predictable parameters. Tet revealed that it was time to focus on the limits of the system. To have pursued the scale of escalation to an even higher level would have wreaked an untold amount of damage on America's economic position at home and abroad, on its military power elsewhere, and on its political life—a price scarcely any serious person proposed to pay.

The offensive brought these processes to a head, and from this viewpoint the Revolution had attained a decisive advantage in its overall struggle. More crucial yet, however, since the wheels of the U.S. political process grind pragmatically and slowly, was its impact on Washington's comprehension of the centrality of the RVN in the war effort. Without exception, all senior officials involved in guiding future policy would have agreed with the CIA when it noted, "The will and capability of the GVN and its armed forces remain the keys to the eventual outcome."[9] The infusion of this understanding more deeply into the American consciousness was perhaps the most important Party goal, and in this regard it succeeded entirely. Even those U.S. generals who later severely criticized the administration's decisions, knew they could not win the war without the RVN's assuming a far greater burden militarily and being far less irresponsible politically. "Vietnamizing" the Vietnam War, ironically, at this late date became the last pillar of American strategy, leaving its position wholly dependent on its own dependents. It was the reluctant acceptance of this unhappy greater reliance on others that guaranteed the Party's eventual victory, for nearly all who were closely connected with the war greatly doubted in private that the RVN could grasp the military victory that had eluded over half a million GIs.

In this sense the Revolution attained the main strategic objectives of the Tet offensive, compelling the United States to leave the realm of desire and confront that of necessity. But the very framework of the epic struggle, for the Revolution as well as for its enemies, was altering. The very process of conflict was disorganizing the entire social order, affecting values and desires. The transformation of the nation, the brutal urbanization, the Americanization of the mores of the youth, and all the scourges of occupation and war were changing the goals of many Vietnamese.

The emergence of new social strata in the burgeoning cities meant that in certain regards both the RVN and the NLF were growing weaker. Yet, while the urban difficulties the Party faced were tactical, and sufficient to undermine its efforts during Tet, for the RVN they were matters of basic survival. As a ruling administrative structure, the RVN needed support and some measure of enthusiasm from those not on its payroll. The passivity and apathy shown to it by the urban population during Tet was extremely ominous. The RVN's potentially fatal dilemma was that it lacked an ideological, economic, and organizational basis for transforming itself into a real political force, able to function and exist independently of the Americans. The very process of egoism and depoliticization which was so troublesome to the Communists was now the RVN's main nemesis, for without a political consensus there could only be cohesion based on repression and avarice. And, given the costliness the economic adhesive of massive corruption which maintained the Thieu regime in power, it was by 1968 quite impossible that the RVN could transcend this fatal contradiction. Indeed, the very nature of the RVN's economic system would eventually produce new issues and grievances around which a new opposition might form. For it had the burden of regulating the social system to minimize the war's dislocations and to meet human needs. In fact it was greatly adding to them.

South Vietnam's rural structure was changing as well, and each mass exodus accelerated this pattern. By the end of 1968 rural Vietnam bore significantly less resemblance to the environment in which the NLF was born. People increasingly desired security from the war's ravages, and this more and more shaped their politics. The collapse or destruction of the NLF infrastructure in many places did not make the RVN any more palatable to the peasants, since what they wanted most—peace—the RVN could not give them. Worse yet, its mounting demands on the peasantry broadened the bases of its grievances even as the land system's traditional economic role altered to make it less onerous. To some extent, and depending on the region, the classic confrontation between the Revolution and its enemies was paralleled by developments in the intricate play of changing peasant values, needs, and politics to which neither the NLF nor the RVN responded wholly. While the NLF's power declined visibly, the RVN could not fill the vacuum. The process of mutual erosion began during Tet, when the Revolution drove the RVN out of a large part of the country yet could not permanently remain there.

Tet was the threshold in the war's development, a major turning point guaranteeing that the Revolution would not be defeated. All the rapidly evolving social, economic, human, and organizational dimensions were increasingly significant for the final outcome, and however nebulous and ambiguous they appeared then, it was clear by the end of 1968 that they would prove decisive.

Part Five

WAR AND DIPLOMACY, 1969-1972

Chapter 27

The Nixon Administration's Confrontation with Vietnam and the World

The Nixon administration came to power carrying with it the full weight of the past—the inherited legacies of earlier assumptions regarding the nature of American power and the world, the overweening desires and ambitions, the same goals and tools for attaining them, and identical paradoxes and frustrations. Continuity rather than calculated innovation is the hallmark of contemporary American foreign policy, and great departures are generally confined to campaign promises and rhetoric, for consensus and vested interests weigh against dramatic variations from conventional wisdom. Changes therefore come slowly, usually as a reaction to forces and factors imposing decisions and actions from outside the immediate control of those in Washington who have the nominal freedom to guide American conduct.

American policy on Vietnam during the first Nixon administration was often tentative and contradictory, reacting both to the changing balance of forces in Vietnam and to the largely unpredictable political and economic compulsions in the United States as well as in Western capitalism. It came to office with a set of objectives, many of which were more a product of its desires than an acknowledgment of the parameters of reality, but no clear global priorities, much less a decisive plan of action. Although it shared the Johnson administration's sense of the war's profound frustrations, it, too, could scarcely admit to defeat. The Nixon administration was no better able to make a real disengagement, for it shared all of its predecessors' ideological and cultural commitments regarding credibility, dominoes, and the dilemma of American military power. All that was basically different was that the context domestically, in Vietnam, and in the world was to evolve far more quickly and decisively than the new administration could ever have imagined at the beginning of 1969.

THE NIXON ADMINISTRATION'S TRANSITION

Richard Nixon brought with him a now thoroughly analyzed and ambiguous personality and set of assumptions and goals, from which came a penchant for procrastination and moodiness. And while it would be too facile to dismiss the new President's individual traits, if only because his role in guiding policy was far larger than that of Johnson, it would be an even greater error to minimize the inherited constraints and dilemmas operating on him both at home and in the world. Nixon was a crucial factor, of course, in defining the tone and tempo of foreign policy, yet ultimately the same forces which had frustrated Johnson also bore down on him.

Nixon had articulated a broad strategy on the war well before he met Henry Kissinger. In its own way, it paralleled the thinking in the Johnson administration. Although Nixon resented the foreign policy establishment, he nonetheless was, like it, bound to a consensus of assumptions on means and ends which was pervasive in Washington. Whatever the personal differences between those from the rarefied Eastern circles and those from the rougher, informal West Coast, they can never be confused with policy disagreements, which were rarely based on geography or class origins. Like most of Washington, Nixon at the end of 1967 saw the war as stalemated. During the Tet offensive he, along with the administration, became committed to the notion of buying time to allow the RVN to take over the main burden of fighting so that the direct American role could be reduced while other factors entered into the effort to sustain a non-Communist South Vietnam. These included new forms of escalation designed to bring pressure to bear on the DRV and also to stimulate other developments. By 1968 he ceased to believe that the war could be won exclusively by force of arms. Nixon's originality lay in his groping for a parallel diplomatic solution to the war which involved the USSR and China. While he was to refine and amplify the policy with time, essentially Nixon intended to link global U.S.-Soviet relations in the world to progress in reaching a satisfactory Vietnam settlement, approaching the Russians with a carrot and stick as necessary. Nixon also saw an autonomous role for China and sensed the possibility of triangular diplomacy designed to capitalize on deepening Sino-Soviet differences.

No less a part of his Vietnam strategy, Nixon believed even before he was elected, was the application of his "madman theory." As he explained it in late 1968, "I want the North Vietnamese to believe I've reached the point where I might do *anything* to stop the war. We'll just slip the word to them that, 'for God's sake, you know Nixon is obsessed about Communism. We can't constrain him when he's angry—and he has his hand on the nuclear button'—and Ho Chi Minh himself will be in Paris in two days begging for peace."[1] Gradually, of course, the impression that the President was consummately irresponsible spread not to the Communists, who were never intimidated, but to his own original supporters and the rest of the world. The weaving together of all the mutually reinforcing components of such an intricate approach would take up most of his first administration, but the elements of its future actions could be detected even before Nixon was elected.

Henry Kissinger played no role in this early formulation of a new strategy. An intensely ambitious seeker of power who had already served both the Democrats and Nixon's main rival, Nelson Rockefeller, Kissinger has correctly analyzed his own initial success with Nixon as being based on the President's mistrust of the State Department and on his desire to control foreign policy himself. But that the new national security adviser was opportunistic or knew how to reinforce the President's ego and amplify his ideas was unimportant—his predecessors and successors were no different. Having pliable, reassuring assistants is one of the prerogatives of being President, and each one finds the advisers he requires for his personal style. Kissinger's originality was not in his sycophancy but rather in his instinctive penchant, developed long before he had a political future, for grossly oversimplifying the nature of the international process and world power relations in a way which reinforced the President's own inclination to make diplomacy central to his Vietnam strategy. Kissinger sincerely believed that great-power diplomacy could produce a mutually satisfying, enforceable consensus that could subsume local problems. Had he been a mere cynic, the administration would have committed itself far less to what was to prove a crucial but erroneous set of assumptions about what China and the USSR could deliver in ending the war. Kissinger had no capacity whatsoever to comprehend how social dynamics in the world and foreign policy crises emerging out of the instability they were creating made diplomacy irrelevant or, at best, superficial. By reinforcing the President's deeply felt assumptions and convoluted strategy with his own, Kissinger was to help the administration embark later on an illusory diplomacy which would make possible a final U.S. troop withdrawal and a precondition for the Revolution's triumph. The

Harvard professor, in brief, was no more perceptive than any of his predecessors.

Kissinger's specific views on the war before being appointed to his strategic post were less imaginative than Nixon's. Equally convinced that the United States could not win the war militarily, he, too, favored transferring a much greater military responsibility to the RVN and strengthening it politically. He believed that America should gear all of its military actions to lead to negotiations; if it failed, then unilateral attainment of as many U.S. goals as possible would have to suffice. For Kissinger, complete withdrawal without the saving of American honor and credibility was quite out of the question.

What differentiated the objectives of the new President and his adviser on the next stage of the war from those of the Johnson administration was Nixon's emphasis on great-power rather than bilateral diplomacy as the key to a settlement. Vietnamization and threats of escalation were scarcely unique approaches. But to bring the strands of the policy together and implement them demanded time. Meanwhile, Kissinger set to work immediately to survey official opinion on the state of the war and the options, the results of which in the form of "NSSM-1" were completed by mid-March 1969. The confidential study revealed a modest split between the military and the rest of Washington, including the civilians in the Pentagon, on the war's prospects. The military naturally defended the effectiveness of its own actions and programs, but in reality it offered only varying degrees of pessimism regarding the future length of the war. Most believed it would last far longer than either Nixon or anyone else thought tolerable. The report deemed the RVN's political future precarious: without a U.S. presence it was unlikely to survive long. It considered the Communists both able and determined to continue the war indefinitely. If what the new administration needed was time to apply its strategy to the war, NSSM-1 revealed immediately that the balance of forces in Vietnam was highly unfavorable and that the ability of American arms to alter it was no more promising for Nixon than it had been for Johnson. But while NSSM-1 was highly realistic in its dismal prognosis, there was a question whether the new government would prove any more rational than its predecessors in confronting facts.[2]

THE ADMINISTRATION'S STRUGGLE FOR TIME

The administration's convoluted initial assumptions regarding Vietnam demanded indefinite time as well as freedom from myriad pressures both at home and elsewhere in the world; its basic dilemma was that it did not know the extent of either its liberty or its constraints. It soon learned how to gain months of freedom from internal political pressures when in March it began to hint that it might soon begin U.S. troop withdrawals linked to Communist reciprocity. The Johnson administration had considered such gestures essentially in order to reduce excessive noncombat forces and economize, but Nixon in June, adeptly responding to political pressures, approved the withdrawal of 25,000 men, followed by a well-timed and somewhat larger number the following September and December—for a total of 115,000 men the first year. The U.S. press's skepticism about the value of such marginal efforts was not long in following. Refusing to reveal its overall strategy in Vietnam, yet publicly asserting it had a plan, the White House eventually began to reduce its credibility until its cavalier approach to the various domestic constituencies helped lay the basis for a major conflict between the executive and Congress and for a historic crisis of the presidency. Meanwhile, the President also had to confront economic and military problems quite immune to the casual manipulation which had temporarily disarmed much of Congress.

Opposition to the war was a political fact of life after Tet 1968, peaking in spring 1970, when Americans by a majority of two to one believed that the sending of troops to Vietnam had been an error. They were patient with Nixon's policies because nothing dramatic was occurring to increase U.S. involvement and because the President's avowed support for Vietnamizing the war and withdrawing small numbers periodically (by April 1970 about 450,000 military personnel were left) made it appear that his professed secret "plan" to end the war was achieving a modicum of progress. Polls produced the seemingly mixed but quite comprehensible results that the majority of the public favored the President's handling of the war but that it was evenly split on support for the goals of antiwar demonstrations. The antiwar movement, which became more active and visible during late 1969, had by then firmly implanted itself in the most articulate intellectual circles and at the prestigious major universities, giving it a visibility which far exceeded its organized numbers. Much more consequential was the enormous reservoir of antiwar opinion which remained inarticulate and which the movement was incapable of mobilizing. Congress was quite aware of the political potential of these trends, which reinforced the latent antiwar sentiment building there. Meanwhile, the war was being demythologized into a brutal, criminal affair demeaning to the nominal values of those who were perpetuating it, and the exposure of the My Lai village massacre in November 1969 played a critical part in that process.

The wholesale destruction of villages and innocent people had been characteristic of the war from the inception, and the matter had received ample publicity from antiwar groups. Earlier expressions of such views of the war were dismissed as extremist until the major media, the *New York Times* particularly, decided that the administration's real intention was to protract the war indefinitely. Its new militancy was due not to fresh information, since it had more such material than the antiwar critics, but to a deepening fear among various layers of the traditional establishment that the war would drag on and that its social, economic, and political cost might become enormous. By the end of 1969 the President's period of grace with such powerful constituencies was over, and there began a persistent shift among the Congress, the media, and other elite elements toward antiwar sentiment.

The major change in the business community came in late 1968 and 1969. In September 1969 *Fortune* polled the heads of the five hundred leading American corporations and found that Vietnam, followed by inflation, urban problems, and campus unrest, was considered one of the most critical problems facing the nation. They regarded Vietnam as linked to all of these, and the failure to win the war had caused the men who counted most in the economy to switch to dovish policies. Inflation in 1969 and 1970 reached a post-1951 peak, and although the fiscal 1969 federal budget balanced after a $25 billion deficit the preceding year, Nixon's first budget, 1970, had a $3 billion deficit, which shot up to $23 billion in both 1971 and 1972. Disquieted, the stock market in early 1970 began sliding with falling profits, inflation, and uncertainty over the war, and during spring 1970, as threats of a widening war in Indochina began circulating, prestigious elements of the business community for the first time began to speak for their prudently silent and pragmatic colleagues. "It seemed to me that the time had come to speak out," Louis B. Lundborg, chairman of the Bank of America, the largest bank in the world, told the Senate Foreign Relations Committee on April 15. "The war in Vietnam has seriously distorted the American economy, has inflamed inflationary pressures, has drained resources that are desperately needed to overcome serious domestic problems . . . and has dampened the rate of growth in profits. . . ."[3] From this point on, opposition to the war engaged not simply an isolated constituency but important power sectors with enormous influence with the media and Congress. "There are few hawks left in the business world," *Business Week* concluded in mid-April.[4] After the widening of the war into Cambodia, including the use of U.S. men on April 30, the President's remaining freedom of action was linked essentially to his ability to cope with a vast public and elite opposition, which by the end of 1970 overwhelmingly favored a complete troop withdrawal from Vietnam within a year. No postwar President had ever been so circumscribed. This did not mean that he could not overcome his immediate political problems, but that opinion was now a powerful challenge to him was unquestionable.

VIETNAM AND THE CONSTRAINTS OF
U.S. GLOBAL PRIORITIES

The challenges before the Nixon administration included most of the prolonged war's accumulated effects on the United States' global military and economic position and priorities. It realized it was no longer possible to postpone facing such issues without a serious eclipse in American power in the world, and despite the symbolic importance of the war, the new administration knew that it also had to meet other needs. Key members of the executive branch responded to this dilemma quite differently, and in principle all agreed that something had to be done, but it was Melvin R. Laird, the new secretary of defense, who was most determined to resolve these challenges.

By fiscal 1969 the war was absorbing 37 percent of the total military outlays, and this money came largely from funds that would have otherwise gone for arms and procurement, including new weapons systems, as well as for greater forces in Europe. Apart from the fact that those branches of the military that were on short rations increasingly resented the war's impact on their missiles, ships, regional jurisdictions, or ability to deal with Soviet power, the overall Pentagon budget had become inflationary and drastic cuts were inevitable. Having increased one-third in constant dollars between 1964 and 1968, the Pentagon's budget was by fiscal 1973 to fall 8 percent below the 1964 level. Both the Pentagon's changing internal priorities and its reduced budget made it the most intractable force the President had to cope with in formulating his Vietnam policy during his first term, for he could not dismiss it as he did students or effete Eastern intellectuals. Moreover, the President never resisted the unimpeachable argument that Vietnam War spending had to be reduced in order that much-needed ships and missiles could be bought.

The administration spent 1969 studying its global military needs and options, which ended in another National Security Council study, NSSM-3, which defined a variety of options, none of which could be achieved unless the United States withdrew its forces, save for a small advisory mission, from Vietnam by 1973. The removal of China from the category of possible major adversaries was also essential to its implementation, which only reinforced Washington's subsequent diplomatic strategy. By early 1970 these policy alternatives for modernizing the entire military were supported by everyone in the administration as essential to the reassertion of the credibility of its strategic power against the USSR and to the ability to fight both a general and one major local war. For the military to become lean and powerful, with more appropriate resources for less money, its personnel would have to drop one million men by 1973 so that funds for their pay would be available for new procurement.

Once committed to this strategy, Laird sought aggressively to carry it out, knowing that failure to do so would leave the military in poor condition because of lower funding. Having spent sixteen years in the House, he was also more exposed to congressional sentiment than anyone in the administration. While he, too, believed that the United States would not win the Vietnam War either on the battlefield or at the negotiating table, he was concerned that public opinion would force it out of the war regardless of the President's desires. At the least, he wanted to both modernize the military and spend less money, and he fought hard for his position publicly and privately. "Laird acted on the assumption that he had a Constitutional right," Kissinger later said of him, "to seek to outsmart and outmaneuver anyone. . . ."[5] Laird's philosophy was that the way to implement a policy was simply to do it, and he did not feel disloyal to the President in relentlessly forcing through administration decisions.

The first troop withdrawals of 1969 had been intended to eliminate superfluous forces and, above all, to win public tolerance for the continuing war. Laird initially proposed only modest withdrawals, but by the time NSSM-3 had been written, he knew that regular withdrawals from Vietnam were essential. Despite the reticence of some key generals preoccupied with the war, Laird steadily pressed on with withdrawals, forcing the President over the next years to implement unwaveringly what was official policy even when he was eager to refocus on the war again. Despite the stormy fluctuations in the war, its cost dropped from $28.8 billion in 1969, the last Democratic budget, to $9.3 billion in 1972. Total American military manpower in the world declined by over 1.1 million men, twice the number in Vietnam at the peak of the war. Having locked troop retirements from Vietnam into the Pentagon budget, Kissinger recalled, Laird neutralized efforts to slow departures by attacking any delay as tantamount to "giving up weapons modernization," thereby putting the hawks in an untenable position.[6]

The withdrawals also succeeded in dampening antiwar sentiment. Even though its first year in office failed to produce an alternative war strategy, the new administration improvised with a variety of ad hoc statements and measures designed to gain time as it experimented with its notions on Vietnamization, diplomacy, and threats of presidential madness to create a new, winning plan. It nonetheless began to formulate more coherent policies on global issues which, in effect, precluded a permanent return to the escalation process. To have done otherwise would have meant not merely losing the war in Vietnam but also leaving American power elsewhere in shambles as well as the ruination of America's position in the world economy.

The White House's war policy immediately collided with the exigencies of its global military strategy, and also with the constraints of the world economic situation and of its relations with its European allies, which had severely inhibited Johnson during 1968. Throughout his first four years in office, Nixon had periodically to address himself to world economic problems. Larger American global interests, which were military, economic, and therefore political, demanded attention far more frequently in the Nixon years than earlier.

No important person in his first administration was willing or able to confront world economic questions. Kissinger, reflecting the myopia intrinsic to the entire political science profession, subsequently admitted that he was wholly ignorant of international economics, and he shrewdly stayed away from the topic as much as possible. "Only later did I learn that the key economic policy decisions are not technical but political."[7] Nixon's first act as President was to exclude the New York Federal Reserve Bank, which had maintained primary responsibility for the issue for decades, from discussions of foreign financial policy. He thereby also created a serious break in informal relations between the administration and New York finance. During 1969 the President ignored the issue, but in January 1970 he appointed Arthur Burns head of the Federal Reserve System. Burns knew and cared little about international finance. The executive immediately embarked on a policy of "benign neglect" of the role of the dollar and the American economy in world finance; this policy was later reflected in the December 1970 appointment of John Connally of Texas as Treasury secretary, which gave to a blunt, defiant jingoist the critical responsibility for economic relations within the American-led alliance. In brief, both the policies and the personnel in Washington assured a turbulent context sure to constrain the administration's Vietnam policy in a manner it had not anticipated.

The basic problem was inflation, which pushed American exports out of world trade and built huge deficits as American businesses invested their overvalued dollars overseas in a way that endangered foreign capitalists. Vast outlays for the war and foreign bases and the soaring budget deficit at home made the statistics appear increasingly frightening. In 1971 the United States had its first postwar foreign-trade deficit, and its foreign net liquidity balance grew to an astonishing $19 billion in fiscal 1972. Both the European capitalists, speaking through their governments, and the U.S. financial interests began to assault its sublime, conscious ignorance. During 1970 both felt that anti-inflationary discipline in Washington was the prerequisite for stanching the flow of overvalued dollars to the world. But rather than treating with its allies, particularly Germany and Japan, regarding the overvalued dollar, Washington preferred to ignore them on the assumption that none would dare precipitate a crisis by challenging it. They were wrong, and the very daring of its approach meant that traumas, involving vast stakes, would dominate foreign economic—and therefore political—relations. Given Connally's periodic provokings of the world with nationalist threats his colleagues thought tactless and given fiscal policies geared exclusively to the needs of the domestic economy, conflict was inevitable. The Europeans insisted that the Americans cease economic programs that irresponsibly eroded the dollar, and the administration felt that the Germans and Japanese should revalue their currencies upward; meanwhile, it refused to discuss the matter for fear its allies, in turn, would attempt to intrude on U.S. economic policies. But the Europeans, who were not helpless, were pushed into confrontation with Washington.

During 1971 the Germans came under increasing pressure to revalue the mark upward. In early May, as $1 billion flowed into the country in only forty minutes in anticipation of a revaluation, the Germans were forced to float the mark, and the world currency structure fell into disarray. Connally had optimistically declared, "The dollar is our currency but your problem," grossly underestimating Europe's resources.[8] To protect themselves, central banks began to redeem dollars for gold in Washington, and $845 million in reserve gold left the country during the first nine months of 1971. The New York Federal Reserve Bank had during the spring repeatedly cautioned Washington that the dollar might collapse—and collapse, of course, meant a world economic and political crisis. By this time virtually all U.S. economic interests with overseas activities were frightened by the trends, and the administration was now compelled to confront the issues. Even the agnostic Kissinger, whose passivity was a mask for his own ignorance, now realized that it was essential "to prevent economic issues from overwhelming all considerations of foreign policy."[9] At the beginning of August, New York Federal Reserve officials were warning Washington of imminent panic. And on August 15, accepting a series of proposals drafted for him by the former head of IBM and reflecting the desires of the major U.S. companies operating abroad, the President adopted a program to defend the dollar which required less overseas spending and an assault on inflation. More important, without consulting its foreign allies or New York financial leaders, the administration withdrew the gold backing of the dollar and ended the Bretton Woods system, which had dominated the world capitalist economy since 1945.

Even this stopgap was now too little and too late. The Europeans deeply resented unilateralism on issues involving their welfare. Seeking to formulate fiscal policies to satisfy domestic needs, the administration remained locked in the classic dilemma between its international and domestic economic roles. On December 18 it formally devalued the dollar. The world economy was now again in a swirl, one which was never to end, and for the next several years it periodically intruded upon Washington's attention and emerged as a persistent factor in its war options. Despite fluctuations in war spending, there was now a limit to how far and long the administration could sustain the war, lest any major increase in its expenses endanger the United States' increasingly precarious position in the world economy. The entirely amoral opinions of key financial and business elements were linked to this question, and during 1972 they emerged to oppose fiscal extravagance, of which the war was now the most visible example. Their potential political weight and campaign contributions were not to be dismissed casually.

The context in which the Nixon administration fought the war greatly reduced its freedom of action. The stark issue confronting the President was the war versus American military and economic power in the world and the health of the economic and political system at home. A deflecting and postponing of the problems in one area still left the President too many others with which to cope. Even when both elite and mass opinion supported him, as it ultimately did in November 1972, this intersection of objective forces precluded either stabilization or escalation of the war, depriving the President of the potentially unlimited time essential to reverse the trend in the real balance of forces in Vietnam. The accumulated problems of American capitalism and imperialism had entered a qualitatively new stage. Just as the logic of U.S. globalism had produced its aggression, stimulating doctrines of credibility and a concern for dominoes in Vietnam when Washington believed it had ample military, economic, and political power, so, too, did it impose its retreat. It was this milieu, these perceptions and problems, pressures and structural constraints, which operated after 1970 to influence American policy concerning a war that was a growing danger to its power and interests throughout the world and to stability at home.

ESCALATION AND VIETNAMIZATION

Its enormous and growing difficulties notwithstanding, the Nixon administration cherished as many illusions and false hopes as circumstances would allow it. It persistently played for time. Its forced confrontation with its restricted choices and limited resources led not to a frank realism, from which it could pragmatically seek to retain as much aggregate strength at home and abroad for its various interests as possible, but rather to a begrudging confrontation with the efficacy of the aspirations and assumptions that have guided postwar U.S. foreign policy down to this day. That America would be gracious or wise before the unrelenting pressures of external forces and its own past failures and existing weaknesses was not to be expected from those who had so mercilessly pounded and transformed the peasant nation that was thwarting them. But despite being elliptical, the retreat was real even though the administration's two most important policymakers,

Nixon and Kissinger, retained sufficient illusions to make every step in the process terribly bloody and painful for the entire Vietnamese nation as well as, on an incomparably smaller scale, their own.

To coherently explain U.S. policy in Vietnam after 1969 requires one to impose a form on what was in fact a series of improvisations and experiments founded on a number of desires and assumptions. For sustained periods the White House itself did not really understand the ultimate implications and goals of its policies, which in retrospect appear often to have been astonishingly casual. Nonetheless, underpinning its actions was a persistent belief that it had to save the "credibility" of American power for as long as it could by protracting the war until the United States obtained an acceptable settlement, without being overwhelmed by other problems and costs. It was a policy from which Laird quietly dissented by withdrawing troops at an increasing speed. Kissinger, however, as an ideologue, thought that convincing European allies of the United States' "staying power" was vital to NATO and essential to maintaining stability and American leadership in the world. He regularly returned to this theme, as did the President, and it doubtless explains his consistent advocacy of periodic escalations of violence during the first term.

Yet credibility was not the only source of the war's protraction, for the administration also sought time to test its policy of Vietnamization and the relevance of great-power diplomacy to a Vietnam settlement. In the process it attempted to apply a number of its new strategies, which in turn postulated public and congressional toleration. Kissinger himself had during 1969 begun to examine various plans for escalating the war, in the belief that he could bludgeon the DRV into negotiating on American terms. Nixon had yet to apply his "madman theory" to a real situation. An opportunity to look irrational, possibly to frighten the USSR if not the DRV, was very much on the minds of Kissinger and Nixon when the Cambodia issue emerged in March and April of 1970. The actual overthrow of Sihanouk by the even more pro-American Lon Nol junta on March 18 was not primarily Washington's doing, though it knew that the coup was coming and immediately aided the new leaders. That the new regime would try to expel Communist forces from their bases in the border areas seemed likely. At the end of March, RVN units, flown in by U.S. helicopters, had set off to attack them, thereby spreading the war to another nation. The opportunity to look tough had arrived.

Both Laird and Secretary of State William Rogers opposed an American invasion of Cambodia, as did several of Kissinger's key assistants, who subsequently resigned in protest. The President on April 20 had announced the withdrawal of 150,000 new U.S. troops over the following year and used it to justify an attack on Cambodia, ostensibly to clean out major supply bases and the COSVN headquarters and protect the troops remaining after the planned reductions. The net effect was to shatter whatever toleration or illusions about the President had existed in the United States; campuses were in upheaval, and protests erupted everywhere, provoked further by the National Guard killing of four students at Kent State University on May 4. Faced with a crucial business constituency publicly impatient with the policy, Congress by the end of the year was seriously considering a spate of legislative proposals to restrict the war.

Militarily, however, the Cambodia invasion turned the war into one for all Indochina, overstretching the unprepared RVN and U.S. military and political resources. The expanded conflict immediately further tilted the new balance of forces in the Revolution's favor, allowing it to fill the vacuum that the diversion of U.S. airpower and the ARVN for mobile warfare outside South Vietnam had created. More important, the White House began the frightfully destructive syndrome which would eventually leave Cambodia the most devastated nation of the entire twentieth century as a consequence of war. Indifferent to such considerations, it then authorized plans for the next ARVN expedition, intending to cut off supply routes passing through southern Laos. The attack, known as Lam Son 719, began on February 8, 1971, with full U.S. air support. Unlike the hastily drawn-up Cambodia invasion, which allowed the PAVN no time to prepare, the Revolution acquired the attack plan long in advance and turned the effort into a huge rout. The implications for the ARVN, and for its inability to engage in mobile combat, were immense. The administration's effort to gain time by expanding the war immediately produced its own contradictions. It was unable to define a coherent military strategy while withdrawing its forces, and this only compounded the military problems it would leave behind.

The convoluted nature of the U.S. objectives was typified by the complicated relationship between "Vietnamization" and troop withdrawals. Until serious negotiations after mid-1972 preempted it, the President's "plan" for the war was simultaneously to improve the RVNAF until it could assume the responsibility for combat, destroy the Revolution's military capabilities as much as possible, and withdraw American forces so as to lower political pressures at home. An end to the war would therefore not depend, ultimately, on diplomatic progress, even though it could help immeasurably, and the administration always made it clear that a residual U.S. force to handle logistics and air and sea war would remain for the indefinite period it took the ARVN to master these functions. In March 1971 Laird and the JCS estimated that this number might be around sixty thousand by September 1972.

The problem is that no informed senior American official was confident that such a Vietnamization program would work without a U.S. willingness to reenter the war if necessary. Kissinger surely was not. The CIA in April 1970 reinforced the dominant impression among U.S. officers in Saigon that the ARVN was unable to improve much more—and that was not likely to be sufficient. Since it was less troop training than technology that the ARVN was now being called on to master, progress was intrinsically more difficult. Kissinger especially thought that Vietnamization was closing off diplomatic and military options, at least insofar as it involved U.S. force reductions. Aware of these risks and determined not to allow the war to wreck his plans for reshaping the entire military structure and priorities, Laird budgeted the troop reductions and made it clear that any delays would be at the expense of American military power elsewhere in the world. To placate those who wanted to get out as well as win, he created a special office to report systematic improvements in ARVN fighting accomplishments and abilities. In due course he locked the United States into a dependency on Vietnamization, quite aware it was unlikely to succeed militarily.

This precarious mixture of policies took sufficient domestic pressure off the President to allow diplomatic wheels to turn until mid-1972. It was, essentially, a successful eclectic response to a variety of national and international considerations. But it was also an acknowledgment that maximum war against the Revolution had failed and threatened to bring down America's economy with it.

Equally haphazard was the effort to define basic U.S. goals and objectives in Southeast Asia, an exercise which had consumed much time as the United States entered the war but very little as it retreated. The formulation of the "Nixon Doctrine" while the President was in Guam on July 25, 1969, was the only pretense of coherence. The so-called doctrine was in fact the result of a fairly casual discussion with Kissinger and of the President's desire for publicity. Kissinger himself was quite surprised. The doctrine became the basis of the administration's subsequent definitions of policy in East Asia. Nixon reiterated that the United States would keep its existing treaty commitments, which, of course, were tolerably vague in regard to SEATO and the Manila Pact. It would expect Asian nations "increasingly" to handle problems of internal security with their own manpower, although America stood ready to provide material aid. The problem was that Dulles had made precisely the same ambiguous declarations of intent after the Korean War, and Vietnam had revealed America's incapacity to keep its troops out of the internal affairs of nations in the region, including those, such as Vietnam, with which it had no treaties at all. Economically, senior U.S. officials made it clear, whatever the security arrangements between America and its regional allies, East Asia would be "increasingly important" to it, especially in terms of trade and investment.[10] The extent of its possible future military commitments, therefore, remained only implicit in its past actions and definitions of its goals, and no great official reassessment occurred. Asia remained an enigma in Washington's calculations of its overall priorities, as events and challenges themselves evoked incremental responses which would become the building blocks of a de facto policy.

Fluid and nuanced within given boundaries, American policy retained a certain flexibility but never accepted the principle of complete withdrawal, noninterference, and, in effect, defeat. To couch the withdrawal of its own troops in sufficient protocol and verbiage to assuage its sense of dignity and its international image was always essential, although expectations in Washington differed as to what would happen afterward. But its stress on the various elements—especially American military power and diplomacy—varied over time, depending on its successes or failures in each domain as well as on political and economic pressures at home and elsewhere in the world.

The growing limitations on the United States after 1969 made diplomacy increasingly the only area in which the administration could seek to attain its objectives without running into material and political constraints. Domestic opposition to the war intensified. In Vietnam there was no way of transcending the realities of the battlefield as well as the finite abilities of America's surrogate in Saigon. In 1972, with the administration restricted in all other domains and facing an election, diplomacy would move from the background to center stage.

Chapter 28

The Crisis of American Military Power

THE LIMITS OF U.S. MILITARY
POWER IN VIETNAM

By the time Nixon came to office, there was nothing to justify the belief that the military stalemate in Vietnam could be reversed. Having failed to win the war at a cost approaching $30 billion annually, the United States could not conceivably expect to succeed by spending less. Almost at once, all of the military lessons and failures of the preceding years began to reemerge. For the White House was also convinced that its "credibility" and diplomatic strategy required it periodically to escalate the war for relatively short durations, even as it was seeking to proceed with troop reductions, cut costs, and deflect the opposition to the war.

All members of the administration agreed that control over military strategy should be transferred from the MACV in Saigon, under the command of General Creighton Abrams, to Washington. Nixon, Kissinger, and Laird now decided issues once made close to the battlefront. But Laird generally won on the controversial issues of the size and the timing of troop withdrawals, sometimes by ramming through his position unilaterally. "He is a hawk on nuclear deterrence," an associate of his explained in 1971, but he "wants to get out of Vietnam . . . so much he can taste it."[1] Laird was not opposed to the war as such, but only to its high cost. When in mid-1969 Kissinger drew up plans for a massive bombing and mining of the DRV, or later considered comparable escalations, he and Nixon generally kept Laird ignorant of them.

Meanwhile, U.S. military strategy in Vietnam adjusted to the troop withdrawals. In 1969 nearly one-half of its manpower in South Vietnam was designated as service personnel, and almost all of the reductions that year were from this sector. Not until 1971 did American and RVNAF combat troops available for offensive operations drop substantially. The United States reduced large-scale aggressive activities on the ground, however, preferring to consolidate its hold over ostensibly "friendly" areas. By 1970, therefore, with manpower over 400,000 most of the year, American combat deaths were less than a third of those in 1968; and in 1971, as manpower fell to half that of 1968, fatalities were less than a tenth. Such a shift reduced the expense of the war and political protest at home, and also accommodated to the overriding reality that the Army was rapidly ceasing to be an effective fighting force.

The administration's alternative was to rely much more on air power and artillery—in a word, on firepower. Well over half the tonnage of the entire war was used during Nixon's first four years. Kissinger's assumption was that it was necessary to reduce the Revolution's supplies and strength for as long as possible to gain time for his other options. In 1969 the United States used 2.8 million tons of air and ground munitions, a shade below the 1968 peak. By 1971 tonnage was slightly over half the 1968 peak. The decline in munitions usage was far more the result of the withdrawal of the artillery after 1971, for a massive air war capacity remained in the region even as it was reduced in South Vietnam. The key to the war's combat was increasingly the U.S. base and fleet system in East Asia.

At the war's peak a quarter of a million Americans participated in the conflict from outside Vietnam, particularly in the Navy. Depending on methods of calculating, anywhere from 125,000 to 200,000 men in Thailand, Okinawa, Guam, the Philippines, the Seventh Fleet at sea, Taiwan, and Hawaii were directly involved in war-related activities in early 1972, roughly equal to the number of Americans still in South Vietnam. Air power remained a card Washington was ready to play and to which the Pentagon, Laird included, had no objection. To the extent that planes were stationed outside Vietnam, the Americans could use them as a threat to reenter the war even if all U.S. forces were withdrawn from South Vietnam. Although Kissinger or Nixon might employ escalation or the menace of it for political purposes against the DRV, American military power was still indecisive. Bombing was ever more a way of concealing defeat rather than of avoiding it.

It was not until about 1970 that the U.S. Army was finally master of its inordinately complex logistical system. The loss of fuel to pilferage fell substantially below the earlier 25 percent peak but remained huge. Extravagance was still common, particularly in the maintenance of equipment, but the war was "winding down." Most officers still ranked sophisticated experiments, such as sensors to detect enemies by remote control, as failures despite the enormous investment of time and money in continued use of them. The American intelligence system was still mediocre. The best information came from defectors, and the most immediately useful for combat from visual reconnaissance, but there was a severe shortage of pilots to fly such missions because the vast majority were injured or killed within six months.

The real dilemma confronting the United States after 1969, as it relied increasingly on air power, was that the effectiveness of its tactical and strategic air forces proved no better than, and in certain regards was inferior to, their earlier performance. Whatever Kissinger hoped for from the bombing, the Revolution still supplied its forces and sustained its needs, and information to this effect passed from the Pentagon to the White House. At least 108 helicopters and planes were destroyed, and another 618 damaged, during Lam Son 719 in Laos early in 1971, by a PAVN air defense system far less formidable than that which existed over the DRV and which was constantly improving. The air war against the DRV largely ceased during 1969–71, but planes previously flying there moved elsewhere, mainly to Laos.

The effort to halt the flow of crucial military supplies failed, for as the United States destroyed more trucks, the numbers the DRV sent south increased. Levels of essential supplies were always sufficient. Not only were American claims to have interdicted traffic publicly challenged in 1972 by former Air Force photo interpreters, but the enormous tactical aviation fleet used to attack the Ho Chi Minh Trail was far less effective than the fixed-wing gunships which flew only eight percent of the sorties but accounted for 48 percent of the trucks hit. Yet the gunships were also the most vulnerable to ground fire. In 1971 the Air Force was once again compelled to build still better planes in the continuous effort to keep its offensive power ahead of its enemy's defenses.

The Air Force's own experts were not so confident of the efficacy of their wares as the proponents of the "madman" strategy in the White House. By the end of the war, the former head of the Air Force's concepts and objectives section conceded, "our experience in Vietnam does not prove or disprove the effectiveness of strategic bombing operations." He admitted, too, that the antiwar movement's focus on tonnages of bombs dropped had created "an unattractive public image."[2] In a political context, of course, such images were extremely important. While both Nixon and Kissinger believed that the use and threat of air power might actually alter the military balance sufficiently to make a difference, or at least affect negotiations, the Revolution and even some military and Pentagon experts denied it had that capacity. As the Army began to decline in numbers and, more dramatic and serious, in terms of morale and internal cohesion, bomb tonnages became the last and only pillar of Washington's crumbling military strategy.

THE CRISIS OF
THE AMERICAN ARMY

The Vietnam War tested every dimension of America's limited-war capacity: its weapons, strategy, and, ultimately, its armed forces. But while earlier experience had shown how finite firepower was in coping with local wars against highly motivated enemies, the United States was completely unprepared for human failures in its own armed forces. By the time Nixon came to office, this was a growing, serious problem; by 1970 it was a major crisis, with obvious implications for America's freedom to protract the war in Vietnam and for its ability to intervene elsewhere in the future.

While the war followed the inevitable logic of U.S. dependence on technology, even within this constraint its officer corps gave weaponry a specific character, making it all the more destructive even though militarily pointless. The average officer, like the enlisted man, served one year in South Vietnam, even if he was a general. About one-tenth of the Army was composed of officers during the 1960s, and for those who were professionals, particularly those from West Point, a tour in South Vietnam was essential to career advancement. Compared with that of earlier wars, the Army senior officer corps was very top-heavy, and so many volunteered that command assignments were restricted to six months in order that they could all pick up experience and, of course, have an opportunity to win promotions. Mainly confined to safe and often extremely comfortable rear bases, careerism became the leitmotif of all of their actions during a glorious half year. Lower-level officers, generally ROTC graduates who were not making the Army a career, were most likely to be sent into the field and exposed to the same risks as common soldiers. From a military viewpoint, they lacked both the experience and the motivation to make good leaders. For the professionals, producing impressive numbers often meant goading men to action, falsifying data on enemies killed or targets destroyed, or both. Once they left, the war was someone else's problem. Deception, cynicism, and brutality were built into such a system. Bombs and shells were dropped to produce results which could be translated into medals, complimentary reports—and promotions. Nearly nine out of ten generals who served in Vietnam thought careerism was a problem, 37 percent considering it a serious one. One of its effects was a huge breach in relations between officers and men. Well before the war ended, critics outside the military and a few disgruntled former officers were airing such problems.

Senior-level officers have always been drawn largely from the middle class, generally from smaller communities. Their class differences with the low-income draftees from rural areas or inner-city ghettos who dominated the ranks were not a new factor. Of the 27,222 Army men who died in the Indochina War between 1965 and 1972, 3,269 were officers; of these, however, 2,348 were first lieutenants or lower, 554 of them helicopter pilots. Of the over 43,000 officers of the rank of major or higher who were in the Army in South Vietnam, only 201 were killed in action, and most of these were majors.

The primary source of junior frontline officers at the start of the war was the ROTC programs on 268 campuses. Apart from engaging in the modestly effective antiwar agitation against the ROTC, educated males voted on the war by ceasing to participate in a program likely to get them sent off to combat. Enrollment dropped from 231,000 in 1965 to 73,000 in 1972, and the Army was forced to replace them with lower-caliber junior officers trained in its own schools. By 1970, moreover, nearly 40 percent of those still in the ROTC were opposed to the presence of U.S. troops in South Vietnam, and fully 60 percent did not intend to volunteer to serve there. These younger men were a very mixed lot both personally and politically, having little in common with the senior professionals over them.[3] Far more serious were the changing relations between officers and their men in the combat zones.

Of the 2,150,000 men sent to Vietnam, a somewhat greater percentage of poor whites and blacks served than usual. Johnson's Great Society program had attempted to enroll disadvantaged teenagers into the armed forces, and a disproportionate number became infantry riflemen—the "grunts" who were most often sent into combat. As a general rule, officers preferred poorly educated soldiers for the front lines. During 1968–70, 62 percent of the casualties were draftees. Those with ten years or less of education had a casualty rate three times that of those with thirteen years or more; those from families with incomes of $4,000–$7,000 had a casualty rate nearly three times that of those from families with $17,000 and over. At the beginning of the war, black casualties were nearly a quarter of the total, but they eventually ended at 13 percent for the entire war, slightly above blacks' share of the population. Half the average combat rifle company, however, consisted of blacks and Hispanics. Race had now become a crucial new part of the U.S. military structure in the war. Although poor and uneducated, the black in South Vietnam was far more likely to have a sense of black pride and solidarity than was ever imagined possible in earlier conflicts, and his mores had also changed. No less important was that an awareness of the controversial political nature of the war partly accompanied class and racial differences to create the first conscious basis for disunity in the military in modern American history.

The paradox of the GI was surely one of the great surprises of the war to leaders in both Washington and Hanoi. A successful strategy requires committed people at all levels, not just in offices and comfortable studies.

The war for the American forces involved great drama and personal trauma, but only for some of the over two million men who went to South Vietnam.

Just as there were two kinds of officers in South Vietnam, so there were two types of soldiers. Soldiers were divided into those who were regularly exposed to combat and the large majority who were in danger only from sappers or remotely fired shells. Most of the Army was spared the infantry rifleman's experiences, and only half was considered combat forces—which included artillery and armor. All of this bare majority took risks, but only roughly a fifth of it served the function of acting as bait to flush out Revolutionary combatants during search-and-destroy missions. Yet, when not in combat, which meant the larger part of the time, the average GI experienced a war that was the most luxurious and expensive in American history. There were bases with astonishing comforts, access to towns and cities, brief "R and R" tours to the brothels of Southeast Asia for many, distractions and vice aplenty. Only the grunt plunging into the suffocating rice paddies and jungles, walking through mud for weeks at a time, exposed to fire primarily so that artillery and air power could target enemies, often being killed and wounded without ever knowing exactly whom to blame, saw something of the horror and terror which for many millions of Vietnamese had become a part of daily existence for years without end. Even when brutalized killers, such soldiers, too, were the victims of their leaders, both in fact and increasingly in their own opinion, and they gradually responded accordingly.

Vietnam's climate was for the average soldier insufferable, and the relatively extravagant efforts to sustain their morale while in the field with food and excellent medical care never compensated for it. The GI was sent out to locate the elusive "VC" in jungles or hamlets where peasants protected them. To kill them with aid of firepower was the objective of the exercise for his superiors, but his own goal was survival. The GI was ready to destroy, and a certain very small fraction became numbed killers with hair-trigger reactions to any threat to their existence. The massacre of the village of My Lai was just one of countless examples. Those who employed firepower from artillery or the air used it impersonally and without remorse. But the GI in combat zones increasingly became a survivor.

American brutality throughout the war was almost wholly the result of superior orders, and the GI was the instrument of his officers. Yet the average platoon and company operation suffered from serious constraints, making them inefficient instruments of warfare. Even junior officers usually spent six months in combat situations, their subordinates one year, and the constant rotation of forces led to minimal group cohesion, with the soldier's primary loyalty, if any, being to his buddies and their mutual passion to survive twelve months and get shipped out. If an officer pressed his men, he was not likely to succeed in motivating them without taking their instinct of self-preservation into account. The most popular officer was the unambitious lieutenant who took no unnecessary risks and was responsible to his men and not his superiors. Such units had high morale and solidarity and minimum losses; if there were dangerous soldiers among them, they tried to constrain them or get them transferred. Senior officers complained that the troops in such units were likely to bunch together and avoid engagements. They could not always do so, but after 1968 it was commonly conceded that whenever possible platoons "[d]on't fight a fire-fight or a contact; they wait it out."[4] " 'Search and evade' (meaning tacit avoidance of combat by units in the field) is now virtually a principle of war," Colonel Robert D. Heinl wrote in a much noticed account in June 1971, "vividly expressed by the GI phrase, 'CYA (cover your ass) and get home!' "[5]

The GI's lack of political commitment was one of the Army's fatal weaknesses. The grunt regarded Vietnam as someone else's country, and he became increasingly sensitive to the immaculate officers back at comfortable bases who were urging him on to greater risks. The soldier soon learned to distrust everyone but those comrades who had shown solidarity with him in battle. Paradoxically, many, perhaps most, grew increasingly to resent the ARVN and the Vietnamese people, and while such blanket hostility is one reason for the countless crimes against civilians that were committed, it also had military implications when cooperation with the ARVN was necessary. Joint ARVN-U.S. units were often dumping grounds for GIs whom their officers thought dangerous or objectionable. Soldiers not only knew that many peasants were NLF supporters but also profoundly resented the ever-present Vietnamese peddlers, prostitutes, and human flotsam the war had made dependent on their money. Outside of combat zones the GI was also alienated in a manner that generated an equivalent response from the Vietnamese people, who increasingly viewed the Americans as the cause of their national humiliation and debasement.

All of these forces and relationships operating in America's military created a grave liability for its entire war effort. However efficient its parts technically, as a human organization the American military was so weak that with time it became more of a factor in the overall military balance. The personal responses of the foot soldier to his predicament and dangers, the class disdain, aloofness, and careerism of his superiors, the soul- and mind-deadening techniques of warfare, the stress on numbers killed, the tension, heat, and degradation—this surreal mélange was destined to create major human problems, which in turn had far-reaching military implications. It was one thing to confront opposition to the war at home but quite another to do so among Americans in South Vietnam.

DEMORALIZATION AND RESISTANCE
IN THE ARMED FORCES

Whatever the personal responses of the GI to his frustration before 1968, morale failed to impress senior officers as a real problem. During 1968–69 troop morale began visibly to break down, and from 1970 onward the human collapse of the Americans in Vietnam ceased to be simply an individual or psychological issue and became a highly publicized major organizational question involving discipline and, ultimately, the very capacity of the U.S. armed forces to function.

The difficulties began with drugs, the GI's anodyne for the minutes and days of terror and boredom. Drug profits were potentially enormous with the troop influx after 1965. Both Air Marshal Nguyen Cao Ky and the RVN navy were central to the bringing of drugs into the country. Thieu played a smaller part. Stopping the drug traffic meant confronting the RVN political structure, which caused the embassy and the MACV in Saigon to take a passive attitude toward the problem. To some extent, however, many senior Americans could not imagine that the use of both hard and soft drugs would become so widespread. Their complicity in protecting their local political allies and the CIA's tacit help in getting opium out of Laos have been fully documented.[6] Heroin and marijuana were cheap and readily obtainable by 1968, when their use began to rise sharply. The drug epidemic that followed was to some extent related to the sheer boredom among enlisted men, as long days on bases replaced search-and-destroy missions. Some generals in Saigon regarded drug use among soldiers as the single most serious personnel problem, even though the Pentagon maintained an embarrassed silence as long as possible, until the press and Congress forced the issue in mid-1971. The Pentagon then attempted to argue that only 5 percent of the GIs were hard-drug users. In 1973 it conceded that 35 percent of all Army enlisted men who had been in South Vietnam had tried heroin and that 20 percent had been addicted at some time during their tour of duty there. Some estimates of its regular use are much higher. The use of marijuana, of course, was much more common. Since the MACV had neither the will nor the capacity to stop the drug traffic, early in 1972 some key U.S. bases began allowing prostitutes into the barracks in the hope of reducing drug usage.

Racial conflict among troops grew out of inherited legacies compounded by the distinctive experiences of blacks in Vietnam. Overrepresented in combat or in menial tasks, and led by very few black officers, blacks in Vietnam were much more under the influence of radical and militant currents than their white counterparts were. Black pride was the rule; Eldridge

Cleaver, Malcolm X, and Cassius Clay were their most admired heroes. One-fifth of all black troops in South Vietnam in 1970 declared they hated whites, and over one-third disliked them but tried to get along with them. Blacks were the most politically conscious group among the GIs, and also the most frequent drug users. By 1968, senior officers were reporting to the Pentagon, "Racial incidents and disturbances have become a serious and explosive problem."[7] The Army did not deny that it had a race problem, but defended itself by arguing irrelevantly that it was one endemic in American society and not of its own making. Still, since armed men were supposed to be fighting a common enemy rather than each other, racism became another factor weakening discipline and morale among already dissatisfied soldiers. Significant riots began as early as 1968, reaching the Navy in 1972. Part of the Army's response was to attempt to restrict symbols of black nationalism.

This combination of the enlisted man's contempt for his officers, the officers' desire to squeeze more combat out of their subordinates, drugs, and racism produced a profound breakdown and the emergence of "fragging," the attempted murder of officers by soldiers, usually with grenades.

Troop attacks on officers occurred during both world wars when troops refused to face the dangers of battles. During the Vietnam War fraggings were expanded to include attacks by black soldiers against white officers for racial reasons as well as the efforts of drug peddlers and users in the military to prevent discipline. The number of actual fraggings, especially in the first category, is difficult to document, but minimum figures for 1969–72 are 788 confirmed cases, resulting in 86 deaths. Other official data raise the number to 1,016, and some estimates are twice that. These levels were far higher than those of earlier wars, which involved many more men. Only a tenth of the attempted fraggings ended in court. Acts of mutiny, insubordination, and disobedience to orders rose from 252 in 1968 to about twice that in 1971, yet it was fragging and the threat of it which most profoundly affected officers. When officers were strong leaders, one general complained in 1972, they "commanded oftentimes at the risk of their lives due to the possibility of grenade incidents." Where new officers attempted to impose discipline in units with racial and drug problems, "there will in all probability be one or more grenade incidents in the first four weeks directed against the commander and the First Sergeant."[8] By the end of the war, fragging had intimidated a large number of officers, whose relationship with their men was shaped accordingly.

Equally disturbing was the spread of disobedience to the Navy and Air Force. In the Navy resistance took the form of sabotage during 1972, particularly on war-related ships. A major fire aboard the aircraft carrier *Forrestal* in July, antiwar petitions with one thousand signatures on another, and myriad incidents produced a House inquiry which reported, "The subcommittee has received a list of literally hundreds of instances of damage to naval property wherein sabotage is suspected. . . . The magnitude of the problem . . . is alarming."[9]

Even more disturbing was the demoralization of the Air Force during the closing months of 1972. "It is an impersonal thing," the commander of the B-52 base on Guam said; the airman doing his job "without too much question about whether he is killing anybody on the ground. I don't think it enters his mind."[10] Still, tactical aviation pilots were concerned that they would be the last to die against the DRV's superb air defenses. In November some began diverting their missions. When the B-52s were sent to bomb Hanoi during Christmas 1972, in the final act of the war, tactical aircraft failed to show up to attack antiaircraft defenses, and fifteen B-52s were shot down. At least one B-52 commander was tried for refusing to fly, but others threatened to follow him. According to one official study, there was a "near mutiny" among some B-52 crews, a crisis only the signing of the Paris accords averted.[11]

On the fringes of the deeply rooted opposition to the U.S. presence in Vietnam, there existed an organized antiwar movement without precedent in the history of the American military. Even though the white GI was not so much antiwar in the political sense as opposed to being in Vietnam for initially personal reasons, in due course such alienation began to take the form of political attitudes. While the "GI movement" by no means created this basically antimilitarist thrust, it certainly reinforced it and at various times helped it emerge coherently. Highly educated civilians of very diverse political backgrounds began the movement, a fact which led to the dissipation of most of its energy in sectarian disputes. Its initial work was around bases in the United States, appealing mainly to GIs with some college education, by way of newspapers and dozens of coffee houses. Minimally effective at the inception, it was watched closely and infiltrated by the Pentagon. Whatever the heavy ideological baggage of each faction of the GI movement, some white GIs absorbed bits and pieces of ideas, which leavened their perceptions. By 1971, civilian organizations were beginning to provide GIs with lawyers, who proved especially time-consuming to the armed services. The emergence of protests and sabotage in the Navy during 1972 was to some extent the GI movement's most important single accomplishment.

However minimal the organizational outcome of the antiwar movement's attempt to mobilize GIs, the effort was a major nuisance to the military. As a symbol of the breakdown of the three armed services, it merely reinforced the gravity of its other problems in discipline and command. In a world gone awry the very existence of a conscious endeavor to subvert the military establishment was symptomatic of the crisis of the entire American system.

The importance of the erosion of the various military services, particularly of the Army, to the military and political evolution of the war should not be underestimated. While political leaders in Washington largely ignored these developments, the generals and admirals fully appreciated them. "Somehow, the Vietnamese communist soldier has absorbed enormous motivation," retired General Hamilton H. Howze, one of the Army's most senior personalities, wrote in 1971. "A force that lacks good discipline will take a terrible shellacking from one that has it."[12] Could the Army be employed again in South Vietnam if necessary? In public the Pentagon avoided the issue, but Peter R. Kann, the *Wall Street Journal*'s authoritative Saigon correspondent, in November 1971 voiced a common feeling that "sapped by problems of drugs, race, discipline and morale, the U.S. military's very ability to fight if called upon to do so is increasingly in question."[13] By that time, moreover, the Pentagon was publicly confessing that the war had weakened the physical and moral capacity of the Army throughout the world, in part because GIs who had been in South Vietnam had transferred their habits and attitudes elsewhere. It was essential, in the view of more and more civilians and military in the Pentagon, to get the vast bulk of its forces out of South Vietnam and to reform the entire personnel structure as quickly as possible. By late 1972, after the intense stress of Navy and Air Force operations off Vietnam seriously cracked the morale and discipline of those two services, there was a virtual unanimity among admirals and generals that solving these problems was a prerequisite to once again making American military power in the world credible.

The withdrawal of troops was therefore essential not only in order to gain political time at home but also to save the military from even graver problems. Had Nixon tried to reverse the process—and Laird was not about to let him, partly for these reasons—he very likely would have produced a far more serious defeat of American power. Such perceptions of the state of the military wove in and about diplomatic and political affairs for the remainder of the Vietnam War. The United States' technology had been its most precious illusion and threat, but that was now disintegrating as the human organization around the machines ceased either to believe or to obey.

Whatever the crisis in American strategy, doctrine, and weaponry before Vietnam, personified in the evolution of limited-war theory, it paled by comparison with that which existed after a decade of effort. For the concept of America's might was based exclusively on the existence and capabilities of tactics and weapons, not on the skills and attitudes of those who operated them; without highly committed personnel the United States, with all its arms, might prove impotent. The steps by which this monumental failure occurred had not been remotely imagined in the strategy seminars of the military, the elite universities, and the think tanks or in the analyses of the entire foreign policy establishment. Now that the inconceivable was a reality, the constraints on those in power were all the greater, their imminent defeat likely to prove yet more monumental. The collapse of conventional wisdom had proved total, as strategy, sophisticated weapons, and well-groomed politicians and generals seemed irrelevant and pathetic before their resourceful, dogged Vietnamese foe.

Chapter 29

The Revolution's Military Policy, 1969-1971

The Tet offensive's impact profoundly altered Washington's perspective on the war as well as its ability to sustain it, and Vietnamization and the erosion of the American Army continued to shift the balance of forces. The Communist Party's military capacity also evolved quickly throughout the post-Tet period, and it was a major challenge to its leadership to assess clearly how changes on both sides were related and to plan how to move toward victory in the relatively near future.

The Tet offensive had been a triumph of daring, revealing the critical importance of the Revolution's military art in its creative merging of surprise, dispersal, the choice of tactics, and realism as to how much was attainable. To have pushed further and harder would have transformed a brilliant strategy into a complete disaster, and Tet's immediate effect was to leave the Revolution in a tactically weakened position. Creativity now required a very high degree of realism, and any error would have to be on the side of prudence, for whatever the existing and the potential balance of forces, objectively the Americans were able quickly to inflict heavy damage on exposed troops.

THE PARTY REASSESSES THE UNITED STATES AND ITSELF

The assessment of America's predicament was the easiest of the tasks confronting the Party's leaders. The "extent of military, political, economic and financial difficulties which the war causes to the Americans in Vietnam, in the U.S.A. itself, and over the world," it believed, would be a key variable in defining the length and outcome of the war.[1] Vietnamization of the war was certain to fail because ARVN was surely not going to achieve the victory which had eluded a vastly superior American army. The Party in 1969 readily described the United States as still very powerful, but its "clear and hold" policy of consolidating its domination over zones and avoiding manpower losses, its gradual reduction of forces, and its isolation in the world left it in a strategically passive position from which the Revolution would win "step by step" regardless of its own problems.[2] Considering all these factors, the Party's leaders decided in July 1969 that the war would end with "a political solution" rather than an outright military victory, for the first time explicitly conceding that the United States possessed the power to affect the form, if not the final outcome, of the struggle.[3]

Whatever strategic consolation the Party had from its quite accurate assessment of the American dilemma, the evaluation of its tactical decisions required flexibility and was more difficult. During 1969 and 1970 the Party's Central Committee met more frequently and issued a greater number of policy guidance statements than in previous years. In the spring of 1969 the Politburo chastised many sectors of the Party and itself more "severely" than usual.[4] The Revolution's considerable weaknesses and difficulties in the period after Tet, a later authoritative Party account admitted, "in some respects . . . were due to the fact that we had not analyzed the enemy and ourselves accurately and promptly [and] . . . to weak organization of implementation, etc."[5] Those who thought Tet would be "a one-blow affair" were criticized along with those who now were too dispirited to act when necessary. In fact, of course, the nuances of the Party's position before Tet were clear only to those who had the time to study it carefully. What is certain is that the Politburo had demanded an optimal effort and that the sacrifices stunned many of those who participated in and survived the effort, their grief having been compounded by disappointment that the offensive had not ended the war. The wisdom of Tet was more widely questioned than was any other decision the Politburo ever took, for the Revolution's tactically much more difficult and dangerous situation did not become easier physically by virtue of its far superior strategic position.

The Party's COSVN Resolution 9 of July 1969 contained a politically comprehensive assessment of the war and a critique of past successes and failures. While it provided guidance on an abstract level, it was quite vague in outlining concrete action. Subsequent policy directives followed, the essentials of which were published for all to read, as the leadership attempted to rectify both its own penchant for equivocal contingencies and the confusion among cadres.

Differences among Party leaders and generals on various questions of military strategy had existed in the past, but they had never been deeply rooted in political doctrine, and few of the older leaders were inflexible over a long period. From 1969 onward there was a larger measure of consensus on strategy simply because their own resources and their understanding of the United States' political and military straits left very few options. "The practical conditions of our fight . . . constantly change and, therefore, do not permit us to mechanically utilize our own combat experience which is no longer practicable," the PAVN chief of staff Van Tien Dung wrote at the end of 1969 in the army's daily.[6] This accord on strategy extended to two crucial points: the nature and meaning of protracted war and the forms of military activity.

CREATING A NEW MILITARY EQUILIBRIUM

Protracted war was accepted as the basic form of revolutionary warfare against a technically superior enemy. The Party knew that its ability to prolong a conflict was its ultimate threat, because this raised the cost to the United States, but it had become increasingly conscious of the considerable price it was paying in lives and economic development. In 1970 it attempted to reconcile its desire for economic growth with the risks and obligations of a war of indefinite duration. It outlined important economic reforms in the DRV to increase the efficiency of the nonagricultural sector. The assignment of a priority to economic development in the DRV had been a source of differences over the Party's commitments to the southern war since 1954, but all agreed that it was mandatory to grasp any new opportunity to hasten the war's end.

The Party's leaders reiterated an eclectic strategy: main forces equipped with modern weapons were to be mixed with guerillas using simple arms, creating a highly flexible offensive capability. While the Party proposed to maintain the initiative in the war, for practical purposes this meant preparing for future combat essentially by rebuilding its position in the south after its Tet losses and by allowing the momentum of U.S. troop withdrawal to continue while keeping the remaining enemies widely dispersed and off balance. The role of local forces in political work was crucial, for the regular army required a political structure which would help it solve its logistical problems. The existence of this guerilla capacity prevented the enemy from concentrating to attack main forces during their period of consolidation, just as main forces drew enemy mobile units away from vulnerable local forces. By 1969, too, the Party made it clear publicly that massed main forces, mobile and operating with optimum technology, would become more important in the future. To develop such an army required time. But whatever the Party's choice of the form of its offensive strategy, it believed that surprise would be vital to its success.[7]

The Revolution decided to concentrate on rebuilding the strength and morale of its military units in the south, conserving both manpower and matériel until a major offensive was both timely and feasible. Since the United States had begun to reduce its troops, nothing was done throughout 1969-71 which might have reversed that process before it was too weak to challenge future offensives. Communist military activity was reduced to a level just high enough to keep the remaining enemy forces dispersed, provide aid to political efforts, and cause sufficient U.S. casualties to sustain political pressure on the administration to continue troop withdrawals.

The U.S. estimate that up to one-half of the Revolution's southern-born armed forces were lost during 1968 is probably as accurate as any, and morale reflected heavy casualties, whatever the precise percentages. The Party sought to improve the work of the political cadres in the military, of course, but in 1969 desertions from the PLAF/PAVN reached a peak. Not until 1971 were they down again to a low level. In 1971 it again outnumbered enemy combat forces available for offensives, although the RVNAF and U.S. manpower was still nearly six times larger overall—a crucial difference being that the Revolution's army was mobile whereas the RVN's was stationary. True guerillas may have dropped to roughly a quarter of their 1966 number. Whatever the exact data, northerners composed a larger share of the Revolution's army in the south than ever before, partly because the inflow of modern technology required the training that only the PAVN soldiers could acquire. Moreover, by 1971 it was a much stronger army and fully recuperated, far better able to play the roles first envisaged for it during 1969.

The Party's inability to rebuild the southern-based guerilla structure was in part due to its need to use as many new southerners as possible for political work. Yet more fundamentally, the population flight to the cities and the RVNAF draft had shrunk its recruitment base among rural youths. To compensate for the reduction of guerilla forces was absolutely essential to disperse the enemy, to leave him strategically vulnerable to massed attacks as well as to retard the pacification program. In the fall of 1969 the PAVN in the south was divided into company-sized bodies, which in turn were partially broken down into sapper units. These companies could be quickly reconstituted to fight as large main forces, but meanwhile they remained elusive and efficient. At the same time, the PAVN consolidated rear bases and communications and reorganized to absorb new weapons and prepare new offensive techniques. Watching the process carefully, American field commanders were impressed by the efficiency of their enemy and reported to Washington that the Communists' new skills were making them more formidable.

Reviewing the future of the war in January 1970, the Party Central Committee cautiously planned to continue improving its military structure, intending toward the end of the year or in 1971 to increase its attacks significantly, especially main-force actions. At the beginning of 1970, indeed, PAVN tanks and greatly improved firepower began to appear in the Central Highlands.

This expansion was possible because of both Soviet and Chinese military aid, which presented the Party with a complex planning dilemma. Military aid from those two countries peaked in 1967, fell dramatically, by nearly two-thirds, in 1969, and was barely a quarter of the 1967 level in each of the next two years. Soviet cutbacks were especially deep, and there can be no doubt that these declines affected the Party's plans. Still, post-1968 equipment contained a far greater component of advanced matériel than did earlier aid, which had satisfied the Revolution's need for simpler arms. The aid equation was both an inhibition and a goad to action, for in 1971 the ominous diplomatic posture of its two allies began to stimulate the DRV to accelerate its plans, lest it lose the initiative. But the Revolution was preparing, in any case, to move to a higher level of military combat. By delaying the PAVN offensive until 1972, it dramatically improved its combat manpower strength relative to the RVN's. Ironically, it was the Nixon administration's desire to exploit diplomacy to preempt a potential offensive that imposed on the Communists the necessity of proceeding with one, confident they could reveal the weakness of the ARVN.[8]

The PAVN's expertise in operating as small components increasingly frustrated the Americans, until U.S. ground operations virtually ceased in 1971. If large units were spotted, they would split up and refuse to fight unless they had no option. Maintaining contact and surprise at its own discretion, the PAVN thereby controlled its losses. And as the Revolution's forces were modernizing, they also turned, out of choice as well as necessity, to a greater reliance on such earlier, primitive forms of guerilla warfare as mines and booby traps.

Simple techniques proved very successful, and neither the United States nor the ARVN ever coped effectively with mines and sappers. Munitions storage facilities were favorite targets, and in early 1969 one U.S. base alone lost 12,000 tons. ARVN bases in 1972 lost 24,000 tons. The final RVN judgment on sapper activity was that it was "a very effective tactic" expertly carried out with a minimum loss of life for the attackers, one which gave the Communists maximum material and psychological value.[9] Equally devastating to the technology on which U.S. and ARVN tactics were founded was the growing improvement in the Revolution's antiaircraft capability. In early 1969, American forces reported meeting far deadlier 51-caliber antiaircraft guns with increasing frequency. In the year ending January 1970, 130 of the U.S. Sixteenth Aviation Group's 223 planes were struck by ground fire. Technology's vulnerability was now integral to its visibility. Not only had technology failed to deliver victory, but the Revolution and the antiwar movement mobilized world opinion in revulsion against indiscriminate, barbaric weapons systems—from chemicals to cluster bombs and saturation munitions tonnages—into a powerful political weapon.

The real strength of a revolutionary army as a political entity appears when it is forced by circumstances or choice to dissolve into small, decentralized units. This was especially true in IV Corps in the Mekong Delta, where local forces still composed a large majority of the manpower. Particularly after the U.S. and ARVN penetration of Cambodia in May 1970, the Revolutionary forces in MR III and IV became yet more heavily dependent on locally supplied goods, which the political infrastructure and supporters among the masses provided. Since nearly two-thirds of its deserters to the RVN after 1968 were from MR IV, the sharp decline in "ralliers" after 1969 was an indication of the relative success of autonomous units, which could operate independently of any contact and aid from the central Party organization for extremely long periods. Given the crucial role of the Delta, this resiliency of the local NLF remained a huge military asset. The Delta pinned down far more RVNAF men than any other region, giving Revolutionary forces elsewhere the time and freedom to develop their military capacity.

Politics therefore supplemented the military efforts in a critical fashion, and it remained essentially the politics of the village Party of earlier years, composed of largely autonomous people who had remarkable tenacity. In the end, whatever the changes in the purely military equation, it was this political context that made possible the Revolution's offensive strategy with what was always to remain inferior equipment. For its strength was not numbers or arms but mobility, and its decisive flexibility was wholly based on the willingness of thousands of committed local guerillas and political cadres to improvise, muddle through, and persist for long periods in a fashion that kept the RVN and American forces distracted and vulnerable. This critical distinction between revolutionary and conventional warfare was to prevail until the war's end. The Party's ability to rely on them was due to the self-motivating as well as autonomous character of local NLF organizations, inculcated into Party members over many decades. Specific directives often could not be sent to them, and they defined the extent and nature of many of their own activities. It was this framework that made the Revolution's strength impregnable during a period of both trial and opportunity, and it was because of it that the Revolution in the south had reemerged after 1954.[10]

THE NIXON ADMINISTRATION
FORCES THE REVOLUTION'S HAND

Caution and pragmatism were the hallmarks of the Revolution's plans and action after 1968. In one crucial sense, the strategic initiative had temporarily passed to the enemy, and it was from this experience that the Party could begin accurately to gauge its own constraints as well as possibilities. Curiously, the superficially planned American decision in April 1970 to turn the war in South Vietnam into a struggle for all Indochina was to foredoom the RVN to failure. Quite apart from its political impact in the United States, the effort spread Saigon's already fragile army over a broader area just when the U.S. was withdrawing its manpower, exposing the vulnerabilities of the Vietnamization program.

The campaign against Cambodia in May 1970 tied up American air power and resources for over three years and also temporarily pinned down an ARVN invading force needed to gain time for the Lon Nol regime to consolidate power. The Nixon administration's calculation that the disruption of the Revolution's bases and logistics along the border would win time for Vietnamization proved correct in terms of months, yet it nourished illusions about virtually all other aspects of the war, encouraging the United States to strike at Laos and Cambodia again the following year.

The first attack on Cambodia had stunned the Communist army, but plans for the February 1971 Lam Son 719 campaign in Laos, and the smaller Cambodian excursion which accompanied it, had been leaked to the Revolution in detail well before the attack and even before the final U.S. approval of it. Yet the administration was confident it could gain at least two years for Thieu's army if it could wreck the Ho Chi Minh Trail around the seventeenth parallel and hold it until late April. American support for it was to be limited to helicopter transport and air cover.

What was intended to be a surprise ARVN offensive proved to be a huge PAVN trap of carefully planned and superbly coordinated defenses, with T-54 tanks and 130-mm guns employed for the first time along with a protective antiaircraft system capable of hitting the crucial helicopters that supplemented the ARVN's large armor force. Beginning on February 8, seventeen thousand of the ARVN's best troops were sent into southern Laos to fight unfamiliar mobile offensive warfare. Thieu issued secret instructions on February 12 to halt the offensive once three thousand men were incapacitated, and around March 8, as his losses of men and matériel mounted, Thieu ordered a retreat without informing the Americans. By this time only massive U.S. air support prevented a complete disaster for the badly coordinated and frightened elite ARVN units. Even so, the ARVN suffered nine thousand killed and wounded and lost two-thirds of its armored vehicles, and over seven hundred U.S. Army helicopters and planes were destroyed and damaged. The campaign turned into a huge defeat for both the administration's pretensions and its plans for the RVN.

During the same period, beginning on February 4, an ARVN force crossed into Cambodia to destroy Revolutionary bases and supplies in and near the Chup rubber plantation. The commander of the operation was killed in a helicopter on February 23, and by mid-April it, too, withdrew in failure.

Kissinger found Lam Son 719 a dismal disappointment, and "Laos exposed many of their [RVN] lingering deficiencies."[11] Thieu had proved duplicitous and a poor military leader. The best ARVN units lacked coordination and were badly led and wholly dependent on American air power and logistics. The RVN was essentially no stronger than it had been before Vietnamization. The event demoralized the RVN's supporters. U.S. generals were certain that only the timely use of massive air power prevented a complete debacle. But while American officials could admit these points both at the time and much later, the President and Kissinger defended the ultimate wisdom of the campaign as one which bought time, discreetly ignoring that events were soon to prove that it was the Communists who gained most of it. The sheer magnitude of the failure made it politically and personally unpalatable, of course, but it also revealed the fatal weakness of the key U.S. strategists as well as of their dependents. Lam Son 719, the crucial battle of Vietnamization, was a total failure. In reality, the Nixon administration's last illusions regarding the RVN's potential had led to the Laos-Cambodia campaign and exposed the RVN's grave military vulnerabilities in the now enlarged Indochina War; they generated, too, mounting political difficulties for the President at home.

The Party's leaders, on the other hand, thought Laos provided the Revolution "very basic experience in the guidance, organization, and development of armed forces, especially the main-force troops." It was now clear to them that Vietnamization was not succeeding, while the PAVN's abilities had advanced greatly. Only U.S. air power was the barrier between it and victory. America's initiative and failure greatly renewed the Politburo's military self-confidence after two years of prudent consolidation and action. In May and early June it met to consider the strategic opportunity and determined to "win a decisive victory in 1972, and force the U.S. imperialists to end the war by negotiating from a position of defeat."[12] Now that the balance of forces had tilted heavily in its favor, the Party's military leaders immediately authorized planning for a major campaign to exploit the American and RVN weaknesses and defensive position. While the Politburo reasserted the need also to focus attention on the parallel wars in Cambodia and Laos as well as on guerilla war in South Vietnam and urban struggle, its major emphasis was on preparations for a main-force offensive employing the modern arms and mobility it had begun to test during Lam Son 719. The destruction of ARVN's main forces would be the primary objective.

By late November, American papers were reporting large convoys moving south, and the game of guessing the time and scope of an offensive began. Most officials mistakenly predicted a far smaller and shorter repetition of the Tet offensive for February. Curiously, many of them, while realistic about the RVN, were skeptical of the extent of the Communists' capacity, and they were still convinced the Party was too shattered to create a major challenge. Some still refused to comprehend the full magnitude of the ARVN's weaknesses. Meanwhile, the DRV's press and Party directives at the beginning of 1972 prepared the public for the new situation and possibilities. The events of 1971 were carefully summarized, ranging from the reduction of American troops and the dismal state of their morale to the reconstruction of the guerilla movement in the south and the failure of pacification. But what was most crucial was Lam Son 719 and the defeat of Vietnamization, as well as the expansion of the war in Laos and Cambodia, creating "profound transformations" in the Revolution's favor on the battlefields. "The victories of 1971 have created an extremely firm, new strategic position. . . . as we begin 1972, we are facing a great opportunity and can develop it quite beautifully."[13] The only thing that the Party left unsaid about the next offensive was its scope, location, and timing.

The Party's perception of its own weaknesses and its enemies' strength had imposed crucial restraints on it after 1968. It was only after the Americans, with their self-deceptions, acted and exposed the fragile state of the RVN's forces that it could accurately analyze its own real power and potential options. It was this demonstration of the new conditions defining the balance of forces that overcame the Party's sustained caution and produced a critical turning point in the war. The problem, of course, was whether the United States' illusions would remain to obscure their vision of reality, or indeed whether it had alternative diplomatic and political resources. The year 1972 proved one of reckoning militarily, but in a conflict so globally significant and against a nation so rich and adroit it was not at all certain that the military balance of power would prove the only critical factor. It might, as the Politburo fully anticipated, merely unlock the door to other developments, especially to negotiations. And that might create another sort of contest altogether.

Chapter 30

The United States and the RVN: Vietnamization's Contradictions

The Vietnamization of the war further increased Washington's dependency on a tiny group of men in Saigon. The ultimate fate of the vast American effort to create a viable alternative to the Revolution rested on their strengths and weaknesses as well as on those of their administrative and military system. Uncertainty whether the shrewd and ambitious political tacticians who ran the RVN would employ their growing power to resolve South Vietnam's seemingly infinite problems or continue to pursue their own private interests was a basic challenge to America's monumental undertaking.

The White House believed that Vietnamization in the right diplomatic context might be sufficient to allow the RVN to survive even with its obvious weaknesses. Politically, it staked the fate of its entire Vietnam policy on one man, Nguyen Van Thieu, in the hope of achieving stability in the RVN's intrigue-prone political universe. The Pentagon, for its part, attempted to create a technically advanced army patterned on American doctrines and procedures even after it became apparent that the model was irrelevant. Given the political imperatives of reinforcing the existing regime, the structure of the entire RVNAF's leadership conformed to Thieu's need to control all possible sources of challenge to himself. When military and political objectives conflicted, as they necessarily did when efficiency and Thieu's power became inconsistent, politics always took precedence.

THE MILITARY ASPECT OF
VIETNAMIZATION

To build the RVN armed forces was essential to the realization of America's commitment to the creating of a counterrevolutionary alternative. By 1970 the effort had no coherent doctrinal basis but was rather defined by accretion and by the pursuit of the most familiar course known to the U.S. military. Functionally, its goal was to construct an army capable of controlling as much of the population as possible, which meant a huge force devoted primarily to static defense and competent to use technology and large quantities of munitions. A part of it, however, they had to train and equip for mobile warfare. The result was a very expensive army, in terms both of the costs to the economy and social order and of its permanent dependency on vast U.S. military aid.

The size of the RVNAF reached 1.1 million men in 1973, absorbing over half the males between the ages of eighteen and thirty-five. The Pentagon continually enlarged its aviation and artillery inventories, on the premise that the ARVN would not only maintain complete air superiority but actively use it as an integral aspect of its operations. Beginning with 75 older-model helicopters in 1968, it possessed 657 of the latest by July 1972. This gave it "one of the largest, costliest, and most modern helicopter fleets in the world."[1] In addition, its air force comprised 740 planes, making it the fourth in size in the world. By 1971 the RVNAF had received at least 1,000 howitzers, 1,650 heavy mortars, over 1,000 M-113 personnel carriers, 300 tanks, and an advanced communications system to coordinate its sprawling army. The exact amount of equipment it received remains a mystery because as the U.S. military withdrew, it left behind vast quantities of matériel. It had been a huge logistical problem to get equipment to South Vietnam, and the Pentagon regarded its removal as no less troublesome, preferring to leave anything that could not be used elsewhere or obtained more efficiently from the United States. Enormous amounts of scrap metal remained in Vietnam, of course, but also much surplus equipment that required maintenance. Whatever the reason, the RVNAF after 1968 moved toward increasing complexity in its armaments. Logistics and maintenance then became vital to keeping the abundantly equipped, technology-intensive army functioning.

The ARVN soon had all of the liabilities of American technology and few of its assets. The training of pilots, mechanics, and technicians was a vast, time-consuming task, and much of the effort was lost trying to teach them essential English. About twelve thousand men were sent to the United States, where language training came first, and special schools were set up in South Vietnam where the men spent up to thirty-six weeks simply learning English. The system never worked effectively, and the more modern the equipment, the more quickly it broke down. Even worse from a military viewpoint was the transfer of American base complexes to the ARVN, a process which followed a fixed scenario in most cases.

The U.S. bases were vast and luxurious, with their own technical maintenance problems. Pilferage immediately relieved them of much of whatever could be sold on the private market, including essential items like light bulbs and roofing. The bases took time and manpower, further immobilizing an already static army. Senior American generals described the process of rapid deterioration very accurately, yet they saw no alternative but to transfer the bases to the ARVN. Logistics and maintenance were regarded by virtually all U.S. officers as insurmountable obstacles.

Such experiences with Vietnamization and the ARVN's actual combat performance merged to greatly discourage those Americans most involved with the RVNAF. They could sometimes cite improvements in specific units, but there remained the essential problem that the U.S. forces were withdrawing faster than the ARVN could or would improve. Ironically, as the ARVN's ranks burgeoned after 1967, its quality declined with growing numbers; the competence of artillery units was diluted, and its few good officers were overtaxed. New equipment had similar effects. Quantity was never transformed into quality. "ARVN's record in the past is not one that instills confidence about its future performance in the main force war," the CIA wrote in April 1970.[2] Despite certain improvements its combat training for over half of its manpower was ineffective and its capacity to fight with large units untried. Time did not alleviate the problem; in various services, such as artillery, it aggravated it. Every effort, when tested in experience, as the U.S. Army artillery experts concluded, disclosed that "little improvement was to be seen in combat."[3] The invasion of Cambodia exposed the virtual dependence of the ARVN on lavish American air support, while the ARVN's artillery simply failed. Lam Son 719 disclosed the inability of the ARVN to coordinate a major campaign and use its superior firepower rationally. Journalists repeatedly reinforced the argument that the ARVN could never replace, much less improve upon, American soldiers.

As many senior RVN generals later admitted, the United States managed to turn an already inadequate army into a yet worse one, making it wholly dependent on American equipment and doctrine. They have correctly argued that the ARVN was simply an appendage to the U.S. expeditionary force, and it was the Americans on whom they relied to solve their problems in case of real need. For the ARVN's condition was the effect of Thieu's leadership, and Thieu was in power, they rightly believed, because the United States kept him there. In reality, of course, the problem went deeper, for the entire ARVN senior officer corps was a political entity and would remain one regardless of Thieu. Ultimately, the purpose of the army was not military but political and economic, and this function was the unavoidable result of the absence of any mass-based political opposition to the NLF, which now was confronted only with the organized violence of an overequipped military machine. While the PAVN successfully absorbed a great infusion of foreign technology, making its army more proficient in modern warfare, technology became an increasing source of dependency and distraction for the ARVN. The difference was the nature of two armies, one politically motivated and the other an artificial creation. In this sense, the ARVN leadership's faith that the United States would bail them out of dire straits was logical, for without the Americans they would never have existed in the first place.

The administration assessed Vietnamization candidly and quite pessimistically from the inception. Remaining illusions declined with time, and in 1969 it still considered the maintenance of a huge American residual force essential to the regime's survival. The Pentagon knew far better than any one else precisely how ill-prepared the RVNAF was to fight modern warfare, and time made it more, rather than less, discouraged. As early as 1970 the Army signed contracts with U.S. civilian contractors to take over and maintain the ARVN's fixed communication facilities. In 1972 it was clear that, because of the crucial logistical failures of Vietnamization, continuous foreign technical aid would be required to keep the ARVN operating. Laird learned very quickly that any reported failure in the Vietnamization program would lead to pressures to slow down troop withdrawals and that training the ARVN would have to become a public relations success regardless of what happened in fact. Praise for Thieu's military achievements came largely from Pentagon press efforts and, of course, from Laird himself, who even in June 1972, after the ARVN's debacles in Laos and in face of the PAVN's April 1972 offensive, maintained that Thieu's forces had "performed quite adequately."[4]

The core of the Vietnamization dilemma remained the quality of the average soldier and the nature of the senior officer corps. The chronic problem of desertions and ghost soldiers only worsened, so that the rapid expansion of the ARVN's size led to a significant decline in the proportion of soldiers actually on duty in the four years after 1968. Growth, which was axiomatic with Vietnamization in Washington's strategy, produced a diluted, weaker army whose destructive social effects mounted without any additional military benefits to offset them. The social impact of this structural process, already great, became increasingly debilitating to the American cause because of the economic premises of the mass army.

The trend of declining real incomes in the RVNAF continued, and both American and ARVN officials acknowledged its effects on morale and desertions. In April 1970, disabled ARVN veterans, neglected and miserable, initiated protests and Thieu's police brutally attacked them, their leaders ending up in prison. Whatever the irony of this episode, it served the ordinary soldier as a reminder, if he needed any, that he was on his own and could expect little from those generals who were milking the economy. As the last vestiges of human solidarity in the RVN areas disappeared, the common people were increasingly subjected to looting and violence, and the regime responsible for the havoc also drafted their sons.[5]

In this larger perspective, it was the social and economic rather than the military role of the RVNAF which ultimately affected the war most profoundly, since mass mobilization and politics were the essence of the Revolution's effort. However weakened the Party's military force or political structure, the RVN's persistent alienation of the population left a growing void which greatly favored the NLF. The expanded, increasingly urbanized ARVN shocked the rural masses, deepening the desire for peace that more and more worked against Thieu's larger goals. Vietnamization was not to make the RVN stronger militarily but only weaker economically and socially, for there was no way to create a large, effective, and less expensive army.

THE POLITICAL ROLE OF THE MILITARY SYSTEM

The ultimate dilemma of Vietnamization and the entire American effort in Vietnam was the absence of any real social foundation for the RVN outside of the military, whose political roles and motives made its warlike functions quite secondary. The tangled considerations which led the United States to sustain the existing military structure for political reasons meant that a transfer of the combat responsibility from Americans to Vietnamese could not succeed. Everyone at the time saw that Washington's backing of Thieu would lead to a further politicization of the senior officers, an economy geared to preserving their loyalty, and a persistent diminution of the RVNAF's military prowess. The alternative to Thieu, as Washington correctly understood, was the mélange of warring cliques, factions, and ambitious men who had emerged after Diem's demise, and therefore a chronic instability from which only the NLF could emerge victorious. Given these two losing choices, the United States selected Thieu, partly because after 1969 it believed it had diplomatic and military options with which to save him. "The present Government will probably remain in power as long as the United States continues to support it," a Senate staff report in December 1969 summarized this opposition's opinion, adding, "If the present Government remains in power . . . Vietnamization will fail."[6]

Thieu solidified his political base by 1969 and spent the next three years gathering up many of the prerogatives Diem had possessed, differing from him mainly in that he gave his key generals a vested interest in keeping him in office. The manner in which he built his machine was typified by the highly publicized case of General Nguyen Van Toan, who in July 1969 was commander of the ARVN Second Division and whose private exploitation of his soldiers and territory for cinnamon smuggling was one of the more extravagant but common enough instances of corruption. Although the anticorruption Censorate, which was headed by Thieu's uncle, had avoided all generals and ministers and existed largely for its highly paid ceremonial function, in mid-1969 it idiosyncratically decided to pursue Toan, releasing details of his various peculations. Thieu, who was legally obligated to take action on the Censorate's recommendations, not only ignored it but even promoted and then decorated Toan. The Censorate dropped the case immediately. Loyal before, Toan became even more devoted to Thieu and eventually was given command of the crucial MR II. "It is generally acknowledged that a rise in rank or change in assignment signifies a change in political fortune rather than a recognition of service on the battlefield," Washington's leading analyst of the RVNAF wrote in a confidential assessment in June 1970.[7]

Thieu worked partly through a crony, military classmate, and prime minister, General Tran Thien Khiem, to administer the vast network of corruption and clip the wings of potential enemies. Thieu managed within a few years not only to eliminate suspect senior officers and province chiefs but also to create the type of neo-Diemist administrative system that the fealty of these men permitted. Running the state apparatus and making money took most of the time of the generals who had power. The real source of authority was Thieu and his loyal men and the increasingly personalized machine based on him.

The Nixon administration's public relations preferred to emphasize the RVN's facade. The 1971 RVN presidential election proved an embarrassing debacle since Thieu rigged a new election law and excluded Ky, so that in the end he was to run as the only candidate. The money for this campaign, an American NBC correspondent in Saigon publicly alleged, came from funds one of Thieu's closes allies, General Dang Van Quang, was raising as the most important figure in the narcotics trade. Former head of the MR IV, Quang was at the time Thieu's chief intelligence adviser.

Meanwhile, Thieu also managed to consolidate power over the National Assembly, either by allowing members to participate in various forms of corruption or by buying votes on crucial issues. In obtaining the assembly's July 1972 approval of martial law, Thieu unleashed every tactic to smash all pretenses regarding his political order. Several Senate opponents to the law disappeared, Thieu offered others $12,000 for their votes, and no one told the remaining opposition senators the time of the vote. The bill passed 26 to 0. By September 1972 Thieu had managed to create a system of administrative control as total of Diem's, with officials at every critical level loyal to him. By then Thieu had dropped all public relations efforts, remaining out of sight and rarely giving interviews. Most important, however, the entire military system led to the presidential palace, the operational command being composed of dozens of men like General Tuan who were directly beholden to Thieu and quite incapable of operating as efficient senior officers. Unfortunately for the United States, this structure had nothing to do with effective political or military warfare against the Revolution.

The schismatic, highly personalized, and opportunistic nature of the anti-Communist groups opposed to Thieu eased his political tasks and to a critical extent kept the United States loyally committed to him. The absence of a large and cohesive Vietnamese elite outside the military was one reason for this opposition's marginality, and Thieu's co-optive talent was another. The sectarian and ambiguous character of the religions of South Vietnam was also important. Buddhism and Catholicism had earlier offered a religious basis for political action, but it proved to be very ephemeral. After 1967 both religions were so divided that five Catholic and four Buddhist slates ran for the Lower House in 1970. The Buddhist leadership which had proved so troublesome between 1963 and 1967 was now, with American aid and funds, deftly co-opted or silenced. "Most of the politicians with whom Thieu had to deal, and for that matter still must deal," a group of advisers to Washington on such matters concluded in 1970, "were not political leaders in any real sense. . . . They had no genuine following, no program or policies—only personal ambition and an addiction to conspiratorial politics. Each wanted to be Prime Minister with maximum freedom and powers."[8] These caucuses rarely cooperated with each other, so that sixteen slates presented themselves in the 1970 Lower House election, all of them anti-NLF. Thieu could easily buy sufficient support and ignore the remainder.

The articulate but internally divided constituency that Thieu managed to alienate had no wide class basis. Much of it was a residue of the French educational and bureaucratic era, connected with the traditional Vietnamese elite that sought a return of French influence. This element became more visible with time, eventually causing outspoken, educated groups of mainly Catholics to withdraw their backing for Thieu, but it was never able to attract a mass following. Until the war ended, this collection of diverse groups and individuals, some of whom were being radicalized, was largely confined to Saigon, but its public prominence there did not overcome its fatal disunity. The official American assessments of its ephemeral, opportunistic nature paralleled those of the Revolution, but the latter actively sought to relate to this amorphous phenomenon, and it was primarily this group which it designated as the Third Force. By 1972 this opposition to Thieu reflected, to some extent, a real and growing national sentiment that the attaining of peace was imperative, and the RVN's truculent hostility to any dealings with the NLF reinforced it. Yet the opposition differed profoundly on how best to attain peace; all it had in common, ultimately, was its opposition to Thieu. Its emergence after Thieu had completely imposed his control over the military and civil bureaucracies made the RVN's internal political life a hopeless, futile affair, one not likely to give the United States a viable alternative to Thieu.

Thieu understood the American dilemma and mood perfectly, and it took very little cunning to play on it. His ability to consolidate his position with the United States greatly reinforced his standing in the eyes of those military and economic elites who were more impressed by the material advantages of being a part of success than by the larger issue of effective anti-NLF politics. "It was our impression," the experts of the Senate Committee on Foreign Relations wrote in June 1972, "that Embassy officials tended to discount the opposition's criticism of the Thieu government and believed that, even if that criticism had any validity, there was no alternative."[9] Most non-Communist Vietnamese who were not part of the Thieu machine believed that the Americans would continue to support Thieu against all rivals; once Thieu and Washington became synonymous in their eyes, a significant anti-American tide emerged.

It was quite clear by 1971 that Thieu and his circle's shrewd political mastery and relentless peculation would produce a hopelessly fragile ARVN, for the RVN's political and military imperatives were absolutely irreconcilable. Thieu's grave deficiencies as a military leader emerged strikingly at that time. His most important commanders in the field were political loyalists, and the nominal head of the Lam Son 719 debacle, Lieutenant General Hoang Xuan Lam, then in charge of I Corps, was both notoriously corrupt and incompetent. The result was what one RVN general later called "dissension verging on insubordination," as the crucial generals failed to work with each other adequately.[10] As bad as Lam Son was destined to be, it was worse yet because the ARVN lacked an integrated command structure capable of operating autonomously of Thieu during the pressures of battle. The command system which existed was perfect for Thieu's power, and he kept it until the final deluge in 1975. General Lam remained head of I Corps until the spring 1972 offensive forced Thieu to remove him and the equally incompetent head of II Corps, whom he replaced with "the Cinnamon King," General Toan.

Thieu tacitly assumed that his primary task was politics and that the Americans would maintain responsibility for military matters. The RVN's essentially political character made it militarily untenable, and since Washington ultimately sanctioned its political role, it also had to confront the military implications. In the end, the United States failed to attain either political stability or military effectiveness.

Chapter 31

The Struggle for a Changing Rural South Vietnam

THE PHOENIX PROGRAM AND PACIFICATION

The pacification program of the United States and the RVN from the start suffered from irredeemable dilemmas. Washington never separated its political from its military functions, and the inability of the program to operate effectively on a political level made it primarily a military effort committed to the physical control of the rural population. Those RVN officers and civilians who ran it were loyal only to themselves and their patrons, and their corruption and incompetence permeated the system. The peasantry's political consciousness reflected the harsh lessons the pacification program's carpetbaggers and officials constantly taught them.

American officials had hoped that the RVN would assume primary responsibility for pacification, destroying the NLF's political infrastructure while U.S. forces fought its military units. They were repeatedly disappointed that the program was inefficient, corrupt, and given low priority in Saigon. Their own firepower also produced fatal contradictions in the program, for pacification was the inevitable victim of the American way of war and of the military order Washington had installed in Saigon as its surrogate. Nonetheless, the United States still knew that an effective rural strategy was a precondition of the RVN's survival, and by 1969 it had few illusions about its deficiencies. When the Nixon administration reviewed the matter on coming to office, it worried that "continuing inefficiency, corruption, and the parochial concerns of the GVN" might very well undermine a renewed effort.[1]

As the Revolution reduced its military activity and entered into a period of consolidation, the very same RVN pacification functionaries who had failed earlier now fanned out into the rural areas and continued to operate as before, or even more corruptly because of the pressures of rising inflation. The data the United States collected automatically showed remarkable improvements in pacification efforts, given the vacuum the Revolution had left. Most knowledgeable Americans regarded the gains in 1969 as fragile and admitted that numbers said little about the peasantry's true loyalties. Any NLF offensive, many believed, would reverse all that had been attained on paper, but until 1972 the figures remained reassuring, and confidence in the program among some Americans increased. Senior ARVN generals later admitted that pacification during the three years of 1969–71 was in essence the same program, premises, and personnel of the earlier period, and wholly linked to military security. The CIA in April 1970 warned that despite the Party's setbacks, it was still very much able to spring back. For the CIA the key element was the condition of its infrastructure.

For reasons like these the RVN always refused to allow villages to choose their own officials; it was aware, as the National Security Council's experts put it in early 1969, that peasants had to be "manipulated by Saigon authorities because of the prospect of success therein for VC and/or oppositional elements."[2] Pressure to confirm pacification's triumph eventually goaded Thieu to take action, and in 1971 he instituted village and hamlet elections. Journalists dismissed them as a complete charade. Villages were forced to vote only for men the district governments nominated, causing one former ARVN general later to comment, "The electoral process thus degenerated into some sort of wholesale appointment under the cover of ballots."[3] A means for establishing much greater provincial control over village affairs than ever, favoritism and corruption now penetrated even more deeply into rural life. In September 1972 Thieu merely dropped the facade and replaced it with the direct appointment of village officials. Not only would the RVN not trust the peasantry, but its growing manipulations and exactions indeed increased mass hostility toward it.

Pacification during the Nixon administration differed from that of the earlier period only insofar as it applied two innovations. One, ostensibly the carrot, was the land reform program, which Thieu rather then the United States initiated in 1970. The second was the stick, the Phoenix program, which the Americans introduced in 1967 but did not formally organize until July 1968. Phoenix was surely one of the most controversial programs of the entire war and, despite constant official efforts to whitewash it, one of the most brutal. Measured by numbers killed and injured, it was small when contrasted to bombing and artillery, yet it revealed the magnitude of the United States' weaknesses in fighting a war against political enemies.

The Americans created Phoenix as a coordinating program for nine RVN and U.S. agencies attempting to eliminate the NLF's cadres and infrastructure. Such a multi-agency effort had aggravated bureaucratic turmoil built into it and presented opportunities for corruption. Phoenix's progress, like that of all U.S.-organized efforts, was assessed quantitatively, and a monthly quota of "VCI" was assigned to the 247 district offices working under the program. If no real or suspected NLF cadres were apprehended, people were arrested anyway. The quota was always filled because, as one former RVN general explained, "the official reasoning went, it was better to detain the suspect than to free the criminal, even at the expense of incurring some wrath."[4] The majority of the cadres spent less than a year in jail, but their ability to bribe local Phoenix operatives often determined the length, $25 to $50 being the usual fee for peasants without real taint of suspicion. The use of the power of arrest to settle personal scores was widespread. Abuse of prisoners and torture were documented repeatedly and were undoubtedly routine; the claim that not all those arrested were maltreated was offered as a feeble defense. Precise information does not exist, because there was no need to collect it. "We do not deny that the program was riddled with serious errors such as the arrest of the wrong suspects, indecent treatment toward detainees, and accidental killing of suspects during skirmishes," senior ARVN generals later admitted.[5] Whether the twenty thousand persons American officials listed killed under the program were already dead when taken or whether they died thereafter was a moot point, even though the CIA director William Colby admitted that three thousand were killed after capture.

Official U.S. disclaimers regarding Phoenix's actual operations are highly suspect because the inherently repressive nature of such a program forced the CIA to try to downplay its crucial role even as it attempted to improve its efficiency. While Foreign Service and Army officers were among the 450 Americans involved, Phoenix's most ferocious section, the Provincial Reconnaissance Unit, was directly under CIA command, which trained and paid for it. The 4,400 PRU operatives, unlike the other RVN agencies involved in Phoenix, had no distractions from their task of listing Vietnamese to target. Highly paid and aggressive, they were the Phoenix's elite action arm and also its most efficient section. "I want to kill as many Communists as I can," one PRU told an American AID worker in a village, boasting, "We killed at least 20 here."[6] The RVN tried to get the bloody PRUs under its jurisdiction and partly succeeded in 1970.

The true impact of the Phoenix program was difficult for the United States to estimate, and only the Revolution could do so. Although American officials claimed to have arrested 86,000 persons under the program between 1968 and 1972, in addition to those killed, the results disappointed them.

They believed that NLF penetration of Phoenix allowed it to warn important cadres of imminent arrest, and that this explained the absence of senior officials. At that rate, they felt, the infrastructure could persist with very little difficulty, even at the lower levels. Americans also suspected that the NLF was buying the release of many of its captured personnel. Some junior U.S. Phoenix operatives were more confident in the program's success, but even they admitted that it was uneven. But most Americans involved in Phoenix were convinced its arbitrary use of arrests, torture, and deaths required some distancing between themselves and the organization they had conceived. A few CIA advisers warned that Phoenix's casual arrests were profoundly alienating many peasants: "The net effect of the program in some provinces has been to create new Viet Cong rather than to 'root out' established operatives."[7] U.S. officials never believed that they managed irreversibly to hurt the Revolution's infrastructure, but it was a quite common impression that Phoenix was widening the already huge gap between the population and the RVN. Save for a small number of RVN supporters, few Vietnamese favored an arbitrary police state.

THIEU AND THE COMPLEXITIES OF LAND REFORM

The struggle for land had been the engine of the Vietnamese Revolution from its inception, and the critical link between the peasantry and the Party. But the RVN's politics and American skepticism and deference to the wishes of its Saigon allies had kept the issue of reform off the pacification agenda under the Johnson administration. By the time the United States and the RVN returned to the issue, the nature of the land problem had greatly changed.

This transformation was due to several factors. First, the NLF had reformed the land system, in terms both of distribution and of rent levels. This fact alone was to keep a large section of the peasantry on its side, in varying degrees, until the war ended. Second, the economics of land had changed dramatically with the impact of the war. Peasants abandoned land as they sought refuge, and the RVNAF's absorption of over half the eighteen- to thirty-five-year-old males, as well as civilian casualties, created a serious labor shortage. So too did the destruction of vast numbers of water buffalo. Rents in the Mekong Delta in 1966–67 averaged 5 to 10 percent, compared with 40 to 60 percent before 1939. Even this sum was often not collected, and land prices in the upper Delta after 1958 had fallen by half by 1967. There was still money to be made in agriculture, given the growing urban market, but it could be done best by capital inputs in the form of technology and seeds, and landownership was now less important. But in the Delta the peasant simply no longer needed land reform, however strong his traditional desire to own his own land. Reform was ceasing to be a critical issue. Landlords, on the other hand, stood to gain from any measure which would allow them to transform their nominal land titles into capital, which could then be profitably invested elsewhere.

On September 21, 1968, Thieu was in Kien Hoa, a province in which the NLF had already redistributed the land. By this time he was well aware of the changing nature of the agricultural economy, and he had often heard American complaints about his troops reinforcing the Communists' power by acting on behalf of landlords after occupying a region. Still insecure and in the process of seeking to build his constituency from civil servants and officers, he decided to make an overture to the peasantry and score a public relations coup by vaguely declaring that peasants who held land distributed by the Revolution could keep it free and that he himself would embark on a program of free land distribution. Those Americans working on land issues had no advance notice of the idea, and indeed they remained largely opposed to it until well into 1969. Over the subsequent months, however, Thieu and his staff skillfully amplified what was to become the "Land to the Tiller" program, which was finally enacted into law in March 1970.

Thieu's carefully crafted land reform was intended to have the maximum political effect and reinforce his power, and the second plank in the law was the compensation of landlords who were to have their legal titles transferred to the peasants, most of whom had already received land from the Revolution. In one fell swoop Thieu removed the landlords' opposition that had earlier stymied reform. Americans who polled them now found that over half were either for reform or at least not opposed to it, especially if their lands were in NLF areas or in regions with labor shortages. Fewer than one-quarter were against it, and these were concentrated in regions where lands were still valuable or where there was no alternative use for their capital, as in Annam. The land reform was therefore tailored to take them into account, and Thieu decided to focus the program almost entirely on the Mekong, where the NLF had to a large extent already redistributed the land, where a labor scarcity existed, and where landlords were eager to sell out. For public relations purposes, Thieu fixed a round one million hectares as the redistribution goal. In effect, the region which had both the greatest land scarcity and the strongest NLF base, with the highest levels of combat, was to be least affected by reform.

During 1969 the American land experts were converted to Thieu's strategy, which was crucial since he could not implement the program without money. Both U.S. and ARVN officers now agreed that the eviction of tenants and the collection of rents by landlords when they captured NLF territory was a formula for allowing the war to continue indefinitely, justifying the reform in terms of military security at least in the Delta. In a sense, Thieu had managed to come up with a hybrid measure that made gestures, even if only partial, in every direction. Americans did not draft the law, and the Saigon mission did not even endorse it until spring 1969. Even then, a significant group opposed it for fear of alienating landlords, though events were to show that Thieu was not about to do so. Quite the contrary, he had shrewdly planned to win them to his cause.

The reform program was applied almost wholly in the Delta, MR IV and MR III, where even after its completion there remained well over half a million hectares of abandoned land. In the two land-scarce regions in the north, the status quo remained intact. Thieu, of course, had promised reform nationwide, but being from Annam himself, he understood that the existing elite was against reform, and he made no serious effort to apply the program there. Only 5 percent of the land targeted for redistribution was in that region. Americans in charge of pacification there strongly supported his conservative approach, for the landlords in the north were linked with the entire local administrative structure and the heads of the army, through which they exploited communal land as well as their own holdings, and given their lack of investment outlets land remained the basis of their wealth. Peasants who applied for land found village officials ignoring them, and they were sometimes directly threatened by ARVN officers. As the U.S. adviser to the program in MR I later concluded, Land to the Tiller was "a miserable failure in Central Viet Nam."[8]

AGRARIAN CHANGE AND THE INCIPIENT RURAL CRISIS

The RVN's land reform law came ten years too late to have a political effect, but it was welcomed by landlords and accepted by peasants. It created the basis for a new land crisis which only the end of the war in 1975 averted. Each landlord was permitted to retain fifteen hectares. With a bit of ingenuity he could keep more, though few chose to do so. Land used for industrial crops and orchards was exempted from reform, as was all owner-operated land falling within urban boundaries. The latter category, comprising a million hectares, was the most valuable. The land's value was calculated at two and one-half times the average annual paddy yield, equal to a rental of 40 percent at a point when most were fortunate to be receiving 10 percent, and some American experts argued that it was overvalued. One-fifth of this sum was paid in cash and the rest as eight-year bonds paying 10 percent interest. The program would have cost at least $500 million over time, depending on exchange rates. During the next three years 1.1 million hectares, one-third of the cultivated land, was transferred free to 40 percent of the rural population, or 800,000 tenants. Those in the Delta could receive up to three hectares. Some 85,000 expropriated landlords still kept, however, 1.7 million hectares, and now they also had capital.

Landlords were delighted. Many had held titles on which they had collected nothing for years, and rents were often lower than the interest they were to receive. Land in insecure zones was given preference for free distribution. Some bribed land reform officials to take their land or expedite the expropriation process. The proportion of the rural population made up of landowners increased from 29 percent at the end of 1970 to 56 percent two years later. Polling six thousand peasants regarding the program, American experts found that the "Vietnamese peasant . . . wasn't as impressed as the outsiders."[9] They were dismayed to learn that land reform did not create a decisive shift in political support for the RVN and that the large majority of those who received land refused to identify with it. So many had obtained the land from the Revolution years earlier that their position was not altered in any manner, save in the RVN's records. Only a quarter believed that the law was being administered fairly. The reform had not affected the peasant nearly so profoundly as it had the landlords, who were now far better off. In a situation of labor scarcity and land surplus, reform ceased to have any real meaning.

Far more important to the peasantry was the credit and marketing institutional framework which historically defined land distribution. The ability of merchants to buy paddy when it was cheap and sell it when it was dear had, along with usurious interest, been a continuous source of exploitation. Nothing was to be done about these traditional peasant grievances throughout the American occupation. In 1973, after land reform had been implemented, the AID's experts thought that not more than a dozen firms and individuals dominated the distribution of the Delta's rice to retailers—a pattern much like that of a generation earlier. Despite the desire of Thieu and the Americans to build a large class of prosperous peasants supporting the RVN, they merely created a rural economy more vulnerable to the world economy in a way no one could have foreseen in 1970.

There was plenty of land for those with machinery, fertilizer, and resources. At first the RVN planned to absorb the new capital by divesting itself of the state-owned firms Diem had created, most of which were now losing money. But a new bourgeoisie began to emerge quite spontaneously, based increasingly on the expropriated landlords, which began to go into trade, business, and lending, reestablishing its hold over the agrarian economy through new forms. With typical interest rates running 60 to 72 percent annually, it began to reproduce the traditional system of mastery over credit-dependent peasants. The reform program also granted expropriated landlords access to cheap credit and virtual domination of the RVN-funded banking system established in the Delta. At the same time, they began to modernize their own farming and moved to exploit changes which occurred in the south's agriculture as a result of the introduction of miracle rice strains and the use of fertilizers. Although this trend toward capital-intensive agriculture had been under way well before land reform, the reform accelerated it considerably.

Ambitious new landholders were also ready to risk using new tools and techniques, which created a new loan market that former landlords now could fill as well as a rental potential for equipment essential for rice culture. Large numbers of tractors, rototillers, and agricultural machinery were imported, so that nearly half of South Vietnam's cultivated surface in 1973 was mechanically plowed. It was not long before real economic power in the Delta was based not on land but on the ownership of horsepower and control of the credit market, and in both areas the former landlords were again masters. Nearly a third of the south's rice was of high-yield varieties in 1973, and these required machinery and credit. By 1972, peasants were beginning to complain about the rising prices of essential imported fertilizers and insecticides and about the difficulties of the high-cost modernization the United States and the RVN were encouraging; in the following year these problems were to explode into a full-scale crisis.

Some American experts soon perceived the problems that were emerging. Since the land reform was implemented in the context of the traditional credit system, the importance of which had grown with modernization, thousands of peasants began to lose their land again to their creditors, many of whom were former landlords using the capital with which they had been compensated. Many tenants' titles, in addition, were withdrawn when former landlords managed to get their expropriated lands declared as falling within urban regions. One-third of Bien Hoa Province east of Saigon was redesignated as urban and the new owners displaced. Had the pattern continued, the mastery the new elite over capital and technology would have reconcentrated as much land as it chose to repossess.

Land reform, in brief, was quickly breaking down and surely did not eliminate the economic basis of peasant radicalism. For several years after 1969, however, this new combination in the factors of production caused a sharp rise in rice and agricultural output. This significantly increased the income of the more privileged landowners, and especially of those who lent or rented to them. The most ominous problem was that the new system was heavily import dependent. Beginning early in the war, the United States dumped subsidized fertilizer on South Vietnam. With the 1973 oil price crisis, the entire agricultural system was gravely threatened; fertilizer prices tripled between 1972 and 1974, even though they were kept below world prices. Pesticide and fuel costs followed. As the war ended, the entire southern agricultural structure was sinking into a profound crisis. It was this condition which the Revolution was to inherit. Land reform only accelerated the transformation in the agricultural system, destabilizing it while making it more vulnerable to the world economy. Change, rather than basically improving the lot of the peasant masses or the political support for the RVN, helped weaken the position of both and hasten the demise of Washington's dependency.[10]

THE DILEMMA OF PROTRACTED WAR AND THE PEASANTRY

It is impossible to describe the total impact of the prolonged, bloody war on the southern peasantry and its society, for the many years of destruction, population movements, and terror had seriously modified the political universe to which both the Revolution and the United States had to relate. One should not underestimate the material or structural aspects of the long conflict, particularly the role of land, in preparing the way for effective Revolutionary mobilization, but it would be equally fallacious to minimize the effects of the war on the political consciousness of the peasantry. Few peasant families did not suffer an irreparable loss, or even many: death, homes destroyed and abandoned, ignominy . . . the toll cannot be measured, or remotely felt, by those never a part of it. For more and more of them, the relentless, interminable pressures began to fashion another way of reasoning; the goal, simply, was to survive and minimize losses. Both the Party and the United States were profoundly aware of this psychology, and tried to cope with it and relate to its challenges.

The politics of withdrawal and survival remains politics nonetheless, because beneath the external posture of caution exists a set of residual attitudes, including perceptions of reality. While a drifting with circumstances may result from a belief in the futility of commitment for daily existence, it often is based on an accurate sense of the nature and origins of constraints on a person, whose alienation includes hostility and desires, however unlikely the individual believes it to be that he or she may hope to fulfill or express them. Nonengagement is not necessarily neutrality, devoid of judgment. Withdrawal merged with alienation is an intermediate political stance fully capable of being organized at the right time and if leadership exists. That none does at a given moment does not alter the fact that forces and events affect people and produce a potentially radical consciousness among those who have lost the material preconditions for survival or are exhausted.

This pervasive passivity posed a far greater challenge to the United States and the RVN in the short run than to the Communists, for the U.S. pacification program made a fetish of control of territory and population, while the Revolution was far more flexible in its methods of relating to the masses. Given the American objectives, active cooperation from the people was crucial or else pacification would inherit intolerable long-term military ar economic burdens, which is exactly what happened. This fatal flaw in America's efforts was the consequence of its basic mode of conducting both military and political warfare. In dealing with the loyalty of the exhausted population, the United States was the victim of its own contradictions, whereas the Revolution had mainly to confront the constraints on its own material resources.

To the extent that there had been politics among the peasantry in South Vietnam after 1954, the Revolution had led it, and though a huge reservoir of sympathy existed for it, particularly among the poorer third of the peasants, the politics of survival had begun to erode the NLF's ability to rouse the peasantry to take action. To some degree the NLF's very success with land reform and rent reduction, along with the improvement in the economic position of those able to remain on the land, decreased the motives for struggle. The essentially marginal 1970 RVN reform, which the peasantry justly credited to the pressures the NLF had created, further minimized economic incentives. Until 1970 it remained in most of the peasantry's interest for the NLF to maintain some sort of presence, since land rents were often proportionate to its proximity. And a nagging economic issue which was never eliminated, usury and credit, continued to infuse class questions into the countryside until the war ended. Indeed, even by 1967 the peasantry's desire for reasonable credit equaled its aspiration for more land, and that it was never to get in the RVN zones.

It was the decline in the relative importance of land issues that permitted peasants increasingly to relate to politics on the basis of their other needs. Here the emerging politics of survival undermined the RVN's pacification efforts and prevented what it needed most for success: positive affirmations of support and cooperation from the population. For the Revolution was, essentially, a movement of the people, while the Americans and the RVN were, overwhelmingly, outsiders, and the vast bulk of the masses' losses in the war were a result of the United States' immeasurably superior firepower and size. Whatever else it was, the Communists' use of surgical violence against landlords and RVN officials was never indiscriminate. In fact, it was generally very popular. The NLF tried to keep the masses within their villages; the United States and the RVN often forced them out. After 1969, the RVN took virtually all the sons who were absorbed into the military. Until 1971 defoliation had been an important cause of peasant complaints, particularly in the peripheral provinces. Phoenix, of course, was a constant source of terror to the masses. Even when the standard of living rose and combat lessened, there remained the routine daily corruption of RVN officials and the constant depredations of its underpaid soldiers, a huge tax on the people and a constant insult to their dignity.

In a word, as peasant politics increasingly moved from economic to survival issues, the hostility toward the RVN and the United States increased, for land without peace was largely useless. It is indisputable that even those no longer under the same economic pressures as earlier saw problems increasingly in terms of preserving not so much a traditional legacy as a coherent one, in which stability also meant physical security for the individual and for the family. One may perceive this response as the politics of the moral society, as opposed to a moral economy founded on traditional visions of equity, evolving from a normal human being's instinctive sense of the preconditions for survival. This amorphous amalgam of the politics of peace—survival, tradition, more-customary economic grievances, and a desire to preserve reforms—merged and deepened, becoming the peasantry's universe of values and action as well as the basis of a largely conscious suspicion toward the RVN's efforts. And beneath it there existed a reservoir of support for the NLF to tap if it could do so.

The Americans dealing with pacification, and even senior ARVN officers, understood the magnitude of this challenge and always appreciated the extent of their own failures. The peasants were "candidly apathetic," the command of the U.S. Eleventh Armored Cavalry reported in late 1969, and this concealed "obvious sympathy for the VC and VCI," most of whom were their relatives.[11] Above all, people wanted peace and to be left alone, even though many were quite ready to supply moral or physical support to the NLF. Both the CIA and the American military experts felt that the peasant was withdrawing, adjusting to power realities, but unwilling to turn in NLF cadres. Economic improvements notwithstanding, the CIA reported in April 1970, there was no "substantial degree" of support for the Thieu regime in the countryside.[12] When Americans asked a large sample of the population between 1970 and 1972 whether it was wise for U.S. troops to leave the country, fewer than a fifth thought it unwise that they were departing. This dislike for the foreign invader spilled over to those who collaborated with them, and a crucial residue of patriotism never ceased to be a force to reckon with.

However much the United States hurt the NLF's efforts, Robert Komer regretfully concluded in 1974, "we never were able to translate this into positive and active rural popular support for the Government of Vietnam. . . . we were never able, ourselves, to generate a counterattraction in Saigon that ever had the charisma, the capability, the administrative effectiveness. . . ."[13] A few of the RVN's more thoughtful officers admitted the same point later: "As to the general population, hardened and disenchanted as they were by the long, destructive war, disillusioned and frustrated by an elusive peace, and ever worried about an uncertain future, many naturally remained uncommitted to the GVN cause and its efforts."[14] This reality, despite all the difficulties it posed, left the initiative for relating to the people with the NLF.

THE REVOLUTION'S RESPONSE TO PACIFICATION

The United States' dilemma was that it had far more to accomplish in pacification if it was to salvage anything out of its massive intervention, whereas for the Revolution it was more a question of tactical adaptations and the option, ultimately, whether to emphasize military more than political struggle. While the Revolution was basically able to use its time to rebuild its forces and assure that it would not fail in either area, it nonetheless suffered from serious problems.

The Americans were convinced that the NLF's penetration of the RVN was by the end of 1970 too deep to be undone, but the Party regarded many of its collaborators as opportunists. The Americans considered the Party infrastructure as highly resilient, and at the end of 1972 they believed that it still had access to over two-thirds of the population. In the traditional NLF strongholds south of Danang, the U.S. military correctly estimated, in mid-1971 the NLF had the "persistent and deeply rooted sympathy and active participation of a large segment of the Binh Dinh Province population," and elsewhere in the region it had "a substantial minority."[15] The Party, too, thought that it still had the firm support of perhaps a third of the nation's peasantry but that the middle third would accommodate to whomever was winning. The U.S. and the NLF perceptions notwithstanding, it was too early to determine whether either was correct.

The Phoenix program was certainly more successful than its organizers ever knew. It did round up sufficient low-level cadres to make an important difference to a highly decentralized political movement. Persistent RVN and U.S. offensives wore down many of the local guerillas, and those who replaced them were not so experienced. The main problem was less actual capture or expulsion from former solid strongholds than the general exhaustion and lowering of morale that began to permeate the local NLF forces. With these came the declining willingness of peasants to take so many risks to help, let alone to volunteer their children to fight. To a critical extent, the military and political aspects of the southern effort had always reinforced each other, and now that the regular military was avoiding combat the caution and loss of élan among political workers was inevitable and understandable. The Party's emphasis at this time on military rather than political work, as it later admitted, led to its losing control of the situation; the United States and the RVN "created many difficulties for us in 1969 and 1970."[16] Despite the continuing progressive, systematic weakening of the RVN in all domains, it was stronger relative to the NLF during this period than at any other time since 1964. Only Lam Son 719 in early 1971 proved it was still, despite all the Revolution's problems, far weaker in absolute terms.

The NLF had to cope with pacification in the period after 1969 from a defensive position until it could protect its political workers with a minimum of armed forces. Although it had few problems in the important populous regions north of Saigon, which became the locus of its military activity, in the Delta its work was badly hurt and in many areas temporarily abandoned. The exhorting of cadres to work harder and better produced few results. Unless they were able to defend themselves, they could not succeed in the beehive of armed RVN functionaries that was being installed in the critical rice belt. While the shell of the NLF organization was considerably smaller, those who remained, despite their losses and the enormous risks and greatly reduced activity, still compelled the RVNAF to commit a huge armed force spread over the vast terrain to prevent them from springing back to full strength. In this sense its role was primarily military, serving as a vital diversion, rather than political. But several developments partially relieved this pressure on the NLF. The first was the use of the ARVN outside South Vietnam, which reduced the forces available for offensives against NLF strongholds. The second was the active deployment of more guerillas throughout the Delta to thin out ARVN ranks and offer the political cadres protection. By 1971 the NLF had begun to return quietly to some Delta areas it had been forced to abandon.

There is no evidence that RVN land reform significantly influenced these trends. Not enough peasants were affected by it before the end of the war to alter the political balance, and the NLF's claim to have been responsible for land reform still remained far stronger. The peasantry's willingness to take risks on behalf of the NLF declined, but this was due mainly to the greater physical dangers involved rather than to political conversion.

Until the pressure of military events could be brought to bear on political activity, before 1972 the Party's strategy remained an improvised one and essentially passive. To some extent, it never fully recovered from the losses of political cadres during the Tet offensive. In the larger context of revolutionary struggle, the party leads but also interacts with forces and currents in the society, economy, and world. Until these were more apparent, it cautiously explored possibilities unless, as with Lam Son 719, it was compelled to convert a challenge into an opportunity.

One option which won renewed interest was its urban efforts, despite the weakness of the NLF in the wake of Tet. The NLF proclaimed itself to be a coalition of various southern elements, although the Party was the controlling heart of it. The urban elements who had emerged in the Alliance of National, Democratic, and Peace Forces during the Tet offensive represented a slice of the still relatively few but highly articulate urban educated individuals whom Thieu had alienated and who wanted peace. In June 1969, in part for purposes of future negotiations but also to stimulate its urban efforts, the NLF and Alliance proclaimed the Provisional Revolutionary Government (PRG), realizing an American anxiety that the Party would embark on some form of coalition with the non-Communist elite opposed to the Thieu regime. Relating to urban trends became more important for the Party as its rural work faltered, despite its desire to place more emphasis on the countryside. The very size and visibility of the urban opposition made this inevitable, and its strengthened position among students made it more promising. Every time Thieu consolidated his power, the political gap between his regime and all those not in it widened. The educated urban elements, mainly marginalized middle class in origin, responded to the war with growing hostility and energy. The Party had often discussed the national bourgeoisie's progressive role in the history of national-liberation movements, but after 1971 its desire for a coalition in the south led the Party to emphasize its possible functions more strongly. By 1972, in any event, the Party was too weak in the cities to pursue any other than a united-front strategy.[17]

The irony of the new balance of forces between the United States and the RVN on one side and the Revolution on the other was that both were weaker politically at the end of 1971 than in 1969. The only question was about the nature and gravity of each side's malady and its capacity to heal it. The problems the RVN confronted were rooted in events in the United States and elsewhere, and many were social diseases intrinsic to its specific social system. The Revolution's weaknesses were partly organizational, and mainly the outcome of Tet, but primarily military. Above all, they were temporary. Politically, it had been weakened not by the RVN's land reform efforts but rather by its inability to protect all of its cadres against Phoenix, a weakness which reinforced the deepening peasant impulse to withdraw from the struggle. Until the spring 1972 offensive, which reversed this overall equation in the political struggle, the Revolution's main gains were from the irreversible, continuous decay of the RVN's military forces, economy, and leadership—all of the developments which so rightly impressed American experts. Yet, before the full implications of the economic, political, and social crisis of the RVN system were revealed, diplomatic and military forces shaping the outcome of the very long and complicated war came to the fore.

Chapter 32

The Communist Party's International Strategy

Like some highly elaborate minuet, the nuances and possibilities of Chinese and Russian behavior defied easy comprehension, for both states found it very difficult to resolve the traditional internal tensions between their national interests and their ideological commitments. And given China's intrinsic instability and the problems of orderly leadership succession within the USSR, the difficulties of both coherent analysis and responses to trends in the Communist world reinforced an instinctive tradition in Washington until 1969 to simplify its interpretation of world communism and consider it essentially monolithic, devoid of differences sufficient to affect the outcome of the Vietnam War.

The ambivalent efforts of Russia and, above all, China in defining their state interest in Vietnam were to a critical extent the result of their evolving perceptions of each other. The possible relationships between the three giant states most interested in the Vietnam War were always shifting, often dramatically, both because of their dealings with each other and because of internal political changes. Until someone in Washington was prepared to attempt to integrate this extraordinarily complex matrix of nations, factors, forces, and power relations, diplomacy lingered in the margins of a war which military events as well as political and social dynamics were shaping. The question of the degree to which international relations and diplomacy could alter the outcome of such realities in Vietnam would in due course arise after all of the United States' other efforts had failed. Whether it would prove as great an illusion as the other means of gaining its goals was crucial to the last phases of the war.

CHINA AND THE WAR

The differences within China's ruling elite as well as the threats and incentives from the United States made China the most unpredictable of the major powers involved in the war. After 1964 the deterioration in its relations with the USSR guaranteed that it would be most susceptible to major shifts in policy favoring its state interests as opposed to its historical internationalist commitments. China after 1950 had shown moments of great flexibility, which France had welcomed at Geneva in 1954, yet its responses to the United States were profoundly colored by Washington's unmitigated hostility in the wake of the Korean War. To the extent that America's intervention in Vietnam was due to its obsessive vision of the war as an effort to control Chinese expansionism, China's potential roles were increasingly circumscribed not by its own desires but by those that outside powers imposed on it.

With the consistent aggravation of Sino-Soviet relations from the late 1950s onward, which blunt Russian economic boycotts reduced to something scarcely more lofty than blackmail, China began to play a role which reinforced both its vision of itself as an autonomous world leader and its desire to advance its state interests. The Laos agreement in July 1962 was a threshold in Peking's policy, as opposed to its rhetoric, since it revealed that keeping the war away from its borders and avoiding a direct confrontation with the United States would remain, as at Geneva in 1954, a cardinal principle of its diplomacy regardless of ideology. There can be no doubt that American analysts saw the Chinese-Soviet split over Laos as reflecting the greater division between the two nations, yet they concluded that a policy that left China isolated would eventually make it more tractable. In fact, China was striving not merely for an independent foreign policy but also for regional hegemony. Soviet efforts after 1957 to reduce it to subservience were surely not the cause of China's new role, which had its roots in a thousand years of history, but Moscow's hostility removed all inhibitions on its returning to its classical place in the Asian firmament. Uncomfortably and inconsistently, China's policies embodied a theory of national-liberation warfare based on small units and protracted war, a desire to form and lead a new Marxist-Leninist international, and adherence to the 1955 Bandung principles of neutrality. At the 1954 Geneva Conference it had staked out its place as the nation crucial to the peace and stability of the entire region. It subsequently attempted to reduce the possibility of an accidental confrontation by making it repeatedly clear to Washington in its statements and actions, and also via confidential direct channels, that it would not enter the war unless the United States invaded the DRV and threatened to move its forces toward the Chinese border. Despite its tough declarations regarding U.S. escalation after 1964, American analysts easily perceived the many loopholes China left in all of its statements.[1]

The United States stumbled over a great deal of contradictory evidence of trends in Peking's policy because the Chinese elite was itself profoundly divided at this time as well as later, making doubt the safest position. American experts subsequently concluded that three factions were struggling for mastery of policy, and whatever the many caveats, events later confirmed this interpretation. The military most feared a U.S. escalation, for which it was not prepared, and sought to avoid a confrontation with the Russians. It supported a protracted, inconclusive war in South Vietnam which would keep the Americans distracted and not require the kinds of arms that would improve Soviet leverage over the DRV. The radicals, emerging from the Cultural Revolution and dominant during 1966–67, were for a purely ideological line of equal hostility to both the Americans and the Soviet "revisionists." And the moderates, led by Chou En-lai, saw the USSR as the greater menace to China and favored an effort to normalize relations with Washington in the hope of working with it to weaken the Russians. The Tet offensive, which made America appear less formidable than ever, reinforced Chou's faction. All of them opposed DRV-U.S. negotiations, but for very different reasons. The radicals and the military rejected them in principle, but the moderates were essentially for the Balkanization of Indochina, fearing that a total victory for the Revolution would give the Soviets more influence over the DRV than Peking thought tolerable. These factions remained fairly balanced until 1968, when Mao Tse-tung's deeply anti-Soviet heritage caused him to add his weight to Chou's position.[2]

The United States' experts perceived the intricate dimensions of China's role in the region and war, the significance of its growing split with the Soviets, its dual if not yet duplicitous strategy toward the DRV, and its internal divisions. Later, officials were to fault the Johnson administration for failing to grasp the historic importance and enormous possibility of these facts, and there is no doubt that the profundity of the Sino-Soviet schism was never fully understood in Washington. Despite the impressive grasp of the details of Soviet and Chinese policies and tensions which the intelligence community possessed at the time, no one had an analytic framework for transcending mere information and producing the obvious hypotheses capable of exploiting the trends. This was due not simply to a lack of imagination but also to the belief, understandably widespread, that China's ideological pretensions were a crucial guide to its actions as a state. But the residues of past myths regarding the China ogre and the absence of insight cannot obscure the reality that China's internal political dynamics and goals were too fluid to be comprehended clearly at this point. But once China's leadership was able to form a cohesive caucus for Chou En-lai's position, it was quite evident that any American exploration of the implications of China's shifting position in the region might quickly become a factor in defining Peking's real policy—assuming China were stable and decisive enough to play a sustained role. To think about such a convoluted process clearly is not possible, because it is not a situation that lends itself easily to rational analysis. To grasp it in its essence would take an important element of guessing and a gambler—in brief, a creative decision to seize the immense possibilities of this situation, including all of its risks of self-delusion and failure. No such diplomatic speculator could be found in the Johnson administration.[3]

THE SOVIET UNION AND THE WAR

Soviet policy was intimately associated with the sparring factions which existed in the USSR until October 1964 and Khrushchev's removal. But given the incomparably greater stability in the Kremlin than in Peking, Moscow's policy was less subject to inconsistencies and manipulation. Until Khrushchev's departure the United States felt that the Russians were not much of a problem and, indeed, believed that they, too, were apprehensive about Sino-Vietnamese actions. Washington saw Russia's symbolic and verbal support for the Vietnamese as an aspect of its need to maintain prestige in the world communist movement. From 1965, when the Soviets substantially increased their economic aid, until mid-1967, the United States tended to regard the Russians as quite acquiescent objects whom the Vietnamese were maneuvering to advance their independent interests. During this period Washington believed that the Russians would restrain the DRV whenever possible.

In 1967 Soviet military aid to the DRV reached a wartime peak, and while its public and private statements of support for the Revolution increased dramatically, Washington did not expect that the Russians would go beyond words in the event of another escalation. Nor did it consider Moscow capable of influencing Hanoi's basic diplomatic strategy, for it perceived Soviet policy as passive and intended to keep the DRV independent of China as well as to protect Russia's image in the eyes of the now huge world antiwar movement.

The Johnson administration believed that the Russians were cautious, and it also knew that the Chinese were eager to avoid a direct confrontation with the United States. It did not think it could exploit Sino-Soviet tension to manipulate one or both of the DRV's allies into forcing the Revolution, which it considered fiercely autonomous, to negotiate on American terms. China's major elite factions, for one thing, were not yet ready to provide the needed leverage. Before 1968 the administration, too, had not yet exhausted its reliance on arms, and after Tet it felt it could not negotiate from a position of weakness. Moreover, it was unwilling to offer the USSR concessions on issues transcending the war or its relations with China, in return for its cooperation on Vietnam. All told, the sheer complexity of exploiting the split in the Communist world defied careful analysts and professionals. Clearly, only an enterprising amateur would dare to ignore the odds in order to play such a diplomatic game.[4]

TOWARD AN ALTERNATIVE REVOLUTIONARY WORLD ROLE

The DRV needed acute analysis and brilliant finesse to maneuver between the treacherous shoals of the Sino-Soviet rivalry and the potential for the Americans to exploit it. The Party was in the precarious position of not wholly trusting its allies but of being unable to fight the war, save at a far more rudimentary level, without their aid. The need to assuage its increasingly disputatious supporters, exploit their differences to extract maximum aid, and avoid an intimate alliance with either side was an immense challenge. While the Sino-Soviet split now worked in its favor, the Party knew that in the long run it was inherently dangerous.

The 1954 Geneva Conference and the 1962 Laos treaty had proved that the Chinese were potentially unreliable. Even so, contacts between the DRV and China remained especially close, and China's influence stayed great even after Hanoi's improvement in its relations with the USSR in 1965. China's logistic forces in the DRV during 1965–68, though probably not as large as the 320,000-man contingent they later claimed, was unquestionably very substantial and vital to the maintaining of transport. The very intimacy of the long relationship, as well as an inevitable condescension in dealing with those at least partially influenced by its culture, made Peking all the more testy as the Vietnamese moved toward a more neutral position in the Sino-Soviet dispute and began to translate their desire for an autonomous foreign policy into practice. Any DRV call for unity against the United States irritated the Chinese, who in mid-1965 occasionally began to rebuke the Vietnamese for "unprincipled flexibility."[5] The Chinese were far less ready to accept an independent DRV than the Russians were.

China's Cultural Revolution accelerated the DRV's movement toward independence. From an ideological viewpoint the Vietnamese found it abhorrent; practically, they thought it so distracting to the Chinese as to make the escalating war a tertiary issue for them. The image of the Red Guards and a nation on the verge of civil war especially shocked the Vietnamese.

Even worse, China's public position throughout this period against any form of negotiations with the United States, for whatever reasons, struck the Vietnamese as a frivolous exploitation of their fate by the various Chinese factions, all of which vied with each other to appear the most militant. By no later than 1967 the Politburo decided that both the Soviets and the Chinese would put their own national interests before the DRV's and that it would have to define a diplomatic line without excessive concern for their hopelessly contradictory suggestions.

The Revolution's relationship with Moscow was inherently less encumbering. The USSR had no direct interest in the region and was content to allow the DRV the freedom to reduce its dependency on China and enjoy an independent position, a role which also greatly reduced Chinese pretensions to guide the world communist movement. It was obvious after February 1965 that the DRV would make the most of the deepening division between its two giant allies in order to optimize aid, and from this time onward both the Johnson and the Nixon administration firmly believed they would continue to attempt to do so.[6]

The Soviets had the ability to give aid well beyond China's capacity, and in sheer volume it was far larger. By 1966 this fact was reflected in a slightly greater emphasis on Russia whenever the DRV issued declarations of appreciation. The Vietnamese never ceased to believe that the Russians could and should provide more, but they were unable to state this publicly. Indeed, as long as Vietnam had its China option, it could deal with the Soviets on a more equal basis. Given the enormous gains to the USSR from a war that tied up U.S. manpower and resources, divided it from its friends, and greatly reduced American pressures on the USSR, the DRV could expect a continuation of aid even as it rejected Moscow's advice on negotiations or kept it in ignorance of its plans, which it did constantly. Privately, the Party continued to criticize residues of revisionism in Soviet foreign policy, for the Kremlin still adhered to the coexistence doctrines initiated under Khrushchev. Although it had initially endorsed the 1968 Russian invasion of Czechoslovakia, with certain reservations, it soon backed away from its implications and in early 1969 categorically came out against "big-country chauvinism" within the communist world and against interference in the affairs of local parties.[7]

While ample experience undermined the Party's naive trust in its allies, for ideological reasons it favored the restoration of international unity. But disunity was an irrevocable fact of life, and once the DRV chose to relate to the split for its own advantage, it did so with increasing expertise. From 1963 to 1965 it carefully avoided aligning itself with either Chinese or Soviet endeavors to build a world communist movement under their respective hegemonies. It interpreted unity in the world movement to mean cohesion among equal partners free to guide their own development toward socialism as they saw fit. It was for this reason that it shifted its position on the Czech invasion. The problem, of course, was that neither of its two allies agreed with this definition and that each was far more likely to cooperate with the United States than with each other. The Party then began to broaden its views to include unity of the world movement behind its own struggle.

This effort can be taken at its face value, as a sincere attempt to restore the toll that time and events had taken of the idealism and purity of international Marxism, but it was primarily an attempt to forestall the dangers of irrevocable disunity for its own cause. So long as China was distracted internally, it was unlikely to trade with the United States for advantages. The Soviets were already committed to a coexistence strategy and open to a diplomacy capable of sacrificing Vietnam's interests. The Party began to argue with increasing passion after 1969 that world communist unity existed only in its support for Vietnam's battle and that without this the world revolutionary movement and proletarian internationalism would be empty shibboleths. Its struggle was symbolically and in fact the personification of the last shred of a noble ideal, one which united a vast number of diverse parties, movements, and people throughout the world whose common denominator was Vietnam and the issues and causes the war embodied. This theme reached its peak after 1971, when the United States' détente diplomacy was eagerly attempting to exploit Sino-Soviet contradictions. Vietnam stood on the world revolution's front line, the Party insisted, confronting its common enemy with "independence and creativity," bound to no one nation but rather to a larger ideal which everyone who claimed to be a socialist was obligated to support.[8]

Whether this evocation of ideology over national interest could still be effective remained to be seen, for in a world in which both China and the USSR had betrayed ideals so often it must have appeared somewhat quixotic. Yet Vietnam had indeed become a personification of a new international cause far transcending either pro-Soviet or pro-Chinese parties, and it embodied a vast and highly pluralist world movement which symbolized an unsullied idealism around which countless millions of people had responded and mobilized. However amorphous, Vietnamese Communism's claim to special legitimacy was also a reality and a political fact, and for China and the Soviet bloc to rupture with Vietnam as the vanguard of social transformation in the modern era was to court a political disaster of untold implications. Both Peking and Moscow, whatever their differences as national states, still contained men whose ideological inheritances, however dusty and abused, forced them to consider such issues seriously. For the Vietnamese Revolution this residue was an admittedly intangible but potentially enormous asset, and it used it.

THE EVOLUTION OF THE
COMMUNIST PARTY'S DIPLOMATIC
STRATEGY

The Party staked out the broad contours of an independent stance after 1955, when its own experiences and its reaction to domestic failures in China and Russia caused it to refine its ideas throughout the next decade. Such a definition of its own road to socialism was essential, lest any of its own members, or students sent there for training, look to those two nations for guidance. Since the Party never fully trusted the diplomatic advice and motives of either nation, distancing itself was crucial to maintaining a consensus at home for its own alternative diplomacy.

Internally and externally, Party members were told with increasing frequency after 1966, the DRV had an autonomous policy relevant to the specific Vietnamese development. It was, the Party claimed, inherent to an international movement that each national party define its own perspective on crucial issues, and learning what it could from others was only a feeble concession it increasingly added on as an afterthought. While the Party began with the common principles of Marxism-Leninism, their creative application to Vietnamese conditions had been the key to success, and the leitmotif of all of the writings on this critical matter stressed "independence and autonomy" as well as "self-reliance."[9] On the other hand, as internationalists, the Party leaders sought to avoid any hint of nationalism or exceptionalism, and Le Duan's authoritative 1970 summation of the Party's theory and practice described the Vietnamese Revolution as an integral part of the world revolution, from which it had received much aid in its pursuit of an independent, creative strategy. Conversely, because it was an aspect of a world movement, Vietnam had an inviolable claim on that movement's continued support.

By mid-1971, as Nixon's détente diplomacy was beginning to succeed, the possibility of betrayal by one or both of its allies made the DRV increasingly anxious, and it obliquely criticized its allies while preparing its own people for a possible rupture with one or both of them. It increased the stress on independence and deplored the "crafty diplomatic trick[s]" the Nixon administration was employing.[10] The DRV's journals began to reiterate frequently such themes as the absolute autonomy of the Vietnamese Party, its complete adherence to Marxism-Leninism, and its equal and sovereign relations with other members of the "socialist camp" along with their duty to support Vietnam's vanguard role in the world anti-imperialist struggle. Even if there were to be continuity of support from its allies, the Party was educating its members. And if there was an open break, it was justifying its position.

If the Party's descriptions of its own role in the world were at the core a consistent reflection of its own experience, their timing and form after 1969 was a direct response to American diplomacy. Washington's experts on the tensions between the DRV and its allies obtained from such statements confirmation of the success of their efforts to capitalize on the differences. Indeed, the very fact the DRV was so autonomous caused them to believe that the White House's diplomacy could triumphantly exploit existing schisms. The tracing of such nuances and trends in Vietnamese Communism was a matter of the highest priority for Kissinger, and his principal adviser in his secret negotiations with the DRV was also a leading authority on the Party's troubles with its allies and its definition of an independent position.[11]

The United States and the Revolution until 1969 shared some critical common assumptions and dilemmas. They felt that any diplomatic accord would reflect the military and political balance of forces in South Vietnam. Until these were fully tested, diplomacy was essentially an effort to mobilize or neutralize domestic and world opinion or the pressure of allies. The long, convoluted chapters in this period of contacts came to nothing because neither side was prepared to negotiate. Until the United States lost confidence in the efficiency of its armed forces, particularly in the capacity of air war to extract a submission to its basic political goals, it had no consistent diplomatic strategy, much less a willingness to compromise on its increasingly chimerical war aims of sustaining its credibility and keeping the RVN in power. Indeed, Washington's use of "peace overtures" as justifications for intended escalations only greatly intensified the DRV's skepticism as to what precipitate talks could accomplish. For the DRV, moreover, a reduction of bombing over its territory meant an increase in American bombing over Laos and South Vietnam, for the planes were never idle. But because of the sheer ineptness and insincerity of Washington's efforts, the Americans remained on the diplomatic defensive until 1969. The Johnson administration never thought serious negotiations were possible, and all it managed to do was alienate its NATO allies as well as many of its own citizens. The Party was therefore never compelled to reveal its basic objections to untimely negotiations.

The DRV strongly believed that the war would pass through three stages: first, fighting; next, fighting and talking; and, finally, negotiations leading to an agreement. It refused to tolerate illusions that diplomacy would reflect anything other than the real balance of forces because premature optimism which relaxed the fighting spirit of its army and political cadres would itself affect that equilibrium. To sustain morale was critical, and the DRV was unwilling to permit public relations to define its diplomatic position.

Even within this constraint, however, the DRV had scope for initiatives, but both enemies understood that diplomacy's function was to gain time for the military to operate. In 1964 the DRV regarded the United States as powerful and as naturally unwilling to negotiate until it understood the limits of its own strength, a process that would require years. It therefore maintained a succession of minor, often ephemeral initiatives which it knew would only embarrass and isolate the Americans. It was not until April 1968, when Johnson announced his equivocal bombing halt and acknowledged the limits of escalation, that the United States scored its first major propaganda coup and forced the skeptical Communists to begin the Paris talks. But open disagreements within the administration, as well as the RVN's constant obstacles, spared the DRV any diplomatic embarrassments. As the Paris Conference droned on meaninglessly, fighting and talking remained the basic DRV strategy until spring 1972. By that time, of course, the balance of forces had shifted radically.

The DRV's problems came not from the United States, which under Johnson had no desire for a negotiated end to the war, but from its friends and potential allies. One patient U.S. official counted as many as two thousand individual peacemaking attempts during 1965–68 alone, and some of these were the work of people who could be useful to the DRV or were simply too important to ignore. Various efforts from Eastern European states caused considerable grumbling among the Party's leaders, who could not always deflect them. At the same time, China opposed any hint of the DRV's readiness to negotiate with the Americans, and Hanoi had to tread a wary path. Such challenges could be handled deftly because the Russians remained fairly restrained in pressuring Hanoi. They felt that the prospect of successful diplomacy with Johnson was slight, and they feared increasing Chinese influence over the DRV. The Russians were often intermediaries, but they made it plain that they had no decisive leverage and that they would increase aid to the DRV should Washington continue to escalate.[12]

By the time Nixon entered the White House, Hanoi's diplomacy had reached a high level of sophistication both in theory and in practice, and it had helped to isolate its enemy internationally. The DRV had prevented the illusions of negotiations from dampening its military efforts, fully aware that until the trial by arms was exhausted no serious talks were possible. At the same time, it kept its realism from looking like cynicism or insincerity. It maintained the initiative in public relations because the United States' air war and military offensives, particularly in Cambodia after 1970, belied its political proclamations. The Revolution's diplomacy bought time to consolidate its military power, while time eroded the RVN's economic, military, and political systems. Although the DRV comprehended the essential relationship between power and diplomacy, its main concern was the constancy of its allies. Balancing one against the other while asserting the independence of its own position had proven successful beyond all expectations until 1969. Whether it could continue this virtuoso accomplishment until it had an opportunity to exert optimum military pressure on its enemies was one of the fateful questions of the entire war. And it was an issue which the United States would try intently to influence.

Chapter 33

War on Two Fronts: Diplomacy and Battlefields, 1971-1972

NIXON'S SEARCH FOR A DIPLOMATIC STRATEGY

Diplomatic negotiations to end the war before Nixon came to power had provided the new administration with a long legacy of frustrations. While both the Revolution and the Americans shared a consensus that a negotiated end to the war would reflect the existing military balance of forces, their conceptions of the extent to which it might still be altered through further combat differed greatly. The American decision makers were too deeply divided until 1969 to pursue a coherent, consistent negotiation strategy. This division had become especially evident after March 1968, when key administration leaders publicly contradicted each other on the exact meaning of the President's September 29, 1967, offer to stop or limit bombing the DRV if it did not take "advantage" of the reduction while "productive" talks were under way. When Johnson reneged on his March 31 pledge to virtually stop bombing the DRV, the subsequent Paris Conference had no chance of success. The President agreed with those who argued that the United States must negotiate from a position of strength and that it could still use air power materially to shift the military balance. "Our most difficult negotiations were with Washington and not Hanoi," one American diplomat in Paris later recounted, and it was this fatal ambivalence regarding talks, as well as interpreting DRV concessions as signs of weakness warranting yet more military pressure, that foredoomed all of the Johnson administration's feeble diplomatic gestures.[1]

Richard Nixon had carefully watched this frustrated diplomatic charade. While he, too, instinctively believed that the application of military power might revise the negotiating context, he began to contemplate alternatives as early as 1967. At the very least, he was determined that a coherent diplomatic strategy not be undermined by open disagreements within the ranks of his administration and that real power over such matters be concentrated entirely in his own hands. He had not only bureaucratic designs, but also more creative conceptions of how to end the war. While the exact form of a new strategy was never fixed in his mind—it varied as fresh opportunities developed—Nixon's self-confident audacity and distaste for the inhibiting complexities which a deeper knowledge of the Vietnamese, Chinese, and Russians was likely to encourage made for more decisive action, both diplomatically and militarily.

Nixon believed that the DRV was an independent nation with inflexible objectives and that dealing with it directly was highly unlikely to succeed in saving the RVN unless its Soviet and Chinese supporters could be cajoled into reinforcing U.S. pressures. Such a view began to emerge in Nixon's mind in 1967 and 1968. The war, he concluded, was stalemated; further escalation would not succeed unless linked to a parallel diplomatic strategy. Moreover, the great range of U.S.-Soviet mutual interests elsewhere in the world, including the containment of aggressive Chinese policies, would make it responsive to U.S. initiatives. At the same time, China had to be offered the opportunity to break out of its isolation, and thus given an incentive to cooperate on the Vietnam War, though Nixon had yet to reconcile the elements of fear and hope in his assessment of the China question. He considered the triangulation of U.S.-Soviet-Chinese relations as a possible way to bring pressure on the DRV, but initially he had no great hopes for it. Bilateral U.S.-Soviet efforts, however, were considerably higher on the president's agenda. Nixon saw the Soviets, whose aid was most important and allowed the DRV to resist Chinese advice, as the major problem. He felt that the DRV had been extremely successful in playing off its two allies against each other to maintain their support and that the USSR had the least to gain from it. To a critical extent, the White House regarded an opening toward China and the emergence of triangulation as a means by which to pressure the Soviets into cooperating with Washington. In essence, the road to Moscow led through Peking. Kissinger himself, like many others, had also been thinking about such proposals, but Nixon reached his own conclusions before meeting his new national security adviser, and he always remained the principal force behind it.[2]

The crux of Nixon's diplomatic analysis was that the Sino-Soviet split created an important opportunity for the United States to explore and exploit and that it was the ability of the DRV to impose its own priorities on its supporters that made it worthwhile to seek to divide or minimize backing for the Revolution. In addition to making diplomatic or strategic concessions elsewhere to Russia or to China in return for their help in Vietnam, Nixon was prepared to combine creative diplomacy with a threat of renewed force to compel one or both of the DRV's allies to risk greater direct involvement in the war or suffer humiliation. Precisely because Nixon cultivated his reputation of being a die-hard anti-Communist devoid of inhibition—his own "madman theory" being the ultimate reflection of it— he thought the specter of military disaster might cajole not only the DRV but also Russia and China into cooperating with him.

How the new administration would create a coherent synthesis out of these two parallel impulses of the use of global diplomacy and the threat of further escalation was to depend greatly on the specific events both in Vietnam and in Sino-Soviet relations, but that Nixon's high-risk diplomacy would be far different from that of Johnson was certain. Although the new President respected the role of the military balance of power in defining the outcome of diplomacy, he was sure he had a formula for overcoming the doubtful economic, political, and military capabilities of the RVN while at the same time withdrawing American forces to attain an "honorable solution" which precluded a Communist victory.[3]

Coming to grips with China, which Nixon had publicly urged as early as 1967, was far easier said than done. American experts on China at the beginning of 1969 portrayed its influence on the war as intransigent and its potential authority over Hanoi as limited. But the main constraint was that the administration itself was still unsure of precisely where to fit China into its strategy and that it preferred to explore the Soviet track and hold the China option in abeyance until it had first plumbed Moscow's willingness to cooperate. The Chinese themselves also remained in transition, having followed Chou En-lai's advice at the end of 1968 to make a gesture toward Nixon, only to have the administration rebuff them. It was the Soviet Union's responses and actions that were to define the speed with which the U.S. opening to China might occur, and Moscow was always to remain the primary objective of its convoluted diplomatic efforts.

The new administration immediately made explicit overtures to the USSR regarding the "linkage" of the war to all other phases of Soviet-American relations, ranging from SALT to the Middle East and trade. "To relate events to each other, to create incentives or pressures in one part of the world to influence events in another," became the prime principle of Washington's diplomacy.[4] Kissinger made this clear to the Russians on January 20, 1969, telling them that their aid in settling the war would determine the course of relations everywhere and hinting that, should they refuse to cooperate, he might turn to the Chinese for aid. The position of the Soviets until 1971 was to bide their time, immediately frustrating the White House, making plain that while they agreed to relate issues, they did not believe that a failure to progress on one should hold up agreements on others. By late spring 1969 Nixon and Kissinger were considering the China card, and in July the NSC began a comprehensive review of Sino-Soviet tensions. At the same time, the President and his aide decided that "incentives and penalties" would be required to shake the Russians out of their procrastinating mood, and efforts to approach China began in earnest.[5] In early March, Russian and Chinese troops clashed along the isolated Ussuri River border in northeast China, and serious border conflicts took place elsewhere as well for the remainder of 1969. By the time Kissinger was telling his staff in mid-1969 that China would behave more as a weaker beleaguered state than as one influenced by the imperatives of ideology, sufficient change had occurred within the mercurial Chinese ruling elite to make contacts with the United States feasible. Both Kissinger and Nixon from this time onward sought to focus on that dimension of Chinese practice which reinforced their desires, and while they grasped a critical aspect of Chinese foreign policy, they were to pass lightly over the time-consuming reality of ideology's restraints and the power elite's divisions. Washington now believed that the diplomacy of Marxist-Leninist states could be made to conform to American-defined rules. And if they were not to do so instantly, it was assumed, they would do so in sufficiently good time that America's other problems in South Vietnam would not come to the fore.

The depth of the Sino-Soviet split was reinforced in the minds of the administration when the Russians informally invited it to join them in attacking Chinese nuclear facilities and when they themselves then almost embarked on such an effort at the end of 1969. Every rumor of Soviet threats only further pressured the cautious Chinese leadership to act pragmatically rather than ideologically in thinking about the Americans. After convoluted preliminaries, in December 1969 the Chinese agreed to a regular channel of communication with the United States, and from this time onward a series of small symbolic gestures on both sides restored the administration's confidence in its approach. Triangular diplomacy on Vietnam seemed possible. As Kissinger later noted, "Our objective was to purge our foreign policy of all sentimentality."[6] During October and December the Russians were formally notified that an improvement in U.S.-Chinese relations was now a part of the overall diplomatic picture and that, in effect, it was the outcome of the failure of the two nations to attain progress on international issues, especially on that of Vietnam. The Chinese, for their part, wanted some gesture of support from the United States to inhibit any possible Soviet action against them. Encouraged, the administration by the end of 1969 felt that its three-pronged strategy of diplomacy over the head of the DRV, threats of escalation, and Vietnamization, each of which aided the other by buying time, could succeed, and it was this hope that was to sustain and guide its policy for three more years.

THE MAZE OF GRAND DIPLOMACY

The Nixon administration's diplomatic strategy was never isolated from the American relationship to the rest of the world, and the sheer complexity and importance of that global framework almost immediately confounded its efforts. Bilateral diplomacy is difficult enough, but triangular far more, and it requires infinitely more finesse to prevent it from backfiring. Yet both Nixon and the rest of the administration were acutely aware that the Vietnam War had caused the United States to neglect its relation with its European allies and Japan at a point when they were becoming economic competitors. The common defense agreements which had initially brought them together were falling into abeyance. For so long as the United States coveted global leadership and hegemony, it had constantly to assess its priorities, and from this viewpoint Vietnam was a growing distraction undermining America's power as well as its image in the eyes of its increasingly rich allies.

An indication of this concern was Kissinger's public musing on the character of the world, for as an academic with unlimited pretensions, he thought it incumbent on him that he try to generalize on the nature of the international system he was attempting to regulate. The world was now said to have five power centers—the United States, Russia, Western Europe, Japan, and China, the latter being a factor by virtue of its size. The definition was amateurish, yet often repeated, because the United States was seeking to put both Western Europe and Japan totally under its political and military umbrella, link them economically as much as possible, and reach bilateral accords with the USSR at the same time. Kissinger now deemed China significant mainly as a lever with which to exact cooperation from the USSR. More crucial, as events in the Middle East, Southeast Asia, Latin America, and elsewhere had shown consistently since 1945, the alleged existence of two to five power centers could neither explain nor subsume the dynamics of change and crises in the world order, which made Kissinger's theory building irrelevant from the inception. What was critical about such efforts, however, is that they were symptomatic of both the analytic and the tactical problems and tension weighing constantly on Washington for the remainder of the war—difficulties which meant that getting out of Vietnam transcended mere relations with China and Russia. And whether Kissinger's vision was false or not was less significant than that he believed it, that it influenced Washington's action, and that it sought urgently to attain its objectives.

Whatever his notions of a five-cornered world, Kissinger always believed that militarily the world was bipolar, which meant the USSR was disproportionately crucial to Washington's desires to stabilize the international order. This fact immediately complicated the administration's policy of linkages in settling the war and implicitly raised the question of its willingness to sacrifice its interests elsewhere to the exigencies of a Vietnam settlement. From its beginning the White House's linkages strategy, despite objections from the State Department, threw all important topics into a common basket, considering it essential that progress on them be in unison. It was a perfect bargaining situation of the sort the White House thought it could relish. While the Russians indicated they were willing to talk about a variety of questions in tandem, they were also eager to reach agreements on concrete issues, arms limitations and trade being the most urgent. But triangulation attempts began in 1970 precisely because the linkages strategy either failed or was too slow for the administration's domestic political goal of ending the war before the next election. Precisely because the United States was unwilling to separate issues, the Russians in turn could bait it on one problem with implied or real concessions on others, trapping it in its own game. No progress with the USSR was made on any issue of significance until 1971, by which time the White House had had ample time to consider whether it could postpone the attainment of its other world goals simply for Vietnam. In a word, the administration's initial negotiating strategy held its entire global position hostage to success in reaching a Vietnam solution, an untenable situation, given its awareness of the imperatives of its simplified model of a five-cornered world.

This dilemma frustrated the administration immediately, as it embarked on a détente strategy intended to attain a diverse set of objectives: a Vietnam peace settlement, a stabilization of the arms race, trade, and Middle Eastern peace, among many others. Inevitably, as its initial all-or-nothing strategy stalled amid endless discussions and as triangulating with China had to overcome barriers of communication and suspicion, various members of the administration began to incline toward quick and specific agreements elsewhere. Kissinger, his memoirs notwithstanding, was one of them. From the inception, American diplomacy on Vietnam was boxed in by contradictions between the war and its global interests, by the substitution of desires and illusions for stark realism, and by the President's and his national security adviser's hypersophistication and cynicism in a context which concealed a profoundly amateurish comprehension of the very nature of the war and the extent to which negotiations could affect it.

Pursuing a very high-risk strategy, given the numerous predictable pitfalls, the White House was nonetheless genuinely stunned when progress came slowly. "I had never imagined that at the end of my first year as

President," Nixon later recalled, "I would be contemplating two more years of fighting in Vietnam."[7] To get out of the impasse, the administration determined during 1970 to play the China card to the hilt, but progress was by no means consistent or Chinese receptivity constant. The May 1970 U.S.-RVN invasion of Cambodia challenged the crucial argument of Chou En-lai and his faction that the Americans were irresistibly getting out of the war. China did, however, remove its opposition to negotiations. The Chinese were unquestionably prepared to subordinate the DRV's interests to their own needs, but they did not yet believe that this was possible or necessary, and each escalation of the war increased their concerns that the Americans were trying merely to use them to prod the USSR or were insincere about normalizing relations. There were too many disputes between Peking and Washington for easy or quick reconciliation, and the Chinese also wanted to play their U.S. card to see whether they could improve relations with Moscow.

To a critical extent, Chinese dealings with America improved roughly in proportion to the failure of Sino-Soviet talks, and when by July 1970 the Russians unsuccessfully proposed joint military action with the United States against any "third" nuclear power threatening either of them, it was clear to Peking that it must seek to forestall any possible hostile coalition. In March 1971 Chou En-lai visited Hanoi and, while the Chinese publicly reiterated their support for the DRV, told the Vietnamese that he thought the United States was withdrawing from the war and made clear that China would not allow the struggle to interfere with the improvement in its relations with Washington.[8] The United States had already broached a high-level visit to Peking, and despite continued disputes in the Chinese leadership, Peking was strongly inclined to accept.

To claim that détente and triangulation were intended only to help mobilize the Russians and/or the Chinese to pressure the DRV into ending the war on American terms would exaggerate the meaning of the next phase of Washington's diplomacy, for both U.S. interests elsewhere in the world and domestic politics also defined its form. Unquestionably, no senior administration leader was certain in his own mind about the exact objective of each effort, for each was pulled by conflicting desires and needs throughout the period, and an attempt to untangle them is futile. Nixon knew that his reelection depended on a combination of sufficient toughness in the war to appeal to conservatives and enough creativity in diplomacy likely to win him centrist votes. His desperate desire for at least the appearance of progress in ending the war and achieving détente had an obvious political basis. The problem of what either of the DRV's allies could do was in doubt because the United States' best informed experts remained convinced the independent Vietnamese would not buckle under pressure and would manage successfully to play off both of its allies. Kissinger ignored this opinion because he felt China needed a counterweight to the Soviets; being well informed about how the DRV had managed to keep its allies behind it, he was certain its very success would lead one or both to refuse to subordinate their national interests and mutual fears to the Vietnamese Revolution.

The public "ping-pong" diplomacy which began with China in April 1971, subsequent measures to normalize trade, and Kissinger's trip to Peking in July to formalize the President's agreed-upon visit the following February were used to apply increasing pressure on the Russians. The Chinese tried to reassure a Hanoi at once irate and anxious that they were not out to sacrifice the interests of Vietnam, granting it supplemental aid just days before Nixon's adviser arrived in Peking. Kissinger raised the question of Vietnam when he saw Chou in July. Later he reported, "I doubted that the Chinese leaders could or would do much to help directly, [but] my trip would be a major defeat for Hanoi" because it would make the American public think its leaders were taking bold steps for peace rather than appearing passive.[9] But once the Chinese agreed to play the game of triangulation, the Soviets immediately became interested, and in October the President announced his trip to Moscow the following May 1972. It was true that the Chinese decision to accept America's initiatives was at first intended primarily to prevent U.S.-Soviet collaboration elsewhere and to obtain various concessions on Taiwan and UN membership. What both China and Russia did do was assure Nixon's reelection and the elimination of many of the internal political constraints on his Vietnam policy. But however modest triangulation thus far, it shifted the burden of diplomacy back onto the DRV, which knew that, whatever the intentions of the Soviets and the Chinese, either or both were increasingly in a position to barter away their commitments to Vietnam against their interests elsewhere, and that Nixon had managed to create the competitive framework for this possibility.

Reasoning geopolitically, the key planners of U.S. strategy became convinced that China did not want the DRV to win the war, because they did not trust its leaders' attitude toward the USSR and because they feared they might become a Soviet satellite and help complete the encirclement of China. Although both Soviet and Chinese aid increased, the Chinese in late 1971 began to advise the Vietnamese not to press their luck, wait for the United States to leave, and then rely on political struggle in the south for an indefinite period. To the Vietnamese this hinted at everything from betrayal to a simple loss of commitment. Meanwhile, Hanoi successfully managed the two sides to gain maximum aid. While Nixon's diplomatic coup gave him the capacity finally to intensify the attempt to divide the Revolution from its suppliers, the DRV, in turn, retained the ability to continue the war on the battlefield against an enemy whose growing diplomatic successes also increasingly encouraged it, ironically, to speed the withdrawal of its forces from South Vietnam.

The Vietnamese on the basis of past experience had ample cause to fear treachery from elements in Peking. In 1971–72 the dominant tendency in China was to use the Americans as a foil against the USSR. Washington believed a triumph was now within its grasp, and this made it willing to assume greater risks. The growing readiness of both Moscow and Peking to triangulate only encouraged it, but their new willingness related overwhelmingly to other issues. Although Vietnam had been the origin of the strategic triangle, it was increasingly a sideshow for both the Soviets and the Chinese, even as it remained the primary, though not exclusive, focus for the Americans.

NEGOTIATIONS—AND PRESIDENTIAL POLITICS

The White House could not conceive that the United States with the aid of China or Russia or both would be unable to define the war's outcome, much less entertain the notion that great powers cannot successfully regulate the destinies of smaller nations. Without this diplomatic myopia the administration would have been forced to admit defeat or else remain in Vietnam indefinitely to cope with the social, economic, and military failures of the RVN system. Deluded by its simplistic visions of the components of war as well as grand diplomacy's potential, it turned with renewed confidence and daring to the protracted, frustrating task of negotiations.

It was in this emerging context that negotiations were to proceed both in public and, sporadically, in secret. Until his détente strategy began to bear fruit, the President believed that only the military balance would affect negotiations favorably, and this required both periodic escalation and the success of Vietnamization. Only Kissinger among his advisers endorsed his larger strategy, tactics, and temporary whims. Nixon considered Secretary of State William Rogers a fuzzy-minded dove and ignored him, while Laird implacably pursued a withdrawal strategy despite the reticence of the President and Kissinger. Transcending all of these beliefs were the administration's political imperatives, which required it periodically to concoct peace proposals aimed at its detractors at home. These reached demogogic levels, as in Nixon's October 7, 1970, plan for a cease-fire in place which was wholly unenforceable technically and unacceptable politically to either Hanoi or Saigon. Thieu openly rejected Nixon's ideas and made it plain that "peace in victory" would come on the battlefield.[10]

The administration believed that it was the visibility of its successful détente diplomacy after 1971 that would truly mobilize the public, whatever
else it accomplished.

Notwithstanding détente diplomacy, the United States continued the
weekly negotiations in Paris, which no one took seriously. The secret talks
between Kissinger and Le Duc Tho and Xuan Thuy during 1970–72 were
soon stymied, less by military than by political issues. Thieu had made it
explicit that he opposed negotiations with the Revolution, saying that "the
Communists use coalition only as a ruse to fool innocent people and to
achieve a silent takeover."[11] It was America's continuous backing of Thieu
with arms, money, and support since 1968 rather than troop withdrawals or
the modalities of a cease-fire that became the biggest obstacle for three years.
The Americans stated that the DRV was demanding that it get rid of Thieu,
but in fact the DRV was asking the United States to stop supporting him,
so that the Revolution might hope for the implementation of whatever peace
plan they agreed on. Had the Americans been merely neutral toward Thieu
and prevented his exploitation of aid to the RVN to stay in power, an
internecine period of political turmoil comparable to that of 1964–67 would
have followed, and Thieu would have been forced out of office. Thieu did
not conceal his rejection of any accord that accepted the NLF's presence,
and the Party neither could nor would leave the Revolution in the south to
his mercy. In any case, there would be no political contest with Thieu, who
had neatly eliminated all rivals to his presidency in October 1971. Washington understood that its support for Thieu would require Soviet and/or
Chinese help to achieve an agreement.

Kissinger gave his assurance to both of the DRV's allies that they might
tell Hanoi that if the NLF challenged Thieu politically rather than militarily
after the GIs left, the United States would not back Thieu unconditionally.
He refused, however, to make even this vague pledge to the DRV directly.
This meant that the Revolution was called on to trust Thieu to agree to
peaceful political change. So long as this basic point remained, the tangled
military issues of the secret talks were incidental. Since the White House
regarded serious negotiations with the Revolution as premature until its
successes with the DRV's allies were attained, the President bided his time
through 1971. Then, to reverse his declining standing at the polls, on January
25, 1972, Nixon revealed both the existence and the content of secret negotiations with the DRV since February 1970. The Party realized that it had been
outflanked in an election ploy and could scarcely trust the Americans to
negotiate seriously. At the beginning of 1972 the administration had attained
three tactical successes with a disillusioned American public, giving the
impression that it was sincerely seeking peace in Moscow, Peking, and Paris,

and the result was a sharp increase in Nixon's political popularity. As his support at home increased, Nixon's confidence in the overall wisdom of his strategy grew with it.

The Party watched with mounting trepidation the United States' efforts to woo its allies. Nixon's use of "contradictions" between Russia and China as a means to impose America's will on "smaller nations" surfaced as a theme in the DRV's press in August 1971 and remained throughout 1972.[12] The pressure on the Party to act speedily and decisively with its own power to tip the balance of forces in its favor had never been greater.

CHANGING THE BALANCE OF FORCES: THE REVOLUTION'S SPRING 1972 OFFENSIVE

Lam Son 719 confirmed that the ARVN was decisively inferior to the PAVN, and it buoyed the Party's confidence in its own main forces after three years of carefully reconstituting and training them for large-scale war employing advanced arms. This reliance on main forces was by no means intended to denigrate its guerillas, whose critical function in pinning down a large part of the RVNAF and whose responsibility for protecting political cadres and retarding pacification were indispensable to the entire war. In calculating its next offensive, the Party's leaders did not focus merely on the battlefield. The primary objectives of its forthcoming effort were to show that Vietnamization was a military failure and, especially, to reverse the United States' pacification successes in the Mekong Delta and strengthen greatly the NLF's political presence, both directly and psychologically, in many areas where it had been weakened. The Party's renewed ability to fill the political vacuum was essential to the exploiting of its military triumphs. The ARVN's defeat would make it clear to many groups, including the urban population, that the NLF remained the decisive force in the future of the south.

The Party planned its 1972 offensive to control its own losses, relying almost exclusively on main forces. Urban uprisings were excluded, and it was sufficient merely to shift the balance of forces so that the urban struggle movement might develop later. By revealing Vietnamization's weaknesses, the Party expected to win "a" decisive victory in 1972, convincing the United States of the hopelessness of its position and further accelerating the military, economic, and psychological decline of its RVN dependents.[13] While the Party thought the RVN might capsize completely, it believed that it was more likely the RVN would simply become much weaker and set the context for diplomacy and for a later final victory. This meant taking and holding a large territory. There was a distinct element of prudence and caution, compared with Tet 1968, in the planning for the offensive, and this was to shape its execution. But Lam Son 719 had convinced the Party that it could count, at the very minimum, on an unequivocal victory visible both to its friends and to its enemies. It prepared its members for at least that much, but not more, because it did not want once again to raise expectations too high. Were diplomacy to fail, the balance of forces would still decisively favor the Revolution and the war would end in eventual victory.

Diplomatically, the Politburo believed, success on the battlefield would preempt the American efforts to gain Soviet and Chinese acquiescence in a settlement which transcended the power both Washington and its surrogate really possessed. The RVN was still growing weaker, and there was no indication that time was going to treat it or the Vietnamization efforts any more kindly. But it was not the Party's desire to allow the slow wheels of time to work, least of all diplomatically, for its own needs and the unsettling transformation of the southern social system made it imperative to bring the war to an end as soon as possible. The 1972 offensive therefore proved to be fundamental to the war's outcome.

The United States expected the offensive, but again failed to predict its time, scope, and location. The White House shared a common belief that the assault could not upset its basic strategy of applying diplomatic pressure, Vietnamization, and threats of escalation. But General Creighton Abrams, who thought an attack would most likely come during February in the Central Highlands, correctly understood that the basic test of the offensive would "be whether Vietnamization has been a success or failure."[14]

The CIA and various Pentagon offices were made increasingly pessimistic by the NLF's rising rural strength. Americans in Saigon most familiar with the ARVN became depressed after Lam Son 719 revealed the obvious failure of their years of Vietnamization efforts. The remainder of 1971 was no better; at best, their operational performance was "spotty."[15] Desertions and demoralization continued, and in the regions expecting an attack the command officers were Thieu's political cronies and poor military leaders. During the Tet 1972 holidays the ARVN kept its soldiers on alert with fewer than 140,000 U.S. forces to help them. The White House thought only its diplomacy might stem the tide, and Kissinger made Nixon's May visit to Moscow conditional on DRV military restraint. Reasonably confident that they were isolating Hanoi from its allies, Kissinger and especially Nixon throughout early 1972 became increasingly sensitive to the United States' symbolic credibility.

The Party's generals opted for maximum surprise when on March 30, forty thousand PAVN troops raced right over the flat demilitarized zone on the seventeenth parallel at a time and place that they were least expected.

Striking as well in the Kontum–Dak To region of the Central Highlands and in the Loc Ninh area north of Saigon, the PAVN were backed by large numbers of tanks for the first time as well as by antiaircraft weapons and abundant artillery. The United States, with all of its advanced technology, had failed to detect the movement of this equipment down the Ho Chi Minh Trail. All of the ARVN's accumulated deficiencies immediately emerged. In the words of General Cao Van Vien, "The enemy's offensive of 1972 dramatically brought to the surface the basic weakness of the Vietnamization process."[16] "The first two weeks of the offensive were disastrous for the South Vietnamese forces," the U.S. Army's artillery expert, Major General David E. Ott, concluded.[17]

As throughout the entire war, the Revolution retained mobility and initiative everywhere while the RVNAF were pinned down in static holding and defensive positions. Wholly unprepared for the direction of the attack, I Corps bases were improperly defended. It was immediately obvious that most of the ARVN's senior officers were incompetent. Stories of cowardice and poor judgment, themes that also dominated the later official U.S. histories, were rampant. Whatever they could do for Thieu politically, the ARVN's generals had no serious command and control system. Units which normally should have been coordinated began to operate independently. The air force (VNAF) began to crumble and proved among the least willing to expose itself to the PAVN's fire.

Discipline now emerged as a critical ARVN defect. The problem immediately became entangled with the huge numbers of troop dependents in the fighting areas, who had from the start gotten in the way and who within a few weeks created terror among the soldiers and hopeless congestion on the roads. The massive use of American air power prevented a total collapse along the seventeenth parallel until April 18, when the ARVN troops began to panic and abandoned their defensive lines. By the end of April the entire ARVN north of the large city of Quang Tri had disintegrated, and on May 1 the PAVN captured it and the entire province. The ARVN had been badly defeated and demoralized, losing immense quantities of matériel. The fall of Quang Tri left the ARVN ready for yet bigger defeats. Hué was now virtually undefended. "The whole thing may well be lost," Kissinger paraphrased Abrams's opinion.[18]

The PAVN, too, revealed some problems. Its forces were badly exposed to U.S. air attacks, and it lost large numbers of its tanks. While it had perfected its use of artillery, its armor was still inexperienced and poorly coordinated with its infantry, and it never adequately linked its three regional fronts to exploit the ARVN's exhaustion of its general reserve. Had the PAVN attack been concentrated, it might have been more decisive. Some Party generals strongly criticized the failure to capture Hué before

Thieu could organize his last and best troops to defend it. Even American generals thought the PAVN might have attained far larger successes. It was perfectly clear that the PAVN had come a long way and had learned much, but not enough, while the ARVN had made no basic progress. Its perform-ance in Laos in 1971 and its much more dismal conduct in 1972 were symp-toms of a terminal malady.

Official U.S. analysts then and later felt that the war would probably have ended in spring 1972 had America not employed huge amounts of air power in South Vietnam. Even though Quang Tri City was recaptured, the PAVN retained most of the vast zones it had attacked, including most of Quang Tri Province. The immediate, lavish use of U.S. air and naval power inflicted heavy losses on the PAVN and brought the ARVN the critical respite it needed. While air power in the south had a military justification insofar as it saved the RVN from its own failures, the PAVN's offensive raised in the White House the basic issue of credibility in regard both to its détente diplomacy and to its global power. It had expected the Soviets in particular to help it end the war, and now, at least in the opinion of the President and his aide, America appeared supine and helpless.

Instinctively, Nixon favored the massive use of air power. The number of U.S. Navy ships stationed offshore by the end of May reached a wartime peak, and that of B-52s more than doubled in two months time. Laird resisted this trend, fearful that the President would reintroduce the Army in South Vietnam at the very time Vietnamization had proven a failure, and in fact he quietly managed to slip 27,000 troops out of the country during April. The U.S. military command in Saigon wanted more air power, but it thought the planes should be restricted to helping the ARVN in the south, where aviation was the slim difference between defeat and survival. To Nixon and his assistant, however, saving the RVN was less important than avoiding a humiliating defeat through Soviet arms just when he was to go to Moscow, and now the "madman" dimension of his strategy—of Nixon the angry, irrational head of the world's leading power—came to the fore. The confirmation of the United States' capacity to act required draconian measures, and the President chose to resume bombing the DRV and to mine its harbors, thereby challenging both Russian and Chinese shipping. The administration also hardened its position in negotiations with the Soviets on mainly economic issues.

But the administration split on the issue of escalating the war. Laird was against it, as was Abrams in Saigon, but the JCS was enthusiastic even though it would not refute the CIA argument that escalation would not materially affect the war in the south. This battle was increasingly irrelevant insofar as diplomacy was concerned, and the President publicly stated on April 30 that the international credibility of American power against a nation "massively assisted" by "two Communist superpowers" was now the prime issue. More ominous, he not only raised the possibility of increasing the air war but also described the dams and dikes in the DRV as "a strategic target, and indirectly a military target," though one that would produce "an enormous number of civilian casualties" if destroyed.[19] When on May 8 the President ordered the mining and blockading of the DRV and a sharp intensification of the air war against old and new targets, the DRV began to evacuate Hanoi and reinforce the dikes. It almost immediately managed to circumvent the single most important effect of the blockade by building a pipeline from the Chinese border to Hanoi and by developing its own effective means of neutralizing mines. B-52 sorties against the DRV over the next months reached a wartime peak, and planes bombed the dikes extensively, failing to do serious damage only because of repairs and unusually low rainfall. Militarily, this meant that as attacks on the DRV increased and served a primarily symbolic rather than military role and the function of putting pressure on the Russians and Chinese, U.S. air power in the south was substantially less than it might have been. With the RVN so badly defeated, the White House believed that much more now depended on its diplomatic rather than its military initiatives. The attack against the DRV was symptomatic of the failure of Vietnamization.

As the White House shifted its focus away from events determining the fate of the RVN, American generals and experts analyzed the 1972 offensive's implications to Vietnamization and the military balance in the south. Deepening pessimism was the outcome. Most disappointed of all was General Abrams, whose five-year tour of duty ended on June 30. Nixon had often cited his opinions as proof that Vietnamization was working, but privately Abrams had been less sure, especially after Lam Son 719. The magnitude of the ARVN's failures during 1972 surprised him, and most of his senior officers shared his keen frustration. The morale and combativity of the ARVN's officers especially shocked them, since these were the men with whom they were closest; after surveying the ARVN's huge losses and lapses, many Americans in South Vietnam thought that at least three more years would be required to turn the ARVN into an effective defensive force. Some of the best informed, however, concluded that the ARVN had deteriorated in the use of heavier weapons and that, implicitly, there was slight hope for it.

All of the ARVN's defects, from desertions to officer incompetence and generally dismal morale, added up to a far weaker RVN when compared with the Revolution militarily. The attempt to fathom the extent of the PAVN's difficulties publicly no longer appealed to a once assured American mission in Saigon. For the Revolution now held a vast new expanse of territory and was strong in the knowledge that both in 1971 and in 1972 a badly mauled ARVN had been saved from total defeat only by U.S. intervention. The MACV's pessimistic reports to Washington shaped its views of the new military balance and of the impact of Vietnamization. Thieu's basic military premise, from the time he took power, had been to hold as much territory and population as possible, and now that his static defense was exposed as mortally vulnerable, he refused to change it or adapt to his own or the Revolution's capabilities. As he failed in his effort to recapture as much lost territory as possible after the PAVN offensive halted, his weaknesses shattered any lingering illusions in the White House.[20]

POLITICAL AND DIPLOMATIC CONSEQUENCES OF THE OFFENSIVE

Not only was the RVN's military position weaker, but its rural power and political life were seriously undermined. A major objective of the Revolution's offensive had been to strengthen its political and guerilla structure wherever possible, especially in the Mekong Delta. The Party had by no means abandoned its strategy of mixed main and local forces, much less its belief that military gains must produce political results. During 1969–71 it had almost foresaken large-unit operations, which, increased tremendously in 1972, but small-unit activities also attained a wartime peak in 1972. While most public in 1972 attention was drawn to the combat in Military Regions I, II, and III, which is where big units operated, the largest number of actions occurred in MR IV, the Delta, where they increased dramatically as the ARVN dispersed many of its men there to the northern provinces for the remainder of the war. The Revolution's small units began to fill the vacuum in many populous areas, and in provinces the United States had previously considered secure, many RF/PF units and even the ARVN responded to the new military balance and reached local accommodations with the NLF. One measure of this change was the drastic decline in desertions from the Revolution's military and political structure during 1972, to less than a quarter of those in 1969, and the huge surge in RVNAF desertions during the second half of 1972, to the highest levels of the war. During 1972 sixteen times as many RVN troops as Revolutionaries abandoned their posts. The destruction of many villages by RVN planes and artillery also accelerated greatly the willingness of many peasants to support the Revolution. The NLF's targeting of RVN officials for kidnapping reached a wartime peak, nearly tripling over 1971. The Revolution was now in possession of vast new territory in MR I, II, and III, allowing it to expand its manpower and logistics. As the NLF's forces in the Delta grew dramatically, the pacification program disintegrated with a speed difficult to estimate, but two influential U.S. experts reported "that the overall enemy position in the delta had been greatly strengthened in terms of freedom of movement, access to population and food supplies, and a weakening of the faith of the rural population in the ability of the government to protect them."[21]

Thieu's political standing was further undermined by his policy of arrests and repression, which intensified at the start of the offensive, 3,300 persons being picked up in the Delta in a six-week period, and 600 in Danang alone. With a combination of U.S. embassy lobbying, chicanery, and bribes, Thieu persuaded the National Assembly to allow him to declare martial law till the end of 1972, muzzling the press even further and ending all remaining pretenses as to who held power. The immediate effect was to galvanize the urban non-Communist opposition to Thieu, including, for the first time, Catholic elements that had once been Thieu's staunchest supporters. The embassy in Saigon argued openly that there was no alternative to Thieu, but it was clear that the offensive had further tipped against him the balance in both the urban and the rural areas. Apart from the existence of a large, and now growing, number of *attentistes* everywhere was the overriding reality that Thieu had failed to create a military system able to succeed on the field of battle. This fact alone meant that unless there was a peace settlement the war might be protracted and that the RVN's defeat was inevitable. Far greater clarity among various urban constituencies regarding the options began to transform the nature of the RVN's urban politics throughout 1972. Peace and reconciliation immediately emerged as issues of critical importance.

The Revolution during the spring and summer of 1972 attained a monumental triumph militarily and politically in Vietnam, and Washington knew it all too well. It had successfully proven that the United States could not rely on Vietnamization of the war to save its position. Both publicly and privately it was wholly satisfied that it had decisively shifted the balance of power to its side and that nothing could reverse it. Given this context and their alternatives, the Party's leaders believed they could for the first time depend on diplomacy as the primary, though surely not the exclusive, means of bringing the war to an end.

Curiously, despite the RVN's obvious failure, Nixon's confidence in negotiations also grew. Although everything was going badly, he was more and more convinced that his strategy of isolating the DRV from its allies was beginning to succeed admirably. Insofar as both China and the USSR were willing to meet with the United States throughout this period of escalation against the DRV, the American leaders were justifiably optimistic, and there is no doubt the DRV became increasingly irritated and anxious as Nixon went to Moscow in May and Kissinger to Peking immediately thereafter. Kissinger, however, has described the Chinese throughout this period as being quite unequivocal. A Chinese note in April "expressed solidarity with North Vietnam," and when Kissinger was in Peking during late June, Chou "repeated the standard line of China's historical debt to Hanoi," in which Kissinger found a hopeful "undercurrent" and "implication" regarding China's concern over the DRV's future role in the region.[22]

The need to "isolate Hanoi" or "separate Hanoi from its allies" increasingly dominated Nixon's and Kissinger's thought as events went from bad to worse in Vietnam. In his later assessment of this period, Kissinger was justifiably convinced "the Kremlin therefore [had] cut loose from its obstreperous small ally." "By proceeding with the summit," he also stated, "Moscow helped neutralize our domestic opposition, which gave us freedom of action to break the back of North Vietnam's offensive. Our strategy of détente—posing risks and dangling benefits before the Soviets—made possible an unfettered attempt to bring our involvement in the Vietnam war to an honorable close."[23] The Russians had not canceled the summit while B-52s were raining bombs on the whole of Vietnam, destroying Soviet lives and boats in the process. Unquestionably, Nixon's political gains from the meeting were enormous, and it was clear that Soviet-U.S. relations had a momentum that went far beyond Moscow's commitment to the DRV. Soviet interests in other questions were obviously very great, and since, as Undersecretary of State U. Alexis Johnson put it several months later, "the decline in tensions between ourselves and the major Communist powers also tends to threaten the stability of the Western alliance," the Soviets, too, had something to gain in Europe regardless of the implications for the DRV.[24] As Kissinger remarked, "The summits helped us complete the isolation of Hanoi," and they lowered domestic opposition at home by making Nixon look like a peacemaker.[25] To the extent, at least, that its allies guaranteed Nixon's reelection, the Revolution was worse off. But summits did absolutely nothing about the physical balance of power and the failure of Vietnamization, or about the other contradictions in America's role in the world, and unless the United States could reverse this reality, it would sooner or later lose the war.

Both the Chinese and the Russians sought to exploit the White House's diplomacy to advance their own interests. But there is no evidence that either did anything important to undermine the Revolution's physical capacity to consolidate its gains by significantly reducing aid, which is what Washington needed most. However debatable the data, official U.S. sources indicated that Chinese military aid to the DRV in 1972 was double that in 1971. Soviet arms aid more than doubled. Only their economic aid fell off somewhat. Both nations overcame their past wrangling by speeding supplies by rail, including heavy Soviet weapons, to circumvent the blockade. The fact is that their rivalry was their primary obsession, and it was predictable as well as understandable that they would seek to line up the United States against their enemy if offered the opportunity, or at least to neutralize it. Each used the Vietnam War as a lever for its dominant concern.

For Nixon, however, the primary goal of détente was to win the war, or at least, after May, to prevent a defeat. Given the basically different and obvious priorities motivating the United States, China, and the Soviet Union, the White House found détente and triangulation an exceedingly difficult and slow, if not impossible, means of succeeding in Vietnam. Most of Washington's foreign policy experts, who had believed this from the inception, thought the effort was failing. But in matters of policy the White House standing alone was quite sufficient to decide an issue. Apart from the more fundamental fact that diplomacy could not reverse realities in South Vietnam, and that the DRV was also able to exploit Sino-Soviet differences, was the remarkable eagerness of Nixon and Kissinger alike to grasp any hint or implied gesture as proof of successes. The White House increasingly succumbed to this self-intoxicating, hypnotic belief in the efficacy and transcendent importance of détente and triangulation, minimizing the obvious failure of Vietnamization and air power to constrain the Revolution's strategy or undo its gains.

In theory Nixon's vision might be justified, at least to the extent that the publicity which accompanied it was an enormous political help to him. However, winning an election required one skill and winning the war another. The opening to China was still premature insofar as Vietnam was concerned and too complex regarding the USSR because of the vast range of differences and conflicts between the two nations. The assumptions which made Nixon a triumphant politician did not make him a successful global diplomat. Public relations coups cannot define the outcome of a war. Kissinger's long-standing academic penchant for the international game the President wished to play was sufficient to assure that the end of America's thirty-year involvement in Vietnam would come amid illusions and hopes more convoluted, but no less erroneous and futile, than those which had drawn it deeper into the conflict. In the end, while the readiness of the Soviet and the Chinese to use the DRV's struggle to serve their own interests hurt the Revolution, the damage scarcely proved crucial to it. Ironically, it was its allies' sincere encouragement of White House ambitions that inadvertently allowed the Revolution to consolidate its military triumphs with diplomatic success. Barely half a year after the 1972 offensive, Nixon accepted the Paris Agreement convinced the Soviets and Chinese both would and could help enforce it by decisively cutting military aid to the DRV. Without this mirage the United States would very likely not have signed the accords when it did.

Chapter 34

The Diplomatic Process: Illusions and Realities

Appearance and desire, illusion and reality, all merged during the remainder of 1972 to produce an intense, convoluted period during which diplomacy took center stage in the war for the first time. As the White House operated on many levels in its global geopolitical gamble, its spectacular efforts caused the Communist Party to be both anxious and angry, for the administration was successfully buying the time and freedom to attack the DRV, escape domestic political pressures to settle the war, and follow its intricate diplomatic strategy. The only solace to the Revolution was its confidence that objective material and political forces in South Vietnam would decide the eventual outcome of the war, and diplomacy's necessary function was to ratify the new balance of power its successful offensive had created. By May it was ready to let diplomacy play a central role in its efforts.

Until May 1972 the United States had accused the DRV of refusing to separate political from military issues in the war, but in fact neither side could afford to divorce them. Even the avoidance of political discussion carried with it explicit political results; by seeking ostensibly to divide political from military issues, the White House was merely attempting to keep Thieu in power while it took care of its own military, domestic, and global political needs. War without politics is an impossibility, but it was a position the United States maintained in all of the futile negotiations during 1970–71, fully expecting that the war would ultimately end by a combination of great-power diplomacy, Vietnamization, and escalation. The Revolution would be compelled to accept an ostensible "military" solution which would allow an American-backed political structure to continue in South Vietnam. The cease-fire, troop locations, or governmental questions endlessly debated at secret and private talks were really quite secondary until May 1972, for both sides felt that power alone would define such technicalities. As a keen

student of games diplomats have played, Kissinger always presented ambiguous and exploratory positions to the DRV during his talks with them, and
Nixon heartily endorsed these efforts. Such successive bargaining ploys,
which began in 1965, were directed far more at the American public and
world opinion than at the DRV. As Johnson's September 29, 1967, formula
or his March 31, 1968, "bombing halt" revealed, the United States retracted
its proposals whenever this suited its purposes. Such reversals naturally
made the DRV suspicious of American intentions, but in May 1972 the Party
knew that a new round of diplomacy could not hurt, and might possibly
strengthen, its position.

THE BEGINNING OF SERIOUS NEGOTIATIONS

Nixon's May 8, 1972, speech announcing the mining and bombing of the
Hanoi-Haiphong region also set a train of diplomatic events in motion,
focusing on a cease-fire in all of Indochina (which meant ending three wars
rather than one), as a precondition of complete U.S. troop withdrawal
within four months after an agreement. The DRV quickly responded with
a plan for a three-part government in South Vietnam, including the RVN
without Thieu, the PRG, and a neutralist "Third Force" holding the balance. Just as Nixon sought merely to mollify outraged world opinion over
his escalation, the DRV attempted to demoralize the RVN and encourage
the numerous Third Force groups emerging at that time. The White House
renewed its recurrent attempts to involve the USSR in the negotiations,
simply as a way to isolate the DRV from its allies. This combination of
public posturing and diplomacy intensified throughout the summer.

Kissinger met Le Duc Tho frequently after mid-July, but henceforth the
political context of the talks was far more important for both sides, especially for the United States, than the substance. That negotiations were
taking place was public knowledge, and this meant votes for Nixon in his
reelection effort. By summer the increasingly self-confident President was
strongly inclined to put the negotiations off until after his reelection. From
this point on, neither the timing nor the content of the talks ever took place
with the American election as a leading factor in the administration's negotiating position. Much more important now was its broader political vision
of its global diplomacy and the highly complex context in which it attempted
to reach a final settlement of the war.

The exploitation of the Chinese and Soviet leverage on the DRV with
détente and triangulation had, by the summer of 1972, completely obsessed
the President and Kissinger. This profound illusion regarding the power of

Moscow or Peking decisively to help the administration attain its war aims, notwithstanding only circumstantial evidence to sustain it, was as vital a source of American conduct leading to the end of the war as any. The fact that both sides were willing to talk to the United States even during the escalation of bombing and to show something less than total solidarity with the DRV was a powerful encouragement. During the spring and summer of 1972, both the USSR and China began to show a greater readiness to serve as intermediaries.

In July the French informed Washington that Mao Tse-tung had advised the PRG to alter its stance on the issue of Thieu's removal, an initiative which bolstered the administration's confidence in its ability to isolate the Revolution. Ironically, it was the DRV itself that seemingly confirmed to the White House the success of its efforts, for as it increasingly criticised its allies, the United States was greatly encouraged. On August 17 *Nhan Dan* published a prominent attack on both the Russians and the Chinese, condemning their cooperation with détente as giving America a free hand to attack national liberation movements and "throwing a life-buoy to a drowning pirate: this is a harmful compromise advantageous to the enemy, and disadvantageous to the revolution."[1]

In dealing with the USSR and China, the White House was so eager to justify its basic détente strategy that it minimized, even ignored, evidence that did not support its plans for the two nations. Although during October the White House asked the Russians for an explicit assurance that they would cut arms to the DRV after a peace settlement and received only evasive replies, when Kissinger saw Thieu at the same time he told him sincerely that China and the USSR had already given promises to reduce the shipment of arms to the DRV. The administration had convinced itself that it was triumphantly exploiting Sino-Soviet differences to gain an alleged tacit or secret accord from both of them to reduce arms shipments. But while the DRV had many complaints regarding its supporters, the encouragement that Peking and Moscow gave to Washington was still not sufficient to diminish Hanoi's basic power; it only reinforced the American illusion of success.

During the summer of 1972, meanwhile, relations between Washington and Thieu became increasingly tense as the Revolution in the south became stronger and as Thieu could less afford to tolerate its challenges. The administration had given Thieu ample reason to think it believed that its goals required him to remain in power and that a common set of interests existed. Nearly five years of loyal cooperation had elapsed since the United States began to accept anything Thieu did, ranging from gross corruption to military incompetence, and during May it helped Thieu impose martial law. Before the President went to Peking, he assured Thieu that there would be no settlement of the war over his head, or at his expense, on matters of concern to the RVN. At the same time, regardless of negotiations, the United States was committed to restoring the RVN's military strength after its stunning defeat, providing him the resources to sabotage any treaty. During the summer of 1972 Thieu declared his "four no's" policy, from which he was never to deviate save under duress: "no negotiating with the enemy"; "no Communist activity in South Vietnam"; "no coalition government"; "no surrender of territory to the enemy."[2]

There was never the slightest doubt what Thieu would do if a peace accord was signed, and it was this fact that had caused the Revolution to demand he be excluded from any future political structure evolving out of a settlement. Publicly and privately, U.S. officials working with Thieu made it clear that they would support his remaining in office, regardless of a treaty or urban opposition. In direct talks with Alexander Haig and Kissinger during the summer, Thieu reaffirmed his opposition to any cease-fire, and on August 3 he publicly declared that the way to achieve peace was to sustain the air war against the DRV—a theme he repeated to Kissinger several weeks later.

Later Kissinger recognized that Thieu was "not ready for a negotiated peace" but wanted "an unconditional surrender."[3] And while he would ascribe this to a species of madness, and justifiably believed Thieu would not present an insurmountable obstacle, the dictator was only taking all he could get. On August 31, after Kissinger discussed the matter with Nixon, the President wrote Thieu a letter guaranteed to reinforce his obstinancy. Claiming that the United States had made a number of "substantive" adjustments as a result of Thieu's views, he also affirmed that the United States could not "purchase peace or honor or redeem its sacrifices at the price of deserting a brave ally." Nixon's effusive praise for Thieu's "sterling leadership" was exactly the endorsement the dictator desired for use against his growing opposition at home.[4] In the end, Thieu had reason to believe that the Americans were irreversibly dependent upon him. His opposition to all that was to occur over the subsequent months was the predictable logic of the United States' relationship to him from the very first.

Full-scale air war against the DRV resumed in April 1972 and by the summer reached massive proportions, including attacks on the most vulnerable dikes in the eastern Red River Delta. With the exception of Hanoi and Haiphong, numerous cities were being systematically destroyed. In the first twenty-five days of October, the United States dropped 31,600 tons on the DRV, making this the most intense period of daily bombing of the north until then. The President was attempting to make the DRV negotiate under extreme duress, implementing his scheme to portray himself as a "madman." By the time the attention of the United States and the world was

turned to the bombing, during Christmas, the DRV had already been subjected to Nixon's wrath for well over a half year. Just as the administration
would not negotiate under the pressure of an election it felt it was certain
to win, so the DRV would not parley out of fear of terrible new destruction
—because the threats that the United States could make they had long since
implemented. The bombing of the north simply bore no relationship to the
military and social equation in the south, and this made the DRV ready to
negotiate from a position of strength. In essence, none of the crucial premises on which the Nixon administration had based the war, from détente
diplomacy to Vietnamization and mad escalation, were successfully holding
up when serious bargaining finally began in September 1972.

THE PARIS TALKS: MAKING AND
BREAKING AN AGREEMENT

Until September 1972 both the Americans and the Communists had directed
their proposals to end the war not to each other but to opinion either at
home, as in the case of Washington, or in South Vietnam. The Revolution's
May plan to form a three-part coalition that included the RVN without
Thieu was its final exploitation of diplomacy for propaganda. By summer
it was clear that it had tilted the military balance sufficiently in its own favor
but that the costs of staying on the battlefield against U.S. air power would
prove very high. The 1972 offensive had brought out all the tensions and
failures of the RVN political and military order, and Thieu's imposition of
martial law reflected the increasingly formidable resistance he confronted
from rising urban middle-class opponents. From its inception the war had
been primarily an international intervention. Without the presence of foreign troops, the Revolution was certain of eventual victory under almost any
reasonably plausible peace treaty.

The White House insisted on separating military and political questions
in negotiations and on resolving the military specifics first. This was its way
of leaving the political status quo. Since the United States during the summer was ready to present nothing more than old plans in new forms, only
fresh DRV proposals could break the impasse. "For once his charge that I
was offering 'nothing new' was accurate," Kissinger admitted of Le Duc
Tho's August 1 rebuke.[5] The DRV now submitted major innovations Kissinger thought would lead to a separation of military from political issues,
and it was at this time that Nixon, confident of reelection, indicated he
would just as soon suspend negotiations until after the elections. Seymour
Hersh has convincingly argued that Kissinger from this point on unilaterally
sought to achieve a treaty in order to shore up his declining relations with

the President. Success in ending the war would allow him not only to keep his job but also to become secretary of state in the next administration. Kissinger was aware, too, that the longer the United States took to reach an accord, the less able it would be to affect future military events should a peace not be attained. Despite the President's uneasiness, the Pentagon under Laird was relentlessly retiring American forces and budgeting Vietnam out of its commitments. On August 29 Nixon announced a further troop withdrawal, leaving only 27,000 men, and Kissinger feared the United States would withdraw its forces unilaterally. He now challenged not just the President and Thieu but also those who were silently bent on getting the United States out of a losing situation.

Despite mounting opposition from Thieu, when the PRG on September 11 released a public position accepting the RVN as a fact and implying a separation of military from political issues, Kissinger knew that Thieu would stay and that major progress would follow in the talks. "This same prospect filled Thieu with renewed dismay," Kissinger has recollected, but he was not deterred.⁶ And though Thieu's opposition increasingly irritated Nixon, over the subsequent weeks he was himself unwilling to conclude an accord before the election if it did not contain precisely what he wanted. Kissinger made a final offer to the DRV on October 8, and he informed it via the Russians that if it rejected the proposal, he would suspend the talks until after the elections. The same day, however, Le Duc Tho gave Kissinger the text of the first complete draft treaty presented by any side since the start of the war, one embodying all the points in the PRG statement. The treaty clearly separated military and political problems, so that rapid progress could be made on military questions while the PRG and the RVN independently attempted to resolve the infinitely more complex political issues. Le Duc Tho felt that the DRV had accepted the essence of the earlier American proposals, and the exultant Kissinger immediately informed Nixon that he agreed. The President concurred—"they were accepting a settlement on our terms."⁷ One important but not insoluble problem, as it was to emerge with clarity over the next harried weeks, was Thieu's determination to block any agreement. Far more critical was Nixon's readiness to postpone the talks, which had been his basic position for some time, despite his assistant's intense desire to see them concluded.

Kissinger knew that Nixon was not eager to end the war that month, but he also felt the dangers of postponement. "One could imagine the public outcry if we rejected Hanoi's acceptance of our own proposals," he later wrote, and in the end "accusations of cynicism and bad faith in welshing on our own proposals" would make it impossible to get better, or perhaps even equivalent, terms later.⁸ In this framework, predestined to frustration, Kissinger and the DRV negotiated in Paris.

The White House sought and received a number of modifications in the DRV draft. The only complicated issue was a cease-fire for all of Indochina as opposed to simply for Vietnam. The remainder consisted of minor technicalities, and these were resolved with breathtaking speed. Principally, there would be no coalition government—but only a nonbinding framework for future discussions of all political issues, albeit one which acknowledged the existence and legality of the PRG. Nothing was said about the withdrawal of DRV forces from South Vietnam, a point Washington had abandoned in October 1970, and the DRV agreed to allow America to replace arms to the RVN on a one-for-one basis. Essentially, the United States would leave South Vietnam and dismantle its bases, the Communists would return its captured soldiers, and it would leave its massively aided surrogate behind to fend for itself. The main substance of the accord was quickly formulated and agreed on in Paris during these few days. The real problem was not its terms but the President, Thieu, and the maze of intrigue and resentment that was building in Washington and Saigon.

Thieu, of course, was altogether predictable, and he immediately threw down the gauntlet and forced Kissinger to go to Saigon on October 19 before continuing to Hanoi for the initialing of the agreement before the scheduled signing on October 31. Kissinger found Thieu intransigent but also eager to milk the United States for military aid while he had it on the defensive, though he made it clear that he opposed both the details and the principle of the treaty. When Kissinger arrived in Saigon, he carried with him a detailed letter from Nixon which explained that Thieu's basic political objective had been attained and "that your Government, its armed forces and its political institutions, will remain intact after the ceasefire has been observed." It would continue to get military and economic aid. "We have no reasonable alternative but to accept this agreement," Nixon made plain. And he not only thought "it was the best we will be able to get" but also assured Thieu that Kissinger had his "total backing."[9] His assistant had known that the President was still not eager for an accord that month, but he thought he could persuade Nixon. Little did he count on Nixon's instability or on the influence of his other White House political advisers, who now argued that the agreement should be delayed—since he would win the election in any case. The President's excuse was his desire to avoid a confrontation with Thieu, but far more important were a variety of political, bureaucratic, and personal reasons which all amounted to the same decision: refusal to sign a treaty based largely on the U.S. position. Kissinger did not believe that this would occur, despite the growth of evidence to the contrary after October 19. As Kissinger kept postponing the date of the meeting in Hanoi, eventually canceling it as well as the scheduled initialing, Thieu on October 24 issued a public denunciation of the talks.

Betrayed, the DRV two days later released the history and text of the negotiations.

The revelation of the White House's astonishing deception of the DRV did not hurt Nixon, who was reelected with the largest majority in American history. Thieu, meanwhile, had managed to extract a huge aid commitment during October as an additional consolation, a reward that only encouraged future obduracy. During the summer the Pentagon had begun to replace key U.S. military technicians with civilians, many of them former military personnel. Project Enhance, as it was called, was at the end of October followed by Enhance Plus, involving 260,000 tons of war goods over a two-month period. At a cost of nearly $2 billion, Enhance left the RVN with the world's fourth-largest air force and a huge quantity of tanks, artillery, and helicopters. It now had overwhelming firepower superiority over the DRV, and in early November, in the words of a U.S. official military history of the event, "the United States violated the spirit of the provisions of the Paris agreement" and transferred ownership of its bases to the RVN so that when the time came to dismantle them, as required, it could claim it had none.[10] Everything was done to prepare Thieu for a protracted war during the post-treaty period.

In a war in which the United States had from the inception committed countless dark deeds, the events of the next two months rank among the most evil. Nixon was the main architect during this sordid period, and Kissinger was, as he had essentially been since the start, his loyal and consummately ambitious sycophant, concerned with his own career above all else. At the end of October the President had thoroughly embarrassed and intimidated him so that he would not prove independent again. Nixon's actions revealed all of the perversity of character that ultimately led to his being forced out of office. Power had made the President drunk.

Thieu was the first to feel the bite of his tongue, even as the flow of arms and money to the RVN grew larger. But Thieu was not the basic problem, for his attitude toward the negotiations had always been clear, and he had made no secret about his "four no's" strategy to prevent the implementation of any agreement. It was sufficient for him to have arms and funds to thwart it, and these he was receiving. Thieu most certainly was not to dictate White House policy at this or any other time, because everyone knew he could not exist without American money. He only served as a convenient excuse for American procrastination. Nixon on October 29 told Thieu, "You should harbor no illusions that my policy with respect to the desirability of achieving an early peace will change after the election." On November 8 he made it plain that while the United States would try to obtain changes in "an agreement that we already consider to be excellent," it would adhere to it.[11] Increasingly irritated by an antitreaty rumor campaign that Thieu was orchestrating, Nixon warned him on October 29, that should "the dangerous course which your Government is now pursuing" continue, there would be "an inevitable cutoff by Congress" of funds. From that time until the final signing of the agreement, the President repeatedly minced no words about Congress's refusing to fund Thieu should he remain recalcitrant, and his numerous threats to Thieu of a total reduction of aid were brutally pointed. Indeed, he made explicit after late December, he would not be able to prevent Congress from stopping aid even if he tried. But to soften these blunt admonitions, even though it was really for the purpose of attaining his own objectives, on November 14 Nixon wrote Thieu, "You have my absolute assurance that if Hanoi fails to abide by the terms of this agreement it is my intention to take swift and severe retaliatory action."[12] Comparable pledges, which I detail later in this chapter, were given Thieu the following January as well. Should he resist the treaty, Nixon threatened him on November 23, "I will proceed at whatever the cost."[13] Warnings to Thieu regarding Congress were not idle words, for the White House at the end of November concluded after sounding out its friends there that Congress would indeed cut off aid if the settlement was not signed quickly after its return at the end of January. The President's real problem was that he was running out of time as a result of his own procrastination, for which Thieu was only tangentially responsible. Nixon had refused for a combination of frivolous and ulterior reasons to approve the signing of a document he endorsed strongly in principle, and now he had to resolve a major dilemma.[14]

THE CHRISTMAS BOMBING AND THE SIGNING OF THE PARIS AGREEMENT

The White House wanted the DRV to solve its predicament, and it managed to persuade the Vietnamese to resume talks on November 20. B-52s were at that time savagely bombing the DRV south of the twentieth parallel, so that the only new threat left was to bomb north of it. The Party's leaders had taken pains to reinforce Sino-Soviet support at a time when U.S. officials were openly claiming success in getting it diplomatically and materially isolated. The Party had a sufficiently clear idea of the overall situation to know its own strengths and weaknesses, and so when it returned to Paris and the duplicitous Americans confronted it with a long list of demands for changes, some of them of fundamental importance, it agreed to several minor alternations and hesitated, and after several weeks began to withdraw concessions it had made earlier—an obvious bargaining ploy. Its basic stand was that the October text should be signed intact. Over the same weeks it evacuated its two largest cities as Kissinger repeatedly threatened to attack them. Apart from the fact that a resolution of the proposed revisions would have required prolonged talks even if the DRV had been weaker, which it was not, was the utopianism of Nixon's effort to obtain at the negotiating table what had eluded the United States for ten years on the battlefield. There was simply no question in Hanoi of relying on the Americans, given their reneging on the October agreement, their vast arms shipments to Thieu, and their stepped-up bombing.

Kissinger's reputation and job were now on the line. Were he to accede to the October text, he believed, America's credibility to "police" the agreement with the threat of reentering the war with air power would be dissipated.[15] The President's assistant, after straining to make peace in October, now swung to the other extreme and favored increased military pressure. He also attempted to have the Chinese and Russians influence the DRV, strongly implying that attacks north of the twentieth parallel would follow if the DRV did not back off and accept the American demands. The Soviets, however, preferred only to transmit the DRV's proposals, evasively hinting they might be more helpful in due course. Le Duc Tho, rather than insisting the Americans go back to the October agreement, tried to keep them at the bargaining table with compromises, but with far fewer than Kissinger demanded. Kissinger, unwilling to make any concessions yet convinced, as was the President, that Congress would end the war if the White House could not, now recommended the bombing and mining of Hanoi and Haiphong. The President knew he had a serious problem in maintaining political control at home, and when he instructed Kissinger to break off talks in Paris on December 13 by making unacceptable demands in order to provoke Le Duc Tho, he was already becoming inaccessible to the outside world. Since early October he had suspended press conferences, and he increasingly restricted his daily contacts to Erlichman, Haldeman, and Kissinger, who were to help ease him into the greatest crisis of the U.S. presidency.

On December 16 Kissinger met the press and attempted to evade the specifics of the problems at Paris, confessing only after a loquacious effort, "It is an agreement that is substantially completed but . . . that alone is not the problem."[16] By that time the President favored a renewal of the bombing, even though he had preferred a softer negotiating policy than his assistant. But the White House was now clearly isolated both at home and abroad, and opposition mounted as details of its tougher negotiating demands made it appear that the President was going too far to woo Thieu. Nixon authorized attacks on Hanoi and Haiphong beginning December 18; he did not expect a great furor, if only because the escalation against the DRV over the preceding months had been virtually ignored. "We were already doing everything to North Vietnam we were capable of doing except massive B-52 bombing in the northern third . . . ," Kissinger had earlier calculated.[17]

The twelve days of sustained bombing against the Hanoi-Haiphong area was designed to intimidate and terrorize the DRV regarding the future but also somehow to put pressure on the Russians and Chinese to force the DRV into line. That B-52s were highly inaccurate, and that the bombing would have no durable or decisive military impact was widely conceded at the time even by the Air Force. Worse yet from the United States' viewpoint, the Hanoi-Haiphong area was among the best defended in the world. The DRV aviation was now in superb form. The Air Force by this time was overtaxed, after months of intense activity, and lacked sufficient tactical air cover and defensive equipment. Coordination of tactical and strategic aviation was also poor because of the rampant demoralization that imminent peace and over-work created. Discipline was a serious and growing problem. When the B-52s began their twelve days of terror, the DRV had spent over three weeks preparing for them, evacuating well over half a million people from Hanoi alone. As the planes began their missions, they exacted a fearsome toll on civilian targets but also paid an unprecedented price themselves. The administration's first response was to minimize losses both to the DRV civilian sector and to the Air Force, but neither contention was accurate. About two hundred B-52s were used in the raids, protective tactical aviation being far more absent than the B-52 pilots thought honorable, and the United States admitted that fifteen were shot down, whereas the DRV put the figure at thirty-four. At least six B-52s were incapable of flying again, and informally some Pentagon personnel conceded that the losses approached the DRV claims, not to mention tactical fighters, of which the DRV boasted downing forty-seven. More embarrassing for the United States, the Vietnamese captured forty-four pilots. "We've lost a lot of planes and I don't think we realized the cost would be so high," one officer admitted.[18] Even the losses it acknowledged meant that the loss rate of B-52s was over 10 percent every ten days, a figure higher than the flyers were willing to tolerate and which further shattered their morale. The administration claimed that Hanoi was on its knees, its SAM missiles exhausted, but it was more certain that the Air Force was unable to function much longer. Even its supply of bombs was low. The DRV, for good reason, treated the battle over Hanoi as a great triumph.

All that the Christmas bombing did was isolate the administration politically and put it on the defensive. Inexplicably, given indifference toward nearly comparable bombing in the earlier months, a large majority of the American press found it especially horrifying during Christmas: "terrorism on an unprecedented scale," in the *New York Times*'s opinion.[19] The reaction in normally pro-American nations was equally critical. Much more important, Congress joined the protest. Forty-five of seventy-three senators polled several days after the bombing began were opposed to it, and only nineteen in favor. Forty-five declared themselves ready to support legislation to end the war. The President had little option but to order a halt to the bombing north of the twentieth parallel, which he quietly did on December 30. At the beginning of January both the House and the Senate Democratic caucuses voted overwhelmingly to cut military funds for Vietnam, including the RVN, on the withdrawal of U.S. forces and the return of prisoners. Even its strategy of using the bombing to exert Sino-Soviet leverage on Hanoi failed, although Kissinger was later to argue that "If our tea-leaf reading" experts were correct, Moscow and Peking were indeed subjecting Hanoi to pressure.[20] More obvious was Brezhnev's public attack on "the longest and dirtiest" war in American history, one that was threatening the whole course of Soviet-American relations.[21] Reporters thought there were distinct signs of Russian and DRV discussions of military aid at that time. Brezhnev, it was hinted, would postpone a planned trip to the United States because of Vietnam. Not to be outdone, a mass rally in Peking against America, with Foreign Minister Nguyen Thi Binh of the PRG as speaker and both Chou En-lai and Mao's wife attending, received great prominence in China's press. Kissinger's tea leaves reinforced his and the President's growing delusions, but it is much more likely that the DRV's allies had rallied to its support.

The only point the White House had made was that it was fully capable of employing its air power to enforce a peace treaty. This had been the primary purpose of the bombing. Nixon wanted America's "own unilateral capability to prevent violations" as well as to maintain "credibility in policing the agreement."[22] Establishing it was worth the delay, the administration reasoned, and it felt that simply going back to the October terms would dissipate the image of its resolve. The only problem was that the world had become more complex than Nixon or Kissinger had imagined, and the newly elected President now appeared to all to be the very frightening and dangerous person he was. That image was never to disappear.

When negotiations reopened in Paris on January 2, the administration was in a relatively much weaker position. Congress was now entering the picture in a decisive fashion, and the White House was incapable for both political and technical reasons of resuming the attacks north of the twentieth parallel. Nixon also wanted a peace accord quickly, and he was quite willing to accept the October draft; only Kissinger preferred exacting some face-saving concessions to justify the torment the United States had imposed on the DRV over Christmas. Thieu was simply brushed aside. During the November and December negotiations, both parties had made and withdrawn many changes, none of which altered the essence of the October accord. Cosmetic modifications of wording were adopted quickly in Paris, but it was not terminology but rather intent that was to define the application of the agreement. The United States had a certain number of phrases it thought superior and claimed that it obtained them, but in the end they affected form rather than substance. It was unable to obtain the elimination of the PRG from those sections, for example, which implied recognition of its existence, but when the final text was completed Nixon stated publicly that the United States recognized the RVN as "the sole legitimate government of South Viet-Nam," revealing simply that it would apply those parts of the accords which it supported and ignore the rest.[23] There was no concealing the fact the administration now wanted to settle on the October terms. "Were the changes significant enough to justify the anguish and bitterness of those last months of the war?" Kissinger later asked. "Probably not for us; almost surely for Saigon. . . . Obviously, we thought the agreement of October adequate. . . ."[24] But Saigon had not received what it had wanted, which was no treaty at all, and no one in Washington thought it would abandon its "four no's" policy, especially since it now had a huge influx of arms to attempt to impose it. Thieu had merely served as a rationale for the Christmas bombing, which was intended as a threat to the DRV in the future as well as a reassertion to the world of the President's willingness, indeed eagerness, to maintain America's image of readiness to use its military power.

The essence of the Paris Agreement was that it separated military and political questions, the former being quite specific and the latter being subject to future negotiations regarding implementation. The United States sought a way to withdraw its last troops and to obtain the return of its prisoners without conceding that its two-decade effort had ended in military failure. The Revolution wanted the Americans out, and save for a quasi-military group of "civilian advisers" and military personnel in the military attaché's office, this it obtained. The Revolution sought to constrict military aid levels to the RVN to one-for-one replacements and to eliminate U.S. bases, thereby further shifting the balance of military power, and this it obtained only on paper. The entire document depended on the real intentions and objectives of each side and the complex processes of war and power they reflected, but its key points nonetheless created a focus for subsequent debates and events.

A cease-fire was to go into effect on January 27 with the formal signing. Within sixty days the United States was to withdraw its arms and military personnel and dismantle its bases, and the two sides would exchange captured soldiers simultaneously. "The United States will not continue its military involvement or intervene in the internal affairs of South Vietnam." The temporary four-party Joint Military Commission was established to prevent a resumption of the war in the south between the mixed zones of control throughout the country, but its need for unanimity doomed it to impotence. A separate protocol creating the International Commission of

Control and Supervision, which was to comprise Canada, Hungary, Poland, and Indonesia, added to the complexity. While it was to supervise the cease-fire, it was also bound by the rule of unanimity. It was never to serve a serious function.

Politically, the agreement provided for the National Council of National Reconciliation and Concord composed of the PRG, RVN, and a Third Force, but it, too, required unanimity in striving for "self-determination," free and democratic elections under international supervision, and much else that sounded commendable but bore no relation to what might happen. Still, the multiplicity of organizations to implement the treaty meant the RVN would have frequent contact with the PRG. Far more important, of course, was the PRG representatives' authorized presence throughout the country. The one issue between them that was crucial was the release of civilian prisoners, which the PRG and RVN were to "do their utmost" to resolve within ninety days after the cease-fire, but there was no mandatory timetable, and this topic was to remain a serious source of dispute. Article 21 of the agreement required the United States to "contribute to healing the wounds of war and to postwar reconstruction" of the DRV, an American bargaining ploy which was, astonishingly, taken much more seriously by the DRV than its past realism would have suggested was possible.[25]

All in all, in the agreement and the protocols signed at Paris, the United States made an unequivocal commitment to get out of South Vietnam. Despite the complicated story which follows, it did remove most of its remaining personnel; and, much more important, it was prevented from sending more in. As for the rest, events were to prove that revolutionary wars do not end with diplomacy.

EXPECTATIONS AND REALITY: THE REVOLUTION

The difficult task of anticipating the next stages in the war preoccupied the Party's leaders throughout the fall of 1972. Each delay in the signing of the agreements compelled them to reconsider their changing prospects. The ARVN had been soundly defeated during the spring, but by November it was better armed than ever, and its enfeebled morale and leadership might not completely negate its huge firepower. The Revolution's forces, by contrast, had exhausted much of their supplies. As General Tran Van Tra, head of the huge B2 region, occupying the entire southern half of South Vietnam, later recalled, after nine months of combat under American bombs "our cadres and men were fatigued, we had not had time to make up for our losses, all units were in disarray, there was a lack of manpower, and there were shortages of food and ammunition. . . . The troops were no longer capable of fighting" when the agreement was signed.[26] U.S. estimates of the size of the Revolutionary forces in the south ranged from 219,000 to 308,000, while the RVNAF nominally had nearly 1.1 million superbly equipped men. While these numbers differed little from estimates over the preceding five years, it was a fact that the victorious army was temporarily less able to continue combat than the defeated one.

Politically, the situation was moving quickly against Thieu, and the Party believed this trend would continue. Passivity had been a major problem for the Revolution in the cities until spring 1972, but Thieu's intensification of repression galvanized against him as never before a variety of disunited and amorphous but real constituencies from middle-class, student, and religious elements. Many of these people saw that the NLF would not be defeated militarily and might very well be triumphant. Apart from the opportunists there were a growing number, rural as well as urban, who realized that peace would never come without a more conciliatory regime in Saigon, which meant the removal of Thieu. Opposition to Thieu began to unify all of these diversely motivated elements. The growing but chronically disunited Third Force burgeoned after 1971 around the issues of peace and repression, and it was in certain ways more radical than the earlier Buddhist opposition which the Americans had deftly co-opted. The urban sector, where the NLF had been the weakest since 1968, was now extremely promising. The Party was convinced that some form of united front would emerge, perhaps based on the Paris Agreement's vague three-part formula, as a possibly long "national democratic" phase in its transition to total power.

The varied fortunes of the Paris talks had left the Party in the south in a perplexing situation. During October, at the latest, it issued directives to local NLF groups to prepare to implement the treaty, with stress on making their presence known to members of the International Commission of Control who were supposed to observe them. Troops were to avoid combat with the RVNAF if possible, and even to bury their heavy weapons, save that for three days prior to the cease-fire day the NLF would occupy crucial points and as many villages as possible and plant the NLF flag, then press for the implementation of the agreements. The struggle would then be mainly political, and include efforts to demoralize and disband RVNAF units. When the October 31 signing did not occur, the COSVN ordered units simply to observe any cease-fire that was signed and await instructions, and probably none was issued for over two months. Many local organizations, as in the past, began to respond to conditions as they thought best. During that time the Revolution's forces, like the RVNAF and the U.S. pilots, fought as little as possible and reached a number of live-and-let-live local accommodations. Many became confused, some demoralized.

Thieu, on the other hand, was quite open about his plans during this period. "They would try to cut our throats," his powerful cousin and closest adviser, Hoang Duc Nha, told an American reporter, "and we have a right to cut theirs."[27] Using the press and TV, the RVN reminded the entire population during October that prison, loss of property, and death were the penalties for being or aiding a Communist. There was never any doubt that even if Thieu signed a peace agreement, he would not implement it. As soon as the agreements were concluded in January, he ordered his province chiefs to arrest all political suspects, preferably for common crimes, and authorized police to "shoot troublemakers" on the spot.[28] A vast program of repression was outlined in Thieu's press, and, above all, the RVN prepared to prevent refugees from returning to Communist-held villages.

The Party's leaders were unable in this constantly changing context to reach a quick consensus on how best to respond to the new situation, and a variety of analyses and sharp differences colored their thinking. They agreed that the RVN was declining fast politically and weak economically. Politically, the NLF was growing stronger in the Mekong Delta and even in Saigon after the dismal days of 1969–71. For the first time, however, a significant sector of the leadership concluded that the mere departure of the Americans would leave a class of RVN officers and their allies who were both ready and able to fight harder than the Americans, for they had no place to go to and too much to lose. These military men and their resources appeared formidable, at least for the moment. A minority of the Party's leaders believed that the war might last up to a decade longer. While most thought timetables were irrelevant, many felt it would be protracted, an impression the experience with the Geneva Accords reinforced. They shared a consensus that a refurbishing of the Revolution's army in terms of both equipment and morale required a transitional period during which the Party would emphasize political activity and determine whether the Paris Agreement would be implemented and the Americans would cease bombing.

The COSVN's 02/73 resolution reflected this dominant opinion, stressing "political struggle" and the development of a mass movement, yet attempting also to walk a narrow path between passivity and adventurism. A secondary role for military activity was part of this equation, but only to support "political struggle as the base."[29] The party hailed the Paris Agreement as a great victory which had tipped the balance of forces in its favor and which would also gain it the time for a further development in its political and military power. Between the end of January and February 9, the Revolution sought to use small units both to plant its own flags in about four hundred villages and push back RVN efforts to grab territory, but it had largely failed. The attempt revealed it to be momentarily far weaker than it had been for a long time; it also showed that the Party really expected the political clauses of the agreement to be implemented and the flags to have some significance. The Party was clearly in doubt regarding its priorities and power as well as the capabilities and intentions of its two enemies and had yet to define its own objective position. Although it tilted strongly to a political course of action, it nonetheless carefully sought to retain alternatives should it fail. Notwithstanding this, it was probably more divided on its next steps than it had been in many years.

The Party's vacillation between pragmatic realism and wishful thinking was never so clear as on the question of Article 21 of the agreement regarding an American contribution to the DRV's reconstruction. The Nixon administration had begun to study the use of financial baits to the DRV no later than 1971 in the context of various approaches to attempt to buy the DRV's cooperation. By the time the Paris discussions became serious, knowledge of this strategy had been publicized widely. Astonishingly, Nixon took to it, thinking it "potentially the most significant part of the entire agreement," one that would give the United States "increasing leverage with Hanoi," allowing it to win with dollars what had eluded its arms.[30] Even more amazing, the DRV thought it could get the aid without far-reaching compromises, and some of its senior officials drew up economic plans on the assumption that American money would be available. The President played his game to the hilt, sending Prime Minister Pham Van Dong on February 1 a secret note vaguely hinting that $3.25 billion in grant aid over five years and an additional $1.0 to 1.5 billion in food and commodity aid might be "appropriate." The World Bank was also inserted into the glitter of promises. On February 10 Kissinger flew to Hanoi to determine whether he could reach a general agreement on all Indochina affairs, especially the termination of DRV troop movements to South Vietnam as well as their withdrawal from Laos and especially Cambodia. Acceptance, of course, would have been tantamount to surrender, in which case substantial sums would probably have been available. He was so irritated at the response that on his return he urged the stockpiling of bombs for a future resumption of the air war. Meanwhile, the DRV was left hoping that money might be forthcoming, and low-level U.S. officials were assigned to discuss meaningless technicalities with it in Paris over the following months. Within several weeks, after making it clear publicly that aid would be a "tangible incentive" only if the DRV stopped "committing aggression," the administration tired of the aid fantasy.[31] Strangely, unable to separate its desires from reality, the DRV made this the one point in the agreement that it persisted in demanding the United States fulfill even as late as 1977.

EXPECTATIONS AND REALITY:
THE UNITED STATES

Thieu had made it explicit from the inception that he would not tolerate the Communist Party's political claims, much less its activity. No one in Washington expected otherwise. Treating the Paris Agreement merely as a cease-fire, he asserted that it recognized the RVN as the sole government of South Vietnam, an allegation Nixon reinforced publicly at the end of January. His intensification of repression at the beginning of 1973 was expected in Washington. For months the administration had believed that immediately on signing the treaty both sides would embark on flag-planting campaigns and territorial expansion, at least for several weeks. Indeed, Kissinger thought it necessary. The United States was ready to apply every possible pressure on Thieu to sign the Paris accords, but once he did, they planned to give him the means with which to violate it, knowing full well he would do so. The White House never asked him to implement its political provisions—provisions it opposed as well. Thieu systematically blocked the work of the four-party Joint Military Commission from the beginning. Apart from bombing and almost destroying the PRG delegation to the commission during Tet 1973, he at times also refused to aid the American delegation. The commission accomplished nothing, and the administration made no attempt to alter Thieu's ways.

The White House's effort to maintain the RVNAF at peak condition encouraged Thieu's ultimately disastrous delusion that he had the ability to resolve the war by force of arms, although in fact most of his American military advisers knew it was futile. During spring 1972, as withdrawals of U.S. forces began to drain away the technicians vital to maintaining the RVNAF's most advanced equipment, the Pentagon made plans to replace them for an indefinite period with so-called civilian advisers it hired on a contract basis. While it preferred using non-U.S. citizens if possible, it was soon compelled to rely heavily on former American military personnel. The size of the problems they confronted was huge, and after the fall of 1972 it increased even more, as the RVNAF was deluged with enormous quantities of new and transferred equipment. At the basic level, U.S. military experts concluded in October 1972, a large portion of the ARVN could not shoot rifles accurately or maintain machine guns, and its ineptitude was reflected in their excessive use of ammunition. But maintaining and flying the approximately two thousand aircraft or eight hundred tanks the RVNAF possessed at the end of 1972 exceeded its capability entirely. Ignoring quality altogether, the air logistics command was understaffed by 50 percent, and maintenance was wholly inadequate. About one thousand pilots were needed. Every branch of the military had similar problems. The Pentagon, which possessed a very clear image of the true state of the RVNAF, was obliged to deal with this hopeless problem, yet at the highest levels it had no enthusiasm for the task.[32]

The United States had to abolish the MACV under the terms of the Paris Agreement, and in its place was installed the Defense Attaché Office (DAO) of 50 officers plus 1,200 American civilians, most of whom were retired middle- and higher-ranking officers. The DRV unsuccessfully attempted at Paris to prevent the creation of this shadow army. Now the DAO had to get on with its task with a minimum of publicity as it violated both the spirit and the letter of the agreement. Because of this, the precise numbers of additional Americans and others working for it were hotly disputed. At first the Pentagon reported about 10,000 as the target, but in March 1973 it admitted to the presence of 7,200 civilian employees, but about 1,000 AID personnel were involved in other projects. The PRG accused the United States of having 10,000 to 20,000 advisers, and if all official agencies and contracts are combined, 10,000 would be a quite low estimate. Later the Pentagon admitted that it had hired "over" 23,000 in January 1973 through contractors only, "over" 5,000 of whom were Americans.[33] Whatever the exact numbers, Washington's effort to keep the RVNAF operating was very large, violated the Paris Agreement, and enabled Thieu to use his military power.

That the United States and the RVN would together disregard the treaty was certain and calculated. While the White House was committed to this strategy, the Pentagon's civilians, and particularly Laird, worried that the United States was injecting itself back into a dangerous situation. His opinion was shared by many others who felt that the United States had helped the RVNAF as much as possible and that it was incapable of improving and could well get much worse. No one had a lower opinion of the ARVN than those who knew it best. Laird's position was that there was no limit to the money and commitments the RVN might demand and that it was time for the United States to get out of Vietnam. The RVN had received $5.3 billion in new equipment during the Vietnamization phase, and over $1 billion in U.S. facilities had just been transferred to them, along with at least $400 million in usable material. On January 8 Laird declared the RVN to be "fully capable" of defending itself, and this warranted "the complete termination of American involvement."[34] Knowing it was untrue, he made the claim that Thieu's air force was able to operate perfectly over its own territory. His successor, Elliot L. Richardson, was to argue the same position.

The Pentagon's anxiety, which reemerged periodically over the remaining years of the war, stemmed from its knowledge that the White House not only was helping Thieu with equipment which might draw the United States back into the war but had also confidentially pledged to re-intervene in an open-ended way certain to encourage Thieu's aggressive impulses. It was the White House's secret undertaking along with lavish arms that guaranteed that the Paris accords would mark only a short interval, at best, before the Revolution was compelled to abandon its mainly political strategy for a military one.

The question of the "credibility" of U.S. military power had been the single most important reason for the Christmas bombings. Ultimately, Washington was relying on this image and threat to see the Paris Agreement interpreted as it chose to define it, which was essentially as a military cease-fire preventing major military challenges to Thieu while he consolidated his power. Nixon had first written to him in mid-November that he would in some unspecified way punish the Communists severely should they violate the agreement, a pledge he reiterated on January 5. On the seventeenth the President informed Thieu that he would "publicly reaffirm" three "guarantees" immediately *after* the Paris signing by sending Vice-President Spiro Agnew to Saigon at the end of January to announce them. First, the United States would recognize the RVN "as the sole legitimate Government of South Vietnam." This meant the United States was reneging on the basic political premise of the entire settlement—and Thieu would be all the more certain to do no less. Second, "we do not recognize the right of foreign troops to remain on South Vietnamese soil," an even more dangerous rejection of the agreement's military keystone. And, last, "the U.S. will react vigorously to violations to the Agreement."[35]

Taken together, this promise indicated that the White House had abandoned the essentials of the Paris accords, save when it was to its convenience, and that with the crucial exception of the withdrawal of the remaining U.S. troops, the agreement was a stillborn. To entice Thieu even more, Nixon agreed to deliver a unilateral, secret, detailed note to Saigon embodying these interpretations of the treaty, a note which Thieu had helped to phrase and had read in draft but was not to receive formally until the day the agreement was signed. Meanwhile, the President indicated he, too, would affirm these three main assurances in a January 23 broadcast to mark the initialing of the agreement, though in fact he was explicit only on the first. Agnew's speech in Saigon a week later, which went largely unnoticed, was explicit on the first two points, yet remained vague on the resumption of the air war. Moreover, the threat to renew the air war was not an idle menace designed merely to cajole Thieu into signing the agreements. Far more consequential, it was to prevent the United States from losing both the war in Vietnam and its international "credibility" to fight limited wars. Meanwhile, Kissinger pointed out at a press conference the following week, the

United States kept its air and naval power stationed nearby for "what might happen," and its deployment would "be related to the degree of the danger."[36]

The President seriously intended to resume B-52 bombings against the DRV, and against Hanoi especially, should the Communists do anything he thought warranted it. There is no evidence whatsoever for, and a great deal against, the notion that the White House was merely interested in a "decent interval" after the Paris Agreement during which the United States could respectably extricate itself from Thieu's cause and a war it knew it had lost. Kissinger bluntly warned his hosts while in Hanoi of "renewed confrontation" in case they did not busy themselves rebuilding the DRV with American aid and, in effect, abandoned their comrades in the south to their fates.[37] Both he and the President were extremely pessimistic about success on this level, however, and the only inhibition on the Revolution they thought remained, other than bombing, was their détente strategy. Meanwhile, the United States prepared to implement the threat the President again made publicly on the "consequences" of the DRV's sending more troops south. On March 26, in response to Nixon's decision, the Pentagon returned to Congress for a $225 million supplemental appropriation to prepare about 120,000 tons of bombs earmarked for Vietnam specifically "to keep the area stabilized."[38] Defense Secretary Richardson, as Thieu was about to depart to California to meet Nixon on April 1, publicly spoke about the possible resumption of American bombing.

Thieu was delighted with his visit, not only because it proved once again to his detractors at home that he had full American backing and could return with pledges of aid but also because the President made detailed secret verbal commitments to implement his earlier, vaguer written and spoken promises to send air power back into the war should the Communists embark on a major offensive. Thieu was to request U.S. air support through the embassy, which would then submit it to Nixon. After August, when Congress imposed a ban on air war throughout Indochina, the ARVN was to resist long enough to allow the President the fifteen days essential to get congressional approval. Meantime, a "hot line" system between the four RVNAF corps commanders as well as the JGS in Saigon to the U.S. Support Command in Thailand was operational by early 1974, including a constantly updated target list and forward air control system. Thieu therefore had every reason to expect U.S. air intervention, and until Watergate there was always a serious possibility of Nixon's sending the B-52s back into the war. Thieu's actions reflected this assurance, and he could break the Paris accords at will because he was convinced that the Americans would save him in the event of a DRV military riposte.[39] His total belief that this guarantee would operate persisted until Nixon left office, and he never quite expunged it. He found it unimaginable that after nearly two decades of involvement the United States would allow the Communists to take power without using its massive power to stop them. So had Nixon.

Just as important as the threat to resume the air war was the increasingly confident assumption in Washington that Nixon's deft relations with China and the USSR would inhibit the Revolution's action, at least through various pressures and reductions of aid. By the fall of 1972 most of the administration believed that even if no explicit understandings had been reached, both China and the USSR understood the rules of the game: economic and political rewards if they cooperated, tilting to support their enemy if they did not, and as much leveraging and triangulation as their imagination and anxieties could conjure. True, neither side had been helpful during the Christmas bombings, but the President believed he had solved his reelection problems as a result of détente diplomacy, and he therefore retained an abiding confidence that something was working. Exactly what was succeeding was not clear, and rather than confront the possibility its diplomatic strategy had failed, the White House preferred the implicit to the explicit.

Throughout January the problem was widely discussed in Washington, and many members of the administration felt reasonably confident the status quo would continue because both China and Russia would, or at least should, reduce aid to the DRV. A few, such as Kissinger's key assistant at Paris, William H. Sullivan, were certain that they would and that geopolitics would dictate Sino-Soviet behavior. Kissinger was not quite so categorical, but both he and Nixon also believed this. Sullivan ascribed the DRV's decision to opt for a political settlement in January mainly to Chinese pressure, but to the USSR as well. He ignored altogether that the DRV had drafted the basic document and that the United States had been compelled to accept it. Sullivan attributed Chinese cooperation to their desire to see a Balkanized Indochina free of DRV control and not potentially open to Soviet influence—a point he argued for the remainder of 1973. Laird felt that trade concessions had and would get the Russians into line on aid levels. No "formal" understandings with China could or should be made, Kissinger admitted, but over the next months it became the conventional wisdom in Washington that tacit understandings with both the USSR and China existed.[40] The Administration dismissed evidence that the DRV might be able skillfully to balance the Sino-Soviet rivalry to obtain sufficient aid for itself.

For the immediate future it was far more consequential that the United States believed that the policies of the USSR and China would help keep the RVN in power than what they actually did. For the war had now become a question of time, which the Americans thought was on their side. Between its bait of economic aid, the threat to reenter the war, Sino-Soviet help, and Thieu's own arms and power, the Nixon administration was reasonably certain it had applied its four-year policy to end the war on terms tantamount to an "honorable" victory. The peace was admittedly an equivocal one, but the White House was confident it could spend the next four years in office with what Kissinger called "our national obsession," and its terrible tensions and conflicts, behind it. Washington could think again about "a global foreign policy."[41]

Part Six

THE CRISIS OF THE REPUBLIC OF VIETNAM AND THE END OF THE WAR, 1973-1975

Chapter 35

The Balance of Forces in South Vietnam, Early 1973, and the Impact of the RVN's Policies

THE BALANCE OF FORCES, EARLY 1973

At the beginning of 1973 both the Revolution and the RVN were acutely conscious of their own military weaknesses. Yet the military balance of forces was now irreversibly weighted on the side of the Communists. At the time of the Paris Agreement signing, the RVN had an overwhelming equipment superiority, but this was also true in early 1971 and spring 1972, and in both cases only U.S. intervention had saved it from disaster. The RVN was essentially defeatist, suffering from declining morale and discipline. While the Revolution was temporarily exhausted materially and physically, it remained highly resilient and with a vastly greater ability, over time, to become the victorious fighting force.

The crux of the RVN's dilemma was its strategy and internal cohesion. By providing Thieu with an abundance of arms and an explicit oral guarantee to reenter the war, the Nixon administration preordained the aggressive manner in which the dictator would employ his army. Neither Thieu nor the United States saw the Paris Agreement as anything more than a military

457

arrangement, possibly no more than a pause, the substance of which would depend on the extent to which the threat of American air power, Sino-Soviet cooperation, and Thieu's own capability could together cope with the variety of threats to his power. Thieu never believed that he alone could deal with a major Revolutionary military offensive, and he and his officers assumed that the United States would intervene in that case to save him. What was certain was that Thieu's self-confidence would soon confront the Revolution with some hard choices, since it put him, to a great extent, in a position to define initially the level and location of violence.

The Revolution's basic premise at the beginning of 1973 was not simply that Thieu was strong, which it believed, but also that it required time to recuperate and to reorganize its forces to master this reality. Essentially, with the Paris Agreement it became temporarily defensive not because of the success of détente diplomacy or the fear of renewed American bombing but in response to its own material limits. The threat of bombing impressed the Party's leaders less and less with time, and they knew nothing of the U.S. stockpiling of bombs until the war was over. They had played on Sino-Soviet differences more ably than Washington in order to sustain the flow of aid. While they were naturally apprehensive about the future, they nonetheless could anticipate a certain minimum of assistance regardless of U.S. blandishments. With the Paris accords the Party believed it had won a breathing spell crucial to its resolution of immediate problems and its coping with an ARVN whose ability at least some of the Party's leaders tended to overrate tactically.

The Revolution's own material problems also caused it to underestimate the structural and political weaknesses of the RVN's social system. Although a minority thought differently, the dominant Party assumption was that it would go through a period of depending on elements in the Third Force to create the main political opposition to the regime and that it might very well have to share power with them for a transitional period. The Party was still too uncertain of its strength to accept the more likely scenario that the RVN would either win complete power or lose the war entirely but that Thieu would be unwilling to allow a more complex transitional alternative to emerge. The Party's defensive mood reinforced its posture and perceptions throughout the critical months when the Paris Agreement was being concluded. In early 1973 it regarded total victory in the not-too-distant future as a possibility, but not a probability.

Thieu, as usual, planned to deal primarily with politics, and he expected the Americans to confront the Communists should they pose a serious military threat to him. Neither he nor the White House ever fully recognized the inextricable relationship between his military capabilities and the increasingly critical social, economic, and human changes that were occurring with astonishing speed throughout South Vietnam. Although its Marxism nominally made it appreciate that economic and social factors were crucial, the Party's analyses at the time the agreement was signed were often too general or, worse yet, not treated seriously enough at its highest levels. While Nixon and Kissinger naturally failed to understand the critical dilemmas of Thieu's economy and society any better than they could those of their own, many lower-ranking Americans who knew the RVN intimately were more conscious than either the White House or the Politburo that time was not on its side even without military challenges. Ultimately, the greatest threat to Thieu came not from armies but from the society he and the United States had installed, and time, rather than being an opportunity, was his worst enemy.

It was in this nonmilitary domain that the balance of forces was swinging decisively against Thieu and the United States. The Paris Agreement won time for these nonmilitary forces to have an impact while the Revolution repaired its armed and political power. Time permitted contradictions not only in the RVN but also in the United States and the world to emerge more forcefully, and no one in Hanoi could imagine the scope and diversity of changes in its favor that were about to develop, constrain, and define the last phase of the three-decade-old struggle. To the extent that the Paris Agreement brought a respite that could only work against Thieu, it marked a decisive turning point in the balance of forces. The full magnitude and dimensions of this shift would not become wholly clear until the spring of 1975.

Politically, Thieu's actions during 1972 isolated him more thoroughly than ever. Whatever their feelings toward the Communists, the huge majority of Vietnamese desired peace. Anyone who did not try to implement the agreement's political provisions would be certain to evoke their hostility. For Thieu the RVN consisted of a military and organizational system which wholly subsumed politics and also gave a decisive direction to the economy and system of privileges, which reinforced his power. So long as the RVN was synonymous with the military, Thieu was certain to resist political innovations which would accompany the effort to alter his policies. But basic political change was now a precondition to attaining the peace so crucial to the most articulate portion of the South Vietnamese people. By resisting any compromise, yet being able to remain in power, Thieu guaranteed that the Revolution would not have to undergo a transitional period of shared authority.

Thieu's role became more critical insofar as his economic and state system proved intrinsically unable to cope with the vast range of social, economic, and structural difficulties emerging from the war. Although these problems had been growing with time, the American presence and money had mitigated their full implications until 1972. The RVN was not simply a dependent society financially; it was systemically corrupt, and this routinized dishonesty was crucial to keeping Thieu in power. Had he attempted to redirect a significant portion of the nation's resources to meet its social needs, which he never showed the slightest inclination to do, he would have lost his hold on the senior officers who were major beneficiaries of his regime —and thereby have created a strategic armed opposition of the sort that had plagued the RVN between 1963 and 1967. In a word, the RVN's politics were locked into a vise until its final defeat. To the degree that the magnitude of economic and social problems transcended the political mechanism for dealing with them, the entire RVN system was foredoomed to fall into a potentially decisive impasse.

In this setting, the balance of forces in South Vietnam was moving in favor of the Party even more quickly and overwhelmingly than it, the Americans, or Thieu could imagine. To some degree, the accumulated effects of the war and its traumatization of the social system were beginning, more than ever, to define the parameters of change and to accelerate it. The Party's passive role would prove less critical because the movement of history had entered a cumulative phase in which all that it and its enemies had done before now produced its own logic and momentum. Events were the outcome of all the preceding human decisions and actions, their collective wisdom or folly, but at this time took on a life of their own qualitatively.

The relationship between the past and the future is evasive and abstract, yet it is nonetheless crucial, and comprehending the nature of this process is the greatest of all challenges to the mind and to the mastery of events and human destiny. Theoretically, the Revolution conceded the relevance of all the factors—economic, social, or political—vital to this assessment, but it had more difficulty perceiving the general character and contours of the end of the war against Thieu than it had had during the final phases of the war against the French in 1952–54 and the Americans during 1971–72. To some extent, it was impossible to predict all the major variables, since U.S. politics was one of them, and in January 1973 no one foresaw Nixon's political demise. The multiplicity and diversity of history, the nature of war not merely as a conflict of men in arms but primarily and increasingly as a political and social struggle, and the critical importance of the economic crisis and human disorder intrinsic to war, now moved to the fore.

The end of the Vietnam War after thirty years cannot be understood simply in terms of armies and generals, or of the individuals who led them. For by 1973 the war in Vietnam had moved beyond the limits of armies and leaders and was being determined ineluctably by the accumulated experience—human, social, economic, political, as well as military—that thirty years of struggle by literally millions of peasants, soldiers, and political activists had created. The Communist Party was now to be the beneficiary of these larger processes, and whether it could diagnose them precisely was less important than the inability of its adversaries to do anything to reverse the disastrous legacies of their own policies and institutions.

THE RVN'S MILITARY STRATEGY

Ironically, immediately after the signing of the Paris Agreement, it was the Americans and the RVN's leaders who determined whether there would be war or peace. Their decision for conflict intensified the very economic and political processes that increasingly made their role in the remainder of the war strategically passive. From the American viewpoint, the efficacy of its decisions depended on whether military struggle would prove more crucial than economic and political mobilization in permitting the RVN to survive over the long run. Washington had never regarded nonmilitary struggle as decisive, and in the fall of 1972 the White House was convinced that its détente strategy, the very real prospect of its resumed bombing, the DRV's exhaustion, and the ARVN's new arms all provided an umbrella for the consolidating of Thieu's power. Once again a President aspired to a de facto victory over the Communists in the greater part of South Vietnam, opting for a military solution at a point when the Revolution was eager to stress political struggle, quite oblivious that the U.S.'s illusions were certain to intensify all of the accumulated economic and political weaknesses and dilemmas in the RVN social system which had been building for a decade.

Throughout the eighteen months following the signing at Paris, the Nixon administration was wholly responsible for the parameters of Thieu's military actions. Only in the summer of 1974 did the initiative finally pass to the Congress. In terms of combat doctrine and a mode of warfare, the United States had, according to the State Department's definition that I noted earlier, "imparted to the South Vietnamese . . . the concept of achieving maximum effect with minimum loss of personnel. This requires high equipment utilization and expenditure of ordnance. . . ."[1] A series of American offices, beginning with the DAO in Saigon and passing through various military hierarchies, controlled the overall timing and scale of the RVN's military actions during 1973 and early 1974. The MACV had drawn up the RVN's military plans from the inception of the war, and its successors continued after 1973 as well. "DOD guidelines outline the size of the force, sortie rates, etc.," the Pentagon reported to Congress in spring 1974. "The U.S. Mission, using U.S. service approved planning factors, develops the specific quantities of supplies, materiels, equipment and weapons required. . . . The South Vietnam Government does not submit an annual request."[2]

This profound dependency produced what the RVN's officers later described as a passive colonial mentality in which they expected the Americans to do all that was essential in the military domain, including intervening again to save them if necessary. And because Thieu was at the apex of this system, and able to obtain the funding, his political strength in the eyes of the senior officers remained impregnable. The Americans, his former cronies later complained, were ultimately responsible for everything, including Thieu. The RVN's senior officers did what the United States both made possible and permitted.

After January 1973 Thieu had an administration mandate to consolidate his power by force of arms. A sufficient number of decision-making Americans were convinced that the military balance was tantalizingly ready for a profound shift in the RVN's favor and that the moment was ripe to press the advantage. While U.S. officials in Saigon advocated this strategy for well over a year, Nixon, Kissinger, and the Pentagon also publicly condoned the pattern of military action as essential for delineating the control of territory.

During the first week after the cease-fire, both sides had attempted to take strategic points. "Saigon, still the stronger side," as Kissinger later grossly understated it, "gave as good as it received; it expanded its control over more hamlets than it lost."[3] The RVN's effort to take territory continued, however, until mid-1974, particularly in MR III and IV, where the Communist armies were most vulnerable. By May 1974, according to RVN claims, the PRG had been driven out of or had abandoned nearly one hundred hamlets it had firmly held before January 1973 as well as about seven hundred others, losing 15 to 20 percent of the area it had initially controlled. Efforts to terminate the "cease-fire war" in June 1973 caused Thieu to reduce his offensive operations for a few days, but they quickly resumed in full force. During the fall his units were punching into traditional PRG strongholds in the region northwest of Saigon as well as in Binh Dinh Province in MR II. On January 4, 1974, RVN began a sustained five-month offensive as Thieu publicly declared that the war had "restarted" and carried it into PRG zones.[4] Major multidivision operations were executed in both MR III and MR IV, capturing much traditional Revolutionary territory.

Thieu's successful aggressive policy favorably impressed many American officials working on military affairs, and this assured him a continuous supply of munitions. Most, of course, had initially been skeptical about him and his army, but since he was gaining territory and the Revolution was scarcely striking back, he in time substantially reduced the number of his detractors. Without asking any basic questions about the RVN's underlying social health, the American chief of intelligence collection in Saigon during 1974 later admitted, "The perception thus gained was of an efficient, aggressive military force that was capable of defending its territory." In allowing it to violate the Paris accords, he added, "the South Vietnamese armed forces became an instrument of U.S. policy," and the RVN's leaders were explicitly aware of this.[5]

But a small group of U.S. advisers and ARVN officers came to the conclusion that Thieu's policy of both holding and expanding territory was extending his army into vulnerable posts, making it increasingly immobile in static positions, and exposing it to potential massed, mobile Communist attacks. The strategic initiative in the war was therefore passing to the Revolution, which could exercise it when it chose. Some even speculated that Thieu's ability to take and hold land was largely due to the enemy's setting a huge trap. Thieu, of course, had always pursued this policy of maximum possession of people and places, which meant a strategy of passive defense. Its success was dependent on two conditions: first, an absence of sufficient Revolutionary resistance; and second, a very large army to be spread everywhere with the funds to supply them by truck and helicopter. But Thieu's strategy would become a recipe for disaster should either factor change.

Thieu and the Americans, in brief, shared the same strategy. Its monitoring and supplying him with munitions left the administration absolute veto power over his actions. Since Thieu was prone to excesses, U.S. officials found it essential in the first months after Paris to define both his constraints and his freedom. In a sense, transcending everyone's desires were simple physical limits and costs, which appeared in February 1973 when the RVNAF used 78,000 tons of munitions—or twice the amount the United States had dropped during its December 1972 blitz of the DRV. During 1973 the RVNAF managed to explode 326,000 tons of ground munitions, more than it had used in any year before 1970 and equivalent to over two-fifths of the entire U.S. 1973 munitions output. The DAO therefore reduced the RVNAF during 1974 to 205,000 tons for ground munitions, about equal to the ARVN's 1968 consumption. Put another way, during 1973 the RVN fired seventeen times more munitions than the Revolutionary army, and twelve times more in 1974. Even in January 1975, despite the RVN's complaints, its use of munitions was nine times that of the PAVN/PLAF. The RVN strategy, to repeat, was based on offensive firepower, extended control of territory by a large army in static defense positions, and dependency on transport to link its huge system together. It was American-style war, and expensive.

The corollary of this strategy, however, was massive destruction. While the data are inherently debatable, the Pentagon reported 25,500 RVNAF soldiers killed in 1973 and 39,000 "enemies." RVN figures for the same year are 13,800 and 48,200 respectively. Either way, it is clear who did most of the killing. In 1974 the Pentagon claimed that 29,900 RVNAF and 61,000 Communists were killed. In 1973 about 15,000 civilians were killed, 70,000 wounded, and 818,700 created refugees. Whatever other things the Paris Agreement attained, peace was not one of them.

Another crucial consequence of the RVN's actions was its position on population movement, which under the Paris Agreement required both "freedom of movement" and "freedom of residence." The United States and the RVN ignored these clauses, like all of the ones they had signed reluctantly, but they failed to consider the economic and political implications of seeking victory. The economic logic of allowing free population movement was quite obvious. Unskilled workers in Saigon, both male and female, after 1969 made less than those in the Mekong Delta, where there was a shortage of labor. Since virtually nothing was being done for the unsettled refugees still remaining among the nearly ten million the war had created by the end of 1972, many of them hoped to return home or move to where there existed opportunities to re-create a normal life after their shattering experiences.

At the beginning of 1973 there were about 640,000 people living in RVN refugee camps, three-quarters of them from four northern provinces which were in Revolutionary hands or which had supported it for years. As soon as the Paris Agreement was signed, the RVN declared that there would be strict control of population movement and that no one would be permitted to move save under restricted circumstances. The RVN's refugee strategy was to proceed on two levels.

One approach was not only to prevent refugees from returning home but also to continue forcibly to move them out of areas the PRG controlled or "contested." Those who refused and tried to remain often had their homes burned, and some low-level American officials thought the RVN created substantial support for the PRG in this fashion where none may have existed. The RVN steadfastly refused to allow refugees to return to the areas it did not dominate completely. "It would be politically impossible for us to allow these people to go back to the VC," a typical RVN official observed.[6] During 1973, about 285,000 refugees were permitted to return to villages the RVN controlled, but the number left in its camps remained constant.

American officials designed the RVN's second refugee program, involving 200,000 people, which was essentially military. "The people will move into areas that were previously considered marginal," they instructed the RVN corps commanders, "thus secure the area, improve movement and security along major routes of communication. . . ."[7] Situated in unsettled stretches in critical strategic territory traditionally under NLF control, these villages required investments, which quickly produced widespread corruption. Worse yet for the villagers, they were not trusted, were surrounded by barbed wire, and often were even unable to leave temporarily without special permits. The new settlements at least obtained "A" ratings on hamlet evaluation charts. "But it is the kind of control that jailers have over prisoners," a *Washington Post* journalist wrote, "as local officials admit, and not altogether effective."[8]

THE DEEPENING CRISIS OF THE RVN SYSTEM: WAR AS A SOCIAL PROCESS

Despite the Nixon administration's belief that its strategy had an increasingly good chance of success, in reality its policies added to the RVN's political and economic problems and began to produce changes dangerous to its future. Given the desperate longing for peace of a huge proportion of the population, the aggressive continuation of the war produced a serious challenge to the RVN in virtually every domain—economic, military, political, and psychological—crucial to the war's ultimate outcome. For the Paris Agreement's promise of peace was in itself an overwhelming political reality for an exhausted South Vietnamese population, including much of the RVNAF. The politics of peace and reconciliation therefore became a potent new force in the critical arena of political struggle.

The RVN's effort to control population movement and trade did not merely violate the Paris accord, which the masses knew about, but also frustrated their desire for stability. Whatever the political commitments and actions of the peasantry in the past, it still remained capable of shifting in response to any pressures and frustrations the RVN or Revolution imposed on it. Here Thieu immediately embarked on a losing course. While the effects of his policy on the peasantry or educated urban elements could have been predicted, neither he nor his U.S. advisers anticipated the impact of the legal fiction of peace on the attitudes of the RVNAF and on its fighting abilities. The RVN had always been plagued by the dilemma of physical control of the population without gaining its allegiance, but its failure in this crucial domain after 1972 was greater than ever. Although the usual favorable data on hamlet control continued to be collected, there was growing evidence that the RVN could operate in a rising number of places only in daytime and that previously neutral peasants were increasingly willing to welcome the PRG. More and more refused to abandon territory the RVN sought to evacuate, and numerous accounts of how mounting alienation from the RVN was being transformed into toleration and support for the PRG began to circulate both among U.S. officials and in the press.

Beginning in early 1973 the Revolution actively sought to arrange local accommodations with RF/PF or ARVN outposts. While most successful where it was militarily most potent, it also made important inroads throughout the country. Explicit understandings regarding patrolling and contact were reached in many areas, and for the first time fraternization occurred in some sections. Even more ominous was trade with the Revolutionary regions, including fuel and even arms, as the PRG now found it increasingly easy to pay premium prices to hard-pressed RVN officials and soldiers to supply itself. And though the RVN labeled such practices illegal, the peace declared at Paris gave them a powerful sanction. To a critical extent, the agreement's impact went beyond the RVN's policies and directly influenced the actions of the masses and soldiers.

Nowhere were these trends more important than in MR IV, in the lower Delta, with nearly half the south's population. When the Paris Agreement was signed, the RVN had three divisions there, one of which was reputedly its worst, and they embarked on an aggressive policy of using artillery to harass the PRG. By mid-1973 the Revolution was making rapid strides throughout the region with a combination of local accommodations and political mobilization, maintaining only sufficient military pressure to keep aggressive ARVN units at a distance and spread out as much as possible. Indeed, in what was to prove one of its biggest errors in the post-Paris period, the RVN decided to recoup its dwindling strength there by waging a "rice war" that accelerated many of its growing contradictions.

The PRG satisfied its rice needs in the Delta and those of much of its bordering Cambodian bases by buying the bulk of its rice in the local open market. This trade was so large that RF/PF units, the RVN navy, and their officers became involved. Fearing that this drainage would increase already spiraling national rice prices and have obvious military implications, Thieu during August 1973 embarked on a massive effort to end the rice trade with the PRG. The entire Delta was segregated into regions either contiguous to the PRG, not contiguous but accessible, or secure. PRG areas existed in every province, but seven were especially tainted. At least 60 percent of MR IV was open to Thieu's enemy. Households in contiguous areas had all but one week's supply of rice confiscated, and in return they were given certificates, allowing them to withdraw rice every week from RVN stores and receive payment for the surplus at a price that was as much as 50 percent below the free-market price. Those in accessible areas were allowed to retain a thirty- day supply of rice on the same terms. Not only did a vast number of peasants suffer enormous inconvenience and large financial losses, but payments were delayed and rice was often graded below its real quality. The rice war produced corruption on a giant scale which involved the entire RVN administrative system, from province chiefs to soldiers guarding checkpoints. The PRG had no difficulty buying rice, for it paid a large premium to smugglers. Peasants naturally hoarded as much rice as possible rather than lose it to avaricious bureaucrats, increasing the shortages in cities and driving up prices, and discontent with the RVN grew by leaps and bounds. The rice war revealed the innumerable weaknesses of the total RVN system as well as the flexibility of the peasantry and its desire for a normalized society. It also alienated the large *attentiste* element among the peasantry and led much of it to give active support to the PRG. During the first five months of 1974, over eighty RVN posts in the Delta fell to the PRG, though many had in fact been abandoned without orders, and the Revolution operated much more openly than it had in years. Local American officials watched these ominous trends with horror, for Thieu had embarked on a high-risk strategy in the most populous and richest part of the country and failed disastrously.[9]

Meanwhile, Thieu's aggressive policies exploited to the maximum his ostensibly decisive material superiority, but the very nature of his army contained dangers for him far more serious than the now obvious one of too great a reliance on technology and equipment the ARVN could neither utilize nor, eventually, afford. Their dependency on U.S. doctrine and their expectation that the American air armada would intervene if necessary totally mesmerized ARVN's senior generals, who at no time searched for an alternative strategy. The ARVN had never fought without the proximity of U.S. air cover, and a substantial part of its own air force was immobilized by a shortage of pilots and the need to have foreign technicians maintain the remainder. Yet this did not prevent the Pentagon from sending even more sophisticated planes, in clear violation of the Paris terms. In fact, the ARVN could not fight conventional or unconventional war well, and its first instinct was to substitute ground munitions for air power.

While the DAO both designed and supported the RVN's basic strategy and military system, Saigon's obsessive reliance on artillery increasingly disturbed American officials, and the ARVN's exhaustion of U.S. productive capacities imposed a restraint even they had to acknowledge. "Harassment and interdiction" firings were routine until mid-1974, hitting nothing in virtually all cases and sometimes serving as an excuse for the collecting of brass shells which officers could then sell as valuable scrap. However successful some of Thieu's military efforts, almost all Americans involved in the war were increasingly conscious that the ARVN was not making progress with logistics and that it wasted immense amounts of equipment which often, as one official admitted, was "sitting around rusting."[10]

WAR AS A SOCIAL PROCESS: THE RVN'S DEEPENING ECONOMIC CRISIS

By 1973 both American and RVN experts publicly acknowledged that the very size of the army created a serious dilemma. Desertions reached a peak of over 200,000 in 1974 because of economic conditions, and the number of ghost soldiers also rose. To maintain the army at a strength of 1.1 million required 200,000–250,000 draftees annually, and by 1974 the male population growth was insufficient to replace the drainage. The RVNAF probably really had fewer than 800,000 full-time soldiers, but even so it became far too large for even an honest, efficient economy to bear. U.S. and RVN economic planners consciously transferred a large portion of its costs to the population by the simple expedient of an indirect tax: the soldiers were paid so little that they were compelled to live by their wits. Innumerable grave problems grew out of this decision. The least socially destructive were ghost soldiers and desertions, and the most dangerous to the U.S. cause were corruption, looting, and scavenging off the people. This policy was so debilitating that even before the cuts in military and economic aid in late 1974, the RVN had begun to capsize.

The real income of soldiers in the RVNAF, but especially in the ARVN, fell much more sharply after 1972 than in the preceding years, when it dropped by approximately two-thirds between 1963 and 1969. The American troop withdrawal and escalating unemployment after 1972 had dried up the petty jobs which had kept many men and their wives out of dire straits. In 1973 the rice allowance to soldiers was replaced with cash, and between January 1973 and May 1974, it was estimated, soldiers' real incomes declined at least another two-thirds. The average married soldier received only one-third the amount needed to sustain his family at a minimal level. Whatever the exact figures, it was clear that after 1965 the average RVNAF soldier had been squeezed dry economically. The vast majority felt the RVN was cheating them. The average member of the RVNAF became a victim of oppression, and his sense of responsibility to his family, more than any other factor, made him turn to corruption and social scavenging. In the end, the masses were to pay the economic bill in a brutal, dehumanizing process with obvious political consequences.

Soldiers had guns, and the police offered the civilian population no protection. Looting became epidemic after 1972. "The ARVN troopers . . . apparently went plundering again," one AID worker reported regarding a common occurrence in October 1973. "The recently returned . . . villagers . . . allegedly lost half their anticipated rice crop to the ARVN soldiers and their dependents. . . . the soldiers held the people . . . at bay with the use of tear-gas grenades and threats of booby traps."[11] As corruption increased dramatically, so did alcoholism, drug addiction, and instances of fragging. Cases of the selling of arms directly to the Revolution now arose for perhaps the first time, the indirect trade having existed for many years. Helicopter pilots began taxing wounded soldiers fixed fees for evacuation, and even some artillery batteries began charging other units $1 to $2 per round. The need of RVNAF personnel to spend their time earning money was a basic reason for the sharp growth in local accommodations with Communist forces. Economics was increasingly making the war passé. By mid-1974, before Congress had enacted any significant reductions of military or economic aid to the RVN, corruption, demoralization, and economic distress had reached epidemic proportions everywhere. The RVN was visibly disintegrating in the midst of a mounting national debate over the degradation into which a large proportion of the nation had fallen.[12]

The RVN's basic dilemma was rooted in the premises which France and then the United States had defined when they brought it into existence. It was essentially an army with a state and an economy grafted haphazardly upon it, but by 1973, without its indispensable foreign sponsor to defend it, the very nature of such a social system assured its imminent collapse. Its nominal material strength, which was very great militarily, ceased to have any meaning. Its economy was entirely imbalanced and its urban sector wholly artificial. Given this ever more precarious foundation, the RVN's remaining supporters became increasingly distracted with their own daily troubles, and their faith in their leaders and future declined perceptibly. In this context Washington was not to shape events but to respond to them.

Chapter 36

The Nixon Administration's Dilemmas of Power

THE EMERGING FRUSTRATIONS OF AMERICAN GLOBALISM

The United States' fatal obsession with Vietnam, as Kissinger understood perfectly, had gravely disoriented its foreign policy after 1965, and the White House at the beginning of 1973 was intent on redeeming it. His "Year of Europe" speech in April reflected a realization that a turning away from Vietnam was a necessity, and the White House in this and countless other ways helped to move both Congress and the Pentagon toward other concerns and priorities. It had not intended to reduce its commitments to Vietnam in the process, for it was firmly convinced its policies could gain time for Thieu to consolidate his power. But by focusing on more important issues, it reinforced everyone's inclination to reduce Vietnam's relative significance.

The Pentagon, for its part, needed very little prompting, for the war had left it seriously underfunded for its other global requirements. Its share of both the federal budget and the gross national product declined dramatically after 1969, and it was convinced that it was losing its technological superiority over the Russians. Moscow's successful testing of multiple-warhead missiles in the summer of 1973 especially upset it. To right the balance would require greater spending, and since the Pentagon was unlikely to get more from Congress, it was axiomatic that it must reallocate its existing resources to meet such challenges. The Defense Department did not pose the problem publicly in terms of Vietnam versus the remainder of American priorities in the world, but its public expositions consistently reinforced the logic of avoiding a repetition of past errors. Privately, however, it pressed for a discreet withdrawal from the region. Kissinger has recalled, "I was fighting a desperate but losing struggle against the Pentagon's desire to redeploy air and naval forces out of Southeast Asia in order to devote scarce funds to the procurement of new weapons."[1]

"In our relations with our friends in Europe," Kissinger admitted at the end of 1973, "the year has been disappointing."[2] Economic and military issues remained divisive, and after the October war between Israel and Egypt, they became openly irritating. The European leaders did not take to Kissinger's authoritarian, professorial manners, nor did they feel bound to American hegemony on such vital economic issues as Middle Eastern policy during the traumatic oil embargo. These questions have yet to be resolved, but their emergence in stark form during 1973 reinforced Washington's need to concern itself less with Indochina.

Had Kissinger been capable of pursuing a coherent policy of reorienting American priorities throughout 1973, the administration might have attained some of its goals, but Vietnam lurked as its continued obsession. The White House emerged from the electoral triumph of 1972 more self-confident and arrogant than ever. Nixon was openly considering means by which to reduce the power of the media, and Kissinger was increasingly contemptuous of Congress. Aside from immediate sustained, acerbic disputes over blatant executive circumvention of congressional budget decisions on monies for Indochina, which helped set the backdrop for the fatal crisis of the presidency the following year, were the White House's repeated threats to use its air power again in Vietnam. Kissinger's continual public warnings to the DRV throughout the first half of 1973, ironically, frightened Congress far more than Hanoi. Congress knew both from hearings and from its knowledge of massive preparations in the Far East that the President was deadly serious about the resumption of the air war. A collision between the two was inevitable because, despite the huge vote for Nixon, the Senate's political composition had shifted decisively toward liberal antiwar politics, and it appeared virtually certain that Congress would mount a frontal attack on the President's war-making powers. The White House fatally misread the complex outcome of the November vote.

The Watergate trials, which were in full swing by March 1973, reinforced Congress's willingness and ability to challenge the administration, but to some extent its new militancy was also a by-product of its now intense frustration with the cynical presidential manipulation of foreign policy, which Johnson had begun but which Nixon had continued with a vengeance. Kissinger had blatantly challenged the last shred of congressional power and self-esteem by frequently asserting that the success of his foreign policy made the niceties of form quite incidental. "The final judgment on foreign policy is the substance and not the procedure," he could not refrain from arrogantly repeating even at the end of 1973, by which time Congress's toleration of subterfuge and secrecy had evaporated.[3] The continuity of his principles, synonymous with his own prerogatives, appealed to him notwithstanding their repeated failures in Southeast Asia and, increasingly, in Europe and the Middle East. Congress was simply not prepared to be ruled out of the constitutional process by self-congratulatory rhetoric used as a justification for the concentration and abuse of personal power. Watergate became a mere vehicle in its defense against the White House's effort to circumvent its authority. As the self-righteous pretensions of the executive evaporated before the unrelieved exposure in the press and hearings of personal dishonesty, wiretapping, false testimony, and miscellaneous chicanery, Congress's passivity and acquiescence on larger issues melted with them. The lies, secrecy, and deception that had always marked the war now began to implode on some of the men who had crafted them.

At the beginning of 1971 Congress prevented the use of American ground forces in Cambodia, and in June 1973 the Senate voted, by a large margin, to cut off funds for any form of U.S. combat anywhere in Indochina. This would have not only stopped the air war then taking place against Cambodia but blocked its resumption against Vietnam. Nixon vetoed the bill on June 27, when it passed the House by a large margin, and the Senate merely resurrected it as amendments to various bills that threatened to paralyze government operations. At Laird's insistence and despite Kissinger's objections, Nixon relented, in return for the face-saving gesture that the law take effect August 15. The White House had lost its biggest card in its Indochina strategy. Both privately and publicly, Kissinger deplored his defeat, making it clear, as he was correctly paraphrased, "I wanted to bomb the daylights out of Hanoi, but Congress wouldn't let me. That would have made it [Paris Agreement] stick."[4] But rather than preventing further congressional assaults on the power of the President, Kissinger's uncontrollable candor guaranteed that more would follow.

The administration tried vainly to maneuver around Congress's blow by stating publicly it was aware the President must return to it for authority to resume bombing, implying he was ready to do so. While the White House sought to keep Hanoi worried, it was now quite clear that Congress and a barely concealed group in the Pentagon would prevent this attempt. In mid-January 1974 Laird announced that Congress both would and should reject a White House request for resumed bombing. All that the administration's threats managed to do was to frighten more of its former supporters into joining the opposition.[5]

THE ROLE OF DÉTENTE

As the Nixon administration lost its freedom to renew the air war, détente, another of the three pillars of its Vietnam strategy, began to crumble. Détente did not die suddenly; it simply became engulfed in the durable realities of a world too complex to submit to great-power control as well as in the deeply rooted legacies of half a century of anticommunism. Apart from the inherent intricacy of its deftly triangulating between the USSR and China, the administration had too many domestic pressures from Congress to reconcile and too many commitments in Europe and the Middle East. These soon caused Sino-Soviet-American relations focused on a resolution of its Vietnam dilemma to be irrelevant. But because détente's demise was a quite slow and lingering process, it nourished residues and hints of progress which continued to feed the hopes, desires, and illusions of the President.

Kissinger's attempts to exploit détente to regulate the Vietnam question persisted until the war finally ended, but were particularly prominent in 1973. Thieu himself encouraged this effort, and Kissinger fancied during 1973 that he was succeeding to an important degree. To have thought otherwise would have been to admit the failure of the White House's basic strategy since 1969, and he was unable to do so—even privately.

But the administration needed the cold war, in particular with the USSR, to mobilize congressional votes on new weapons, such as the Trident submarine, and to sustain funding for the maintenance of U.S. troops in Europe. Once the specter of Soviet expansion was again refurbished on demand, specific interests like the Jewish lobby working on Soviet emigration policies scuttled its trade policy with Moscow. The mirages of peaceful coexistence were dissipated in the process. Soviet shipments of arms to the Arab states during the October Middle Eastern war greatly accelerated this process. "Selective detente," Kissinger ruefully noted at the end of 1973, was not possible. Vietnam by now was only one of a growing number of issues between the Soviets and the Americans—and no longer the most important.[6] Vietnam's shift from the center to the periphery of American interests made it a source of disorientation for the administration, which was increasingly held in thrall by its illusory hopes when dealing with the Soviet Union.

The problem of China in this strategy was more straightforward. Kissinger, who visited Peking in February 1973, couched his appeals to Chou En-lai in intimations of a de facto strategic collaboration against the USSR in Asia, an arrangement that would maintain a balance of power in the area but that presupposed a continued American presence and the Balkanization of Indochina. He found Mao Tse-tung a real cynic on the question of China's public ideological commitments and fancied he could extract something from Peking, thereby applying pressure on Moscow. But Chou and Mao had to retain influence at home; given the precarious balance among China's leadership factions at that time, they had to defer to the powerful opponents of such profound cooperation with a traditional enemy. A basic compromise with the United States was premature, too, because of the Taiwan question. There were other irksome complexities. Not the least was Kissinger's incessant braggadocio, which in February 1974 came out in his assertion that he was mainly playing China off against Russia to extract more concessions from Moscow. Afraid of appearing outwitted, Chou swung behind the dominant current in Peking, which emerged in the same month as Kissinger's publicized boasts, in the form of the temporarily ascendant "three worlds" theory, which advocated unity against both American and Soviet hegemonism.[7]

By the fall of 1973 many members of the administration were openly skeptical about the success of détente and its false promises. The traditional cold war competition at least had the benefit of mobilizing Congress and European allies behind the President. The White House chose to continue both approaches, and for the remainder of the war Kissinger insisted that détente had caused the USSR and China to be helpful in Indochina, particularly in reducing aid to the Revolution. The problem, he admitted only in February 1975, was that though the volume of aid had declined substantially, the American effort to interdict its southward movement had stopped entirely. Less, he implied, was still too much. In fact, its partial success had made the administration overconfident, and this was also to prove disastrous for its ambitions.

The DRV watched these developments and responded to U.S. efforts to win over its allies in essentially the same fashion as it had before the Paris Agreement. The Vietnamese were particularly concerned about China, and relations with it in 1974 declined as Peking began to maneuver to expand its influence in the region. The DRV sought again to reassert the historical meaning of the Vietnam struggle as the convergence and testing of world revolution and counterrevolution in the contemporary era, which it in fact was, but such reminders surely irritated the cynics both in Peking and in Moscow who read the Vietnamese's plaintive statements. The dilemma of their ideological pretensions remained, and in the struggle for world leadership, both allies of the DRV had to pay public obeisance to them as well as to test the diplomatic waters in Washington for any possible gains for their state interests elsewhere. This problem was insoluble, and in fact led to a pattern of cooperation and tension between the DRV and its allies until the war ended.

Moscow and Peking had both admonished the Party's leaders not to precipitate a crisis in the south and had warned that they would not provide arms for any escalation. On the other hand, they reassured the DRV that they would give it enough to protect and consolidate its power. The Party explicitly understood the material constraints on its military options and acted accordingly. Military aid to the Revolution fell by over half during 1973 and increased to slightly over half the peak 1972 level in 1974. Economic aid, on the other hand, grew sharply and in 1974 was three times the 1972 amount. Compared with that in 1972, overall aid was slightly lower in 1973 but 40 percent higher in 1974. Since the United States, with at least some justification, boasted that before 1973 its air power had destroyed most military equipment before it could be used in the south, the Revolution still had access to more arms after 1972 than ever.[8]

In this sense, the Soviets and Chinese had done their part by both the Americans and the Revolution. What they could not do, of course, was maintain the administration's rapport with Congress, much less keep Thieu's social system from disintegrating. Yet, unless all dimensions of its policy succeeded in tandem, it was clear that the White House's grand strategy would fail. Moreover, while Russia and China were indeed fairly helpful, they could not abandon or regulate the DRV beyond military aid reductions. And ironically, though the Vietnamese Communists refused even to consider it, America's self-delusion on the decisive role of aid to the DRV was a vital asset. In the end, the administration's simplistic view of the importance of aid reductions made it less dangerous. Had it not believed it was succeeding in its project to cut aid, it would probably have made a greater effort to gain congressional approval to resume the air war or, at the very least, to send more arms to the RVN. Its myopia therefore caused the White House to lose time, during which events both in Congress and in South Vietnam made its diplomacy and its military intervention increasingly chimerical.

Chapter 37

Recovery and Response: The Communist Party's Strategy until Mid-1974

THE REVOLUTION'S MILITARY
STRATEGY UNTIL JUNE 1974

When the Paris Agreement was signed, the Communist Party expected difficulties from Thieu, but when it sent Resolution 02 to all its branches in the south, it anticipated a primarily political struggle. While it had no illusions about the need to protect itself, it believed that the very existence of the agreement and the control commissions would impose considerably more restraint on Thieu than it in fact did. What the Party then needed most was time to consolidate its position and recover from its exhausting 1972 offensive. To a large degree its military policy throughout 1973 reflected this imperative. In Resolution 03 during March the Party reasserted its political emphasis. But while it moved to a much lower level of military activity and strictly discouraged an emphasis on military force as it tested the political potential in South Vietnam, the Revolution also reconstructed and rearmed its local units and guerillas. Yet the RVN was able to reduce the Revolution's power and territory significantly in the first half of 1973 because it avoided combat. U.S. estimates of enemy troop strength in the south ranged from 200,000 to 253,000 in spring 1973, dropping to 184,000 in April 1974.

The Revolution successfully used primarily local forces to tie down as many RVNAF forces as possible and maneuver them into a passive, defensive, vulnerable position. Given Thieu's insistence on holding territory, this was quite simple. As the DAO correctly perceived, the Communist military policy was essentially a defensive holding action designed mainly to perfect its logistical structure and rear areas and to improve the quality of its forces. The one exception was in the lower Mekong Delta, where survival required local forces unilaterally to take unauthorized military action and mount an increasingly successful resistance that exceeded their political activities. "Those specific acts were completely contrary to a whole series of policies at that time," the Communist general in command of the region later admitted, and Hanoi was too distant to do much about "the rectification of mistakes."[1] On the other hand, only in the Delta was the Revolution's position to improve substantially throughout this period, if only because Thieu's rice war and offensive operations had managed to alienate many formerly passive peasants.

In essence, the Party's strategy until August 1974 was to build its strength and bide its time in a context in which Thieu was becoming politically and economically weaker and the Americans more distracted. The Politburo met in June 1973 and heard from senior generals, local Party leaders, and some of its own members who had gone south to study the situation; not until the following October did it reach a typically very eclectic policy, which revealed there was still no clear consensus among the leadership. Its Resolution 21 ordered the Party largely to pursue the political route while intensifying its military preparations. It focused on maintaining and expanding power in the Delta, where the initiative of the local Communists had revealed new possibilities, and on tailoring tactics appropriate for each region without becoming either too aggressive or defensive. In a real sense, it returned an indispensable degree of autonomy to local units, demanding only that they emphasize political work and not embark on any dangerous adventures. U.S. intelligence interpreted Resolution 21 also as a holding action and a continuation of earlier policies.

Part of the Politburo's problem at this time, aside from its other priorities and political expectations, was that it regarded the RVNAF as considerably stronger than it was in fact. Indeed, many in the DRV, too distant to comprehend realities on the ground but still able to influence policy, overrated the RVN's viability in numerous domains, especially its leaders' capacity and willingness both to lead and to fight, and this inhibiting perception lasted until mid-1974. But to the extent that Thieu thwarted the political mechanisms and hopes in the Paris Agreement, the Party, as a Senate study predicted in April 1973, might "see no alternative but to renew the military struggle."[2]

In fact the Party's cautious policy was to change only because repeated successes revealed that it had recovered its strength quickly while the RVNAF, even as it attempted to maintain the initiative, was weakening far more rapidly. At the beginning of 1974 U.S. intelligence correctly predicted that the Communists would concentrate during 1974 on perfecting their logistical structure and keeping the RVNAF overextended and demoralized. In the lower Delta, however, the Revolution continued to fill what was essentially a political vacuum. Elsewhere, it had by May 1974 abandoned or lost a number of hamlets, though nowhere near the eight hundred the enemy claimed. The RVN regarded it a sign of its own growing strength rather than as a further dilution of its already weakening forces. During March 1974, indeed, the Party's Military Commission decided to continue what appeared a successful mixed strategy outlined in Resolution 21 "for the next few years."[3]

Other considerations inhibited the Politburo from testing Thieu at this time. In mid-1973 the PAVN did not hesitate to describe the RVNAF as "strong and very obstinate."[4] Both the quality and the quantity of the ARVN's arms impressed it, even as the vulnerability of its weaponry was extensively discussed in its military journals, stressing the need for surprise and mobility, as well as skill, to neutralize the ARVN. The mixture of forces and the use of guerillas to disperse and whipsaw the enemy still had its advocates. While most analysts emphasized the role of morale and politics, for the first time in the history of the Party an essentially technocratic and technological vision of war was endorsed by no less a figure than General Van Tien Dung, the head of the PAVN. "Regularization has been an essential step for every standing army of all states in history," Dung asserted while bypassing the heterodox concept of the Revolution's military theory and successful practice until then.[5] "The advanced methods of a conventional and modern army" became quite acceptable, if not yet dominant, in PAVN definitions of the ideal structure of the army.[6] At the level of military theory, the Party was now seriously divided. This vision was intimately linked to its new economic strategy after the signing of the Paris Agreement, and the two combined after 1973 to constrain its leadership from acting decisively in the very near future. For one thing, the balance of military forces materially was never in the Party's favor if all one did was to count modern weapons. Dung's implicit discounting of the centrality of morale and politics at a point where these factors were overwhelmingly against the RVN was to adopt a strategy of delay.

As might have been expected after a decade of war, the Party's leaders had again to weigh the relationship of the needs of the people and economy in the north to the requirements of the war in the south, and they shifted strongly in favor of reconstruction of the DRV and protraction of the war. The sheer volume of economic aid from the USSR and China, and cunning U.S. enticements, led to ambitious economic programs predicated on a divided nation and on minimal costs in the south. While this policy was compatible with support for the struggle in South Vietnam up to a certain point, during 1973 and early 1974 its priorities were explicitly and overwhelmingly to make the DRV "a base area for our country's entire revolution. . . . In the new phase the economic front in the north has become the most decisive front of the revolution."[7] The emphasis in DRV public statements and analyses during the first eighteen months after the Paris accords strongly reinforced this position. Le Duan's authoritative statements pointed to the need to terminate inefficient, war-imposed decentralization and to move toward large-scale production techniques incorporating modern technology. After a projected two-year period of reconstruction, the Party was to give priority to heavy industry, and a scientific and technological revolution as the basis of the economy was also the overarching conception within which General Dung was seeking to reorganize the army.

The Party, in effect, was still attempting to resolve its classic dilemma of transcending the material imperatives of protracted war to attain far greater economic development. Its new vision was wholly incompatible with impending victory in the south, which would create a quite different set of economic priorities and conditions. It surely was not a scheme which stressed terminating the war, the very existence of which made serious economic planning impossible. Economically, the quickest way to reconstruct was first to achieve peace, and this meant either abandoning the south or opting for complete victory, and until mid-1974 the Party planned neither. It was for this reason that for about a year and a half there was very little coherence between the Party's economic priorities and military possibilities, and the majority of its leaders and senior members did not envisage an imminent victory. And the dominant faction of the military itself was committed to a modernization program which required both time and resources to implement.[8]

Put another way, events were now transcending the Party's plans and imagination.

THE REVOLUTION'S POLITICAL STRATEGY

The Communist political organization in South Vietnam had been brutally damaged after 1968, and with the signing of the Paris Agreement its leaders were eager to see it reconstructed, believing that success in doing so was a precondition for all of their other efforts. The Party's work in RVN-controlled rural zones, particularly in the Mekong, succeeded quickly. It intensified the symbiotic integration between the RVN, the liberated areas, and the larger shadow region which in certain ways belonged to both sides and which the Party preferred to keep that way in order to both supply and protect itself. Economic conditions, the ARVN's alienation of the peasants, and Saigon's heavy reliance on its soldiers and firepower to traumatize large areas, prompted people to trade with the PRG and to become increasingly hostile to Thieu's regime. Thieu managed to anger a sufficient number to permit the PRG to resume recruiting, and some former RVN supporters became *attentistes,* and *attentistes* became open friends of the Revolution. The accumulated residues of the Party's work in the villages over thirty years began to bear fruit again as it adapted to the new conditions. To claim that it had planted a deep radical culture, at least among the poorer peasantry, would not be excessive. Only this context explains the ease with which lower-level Party workers, often acting autonomously, rebuilt the Revolution in the Delta. Whatever the profound mutations that accompanied the war's material and psychological effects, certain patterns of peasant radicalism remained.

The PRG also possessed a region it administered openly, which American officers at the beginning of 1975 admitted comprised 25 to 30 percent of South Vietnam's landmass and about 1.2 million people. The PRG itself at the end of 1974 calculated that it had 3.4 million people in its B2 region alone, in both liberated and contested areas, bringing the Revolution's organizations "not far below the 1968 level."[9] These trends were crucial because, ultimately, the Party had to make plans to conform to them, and the Revolution was not inclined to overestimate its real strength. If anything, it tended to underestimate it.

The wholly controlled PRG zones obtained large amounts of scarce goods from the DRV, and an effort was made to attract people to them. Commodities from RVN-controlled zones circulated freely in an essentially dual economy, and many peasants were ready to enjoy the advantages of both sides as the RVN's economy declined. To some extent, the speed and extent of all its political successes surprised the Party's leaders in the DRV. Even those who had contemplated a decade-long, protracted war with emphasis on building the north, and concentrating on a modern conventional army, were compelled to reflect on such trends.

The cities presented the PRG with a much more complex challenge, but every political and especially every economic crisis in the RVN made the urban context also seem more promising. The opposition to Thieu developed in cities much more quickly than the PRG's own organizations. Given its united-front heritage and traditional definition of the working class's role in the revolutionary process, its attempt to reach out to those in cities was logical and predictable. It would have been far more successful had the countless sections of the Third Force been able to cooperate in a coherent manner. Its sheer diversity defied the Revolution, even though it was able to establish contact with many of its constituencies.

The PRG was quite prepared to collaborate with these groups as part of the Paris Agreement. The national bourgeoisie, to the extent one existed, had been passive before 1973, but economic hardships galvanized certain elements within the trading middle class, although the Party itself did not appeal to them. Their children, mainly students and intellectuals who were ready to transcend their class origins and make political commitments based on ideas rather than on interests, were much more responsive, and the Revolution's major success was among them. Legal trade unions, which had supported the RVN, been corrupted, and behaved conservatively, nonetheless had a small membership with bread-and-butter interests. The Party made a special effort to contact them and succeeded in doing so on mainly quite narrow economic issues. In the end, workers were the urban group most ready to take physical risks when the war ended, and in certain regards proved the most useful.

By dint of hard work and political flexibility, the Party was able to rebuild a structure in the objectively ripening urban environment after 1972. Its solid core of urban Party members never approached its pre-1968 numbers, largely because Thieu's repression was far more effective. Given the enormous dangers, the Party sought pragmatically to encourage the non-Party but anti-Thieu Third Force to emerge around the transitional coalition politics of the Paris Agreement. The Party itself was unprepared to risk too great a section of its members to urban work, and so it regarded the Third Force as an important complement to its now basically rural emphasis. While it never formally abandoned its commitment to the rural-urban general uprising, it ceased to expect the cities to play a critical, let alone a decisive, military role.

There was unquestionably a radicalizing trend among the urban intelligentsia after 1972, but Vietnamese intellectuals in a political context are no more stable and reliable than intellectuals anywhere, and many were both vacillating and *attentiste,* frustrating the Party and themselves as well. Their sheer numbers, however, could not be ignored in the cacophony of opposition politics, and this compelled the Party to tolerate their idiosyncrasies in the vain hope they might eventually prove more decisive.

By mid-1974 the Party managed to create a substantial presence among a minority of the student organizations, the trade unions, and sundry intellectuals and religious elements. It was never in a position to lead the overt opposition to Thieu—in the end no one could accomplish that task. Because so many in the Third Force were *attentistes* conscious at once of Thieu's growing weaknesses, of their own fragility, and of the immensity of the PRG and the DRV beyond their own finite neighborhood, they too were often ready to touch base with Party fronts, if not with the Party itself. It is a standard characteristic of all wars that the longer they last, the more *attentisme* as a mode of surviving increases. The PRG's strength, therefore, was both real and incipient. The count of its reliable activists in 1975, not necessarily all Party members, may have been as low as five hundred members in Saigon, according to one Party source, with a maximum of ten thousand members and twenty thousand sympathizers probably the highest estimate. One to two thousand people in or deeply involved with the Party is a guess by one key Party leader in Saigon throughout this period, and this seems as reliable a figure as any. Those ready consciously to relate to the PRG exceeded the real militants at least ten- to twentyfold, and so the Party was a serious force without being the leader of the urban political opposition. While its strength and potential in the cities was not directly proportionate to the vacuum that was emerging in the RVN with growing speed after the Paris accords, it had by late 1974 reestablished a significant political existence in the cities. Equally important, it now knew with whom it could work and how much to expect from them. In 1975 it was able to list those non-Party people, including many *attentistes,* who might help before and after its armies entered the cities. As it turned out, they proved to be a major asset.[10]

Chapter 38

The Deepening Crisis of the RVN Social System

THE RVN POLITICAL ORDER UNTIL SUMMER 1974

The RVN's entire military capability depended decisively on the nature and strength of its political and economic order. In wars against revolutionary movements, between social systems and ideologies as well as armies, major changes in either side's social and economic power can critically affect the outcome of the struggle. The United States had been at a grave disadvantage in this part of the contest from the start, but after 1972 its situation became far more precarious, for while it could supply the RVN with military equipment, it had no way to sustain Thieu politically in a situation where the entire anti-Communist effort was no stronger than its weakest link. Politics had been the Achilles' heel of the American war effort since its support of Ngo Dinh Diem and its subsequent need to send in its own forces to save the chaotic regimes of his successors, and the triumph or failure of its monumental effort was still wholly contingent on the ability and role of one man—Nguyen Van Thieu.

The White House at the beginning of 1973 was committed to maintaining Thieu in power. "The attempt to force-feed constitutional government can hazard what little cohesion exists," Kissinger was later to write, by way of justification. He thought it a typically American, maudlin, and erroneous illusion "that a government under siege can best maintain itself by accelerating democratic reform and by expanding its base of support by sharing power," and he endorsed Thieu's authoritarian regime until the end.[1] The problem, however, is that while the RVN proclaimed itself the state in South Vietnam and had all the responsibilities of one, it had no broad social basis or legitimacy, and Thieu had no interest in creating it. He ran the RVN

483

entirely as a political instrument to maintain himself in control. The prerequisites of statehood did not exist, because the RVN, from Diem through Thieu, had always been a successively distinctive but highly person-alized machine whose final mandate and function came from Washington, along with the arms and money to uphold it. Given the specific elitist nature of the RVN and the unstable class structure underneath the small circles in power, the American undertaking had been doomed from the beginning.

White House support was Thieu's most precious asset, and so long as it was translated into adequate material aid, he could sustain the organization keeping him in power. Whatever consensus for Thieu existed had been created not simply by his cunning as a political actor in the Byzantine milieu of rival elites but also by his willingness and ability to divide the spoils of office with a fairly substantial group of loyalists. Thieu was far less greedy than Diem, though he was avaricious enough, but he was plagued after 1972 by insufficient lucre to pass around, and the less there was, the greater his problems. While Thieu had always faced substantial political challenges, these mounted with the decline of funds that encouraged those who had earlier been relatively honest to turn to corruption. In the last analysis the political crisis of the RVN system came from many directions—economic, organizational, and ideological—all merging so that by the summer of 1974 the regime reached an impasse.

Without political or ideological legitimacy, but with economic and ad-ministrative responsibility and power, a state can only increase repression, which in turn will create diverse levels of resistance to defy it. During 1972 and early 1973 Thieu could easily refuse to tolerate the antiauthoritarian Third Forces. Although there were pockets of effective public opposition in Saigon, Thieu's system was still very much a police state. It was less compre-hensive in practice than on paper because the 120,000 policemen and mili-tary courts often were corrupt, somewhat mitigating their brutality, but the legal structure was highly repressive. An August 1972 press law closed fourteen of forty-one papers, and the remainder, including two vaguely opposed to Thieu, were forced to post large bonds with the RVN's censors as security. The power to suspend publication kept the press tame for the next two years insofar as Thieu personally was concerned. Martial law after mid-1972 gave the RVN draconian powers, including that of holding anyone in prison for years without trial for "incitement of neutralism" or "jeopard-izing public safety."[2] Apart from an unknown number already in prison by mid-1972, Thieu's aides acknowledged that at least 40,000 were arrested in the fall of 1972. Many more were rounded up after the Paris signing and charged with common crimes. The number killed outright is unknown. While the exact figures regarding repression are debatable, its overall nature was quite public. Because there were prisons throughout the country and because those outside of Saigon were the most brutal, even the CIA claimed it had lost track of the numbers in them although the United States still had 160 police advisers in South Vietnam in 1973. The issue of political prisoners had been left in abeyance at Paris, beyond a nonbinding proposal to resolve the issue within three months, but it was never settled and the problem only grew with time.

Thieu conceded that he had 32,000 civilian prisoners of every type when the Paris treaty was signed, but the CIA believed the number was much larger. During the first weeks after military prisoner exchanges were to begin, Thieu began to alter the numbers involved and almost brought the entire process to a halt, threatening to abort the return of captured Americans and revealing that he would ignore the Paris commitments as much as possible. At the beginning of February 1973, he claimed to have already freed 20,000 civilian political prisoners, despite the agreement that these releases were to have been verified, and declared himself no longer accountable for their whereabouts. From this point until the war ended, the numbers of political prisoners became a source of endless controversy. Thieu made an accurate accounting impossible, and he persisted in labeling political prisoners as common criminals. The PRG utilized a Third Force committee's figure of 202,000 but never claimed it as its own. The U.S. embassy replied by arguing that the RVN's prisons could hold only 52,000 people, as if that made any difference, asserting there were no more than 1,000 political prisonrs among the 35,000 allegedly in them. It is pointless to guess at the exact number between 35,000 and 200,000, for arrests and releases were constantly occurring. American journalists and Congress fully documented that the number of political prisoners was very large, many of whom suffered torture and terrible abuse. That Thieu ran a repressive police state with Washington's money and technical assistance was beyond any doubt whatsoever. An increasing proportion of those in prison were non-NLF Third Force people.[3]

Thieu's effort to create an administrative structure he could better control paralleled the increased repression after 1972. He first organized his own, semisecret Democracy party in November 1972, and through it Thicu hoped to gain mastery over the state bureaucracy largely as Diem had done with his Can Lao party. Having altered the laws on political parties along with the procedures for village elections in September 1972, his Democracy party was now the only legal national party. During 1973 he revised the constitution so that he could be reelected for another five-year term in October 1975. While he was careful to keep RVNAF officers and police out of his party, he welcomed state officials and civil servants, and it was deluged with ambitious people who eventually presented Thieu with an unanticipated nuisance.

Far more important was his effort to consolidate control over the civil service in much the same way as he had over the senior officers, for they alone possessed skills and residual powers capable of sustaining a serious rival for political power in the RVN system. Often highly educated and from established families with prestige and money, senior civil servants had created a problem for Diem, too, and their share of corruption was very substantial. Ironically, Thieu had greatly enlarged the civil service, and initially it had been an integral part of his machine, but now he was prepared to drive a significant portion of it into the opposition. In July 1973, after obtaining enthusiastic U.S. endorsement, Thieu proclaimed a program for an "administrative revolution." He would give each province chief complete control over all civil servants within his domain, including the power to fire and hire, as well as responsibility for virtually all governmental functions. Decision making was to move from ministries in Saigon to the province chief's office, and the plan scheduled many in Saigon to be transferred to local towns. It was, in effect, a duplication of the RVNAF organization, and apart from the fact that most province chiefs were military officers, Thieu appointed them all. Each, however, was to become the effective political boss of his territory, working directly with local elites and eliminating their need to go to Saigon for action, where they lost both time and money in making required bribes.

Theoretically, the new plan was more efficient, since it removed one level of corruption. In practice, however, it would have guaranteed Thieu a total monopoly of power, with all the strings in the military and civil hierarchies reaching into his office. An organizational transformation of this nature required a fairly long transition if chaos was to be avoided. Thieu appointed one of his colonels to begin its implementation, but until the end of the war the plan existed only as a potentially catastrophic menace to the senior civil service and those under them. Not only were his province chiefs notoriously inefficient and corrupt, netting an average of $100,000 a month according to a *New York Times* report, but by opting for total control Thieu also undermined a crucial segment of past supporters of his power. He surely created the basis of a long, exhausting period of political turbulence, and a few of the abler American advisers saw this most clearly.[4]

Thieu's politics after 1972 became increasingly corrosive to the very efficacy of the huge war machine the United States had given him. His actions were so blatantly self-serving that he placed himself in an extremely assailable position for rivals wishing to defend or enlarge their own interests in the RVN system. Thieu had to protect himself by maintaining the mutual loyalty of key corps commanders and province chiefs. His willingness and obligation to tolerate their corruption grew just when he needed to improve his image against his detractors in RVN circles. As corruption scandals multiplied, they undercut his image but reinforced the devotion of his most venal subordinates. Exposing the corruption of their opponents soon became a means by which aspiring elites began to score points against Thieu and each other. Thieu's assistant for security, Lieutenant General Dang Van Quang, had been publicly accused of opium and rice smuggling, and most of the corps commanders were involved at one time or another in malfeasance. Generals were to have very little time for military affairs throughout the post-Paris period. Indeed, this was the inexorable logic of Thieu's system.

Cracks in Thieu's order were the inevitable outcome of his own vulnerability, the ambitions of those around him, and his own greed for yet more power. The Democracy party quickly attracted a number of climbers under Thieu's assistant and its head, Nguyen Van Ngan, who soon thought the party should dictate government policy. Clashing with Thieu's cousin Hoang Duc Nha, who was also his assistant and architect of the "administrative revolution," Ngan accused him of corruption. The result was a cabinet shift in February 1974 which revealed a huge and largely self-imposed fissure in Thieu's inner circle. The net gainer was Prime Minister Tran Thien Khiem, who had been in the shadows for some years and was now ready to reappear. Nha was ostensibly demoted, but biding his time he eventually had Ngan labeled a Communist agent and fired. Khiem was now consulted on the appointment of province chiefs. By spring 1974 Thieu's unlimited ambitions were backfiring, and politically he was weaker than he had been at any time since 1968.[5]

THE RVN'S DILEMMA OF POLITICAL LEGITIMACY

By spring of 1974 the carefully balanced political world around Thieu was disintegrating, with the military more than ever becoming his principal support while the civilians who had collaborated with him for years increasingly began to jockey to both his left and his right. The sheer diversity and complexity of this mounting opposition, dubbed the Third Force, went far beyond the urban intelligentsia ready to fight for the implementation of the Paris Agreement or the immeasurably larger but wholly unorganized people who wanted peace. Precisely because many of his new adversaries came from among those who had always supported him, Thieu was confronted with a far more dangerous challenge.

His threatening the civil servants was Thieu's major tactical error, because there were enough of them potentially to provide significant numbers to almost any opposition group. Economically under pressure and reduced to demanding higher payoffs for their services, Thieu unsuccessfully tried to mollify them by increasing their salaries on June 1, 1974. It was mainly individuals of this element who were to support a substantial pro-French Third Force which was to re-form around a vague nostalgia which was both anti-American and elitist, but divided as to how to deal with the PRG. The French embassy, instructed to encourage developments which might restore glory to France's civilizing mission, became extremely active. In April 1974 Thieu attacked the Third Force as being a creature not merely of the Communists but also of the "colonialists," from whom it was allegedly receiving money.[6] Much more potent as an opposition were the Catholics, who remained divided between right and left factions.

Thieu had begun to lose support from Catholic elements in 1972. The following year the Vatican endorsed a policy of accommodation with the PRG, stimulating a minority of Catholic "progressives" to become more active on behalf of peace. Far more important was a right-wing resurgence under Father Tran Huu Thanh, one of Diem's close intellectual collaborators and organizer for Nhu, who in June 1974 issued a proclamation against corruption and social decadence signed by 301 priests. Father Thanh was convinced that only a purified state could defeat Communism, and many considered him even more hawkish than Thieu. In contact with diverse aspiring leaders who lived in a heady atmosphere of growing rumor and intrigue, and claiming three thousand senior officers as his former students, Father Thanh became a major opposition figure. Even Thieu's own Democracy party was a magnet for potential opponents; after May 1974 it was run by Tran Van Don, who was born in France and had a long record of conspiracy and opportunism.

Thieu was also in growing difficulty in the provinces. The Hoa Hao sect in the deep south of the Mekong Delta was beginning to reestablish its private army with guns purchased from the ARVN. The need to confront them was a serious matter, compelling Thieu to invade their territory in February 1975. In the strategically vital Central Highlands, as Thieu's minister in charge of them reported later, the Montagnards were becoming restless because ARVN soldiers "stole the chickens and killed the animals, destroyed crops, burned houses and arrested . . . villagers."[7] U.S. experts in Saigon watching these trends were alarmed, for Thieu was for them the foundation of America's effort. As one observer told Senate analysts in May 1974, "if the day ever comes when other Vietnamese believe that Thieu can no longer deliver American aid, he will be finished."[8]

So long as the Third Force was disunited, it was destined to remain only a source of schisms and distraction as well as of demoralization, unable to attract a sufficiently large or critical elite behind it. Since neither the conservative, other opposition tendencies, nor Thieu had a mass basis, it became highly unlikely that any of them could impose its hegemony over the others. The RVN was entering a long period of discord and instability.

For two decades the RVN had scarcely attempted to mobilize the urban population behind its cause. Urban ideology, apart from an ineffectual, shallow rhetoric inculcated in schools and on posters, was a spontaneous result of the consumerism and narcissism which affected the larger part of the city dwellers, especially the youth. Washington's immediate dilemma, however, was that elite politics was the only alternative for the RVN, since there existed no social consensus for Thieu, even though the bulk of the urban population remained circumspect, at least until then, in its attitude toward the Revolution. Thieu, like most such dictators, had power without legitimacy. When this became apparent after mid-1973, it was manifest that his survival was wholly dependent on American money, essential for the backing of the officers and elites who had profited from the system during the fat years. Even more ominous, he still had the increasingly awesome responsibility of keeping the urban masses fed and acquiescent, and to fail to do so was to court their eventual radicalization.

Forging a durable political alternative to the Revolution out of a welter of factions, marginalized elements, self-serving functionaries, and generals presiding over an alienated, passive urban society was wholly impossible. Between 1973 and 1975 the RVN revealed once again the long-standing and the new reasons for the absence of a broadly based non-Communist opposition to the French as well a key source of the ultimate political failure of the long American effort. The concentration of the population into cities accelerated the process of the RVN's disintegration because it was now far more difficult to sustain the social order the United States had created both consciously and by default. The only way to fend off the multiple contradictions of such a system was to buy the loyalty or, much more frequently, the passivity of strategic elites and the urban masses. And this involved the economic viability of the entire American effort.

THE ECONOMIC CRISIS OF A
DEPENDENT ORDER

The RVN fell into a fatal syndrome after 1972 in which its military ambitions gravely undermined its economy, economic failures eroded its already narrow political support, and economic and political trends quickly sapped its military structure. The RVN system was sinking as a total entity. Its most obvious dilemma in 1973 was Thieu's war aims, which carried with them inevitable economic consequences. The funding of the war, obviously, was a key to the attainment of his military goals, and the failure to solve this problem would be a major factor in the RVN's military defeat. There were many ways the RVN could capsize, any one of which would be decisive, but while the economy was a sufficient condition for its eventual demise, over the medium run it constantly exacerbated and compounded a myriad of other problems.

That every conceivable indicator of the economy was down after 1972 was no surprise, but Thieu also had unpredictable bad luck. The urbanized, import-dependent system after 1973 began to dissolve in its overwhelming contradictions despite huge amounts of American aid. While data on the RVN economy are mediocre, there is no dispute about larger trends. Industrial production in 1972 fell slightly below the 1971 peak; it dropped 8 percent in 1973 and 23 percent in 1974. Agricultural output increased even though the country imported 382,000 tons of rice in 1973 and 319,000 tons in 1974, nearly double the amount imported in 1971–72. The economy's basic problem was that over half of the RVN's national product was attributed to services, and over 27 percent of all those employed were in strictly service occupations. This fatal economic distortion, which the United States had created, made the economy largely dependent on the fate of the artificial, urbanized sector. U.S. agencies' employment of Vietnamese fell from 145,000 in 1969, or three times the number of those in manufacturing, to 15,000 by the end of 1973, and official American piaster purchases fell from $347 million in 1969 to $97 million in 1974. Indirect employment—maids, prostitutes, pimps, and such—fell by at least as much.

Inflation proved the most urgent problem, especially to the bureaucracy and the army. Prices in Saigon increased 26 percent in 1972, 45 percent in the next year, and 63 percent in 1974. Far more consequential to an import-dependent nation was the impact of the October 1973 Middle Eastern war on world prices. In 1973 import prices were 35 percent higher than in 1972, and in 1974 they were 53 percent higher than in 1973—that is, they more than doubled in two years. Put another way, U.S. import support programs of every sort came to $591 million in 1972 and $532 million in the following year, rising to $727 million in 1974. Although the RVN imported substantially more in 1974 than in 1971 in dollar terms, the volume of imports in 1974 was only 54 percent that of 1971. The economy went through a traumatic decompression not because of a decline in direct U.S. aid but because the withdrawal of U.S. troops was followed by a world inflation over which neither the RVN nor Washington had any control.

The result was a deepening crisis of the RVN budget, the overwhelming portion of which was directly and indirectly funded by foreign aid. Half of the RVN's budget, which was usually at least 50 percent in deficit, went for military expenses, though with indirect costs the military allocation consumed far more. Employing over 1.4 million people, the RVN saw its budget rise from 19 percent of the GNP in 1960 to 30 percent in 1973. The military's share of the GNP grew from 9 percent to 18 percent over the same period. The RVN's own exports were never more than one-tenth of its imports, and often around one-twentieth. Its domestic revenues came from a general tax on mass-consumption items and imports, which were declining. Taxes on tobacco were far greater than direct income taxes, which corruption made too difficult to collect. By any criterion, the RVN economy was in wretched condition, incapable of sustaining itself. The RVN was unwilling to cut the expenses of the huge bureaucratic machinery and unable to obtain sufficient foreign aid to maintain the economy at anything approximating 1969–71 levels.[9]

These raw measurements cannot convey the flavor of the economic crisis which helped dramatically to accelerate the end of the war. The crisis was felt most sharply in the cities. As inflation forced cutbacks in imports and as layoffs followed, unemployment rose to all-time levels. The AID estimated that one-third of the urban labor force in 1974 was unemployed, surely a conservative figure, and that urban per capita income fell between 36 and 48 percent from 1971 to 1974.

This economic crisis, along with lurid tales of corruption and malfeasance, was the context in which Thieu faced growing urban opposition. How long the political and social fabric could survive was now a fundamental question discussed in conservative circles in Saigon for the first time. In mid-April 1974 an exclusive gathering of key RVN officials and economic policymakers heard Nguyen Huu Hanh, a highly respected senior International Monetary Fund official, assess the future. He expected foreign aid to fall, intensifying the import deficit. At the end of 1974 or early 1975, Hanh predicted, foreign-exchange shortages would force drastic cuts in imports. Then, as someone summarized his prognosis, "economic activities will come to a standstill . . . inflation will get out of control, business and industries stop operation for lack of raw materials, unemployment reach massive proportion and social and political chaos begin."[10]

RURAL VIETNAM AND THE CONSEQUENCES OF DEPENDENCY

While the RVN economy in 1973 was preponderately nonagricultural, the rural economic crisis was even more ominous because any possible remedy for the depression would be found in the countryside or not at all. But the imbalances the U.S.-sponsored economy produced were creating irremediable agrarian structural dilemmas. Apart from the huge labor surplus in the urban areas and an acute shortage in the rural regions, there was the agricultural economy's new dependency on the world economy for imports. The so-called modernization of the rural areas, rather than producing a new class of kulaks who might provide the RVN a social base, created a temporary prosperity which both installed and concealed a systemic vulnerability which in 1973 began to emerge and point toward a catastrophe. Only the end of the war, which this weakness helped to accelerate, prevented it from becoming a full-blown disaster.

The peasants had been encouraged and subsidized to modernize. The RVN drafted their sons, and women, who in 1971 composed nearly three-quarters of all hired agricultural labor, earned more in the Delta than their city counterparts, thereby forcing them to adopt labor-saving innovations. Machinery and pumps, fertilizers and insecticides, along with high-yield rices demanding these intensive capital inputs, left a significant portion of the peasants with varying degrees of debts and fixed costs. Although the continuation of markets for rural output and stable costs of production could doubtless have eventually created kulaks, the inexorable workings of the system first produced overextended peasants ripe for a renewed radicalization.

On the cost side of the peasantry's ledgers, the price of needed inputs had spiraled. Fertilizer became the focus of the peasant's concerns and the symbol of his dilemma. Largely because of U.S. aid, South Vietnam's rural economy used more fertilizer per hectare than did that of any other nation in South or Southeast Asia, and so long as the cultivated area declined but the need for food grew, the AID sponsored this costly policy. The new rice strains the Americans introduced required twice the amount of fertilizers per hectare as traditional rice. During 1972–74 the price of fertilizers in South Vietnam shot up 285 percent, and there was a world shortage. Even exports from the United States were banned during part of 1974 in order to supply American farmers. Despite RVN and U.S. reintroduction of subsidies at the end of 1974, consumption and real imports dropped drastically. As fertilizer use fell, the RVN anticipated a steep decline of output after 1975, which in fact occurred.

Peasants also required fuel for their pumps and machinery, and between 1973 and 1974 fuel oil prices increased 250 percent and those of diesel fuel doubled. To conserve foreign exchange the RVN slashed imports by one-quarter but still ended up with an oil bill twice that of 1973. Kerosene and gasoline consumption, most important to peasants, fell by over one-half in 1974. Overall, costs rose decisively and shifted the terms of trade against the peasants. With ducks beginning to replace imported pesticides and with far less fertilizer and petroleum available to an agricultural system the United States had made absolutely dependent on them, South Vietnam was heading straight toward a rural crisis.

In essence, the RVN was an urbanized system which treated the rural areas as both an afterthought and a necessity, but its ultimate responsibility was to the huge army and bureaucracy linked to the cities, which meant it had to keep the cost of food as low as possible. While it still proved far too high for the army, fear of urban social unrest nonetheless kept food prices far lower than they would have been had the RVN not decided to make the peasants bear a substantial part of the cost of inflation. Balancing the growing alienation of the peasantry against the needs of the remainder of the country was perhaps the greatest long-term political challenge confronting the RVN in late 1974.

While substantially worse off than earlier, the peasants were still better able than the city dwellers to survive the economic crisis. Their most urgent problems were liquidity and adaption to a costly, U.S.-sponsored mode of agriculture. The peasants who had cooperated most with the American programs were now in the worst condition. Many peasants returned to the traditional ways of agriculture burdened with debts and new problems. The decline of credit and markets meant a reappearance of the old land system beginning in 1974.[11]

Though the price of rice rose 143 percent between the end of 1972 and the end of 1974, it was not sufficient to meet the peasants' rising costs. Meanwhile, the world price of rice climbed much more rapidly. Rather than increase the price of domestic rice further and cut its over 300,000 tons of rice imports to encourage production, the RVN preferred to maintain U.S. rice imports as leverage to restrain prices, in effect subsidizing consumers. Its rice war in late 1973, on the other hand, forced the peasants to sell rice at artificially low prices. They retaliated in the second half of 1974 by hoarding rice in preference to selling it for devalued money. A confrontation with the peasantry was inevitable. Meanwhile, the relatively quiescent and increasingly prosperous peasants of the 1969–71 period were once again being subjected to radicalizing pressures.

The rural and food problems could have been solved by the utilization of half a million hectares of the uncultivated rice lands included in the million hectares of unused arable land that the AID's economists claimed existed in 1973. But both RVN and U.S. officials thought it impossible because the PRG controlled most of this territory. The economically most rational solution was rejected in 1974, just as it had been for decades, for political and military reasons.

The other major dilemma was corruption, and its economic costs in 1974 were larger proportionately and probably absolutely. It was, the AID later admitted in its private assessments, "enough to have been a key factor in the 1973–74 recession. . . . Without wishing to down play the effect of declining American aid and support, there is little question that corruption, especially high level corruption, was a critical factor in the deterioration of national morale. . . ."[12] Fertilizer was the most crucial imported input in food production, and the eruption of the fertilizer scandal in April 1974, implicating Thieu's family, his minister of trade, ten province chiefs, and various cronies, revealed the nature of the contradiction. Thieu's brother-in-law and intimate was the key organizer of the affair. Details were made public precisely because Thieu's political enemies knew that this issue made him very vulnerable. Thieu's unlimited avarice in so vital a matter exposed a gangsterism certain to hasten his overthrow.

As world fertilizer prices rose in 1973, the RVN importing agency allowed over two-thirds of it to be diverted outside the official system. It was both hoarded and sold at whatever the market could bear, possibly even exported. Its sales price was at least double the subsidized rate, but most apparently was retained for future speculation. While Thieu's allies managed to suppress most of the details, the affair became the major cause célèbre of 1974, and Thieu could not escape it. Since fertilizer imports in 1973 cost $85 million, far more than that went into his collaborators' pockets.[13]

The French first commercialized the rural economy, the only economic sector capable of supporting South Vietnam, and made it export dependent. The United States later forced an import dependency, leaving it vulnerable to any changes in the world economy or to a decline in aid. French policy had helped the Revolution organize before 1954 because it created an inequitable land system, and the changes the United States imposed had also begun to traumatize the peasantry. The short-lived prosperity required war to fuel it, but it was purchased at the price of the peasants' security and social cohesion. So long as the system worked well, a portion of the peasants was fairly quiescent, and many were prepared to avoid politics and live for the moment, but meanwhile they were being increasingly taxed directly and indirectly by the army. For the U.S.-sponsored formula to succeed, it required stability, which in turn demanded peace and a prosperous market, and neither existed. By 1974 the peasants had the worst of all worlds, being devoid of children and peace as well as of foreign money. They could see only Thieu and his soldiers stealing, prices climbing, and insecurity and disaster looming in the future. By any criterion, operational or human, the rural economy in the south was declining with astonishing momentum. Had the war lasted any longer, even the more affluent peasants would have been ripe for Revolutionary mobilization. They were being forced to reconsider their passivity toward the RVN system and either collaborate with or support the PRG to an extent they had been unable or unwilling to do since 1968.

Compared with the rural structure, the urban economy was far closer to collapse. The immiserization of the cities was advancing at a breathtaking speed. As the war after 1972 made economic issues much more crucial than they had ever been, the Nixon administration had to solve them. To fail would lead to an American defeat far more certain than any on the field of combat.

AMERICAN PLANNERS CONFRONT
THE ECONOMIC CRISIS

The RVN's economic troubles were the irreversible legacy of the traumatizing American presence after 1964, for which no cure existed. The economy's decline caused the political and military situation to deteriorate with it. While U.S. officials dealing with the war tried publicly to maintain a modest optimism, occasionally they admitted, as did the Joint Chief's Admiral Thomas Moorer in February 1974, that Thieu's "primary problem is economic."[14] The effort to deal with it had preoccupied a small number of AID economists, who in turn consulted the government's think tanks and several marginal academics who knew precious little about the topic. The best-placed of them, Harvard's Arthur Smithies, was always a cautious pessimist regarding the RVN's economic future. In 1971 he predicted it would remain dependent on aid for at least one to two decades.

This group of Americans along with the World Bank, which the United States brought into the picture in 1973, charted the RVN's economic future. They premised their analyses on the continuation of military activity at the 1972 level, diminishing over the next several years to "manageable proportions."[15] They understood the difficulty of combining development with optimum mobilization, since it made the RVN dependent on very high levels of aid, but they hoped that the size of the army could be slightly cut when Thieu consolidated power. This core group was aware that the reigning Chinese businessmen would prevent urgent organizational changes in the economy. The clear regression of the RVN economy after 1973 increasingly discouraged them, and their prognosis was therefore dismal.

The RVN's own economic planning was one of the most ominous elements in this situation, for there was no system worthy of the name. Every ministry involved with money was essentially a center of patronage and corruption, and Thieu carefully handpicked those in charge. The economy minister during 1973, Pham Kim Ngoc, was linked to Ly Luong Than, the most important Fukienese in Saigon and a major conduit of funds to Thieu. Although a favorite of the head of the AID and owner of its building in Saigon, Ngoc was blamed for the 1973 inflation and transferred to head the planning commission. He was replaced by a thirty-three-year-old MIT graduate, Nguyen Duc Cuong, who then collaborated with him to mastermind the fertilizer scandal. By the summer of 1974, as one economic official after another was purged for corruption or incompetence, Thieu began to rely on obscure officials who seemed free of taint and whom the AID regarded as even less able than their predecessors. While there was precious little of a guiding economic organization to break down, even this began to occur.

There was no RVN plan, save to obtain foreign aid. Each ministry went to the AID official in charge of its work and negotiated a specific program, then returned to the other ministries to have their U.S.-endorsed activities collectively merged into a "plan." Since the AID itself had no plan, but only a budget from Washington, it regarded this procedure with horror. "The lack of leadership came to be regarded as an extremely serious matter," it wrote later; ". . . it became difficult to get action on important measures. When action was taken, it was liable to be so late that circumstances were already dictating an alternative course. . . ."[16]

This economic bureaucracy paralleled Thieu's military organization, both being private machines in his power structure. Increasingly concerned, American economic experts, who did not have the competence themselves to draw up a plan to impose on the RVN, in 1973 asked the World Bank and the IMF to assess the situation. The bank learned that the RVN was able to draw up sectoral programs but unable to coordinate a single plan, and even that left "much to be desired."[17] Indeed, it found it impossible to project future economic development without high aid levels. The RVN would still need, bank experts predicted, $770 million in aid in 1980 (more than it seemed likely to get in 1974) and $450 million in 1990.

The RVN's only concrete strategy was to receive aid indefinitely, and that was a purely political calculation. This was all the more dangerous because, unlike military aid, which the RVN could adapt to by reducing the fighting, economic aid had to increase in volume in order to keep pace with a rapidly deteriorating situation. Attempting to compensate for the decline of piaster purchases for U.S. military activities during the war, the AID did in fact manage to increase economic aid to the RVN, from $502 million in fiscal 1973 to $653 million in 1974 ($727 million if the piaster procurements are included, making it the third-highest year for economic aid). Adjusted for inflation, of course, this amount bought far less. The problem was that neither the U.S. Congress nor the White House itself was willing to pay for the disastrous economic conditions they and their chosen surrogate had imposed on the RVN. The sums required to implement the administration's policy to keep Thieu in power and his army both large and active were far greater than anything it ever requested. The White House instead sought to improvise by seeking funds from new sources.

The Johnson administration had discussed using international banks to provide economic aid to the RVN, and early in 1973 its successor moved to implement this strategy. The AID hoped that the World Bank and the Asian

Development Bank might supply from one-third to one-half of the RVN's requirements within two to three years. The ADB and several countries, Japan and France especially, had increased their grants and loans to the RVN, from $33 million in 1970 to $168 million in 1973, and slightly more the following year. These sums aided the RVN substantially. The impressive success of the strategy encouraged Washington. In principle, the administration preferred that a World Bank–led consortium assume responsibility for all economic aid since this would not only enlarge funding but also sanctify aid among liberals in Congress. It also offered an alternative should Congress attempt to reduce its direct aid, and a method of avoiding congressional control over foreign policy that it was subsequently to use in Latin America. The bank immediately began to examine the RVN's economy, and its two confidential reports, which gave a portrait of a sick economy without a plan, indicated that for political reasons the bank would provide funds merely to remedy the chronic payments deficit.

Such schemes immediately ran into time-consuming difficulties which proved fatal. The bank's members were divided, and virtually every one of its private documents quickly fell into the hands of antiwar activists, whose revelations interfered with speedy action. More important, the United States in July 1973 made its allotment of $1.5 billion in renewed aid to the bank's soft-loan affiliate, the International Development Association, contingent on the bank's agreement to create a consultative group and an IDA loan to the RVN. Congress, as usual, delayed the IDA appropriation until July 1974, and until then the bank postponed any action on the RVN in the hope of goading the Americans to allocate the money. When the bank again met the following October to resume the effort, *Le Monde* published full details of its confidential discussions, causing yet more embarrassing delays until the war ended. Had U.S. plans succeeded, at least $200 million from non-American sources would have gone to the RVN in 1975. The failure to finalize bank aid during 1974 was important psychologically in Saigon.

Far more curious and quixotic were fantasies of saving the RVN from disaster with the help of oil. U.S. companies had explored Vietnam's offshore area in the late 1960s and found it geologically promising. During 1971 publicity in the antiwar movement and Congress discouraged a number of companies. The RVN wanted foreign investment, however, and it knew oil was the only way to attract it. In the summer of 1973 it asked for bids but received far fewer acceptable offers than it had expected. In May 1974, after the oil price hike, it reopened bidding. Altogether it received $47 million in signature bonuses, but not until November 1974 did anything tangible result from the drilling, and the exception was neither definite nor highly promising. Objectively, there was no justification for the RVN's oil fever, and it was to serve only as a measure of the growing desperation of Saigon and Washington.

The AID helped to fan the enthusiasm, and as the economy declined, hopes for oil rose. Smithies's assessments began to include references to possible oil. In the summer of 1974 AID began intimating that economic aid was justified because oil would in five years reduce or even eliminate future need for it. During its final appeals to Congress for aid in early 1975, the State Department and the Pentagon held out the promise that oil would come to the rescue. Throughout the final months of the RVN's existence, its leaders fervently believed that oil would fend off disaster, supplementing and even replacing all aid and also building a powerful bloc of supporters in the United States: "We must rely on Shell, Mobil and Esso and their anti-Communism," as one elated official remarked.[18] When the first trace of oil was discovered in August 1974, Thieu was exuberant. The illusion, as one of Thieu's closest aides put it, "that the discovery of oil might hold the magic power to solve all the country's economic problems," only increased with the mounting despair.[19] Instead, it merely further encouraged catastrophic policies, deepening the RVN's endemic inability to confront reality. In the surreal atmosphere which every disintegrating nation generates, belief in the promise of salvation by oil was only an exotic manifestation of a moribund culture.

Chapter 39

Saigon and Washington, Mid-1974: The Conjunction of Two Crises

THE CRISIS IN WASHINGTON

Watergate, the most traumatic American political experience in over a century, profoundly influenced the entire spectrum of U.S. foreign policy. As the administration's room for maneuvering shrank, it was tactically unable to rally support for its policies, or even to think about them after spring 1974. But its real problem was that most of its global difficulties were inherited and insoluble under any conditions. Watergate was not the cause of the crisis of executive power and political legitimacy in the United States, much less of that in Saigon. That crisis was only partly the effect of the increasingly closed and manipulative structure of policy formulation and implementation which had been created in the period after 1946 and applied to its extreme degree in Vietnam. The confrontation in executive-congressional relations was not primarily the result of the massive deceptions that had accompanied that foreign policy process, for Congress was fully capable of acquiring basic information if it chose to do so. Rather, what was originally a consensual bipartisan foreign policy not only was failing but also gravely interfered with a rational allocation of limited resources to other domestic and foreign needs. By 1973 the most important residues of two decades of collaboration between the presidency and Congress were the decision-making powers concentrated in a White House whose only justification for them, the efficacy of the system in advancing the national interest, was now patently false and unconvincing. Watergate became Congress's chosen vehicle for redressing the imbalance between itself and the institution

499

of the presidency, and it thereby speeded a conflict that had begun under Johnson in 1968 and has continued to this day.

Even without Watergate there would have been a crisis in executive-congressional relations. Watergate erupted simultaneously with Thieu's gravest dilemmas, but it was surely not their cause. The executive naturally became vulnerable more quickly because of Nixon's difficulty with Watergate and his moralistic but tainted Vice-President, but essentially the cause was Nixon's attempt to take the inherited presidential powers beyond the permissible limit at a tactically inopportune moment. He was goaded into doing so primarily by his own consummate desire for power and dislike for the constraints of the constitutional system, but also by the unquenchable ambition of Kissinger, whose open disdain for the opinions of others and unconcealed desire to monopolize foreign policy decision making guaranteed that the legacies of Watergate would continue after Nixon resigned on August 9, 1974, bequeathing Thieu a fatally weakened but crucial ally in Washington. As Watergate consumed the President's attention, Kissinger attempted to dominate all the means of directing foreign policy. Adroitly squeezing the passive William Rogers out as secretary of state at the end of 1972, arranging only that he serve as a lame duck for six months, Kissinger by the summer of 1973 was unprecedentedly both secretary of state and national security adviser. His efforts to eliminate all other influences on the distracted President helped accelerate Nixon's political demise and build hostility toward Kissinger as the personification of overweening executive authority.

During 1973 and 1974 Kissinger virtually eliminated the foreign policy advisory committees of key business and establishment leaders, which in the past had won well-placed supporters for preceding administrations. By late 1973 Nixon had alienated his business backers to a remarkable extent, as he retreated to isolation and dependency on a handful of people. Refusing to decentralize even the most trivial details, publicly vain and contemptuous of critics, Kissinger was very much a part of Nixon's problem. He confessed his own failings sufficiently often to undercut his appeals for the reemergence of a foreign policy consensus ready to accept "the substance" but ignore "the procedure" of his diplomacy and thereby confirm his virtual control of foreign policy.[1] In January 1975 he thought the world was at a "watershed" of "chaos" in international relations. In one of his final press conferences, he appealed for toleration of men "as confused as I was" but "grappling with events emerging from a fog of confusing reports and putting forward policies which they believe to be right, but which they cannot *know* to be right until the time for decision is past."[2] So long as Nixon was in office, many congressmen saw Kissinger as a useful inhibition; the moment he quit, however, Kissinger increasingly became the focus of Congress's hostility, denounced for his "one-man authoritarianism" and for having placed himself "above the dictates of law" while pursuing a foreign policy of "bribes, false promises and gesticulations."[3]

From early 1973 until the time Nixon left office, the White House sought to deny Watergate's impact on the conduct of foreign policy in order "to salvage anything," but the administration was increasingly on the defensive.[4] At the beginning of 1974, as Nixon later recounted, the preceding eight months had seemed "brutal," "an endless cycle of blows and rallies followed by further blows." He added, "Now I was reduced to analyzing my situation in the stark terms of the possibilities of simple survival."[5]

It was not only the restoration of congressional power, especially the passage of the War Powers Act during October 1973, and Watergate that created the large crisis in American power in the world at the end of 1973. The October 1973 Middle Eastern war and oil embargo compelled it to reconsider the benign neglect and ad hoc improvisations which had become the basis of its policies. This was all the more true because the economic jolt of the oil price increase was overwhelming. Prices in the United States rose 6.2 percent in 1973, almost twice as much as in the preceding year and the most since 1948, but in 1974 they shot up by 11.0 percent. The 1975 budget deficit, beginning July 1974, was $71 billion, the largest in history and equivalent to all the deficits since 1960 combined.

Growing economic problems and foreign policy dilemmas intersected. The year 1973 also marked the beginning of a new stage in the strategic-arms race, ostensibly because of the Soviet development of new missiles, and the administration still desired to attempt once again to define and construct a superior conventional, local-war capability. These persistently frustrated aspects of American defense policy required funding even under normal circumstances, but the impact of inflation on weapons procurement was disastrous, causing the price tag of existing major programs to leap $17 billion in the three months ending in June 1974. Something, in brief, would have to be cut.[6]

Vietnam in this context dropped out of the administration's sight, to be dealt with by lower-level officials without final power. Vietnam policy did not and could not adapt to changing circumstances, for the White House had a vast number of intersecting challenges, all far more urgent, ranging from the survival of the presidency to the health of the economy and the future of American power in Europe and the Middle East. Even without Watergate these issues would have demanded all of its time and budget priorities. When Nixon resigned and Gerald Ford replaced him, the new President had neither the time nor the predilection to confront Congress on

Vietnam or, indeed, on any other issue. His secretary of state, whom many regarded as a discredited remnant of a bankrupt past, ceased to have any significant influence over events.

. . . AND IN SAIGON

The RVN was by mid-1974 politically and economically brittle. The volume of aid in no way explains its political weaknesses; its real economic dilemma was intrinsic in the countless structural distortions the United States had built into the RVN system over a decade. Its military fragility was the consequence of a collapsing army, underpaid and without morale, which traumatized the peasants, who increasingly turned against the RVN and toward the Revolution. Given also the other American dilemmas, it was certain that the balance of forces in Vietnam by the summer of 1974 had tilted overwhelmingly against the RVN, and it would not take much more to shatter its institutional layers and create fatal political traumas and economic upheavals. Nixon's demise obviously hurt Thieu, and though Watergate was not the decisive element, it intensified Thieu's difficulties at a point where he could least afford more.

THE STRUGGLE OVER MILITARY AID TO THE RVN

Thieu's order had too many fundamental human and organizational weaknesses for money alone to cure, but American military aid was one of the crucial factors influencing the pace of events in South Vietnam. The Revolution's defensive military policies during 1973 and 1974 had misleadingly concealed the huge and growing disparity between the military successes and the underlying weaknesses of the ARVN. Meanwhile, the annual question of military aid to the RVN remained the residual issue defining the relationship of the administration to Thieu. It was all the more disturbing to the dictator because the White House also sought desperately to focus on policy issues elsewhere in the world and reassign Vietnam a lower priority in its concerns.

The sheer complexity of military aid to the RVN guaranteed that it would remain a contentious issue, and it was a nightmare both to accountants and to lawyers skilled in such matters. This fact alone increasingly distressed the Pentagon and infuriated Congress, including many members who favored the sustaining of aid, which even under normal circumstances rightfully believed that the Constitution guaranteed it control over the budget. The heart of the problem was that the RVN's military aid funds for years had come directly from the budgets of the Army, Navy, and Air Force, labeled MASF. The normal source of military aid to nations, under which they received no more than Congress allotted, was the wholly independent and visible Military Assistance Program (MAP). Under the MASF there were innumerable devious ways the White House could obtain funds should Congress fail to appropriate them or should the RVN need more. Reliance on the MASF proved to be a major administration error.

The State Department in early 1973 wanted to see the military aid program transferred to the MAP. The Pentagon was indifferent, though sections of it were increasingly concerned that should aid exceed the amounts Congress approved, it would be taken out of their other programs. The White House opted firmly for keeping aid under the MASF. In 1973 it was policy simply to pay for what was actually being spent, and by the end of the year the administration, prodded by Ambassador Graham Martin in Saigon, reluctantly returned to Congress for supplemental aid to the $1.126 billion ceiling Congress had imposed on an initial request of $1.560 billion.

The RVN's extravagance became entangled with Martin's irritating and counterproductive lobbying for greater aid and forced a subtle new realignment within the administration on the military aid question just as the overall U.S. military budget was undergoing a serious crisis of priorities. Martin's penchant for exaggeration and didactic lectures to the White House and State Department managed quickly to polarize Washington's decision makers. At the end of 1973 he asked for $494 million to supplement the miltiary aid commitment for the remaining six months of fiscal 1974, arguing that it was the "minimum safety position" against alleged Communist capabilities and aggressive intentions.[7] Apart from the fact that both the CIA and the Pentagon had carefully examined the Party's Resolution 21 and that neither thought an offensive likely, Thieu's military spending by the end of 1973 was already exceeding even the $1.6 billion ceiling for which the administration, after some hesitation, decided to ask Congress in January. Munitions usage, particularly, was again increasing. More disturbing, Martin, indifferent to the RVN's ability to absorb new equipment and manage its existing stocks, was also aggressively pushing for a $1 billion list of advanced equipment to supplement the regular aid budget. Having grossly underestimated Vietnam spending and now needing to fund it from its rising obligations elsewhere, the Pentagon was losing control of it to the embassy.

Martin's want list included over $500 million for F-5Es to replace existing models and much greater sums for munitions. His 1974 supplemental request was largely for just these two items. The Pentagon believed that new equipment given to the RVN would be a total loss and that the ARVN's most immediate problem was to learn how to use what it already had on hand, much of which was still in crates. "DAO," the comptroller general

reported on its policies until 1974, "with minor exceptions, was replacing all
ARVN losses and turn-ins, without regard to whether the equipment was
needed or qualified for replacement under the terms of the cease-fire agreement."[8] The head of the DAO, Major General John E. Murray, also shared
Martin's passionate commitment to aiding Thieu, but an important section
of the Pentagon was quickly losing its toleration for the ambassador's grandiose, costly projects. Reports of astonishing waste of military equipment
reached Washington with increasing frequency. When it was confirmed that
ARVN generals were selling huge quantities of brass from shell casings as
scrap, the Pentagon insisted that the ARVN curtail use of munitions, since
it was exceeding both available funds and stocks. Allegedly scarce helicopter
components, too, ended up on the scrap-metal market during 1974, much to
the horror of officials in Washington. As Congress considered the 1974
supplemental during spring 1974, the Pentagon, unquestionably goaded by
Martin and Murray with false alarms concerning RVN resources and DRV
threats, discreetly confessed that the ARVN would require large numbers
of civilian advisers indefinitely. Even so, it could not use a substantial part
of the equipment it already had. Nor did the RVN have enough pilots for
the planes on hand, and those it had were not overly competent. Even
members of Congress sympathetic to Thieu were now eager to reassert
control over the budget process, for although Congress had refused to pass
the supplemental aid, the Pentagon still had given the RVN at least $1.4
billion in military aid by June 30. Trapped by White House pressure and the
excesses of its own personnel in the DAO in Saigon, the Pentagon now
reached a tacit consensus with Congress. It, too, was prepared to reduce
military aid to the RVN.

While the Pentagon's quiet but critical shift against high levels of military aid to the RVN partly reflected its realistic assessment of the RVNAF,
it was mainly the result of the overall crisis of military spending which
followed in the wake of the vertiginous 1973–74 inflation. Beginning with
Laird, the Pentagon had been forced to choose between the war in Vietnam
and its other needs, resulting in a scarcely noticed but de facto alliance with
the growing anti-aid coalition in Congress.

The Pentagon argued that its real spending in 1973 was $34 billion less
than in 1968. Because over half of its budget was committed to inflexible
salaries and only one-quarter to new weapons, inflation caused havoc on this
discretionary share of its funds. Fighting within and between services for
funds, always traditional, was never fiercer than during 1974. With the
Soviets allegedly outspending the United States by huge margins in research,
procurement, and strategic nuclear offensive forces, the federal budget in the
deepest deficit in history, and the President opposed to any increases in
military spending and committed to cutting the federal budget by $5 billion,

the setting for the debate over more aid to the RVN was hardly propitious. The conservatives in Congress, even more than antiwar liberals, were now on the side of fiscal restraint, and it was in the context of huge congressional slashes of all Defense Department funds, reaching up to $5 billion in the conservative-dominated Senate Appropriations Committee during August, that aid to the RVN was considered. The President's incapacity was far less important than the financial pressures on Congress and the Pentagon alike.[9]

The administration initially requested $1.6 billion in 1975 in military aid as a bargaining figure, but Martin thought $1.45 billion absolutely essential. He and Murray lobbied for it in Washington after April, alienating important potential allies. At the request of the Senate Armed Services Committee, Schlesinger sent Erich von Marbod, his ablest civilian logistics expert, to Saigon to examine the RVN's real situation. In May the Pentagon asked Murray to project what might happen to the RVN should money be cut back to various levels. Murray and Martin decided to outline a variable sequence of ominous scenarios should sums fall below $1.45 billion, and at $750 million they predicted the division of the country and inevitable calamities. Von Marbod, meanwhile, found that the ARVN had vast stocks of artillery and routine munitions, approximating the huge January 1973 levels, and was indifferent about conserving it. Much of its gasoline was going into the black market. The ARVN, Martin was told, was too profligate. Murray had managed only to again irritate rather than to convince the Pentagon, and von Marbod reported that the aid request was unnecessarily high. The key conservatives in the Senate were given the facts and told that in case of shortages the Pentagon would request a supplemental. The Pentagon now expected the RVNAF to accept a budget adequate for an efficient, well-managed army utilizing only equipment it could operate and maintain itself. The conservatives in Congress accepted the new approach as consistent with their larger reductions of the national budget. It was this reasoning, not the antiwar minority of both houses or the President's resignation, that shifted the attitude of Congress decisively.

On August 5 a House and Senate conference imposed a $1 billion military aid limit on the RVN for fiscal 1975. One member then proposed an amendment to cut it another $300 million, and various conservatives asked the Pentagon for its opinion and received only the enigmatic response that "the military situation is far from critical."[10] The Pentagon did not lobby to keep the $300 million, which was thus removed by a large majority. The Senate came within three votes of cutting an additional $150 million. Everyone close to the issue understood that the Pentagon wanted the money for more pressing needs, and since these were permanent, the aid reductions were likely to be also.

That the Pentagon was as eager as Congress to remove the potential and real RVN millstone from around its neck was also apparent from its strong support for the switching of aid from the MASF to the MAP, which was passed to begin fiscal 1976. Accounting complications delayed an immediate transfer. In the interim it introduced its own unified account for 1975, making covert aid from thirteen funds, as in the past, much more difficult. The aid law also substantially decreased the numbers of U.S. military and civilian personnel allowed in South Vietnam, but the Pentagon far exceeded the required reduction of its own volition, cutting the number of American civilian contract employees by over half during the latter part of 1974. More onerous, the Pentagon then slashed $110 million from aid to pay for shipping, the DAO's expenses, and a variety of bills it usually covered from other funds, including undelivered items from earlier budgets. All told, the RVN now had under $500 million in uncommitted funds for operational needs.[11]

Murray in Saigon had made numerous enemies in the course of this battle, and since he was eligible for retirement, the Pentagon chose to recall him. Before leaving Saigon, he publicly denounced Congress for its cuts until the Pentagon muzzled him. Returning to Washington, he unsuccessfully attempted to persuade the Pentagon to cancel its deductions. Meanwhile, one of his fellow senior officers anonymously attacked the Pentagon as "fiscal whores" for further reducing the $700 million by one-third "for stuff we didn't want, didn't need or didn't expect to be charged against aid."[12] Thieu had lost a friend not simply in the White House but in the Pentagon as well, which further reduced his popularity with Congress.

"News of U.S. military aid cutbacks propagated through the RVNAF hierarchy with the effect of a gigantic concussion bomb," one senior ARVN general recalled.[13] Thieu's most pressing immediate problem, therefore, was not military but political. The myth of Nguyen Van Thieu was shattered in Saigon, for he no longer infallibly controlled the American cornucopia. The effort to deal with this dimension of the military aid reduction was to preoccupy the RVN until the last days before its fall, adding immeasurably to the political and psychological malaise.

THE RVN'S ECONOMY ENTERS ITS FINAL THROES

During the late summer of 1974 the handful of responsible American economists and aid officials initiated a major reassessment of the RVN economy's rapidly declining condition. In September RVN released its 1975 budget; its implications were ominous. The 1974 budget had been planned for VN$561 billion but ended at VN$720 billion, which accelerated the rampant inflation. RVN officials fixed the 1975 budget at VN$825 billion, while AID experts were confident it would reach at least VN$975, about two-thirds of which would be deficit. Since it was impossible to find $1.5 billion in foreign aid to fill this void—total economic aid from all sources in 1974 was already a huge $913 million—the American advisers confronted the prospect of reliance on the printing presses sharply to increase the money supply.

Unlike its military situation, the RVN's economic perspective and crisis constantly affected the entire nation and, ultimately, the military balance. The AID mission had the responsibility of coping with the phenomenon in large part because Thieu and his ministers would not. The United States had always stepped in to save the situation, and Thieu fully expected this to occur in the economic as well as the military realm. So, too, did his supporters, and he needed aid to retain their backing, particularly after the military aid cuts. The AID's experts, on the other hand, now expected runaway inflation and profound economic instability in 1975. In the fall of 1974 they made a comprehensive general review of the RVN economy in the hope of finding solutions.

The AID consulted its advisers and the IMF. While they could agree on the nature of the problem, they disagreed strongly on the solutions. Smithies and Rand Corporation experts thought the piaster had been devalued too rapidly, but the IMF, applying its standard recipe for every nation, wanted much more rapid devaluation (to encourage exports and discourage imports), a balanced budget, and even a reduction in the size of the army. These differences, along with the sheer magnitude of the challenge, discouraged the AID from further attempts to resolve the RVN's economic dilemma.

During October, Smithies publicly and privately described the RVN's economy as being in a "state of deep depression."[14] While AID officials in Washington quite sincerely told Congress that chaos would occur in the economy if it did not grant sufficient funds, its experts in Saigon now confronted the fact that the accumulated structural problems bearing down heavily on the RVN far transcended the probable level of funding. "By the end of 1974," the AID wrote shortly thereafter in its internal assessment, "virtually all of the best efforts of the policy-makers were on the verge of being undone by the combined effects of world-wide inflation and declining real aid levels."[15] Total incompetence among the RVN's officials aggravated the problem. In an exhaustive report on the RVN economy at the end of 1974, the AID in Saigon predicted that "1975 may, by comparison, soften the memory of the 1973–74 period."[16] Privately, the AID's keenest analysts in Saigon felt the end was near: "The dimensions of a potential monetary disaster were becoming clear to all before the fall of Phuoc Long [January 6, 1975]."[17] They expected 1976 and 1977 to produce untold crises. This vision of imminent, portentous economic events pervaded the entire RVN political structure as well.

While Congress had reduced military aid drastically, there was initially no reason in the summer of 1974 to believe that economic aid would suffer the same fate. The first administration proposal had been for $600 million, linked to a five-year plan for which it unsuccessfully sought to win congressional acquiescence. It raised the request to $750 million plus $150 million in PL-480 food surpluses—a generous sum but still far less than the RVN needed. When the bill reached various committees, they attached drastic riders to it, and the administration decided to defer passage until after the November elections. Meanwhile, it funded aid to the RVN at 1974 levels on a "continuing resolution" basis. Time was initially not crucial, but time nonetheless treated the RVN badly.

Kissinger, distracted by myriad other problems but unwilling to delegate responsibility for dealing with Congress to his assistant secretary for congressional relations, was part of the problem as his rapport with the legislative branch fell to an all-time low. Not until mid-December did Congress appropriate a maximum of $575 million in aid to the RVN, or far less than the amount needed to postpone the breakdown the AID was predicting. Even then the necessary authorization was postponed until March 24, 1975, when, as the regime was collapsing, the sum was slashed to $446 million. In effect, congressional delays allowed the administration to sustain the RVN at 1974 levels during the critical final half year of the war. Had the RVN not been defeated militarily, it would have confronted a drastic cut in absolutely imperative aid and the AID's worst expectations would have been realized no later than 1976.[18]

SAIGON'S POLITICAL CRISIS AND THE ADMINISTRATION'S RESPONSE

The erosion of Thieu's political stability, which had begun earlier in 1974, the outcome of his threats against the civil service as well as worsening urban economic and social conditions, reached crisis proportions by late summer, and political stresses within the RVN were increasingly to dominate its final months of existence. More and more of the elite that had supported Thieu until then sought to find salvation by turning against the military dictator. During its two decades the RVN had experienced intense periods of infinitely complex political machinations and possibilities, exhausting both to those involved and to the Americans. The last half of 1974 was perhaps the most convoluted of them all.

It is impossible to chart the intricate combinations and plots that emerged throughout this time. The dominant characteristic of the serious new opposition was that it was now largely from those within Thieu's own ideological orbit, and it included not just senior civil servants but an increasing number of senior officers who were now conscious that he no longer had the ability to open the American cornucopia of military and economic aid. Congressional reduction of military aid galvanized sufficient skepticism toward Thieu within the highest ranks of the ARVN to require him to focus all of his energies on stabilizing his power. As rumors abounded, many of them unquestionably well founded, Thieu sought first to neutralize the growing accusations of corruption that Father Thanh had initiated the preceding June. Such charges reemerged in early September in the form of a highly specific indictment, signed by three hundred priests, itemizing Thieu, his family, and friends' personal involvement in corruption and chicanery, ranging from fertilizer speculation and the heroin trade to rice price manipulation. Senior political figures, including Tran Van Lam, Thieu's former foreign minister, General Cao Van Vien of the JGS, and Tran Quoc Buu, head of the trade unions and closely linked to the CIA, now weaved in and out of the heady intrigues, ready to exploit the corruption issue as a convenient foil. Father Thanh's movement, however, was the most visible center of opposition, but since it attracted an array of known opportunists and former Diemists and since the worldly cleric had managed to create an alliance with Nguyen Cao Ky, its effectiveness was limited.

At face value, Thieu's handling of the challenges to him was deft: he made some superficial concessions to his critics and weeded out possibly disloyal elements in his administration. In mid-September he replaced six province chiefs whose allegiances he questioned, and while promising greater freedom of the press, he cracked down on those papers that printed Father Thanh's accusations. In a public response to the detailed charges of personal corruption on October 1, Thieu lamely replied, "There is a little something that has been exaggerated."[19] While his critics saw this as an admission, in fact Thieu rightfully felt that many of those seeking to oust him had records that left them vulnerable to charges of dishonesty. Corruption had been built into the RVN since its inception, and Thieu was not about to go on the defensive. But the system's inability either to pay for peculation or to survive without it was now very much a part of his problem.

On October 24 Thieu fired four of his cabinet ministers, only two of whom had been charged with graft, and dismissed 377 field-grade officers, none of them generals, from the army. More important, he removed three of his four military corps commanders, installing them in the military academies. The most crooked of the three, General Nguyen Van Toan of "cinnamon" fame, was brought back as head of the crucial MR III the following February, when Thieu further consolidated control over the army and police commands. For the remainder of 1974 and the RVN's existence, Thieu was able to fend off his challengers. He retained virtually all of his thoroughly corrupt, sufficiently loyal underlings, in part because of the careful way he had established and maintained his machine since 1968, but primarily because of his American sponsorship. In the end, his fate and that of the United States were inextricable.

The political crisis in Saigon after mid-1974 presented the administration with ample headaches but few opportunities. The background and motives of Thieu's conservative detractors left too many doubts about what they would or could do if they assumed power. It was the responsibility of the U.S. mission in Saigon to follow the Byzantine political events which emerged after May; thanks to its electronic listening devices throughout Thieu's palace, it was privy to his most private affairs. While there can be no doubt that some officials, especially in the CIA, favored Thieu's removal, they were unable to alter the existing policy but were sufficiently conspicuous to attract a great deal of notice. Martin himself rather equivocally went on public record during July as being against the elimination of Thieu, but should it occur, he added, he did not believe the turmoil would prove more than temporary. While Martin never turned against Thieu, he believed it imperative to bring competent people into his government and retain those already there. He openly supported Chau Kim Nhan, the finance minister and a particularly competent technocrat, but as rumors of an American-backed change mounted and Nhan was reputed to be the heir apparent, Thieu singled him out for retirement. When he fired four ministers in late October, Nhan was one of them even though he had never been accused of corruption. Once it became clear that Thieu would resist, Martin and most senior Americans in Saigon preferred a peaceful transition, possibly by means of the late 1975 presidential election, to a fatal split within the anti-Communist elite. But since Thieu controlled the only legal party, the RVN's political future appeared extremely complex.

Kissinger, in particular, opposed policy innovations, and that was sufficient to prevent them. In effect, the administration undercut Thieu's position, because while it would not actively support a rightist challenge to Thieu, it did far too little to discourage it. Because the RVN's entire destiny until then was the outcome of American actions and guidance, the very fact of its apathy confronted Thieu with unprecedented political pressures from his former supporters. Worse yet, several members of the U.S. Senate publicly advocated alternatives to Thieu. By early October they were openly criticizing the White House for its failure to formulate a clear policy on the RVN's political future. Kissinger, overwhelmed by Watergate's legacies and busy gathering in his own hands all the cords controlling foreign policy, publicly regretted that "so much of the time had to be spent on the Viet-Nam war" in the past, and he was hardly inclined to return to it.[20] He knew as well as anyone that the options were likely to prove infinitely time-consuming as well as equally unsatisfactory in coping with the economic and military realities facing the RVN. More realistic about the balance of forces in South Vietnam than were his more adventuresome subordinates in the CIA and the State Department, Kissinger did not wish to appear as if he were unceremoniously abandoning Thieu, as Kennedy had dropped Diem. An orderly transition appealed to him, but a coup did not. Every consideration favored maintaining the status quo.

The problem, however, was that during October and November the CIA and many lower-ranking members of the embassy continued to make sufficient disparaging comments about Thieu to keep open the possibility of a new regime, encouraging local opposition. Some of the CIA's most senior Vietnam specialists arrived in Saigon during September and October to renew contacts with key opposition figures. Journalists with long experience became aware of the policy options they were considering, particularly focusing on the CIA's Tran Quoc Buu as a likely successor, if not by means of an immediate shuffle then perhaps during the October 1975 election. The efforts of ultimately powerless Americans to explore alternatives greatly undermined Thieu's alliance, and on October 21 the embassy issued a strong statement denying it supported any opposition group and renewed its commitment to Thieu. The following day Martin made an unprecedented visit to Chau Kim Nhan's office in an open, and unsuccessful, effort to prevent Thieu from firing him. The rumor mills therefore kept turning, politically undercutting Thieu. Trying to maintain all options, the administration had worked itself into an ambiguous position just as Congress was reducing the RVN's military and economic aid funds. Its apathy and incompetence had seriously embarrassed Thieu at a moment when he could least afford it. For the first time in the history of the war, Washington was following a passive strategy in Vietnam, content to allow events to bypass it. It was an ambiguous stance, ripe for frustration and ignominious failure.[21]

Thieu was now left exposed to his fickle friends and supporters, whose commitment to him declined along with the volume of American aid. The rightist opposition by itself had not been formidable, because it had no mass base and very little credibility. Its most prominent members were tainted, dispossessed politicians, ambitious generals, and dubious claimants to the mantle of purity. But the CIA's and the embassy's flirtations with them, and the open conspiracies against Thieu, had hurt Thieu nearly as much as Congress's reduction of military and economic aid. Thieu did not conceal his anxieties regarding American designs. Since the administration merely preferred to avoid a distracting crisis, it finally decided that the easiest way to do so was to make some symbolic gesture of support for Nguyen Van Thieu. In practical terms, this meant to restore his image among officers and functionaries as a personality who could still obtain money from Washington. When the White House initiated this effort as a supplemental aid request in January 1975, it had no idea how large and dangerous an undertaking it was embarking on. For just as its casual flirtation with change in Saigon proved more destabilizing than unwavering support for Thieu and his corruption, so too would its failure of the test of its ability to raise small sums for Thieu threaten to produce far greater demoralization in the American-backed system in South Vietnam.

Chapter 40

The Revolution's Perceptions and Plans, Late 1974

By the summer of 1974 the magnitude of the RVN's political and economic stresses had begun to transcend the Communist Party's analytic grasp. The entire RVN structure was losing strength far more rapidly than the Revolution was gaining it, and the latter most influenced the Party's dominant perceptions. Clearest of all it saw the balance of military power, which it could easily measure in terms of land controlled and combativity of RVNAF forces. But the speed, complexity, and intensity of Thieu's decline after late 1973 had no precedent, and few of the Party's leaders fully comprehended it.

Up to a point, certain aspects of the RVN's descent were obvious. The economic trends were clear, and the Party discussed them very generally. It appreciated the importance of the drop in American aid, of course, but AID economists familiar with the RVN's economy were far closer to being apocalyptic than the Party. To a large degree, the type of understanding needed at this point neither can nor even should emerge from a highly rational and essentially prudent revolutionary movement that cannot allow the romantic possibilities of sudden disintegration and instant victory ever to enter into its thinking, lest it paralyze its patient and necessary organizational efforts. And the rare historical precedents for total collapse hardly encourage others to envisage its likelihood. Yet the problem was that the seemingly impossible was about to occur, and relating to it economically and organizationally was soon to become imperative and unavoidable. A creative, imaginative vision of imminent historical possibilities was necessary to exploit the rare opportunities of a long-awaited situation.

In part this absence of a dynamic social analysis was due to the fact that the objective conditions in the RVN areas, particularly urban, were not being translated into a subjective radical consciousness the Party could channel. Throughout the latter part of 1974, even as it described the contours of the economic and political crises unfolding before its eyes, the Party complained that its urban organization was still far weaker than it should or might be. Its political progress in the rural areas, building in part on the accumulated legacies and residues of a Revolutionary tradition and culture that was now thirty years old, was much more rapid. To some extent, the PRG was no longer capable of influencing the visible, organized urban opposition to the Thieu regime. Most of the rightists who emerged by mid-1974 were at least as hostile to the Paris Agreement as Thieu himself, and their only value was in accelerating the disintegration of the total RVN system. A united-front coalition was therefore less likely than ever. The Party still energetically sought to relate to the diverse elements in the propeace Third Force, assigning them a role in fulfilling the Paris Agreement's terms, yet that movement remained disunited and at an impasse while the rightist Third Force gathered momentum until the fall of 1974. By the summer of 1974 most of the Party's leaders were convinced that a U.S.-backed replacement of Thieu was increasingly probable, and that it might temporarily neutralize opposition to his successors. Watching the CIA's and the embassy's ceaseless activity, they found it difficult to imagine that so many officials could act without the White House's endorsement of the logical outcome of their machinations. In brief, the Revolution's perceptions of the dynamic elements in the balance of forces shifted toward a greater emphasis on its military component as the one it could best control. The growing alienation in cities, so dangerous to the American cause and to the Revolution, now left a power vacuum the Party could not easily fit into its conceptions. For the time being, the Revolution was now largely a rural-based movement in a vast area, most of which was administered by the RVN, whose urbanized sector was rapidly disintegrating. It greatly underestimated the potential impact of its military force precisely for these reasons.

However reluctant the Revolution was to overdramatize the cataclysmic crisis of the Thieu system unfolding before it, its perceptions of the RVN's military decay after mid-1974 was nonetheless sufficiently comprehensive to encourage it to act. Indeed, the full extent of the RVNAF's difficulties emerged only after the Revolution abandoned its hopes that the Paris Agreement would be implemented. In the spring of 1974 it began actively to probe the RVNAF positions and respond to its attacks, particularly in the Mekong Delta and the Central Highlands. While the ARVN retained huge firepower and superior equipment, its efforts after mid-1974 to conserve its resources struck the PAVN's officers as an important shift in the physical balance of forces. They quickly concluded that the RVNAF was passive and confused, defensively committed to holding terrain and increasingly vulnerable as it lost access to roughly half of its essential helicopter and tactical air support. Without high mobility, the RVNAF could be defeated with astonishing ease. The PLAF/PAVN mounted many small attacks on isolated outposts, relying also on its guerilla and local forces to clear out huge corridors in the Central Highlands. Even though the Revolution during the first half of 1974 also lost territory, in the Delta PLAF units combined to destroy pregnable RVN positions and then retreated quickly to avoid becoming exposed targets. While it had been obvious to the Revolution during 1973 that the RVNAF was increasingly demoralized, the extent to which it now refused to fight surprised it. With at least five hundred PRG hamlets in the Delta by late 1974, guerillas now appeared on roads during daylight for the first time since 1968.[1]

Throughout 1973 the Party's leaders had sought to focus on reconstruction in the DRV and political struggle in the south while rebuilding its military forces and capabilities. Events, however, began to transcend its plans. Even as the RVNAF's desertion rate increased dramatically and morale dropped, Thieu, paradoxically, not only was aggressive militarily but began to lay plans for major offensives in 1976–77. The Party followed these closely. Meanwhile, some local Revolutionary units simply refused to remain passive, and their easy successes revealed the superficiality of Thieu's power. The Party's March 1974 policy amendment, typically, had sought to satisfy all the major tendencies within the leadership, from those favoring emphasis on the reconstruction of the DRV to those calling for an offensive in the south. The Politburo's effort at eclecticism was soon irrelevant. Thieu's weaknesses and the relentless economic and political developments in the south deprived it of real choices.

By mid-1974 the DRV had managed to reconstruct its economy to about its 1965 level. While it received aid from the USSR and China in large quantities, Party leaders had forebodings about future aid, especially from China. Protracting the war made sense only if the RVN was militarily able to resist, but by July at least Le Duan was convinced that all factors required a shift in strategy. During July the Politburo began to consider how to relate to the dynamics in the south. Although it did not formally decide to end the war during 1975 and 1976 until early October, that decision was more an acknowledgment of reality than a choice, and for the first time in its history the Party linked its belief in final victory to a precise timetable.[2]

The October decision caught the Party's generals in the midst of intense debate over the technical dimensions of strategy, one which continued publicly long after the war was over. Technically, the RVNAF was still considered superior in terms of numbers and equipment. The key to the Revolution's strategy remained to draw it out, disperse it, and employ massed attacks and surprise against critical fragile points, taking account of its dependency on distant logistics bases. The RVNAF's addiction to the holding of territory required a defensive strategy and left it vulnerable, passing the initiative to the Revolution. Its immobility was the outcome of the Party's prudent use of local military and political forces, which tied down vast numbers of RVNAF troops to protect the extended RVN political apparatus Thieu insisted on maintaining. Concentrated main and mobile forces were therefore capable of striking where the enemy was weakest and least prepared. This strategy had often been discussed publicly, but in October the PAVN's journals reiterated it, offering a general blueprint for the campaigns that were to follow. Despite important nuances in emphasis among the Party's military strategists, they agreed that they could not squander their basic assets or transcend the accumulated wisdom emerging from the southern experience and conditions. These consisted of local military and political units built up over two decades, able to function in diverse crucial ways and exploit innumerable possibilities only they could perceive; a huge RVNAF system in the process of rapid disintegration and vulnerable to external pressures to an extent which seemed immensely promising; and a modern, trained main-force army, overwhelmingly composed of northern soldiers who would provide the primary cutting edge of the offensive itself. The mere fact the war was projected to last until 1976 revealed the Party's own uncertainty over how quickly this combination and context could lead to a total victory.

The initial plan for a two-year campaign focused during 1975 on the Central Highlands, where the ARVN was weakest and the PAVN strongest. The goal was to bisect the country and greatly extend control in populated areas. The Politburo thought that an end to the war in 1975 was possible, but not so probable as to require it to prepare a political and economic plan to administer the liberated areas, particularly cities, in the event of victory. Military preparations for the two-year effort, on the other hand, were highly organized. But the Politburo and most of the general staff, especially General Dung and his advocates of conventional war, did not yet believe their logistics in the south were sufficient. They primarily expected during 1975 to prevent the RVN from withdrawing into defensible enclaves. While they believed the balance of forces was rapidly moving in their favor, they still saw the RVN as a formidable enemy fully capable of recovering its strength if not defeated soon. According to their calculations, 1976 was to be the year for the major, decisive offensive. Even in this context of an expected final military victory, their political vision of the coming years was still unclear. To the very end, most senior Party officials thought a transitional political coalition in the south would be necessary as an aspect of a national democratic revolution, and there was no plan for reunification of the nation into an integrated socialist political and economic system.

The Party, as a consequence, was to win the war before it was ready to cope with the main difficulties plaguing the RVN and making the Revolution's complete victory that much more certain. Total victory was to come as a complete surprise to so many senior Party leaders that it was apparent that the habit of patience over a thirty-year struggle had to some extent dulled their political sensitivities to the factors which determine the outcome of wars. Those who were most committed to developing a conventional military force based on expertise and equipment were least attuned to the intangible factors which made their triumph over a far larger and better-equipped army so rapid and decisive. The first problem of planning the campaign, indeed, evolved from precisely this difference between the technologically oriented, such as General Van Tien Dung, and the more politically sophisticated officers.[3]

SURPRISE AT PHUOC LONG AND THE PARTY'S NEW PLANS

In their initial plan the generals in Hanoi divided the 1975 campaign into three phases. The first was to begin in December and end in February 1975 and remain confined to the western portion of the B2 theater. The next phase was to extend from March until June and encompass the entire country, but particularly the Central Highlands. After August there was to be small-scale activity preparatory to 1976 and the grand offensive. The senior officers planning the campaign first met in Hanoi for a two-month period beginning mid-November to review the entire strategy. At that time only the first phase was wholly ready to be executed. The B2 leadership and the COSVN formed a fairly coherent caucus throughout these crucial discussions. They were so directly in touch with conditions in the populated regions and among the RVN soldiers that they were far more aggressive and coherent than the often divided generals operating in remote expanses or stationed in Hanoi. They alone saw the real possibility of the RVN's collapsing and indeed had military contingency plans drawn up should that occur. But B2, represented by General Tran Van Tra and including the Politburo member Pham Hung, thought it essential that the thrust of the 1975 campaign be national in scope to prevent the RVN from shifting its forces around. In effect, they argued for a more ambitious use of mixed local, regional, and main forces to assault the RVN everywhere and exploit its weaknesses while inflicting on it optimum losses.

B2's spokesmen would probably have lost this debate if their description of conditions in the south and their capacity to translate theories into practice had not been confirmed by the attack against Phuoc Long Province, a huge, sparsely populated area barely a hundred kilometers north of Saigon, beginning on December 13. The central command allowed the offensive forces minimal resources. Their success was all the more significant because the ARVN's generals had known in detail since October that an attack was coming, so that the Revolutionary forces confronted not surprised but apprehensive and demoralized troops. Using a combination of local and main forces, the relatively small Revolutionary army began to succeed immediately, and it greatly influenced the discussions then taking place in Hanoi. RVNAF units fought very badly, and Thieu refused to reinforce them. Losses amounted to over four-fifths of the defenders, including at least twenty aircraft. The capital, Song Be, fell on January 6, and the first liberation of a complete province of the entire war proceeded quickly and easily. The defeat's psychological impact on the RVN was immeasurable. For those planning the next phase of the war in Hanoi, it provided vital reassurance. It eliminated the lingering fears of America's reentry into the war, and it exposed the ARVN's impotence on a much larger scale than ever before. The Revolution's soldiers, on the other hand, had fought very well, having mastered deficiencies of coordination and training that had marred their 1972 offensive. Numerous smaller military objectives were taken throughout the eastern Delta and Tay Ninh Province at the same time.

The Politburo met from December 18 to January 8 to make final plans for the 1975–76 campaign. Until then it had merely a very general plan, the only specific aspect of which was even then being implemented in the B2 region with mounting success. Its own overall estimates of the balance of forces in the south were greatly reinforced by the experiences in Phuoc Long. The Politburo's thinking remained open, however, to current events and arguments, and one of these was also the RVN's assessment of Revolutionary intentions. The CIA in Saigon, which believed it had obtained the essence of the first general 1975 resolution, had concluded that apart from phase one of the offensive in MR III and IV, there would be no offensive on the scale of those of 1968 or 1972 but only sufficient activity to keep the RVN off balance. Thieu received this estimate and accepted it, for it was reasonably accurate, but ignored the fact that the Party had yet to determine its final strategy. The worst possibility Thieu foresaw was a general offensive to coincide with the RVN presidential election the following October, or perhaps with the U.S. election a year later. He concluded that this did not warrant making any changes in his own forces. The CIA also released its detailed assessment to journalists, who published it during late December. While the Party's generals had especially targeted the Central Highlands for an attack, their own detailed knowledge of Thieu's perception of their intentions as well as his decision not to reinforce MR II reassured them that it was the place to concentrate their initial major effort.

It remained only to select the main location for the first assault. B2's representatives argued for Ban Me Thuot, a town much closer to Phuoc Long and considerably to the south of Kontum and Pleiku, both of which had been attacked in 1972. It was a target likely to cause the greatest surprise, and it was the least defended in the region. They were convinced that by moving the main axis of the war much farther south and by linking it with the B2 region, they would make the victory all the greater and possibly shorten the war. Since the Phuoc Long engagement had already proved that the RVNAF was weaker than many in Hanoi realized, the B2 argument carried the day. General Dung, for his part, believed not only that the opening campaign in the Central Highlands would succeed anywhere in that huge region but also that its main thrust would not move farther south until the following year.[4]

The Party's final plans were therefore not the product of a comprehensive, detailed, long-term strategy but rather the outcome of both a desire to exploit what was clearly a far more favorable balance of forces and specific opportunities. In one sense the discussion of campaign strategy was increasingly irrelevant, for what was being tested was the strength of two social systems and conceptions of society, and the Revolution's real power lay both in its own coherence and relationship to a decentralized mass movement and in the RVN's compounded weaknesses. The B2 strategy maintained the Party's traditional commitment to the mixed theory of warfare and politics, and its sense of the specific southern needs and potential of the situation was highly accurate. The RVN was now very weak at all levels, and there can be little doubt that the more technocratic and quite non-Marxist conceptions then gathering momentum in Hanoi were also likely to succeed in battle. To some extent, the two were applied in tandem. All a military assault would do was reveal the fatal vulnerability of the social order the United States had installed to represent its interests. That it would collapse by one means or another was now certain. The Party's generals would merely become players in history, but not its creators. All the pieces in the final act of the war were set; none were the result of accident or individual brilliance, and even the RVN's most spectacular errors were quite predictable, because Thieu was a known quantity. At the beginning of 1975 all the factors deciding the outcome of the war were the accumulated results of events and processes, some of immense proportions and others quite banal, which had preceded them: of RVN soldiers spread out everywhere and lost in deprivation and demoralization, of stubborn peasants who caused province chiefs anxiety and had to be constantly watched, of exhausted American leaders who rankled at the very mention of the word "Vietnam" and were determined to avoid a renewed dissipation of their energy and money there, of venal generals with bejeweled wives, and of much else.

Vietnam's destiny, two decades overdue, was finally to be realized.

Chapter 41

The End of the War

AID TO THIEU AND THE RVN'S FUTURE

The political crisis which racked the RVN after mid-1974 confronted the Ford administration with the increasingly unavoidable reality that all of the United States' monumental past and present efforts in Vietnam were being endangered. The administration's apathy, incompetence, and maladroit efforts had combined by the end of 1974 to leave it in the worst of all situations—one with a seriously weakened regime and no viable alternative to Thieu.

The question of supplemental military aid for the RVN became a far greater issue for Thieu and the administration than either had anticipated when the White House requested the funds during January. Far more significant than the material consequences of the initial reduced aid appropriations for fiscal 1975 were the obvious political implications to the future of Thieu and the RVN. Designed originally as symbolic reassurance, the supplemental turned out to be a congressional refusal to back Thieu unequivocally, requiring him to concern himself entirely with his enemies in his own military. It revealed the divisions and impotence of the Ford administration in a way that precipitated a crisis in its Vietnam policy. By ineptly creating a major test of its position at a time when the White House was certain to lose, Kissinger was to harm Thieu immeasurably.

Thieu by late 1974 needed some psychological gestures to prove that his relationship with Washington was as strong and effective as ever. Virtually everyone understood that this, rather than some marginally useful arms, was the main purpose of the supplemental request. The senior officers, the only force able to overthrow Thieu, were the most directly concerned with his inability to guarantee funding. "There is a lot of grumbling about his leadership," as one of them put it in February 1975.[1] This fact caused Thieu early that month to install the infamous General Toan as commander of the critical III Corps around Saigon and to tighten his grip over the police and various key commands. While politics had always set the ultimate limits on the army's military functions, it was never more obvious than during the months preceding the RVNAF's final test on the field of battle.

Kissinger, for his part, handled the supplemental and Vietnam issues in a frivolous manner at the very point he was least able to charm his way out of difficulties, treating it as a symbol of both his own and the nation's credibility in the world. Extremely distracted by Middle Eastern issues throughout this period, he publicly confronted Congress over Vietnam at a time when the Pentagon scarcely concealed its growing opposition to additional aid. These two problems were to merge during the final months of the war to paralyze the White House's Vietnam policy and drastically undermine Thieu's prospects for political survival.

The seventy-five new House members who joined the Ninety-fourth Congress in January 1975 were strongly antiwar and dedicated to reforming the committee system, which had helped successive administrations implement foreign policy. Unwilling to make traditional bargains, openly disparaging of Kissinger as a pretentious seeker after power, both the House and Senate let it be known from the very beginning of the supplemental request on January 28 that the possibility of passage was slight and that quick passage was even less likely.

The $300 million figure was selected arbitrarily, and the CIA in Saigon believed that since it was intended for psychological effect and since the arms it was to buy were less urgent, a much smaller sum capable of swift approval would have sufficed. During these weeks, a confidential comptroller general's report on excess equipment and munitions usage of the ARVN was leaked to Congress and then to the press. The Pentagon also quietly released information on the large supplies the RVN had stored away. Although the Pentagon had diverted $36 million in munitions to the RVN, much to Congress's fury, it stoutly refused to share the apocalyptic visions that Martin, who had returned to lobby for the bill, was broacasting throughout Washington. The public data the Pentagon issued were not helpful to the White House. They revealed that with more money the RVN would be able to stockpile munitions or greatly expand the war. Since the State and Defense Department experts who went to Saigon to study the situation reported that the economy and the army's morale were far more serious problems and since there was a consensus on the lack of military threat comparable to 1968 or 1972, the Pentagon began subtly but publicly backing away from the supplemental request for a variety of reasons.

By this time Schlesinger and Kissinger intensely disliked each other, and, by March, Kissinger was able unprecedentedly to exclude the defense secretary from critical meetings. At the beginning of January, Kissinger had chastised the Pentagon for refusing to send a nearby naval task force into Vietnamese waters to intimidate the DRV. The immediate Pentagon leak of the fact embarrassed the secretary of state, compelling Ford on January 21 to declare that he could not foresee circumstances that would cause the United States to reenter the war. During the first hearings on supplemental aid, the Pentagon provided data showing that the RVNAF still retained an overwhelming superiority of material power. The White House, belatedly aware it was unlikely to obtain the supplemental, began to formulate a $6.4 billion combined three-year package of military and economic aid, at the end of which all aid would terminate. This prospect of throwing much more money into the Vietnam War compelled the Pentagon to act even more directly than it had the preceding summer. It wanted funds with which to modernize its own armed forces, and Schlesinger argued that if the administration was ready to allow the RVN to collapse in 1977, it might just as well do so immediately. Even before the three-year plan was released, the Pentagon began to tell Congress that the RVN would fall if it did not receive aid for up to another decade. It systematically undermined the White House's three-year alternative to the supplemental. Schlesinger himself refused to predict the RVN's defeat should the supplemental request fail, and during March he publicly urged that the American military shift its focus to Europe and modernization.[2]

The administration was now gravely compounding both Thieu's and its own problems at least as much as Congress's refusal to give superfluous military aid was, and this plunged the RVN into a psychological and political crisis during the final period of its existence.

THE MILITARY BALANCE AND THE RVN'S DEEPENING CRISIS, EARLY 1975

Materially, the RVNAF at the beginning of 1975 had a huge numerical superiority over the Revolution in all domains. Despite its complaints, the figures showed that the RVNAF was a formidable army, if only it would fight. It possessed 1,400 artillery pieces against 400 for the Communists, and 1,200 tanks and armored personnel carriers against 600 tanks in the PAVN. The Pentagon estimated there were 185,000 combat troops, 107,000 support troops, and 45,000 guerillas in the Revolutionary army, giving the RVNAF a two-to-one advantage in combat troops and an overall superiority of forces of three to one on paper. The RVN air arm still had over 1,400 aircraft, though the PAVN's antiaircraft system was now also very powerful. The RVNAF's real troop strength was by then a mystery even to its highest officers. They knew only that they were getting about one-half of the 250,000 men they needed annually to replace deserters and normal losses, and this made constituting a strategic reserve all the more urgent. Despite Martin's plaintive appeals, even as the RVNAF was firing nine times as many shells as the Communist side, the RVN's munitions supply rose from September 1974 until March 1975 to two-thirds of the huge stocks which existed when the Paris Agreement was signed. "But combat units never lacked ammunitions during an engagement with the enemy and no operation was delayed for lack of ammunition," the ARVN's head of logistics was later to admit.[3] On paper, the RVNAF was a large, powerful army capable of commanding the respect of the Revolution.

While the morale of the RVN was too debilitated to be remedied, technically Thieu's commitment to the "four no's" strategy of holding as much territory and population as possible militarily squandered its potential assets. For this reason the Revolution could define the time and form of battle and consistently defeat the RVNAF. Many U.S. officers had for years urged their RVN counterparts to concentrate their armies in defensible regions, and this alternative strategy had always had a respectable following. Thieu's generals also debated it, and during August 1974, after it became obvious there would be less equipment to spread throughout the country, an ARVN committee studied the possibility of abandoning the poorer regions in MR I and II and concentrating on the coastal cities and on the territory south of Nha Trang near the twelfth parallel. Martin and the embassy encouraged the truncation option mainly as a threat to Congress should it persist in cutting aid, but it had serious advocates as well. It was far from being an obscure or eccentric strategy, and only Thieu's opposition stopped it. General Murray was the most important American to favor it, and the DAO was familiar with the status of the strategy review long before Thieu decided under pressure to implement the change the following March.

By the end of 1974 Thieu agreed that creating a strategic reserve was desirable in principle, and the proposal was again given to a committee to study. Generals Vien and Khiem both strongly favored the reform. This alone caused Thieu to be cautious about its implementation, since Khiem was his chief threat in the military. Pushing them, in turn, was an Australian who had been a CIA and a Rand employee, Ted Sarong, who now worked for the RVN as an adviser. Seven of the ARVN's thirteen divisions were defending one-sixth of the population, he argued, and he advocated abandoning the upper half of South Vietnam. Most Americans in Saigon thought calculated withdrawals prudent; when Thieu and his aides consulted them, they all made it clear they would support him whatever his decision.

Implicitly at stake in the question was the broader strategic guidance Thieu had given since coming to power, and this alone was sufficient to force him to hesitate until he had protected himself from the political repercussions of admitting his own past failure. At least as important, in a context where control over military commands had major political implications, were the risks to Thieu's power and the stability of the existing system from a repartitioned military structure, with its new and invariably disgruntled generals and divisions entering the populated southern regions. Thieu, as always, calculated not as a military leader but as the dictator of a troubled political order. The RVN's desperate need for a strategic reserve and its immobility were therefore to persist until the last moment. The belated attempt to rectify these difficulties was delayed until it was certain to produce total disaster.

The RVNAF's immediate problem was not its matériel but its morale and leadership. Inept officers and strategies and less abundant supplies undermined it, but ultimately the RVN's fatal weaknesses were rooted in the more fundamental nature of its social system and the war itself. "The morale of the ARVN soldier was adversely affected by so many factors that it is remarkable that he was able to fight at all," a Rand summation of the opinion of key RVN leaders later accurately phrased it.[4] The soldiers' morale had been low for years. Although it was worse in January 1975 than ever, this alone cannot explain the subsequent events. What was unique was the disintegration of Thieu's political system in the wake of interrelated anticorruption protests, the economic crisis, congressional aid cuts, and the profound split within the coalition Thieu had welded during the prosperous years of 1969–72. The turning point for the traditional elite was the loss of Phuoc Long Province, followed by the failure of the supplemental aid in Congress. A desperate pessimism and sense of impending doom descended on Saigon; it only deepened when Tran Van Lam, head of the RVN senate and former foreign minister, went to Washington during February and returned to opine, without real justification, that all aid would end that fiscal year. By this time Thieu had unsuccessfully attempted to ship the RVN's gold to Switzerland, presumably as collateral for loans to buy munitions, and also tried to borrow on future oil revenues. Saigon's morosity turned into a veritable panic when a distinctly cool congressional delegation quickly passed through at the end of February. It was this mood, "the atmosphere . . . charged with rumors and speculation," as General Vien described it, threatening Thieu's hold over the reins of power, that gripped the RVN, its leaders as well as its soldiers, as the Revolution's armies prepared their offensive.[5]

THE BEGINNING OF THE END:
MARCH 1975 AND THE MILITARY DEBACLE

At the beginning of March 1975, the outcome of the war was destined to reflect the totality of over two decades of experiences in South Vietnam, but the precise form of the end was linked to a remarkable extent to the judgment and behavior of Nguyen Van Thieu. It was on Thieu that American foreign policy's symbolic credibility and efficacy was now wholly reliant, making its long effort no stronger than a man and a structure that had since its inception been America's utterly dependent surrogate in Southeast Asia. It was a relationship fraught with danger for both the Ford administration and America's collaborators in Saigon.

The Party's decision to attack the Central Highlands came at a time when the RVN's position in the region was especially vulnerable. The Montagnard tribes in the local RF/PF units, particularly around Ban Me Thuot, were, as so often in the past, in open rebellion against the RVN, particularly because of the ARVN's depredations. They were therefore unwilling to report the large PAVN troop movements into the region throughout February. ARVN troop morale in the Highlands was as low as in any place; the rate of heroin addiction was reported to be 30 percent in the Pleiku region, some of the supply being sold by officers to their men. The ARVN's intelligence nevertheless decided in mid-February that a major offensive in the Highlands was imminent and that Ban Me Thuot was the primary target; but the commander of the II Corps was convinced that Pleiku was the main objective, and he prepared his defenses accordingly. The PAVN, meanwhile, reinforced his impression by diversionary actions both in the region and around Hué and west of Saigon, once again pinning the entire RVNAF to static positions. It carefully prepared to cut all the major routes so that reinforcements could not be sent into the Highlands or from Pleiku and Kontum to the relief of Ban Me Thuot, and to prevent the troops there from escaping should Thieu order the strategic withdrawal from the region—a withdrawal they knew had been under discussion for many months. The RVNAF in the Highlands had sufficient supplies to fight for two months. While the PAVN's generals also imagined a shorter operation, they prepared for the likelihood of a two-month campaign before the rainy season bogged down their heavy equipment. Their estimate was based on the RVNAF's capabilities. As one U.S. officer later concluded, "the North Vietnamese did not start the campaign with overwhelming force superiority."[6] Their most optimistic prognosis was that the entire Highlands might be conquered in 1975, though 1976 was the more likely target. Unless Thieu ordered a withdrawal, they expected, they would require time to take the major Highlands cities.

The attack on Ban Me Thuot came during the early morning of March 10. The PAVN units fought very well, achieving surprise and preventing reinforcements from reaching the city. When RVN aircraft were sent to retaliate, one scored a direct hit on the defending ARVN division's tactical-operations center, completely destroying it and ending any organized defense. It was the first omen of a series of events exposing the basic structural weakness of the RVNAF throughout the country. The PAVN took the town the next day, and Thieu ordered the head of MR II to recapture it, regarding it as more important than Pleiku or Kontum. Two regiments of ostensibly highly motivated ARVN troops were airlifted into a town thirty kilometers east of Ban Me Thuot on March 14, and they were expected to fight because their families were supposed to be in the city. But since many of their relatives had already left and were scattered in many directions, the ARVN soldiers simply abandoned their units and arms to search for them. This display of primary loyalty of the RVN's soldiers to their families living near most of them, which caused a total collapse of military cohesion and discipline, was constantly repeated elsewhere over the next weeks and was a basic source of the RVN's defeat. The commander of the Twenty-third Division also deserted his post to send his family out by helicopter. As the mass of soldiers and dependents cluttered the roads, seeking to escape to the coast nearly a hundred kilometers away, fear and panic began to set in throughout the region.

The opening of the attack in the Central Highlands was accompanied by a series of smaller offensives elsewhere which confused Thieu as to the Revolution's major goals and capabilities. In this sense the Revolution's existence throughout South Vietnam created the pressures and context for Thieu's fatal strategic error, without which the Party's original expectations regarding the length of the war would have proven accurate. While the large bulk of the Revolution's armed forces were regular units, mainly from the DRV, the existence of local forces spread around the country had a qualitative importance to Thieu which affected his calculations as well as his deployment of soldiers. Pinning down huge numbers, local militia and guerillas immediately presented Thieu the crucial problem of space and priorities and shaped his decisions both at the start of the campaign, when his errors were decisive, and then over the subsequent weeks of denouement. The PAVN was free to concentrate its men to attain superiority precisely because local units in MR I or in the Delta threatened the RVNAF in the days before the opening attack on Ban Me Thuot and in the following weeks, when local forces administered the major northern cities of South Vietnam.

It was the disturbing necessity to deploy throughout the nation, even against numerically weaker and poorly equipped guerillas, that led to Thieu's strategic blunder and the stunning end of the war in just six weeks.

Thieu had managed the RVNAF as a political arm for so long that it was difficult for him to change, yet with the opening of the Tay Nguyen campaign he had few choices before him. Both Lam Son 719 and the 1972 spring offensive revealed his instability and incompetence as a military strategist. For obvious political reasons, Thieu had resisted the strategic shift of his forces which had been under discussion since August 1974, and now the Communist offensive exposed the RVN's vulnerability. On March 10, after a final consultation with the embassy—Martin was in the United States until the end of the month for dental treatment—Thieu made his decision to redeploy his army. On the morning of March 11, with Ban Me Thuot lost, he informed his senior military advisers of his plan to hold only the key coastal cities in MR I and II and abandon all of the Highlands save the Ban Me Thuot region, which they were to reconquer. Along with the southern half of the country, it would form the basis of a territorially more defensible RVN possessing a strategic reserve. Reinforced by both his military sycophants and quite minor officials in the U.S. embassy, Thieu made his most fateful decision of the war as a desperate attempt to respond to the Revolution's offensive. Over the next two days he contemplated the plan, parts of which were in fact already in motion, and consulted his astrologer and Ted Sarong—both of whom were skeptical. Then, on March 14 he flew to Cam Ranh Bay to order Major General Pham Van Phu, head of the II Corps, to abandon all of the Highlands within two days. They would use the forces withdrawn from the Kontum-Pleiku area to retake the Ben Me Thuot region. Phu was to tell no one of the evacuation except the most senior officers, and he was not to inform the RF/PF units at all before the withdrawal began. Unplanned and impulsive, the scheme was improvised even as General Phu's effort to retake Ban Me Thuot had already begun to fail. All the ingredients made disaster a virtual certainty, yet the enormity of it could hardly be imagined.

While no U.S. officials were involved in the plan, they knew it was imminent; immediately after it began, Westmoreland in Washington called it a "prudent action."[7] Only when it proved catastrophic did they seek to distance themselves from it. Although no senior Americans participated in the specific decision, they had been instrumental in the discussions after August 1974 which had inspired it. Above all, they had selected Thieu as commander in chief and made his word fiat.

The withdrawal began on March 16. After General Phu had met his officers in Pleiku, he returned to the safety of Cam Ranh, leaving them to their own devices. One officer had asked about the fate of RVN employees,

RF/PF forces, and the dependents of ARVN troops. "Forget about them," Phu commanded, in accordance with Thieu's orders. "You have no responsibility to take care of them! . . . If you tell them about it, you can't control it and you cannot get down to Tuy Hoa because there will be panic."[8] Yet when the ARVN began to withdraw down an abandoned, unreconnoitered road to the coast, their families fled with them, and there was immediate pandemonium. Rioting, looting, and rape accompanied the entire exodus, and they were to occur constantly elsewhere as the panic generated by the abandonment of the Highlands spread throughout the region as far as Hué. The tidal wave of the military forces, their families, and civilians pushing down an overgrown route without critical bridges disintegrated completely, at one point being bombed by their own air forces. At least three-quarters of the II Corps' military strength was lost during this debacle, and of 400,000 civilians who tried to reach the coast only a quarter arrived. Yet the survivors were able to spread such tales of RVN horror and duplicity that panic followed them like a plague. From this point onward, the vast bulk of the RVNAF, officers included, chose loyalty to their families rather than to their commanders when subjected to any Revolutionary attacks, and a very large part of its equipment was discarded in the process.

Meantime, relatively small PAVN units applied pressure on ARVN installations near Hué, which easily held their own until news of the debacle in the Central Highlands began filtering through. Even more crucial, the elite Airborne Division north of Hué was ordered on March 12 to Saigon for essentially political reasons, threatening fatally to weaken the defense of MR I. On the thirteenth the commander of the I Corps, Lieutenant General Ngo Quang Truong, met with Thieu and pleaded for a reversal of the order, and Thieu informed him that he would evacuate all of MR I, concentrate defenses around Danang, and build a strategic reserve from the surplus forces. When Truong returned to Hué, Thieu instructed him to speed the withdrawals; as soon they began, ARVN in the I Corps began to dissolve. Dependents of troops followed them, civilians panicked, and soon the sea of distraught people made roads impassable. Plundering broke out everywhere; units simply melted away as some soldiers set out to find or help their families. The population was terrorized by ceaseless robberies, rapes, and shoot-outs between various RVNAF soldiers. As the terror spread, ultimately two million people crushed into Danang, and a huge scene of endless chaos and depravity unfolded. Thieu called Truong back to Saigon on the nineteenth and gave him complete freedom to choose his own strategy. By that time the dissolution of the army and mass hysteria left him few alternatives. Truong urged that they defend Hué, and Thieu agreed. Going on TV early the next afternoon, in an astonishing four-minute speech intended to reassure his followers but whose brevity only further unnerved them, he declared that they would hold Hué at all costs. But the very same afternoon he secretly ordered Truong once again to concentrate only on the defense of Danang and also to fly a final airborne brigade to Saigon immediately. In effect, in the ten days after the attack on Ban Me Thuot, the RVNAF in the northern half of the country disintegrated as Nguyen Van Thieu imposed absolute confusion on it.[9]

THE REVOLUTION OPTS FOR TOTAL VICTORY

The Revolution's leaders were astounded by the swiftness of events and the new possibilities which had suddenly opened up in the vast void before them. They had resolved definitively to shift the balance in the Highlands but scarcely imagined that within a few days Thieu would commit multiple, compounded errors and fail to use his formidable defensive forces. Now conventional criteria of warfare became irrelevant and even dangerous; the factors of morale and command became decisive.

The Politburo met on March 11 and considered the possibility of quick, total victory and urged the PAVN not to allow the remnants of the RVNAF to escape the Highlands and regroup elsewhere. At this critical moment the Party's military doctrine, which had by then increasingly emphasized a regularized fighting force using standard techniques characteristic of all armies, was shifted to stress speed, flexibility, and creativity against a disorganized enemy which could no longer fight conventionally. The PAVN abandoned much of the technological fetishism of the preceding two years and discarded cumbersome equipment, such as the huge SAM 2 missiles which they had sent south. Rapidity and mobility were of the essence to exploit the ARVN's panic and disorganization. General Dung himself, the key advocate of regularization, immediately switched back to fighting the war without concern for his recent theses, realizing that in a rout only creativity would suffice to exploit time. He now urged that the PAVN take the northern section of South Vietnam at once.

As soon as Thieu gave his command to abandon MR I and II, all of the Party's options were likely to lead to the RVN's total defeat. On March 18 the Politburo resolved to move on Saigon and end the war, first consolidating control over the I Corps. The decision had monumental implications to the DRV's policies on reconstruction and overall priorities, yet to end the war when it was possible to do so was an opportunity it could scarcely forgo. Speed was therefore essential. Had the remnants of Thieu's forces been able to regroup and resist, protracting the affair, the costs to the DRV could have become extremely onerous. On March 25 the Politburo fixed a timetable for victory by the end of the dry season in mid-May. For the first time, it prepared a plan to take Saigon. The entire PAVN was committed to the war, and all resources were diverted to win it.

To quickly end a thirty-year war, spread over a vast territory, required daring and improvisation. General Dung urged his generals to solve their huge new logistics difficulties in much the same way as the Revolution had since the inception—by taking them from the enemy. As it moved beyond the Highlands regions where it had prepared to fight for some time, it shifted increasingly to a policy of supplying its needs on the spot, and here local political and guerilla units proved important. The Danang PRG fetched the first PAVN units and brought them into the city because they had run out of gas. The retreating ARVN failed to destroy huge stocks of fuel, trucks of every sort, munitions, and guns—and close to a half of the PAVN's transport in the last days consisted of U.S. trucks. They even pressed many former ARVN drivers into service and extensively utilized captured artillery. Cam Ranh Bay, with its vast facilities, became a vital source of supplies for the attack on Saigon, and instead of relying wholly on their own laboriously constructed roads, the advancing PAVN time and again found the American-built highways extremely valuable. The Revolution had always been symbiotic with its enemy, and the final days of the war were no different —only the scale was grander. As the huge void opened, transport was a key to winning, and the Revolutionary forces, combining their own resources with what they seized, were better equipped at the beginning of April than at any time in their entire history. Despite inevitable lapses of coordination and matériel, they were able to sustain the essential momentum and élan, aided immeasurably by the RVN's ever-deepening descent into defeat. To a vital extent the Revolution was by mid-March winning with very little combat, simply entering immense areas which the disintegration of its enemy had opened quite independently of the manpower arrayed against it. When fighting became essential, it was from such an unequal balance of material forces that it rarely lasted long.[10]

SAIGON'S FINAL DAYS: POLITICS TO THE FORE

Nguyen Van Thieu's military structure was organized to preserve his political power, and that it failed, and indeed immeasurably accelerated its own demise in the face of a serious but not yet decisive military challenge, was the logic of the system the Americans had installed. It was not merely that Thieu had parcelized the entire military command into four corps, all but one of which was in March 1975 in the hands of a corrupt crony directly responsible to him alone, but that they could not communicate with each other even in case of extreme need. The JGS under General Cao Van Vien was excluded from command decisions; moreover, Vien, ever supine but financially successful, always reinforced the inclinations of whomever he served and remained silent when Thieu outlined his disastrous Highlands withdrawal scheme on March 11. Thieu, for good reason, no longer trusted him. Thieu had ample contempt for all his generals, corrupting and constantly spying on them, lest any be drawn into a cabal against him. Since mid-1974 his fears of being overthrown obsessed him and completely overshadowed his concern for purely military questions. He had always been a political person first and a general by convenience, and that he was an extremely poor judge of military matters had made no difference so long as the Americans were there to save him. The entire regime was the outcome of a political process, and during the final weeks it was inevitable that politics motivated many of Thieu's military decisions. To divorce the two dimensions was impossible, because those to whom he delegated key military responsibilities, such as General Phu, were linked to Thieu politically. The one exception was General Truong of MR I, who was considered efficient and who commanded the best troops on the RVN's side. To some extent, Truong's experience illustrated the magnitude of Thieu's role in the debacle.

The RVN might have survived somewhat longer if Thieu's general March 11 plan to abandon the Highlands and hold the coastal cities of MR I and II had been applied in an orderly fashion. But unraveling both MR I and MR II at the same time made it impossible to avoid total defeat almost immediately. His March 12 request to General Truong to send a division to Saigon was therefore the critical decision, in conjunction with the abandonment of the Highlands, guaranteeing the vast upheaval. Thieu wanted the troops in Saigon for political reasons. On the one hand he needed them to protect himself against a possible coup from forces near Saigon. On the other he feared Truong as a possible American-backed replacement and wanted the elite troops out of his hands. Truong's meeting with Thieu on March 13 so horrified Truong that he brashly told confidants that he might organize a coup should the dictator change his plans again—which was precisely what Thieu did. Thieu therefore regarded him as a dangerous man. The withdrawal of the Airborne Division was the critical trigger of the immediate debacle in MR I, and the end of the entire war.[11]

While it oversimplifies events to claim that the coping with cabals and internal political threats was all that preoccupied Thieu and his generals and conservative rivals, politics was surely more important than their time and effort spent on purely military questions. Indeed, even politics took second place to personal matters for most. The DAO was chagrined that so many of them were so distracted with their own private and family problems that they did almost nothing to reconstruct the RVNAF from the remnants filtering from the north. Many were busy preparing their own departures. They simply issued orders and did nothing to carry them out. Only the DAO attempted to reconstitute the ARVN to enable the war to continue. The Saigon generals knew all too well that the Americans were still dreaming. Thieu went into virtual isolation, refusing to see his ministers, talking to only a few people, making rare public appearances, and saying nothing to reassure the population he still controlled. His relationship to his soldiers was personified by the local RVN troops in his native village who bulldozed his ancestral grave site and removed all trace of it.

During his last weeks Thieu nonetheless had to confront serious, time-consuming political challenges from the conservatives who had opposed him since mid-1974 and who now claimed they both could and would fight the war until the bitter end. The arch-conspirator was, as usual, Nguyen Cao Ky, who had Father Thanh and an assortment of aspiring ministers behind him. Even General Vien maintained cordial, if discreet, contacts with him, and Prime Minister Khiem also became involved. Spied on by Thieu and the CIA alike, Thieu outflanked them all by inviting Ky and two others to recommend governmental changes and then arresting seven of his collaborators. On April 2 the senate, a traditional conservative bastion, overwhelmingly voted to demand a new government, and Thieu deftly outmaneuvered them by ousting Khiem, once his only real threat, and co-opting some of the senate's leaders into a new rubber-stamp cabinet. He then arrested at least six more key plotters, including Nguyen Van Ngan, his former assistant and head of the Democracy party. As he moved through this Byzantine maze of intrigue, the embassy consistently supported him. With Ky's cohorts scheming until the final days of the war, whom Martin betrayed at least once, Thieu proved he was still the consummate master of Saigon politics. But he could do nothing about his army. On April 8 one of his own F-5 aircraft attempted to bomb the Presidential Palace but, typically, missed.

Saigon's political life ended as it had begun, a mixture of opera buffa, avarice, egoism, and treachery. Thieu's generals were not to oust him, ultimately, or to help him deal with the armies now descending on Saigon. Superb political tacticians, Thieu and his officers failed utterly as military leaders, and their talents were now wholly self-destructive.[12]

PARALYSIS IN WASHINGTON

The pain and anguish the collapse of the RVN's armies caused in Washington was both anticlimactic and profound. The twenty-year effort to maintain a surrogate in South Vietnam was now visibly coming to an end in a way that made America, its commitment and power, look supremely impotent and pathetic. The global symbolism of this image weighed most heavily on Kissinger and the White House. The spectacle the administration was witnessing was one entirely of its own making, but it was quite unwilling to face that fact. It confronted the end of its own enormous investment of time and blood over two decades by treating the culmination of the most important foreign policy and military defeat in its entire history as a matter to be relegated to the embarrassing past as quickly as possible.

When Thieu's army began to disintegrate, Congress was still discussing the supplemental aid request, and the debacle only convinced it that any new funds would be wasted. The House Democratic caucus on March 12 voted over three to one against it, and during the subsequent days of March, as Thieu's cause looked even more hopeless, many Republicans and conservatives joined them on the assumption that they would now merely be pouring money down the proverbial rat hole. The administration exploited the opposition to transfer the blame for the loss of South Vietnam to Congress and chose to press harder for its three-year plan of $6.4 billion. The only difficulty was that money was now quite irrelevant to the RVN's problems, and the Pentagon was more than ever opposed to squandering such amounts on symbolic and political gestures. These profound disagreements guaranteed that the war would end in much the same way as it began and that it would remain the most divisive, acrimonious event in American history since the Civil War.

The dispute in the administration soon provided the press with colorful gossip, and Kissinger's ability to get Schlesinger excluded from the highest policy deliberations on Vietnam only reinforced the de facto conservative-Pentagon-liberal alliance in Congress opposed to aid. To conjure up backing for its efforts, the White House decided to send General Frederick C. Weyand, Army chief of staff, to Saigon to make a direct assessment of the war and gain support for its aid appeal to Congress. Weyand's task was difficult, not least because both the DAO and the CIA had already filed highly informed analyses of the situation which predicted imminent military defeat for the RVN. From his arrival in Saigon on March 26 until his departure, Vien and Thieu urged that B-52s be sent to their rescue, making air power the key to the RVN's survival. Weyand, in turn, suggested that Thieu transfer power to direct the war to the JGS. Vien's outright dismissal of the idea merely reinforced his pessimism. Weyand reported to the administration that only strategic air power might save the RVN from defeat should the Communists commit three more divisions to MR III. Otherwise, he predicted, even the delivery of all necessary arms would not stave off defeat within three months, because of the monumental errors Thieu had made in mid-March. The Pentagon's intelligence agency was less sanguine—it gave the RVN just one month under any circumstances.

The Pentagon openly refused to cooperate with the White House, making public the main facts which had led it to oppose excessive military aid since mid-1974. During the end of March and early April, it released all the information needed to scuttle the White House's efforts. There were sufficient arms and fuel in RVN-controlled areas for the RVN to resist, with $270 million still available to it from the 1974 appropriation. Schlesinger himself on April 2 argued publicly that the ARVN was simply not fighting and that the problem of leadership and command had nothing to do with supplies. Kissinger, however, regarded the unquestionably accurate Pentagon pessimism as irrelevant, for Thieu was the United States' chosen instrument in Vietnam, and his army was the product of American training and policy. Aid was not a matter of preventing defeat or saving scarce resources but rather a symbolic defense of U.S. commitments and credibility. But he was boxed in by Congress and the Pentagon, and his last major effort on behalf of his Vietnam policy was to prove as futile as all of his earlier attempts to redeem the nation's sustained failure in Vietnam.[13]

THE REVOLUTION ENTERS THE VOID

After Ban Me Thuot the Revolution had to fill the huge void opening up before it with breathtaking rapidity. The entire RVN administrative and military structure outside Saigon was destroyed, for all practical purposes, by early April. Soldiers threw down arms, and civil servants failed to report to work, and those who could moved toward Saigon. More important officials and businessmen began to leave the country or send their children abroad. Airports were jammed; visas and tickets commanded fabulous prices. Thieu's air force melted away as pilots and mechanics sought to escape. At the end of March the Party's leaders estimated that the RVN had lost half of its army and that much of the rest was ineffective. Some U.S. analysts calculated that not more than a fifth of the RVNAF would fight, and even that assessment was soon outdated. By the end of April the Revolution had eighteen divisions massed around Saigon against three demoralized ARVN divisions.

During the final weeks of the war, the RVN increasingly fell apart in innumerable areas more quickly than the regular PAVN forces advanced. The collapsing army and bureaucrats left many areas in limbo for terrifyingly long periods, during which RVN soldiers could impose their wills and desires at random. The arrival of Revolutionary forces in Danang was welcomed by many former anti-Communists as a salvation from the ravages Thieu's troops wreaked on their property and lives for two traumatic weeks. Saigon declared a location captured as soon as it lost contact, while the

Revolution claimed only those places it actually entered. The important coastal cities of Nha Trang, Phan Rang, Qui Nhon, and Phan Thiet were abandoned without a fight. Local Revolutionary forces threatened to pin down the overextended RVNAF until regular troops arrived to destroy them, thereby persuading them to move on quickly. Local forces played a critical role from the beginning to the end of the campaign, swelling with new recruits during the final months as many surfaced to take up arms. In the Highlands they cut supply and communications routes and rounded up and harassed retreating troops, freeing regular units from all such distractions. In Danang and Hué they captured crucial installations and utilities. In Saigon they took key utilities, guiding the PAVN units through an otherwise confusing city. Their greatest importance was in the Delta, where three ARVN divisions existed amid vast food supplies and a population that would have been essential to a possible defense of Saigon and the implementation of Thieu's March 11 plan to consolidate his power in Cochin China. Keeping these divisions pinned down and off balance was vital to shattering Thieu's illusions and to preventing him from reinforcing the capital with men and supplies. Successfully applying mainly guerilla tactics, local Revolutionaries managed to cut roads linking the Delta to Saigon, foreclosing the one option that might have protracted the war or given Thieu's generals some tangible reason to resist.[14]

Throughout South Vietnam the end of the war saw a mixture of local militia and guerillas complementing regional and main forces in ways indispensable to both. The local forces in many areas would surely have been destroyed had it not been for the presence and imminent arrival of regular soldiers and their effect on RVNAF morale, but the main forces urgently needed the help of local fighters to take over policing and support operations, lest they themselves be diverted to less urgent tasks. In a conventional war that almost immediately became unconventional, the poorly armed local units performed a far greater function than they had at any other time since 1968, save in the Delta, where they played a primary role of immense strategic value.

Its coping with the administrative problems of success reflected the major gap in the Party's basic plan for the 1975 offensive. Not until a week after its first attack had produced the opportunity for total victory did it draw up a military plan to reach Saigon, but throughout this period it had no economic and political scheme for administering the south. Even when at the end of 1974 it projected complete victory in 1976, much less 1975, its political meaning was far more vague than its military meaning, and it included the possibility of a coalition with the Third Force, with PRG dominance, as an interim transition before reunification. Indeed, for some it meant little more than Thieu's being removed from power and replaced by less hostile elements and a Paris-style coalition. There was no economic plan or even a staff capable of formulating one for the south. The Party was not, in brief, prepared for the kind of total victory—and responsibility—it was to attain. This absence of a sense of imminent complete victory affected the best and ablest of the Party's leaders, including those who knew most about the south.

The Party's oversight was greatly complicated by the large number of people who surfaced and claimed always to have been part of the Revolution. Some were sincere, having merely been relatively inactive. That they had not worked steadily over many years did not decisively affect their ability to assume responsibility. Many joined new guerilla units and took over villages and towns, sometimes before any NLF political or military cadres appeared on the scene. To say that such people were opportunists ignores the fact that absolute heroism would have led many of them to death, and the Party understood well human limits in the face of protracted adversity. Revolutionary morality did not require sainthood. The Party's leaders were acutely conscious of the unbearable tensions and pressures that had driven many former NLF supporters to withdrawal and even collaboration. They now encouraged them to return to the Revolution and supplied them with arms to create local forces. Many who had never been involved on either side, particularly students, now were eager to join. During the euphoric days of liberation, the Party had no desire to raise too many questions. Obviously, senior Party people had confronted such issues after 1945, and they comprehended the scope of the problem—and the Revolution's immediate needs.

On the other hand, true opportunists and *attentistes* also emerged from the very beginning of the offensive, and this problem became more acute as victory became more certain. Even members of the Hoa Hao sect, classic survivors who had worked with the Japanese, the Communists, the French, and the Americans, now were ready to join forces with the Party. When various military units arrived in abandoned villages and towns, the local liberation committees running them often included *attentistes* and opportunists of various sorts and degrees. The Party's line was to create a coalition, and local NLF people, especially where they were weak, were quite ready to accept such elements, though they were realistic about their motives. In Danang the ARVN had so terrorized the local residents that mass support for the NLF as a force of order was often frankly nonpolitical, and they criticized the NLF for being too permissive with former ARVN soldiers, some of whom were still common bandits. To the extent that local self-governing committees relieved the advancing army of responsibilities, they were encouraged to function.

Military management committees were prepared to assume final responsibility where essential. But they, too, were overwhelmed with duties as the military moved south. During April thousands of civilian experts from the DRV were sent down to take charge of crucial duties, often only because they were dependable rather than because they were equipped for the tasks. Reliance on some former RVN functionaries was therefore another expedient the Party adopted immediately. Victory had caught the Party breathless, unprepared for the vast range of new work before it. This fact, perhaps more than any other, revealed the extent to which it had underestimated its own power, exaggerated that of Thieu, and misunderstood the total social dynamics of the conflict.[15]

THE END OF THE WAR: WASHINGTON AND SAIGON

The United States now had to confront the end of its decades of involvement in Vietnam, its failures and tragedies, its lost lives and riches, in a hopelessly futile effort that was ending ignominiously, without the hope of the slightest shred of dignity or honor for it to hide behind. Because this was the longest foreign war in American history, and the costliest in its impact on the internal cohesion of the nation, the significance of the imminent defeat was monumental in terms of the failure of a policy and technology. Potential replicas of Vietnam existed everywhere, and the United States would have to confront them with the same goals and resources. The identical considerations that had caused preceding administrations to enter and to persist with the war now affected Kissinger as he contemplated the total wreck of the RVN system on which the United States had depended to fulfill its mission in Southeast Asia and, implicitly, in the Third World.

At the end of all wars, very brief periods of time are filled with complex, multiple experiences which desperation and vain hopes produce, and the futile efforts to snatch some consolation from the inevitable, iron mechanisms of social processes and events bearing down on all those involved in the great drama are always convoluted and often wholly absurd. It would be wrong to focus on these marginal adventures, for however fascinating they may be, they should never obscure the simple, irreversible logic of the situation: the Communists were militarily and morally on the verge of victory because of the strength of their own forces and the weaknesses of their enemies, and Americans were witnessing the complete, unequivocal failure of their most important, sustained foreign intervention in over a century. The Party's leaders saw increasingly that the balance of forces now allowed them freedom to dictate the precise form of their ultimate triumph. Kissinger, too, very clearly appreciated the Revolution's strength and the symbolic meaning of the entire event for American power in the world.

Kissinger knew by mid-March that the United States' position of weakness condemned to futility any of its efforts, ranging from negotiations, aid to the RVN, or replacement of Thieu with another leader. If the Communists agreed to talk, it would be only because they might gain something and not because they were under any pressure. Thus all his efforts were devoted to the symbolism of defeat and to the need to maintain U.S. dignity and credibility insofar as it was possible under the circumstances. Proceeding within these constraints was essentially a technical matter for him. The Party's leaders, on the other hand, had the opposite problem of making certain that negotiations did not delay their increasingly irresistible military advance. Despite some involvement in oblique, convoluted negotiations, both sides knew that armies and people would define the outcome of the war. Diplomats could maneuver around this reality, but they could not overcome it.

In the diplomatic domain there was a ceaseless round of activity. The French now aggressively entered the picture, and they were aided by the instinctively intriguing Saigon politicians who flourished in cabals and welcomed an audacious French effort to reestablish influence in their former colony. The Party, on the other hand, had long favored the implementation of the political sections of the Paris Agreement, partly because its own political scenario was imprecise. They had yet to resolve differences among leaders on this point, and until the new military balance was established, they could not decide what was possible or necessary. After the fall of Ban Me Thuot, the French proposed to the Communists a new scenario that eliminated Thieu and implemented the Paris Agreement. U.S. and RVN refusal to discuss the idea saved the Party from much potential embarrassment later, but the fact it did not reject the scenario spurred the French to greater efforts. Working both in Paris and in Saigon, the French pressed for the removal of Thieu as a precondition for serious bargaining.

Kissinger dismissed these exertions as irrelevant. The Party simply decided to listen to them politely and not discourage any effort that would further weaken the RVN and possibly save it unnecessary loss of life. The Party did not, however, direct any of its diplomats to promote bargains; it merely left them without instructions regarding any departures from its existing commitment to the Paris Agreement. The Party's diplomacy at this time remained highly flexible; complete and total victory was only one of the possible outcomes to the war it had contemplated. Grasping the full implications of this prospect took most of March, and over the next weeks prudence and especially habit dictated that they retain every possible option. It was well into April before the Party realized that it would not have to share power. Meanwhile, many negotiating tracks were already operating.

By early April the French and some Americans, particularly the CIA in Saigon, came to believe that the dumping of Thieu and the arranging of a political settlement might stop the offensive. This hope galvanized most of Saigon's aspiring prime ministers and cabinet members into motion. Even though many strongly disagreed on the basis of a new regime, they were united mainly by their hatred of Thieu or, in most cases, by ambition. Neither Kissinger nor Martin thought these efforts would succeed, and the secretary of state was more concerned that America's reputation for constancy to its old friends not be soiled prematurely.

While the French and Saigon politicians indulged their fantasies, the administration turned to the more immediate problem of symbolic aid to the RVN. This was far more important to Kissinger because it was the sole concrete gesture to the world the United States could hope to make, and the chimera of a negotiated peace could undermine it. However, not only did the Pentagon think additional aid would be a waste of money, but President Ford, unlike his predecessors, was not ready to tarnish his prestige on a war that was nearly over. Only Kissinger attempted to obtain further aid after Ford's request to a cold and silent Congress on April 10 for $722 million in emergency aid. It was a sum sufficiently large to make it appear as if the United States were ready to stake something tangible on its doomed ally, but quite irrelevant to the RVN's real needs. The speech was rather an appeal to protect American credibility and its global image than an attempt to decisively help the RVN. Ford demanded the whole sum with the argument that a halfhearted gesture would be worse than none at all. The main point was not success or failure, Kissinger had the President state, but for America to make an effort. Even so, Ford gave Congress until the nineteenth to act, knowing full well it would not.

During the next days Ford's aides revealed that he would not seriously lobby for the money against what was overwhelming congressional opposition and overt Pentagon skepticism. The President applied no pressure on Congress and over the subsequent days said less and less about Vietnam. A fight would only lead to defeat and hurt his reelection prospects in 1976. The only serious question facing the administration was how to extricate the remaining six thousand Americans from South Vietnam along with the large numbers of Vietnamese who had worked for the United States. It was this sordid issue, with bureaucratic intrigues and personal rivalries involving the President, Martin, the CIA, Kissinger, and the Pentagon in ceaseless activity, that became the major focus of Washington's attention. Congress, too, applied pressures and added to the imbroglio's complexity. Uppermost in the minds of congressmen was the risk that the symbolic posturing of Kissinger and Martin would lead to the loss of American lives. Kissinger, obsessed with appearances, wanted America's departure to appear dignified and consistent with its world position. His support for Martin produced the final scenes of hundreds of empty-handed Americans clambering up rooftops in single file to helicopters to take them to aircraft carriers while hordes of ARVN soldiers and police rampaged through American housing, looting all that was left behind, a few firing shots at their escaping benefactors. The growing fear confronting the Americans in Saigon during their last two weeks was whether they would be killed by RVN troops or by bureaucrats now abandoned to their own devices. At the beginning of April, ARVN generals made explicit threats to this effect. The Americans in South Vietnam were in the position of hostages, a fact which the White House used to mobilize congressional support for its aid proposal, treating it as something of a ransom. Sustained American efforts to evacuate the best placed or most vulnerable of this group, who were among the 130,000 who managed to leave, partly reflected this fear of a massacre at the hands of those the United States had supported for decades.

As the administration groomed itself for the RVN's demise, French attempts to save some role for non-PRG politicians in Saigon reached a climax. While its ambassador in Saigon, Jean-Marie Mérillon, and the Quai d'Orsay tried to orchestrate it, they were aided by a bevy of aspirants to power in and around Thieu's circle, the CIA station and Martin in Saigon, Russians, Hungarians, and the DRV and PRG itself. The latter merely repeated the Party's past position that the Paris accords be applied and that Thieu's departure was a precondition. Kissinger on April 7 rejected the expulsion of Thieu, believing it would not make much difference and only further smudge the American image when the inevitable collapse came. The secretary of state now lost control of the situation. Although the French had many contacts, their two most important were Tran Van Don, then Thieu's minister of defense, and Duong Van Minh, or "Big Minh," who had been something of a neutralist when he was head of the Saigon junta in 1963. Minh was in contact with the French, Don, and the NLF, playing a different game with each of them.

To further complicate the picture, on April 8 the CIA obtained a Party directive to those in the south stating that the goal now was total victory and that they would use negotiations only as a stratagem. The significance of the document was disputed both within the CIA and by General Vien, who understandably interpreted it as an indication that the Party wanted to win a military victory rather than to end the war politically.[16] The Party, however, was not going to permit rumors of imminent peace to blunt the offensive mood of its armies by revealing to them that their combat might prove superfluous, even though in reality its final strategy was not irrevocably fixed. The true intentions and realism of their fast-dealing French and

RVN contacts as well as their own real options would certainly shape their ultimate responses to settlement offers.

Minh believed that a variety of supposed considerations, ranging from an alleged PRG-DRV split to Chinese opposition to a reunited Vietnam and the French role, might prove successful. So too did those around Thieu, who by this time had sent his wife and daughter to Bangkok and was himself less and less inclined to forgo his past gains to lead the remnants of his cause to a fiery end or, much more imminent, confront a coup led by Don and Vien. Kissinger now wobbled, the intricate brilliance of the French-backed maneuver momentarily causing him to abandon his earlier realism. On April 20 Martin saw Thieu in order to survey the entire military, political, and aid situation, claiming later that he did not ask him to resign but simply explained facts to a highly pragmatic man hoping that he would do so of his own volition. The next morning Thieu informed Khiem and Vice-President Tran Van Huong of his decision to quit, and that night he announced it publicly. Keeping Huong in power for a critical week so that it would not appear as if the United States had knuckled under to Communist or French pressure was the price Martin and Kissinger had exacted from Thieu's rivals. Huong, a man fully associated with Thieu policies and wholly unacceptable to the Party, became the senile new head of state. Four days later, with two huge suitcases full of gold in his baggage, the CIA flew Thieu to Taiwan. The appointment of Huong led to a week of ceaseless caballing for Saigon's plotters. Ky, Vien, Khiem, Don, and all the others met with Minh and the French, and every conceivable deal was struck. In this jungle it was left to the French to sort out the rivals. The provision of Minh with support against other ambitious generals, particularly Ky, depended almost wholly on them. He was now France's man as Thieu had been the United States'. Martin therefore greatly accelerated the departures of Americans and their Vietnamese collaborators and friends during this week of consummate intrigue, possibly the most intense since the death of Diem.

For the Party the appointment of Huong was the final straw. Several days later it informed the French that time had run out and that no coalition was possible, a fact which did not deter the French at all. On the twenty-sixth Huong suggested to the National Assembly that they replace him with Minh, and the next day they did so. By that time Minh had struck many bargains, and whether he would abide by those with the French or those with the PRG was his crucial decision. He was unsure what the Communists' policy toward himself would now be, and they in turn were aware of his many convoluted agreements. These, of course, made them very chary, and it was certain that the Communists would not forgo the option of quick and certain military victory should Minh make the slightest false move. On the afternoon of April 28, during a thunderstorm, Minh in his inaugural speech called for a negotiated peace but also asked the Revolution immediately to cease hostilities. His own troops he urged "to defend the territory which is left and to defend peace," adding, "Keep your spirit high, your ranks intact, and your positions firm. . . ."[17] He drew up plans not only to continue resisting but also to counterattack the Communist forces.

Minh's speech confirmed to the Communists that the French had him well in hand, and it ordered captured U.S. planes to strafe the Presidential Palace and its divisions to move toward Saigon. Minh's utopian message reinforced definitively the Party's natural reluctance to continue the charade with another puppet. Minh had agreed to ask the Americans to get the DAO out of South Vietnam within twenty-four hours, but Martin managed on April 27 to talk him into prolonging it until the thirtieth. It was another error at a time when his crumbling divisions allowed him precious little freedom of action. On the morning of April 29, the offensive against Saigon began, quickly cutting off the city on all sides. Martin ordered the final evacuation by helicopter, and the last Americans left by 5 A.M. on April 30. By that hour all of the key approaches to the city were in PAVN hands, while local forces, sympathizers, and sappers fanned throughout the city itself.

For the first time in well over a century, no foreigners occupied Vietnam to run its affairs.

Nguyen Van Thieu had constructed himself a worthy Presidential Palace set in the middle of a great park in the center of Saigon, with a vast ballroom, a swimming pool, game salons, a cinema, and a complex of halls for appropriate occasions. His furnishing it with plush and rich textiles, marble, and rare woods, with polished and heavily carpeted interiors, with lacquer panels and overstuffed couches, created a mood he thought essential. His own office was a vast chamber with a throne-like chair behind a huge desk. His private apartment was installed around a lush garden set deep into the interior of this massive edifice. For all practical purposes, on the morning of April 30 the palace was the symbol of all that was left of the American effort that had begun twenty years earlier and consumed the lives and commitments, emotions and existences, of millions of people. South of Saigon, in the Mekong Delta, the remnants of the RVN's armies were surrendering and disintegrating to local NLF units, sometimes several guerillas capturing hundreds of superbly equipped soldiers. At 10:15 Minh broadcast a cease-fire to his own forces, urging them also to remain in their positions and asking the Communists to do the same until there was a discussion of the orderly transfer of power. It was a surrender, but scarcely an unconditional one which acknowledged the reality of the battlefield. Minh and his cabinet then repaired to Thieu's palace and waited.

Thieu was in Taiwan; the Americans were on aircraft carriers heading toward the Philippines. As the first units of the PAVN entered the city, they confronted sporadic shooting and wiped out a few pockets of resistance, and a team of three tanks went straight to the palace Thieu had built. By this time the entire nation knew the end was imminent. The radios had ceased to operate, and for several hours the city was suspended between the old order and the new. The tanks reached the palace, which was undefended, and, after smashing through the huge iron grill protecting it, sped up the vast lawn to the broad stairs. A soldier with a PRG flag ran to a balcony, euphorically waving it back and forth, and then raised it up a flagpole at about 11:30 A.M. He and a comrade next searched the rooms and quickly found Minh and his cabinet seated around a table, silent. No one moved. One soldier stood guard while the other ran to find his officers. When a political cadre arrived, Minh declared, "We have been waiting for you so that we could turn over the government." "You have nothing left to turn over," he retorted, "You can only surrender unconditionally."[18] Minh immediately went to the radio station and did so.

The Vietnam War had ended.

Conclusion

Victory in war is not simply the result of battles, and nowhere in the twentieth century has this been truer than in Vietnam. To measure only the military balance of forces is misleading. To estimate the explicit designs of each of the contestants, while crucial, is by no means sufficient. Human goals and weaknesses are obviously critical, but in the social context which existed in South Vietnam between 1973 and 1975, far more was involved than conscious decisions. These were scarcely more than the sparks which led to the denouement neither side predicted, much less controlled. After the signing of the Paris Agreement, the fundamental change which occurred in South Vietnam was the general crisis of the entire social order the United States had installed. Its innumerable political, economic, and human consequences telescoped time and ended an epic, thirty-year war in a few stunning weeks in complete victory for the Communists.

The United States constructed a political and economic order in South Vietnam similar to the one it has repeatedly encouraged throughout the Third World. America's defeat was not merely a failure of its arms. Indeed, while partly successful in transferring military power to its surrogate, the Americans established institutional forms that were totally incapable of challenging the Revolution. The United States utterly failed to develop a credible limited-war doctrine and technical capability to intervene in the Third World, a crucial symbolic objective of the entire campaign for three administrations. Yet ultimately this was even less decisive than its intrinsic inability to create a viable political, economic, and ideological system capable of attaining the prerequisites of military success. This nonmilitary defeat makes Vietnam so significant for the limits of U.S. power in the Third World. America, locked into its mission to control the broad contours of the world's political and socioeconomic development, had set for itself inherently unobtainable political objectives.

Whatever the human and physical toll of the war on the Revolution throughout Vietnam, it was the myriad weaknesses of the foreign-sponsored society and the Communists' own strength which produced the decisive equation in the war. The individualism and egoism the Americans sought to implant were reflections of their own ideology and social system. Their encouragement of the private accumulation of possessions and wealth did not require an explicit counterrevolutionary ideology but only a lifestyle incompatible with the Revolution's essential values regarding personal behavior and social institutions. Washington's alternative, like its military doctrine, was capital intensive, since it purchased a corrupt, fragile, and fickle constituency, but it was also inherently self-destructive. The moment the amount of money to pay for the RVN system declined even slightly, the entire order began to tremble so that almost any challenge, military or political, would shatter it. Party decisions in 1974 and 1975 could operate only within this framework. Alone, they were important merely insofar as they created a confrontation of the two forces, in which the total power and disabilities of the two systems could be fully tested.

By 1974 the RVNAF was disintegrating amid the ravages which inflation and the demoralizing prospect of interminable war imposed on its soldiers. The army was ready to capsize at the first significant challenge, and the RVN's collapse after over two decades of assiduous, costly American efforts to build its military says more about each side's human resources than about the Communist army's specific strategy or equipment.

No less critical was the role of the people in the RVN-controlled rural and urban areas. To the extent that a radicalizing process was again well under way among them by 1974, it assured the Revolution's eventual success with or without the test of arms. For had the PAVN not attacked in March 1975, the war would have ended in the very near future with economic and political upheavals from which the Revolution would have emerged victorious after a period of social chaos. When the attack came, it quickly upset a house of cards.

The United States had installed a military system as a mechanism for controlling the political structure and, above all, the American-subsidized economic order. Fear of a coup or rivalry colored every aspect of its organization and action under Nguyen Van Thieu, and the total failure of its leadership in March 1975 revealed that an initially successful political apparatus posing as an army will not suffice in the long run. Thieu's key generals, while politically reliable, proved incompetent and powerless as military leaders. The RVN was not, as some Americans later argued, a military machine with an annexed political structure. Rather, it was an intrinsically dysfunctional hybrid order that the United States had constructed both by default and by accretion: an army, in the final analysis, that could not make successful war or politics, much less operate an economy. Almost all Americans watching the RVN closely after 1973 knew that its ineluctable demise was not far off, and some of them were less surprised at the speed and form of the collapse than many of the Party's leaders. Wars often end when the social, human, and political conditions are ripe, and the nature and tempo of the Communist military triumph in Vietnam was primarily a consequence of them. The Communist Party was to inherit this social system's immense disorganization when it came to power.

America's losing the war had little to do with the crisis of its politics connected with Watergate. Given the dilemmas it confronted in the world economy, the administration's problem in South Vietnam was one that would have arisen even if Nixon had been at the peak of his powers. It had to impose priorities on its global objectives in order to attain any of them. Economic difficulties at home and constraints on resources and manpower finally compelled the United States to make the RVN conform to American norms of efficiency—an obligation that merely triggered a crisis in Thieu's system.

Ultimately, the weakness of the RVN's social order was also the recurrent dilemma of the United States' relationship to all of its Third World clients, on which it has become fatally dependent as instruments for applying its foreign policy. The inevitable choice of Thieu as its surrogate made Washington's position increasingly precarious. It was impossible to meet this challenge, because the notion of an honest puppet was a contradiction Washington has failed to resolve anywhere in the world since 1945. In effect, while the White House had to cope with the problem of its own legitimacy and relationship to Congress after 1972, it still had to deal with this enduring, universal paradox of the relevance of the impotence of its dependents to the advancement of American power.

The Vietnam War was for the United States the culmination of its frustrating postwar effort to merge its arms and politics to halt and reverse the emergence of states and social systems opposed to the international order Washington sought to establish. It was not the first serious trial of either its military power or its political strategy, only the most disastrous. Despite America's many real successes in imposing its hegemony elsewhere, Vietnam exposed the ultimate constraints on its power in the modern era: its internal tensions, the contradictions between overinvolvement in one nation and its interests and ambitions elsewhere, and its material limits. Precisely because of the unmistakable nature of the defeat after so long and divisive an effort and because of the war's impact on the United States' political structure and aspirations, this conflict takes on a significance greater than that of either of the two world wars. Both of them had only encouraged

Washington's ambition to guide and integrate the world's political and economic system—a goal which was surely the most important cause of its intervention in the Vietnam conflict after 1950.

While the strategic implications of the war for the future of American military power in local conflicts was the most obvious dimension of its defeat, it had confronted these issues often since 1946. What was truly distinctive was the collapse of a national consensus on the broad contours of America's role in the world. The trauma was intense; the war ended without glory and with profound remorse for tens of millions of Americans. Successive administrations fought the war so energetically because of these earlier frustrations, of which they were especially conscious in the early 1960s, scarcely suspecting that rather than resolving them, they would only leave the nation with a far larger set of military, political, and economic dilemmas to face for the remainder of this century. But by 1975 the United States was weaker than it had been at the inception of the war in the early 1960s, a lesson hardly any advocate of new interventions could afford to ignore.

The limits of arms and armies in Vietnam were clear by Tet 1968. Although the United States possessed nominally good weapons and tactics, it lacked a military strategy capable of overcoming its enemy's abilities and appropriate to its economic resources, its global priorities, and its political constraints in Vietnam, at home, and in the rest of the world. Although its aims in South Vietnam were never to alter, it was always incapable of coping with the countless political complexities that irrevocably emerge from protracted armed conflict. America's political, military, and ideological leaders remained either oblivious or contemptuous of these until the war was essentially lost. Even today they scarcely dare confront the war's meaning as Washington continues to assert aggressively its classic postwar objectives and interests in Latin America and elsewhere. America's failure was material, of course, but it was also analytic, the result of a myopia whose importance greatly transcended bureaucratic politics or the idiosyncrasies of Presidents and their satraps. The dominating conventional wisdom of American power after 1946 had no effective means of inhibiting a system whose ambitions and needs increasingly transcended its resources for achieving them. They remained unable and unwilling to acknowledge that these objectives were intrinsically unobtainable and irrelevant to the socioeconomic forms much of the Third World is adopting to resolve its economic and human problems, and that the United States' effort to alter this pervasive reality was certain to produce conflict.

That America's destiny in Vietnam should have been inextricably tied to two venal men is by itself a remarkable fact, but scarcely unique in the postwar era. Nor is it surprising that the nature and role of Thieu and the society he and the Americans fashioned became the critical variable in the war's astonishing end. Since there was no durable social, economic, and political basis for any of the French- or American-imposed regimes, their demise was inevitable despite the quite unforeseeable quality of the RVN's final weeks. In retrospect, it is extraordinary that four administrations attempted at immense cost to impose American hegemony on Vietnam while totally dependent on such vulnerable surrogates.

The United States had no way out of this hopeless trap short of a readiness to concede an early defeat of its aim to create an anti-Communist South Vietnam. It always favored erstwhile strongmen in the hope they would provide stability and an effective alternative. The size and the political and economic functions of the RVN military left no space for any of the largely ephemeral, disunited, non-Communist social forces. In every sense there was no serious option to the Revolution, and none would have emerged even if the United States had sought to encourage one. America's sponsorship of the military's central role in every dimension of the RVN system created a recipe for social, economic, and political disaster. In the end, this unavoidable policy was certain to produce a wholly artificial society which traumatized the masses and expanded the Revolution's objective potential, notwithstanding its large losses.

Linked to this problem of translating its armed might into political success was the fact that in the very process of fighting a war utilizing titanic firepower, the Americans created vast demographic and human upheavals, with their searing psychological and economic impact, resulting in an urbanized society that was not viable either economically or politically. The very consequences of its technological premises stretched South Vietnam's entire social fabric far beyond the control of the American surrogates in Saigon. It was the irony of U.S. local-war strategy, and then of Vietnamization, that its intrinsic effects imposed intolerable and fatal burdens on the social order. These far outweighed the importance of its nominal victories in battles. It suggests, as well, why the American military cannot enter any society without accelerating the corrosive dynamics and problems sure to lead to political failure for its local allies.

Technology in the war played a profoundly different role for each side. Applying its existing weaponry and technological potential to define and develop a limited- and counterinsurgency-war strategy applicable to Third World contexts was far more complex then the United States had ever imagined in the early 1960s. America's leaders and generals substituted confidence in the quantity of their arms for cogent strategic and political analyses. They failed to make an accurate assessment of their prospects for success, or even of the economic costs of their doctrines, until well into the war, when symbolically important considerations, such as "credibility," paralyzed their thinking in additional ways. Only the Communists fully appreciated the larger context of the struggle. They overcame the most formidable array of arms in history with a protracted war based on decentralization, mass mobilization, and highly adaptive military tactics tailored to technology's specific vulnerabilities. Indeed, just as the United States hoped to develop a limited-war capability relevant throughout the globe, the Communists articulated political, organizational, and technical responses to American intervention and arms valuable to revolutionary forces everywhere. This fact is likely to compound the difficulties of America's self-appointed counterrevolutionary mission in the Third World for decades to come.

The Communist Party is the easiest contestant to understand in the Vietnam War. Its passion for theory and analysis was quite introspective, constant, and invariably public. Its role and decisions were always manifest both from its deeds and from its words. It is simpler to fathom because it succeeded, and the causes of a system's triumph are much more obvious than those of a system's failure. For the Party's victory is a testimony not only to the malleability of history as a general process but also to the wartime efficacy of the institutions and ideas of the winning side as well as those of the nation that lost.

The Party's power, especially before 1949, was intimately linked to the void which the breakdown of French colonialism and the nature of the class system did so much to create. The thread of its success by default, due largely to its existence and endurance and to its enemies' follies, weaves through the entire thirty-year war. The Party's carefully calculated political and military initiatives, of course, made it assume an increasingly activist leadership. But the disastrous structural impact of the actions of the United States and the RVN throughout South Vietnam meant that the Party would always be able to exploit the consequences of its enemy's innumerable weaknesses. The Party was highly creative and pragmatic in its attempt to make the most of the possibilities before it. The worst error anyone studying it can make is to try to explain its actions, policies, and resilience simply as a predetermined, deductive consequence of its Marxist-Leninist ideology. To a crucial extent, the diversity and richness of the Party's practice and success transcended its own formal theoretical system.

The Revolution had to organize large sectors of Vietnamese society. In the process it recorded errors as well as accomplishments. Most important, though, was its ability to survive both as an organization and, at the very least, as a cause in the minds of the people. It thereby retained the ability to reassert itself when there were new opportunities to do so. The Communist Party leadership's ability to analyze and adapt, to relate its resources to reality, and to avoid a sense of omnipotence as well as excessive caution was the essential link between its existing and potential forces and the future.

To a critical degree the Party's power to rally vast numbers was due to the corrosive impact of wars on the traditional rural order and to its own integrative role. The French-imposed land system and economy drove the masses to desperation by the time of World War Two, and the Communists offered them an organized revolutionary response to common social problems. It was from this assertion of community and class in the face of famine and war that the Party's organization became durable. And it was the economics of peasant discontent, more than any other single long-term issue, which gave the Party a capacity to mobilize the masses, its ultimate reservoir of power. Time and again the peasantry profoundly influenced the Party's grand strategy—most decisively during 1953–55 in the north, in 1959–61 in the south, and thereafter in various localities in the south. Adherence to the poor-peasant line made mass mobilization possible, and it was repeatedly the price of success.

Such concessions to pressures from below often conflicted with the Party's continuous advocacy of a united-front line against the French and Americans. Reconciling the tensions between class conflict and political unity was a perpetual challenge to it—one which it never wholly mastered and which compelled it at times to go against its preferences. Still, the Party's ability to employ nonclass appeals like patriotism and to absorb better-educated revolutionaries of bourgeois origins at all levels proved an inestimable source of strength to it over the years. Although its united-front strategy was never as successful as the Party hoped after 1961, particularly in the cities, its minimal achievements were sufficient to provide the Party with the support it needed.

In coping with these and countless other challenges, the Party committed errors, but none, obviously, that were fatal to its entire effort. If the Party's leaders sought to portray themselves as performing a greater role on the road to power than they in fact played, their accomplishment as a guiding force was nonetheless exceptional in the twentieth century. Extremely careful students of social dynamics, essentially cautious, deliberative analysts both by inclination and because of the checks inherent in their collective decision-making structure, they were far more adept at making rational, logical assessments than any of their French and American enemies, whose penchant for illusions and symbolism made them the only total ideologists of the war. While ready to take risks to move toward their ultimate goals, the Party's leaders always carefully estimated the balance of forces they confronted at home and abroad and the long-range implications of various actions. Such realism prevented decisive mistakes.

The Party's leaders repeatedly responded to pressures from the masses, ostensibly to guide them along a coherent route but in reality sometimes only after recognizing that their demands were irresistible and would find expression with or without guidance. Given the immense length of the nation and the difficulties of communication, the process of both leading and following the people was an inherently slow one. Space and time imposed their own imperatives on both sides during the war, but particularly on the materially poorer Communists. While the Party's leaders articulated an ideal organizational form, realities forced them repeatedly to conform in an ad hoc fashion to the local imperatives of economic underdevelopment and of protracted war. Their ultimate wisdom was to accept such inhibitions and define the nature of revolutionary commitment in a way that transcended predetermined organizational concepts but touched the essentials of revolutionary politics in a long war.

The Communist Party's genius was in its ability to survive and adapt to the most incredible challenges and reemerge sufficiently powerful to fill the vacuum that the United States and its dependents created. Its retention of the loyalty of its most committed members, who endured astonishing personal losses for long periods, was the core of this resiliency, and it could do so because of its ability to relate to the most pressing social problems facing the people. This effort after 1968 became far more complicated as the problems of peace and the preservation of a coherent society against the onslaught of the American presence and the traumas of war surpassed obvious class issues as the burning mobilizing questions. The Party's tasks in coping with this new, broader consciousness in both urban and rural areas posed a much more subtle challenge. It knew that the war's physical and psychological toll on the people had been profound, though most of its leaders failed to perceive that the true balance of forces had overwhelmingly shifted in their favor.

The Party therefore underestimated the distinctive transformation of political attitudes which was then taking place among the urban elements, quickly leading to an alienation and apathy fundamentally subversive to the RVN's cohesion and future. It understood the RVNAF's demoralization better, but, even here, the implications did not become apparent to most of its leaders until December 1974, when they realized resistance to an offensive might be minimal and ineffective. That a large and growing vacuum existed, which any concerted effort could fill, seemed possible to the Communists, but little did they imagine the monumental occurrences of March and April. To the degree that these were the outcome of Thieu's priorities and commitments to himself, they were predictable, however, and the precedents of Lam

Son 719 and the 1972 offensive were powerful indicators of his incompetence and of the fragility of his soldiers and officers when confronted with danger.

To some extent, then, although the astounding events of the final chapter of the war were unforeseeable to the Communists, their results were the inexorable and predictable outcome of their own efforts and of the nature of the forces arrayed against them. When the moment came, they seized the opportunity and entered the enormous void during the most remarkable seven weeks in the entire history of the war. But that astonishing drama was merely the culmination of a political, social, and human struggle that had begun two decades earlier and that the Revolution had used to build its ranks and establish its legitimacy in a slow, patient, and painfully cumulative process. It could only predict that this vast, interminable chain of sacrifices and efforts would produce total victory. And at times it offered those who stayed with it throughout the long ordeal only the often abstract and all-too-distant proposition, grounded in its Marxism, that people and social processes can intersect and interact to determine their own future and shape the outcome of their history.

The Vietnam War, in the final analysis, was a contest between the U.S. with its abundantly subsidized, protected surrogate and a Revolutionary movement whose class roots and ideological foundations gave it enormous resiliency and power. The way individuals behaved both in war and in peace reflected the social norms and the nature of the two competing systems. The Communist Party's most important source of strength over thirty-five years was its conception of a socialist and revolutionary morality and its insistence on the primordial significance of radical values and conduct to the achievement and implementation of a socialist society. Its capacity to develop an organization whose members' lives conformed sufficiently to these principles attained this objective functionally, if never perfectly. This notion of the critical role of the individual was Vietnamese Communism's most distinctive and fundamental addition to Marxist-Leninist theory and an implicit major revision of the relative importance of leaders and purely organizational forms. No one can comprehend how countless tens of thousands of men and women struggled for decades—usually under conditions of extreme privation and often in isolation, demanding extraordinary personal commitments, patience, and sacrifices—without appreciating the influence of such revolutionary commitments and values as well as the attraction of its social and political program. For while the Party's tactics and strategy throughout the war had to be correct far more often than not, that was a necessary but not sufficient condition of success. In a protracted struggle in which a multidimensional crisis affected events in a manner exceeding the capacity of anyone—including its leaders—to anticipate, the Party's ultimate power was its ability to endure and thereby, either wisely or erroneously, to continue to relate to events. The very existence of its persistent, devoted members gave the Party the freedom to assume mastery of the nation's future and to fill the void the French and American experience left in Vietnam.

Revolutionary morality postulated that consciousness affects the historical process by its very being. It did not, lest it become radical mysticism and romanticism, ignore the material balance of forces, but it asserted the critical role of personal responsibility and action. Whatever the exact internal nature of a party, which requires discipline in some measure to address itself to difficult circumstances, the very existence of such a degree of optimism assumes an element of freedom in social processes. A conception of the masses' role in great events and history produced a self-consciousness which itself became an ingredient of power. However strict Party control, the very existence of the Party is an affirmation of the role of will and choice in history, and its cohesion became the precondition of eventual freedom from the constraints of a historical process which makes the need for unity and morality essential in the first instance. Conscious of the risks of excessive discipline as well, the Party sought to minimize them with an essentially institutionalized antibureaucratic campaign which, though far from solving the problem, lessened it significantly.

In analyzing the Communist Party's remarkable and often unique efforts on behalf of a revolutionary morality and personal socialist values, one must make a clear distinction between total success and sufficient attainment of its goals. It never became a Party of revolutionary saints, nor did it proclaim total triumph for its efforts to achieve its ideal standards, but it did manage to bring together a great number of men and women whose morals and dedication to a cause were very high, who made monumental sacrifices and underwent incredible deprivation, and who alone made the Party play its role in history. These people, as well as a substantial number who were not so devoted, were the objects of a constant effort at self-renewal and reinvigoration. The Party was, after all, a group of mortals who possessed many of the weaknesses of humankind, but also a great share of its all-too-rare strengths. One could ask little more. The very drive for personal morality was seen as a part of the process to overcome the freely acknowledged faults of its members, and the attempt to deal explicitly with their limitations resolved many of them. In a word, the system worked, thereby confirming revolutionary optimism's relationship to historical change.

It is the extent of the Party's success which is all the more interesting, as if the constant pressure of the long struggle strengthened many of its members and made it easier for them to dedicate their lives to the cause. Underlying the commitment of the Party's best and strongest members was a synthesis of belief and confidence in the future, based on a merger of their own required action with a rational assessment of the nature of social reality and historical materialism—a synthesis of the personal and impersonal that made belief all the more plausible and action all the more necessary. Each could attain personal fulfillment by seeking to change history, but it would be through and for the people—and for a cause in which each person's destiny was linked with that of the revolution. The impact of this conception made the seemingly impossible victory over France and America possible, and the strongest proof of its efficacy is that, in the end, experience vindicated it.

The role of freedom and constraint in historical processes and great events intrudes perpetually into mankind's ideas. The real question in this search for primary explanations is the extent to which both choice and necessity operate over time and, above all, how, when, and why one becomes more important than the other. The significance of these issues, fundamental for understanding the modern historical experience, resists simplifications and does not permit the evasion of contingent conclusions, for living with the tensions of complexity and partial insight is superior to the false security of pretentious final solutions to the inherent, but creative, dilemmas of knowledge.

For the activist the extent of freedom in the face of historical forces is a fundamental question about the meaning of action and about a life's commitments. The comprehension of the limits *and* possibilities of reality is the essence of political strategy and the precondition for optimal social change. Over time, risks of error are constant, their consequences to the destinies of conscious people being easily capable of defining their lives and crucial experiences. The effort to master one's environment and world is integral to the nature and extent of rationality and freedom in modern life. That constraints have and will always operate on people's desires is less contentious than understanding that social change in this century has been astonishingly rapid and traumatic. The external crises of war and multiple internal developments will sustain this transformation of the world in the future. The very inevitability and the impact of such monumental events create both the potential and the need for directed change, making the possibilities of freedom and mastery integral to the human condition.

The interaction between reality and ideals, in Vietnam but also in many other nations throughout this century, has been a critical element in those successes that proponents of deliberate changes have attained. Whatever the precise validity of various socialist diagnoses of the nature of capitalism and the Third World, their ultimate intellectual and political strength has been their keen appreciation of the profound importance of change and crisis in the modern historical experience and of the ability and obligation of organized forces to attempt to influence them. It is this fixation that has renewed socialism's significance time and again after sometimes enormous political failures and errors in analysis, for change is also predicated both on the ability and on the need of people to respond to real opportunities in defining society's affairs. The comprehending of social forces and guiding them in a resilient and patient manner is relevant when existing orders become unstable or fail. The costs of protracted wars to national economies and their social and ideological cohesion have been the most important source of change, especially in accelerating the decolonization of the European and American imperialist orders, but there have been others as well. As the longest conflict of the modern era, the Vietnam War offers a vast panorama for assessing the origins and components of a crisis affecting two major Western nations and for exploring the significance of action and organizations in consciously defining the final outcome of a major historical event.

War is generally the transcendent element in all societies that compels choices and action. Parties of change at such times relate to the masses, attempting to impose ideas and roles on those now increasingly likely to act with or without leadership. When large numbers of people realize that they are unable to evade the personal consequences of their action or inaction—and may indeed pay a much higher price for their passivity—they become a social force, all the more durable to the extent they take an organized form. Evasion is, however, the normal response of most people to the risks about them, and it usually is far less the party with claims of leadership than the breakdown of the traditional order that stimulates their initial consciousness and discontent, conditioning them to act. Evasion will tend to recur as the society's crisis is alleviated, though not without the persistence of residues of earlier ideas and values in mass consciousness. But stability is so rarely permanent that a party's main role in this process is to provide the continuity and linkage between periods of crisis and relative tranquillity, along with such leadership as the masses will accept when their readiness for action returns. In this sense, though a party must not make too many errors, it is less important that it always be correct than that it be able to sustain its existence and relationship to social dynamics and forces so that its influence reemerges with the growth of a society's crisis. Its capacity to persist is a critical measure of the potential of freedom and rationality in history.

This commitment to activism as a way of extracting maximum change from given social conditions becomes integrated with institutional processes and also accelerates them. It does not passively wait for such processes to culminate impersonally at some desired, hypothetical point. To the extent that social forces and movements are underdeveloped, they are galvanized through a merging of objective conditions in the economy and society with the activity of a party. A party's significance may range from utter futility at one period to decisive relevance at another, or to all the intermediate stages possible. Activism, along with organization, is a risk that the assumption of freedom to measurably affect historical forces requires—and one that has produced success so often in this century, and in so many nations, that the numerous occasions on which it has failed in whole or in part should never occlude our comprehension of the parameters of human possibilities and change in our age. This degree of accomplishment does not eliminate all limitations on freedom, but only those which would result if there were no concerted efforts at controlled change. The general Marxist tradition has not, in any event, minimized the domain of impersonal institutional and social inhibitions. But precisely because the Left is aware of the reality of the absence of total liberty, it has also acknowledged the existence of opportunities to transform, and the obligation to exploit, historical processes.

Yet when all of these contingencies are taken into account, events in the twentieth century, in Vietnam and in countless other nations, have shown that those who have pursued the route of action for social change and paid their price in time, passion, and commitments are also those who have most defined the extent to which human choice and freedom affect social developments. The residual legacies and problems of past institutional and social experiences exist throughout the world, of course, and no nation, even when the old regime is totally eliminated, is able easily or quickly to transcend them. Historical experiences are complex and often problematical, and that successes are never total or victories truly final is less important than that they occur often as a consequence of human will and action, with coveted social changes often resulting from combinations of freedom and necessity, desire, action, and insight, but never from apathy and indifference.

The Vietnam War was a monumental event which transcends one nation or time and reflects, in the most acute form, the basic dynamics and trends in the historical experience since 1946. It was scarcely accidental but rather the logical outcome of contemporary U.S. ambition, strength, and weakness. The war once again confirmed the inevitability of social transformations and social movements in the world today, their real vulnerabilities as well as their enormous force, and the awesome potential of men and women to define their own future against overwhelming opposition. To weigh both American resources and ultimate impotence against the capabilities of those adversaries it may very well confront in some other hapless nation in the Third World, this year or in the future, is to gauge the true nature of power and the components of change in today's world. For given all the social and human dimensions which will affect the outcome of warfare between the United States and radical movements and nations, it is scarcely imaginable that another massive encroachment in some recalcitrant revolutionary nation would have an end different from that in Vietnam.

All that the United States has the ability to accomplish today is to impose immeasurable suffering on people whose fates its arms and money cannot control. To do so once more would also demand from the American public a price it eventually refused to pay in Vietnam and is even less likely to give willingly in the future. Profound social change in the modern historical experience is irresistible. But the nature of that process and the manner in which it affects the lives of the masses in developing countries over the coming decades are inextricably linked to the question whether its defeat in the Vietnam War constrains the United States from interventions elsewhere and allows the people of the world to develop their own future.

Sources and Notes

A Word on Sources

The quantity of materials available on both the United States and the Communist Party is monumental. In my attempt to outline and analyze the major contours of the war and the forces shaping it, I have constantly had to avoid extraneous but fascinating or colorful details which shift one's focus away from larger trends and meanings. In dealing with each of the three sides, I have attempted to evaluate available information and facts, not to mention analyses of them, against the broader context of events that would allow me to treat them as credible or dubious. Given the imperative functions which societies at war must carry out and given the kinds of situations and responses which seem possible in the context of total war and the nature and role of the leaders and social systems involved in it, I do not believe it is difficult to differentiate plausible from doubtful information.

Since this book is based not only on documents and printed matter but also on countless conversations, some formal interviews, and experiences, I have attempted to weigh information gleaned from paper against that which I have obtained by sight and sound. In no case have I taken any orally communicated assertions at face value; rather, I have, if possible, checked them against other sources before accepting their veracity. Obviously, an afternoon's exchange with a dozen ARVN deserters, discussions with peasants about their experiences, wandering through the vast Danang air base, or crawling through a tunnel in which people lived for months, let alone observing the momentum of the Revolution's forces in the south at the end of April 1975, makes an indelible impression that is a useful foil for excessive abstraction or impersonality. Still, I have tried to avoid the serious liabilities of both firsthand journalism and academia, of which I am acutely aware. The result, I hope, is a critical, balanced evaluation. The reader should be aware that many of the people and events I discuss in this book I saw with my own eyes or had direct contact with, ranging from dissident GIs and village activists in South Vietnam to some of the men who shaped U.S. policy. For this reason, while the footnotes which follow are a very important indication of sources for this book, they by no means include all of them.

Apart from the primary and secondary works cited in the footnotes, for the

559

United States, the Communist Party, and the RVN, I have found certain documentation especially valuable. For the United States, *The Pentagon Papers* remains the best readily accessible source for the period up to 1968, at least insofar as policymaking is concerned. The National Security Council internal documents collection on the war, 1964–68, is far more detailed and in certain ways more insightful because one does not have to rely on Pentagon writers' interpretations. Covering the CIA, Defense Department, National Security Council, State Department, and White House, the Declassified Documents Reference System has reproduced the most valuable of the voluminous manuscripts released under the Freedom of Information Act, and its military information is much more revealing than that either the Army or the Air Force has so far managed to include in their innumerable and sometimes useful published studies of the war. Thomas C. Thayer's "How to Analyze a War without Fronts: Vietnam, 1965–72" is a very helpful summation of the prodigious analyses the Pentagon's Systems Analysis Office produced during the war; it is a distillation of many of the key data the quantitative fixation the United States suffered from was able to muster. After 1968, House and Senate hearings and documents become increasingly valuable, as elements in Congress moved to a critical position. The U.S. Army War College–sponsored unpublished prolix analysis of the war, "A Study of Strategic Lessons Learned in Vietnam," is mediocre, but a few sections contain new or useful information. Rand Corporation studies of the war are also often helpful in confirming knowledge one may glean elsewhere too.

The United States funded immense translation series of both public and captured Communist Party sources, and I unfortunately began with the captured, presumably confidential and more accurate, series. These consist of the *Viet-Nam Documents and Research Notes,* the State Department's 1968 documents collection entitled "Working Papers," and the Douglas Pike and Jeffrey Race collections. While a certain number of original and inaccessible items may be found in these collections, the U.S. Joint Publications Research Service regular translations of the Party's most important printed publications remain, by far, the single most important body of sources on the Communist Party. Many of the so-called confidential captured documents are merely summations and analyses of the wordier and sometimes far more subtle and valuable public Party statements and discussions, in large part simply the result of a paucity of printed copies in the south. I have exploited all of these materials systematically, as well as the Party's own publications in English and French.

Researching the RVN proved far more challenging, particularly given my focus on its socioeconomic structure. The U.S. Army Center of Military History commissioned senior ARVN officers to write studies of the war, and these were published during 1979–80 in nineteen volumes as the "Indochina Monographs" series. They are sometimes valuable even though part of their data came from the U.S. Army itself. The Rand Corporation synthesis *The Fall of South Vietnam* (1980), by Stephen T. Hosmer et al., is far more candid but lacks details. My effort to obtain U.S. Agency for International Development materials touching the economic and social dimensions of the war was extremely time-consuming but ultimately fruitful, despite my failure to obtain anything under the Freedom of Information Act after five years of attempts. The AID was the major organization privy to the RVN as an economic and political machine. I had very insightful interviews with Americans who were in Vietnam specializing on such matters, from whom I also obtained a variety of helpful documents, and I have deposited all or parts of these with the Echols Collection of the Cornell University Library, along with a copy of the AID's unpublished 850-page "Terminal Report." The latter is the single most valuable and candid source on the RVN economy available. A copy also exists in the AID Library in Rosslyn, Virginia, along with many other documents I have cited here.

The best accessible documents collection on the war is Gareth Porter, ed., *Vietnam: A History in Documents* (New York: New American Library, 1981).

The following code abbreviations are used in the notes:

AID— U.S. Agency for International Development, Asia Bureau, Office of Residual Indochina Affairs, "United States Economic Assistance to South Vietnam, 1954–75," December 31, 1975. Pagination is for the copy in the Echols Collection, Cornell University Library.

BDM— BDM Corporation, "A Study of Strategic Lessons Learned in Vietnam," April 4, 1980, under contract to the U.S. Army War College. Volume and page number follow the code.

DDRS— Declassified Documents Reference System (Carrollton Press). In most cases, only the author, nature of the document, date, and exact microfiche citation are given, but not the title of the document.

DOD— U.S. House of Representatives, Committee on Appropriations, *Hearings, Department of Defense Appropriations,* the fiscal year being considered, date, and page.

DSB— U.S. *Department of State Bulletin.*

EC— Echols Collection, Cornell University Library. Indicates I have deposited copies of the pages I cite in the Collection.

GP— Gareth Porter, ed., *Vietnam: A History in Documents* (New York, 1981).

IM— "Indochina Monographs" series, U.S. Army Center of Military History, Washington, D.C., 1979–80.

JPRS— U.S. Joint Publications Research Service. Author, journal, date, and JPRS number only are given.

NSC— U.S. National Security Council 1964–68 files on Vietnam (University Publications of America microfilm edition). Author, nature of document, and date only. The collection is chronological.

NSSM— U.S. National Security Council Study Memorandum No. 1, March 14, 1969, in *Congressional Record,* May 10–11, 1972, pp. E4975–5066.

NYT— *New York Times.*

PM— Douglas Pike Collection, "Documents on the National Liberation Front of South Vietnam," Center for Research Libraries, Chicago.

PP— The Senator Gravel Edition, *The Pentagon Papers: The Defense Department History of United States Decisionmaking on Vietnam,* 4 vols. (Boston: Beacon Press, 1971).

RC— Rand Corporation, Santa Monica, California.

SA— Thomas C. Thayer, "How to Analyze a War without Fronts: Vietnam, 1965–72," *Journal of Defense Research,* ser. B, vol. 7B, no. 3 (Fall 1975).

VN— Joint U.S. Public Affairs Office, Saigon, *Viet-Nam Documents and Research Notes.*

WP— U.S. Department of State, "Working Paper on the North Vietnamese Role in the War in South Viet-Nam," March 1968. Probable author and date are listed where relevant along with the "item" number in this collection.

A note indicates the source of each preceding quotation or series of quotations. It frequently also includes references for nonquoted information following the prior note. Where there are no quotations, the note documents the information in the preceding paragraphs.

Preface

1. Ho Chi Minh, *Selected Works* (Hanoi, 1961), III, 193.

Chapter 1: Vietnam's Road to Crisis

1. While all accounts agree on peasant conditions, data on land distribution are not wholly consistent. See Erich H. Jacoby, *Agrarian Unrest in Southeast Asia* (Bombay, 1961), 160–64, 175; Pierre Gourou, *Les Paysans du Delta tonkinois* (Paris, 1936), 268–69, 360, 569–79; International Labour Office, *Labour Conditions in Indo-China* (London, 1938), 197; Robert L. Sansom, *The Economics of Insurgency in the Mekong Delta of Vietnam* (Cambridge, 1970), 21–22, 30–32, 261; James C. Scott, *The Moral Economy of the Peasant: Rebellion and Subsistence in Southeast Asia* (New Haven, 1976), 57, 80; Stanford Research Institute, *Land Reform in Vietnam* [summary volume] (Menlo Park, 1968), 3; Jeffrey M. Paige, *Agrarian Revolution: Social Movements and Export Agriculture in the Underdeveloped World* (New York, 1975), 289–90, 303–6; Christine K. White, "Agrarian Reform and National Liberation in the Vietnamese Revolution: 1920–1957" (Ph.D. thesis, Cornell Univ., 1981), 34–37; Ngo Vinh Long, *Before the Revolution: The Vietnamese Peasants under the French* (Cambridge, 1973).

2. ILO, *Labour Conditions,* 146. See also ibid., 18–21, 47, 53, 87, 273–75, 288; Virginia Thompson, *French Indo-China* (New York, 1937), 208; Vo Nhan Tri, *Croissance économique de la République Démocratique du Viet Nam, 1945–1965* (Hanoi, 1967), 38; Jean Chesneaux et al., eds., *Tradition et révolution au Vietnam* (Paris, 1971), 164–88; Duc Thuan, *Nghien Cuu Lich Su,* March–April 1970, JPRS 51,415, 30.

3. David G. Marr, *Vietnamese Tradition on Trial, 1920–1945* (Berkeley, 1981), 40, 303–4; Huynh Kim Khanh, *Vietnamese Communism, 1925–1945* (Ithaca, 1982), 35–36, 54; Chesneaux, *Tradition et révolution,* 189ff.; Jayne S. Werner, *Peasant Politics and Religious Sectarianism: Peasant and Priest in the Cao Dai in Viet Nam* (New Haven, 1981); Scott, *Moral Economy of the Peasant,* 221; Jayne Werner in William S. Turley, ed., *Vietnamese Communism in Comparative Perspective* (Boulder, 1980), 107–36; Alexander B. Woodside, *Community and Revolution in Modern Vietnam* (Boston,

1976), 183ff.; Nguyen Khac Vien et al., *Vietnam: A Historical Sketch* (Hanoi, 1974), 165–66.

4. Bernard B. Fall, "Viet-Nam's Chinese Problem," *Far Eastern Survey,* May 1958, 65–66; ILO, *Labour Conditions,* 243–49; Victor Purcell, *The Chinese in Southeast Asia* (London, 1965), 174–204; Alexander B. Woodside, *Vietnam and the Chinese Model* (Cambridge, 1974), 270–75; Chesneaux, *Tradition et révolution,* 147–63; Tri, *Croissance économique,* 57–70, 94–97; Ngo Vinh Long, [Harvard East Asian Research Center], *Papers on China,* 24 (Dec. 1971), 125–45; Tsai Maw-Kuey, *Les Chinois au Sud-Vietnam* (Paris, 1968), 140–42; Milton Osborne in Walter F. Vella, ed., *Aspects of Vietnamese History* (Honolulu, 1973), 160–90; Khanh, *Vietnamese Communism,* 40–45.

Chapter 2: The Communist Party until 1945

1. Ho Chi Minh, *Selected Works* (Hanoi, 1962), IV, 426. See also To Huu, *Blood and Flowers* (Hanoi, 1978), 58; Huynh Kim Khanh, *Vietnamese Communism, 1925–1945* (Ithaca, 1982), chap. 1; Commission for the Study of the History of the Party, *50 Years of Activities of the Communist Party of Vietnam* (Hanoi, 1980), 22.

2. To Huu, *Blood and Flowers,* 42–43.

3. Ho Chi Minh, *Selected Works* (Hanoi, 1961), III, 195.

4. Khanh, *Vietnamese Communism,* 84ff., 124ff., 168ff.; Ho Chi Minh, *Ho Chi Minh and Africa* (Hanoi, 1980), 95–102; idem, *Selected Writings, 1920–1969* (Hanoi, 1977), 39–41, 103–5; idem, *Patriotism and Proletarian Internationalism* (Hanoi, 1979), 61–62; Commission for the Study, *50 Years of Activities,* 30–32; János Radványi, *Delusion and Reality* (South Bend, 1978), 4–5; Robert Shaplen, *The Lost Revolution* (New York, 1965), 38–40; Le Manh Trinh, *Hoc Tap,* Aug. 1966, JPRS 37,878, 31.

5. Khanh, *Vietnamese Communism,* 153, 191ff., 208ff.; Douglas Pike, *History of Vietnamese Communism, 1925–1976* (Stanford, 1978), 155; Vietnamese Studies, *Nghe Tinh: Native Province of Ho Chi Minh* (Hanoi, 1980), 64–97; Martin Bernal, "The Nghe-Tinh Soviet Movement, 1930–1931," *Past and Present,* no. 92 (Aug. 1981), 148–68; David G. Marr, *Vietnamese Tradition on Trial, 1920–1945* (Berkeley, 1981), 382–85, 392–97; Commission for the Study, *50 Years of Activities,* 40, 49–56; James C. Scott, *The Moral Economy of the Peasant* (New Haven, 1976), 147–49; Ton Duc Thang, *Nhan Dan,* Sept. 13, 1960, JPRS 7,137, 143; Le Manh Trinh, *Hoc Tap,* 31–34; Ho Chi Minh, *Selected Writings,* 42–43.

6. Commission for the Study, *50 Years of Activities,* 58 65; Commission on Party History, *History of the August Revolution* (Hanoi, 1972), 11–29, 58–59; Khanh, *Vietnamese Communism,* 252–56; Christine K. White, "Agrarian Reform and National Liberation in the Vietnamese Revolution: 1920–1957" (Ph.D. thesis, Cornell Univ., 1981), 91–95; Pierre Brocheux in Paul Isoart, ed., *L'Indochine française, 1940–1945* (Paris, 1982), 137–39.

Chapter 3: Vietnam: From the August 1945 Revolution to Protracted War

1. Ho Chi Minh, *Selected Writings, 1920–1969* (Hanoi, 1977), 47; Christine K. White, "Agrarian Reform and National Liberation in the Vietnamese Revolution: 1920–1957"

(Ph. D. thesis, Cornell Univ., 1981), 101ff.; Huynh Kim Khanh, *Vietnamese Communism, 1925–1945* (Ithaca, 1982), 299–308; Commission for the Study of the History of the Party, *50 Years of Activities of the Communist Party of Vietnam* (Hanoi, 1980), 68, 74; Commission on Party History, *History of the August Revolution* (Hanoi, 1972), 24–28, 134–35, 172–75; Vo Nguyen Giap, *Unforgettable Days* (Hanoi, 1975).

2. Nguyen Cao Ky, *Twenty Years and Twenty Days* (New York, 1976), 17. See also Ralph F. Turner, *Vietnamese Communism: Its Origins and Development* (Stanford, 1975), 49, regarding the 1946 consensus.

3. CIA report, Sept. 20, 1949, 23–25, DDRS 76:12E. See also Ho Chi Minh, *Selected Writings,* 62–65; Ho Chi Minh, *Selected Works* (Hanoi, 1961), III, 57–61; Pham Cuong and Nguyen Van Ba, *Revolution in the Village: Nam Hong, 1945–1975* (Hanoi, 1976), 13; Vo Nhan Tri, *Croissance économique de la République Démocratique du Viet Nam, 1945–1965* (Hanoi, 1967), 106–7.

4. Truong-Chinh, *Selected Writings* (Hanoi, 1977), 27, 49–50, 104–5, 127. See also White, "Agrarian Reform," 115–21.

5. Truong-Chinh, *Selected Writings,* 229, 348, 350, 353, 355. See also ibid., 352, 369; White, "Agrarian Reform," 123–34; Tri, *Croissance économique,* 121; Etudes Vietnamiennes, *Politique économique et guerre de liberation nationale* (Hanoi, 1976), 60–66.

6. Truong-Chinh, *Selected Writings,* 108, 111–12. See also Giap, *Unforgettable Days,* 158, 323; Commission for the Study, *50 Years of Activities,* 94–95; Eugene K. Lawson, *The Sino-Vietnamese Conflict* (New York, 1984), chap. 2, for Sino-Vietnamese military differences.

7. Ho Chi Minh, *Selected Works,* III, 146–47. See also Truong-Chinh, *Selected Writings,* 142–49.

Chapter 4: The Internal World of Vietnamese Communism

1. Le Duc Tho, *Hoc Tap,* Feb. 1961, JPRS 8,914, 15. See also ibid., 13; Ho Chi Minh, *Selected Writings, 1920–1969* (Hanoi, 1977), 203.

2. 1948 report, WP, item 1; Commission for the Study of the History of the Party, *50 Years of Activities of the Communist Party of Vietnam* (Hanoi, 1980), 104; Ho Chi Minh, *Selected Writings,* 59–61, 88–89; idem, *Selected Works* (Hanoi, 1961), III, 148–50; Etudes Vietnamiennes, *Politique économique et guerre de liberation nationale* (Hanoi, 1976), 130.

3. Le Duan, March 1966 letter, WP, item 302, 2.

4. Vo Nguyen Giap, *Unforgettable Days* (Hanoi, 1975), 63.

5. Truong-Chinh, *Selected Writings* (Hanoi, 1977), 382 (italics in original). See also ibid., 75, 158–67, 385; David G. Marr, *Vietnamese Tradition on Trial, 1920–1945* (Berkeley, 1981), 362–67; Commission on Party History, *History of the August Revolution* (Hanoi, 1972), 179–80.

6. Ho Chi Minh, *Selected Writings,* 89.

7. Ibid., 203. See also Nguyen Khac Vien, *Tradition and Revolution in Vietnam* (Berkeley, 1974), 47–49; Marr, *Vietnamese Tradition,* 374–75.

8. Ho Chi Minh, *Selected Works,* III, 116.

9. To Huu, *Blood and Flowers* (Hanoi, 1978), 93.

10. Nguyen Chi Thanh, *Nhan Dan,* July 4, 1968, JPRS 46,190, 3. See also Douglas Pike, *History of Vietnamese Communism* (Stanford, 1978), 67–69; W. P. Davidson and J. J. Zasloff, "A Profile of Viet Cong Cadres," RM-4983, June 1966, RC, x, 36; 1949 agent report, WP, item 21, 10, regarding tired cadres.

11. Ho Chi Minh, *Selected Works,* III, 141. See also ibid., 148–50; Truong-Chinh, *Selected Writings,* 76–77; Ho Chi Minh, *Selected Writings,* 88–89; WP, item 21; Vu Tho, *Nhan Dan,* Dec. 29, 1958, JPRS 1,400-N, 3–4.

12. To Huu, *Blood and Flowers,* 49.

13. Ho Chi Minh, *Selected Works,* III, 202. See also ibid., 387–89; Ho Chi Minh, *Selected Writings,* 92, 117–19, 127; Truong-Chinh, *Selected Writings,* 443; WP, item 1, 2; WP, item 3, 1; Le Duc Tho, *Hoc Tap,* 19; William S. Turley, ed., *Vietnamese Communism in Comparative Perspective* (Boulder, 1980), 182.

14. Vu Tho, *Nhan Dan,* 3–4.

15. Le Duc Tho, *Hoc Tap,* 13. See also Nguyen Chi Thanh, *Nhan Dan,* July 4, 1968, JRPS 46,190, 14, on the need to make criticism more "conciliatory."

16. Ho Chi Minh, *Selected Writings,* 119.

17. Nguyen Chi Thanh, *Nhan Dan,* 14.

18. Ho Chi Minh, *Selected Writings,* 127, 146. See also ibid., 141–42, 205; Truong-Chinh, *Selected Writings,* 444.

19. Le Duc Tho, *Hoc Tap,* 19. See also WP, item 21, 5–7; WP, item 1, 2.

20. Ho Chi Minh, *Selected Writings,* 204.

21. Hong Chuong, *Hoc Tap,* May 1967, JPRS 41,648, 80.

22. Ho Chi Minh, *Selected Works,* III, 199; IV, 249, 254, 257.

23. Ton Duc Thang, *Nhan Dan,* Sept. 13, 1960, JPRS 7,137, 156.

24. Ho Chi Minh, *Selected Works,* III, 202. See also Truong-Chinh, *Selected Writings,* 112; Le Duc Tho, *Hoc Tap,* 19; 1951 document, WP, item 2, 5; 1949 report, WP, item 3; Song Le, *Hoc Tap,* Aug.–Sept. 1960, JPRS 6,390, 1.

25. Truong-Chinh, *Selected Writings,* 478. See also ibid., 484, 511, 553; Vo Nguyen Giap, *Unforgettable Days,* 75–81; Song Le, *Hoc Tap;* editorial, *Hoc Tap,* Sept. 1961, JPRS 11,233, 1–3; Roger Darling, "The Unique Capacities of North Vietnam in Achieving Peasant Participation in Revolution," *Military Review,* Jan. 1977, 3–13; Turley, *Vietnamese Communism,* 179–81; Vo Nhan Tri, *Croissance économique,* 126, 277; Commission for the Study, *50 Years of Activities,* 115; Christine K. White, "Agrarian Reform and National Liberation in the Vietnamese Revolution: 1920–1957" (Ph.D. thesis, Cornell Univ., 1981), 175 and passim; Etudes Vietnamiennes, *Politique économique,* 88.

26. GP, 131. See also Truong-Chinh, *Selected Writings,* 480–85; White, "Agrarian Reform," chaps. 4–5, 326–29; Edwin E. Moise, *Land Reform in China and North Vietnam* (Chapel Hill, 1983), 168ff.

27. Ho Chi Minh, *Selected Writings,* 168. See also Truong-Chinh, *Selected Writings,* 540–48; Etudes Vietnamiennes, *Politique économique,* 83.

Chapter 5: The Communist Party's Consolidation of Power

1. The Revolution's imperative need to consolidate after its 1954 offensive is documented in Etudes Vietnamiennes, *Politique économique et guerre de liberation nationale*

(Hanoi, 1976), 130–31; Vo Nhan Tri, *Croissance économique de la République Démocratique du Viet Nam, 1945–1965* (Hanoi, 1967), 171; János Radványi, *Delusion and Reality* (South Bend, 1978), 6–9; Military Institute, *Vietnam: The Anti-U.S. Resistance War for National Salvation, 1954–1975: Military Events* (Hanoi, 1980), JPRS 80,968, 6. China's diplomatic role is analyzed best in the semi-official work of François Joyaux, *La Chine et le règlement du premier conflit d'Indochine (Genève 1954)* (Paris, 1979), 64–69, 85, 142–43, 197, 264, 286–321, 358. See also *PP,* I, 109, 134–35, 173; Melvin Gurtov, "Negotiations and Vietnam: A Case Study of the 1954 Geneva Conference," RM-5617, July 1968, RC, DDRS 76:31A.

   2. Christine K. White, "Agrarian Reform and National Liberation in the Vietnamese Revolution: 1920–1957" (Ph.D. thesis, Cornell University, 1981), 242–50, 265–71, 306–23, is the best overview. See also Vo Nhan Tri, *Croissance économique,* 214–15; Etudes Vietnamiennes, *Politique économique,* 88–92; Ho Chi Minh, *Selected Works* (Hanoi, 1962), IV, 32–35; Edwin E. Moise, *Land Reform in China and Vietnam* (Chapel Hill, 1983), 196–201, 220–21, 240, 254; Douglas Pike, *History of Vietnamese Communism, 1925–76* (Stanford, 1978), 110; Tibor Mende, *Esprit,* June 1957, 941. Professor Moise kindly clarified a number of issues for me.

   3. White, "Agrarian Reform," 309–13, 431–46; Moise, *Land Reform,* 237–48; Pike, *Vietnamese Communism,* 163; Ho Chi Minh, *Selected Works,* IV, 34, 190–93, 359; Vo Nhan Tri, *Croissance économique,* 202, 277–85; David W. P. Elliott, "Political Integration in North Vietnam: The Cooperativization Period," SEADAG Papers 75-2 (Asia Society, 1974); Commission for the Study of the History of the Party, *50 Years of Activities of the Communist Party of Vietnam* (Hanoi, 1980), 131; Etudes Vietnamiennes, *Politique économique,* 84–87; Pham Cuong and Nguyen Van Ba, *Revolution in the Village: Nam Hong, 1945–1975* (Hanoi, 1976), 34; Alec Gordon, "Class Struggle, Production and the Middle Peasant: North Vietnam's Collectivization Campaign," *Economic and Political Weekly* (India), 16 (1981), 459–73.

   4. The basic study is Vo Nhan Tri, *Croissance économique.* See also Bernard B. Fall, *The Two Viet-Nams* (New York, 1963), 139, 177; Pike, *Vietnamese Communism,* 103; Etudes Vietnamiennes, *Politique économique,* 188–89.

Chapter 6: America's Confrontation with the Limits of World Power

   1. Joyce and Gabriel Kolko, *The Limits of Power: The World and United States Foreign Policy, 1945–54,* (New York, 1972), 340. Both in this volume and in my *Main Currents in Modern American History* (New York, 1984), chaps. 6 and 10, I have developed and documented many of the ideas presented here.

   2. *PP,* I, 187, 364.

   3. *PP,* I, 83–84. See also ibid., 375–90; NSC paper 48/4, May 4, 1951, DDRS 77:41C.

   4. NSC paper 141, Jan. 16, 1953, 18, DDRS 77:44B.

   5. Kolko, *Limits of Power,* 685.

   6. Ibid., 684–86; State Dept. memo, July 10, 1953, DDRS 78:278B, 11.

   7. Kolko, *Limits of Power,* 699.

Chapter 7: South Vietnam to 1959

1. Dulles to Frank C. Laubach, Oct. 31, 1950, Dulles Papers, Princeton University Library. See also Gabriel Kolko, *The Roots of American Foreign Policy* (Boston, 1969), 90–101; NSC paper 48/4, May 4, 1951, DDRS 77:41C; NSC paper 141, Jan. 16, 1953, 18, 27, 50–52, DDRS 77:44B.

2. U.S. Dept. of State, *Foreign Relations of the United States, 1952–1954* (Washington, 1982), XIII, 1869. See also ibid., 1122–23, 1241, 1270–72, 1334; ibid., XVI, 682–83, 758, 898–99; Melvin Gurtov, "Negotiations and Vietnam . . . ," RM-5617, July 1968, RC, 69, DDRS 76:31A; Chester L. Cooper, *The Lost Crusade* (New York, 1970), 70–74, 81, 99; Ronald H. Spector, *Advice and Support: The Early Years, 1941–1960* (U.S. Army Center of Military History, 1983), chap. 11; *PP*, I, 144; George C. Herring and Richard H. Immerman, "Eisenhower, Dulles, and Dienbienphu . . . ," *Journal of American History*, 71 (1984), 343–63; William C. Gibbons, *The U.S. Government and the Vietnam War: Executive and Legislative Roles and Relations*, pt. 1, *1945–1961* [U.S. Senate, Committee on Foreign Relations, 98:2, April 1984], 175–216; François Joyaux, *La Chine et le règlement du premier conflit d'Indochine (Genève 1954)* (Paris, 1979), 142, 197.

3. State Dept., *Foreign Relations*, XIII, 1906. See also ibid., 2123, 2286–87, 2407–9; XVI, 565, 603, 845–46, 860–61, 1009–10; Robert Shaplen, *The Lost Revolution* (New York, 1965), 109–13; Cooper, *Lost Crusade*, 128; regarding elections, see also *PP*, I, 146n, and Gibbons, *U.S. Government and the Vietnam War*, 269; GP, 168.

4. Edward G. Lansdale, *In the Midst of Wars* (New York, 1972), 147–48, 216ff., 300ff.; Cooper, *Lost Crusade*, 137–44; *PP*, I, 182–83, 206–11, 305; Shaplen, *Lost Revolution*, 120ff.; J. Lawton Collins to Dulles, Jan. 20, 1955, DDRS 78:295A; CIA estimate, Aug. 16, 1955, DDRS 77:5C; CIA estimate, Oct. 11, 1955, DDRS 76:145F; Gibbons, *U.S. Government and the Vietnam War*, 295–97.

5. CIA estimate, Oct. 11, 1955, 2. See also Nguyen Duy Hinh and Tran Dinh Tho, *The South Vietnamese Society*, IM, 75, 128–31; Tran Van Don, *Our Endless War* (San Rafael, 1978), 50; State Dept. report, May 5, 1959, 5–8, DDRS 77:77C; *PP*, I, 299, 302; Cao Van Vien, *Leadership*, IM, 30; Shaplen, *Lost Revolution*, 130–32; Spector, *Advice and Support*, 279–81, 305; Denis Warner, *The Last Confucian* (Baltimore, 1964), 116–17; Lansdale, *Midst of Wars*, 342–43.

6. Spector, *Advice and Support*, 303–4; CIA estimate, Oct. 11, 1955; Cooper, *Lost Crusade*, 149–51; Kolko, *Roots*, 112–13.

7. *PP*, I, 275, 298, 323; Hoang Ngoc Lung, *Strategy and Tactics*, IM, 63–64; George S. Eckhardt, *Command and Control, 1950–1969* (U.S. Dept. of the Army, 1974), 11–12; James L. Collins, Jr., *The Development and Training of the South Vietnamese Army, 1950–1972* (U.S. Dept. of the Army, 1975), 4–19; Vien, *Leadership*, 163–64; Dong Van Khuyen, *The RVNAF*, IM, 313; Lt. Gen. Lionel C. McGarr report, Nov. 10, 1960, 14–15, DDRS 75:255C; Cao Van Vien and Dong Van Khuyen, *Reflections on the Vietnam War*, IM, 8–9.

8. Tsai Maw-Kuey, *Les Chinois au Sud-Vietnam* (Paris, 1968), 59, 63, 142–49, 199ff.; Tran Van Dinh, *Que Huong* (Saigon), March 1961, 131–53; Bernard B. Fall, "Viet-Nam's Chinese Problem," *Far Eastern Survey*, May 1958, 65–67; AID file on Chinese in Vietnam, EC, item 4A, 2.

9. *PP*, I, 318. See also ibid., 255–58, 311, 338; Carlyle A. Thayer, "The Origins of the

National Front for the Liberation of South Viet-Nam" (Ph.D. thesis, Australian National Univ., 1977), 269, 403; Cooper, *Lost Crusade,* 153–54; Kolko, *Roots,* 113, 157; Lung, *Strategy and Tactics,* 40.

10. Donald Q. Coster speech, March 30, 1961, 4, DDRS 76:139D. See also ibid., 6; State Dept. report, May 5, 1959, 2, 4 and passim; McGarr, Nov. 10, 1960, 3; *PP,* I, 267–68; Robert Scigliano and Guy H. Fox, *Technical Assistance in Vietnam* (New York, 1965); Collins, *Development and Training,* 4–12; NSC memo, Aug. 18, 1959, 7ff, DDRS 79:48A; Nguyen Kien, *Le Sud-Vietnam depuis Dien-Bien-Phu* (Paris, 1965), 148–57; Hinh and Tho, *South Vietnamese Society,* 138–39; Bernard B. Fall, *The Two Viet-Nams* (New York, 1963), 302–8; U.S. Senate, Comm. on Foreign Relations, *Executive Sessions* (Historical Series), XI, 86:1 (Washington, 1982), 853–54; Cooper, *Lost Crusade,* 165; Lansdale, *Midst of Wars,* 357–58.

11. Roy L. Prosterman, "Land-to-the-Tiller in South Vietnam," *Asian Survey,* Aug. 1970, 755. See also ibid., 754; *PP,* I, 254, 400–401; Stanford Research Institute, *Land Reform in Vietnam* (Menlo Park, 1968), 10–15; Jeffrey Race, *War Comes to Long An* (Berkeley, 1972), 57–59, 316–20; Robert L. Sansom, *The Economics of Insurgency in the Mekong Delta of Vietnam* (Cambridge, 1970), 54–59; Cao Van Luong, *Nghien Cuu Lich Su,* no. 2, 1981, 55–62; Le Chau, *La Révolution paysanne du Sud Viet Nam* (Paris, 1966), 56–59; SA, 923; J. Millard Burr, "Land to the Tiller: Land Redistribution in South Viet Nam, 1970–1973" (Ph.D. thesis, Univ. of Oregon, 1976), 7.

12. Sansom, *Economics of Insurgency,* 67; *PP,* I, 255, 310; William Bredo, "Agrarian Reform in Vietnam . . . ," *Asian Survey,* Aug. 1970, 748; Stanford, *Land Reform,* 186–87; Race, *War Comes to Long An,* 8–12, 40–41, 91–94; Tran Van Don, *Our Endless War,* 66–67; Lansdale, *Midst of War,* 356; Stuart A. Herrington, *Silence Was a Weapon* (Novato, 1982), 27; J. J. Zasloff, "Origins of the Insurgency in South Vietnam, 1954–1960 . . . . ," RM-5163, May 1968, RC, 9–10; Nguyen Minh Vy, *Hoc Tap,* Aug.–Sept. 1960, JPRS 7,165, 4–5.

13. Lung, *Strategy and Tactics,* 40. See also *PP,* I, 255–56, 311; Spector, *Advice and Support,* 310–12.

14. Tran Dinh Tho, *Pacification,* IM, 72. See also Thayer, "Origins," 267–68.

15. State Dept., May 5, 1959, 7. See also Spector, *Advice and Support,* 310–11, 332–34; *PP,* I, 255, 312–13; GP, 200–201.

Chapter 8: The Communist Party's Dilemma in the South, 1954–1959

1. Ho Chi Minh, *Selected Works* (Hanoi, 1962), IV, 158. See also idem, *Selected Writings, 1920–69* (Hanoi, 1977), 189–90; Carlyle A. Thayer, "The Origins of the National Front for the Liberation of South Viet-Nam" (Ph.D. thesis, Australian National Univ., 1977), 69, 121ff.; 1948 report, WP, item 1; index to the U.S. government edition of the Pentagon Papers, III, C-14; J. J. Zasloff, "Origins of the Insurgency in South Vietnam, 1954–1960 . . . ," RM-5163, May 1968, RC, 1–7; Pham Van Dong, *Ecrits* (Hanoi, 1977), 27–31; Lt. Gen. John W. O'Daniel brief, ca. late 1955, DDRS R:73B; Ronald H. Spector, *Advice and Support* (U.S. Army Center of Military History, 1983), 303–4; Commission for the Study of the History of the Party, *50 Years of Activities of the Communist Party of Vietnam* (Hanoi, 1980), 133.

2. Military Institute, *Vietnam: The Anti-U.S. Resistance War for National Salvation* (Hanoi, 1980), JPRS 80,968, 16. See also Thayer, "Origins," 203–4; *PP,* I, 263.

3. Thayer, "Origins," 83, 92, 462–63, 530–31; Zasloff, "Origins," 5–13; Spector, *Advice and Support,* 310ff.; Military Institute, *Anti-U.S. Resistance,* 6; *PP,* I, 258; 1958 and 1961 interrogations, WP, items 12 and 26; early 1963 document, WP, item 301, 2; WP, item 29; Jeffrey Race, *War Comes to Long An* (Berkeley, 1972), 37.

4. 1958 interrogation, WP, item 12, 10. See also ibid., 4; Zasloff, "Origins," 12–17; Race, *War Comes to Long An,* 101–4; WP, item 301, 1–10; 1964 interrogation, WP, item 27; Nov. 29, 1954, document, WP, item 29; Spector, *Advice and Support,* 347; State Dept. Report, May 5, 1959, 11–12, DDRS 77:77c; WP, items 18, 31, 201, 204, 210; Ta Xuan Linh, "Les Débuts de la lutte armée au Sud Viet Nam," *Le Courrier du Viet Nam,* March 1974, 22; Thayer, "Origins," 279–91, 355ff.; Military Institute, *Anti-U.S. Resistance,* 19–20; Cao Van Luong et al., *Tim Hieu Phong Trao Dong Khoi o Mien Nam Viet Nam* (Hanoi, 1981).

5. WP, item 301, 10; To Minh Trung, *Nghien Cuu Lich Su,* Jan. 1969, JPRS 48,515, 40–41; GP, 191–92; János Radványi, *Delusion and Reality* (South Bend, 1978), 24–25; Tran Van Tra, *Concluding the 30-Years War* (Ho Chi Minh City, 1982), JPRS 82,783, 53; Cao Van Luong, *Tim Hieu Phong;* Thayer, "Origins," 539–45; Spector, *Advice and Support,* 326–27.

6. *PP,* I, 305, 330–36; Jayne S. Werner, *Peasant Politics and Religious Sectarianism* (New Haven, 1981), 43–69; Race, *War Comes to Long An,* 36–37, 72; Spector, *Advice and Support,* 313–15, 325; Thayer, "Origins," 530–39; Military Institute, *Anti-U.S. Resistance,* 11–12, 20–26; State Dept. Report, May 5, 1959, 10–12; ca. 1956 cell analysis, WP, item 201; report, Oct. 1955 meeting with sects, WP, item 205; early 1965 document, WP, item 301; Ta Xuan Linh, "Les Débuts," 19–22.

7. Nguyen Thi Dinh, *No Other Road to Take* (Ithaca, 1976), 62. See also Radványi, *Delusion and Reality,* 24–25; Zasloff, "Origins," 57; *PP,* I, 263–64; Cao Van Luong, *Tim Hieu Phong,* 58; Military Institute, *Anti-U.S. Resistance,* 28–30, 34–35; Race, *War Comes to Long An,* 113, 120; Tran Van Tra, *30-Years War,* 53; 1964 interrogation, WP, item 36, and esp. WP, item 301, 3, 10, 29; Thayer, "Origins," 669–75.

8. GP, 197. See also VN, nos. 36–37, June 1968, 10; To Minh Trung, *Nghien Cuu Lich Su,* 50; late 1959 interrogation, WP, item 202; Race, *War Comes to Long An,* 116, 126–30; Nguyen Thi Dinh, *No Other Road,* 65, 75–77.

9. March 28, 1960 letter, WP, item 34, 2. See also Dept. of State, *A Threat to the Peace,* pt. 2 (Washington, 1961), 93; GP, 196–99.

10. McGarr report, Nov. 10, 1960, 12, DDRS 75:255C. See also State Dept. Report, May 5, 1959; WP, item 301, 30; U.S. May 27, 1968, memo, VN, nos. 36–37, 10.

11. Interview with Vo Van An in Jeffrey Race Collection, Center for Research Libraries, Chicago, reel 2; Race, *War Comes to Long An,* 121; Douglas Pike, *History of Vietnamese Communism* (Stanford, 1978), 122.

Chapter 9: The U.S. Involvement in Vietnam

1. *PP,* II, 33. See also ibid., 22, 48–49.

2. Ibid., 34.

3. Ibid., 336. See also ibid., 174–75, 663–65, 817; III, 51, 500; NSC report, n.d. [1962],

10, DDRS 80:281A; Guy J. Pauker, "Indonesia's Grand Design . . . ," RM-4080, May 1964, RC, iv–vi, DDRS 75:60A; State Dept. mss, n.d. [early 1964] 20, DDRS 79:90B.

4. *PP*, III, 695. See also ibid., 592; Gerald Segal, *The Great Power Triangle* (London, 1982), chaps. 2–3.

5. *PP*, III, 51. See also ibid., 153, 598–99, 622–23, 683.

6. W. W. Rostow memo, Jan. 30, 1961, DDRS 75:328C.

7. Robert Shaplen, *The Lost Revolution* (New York, 1965), 152.

8. *PP*, II, 250. See also ibid., 228; Ronald H. Spector, *Advice and Support* (U.S. Army Center of Military History, 1983), 339ff., 363–67; Denis Warner, *The Last Confucian* (Baltimore, 1964), 22ff.; Shaplen, *Lost Revolution,* 156ff.; Roger Hilsman, *To Move a Nation* (Garden City, 1967), 447–49; Durbrow to Rusk, May 3, 1961, DDRS 75:318A; U.S. Army, Saigon, report, Nov. 1961, DDRS R:197D; Bowles to Nolting, Nov. 4, 1961, DDRS R:799E; Nolting to Rusk, Nov. 5, 1961, DDRS R:800B; Nolting to Rusk, Nov. 18, 1961, DDRS R:809E.

9. W. W. Rostow memo, Dec. 1, 1962, 21, in James Thomson Papers, Kennedy Library, box 6. See also James L. Collins, Jr., *The Development and Training of the South Vietnamese Army* (U.S. Dept. of the Army, 1975), 18–22; *PP,* II, 134–36; William Colby, *Honorable Men* (New York, 1978), 155, 163–64.

10. Tran Van Don, *Our Endless War* (San Rafael, 1978), 87. See also ibid., 53; *PP,* II, 208ff.; Shaplen, *Lost Revolution,* chap. 6; Nguyen Cao Ky, *Twenty Years and Twenty Days* (New York, 1976), 40–46.

11. GP, 253. See also *PP,* II, 234–35; George W. Ball, *The Past Has Another Pattern* (New York, 1982), 371–73; and esp. William C. Gibbons, *The U.S. Government and the Vietnam War,* pt. 2, *1961–1964,* December 1984, 139–89.

12. U.S. Senate, Select Comm. to Study Governmental Operations, *Report: Alleged Assassination Plots Involving Foreign Leaders,* 94:1, Nov. 20, 1975, 220. See also Shaplen, *Lost Revolution,* 211.

13. Senate Select Comm., *Assassination Plots,* 221. See also Gibbons, *U.S. Government and the Vietnam War,* 189–202.

14. Rusk to Taylor, Sept. 13, 1964, DDRS 79:94E. See also Nguyen Van Tiet, *Thuc Trang Nen Han Chanh Dia Phuong Tai Viet-Nam* (Saigon, 1969), 22–30, 87–166; William R. Corson, *The Betrayal* (New York, 1968), 227.

15. Collins, *Development and Training,* 31–32; Ngo Quang Truong, *RVNAF and U.S. Operational Cooperation and Coordination,* IM, 2–3; Harkins to Felt, Feb. 17, 1964, DDRS 75:167B; State Dept. mss, n.d. [early 1964], 4–9, DDRS 79:90B; Lodge to Rusk, Feb. 27, 1964, DDRS R:836B; various CIA and State Dept. dispatches, DDRS 79:134B, 207B, C, and E; Taylor to Rusk, Jan. 24, 1965, DDRS R:858A.

16. CIA estimate, Sept. 8, 1964, 1, DDRS 78:31A. See also *PP,* V, 338.

17. CIA estimate, Sept. 8, 1964, 3. See also CIA report, Feb. 25, 1965, DDRS R:48G; Shaplen, *Lost Revolution,* 296ff., remains the best guide to this maze.

18. William C. Westmoreland, *A Soldier Reports* (Garden City, 1976), 107. See also *PP,* III, 150–51; V, 321; Gibbons, *U.S. Government and the Vietnam War,* 210–14.

19. William P. Bundy memo, March 2, 1964, 19, DDRS 75:157A. See also Rostow to Rusk, Jan. 10, 1964, DDRS 77:147C; McNamara memo to Johnson, March 16, 1964, NSC.

20. GP, 264; *PP*, V, 321. See also *PP*, III, 176; Doris Kearns, *Lyndon Johnson and the American Dream* (New York, 1976), 170–72.

21. GP, 278; McGeorge Bundy, June 10, 1964 memo, 2, NSC.

22. *PP*, V, 322. See also ibid., III, 144; V, 320–21; GP, 277–80; State Dept. to U.S. embassy, Vientiane, July 29, 1964, NSC.

23. Transcript, Ball on BBC, Oct. 16, 1977. See also GP, 284; Ball, *Another Pattern*, 379; *PP*, V, 321–23; U.S. Senate, Comm. on Foreign Relations, *Hearings: The Gulf of Tonkin: The 1964 Incidents*, 90:2, Feb. 20, 1968, 49; pt. 2, Dec. 16, 1968, 7; Gibbons, *U.S. Government and the Vietnam War*, chap. 5.

24. *PP*, III, 145–46.

Chapter 10: The War and Rural Vietnam

1. Tay Ninh tax schedule, Sept. 1963, PM, no. 876. See also Stanford Research Institute, *Land Reform in Vietnam* (Menlo Park, 1968), 156; CIA report, Sept. 26, 1966, DDRS 76:26G; R. Michael Pearce, "The Insurgent Environment," RM-5533, May 1969, RC, 50, 98–99; Pearce, "Evolution of a Vietnamese Village—Part II . . . ," RM-4692, April 1966, RC, 24–25; Jeffrey Race, *War Comes to Long An* (Berkeley, 1972), 127, 161–62, 177–79; Konrad Kellen, "A View of the VC . . . ," RM-5462, Nov. 1969, RC, 8–9; and esp. James W. Trullinger, Jr., *Village at War* (New York, 1980), 40ff., 91.

2. Douglas Pike, *Viet Cong* (Cambridge, 1966), 251. See also Kellen, "View of the VC," 14–15; Pearce, "Insurgent Environment," 45–48; Stuart A. Herrington, *Silence Was a Weapon* (Novato, 1982), 36, 72; W. P. Davison, "Some Observations on Viet Cong Operations in the Villages," RM-5267, May 1968, RC, v–vi; James L. Collins, Jr., *The Development and Training of the South Vietnamese Army* (U.S. Dept. of the Army, 1975), app. D; *PP*, II, 694–95.

3. For assassinations, see Denis Warner, *The Last Confucian* (Baltimore, 1964), 161; Trullinger, *Village at War*, 92; Stanford, *Land Reform*, 167; Davison, "Viet Cong Operations," vi; Dec. 24, 1965, document, VN, no. 5, Oct. 1967, 2–5; March 28, 1960, letter, WP, item 34, II; interview with Vo Van An, Jeffrey Race Collection, reel 2. For unity and land policy, Le Manh Trinh, *Hoc Tap*, Aug. 1966, JPRS 37,878, 36–37; Stanford, *Land Reform*, 15, 21, 30–31, 139–41, 150–51; Race, *War Comes to Long An*, 127–29; W. P. Davison and J. J. Zasloff, "A Profile of Viet Cong Cadres," RM-4983, June 1966, RC, 5, 8.

4. Robert L. Sansom, *The Economics of Insurgency in the Mekong Delta* (Cambridge, 1970), 229. See also William Bredo, "Agrarian Reform in Vietnam . . . ," *Asian Survey*, Aug. 1970, 743; AID, 256–65.

5. Lt. Gen. Lionel C. McGarr report, Oct. 25, 1961, 4–5, DDRS R:75A. See also *PP*, II, 128–39, 148–49; and esp. Roger Hilsman, *To Move a Nation* (Garden City, 1967), 431ff.

6. U.S. Operations Mission-Saigon, Office of Rural Affairs, "Notes on Strategic Hamlets," Aug. 15, 1963, 2. See also *PP*, II, 150–52; AID, 267; Tran Dinh Tho, *Pacification*, IM, 162.

7. Nguyen Hoai, *Nghien Cuu Lich Su*, Dec. 1969, JPRS 50,553, 7.

8. Hoang Ngoc Lung, *Strategy and Tactics*, IM, 27.

9. William R. Corson, *The Betrayal* (New York, 1968), 174. See also Robert Shaplen,

The Lost Revolution (New York, 1965), 167; Race, *War Comes to Long An,* 132–33; *PP,* II, 153; BDM V, 5–25; Pearce, "Insurgent Environment," 108.

10. Westmoreland to Taylor, Nov. 24, 1964, DDRS 77:288E. See also *PP,* II, 149–57; AID, 267–68; Nguyen Hoai, *Nghien Cuu Lich Su,* 8; BDM V, 5–23; Operations Mission, "Strategic Hamlets," statistical annex; Forrestal to McNamara, Feb. 14, 1964, DDRS 77:109B; Tran Dinh Tho, *Pacification,* 162; McNamara memo, March 13, 1964, DDRS R:89B; McNamara memo, March 16, 1964, DDRS 78:148A.

11. Corson, *Betrayal,* 161–62. See also Pearce, "Insurgent Environment," 107–8; Bredo, "Agrarian Reform," 740–41; U.S. May 27, 1968, memo, VN, no. 36–37, June 1968, 20; Herrington, *Silence Was a Weapon,* 38–39; Trullinger, *Village at War,* 40–42, 110–12, 143.

12. U.S. Senate, Comm. on Foreign Relations, *Impact of the Vietnam War,* 92:1, June 30, 1971, 21–22.

Chapter 11: The Challenge of Defining Military Strategies

1. Early 1963 document, WP, item 301, 6, 41.

2. March 28, 1960, letter, WP, item 34, 4 and passim.

3. GP, 217. See also ibid., 198.

4. NLF central committee resolutions, PM, no. 866, 36, 39 (italics and punctuation as in original).

5. WP, item 301, 41. See also ibid., 31–37; PM, no. 866.

6. L. P. Holliday and R. M. Garfield, "Viet Cong Logistics," RM-5423, June 1968, RC, 19. See also CIA report SNIE-2-61, DDRS 78:141D; 1962 directive, PM, no. 858; Douglas Pike, *Viet Cong* (Cambridge, 1966), 253ff.; CINCPAC to JCS, May 23, 1964, DDRS 76:250C; CIA estimate, Oct. 1, 1964, 10, DDRS 76:229C.

7. Dong Van Khuyen, *RVNAF Logistics,* IM, v. See also *PP,* II, 434–38, 454; BDM VI (1), 1-35ff., 2-44ff.; William Colby, *Honorable Men* (New York, 1978), 166–67; Francis J. Kelly, *U.S. Army Special Forces, 1961–1971* (U.S. Dept. of the Army, 1973), 12; Roger Hilsman, *To Move a Nation* (Garden City, 1967), 424–27; Rostow to Kennedy, March 29, 1961, DDRS 75:329A; Arthur M. Schlesinger, Jr., *A Thousand Days* (Boston, 1965), 341–42; Nolting to Rusk, Oct. 12, 13, 1961, DDRS R:793B, D; Joseph M. Heiser, *Logistic Support* (U.S. Dept. of the Army, 1974), 14.

8. William A. Buckingham, Jr., *Operation Ranch Hand: The Air Force and Herbicides in Southeast Asia, 1961–1971* (U.S. Office of Air Force History, 1982), iii. See also John J. Tolson, *Airmobility, 1961–1971* (U.S. Dept. of the Army, 1973), 104; William W. Momyer, *Airpower in Three Wars* (U.S. Office of Air Force History, 1978) 65–82; George W. Ball, *The Past Has Another Pattern* (New York, 1982), 174, 369; Alain C. Enthoven and K. Wayne Smith, *How Much Is Enough?* (New York, 1971); Gregory Palmer, *The McNamara Strategy and the Vietnam War* (Westport, 1978); Seymour J. Deitchman, *The Best-Laid Schemes* (Cambridge, 1976).

9. Buckingham, *Operation Ranch Hand,* iii, 16–27, 109–13, 134, 148, 172, 200; Robert H. Johnson to Rostow, Sept. 20, 1961, DDRS R:74A; *International Herald Tribune,* May 6, 1983; 1st Infantry Div., operational report, Sept. 16, 1969, 37, DDRS R:217D; reports on defoliants, April 14, 1965, EC; Hoang Ngoc Lung, *Strategy and Tactics,* IM, 111–14.

10. Hilsman, *To Move a Nation,* 442.

11. Tolson, *Airmobility;* Kelly, *Special Forces,* 143–47; Chester L. Cooper, *The Lost Crusade* (New York, 1970), 214–15.

12. Military Institute, *Vietnam: The Anti-U.S. Resistance War* (Hanoi, 1980), JPRS 80,968, 56; M. Anderson et al., "Insurgent Organization and Operations," RM-5239, Aug. 1967, RC, xi; VN, nos. 36–37, June 1968, 12, 20; William C. Westmoreland, *A Soldier Reports* (Garden City, 1976), 98–101; Corson, *Betrayal,* 146–48.

13. *PP,* II, 336. See also Colby to Forrestal, May 11, 1964, DDRS 78:142B; CIA estimate, May 25, 1964, DDRS 78:30A.

14. *PP,* III, 114. See also ibid., 107ff.; McGeorge Bundy to Johnson, Nov. 28, 1964, DDRS 78:130A; Lyndon B. Johnson, *The Vantage Point* (New York, 1971), 120–21; GP, 287–88.

15. Westmoreland, *Soldier Reports,* 115. See also Johnson, *Vantage Point,* 122; *PP,* III, 248–53.

Chapter 12: The United States, the Revolution, and the Components of Struggle

1. McGeorge Bundy to Johnson, Jan. 27, 1965, DDRS 78:131B.

2. Forrestal to McNaughton, May 1, 1964, DDRS 78:129A.

3. William C. Westmoreland, *A Soldier Reports* (Garden City, 1976), 112–13; Lewis W. Walt, *Strange War, Strange Strategy* (New York, 1970), 1; U. S. G. Sharp and William C. Westmoreland, *Report on the War in Vietnam (as of 30 June 1968)* (Washington, 1968), 11; Military Institute, *Vietnam: The Anti-U.S. Resistance War* (Hanoi, 1980), JPRS 80,968, 64–65.

4. U.S. Army Command and General Staff School, *The Principles of Strategy* (1936), 70. See also *PP,* III, 109–12; Vo Nguyen Giap, *People's War against U.S. Aero-Naval War* (Hanoi, 1975), 23; Giap, *Ecrits* (Hanoi, 1977), 336ff.; Patrick J. McGarvey, ed., *Visions of Victory: Selected Vietnamese Communist Military Writings, 1964–1968* (Stanford, 1969), 7–8; Military Institute, *Anti-U.S. Resistance,* 56, 89, 93.

5. Roger P. Fox, *Air Base Defense in the Republic of Vietnam, 1961–1973* (U.S. Office of Air Force History, 1979), 1, 11.

6. Daniel S. Papp, *Vietnam: The View from Moscow, Peking, Washington* (Jefferson, N.C., 1981), 20–21, 36–41; Le Duan, *Ecrits* (Hanoi, 1976), 17, 116ff., 168; Ministère des Affaires Etrangères, [SRV], *La Vérité sur les relations vietnamo-chinoises . . . ,* 1979, 45ff.; W. R. Smyser, *The Independent Vietnamese: Vietnamese Communism between Russia and China, 1956–1969* (Athens, Ohio, 1980), 63–64; CIA memo, Feb. 4, 1964, DDRS 78:228A; William P. Bundy memo, March 2, 1964, DDRS 75:157A; CIA report, Sept. 9, 1964, DDRS 77:27C; CIA report, Feb. 27, 1965, DDRS 75:49A; CIA memo, June 9, 1965, in *Journal of Contemporary Asia,* 13 (1983), 261–71.

7. Sino-Soviet policy and relations with Vietnam were minutely followed. In addition to the preceding references, see the various official analyses and discussions in DDRS 77:26E; R:41C; 77:27D; R:866E; R:45E; R:873B; 77:28B; R:876A; 77:118A; 77:345B; 78:36B; and Smyser, *Independent Vietnamese,* 79.

Chapter 13: Escalation and the Frustration of American Politics

1. McGeorge Bundy to Johnson, Feb. 16, 1965, DDRS 78:131C.

2. *PP,* III, 683; IV, 23, 47. See also ibid., III, 349; IV, 88–89, 613–14, 636, 664; George W. Ball, *The Past Has Another Pattern* (New York, 1982), 402; Doris Kearns, *Lyndon Johnson and the American Dream* (New York, 1976), 257; Lyndon B. Johnson, *The Vantage Point* (New York, 1971), 151–52; Roswell Gilpatric to McGeorge Bundy, July 9, 1965; JCS memo to McNamara, Aug. 27, 1965, NSC.

3. *PP,* III, 433. See also ibid., 319, 338–39, 360, 450; Chester Cooper, *The Lost Crusade* (New York, 1970), 270–71; Roger P. Fox, *Air Base Defense in the Republic of Vietnam, 1961–1973* (U.S. Office of Air Force History, 1979), 11, 19–25; Westmoreland in W. Scott Thompson and D. D. Frizzell, eds., *The Lessons of Vietnam* (New York, 1977), 58.

4. Leonard B. Taylor, *Financial Management of the Vietnam Conflict, 1962–1972* (U.S. Dept. of the Army, 1974), 18. See also Ball to Johnson, April 21, 1965, DDRS 81:113A; Taylor to Johnson, Jan. 6, 1965, NSC.

5. *PP,* II, 471ff.; Johnson, *Vantage Point,* 144–46; Kearns, *American Dream,* 263; *Wash. Post,* June 15, 1969; Henry F. Graff, *The Tuesday Cabinet* (Englewood Cliffs, 1970), 54–59; Rostow to Rusk, May 20, 1965, DDRS 81:119A; Taylor to Rusk, June 5, 1965; McGeorge Bundy to Johnson, June 5, 1965; Ball to McNamara, June 30, 1965; McGeorge Bundy to Johnson, July 1, 1965; Gilpatric to McGeorge Bundy, July 9, 1965; minutes, NSC, July 27, 1965, NSC.

6. Cooper, *Lost Crusade,* 264. See also Paul M. Kattenburg, *The Vietnam Trauma in American Foreign Policy, 1945–1975* (New Brunswick, 1980), 212–13.

7. Ball, *Another Pattern,* 407. See also *PP,* III, 460; Ball to Johnson, April 21, 1965, DDRS 81:113A.

8. Woodrow Wilson International Center, *Some Lessons and Non-Lessons of Vietnam* (Washington, 1983), app. 1; James D. Wright, *The Dissent of the Governed* (New York, 1976), 188–89; Kattenburg, *Vietnam Trauma,* 213; BDM IV, 1-18-28; VIII, 3–9.

Chapter 14: The Continuing Search for Effective Military Strategies

1. *PP,* IV, 293. See also JCS memo, Oct. 14, 1966, DDRS 80:277A; Bruce Palmer, Jr., *The 25-Year War: America's Military Role in Vietnam* (Lexington, 1984), 42–46.

2. Chester L. Cooper, *The Lost Crusade* (New York, 1970), 432–33. See also William C. Westmoreland, *A Soldier Reports* (Garden City, 1976), 128–29; *PP,* IV, 193–96.

3. JCS to McNamara, Oct. 14, 1966, NSC. See also McNamara to Johnson, Oct. 16, 1966, NSC.

4. CIA estimate, Jan. 9, 1967, 3, DDRS 78:37B.

5. *PP,* IV, 391, 420, 428.

6. William W. Momyer, *Airpower in Three Wars* (U.S. Office of Air Force History, 1978), 297. See also Lyndon B. Johnson, *The Vantage Point* (New York, 1971), 245; SA, 835; Westmoreland, *Soldier Reports,* 25–28; *PP,* IV, 308; Palmer, *25-Year War,* 60, 69–70, 178; Roger P. Fox, *Air Base Defense in the Republic of Vietnam, 1961–1973* (U.S. Office of Air Force History, 1979), 25–28.

7. Robert M. Kipp, "Counterinsurgency from 30,000 Feet," *Air University Review,*

Jan.–Feb. 1968, cover. See also Westmoreland, *Soldier Reports,* 139–51; BDM VI (1), 3–26; *PP,* IV, 330–31, 386, 456–62; SA, 772, 834–38; Leslie H. Gelb and Richard K. Betts, *The Irony of Vietnam* (Washington, 1979), 134; Guenter Lewy, *America in Vietnam* (New York, 1978), 68.

8. Momyer, *Airpower,* 81–82, 106–7, 285–86; George S. Eckhardt, *Command and Control, 1950–1969* (U.S. Dept. of the Army, 1974), 43, 74–76, and passim; John J. Tolson, *Airmobility, 1961–1971* (U.S. Dept. of the Army, 1973), 10–14, 104–6; Douglas Kinnard, *The War Managers* (Hanover, 1977), 60–63; BDM VI (1), 6-35-40; (2), 11-40-45.

9. Truong-Chinh, *Selected Writings* (Hanoi, 1977), 604–7; Van Tien Dung, *After Political Failure . . .* (Hanoi, 1966), 15–21, 28–34; WP, item 302, 16, 23; item 65, 5–11; item 303, 8; Patrick J. McGarvey, ed., *Visions of Victory* (Stanford, 1969); SA, 772, 788–89, 800–803, 834–38; Nguyen Van Tran, *Tuyen Huan,* Oct. 1966, JPRS 39, 758, 18–27; Westmoreland, *Soldier Reports,* 139–41, 161, 177–78; Vietnamese Studies, *American Failure* (Hanoi, 1969), 34–37, 68–70; Etudes Vietnamiennes, *Face aux forces armées U.S.* (I) (Hanoi, 1978); W. Scott Thompson and D. D. Frizzell, eds., *The Lessons of Vietnam* (New York, 1977), 24–25, 76, 88–91; NSSM, 4978, 4989, 5027; Leon Goure, "Some Impressions of the Effects of Military Operations on Viet Cong Behavior," RM-4517, March 1965, RC, 1–5, DDRS 77:185C; JCS to McNamara, Oct. 18, 1966, DDRS 80:277A; CIA estimate, Jan. 9, 1967, DDRS 78:37B; CIA estimate, Nov. 13, 1967, DDRS 76:152A.

10. Summary, mid-1966 speech, WP, item 65, 9.

11. March 1966 speech, WP, item 302, 12. In addition to sources in preceding notes, see Vo Nguyen Giap, *Ecrits* (Hanoi, 1977), 368–73; Giap, *To Arm the Revolutionary Masses to Build the People's Army* (Hanoi, 1975), 138–52; no author, *South Vietnam: Initial Failure of the U.S. "Limited War"* (Hanoi, 1967), 28–39; Hoang Minh Thao, *Hoc Tap,* Dec. 1966, JPRS 39, 796, 38–39; *PP,* IV, 305, 321, 325, 406; CIA review, Dec. 8, 1967, DDRS 78:37C.

12. M. Anderson et al., "Insurgent Organization and Operations . . . ," RM-5239, Aug. 1967, RC, x–xi; Hoang Minh Thao, *Hoc Tap,* 39; *Quan Doi Nhan Dan,* June 8, 1966, JPRS 36,804, 24; Cao Van Vien and Dong Van Khuyen, *Reflections on the Vietnam War,* IM, 68–69; Aug. 18, 1966 COSVN paper, VN, no. 6, Oct. 1967, 1–8; VN, no. 24, April 1968, 1–5; no. 40, Aug. 1968, 108; no author [U.S.], "The Viet Cong Infrastructure: *Modus Operandi* of Selected Political Cadres," Dec. 1968, 22; James W. Trullinger, *Village at War* (New York, 1980), 92; *Quan Doi Nhan Dan,* June 5, 1966, JPRS 36,682, 7; 1966 document, WP, item 39; D. W. P. Elliott and W. A. Stewart, "Pacification and the Viet Cong System in Dinh Tuong, 1966–67," RM-5788, Jan. 1969, RC.

13. SA, 788, 829; U.S. House, Select Comm. on Intelligence, *Hearings: U.S. Intelligence Agencies and Activities,* 94:1, Dec. 1975, 1687–95; R. Michael Pearce, "The Insurgent Environment," RM-5533, May 1969, RC, 42; Nguyen Duy Hinh and Tran Dinh Tho, *The South Vietnamese Society,* IM, 111–12; U. S. G. Sharp and William C. Westmoreland, *Report on the War in Vietnam (as of 30 June 1968)* (Washington, 1968), 255; VN, no. 49, Jan. 1969, 15; WP, item 96; Robert L. Sansom, *Economics of Insurgency in the Mekong Delta* (Cambridge, 1970), 222–25; Ralph W. McGehee, *Deadly Deceits* (New York, 1983), 150–55; Palmer, *25-Year War,* 56–57; NSSM, 5030; CIA estimate, Nov. 13, 1967, 18–19, DDRS 76:152A.

Chapter 15: The Dilemma of the American Way of War

1. William W. Momyer, *Airpower in Three Wars* (U.S. Office of Air Force History, 1978), 277. See also William D. White, *U.S. Tactical Air Power* (Washington, 1974), 1–5.

2. Robert M. Kipp, "Counterinsurgency from 30,000 Feet," *Air University Review,* Feb. 1968, 17.

3. William C. Westmoreland, *A Soldier Reports* (New York, 1976), 137. See also Kipp, "Counterinsurgency," 17; Douglas Kinnard, *The War Managers* (Hanover, 1977), 48–49; SA, 826–27.

4. *NYT,* Dec. 31, 1972; White, *Tactical Air Power,* 47; Raphael Littauer and Norman Uphoff, eds., *The Air War in Indochina* (Boston, 1972), 9, 24; SA, 829; Momyer, *Airpower,* 190, 214; CIA estimate, Feb. 4, 1966, DDRS 76:151D; Jack S. Ballard, *Development and Employment of Fixed-Wing Gunships, 1962–1972* (U.S. Office of Air Force History, 1982), 47ff., 111ff., 167–73.

5. DOD, 1972, 92:1, June 1971, pt. 6, 66. See also White, *Tactical Air Power,* 66; Momyer, *Airpower,* chap. 4; U.S. Senate, Comm. on Foreign Relations, *Study: Bombing as a Policy Tool in Vietnam: Effectiveness,* 92:2, Oct. 12, 1972, 9ff.; *PP,* IV, 107–19, 133, 172–90, 223–26; Taylor to Johnson, Jan. 6, 1965; McGeorge Bundy to Johnson, Feb. 7 1965; Taylor to U. A. Johnson, June 3, 1965; McNamara to Johnson, Oct. 14, 1966; CIA briefing book, ca. March 20, 1968, all in NSC; Ball to Johnson, April 21, 1965, DDRS 81:113A; CIA report, Nov. 8, 1965, 3–8, DDRS 77:178C; CIA estimate, Feb. 4, 1966, DDRS 76:151D; CIA report, Sept. 1966, DDRS 77:178D; Oleg Hoeffding, "Bombing North Vietnam . . . ," Oct. 1966, RC, passim, DDRS 78:37A; JCS memo, Oct. 14, 1966, DDRS 80:277A; CIA report, May 12, 1967, DDRS 76:151F.

6. SA, 810. See also Hoang Ngoc Lung, *Strategy and Tactics,* IC, 107–8, 128; interrogations, WP, items 47 and 63; Westmoreland, *Soldier Reports,* 147; Lynn D. Smith, *Army,* Dec. 1969, 16; *Business Week,* Aug. 29, 1970, 58; DOD, 1972, pt. 6, 67; John J. Tolson, *Airmobility, 1961–1971* (U.S. Dept. of the Army, 1973); Bruce Palmer, *The 25-Year War: America's Role in Vietnam* (Lexington, 1984), 168.

7. David E. Ott, *Field Artillery, 1954–1973* (U.S. Dept. of the Army, 1975), 187. See also ibid., 173–75; Palmer, *25-Year War,* 167–68.

8. Lloyd Norman, *Army,* Dec. 1966, 59. See also Hoang Ngoc Lung, *Strategy and Tactics,* 95ff.; Ott, *Field Artillery,* 14–17; Truc Chien, *Quan Doi Nhan Dan,* April 23, 1968, JPRS 45,626, 38–40.

9. *PP,* IV, 456. See also SA, xi, 944; Joseph A. McChristian, *The Role of Military Intelligence, 1965–1967* (U.S. Dept. of the Army, 1974); Patrick J. McGarvey, *CIA* (New York, 1972); Palmer, *25-Year War,* 30, 162–67; Americal Div., operational report, Sept. 5, 1968, 79, DDRS R:211A.

10. BDM VI (2), viii.

11. DOD, 1968, March 20, 1967, pt. 3, 13. See also SA, 845; Kinnard, *War Managers,* 71, 172.

12. U.S. House, Comm. on Government Operations, *Report: Military Supply Systems,* 91:2, Oct. 8, 1970, 5.

13. Ibid., 28. See also ibid., 6–9, 17–18, 24; Joseph M. Heiser, Jr., *Logistic Support* (U.S. Dept. of the Army, 1974), 22–24, 48, 60–61, 81; Palmer, *25-Year War,* 43, 71, 168–69.

14. Westmoreland, *Soldier Reports,* 186–87; SA, 783; Littauer, *Air War,* 100–01; Leon-

ard B. Taylor, *Financial Management of the Vietnam Conflict, 1962–1972* (U.S. Dept. of the Army, 1974), 25–29.

Chapter 16: War and the Transformation of South Vietnamese Society

1. NSSM, 4995. See also SA, 847, 863, 866, 920; *Cong. Record,* May 6, 1974, S7129.

2. AID, 110. See also SA, 866.

3. *PP,* IV, 441. See also William A. Buckingham, Jr., *Operation Ranch Hand* (U.S. Office of Air Force History, 1982), 109, 136; U. S. G. Sharp and William C. Westmoreland, *Report on the War on Vietnam* (Washington, 1968), 148–49; 5th Special Forces Group, report ending July 31, 1967, DDRS R:210A.

4. *Cong. Record,* May 6, 1974, S7129; U.S. Senate, Comm. on Foreign Relations, *Report: Impact of the Vietnam War,* 92:1, June 30, 1971, 22; RVN, National Institute of Statistics, *Viet Nam Statistical Yearbook, 1972,* 357, 378–79; SA, 919–21, 925; Nguyen Duc Nhuan, *Désurbanisation et développement régional au Viet-Nam (1954–1977)* (Paris, 1977), 16; Bryan Roberts, *Cities of Peasants* (Beverly Hills, 1978), 7; Allan E. Goodman, "The Causes and Consequences of Migration to Saigon, Vietnam," Aug. 1973, (New York, SEADAG), 64, 140, 180.

5. John P. Mossler, *Vietnam Economic Report* (Saigon), July 1971, 9. See also Goodman, "Migration to Saigon," 13–14, 153–55; Marilyn W. Hoskins and Eleanor Shepherd, "Life in a Vietnamese Quarter," Southern Illinois Univ. Center for Vietnamese Studies, 1965, 165; AID, 124–25; Nguyen Duy Hinh and Tran Dinh Tho, *The South Vietnamese Society,* IM, 110; *Viet Nam Statistical Yearbook,* 283, 292; RVNAF, JGS, "Report on the Study on Living Standards Republic of Vietnam Armed Forces (Army)," (Saigon, 1968–69), 63–64, EC; Arthur Smithies, "Economic Problems of Vietnamization," Aug. 1970, Smithies Papers, Harvard College Library, A14-15.

6. C. J. Zwick et al., "U.S. Economic Assistance in Vietnam," R-430. July 1964, RC, 10. See also Asian Development Bank, *Rural Asia* (New York, 1977), 33, 44, 327, 340; AID, 124–25, 207; Smithies, "Economic Problems"; Tran Dinh Tho, *Pacification,* IM, 133; misc. psywar documents in DDRS R:840C, 841F, 842B, 894F; 77:348B, C; 78:29C.

7. SA, 897, 936; William Bredo, "Agrarian Reform in Vietnam," *Asian Survey,* Aug. 1970, 740; Goodman, "Migration to Saigon," 188; *Viet Nam Statistical Yearbook,* chart 324; Tran Dinh Tho, *Pacification,* 4, 133, 156–58; Nguyen Duy Hinh, *South Vietnamese Society,* 154; Hoang Ngoc Lung, *Strategy and Tactics,* IM, 90; Roger P. Fox, *Air Base Defense in the Republic of Vietnam, 1961–1973* (U.S. Office of Air Force History, 1979), 171; CIA memo, n.d. (ca. Feb. 1966), DDRS 78:29C.

Chapter 17: Nguyen Van Thieu and the RVN Power Structure

1. Allan E. Goodman, "An Institutional Profile of the South Vietnamese Officer Corps," RM-6189, June 1970, RC, 15, 21ff., 75ff., EC; John Prados, "Generals and Politics in South Vietnam," *Indochina Chronicle,* July 17, 1973, 6–9. See also Cao Van Vien, *Leadership,* IM, 75–81; CIA report, Feb. 25, 1965, DDRS R:48G.

2. Jean Lartéguy, *L'Adieu à Saigon* (Paris, 1975), 73–75; *PP,* II, 395; Goodman,

"Officer Corps," 80; Nguyen Khac Ngu, *Nhung Ngay Cuoi Cung Cua Viet-Nam Cong-Hoa* (Montreal, 1979), 37–72.

3. Stephen T. Hosmer et al., *The Fall of South Vietnam: Statements by Vietnamese Military and Civilian Leaders* (New York, 1980), 74.

4. Clifton G. Barton, "Trust and Credit: Some Observations Regarding Business Strategies of Overseas Chinese Traders in South Vietnam," n.d., EC; Barton, "Credit and Commercial Control in South Vietnam," AID, n.d. (1973) (a similar version exists as a Cornell Univ. thesis, 1977); State Dept., "Overseas Chinese Business Community—Vietnam," March 27, 1972, EC; V. L. Elliott, [AID], "Development Problems in Viet-Nam," April 1973; Nguyen Khac Ngu, *Nhung Ngay Cuoi,* 37–72; Vo Nhan Tri, *Dai Doan Ket,* May 6, 1978, 11–12; Cao Van Luong, *Nghien Cuu Lich Su,* no. 2, 1976, 40–55.

5. *Viet Nam Statistical Yearbook, 1972,* 292; Hosmer, *Fall of South Vietnam,* 74–76; Cao Van Vien, *Leadership,* 120–21; Nguyen Duy Hinh and Tran Dinh Tho, *The South Vietnamese Society,* IM, 115.

6. Cao Van Vien, *Leadership,* 169. See also ibid., 164; Dong Van Khuyen, *The RVNAF,* IM, 77–78, 103, 341–77; Barton, "Credit and Commercial Control," 180–82; SA, 812–13, 816–18; Goodman, "Officer Corps," 52, 80–82, table 19.

7. Hinh and Tho, *South Vietnamese Society,* 111.

8. Tran Dinh Tho, *Pacification,* IM, 181. See also Elizabeth Pond in J. J. Zasloff and A. E. Goodman, eds., *Indochina in Conflict* (Lexington, 1972), 3; Goodman, "Officer Corps," 80; Komer to Johnson, April 19, 1966, DDRS 80:287B; Vien, *Leadership,* 156–70; Hosmer, *Fall of South Vietnam,* 100–03; Hinh and Tho, *South Vietnamese Society,* 145; Cao Van Vien, *The Final Collapse* (U.S. Army Center of Military History, 1983), 169–71.

9. Tran Van Don, *Our Endless War* (San Rafael, 1978), 237.

10. Allan E. Goodman, *Politics in War* (Cambridge, 1973), 48. See also ibid., 117, 129ff.; BDM II, 2–22.

11. Nguyen Khac Ngu, *Nhung Ngay Cuoi,* 37–72; Alan Dawson, *55 Days: The Fall of South Vietnam* (Englewood Cliffs, 1977), 103–05; Alfred W. McCoy, *The Politics of Heroin in Southeast Asia* (New York, 1972), 153–59, 167–210.

12. Memo of conversation, July 16, 1965, NSC. See also *PP,* IV, 390; papers for May 9, 1966 NSC meeting, DDRS 78:63A; CIA report, July 31, 1967, DDRS R:49F.

13. NSSM, 5052. See also Hosmer, *Fall of South Vietnam,* 74–76; draft memo for Johnson, tab B, March 4, 1968; CIA briefing book, March 13, 1968, NSC; BDM II, 5-55-56.

14. NSSM, 5053.

15. Barton, "Credit and Commercial Control," 195. See also State Dept., "Overseas Chinese," 3; file on Chinese community and Ngo Vinh Long March 19, 1984 summation, EC.

16. Barton, "Credit and Commercial Control," 15; Industrial Development Bank of Vietnam, "Problems and Prospects of Small Industries in the Republic of Vietnam," Dec. 1974, 33–35, EC; Clifton G. Barton, "Credit and the Small Farmer," *A.I.D. Spring Review of Small Farmer Credit,* II (Feb. 1973), 31; item 4A in Chinese file, 4, EC; Elliott, "Development Problems in Viet-Nam," 10–11, 16; Simulmatics Corp., "A Study of Commercial Distribution of Agricultural Inputs in the Mekong Delta of Vietnam," 1968, 45.

17. State Dept., "Overseas Chinese," 7.

Chapter 18: The Dilemma of Economic Dependency and the RVN

1. AID, 129.

2. Ibid., 107.

3. J. A. Stockfisch, "The Domestic Tax System," Institute for Defense Analyses, April 1971, 1, EC. See also ibid., 4–5; AID, 72, 107, 109, 152; SA, 933–34; *PP,* IV, 340–45; Arthur Smithies, "Economic Problems of Vietnamization," Aug. 1970, A-7, Smithies Papers, Harvard College Library; data from *Viet Nam Statistical Yearbook, 1972,* and United Nations, *Economic and Social Survey of Asia and the Pacific, 1975,* 28, 33; AID, *Vietnam Economic Data,* April–June 1973, 9; Smithies, "Economic Development in Vietnam: The Need for External Resources," Institute for Defense Analyses (1970), 3; *Cong. Record,* May 6, 1974, S7130–31; John B. Mulvey, [AID], "Report of Survey of the Directorate of Excise Taxes," Nov. 1968, 6, EC.

4. Douglas C. Dacy, "The Value of Imports, Windfalls, and the Foreign Exchange Rate in South Vietnam, 1962–1970," n.d. (ca. 1971), Institute for Defense Analyses, 59–60, EC. See also BDM II, 4–18; AID, *Vietnam Economic Data,* Oct.–Dec. 1974, 26; AID, 452ff., for the basic data; for CIP and currency in general, see AID, 117, 440ff.; Dacy, "Value of Imports," 17–18; U.S. Senate, Comm. on Government Operations, *Hearings: Illegal Currency Manipulations Affecting South Vietnam,* 91:1, Nov. 1969, 533; U.S. House, Comm. on Government Operations, *Report: A Review of the Inequitable Monetary Rate of Exchange in Vietnam,* 91:2, June 25, 1970, 7; *PP,* II, 383; *Xay Dung* (Saigon), Jan. 28, 1966; *Than Chung,* Feb. 7, 1966.

5. AID, 444. See also ibid., 141–42; U.S. House, *Inequitable Monetary Rate,* 4 and passim.

6. Dacy, "Value of Imports," 11, 41; AID, 469–76; my data are calculated from AID, *Vietnam Economic Data,* Oct.–Dec. 1974, 23.

7. Smithies, "Economic Problems," A-10. See also ibid., A-4, 10; RVNAF, JGS, "Report of the Study on Living Standards Republic of Vietnam Armed Forces (Army)" (Saigon, 1968–69), 65, EC; V. L. Elliott, [AID], "Vietnamese Compensation Structures . . . January 1, 1965, through January 1, 1968," 96, EC.

8. Stockfisch, "Domestic Tax System," 2.

9. Industrial Development Bank of Vietnam, "Problems and Prospects of Small Industries in the Republic of Vietnam," Dec. 1974, 60. See also *NYT,* April 22, 1971.

10. *PP,* IV, 351. See also AID, 126, 146; *NYT,* Oct. 11, 1970; Townsend Hoopes, *The Limits of Intervention* (New York, 1969), 118, 188; Cao Van Vien, *Leadership,* IM, 120–21, for a catalog of corruption; Tran Anh Tuan, "Anti-Corruption and the Censorate: The Vietnamese Experience" (Ph.D. thesis, Syracuse Univ., 1973), 20ff.

11. Smithies, "Economic Development," 7, 9; idem, "Economic Problems," D-3. See also *NYT,* Dec. 27, 1970.

12. AID, 234–35.

13. *DSB,* Feb. 15, 1971, 209.

14. AID, 129. See also Smithies, "Economic Development," 17–18; "Economic Problems," B-6; "The Transition to Economic Development in Vietnam," Institute for Defense Analyses, Aug. 1971, F-22.

15. Smithies, "Economic Development," 2, 12–14, 24ff.; "Transition," C 1–4, 14; *Viet-*

nam Economic Report, July 1971, 11; *Cong. Record,* May 5, 1971, E4018–22 [chronology by Gabriel Kolko]; Ruth Russell to Arthur Smithies, Oct. 11, 1971.

Chapter 19: The Building of the RVN's Army and the Struggle for Rural South Vietnam

1. Ngo Quang Truong, *RVNAF and US Operational Cooperation and Coordination,* IM, 164–66; Stephen T. Hosmer et al., *The Fall of South Vietnam* (New York, 1980), 88–89; *PP,* IV, 376, 380, 503; NSSM, 4979, 4991; SA, 819–20; Brig. Gen. Donald D. Dunlop debriefing, 1968–69, 1–3, DDRS R:215A; Komer to Johnson, Oct. 16, 1966, NSC.

2. *PP,* IV, 443.

3. CINCPAC to JCS, May 23, 1964, DDRS 76:250C. See also *PP,* II, 395; IV, 440, 502; Cao Van Vien and Dong Van Khuyen, *Reflections on the Vietnam War,* IM, 47–48, 55; Hosmer, *Fall of South Vietnam,* 88–89; Roger P. Fox, *Air Base Defense in the Republic of Vietnam, 1961–1973* (U.S. Office of Air Force History, 1979), 16; NSSM, 4979; Jeffrey Race, *War Comes to Long An* (Berkeley, 1972), 260–61.

4. U. S. G. Sharp and William C. Westmoreland, *Report on the War in Vietnam* (Washington, 1968), 216. See also Fox, *Air Base Defense,* 16, 120, 162; Charles J. Levy, "ARVN as Faggots," *Transaction,* Oct. 1971, 22; *NYT,* July 4, 1971; James L. Collins, Jr., *The Development and Training of the South Vietnamese Army, 1950–1972* (U.S. Dept. of the Army, 1975), 72–73.

5. Dong Van Khuyen, *RVNAF Logistics,* IM, v.

6. *Cong. Record,* Aug. 20, 1974, S15496. See also NSSM, 4996; Hosmer, *Fall of South Vietnam,* 103–104.

7. Komer, "Clear, Hold and Rebuild," *Army,* May 1970, 23. See also ibid., 24; *PP,* II, 393, 542–43, 596; IV, 386; Taylor to Rusk, July 11, 1965, NSC; record of Honolulu conference, Feb. 23, 1966; State Dept. memo, Feb. 15, 1966, NSC.

8. William A. Buckingham, Jr., *Operation Ranch Hand* (U.S. Office of Air Force History, 1982), 136. See also Rusk to embassy, March 28, 1965, DDRS 79:208D.

9. Quoted in Guenter Lewy, *America in Vietnam* (New York, 1978), 65.

10. "The Bases of Accommodation," *Foreign Affairs,* 46 (1968), 650. See also Lewy, *America in Vietnam,* 125.

11. Chester L. Cooper, "The American Experience with Pacification in Vietnam," Institute for Defense Analyses, March 1972, 26. See also ibid., 15–20; Maj. Gen. A. H. Manhart to JCS, July 23, 1965, NSC.

12. Rostow memo to Johnson, March 1, 1968, NSC. See also SA, 874.

13. Nguyen Duy Hinh and Tran Dinh Tho, *The South Vietnamese Society,* IM, 106–107. See also NSSM, 4979; Sharp and Westmoreland, *Report on the War,* 199; SA, 918.

14. NSSM, 5023. See also Tran Dinh Tho, *Pacification,* IM, 189; Stuart A. Herrington, *Silence Was a Weapon* (Novato, 1982) 193; Robert Thompson, *No Exit from Vietnam* (London, 1969), 137; William R. Corson, *The Betrayal* (New York, 1968), 232–34; U.S. House, Comm. on Foreign Affairs, *Report: Measuring Hamlet Security in Vietnam,* 90:2, Dec. 1968, 5ff.; Douglas Kinnard, *The War Managers* (Hanover, 1977), 108; Robert L.

Sansom, *The Economics of Insurgency in the Mekong Delta* (Cambridge, 1970), fig. 1.7; James W. Trullinger, *Village at War* (New York, 1980), 193-94.

15. Tran Dinh Tho, *Pacification,* 86.

16. Porter to Komer, ca. March 15, 1967, DDRS 80:210C. See also Cooper, "Pacification in Vietnam," 20; Tran Dinh Tho, *Pacification,* 86, 104, 167, 176; *PP,* II, 385-86, 399; IV, 386-89; AID, 272-76.

17. Tran Dinh Tho, *Pacification,* 176-77. See also ibid., 193.

18. Cao Van Vien, *Reflections on the Vietnam War,* 63-64. See also Race, *War Comes to Long An,* 161.

19. USIA, "Facts and Attitudes: Long An Province," Feb. 1965, DDRS R:895A.

20. Konrad Kellen, "A View of the VC: Elements of Cohesion in the Enemy Camp in 1966-67," RM-5462, Nov. 1969, RC, 10.

21. CIA report, April 19, 1967, 2, DDRS 80:136D. See also McNamara to Johnson, Oct. 14, 1966, NSC; State Dept. memo, Feb. 17, 1967, DDRS 80:207A; Porter to Komer, ca. March 15, 1967, DDRS 80:210C.

22. Tran Dinh Tho, *Pacification,* 193. See also NSSM, 4993, 5023.

23. C. J. Zwick et al., "U.S. Economic Assistance in Vietnam," R-430. July 1964, RC, 94. See also U.S. Senate, Comm. on Foreign Relations, *Background Information Relating to Southeast Asia and Vietnam,* 3d ed. 90:1, July 1967, 193, 231; U.S. House, Comm. on Government Operations, *Report: Land Reform in Vietnam,* 90:2, March 5, 1968, 5.

24. For land reform see J. M. Burr, "Land to the Tiller: Revolution and Land Reform in Viet Nam" (M.A. thesis, Univ. of Oregon, 1973), 190-91; idem, "Land to the Tiller: Land Redistribution in South Viet Nam, 1970-1973" (Ph.D. thesis, Univ. of Oregon, 1976), 244, 339; John L. Cooper, [AID], end-of-tour report, Oct. 18, 1968, 6, EC; Sansom, *Economics of Insurgency,* 229-35; AID, 53, 136-37, 585-94; for the changing rural economy see Rex F. Daly et al., [AID], "Agriculture in Vietnam's Economy," June 1973, 150; AID, 470-71; Trullinger, *Village at War,* 168; Willard C. Muller, AID, "End-of-Tour Report," April 1973, 38; AID, "Republic of Vietnam Economy," Nov. 1974, 54, 58; Burr, M.A. thesis, 187; Joseph F. Stepanek, *Land Economics,* 44 (1968), 525-27; Asian Development Bank, *Rural Asia* (New York, 1977), 66, 76-80.

25. W. P. Davison and J. J. Zasloff, "A Profile of Viet Cong Cadres," RM-4983, June 1966, RC, 8. See also Sansom, *Economics of Insurgency,* 130-33; William R. Andrews, *The Village War* (Columbus, 1973), 29; Stanford Research Institute, "Land Reform in Vietnam," 1968, IV, 17, 105; Nathan Leites, "The Viet Cong Style of Politics," RM-5487, May 1969, RC, ix, xii; notes on Nguyen Chi Thanh speech, mid-1966, WP, item 65, 3; Party directive, Feb. 1966, WP, item 43.

26. Tran Dinh Tho, *Pacification,* 166. See also Herrington, *Silence Was a Weapon,* 36, 72; R. Michael Pearce, "Evolution of a Vietnamese Village—Part II," RM-4692, April 1966, RC, 24-26; Davison, "Viet Cong Operations," ix; Konrad Kellen, "A View of the VC," RM-5462, Nov. 1969; David Hunt, "Village Culture and the Vietnamese Revolution," *Past and Present,* no. 94 (Feb. 1982), 150ff.; 1st Infantry Div. report, Sept. 16, 1969, 38, DDRS R:217D; CIA review, Dec. 8, 1967, pt. 1, DDRS 78:37C.

27. *Nghien Cuu Lich Su,* Jan. 1968, JPRS 45,602, 9. See also April 17, 1966, Party

directive, 8–11, WP, item 66; David W. P. Elliott and W. A. Stewart, "Pacification and the Viet Cong System in Dinh Tuong, 1966–67," RM-5788, Jan. 1969, RC.

28. *Pacification,* 192. See also Kellen, "View of the VC," 9–14, 23, 72; Pearce, "Insurgent Environment," 107–108; Herrington, *Silence Was a Weapon,* 38–39, 128–29; Pearce, "Vietnamese Village," 26; Trullinger, *Village at War,* 109ff., 143; CIA estimate, April 19, 1967, DDRS 80:136D; Americal Div. report, Sept. 5, 1968, 77, DDRS R:211A.

29. Dec. 24, 1964, document in VN, no. 5, Oct. 1967, 5. See also May 1966 resolution in WP, item 51, 3.

30. CIA estimate, April 19, 1967.

31. Nov. 27, 1968 directive, VN, no. 54, March 1969, 3; Hunt, "Village Culture," 151; May 1966 resolution, WP, item 51, 6; *Quan Doi Nhan Dan,* Sept. 29, 1965, JPRS 33,006, 34–35; NSSM, 4995; SA, 913.

Chapter 20: The Character and Consequences of Two Vietnamese Armies

1. *PP,* IV, 398; Nolting to Rusk, June 12, 1961, DDRS R:784G; CIA cable, March 20, 1964, DDRS R:40D; MACV, "The Revolutionary Spirit," n.d. (ca. 1964), DDRS 78:236C; Taylor to Rusk, Jan. 24, 1965, DDRS R:858A; CIA report, March 4, 1965, DDRS 81:142B; Cao Van Vien, *Leadership,* IM, 120–21; Dong Van Khuyen, *The RVNAF,* IM, 344–45; Nguyen Duy Hinh and Tran Dinh Tho, *The South Vietnamese Society,* IM, 113; James W. Trullinger, *Village at War* (New York, 1980), 168–69; Tran Dinh Tho, *Pacification,* IM, 178–79; Stephen T. Hosmer et al., *The Fall of South Vietnam* (New York, 1980), 120–21.

2. *Quan Doi Nhan Dan,* March 21, 1967, JPRS 41,025, 20; Jan. 22, 1972, JPRS 55,613, 8. See also *Quan Doi Nhan Dan,* May 23, 1971, JPRS 53,828, 21; *Nhan Dan,* April 8, 1967, JPRS 41,265, 21–23.

3. Konrad Kellen, "A View of the VC," RM-5462, Nov. 1968, RC, 52–53; Dong Van Khuyen, *RVNAF,* 221; Paul Berman, *Revolutionary Organization* (Lexington, 1974), 84; 1965 interrogations, WP, item 86, 15–16, 22.

4. *Quan Doi Nhan Dan,* Sept. 21–23, 1966, JPRS 38,696, 27. See also *Quan Doi Nhan Dan,* July 2, 1965, JPRS 31,476, 33; March 21, 1967, JPRS 41,025, 19–20; May 16, 1967, JPRS 41,721, 12; Jan. 22, 1972, JPRS 55,613, 7–8; Kellen, "View of the VC," 33–36; Melvin Gurtov, "Viet Cong Cadres and the Cadre System," RM-5414, RC, ix–x; John C. Donnell, "Viet Cong Recruitment: Why and How Men Join," RM-5486, Dec. 1967, RC, xvii–xviii.

5. *Quan Doi Nhan Dan,* May 23, 1971, JPRS 53,828, 21.

6. Kellen, "A View of the VC," 36.

7. *Quan Doi Nhan Dan,* July 15, 1966, JPRS 37,565, 2.

8. Ibid., Feb. 16, 1967, JPRS 40,430, 16.

9. David W. P. Elliott and Mai Elliott, "Documents of an Elite Viet Cong Delta Unit," RM-5850, May 1969, RC, ix; RM-5851, ix; *Quan Doi Nhan Dan,* Sept. 20, 1966, JPRS 38,482, 62; March 16, 1967, JPRS 41,025, 9–10; *Nhan Dan,* April 8, 1967, JPRS 41,265, 21–23.

10. Frank Denton, "Volunteers for the Viet Cong," RM-5647, Sept. 1968, RC, summary by RC. See also ibid., 11–21.

11. RVNAF, JGS, "Report of the Study on Living Standards Republic of Vietnam Armed Forces (Army)" (Saigon, 1968–69), 30, 65, 79–81, 106–7, 117, 198, EC; Dong Van Khuyen, *RVNAF,* 224.

12. Captured Diary, VN, no. 10, undated (1967), 11.

13. Sept. 5, 1966 directive, WP, item 112. See also *Quan Doi Nhan Dan,* Jan. 20, 1972, JPRS 55,155, 10–11; VN, nos. 2–3, Oct. 1967, 9–10; no. 19, Feb. 1968; Konrad Kellen, "A Profile of the PAVN Soldier in South Vietnam," RM-5013, June 1966, RC, 36–38.

14. Song Hao, *Hoc Tap,* May 1967, JPRS 41,648, 58. See also captured diary, VN, no. 13, Jan. 1968, 4; interrogations, WP, item 83; item 91; *Quan Doi Nhan Dan,* Nov. 10, 1965, JPRS 33,569, 4–5; *Hau Can,* Jan. 1969, JPRS 51,950, 17–18; SA, 785; William R. Corson, *The Betrayal* (New York, 1968), 147–48; Kellen, "A View of the VC," 33–36.

15. *NYT,* Oct. 28, 1965. See also training plan, VN, no. 15, Jan. 1968, 4; *Quan Doi Nhan Dan,* Jan. 20, 1972, 9; Kellen, "A View of the VC," 67; RVNAF, "Living Standards," 92; Berman, *Revolutionary Organization,* 177; *Quan Doi Nhan Dan,* Feb. 16, 1967, JPRS 40,430, 12–17.

16. SA, 821–22, 909, 911, chaps. 7, 16; Corson, *Betrayal,* 146; Kellen, "Profile of the PAVN," 37; Robert W. Chandler, *War of Ideas* (Boulder, 1981), 92–93; Lucian W. Pye, "Observations on the Chieu Hoi Program," RM-4864, Jan. 1969, RC, ix; Dong Van Khuyen, *RVNAF,* 140–44; Hinh and Tho, *South Vietnamese Society,* 120.

17. Song Hao, *Hoc Tap,* 57.

18. Arthur Smithies, "Economic Problems of Vietnamization," Aug. 1970, A10, Smithies Papers. See also ibid., A4; RVNAF, "Living Standards," 65, 106–107, 198; interrogations, WP, item 86, 15; *Quan Doi Nhan Dan,* July 27, 1967, JPRS 42,469, 17–19; Dong Van Khuyen, *RVNAF,* 223, 238; Cao Van Vien, *Leadership,* 120.

19. Hinh and Tho, *South Vietnamese Society,* 115. See also RVNAF, "Living Standards," 85, 125, 129.

20. Hoang Ngoc Lung, *Strategy and Tactics,* IM, 131. See also ibid., 95, 114; Cao Van Vien, *Leadership,* 69, 118, 121; Dong Van Khuyen, *RVNAF,* 346; *Quan Doi Nhan Dan,* Sept. 29, 1965, JPRS 33,006, 31–35; training bulletin, 15–16, WP, item 38; Sept. 5, 1966, directive, WP, item 112; SA, 806.

21. Dong Van Khuyen, *RVNAF,* 295. See also ibid., 300–301; Tran Dinh Tho, *Pacification,* 167; Pearce, "Insurgent Environment," 108; State Dept. memo, Feb. 17, 1967, DDRS 80:207A.

22. Hinh and Tho, *South Vietnamese Society,* 115. See also ibid., 298–99.

23. NSSM, 4991, 5033. See also ibid., 4994; *NYT,* Jan. 22, 1970.

Chapter 21: The Communist Party's Response to Total War

1. The most useful survey is Etudes Vietnamiennes, *Politique économique et guerre de liberation nationale* (Hanoi, 1976), 150–227. See also Le Tat Dac, *Hoc Tap,* Sept. 1966, JPRS 38,660, 78–82.

2. Etudes Vietnamiennes, *Politique économique,* 194, 200–210, 240–41; Jon M. Van Dyke, *North Vietnam's Strategy for Survival* (Palo Alto, 1972), 100–101; Vo Nguyen Giap, *People's War against U.S. Aero-Naval War* (Hanoi, 1975), 53–56; Doan Trong Truyen,

Hoc Tap, June 1968, JPRS 46,203, 44–45; *Tuyen Huan,* Aug.–Sept. 1966, JPRS 47,273, 10–12.

3. To Huu, *Tuyen Huan,* Aug.–Sept. 1966, JPRS 39,035, 29. See also April 17, 1966, directive, 8–11, WP, item 66; Be Chan Hung, *Hoc Tap,* Nov. 1964, JPRS 28,194, 100; GP, 142; Le Duan, *Ecrits* (Hanoi, 1976), 69, 310, 331–32; Le Tat Dac, *Hoc Tap,* 75–83.

4. *Nhan Dan,* April 8, 1967, JPRS 41,265, 21; Le Duan, *Role of the Vietnamese Working Class . . .* (Hanoi, 1969) 37–38, 49, 56; *Nhan Dan,* Oct. 25, 1968, JPRS 47,026, 36–38; *Tuyen Huan,* May–June 1972, JPRS 56,676, 67–68; *Nhan Dan,* Aug. 30, 1967, JPRS 43,079, 12–14; William S. Turley, ed., *Vietnamese Communism in Comparative Perspective* (Boulder, 1980), 186–88.

5. Le Duc Tho, *Nhan Dan,* Nov. 7, 1966, JPRS 38,814, 46. See also Le Duc Tho, *Hoc Tap,* June 1966, JPRS 36,370, 16, 22.

6. Le Duc Tho, *Tuyen Huan,* June 1966, JPRS 36,370, 5.

7. To Huu, *Tuyen Huan,* Sept.–Oct. 1971, JPRS 54,782, 8. The outpouring on these themes was vast. A few useful samples are *Nhan Dan,* Aug. 26, 1967, JPRS 42,791, 4–5; *Nhan Dan,* Aug. 30, 1967, JPRS 43,079, 15–17; *Nhan Dan,* July 4, 1968, JPRS 46,190, 14–15; Ho Chi Minh, *Selected Writings, 1920–1969* (Hanoi, 1977), 317.

8. Le Duan, *Hoc Tap,* April 1969, JPRS 48,286, 22–23; Le Duc Tho, *Tuyen Huan,* Feb. 1968, JPRS 45,101, 13; *Tuyen Huan,* May–June 1972, JPRS 56,676, 117; Le Duc Binh, *Hoc Tap,* April 1969, JPRS 48,286, 50–57; Le Tat Thang, *Tap Chi Quan Doi Nhan Dan,* Jan. 1971, JPRS 53,248, 30–31; Le Duan, *Ecrits,* 347–49; Hong Chuong, *Hoc Tap,* May 1967, JPRS 41,648, 79–80; Truong Chinh, *Tuyen Huan,* Aug.–Sept. 1966, JPRS 39,035, 12.

9. *Hoc Tap,* April 1969, JPRS 48,286, 10. See also, as a sample, Nguyen Long Bang, *Tuyen Huan,* no. 3, 1969, JPRS 48,983, 23; Le Duan, *Ecrits,* 351.

10. Nguyen Hong Phong, *Hoc Tap,* Sept. 1973, JPRS 60,415, 84. See also Nguyen Chi Thanh, *Hoc Tap,* 3, 16; Vu Khieu, *Hoc Tap,* May 1970, JPRS 50,954, 84.

11. Ho Chi Minh, *Selected Writings,* 330; Tran Quang Huy, *Tuyen Huan,* June 1966, JPRS 37,675, 44; Vu Hong, *Hoc Tap,* April 1967, JPRS 41,044, 99–100; Le Duan, *Role of the Vietnamese Working Class,* 47–48; Le Duan, *Ecrits,* 256, 263–65; Le Duc Tho, *Hoc Tap,* 17.

12. Editorial, *Hoc Tap,* March 1973, JPRS 59,150, 10. See also Trung Kien, *Tuyen Huan,* Jan.–Feb. 1967, JPRS 40,359, 17–19; Vu Hong, *Hoc Tap,* 99–100.

13. Tran Nhan, *Triet Hoc,* July 1974, JPRS 63,796, 16.

14. Nguyen Van Tran, *Tuyen Huan,* Aug.–Sept. 1966, JPRS 39,035, 53.

15. Quang Huy, *Tuyen Huan,* Sept.–Oct. 1972, JPRS 57,853, 13.

16. *Tuyen Huan,* July–Aug. 1970, JPRS 51,678, 70.

17. Ibid., 71.

18. Le Duc Tho, *Tuyen Huan,* Feb. 1968, JPRS 45,101, 10.

19. *Hoc Tap,* June 1968, JPRS 46,203, 11.

20. *Tuyen Huan,* Jan.–Feb. 1972, JPRS 56,123, 15–16. See also Nguyen Vinh, *Tuyen Huan,* Dec. 1969, JPRS 50,116, 17–18.

21. Le Duan, March 1966, WP, item 302, 2.

22. *Tuyen Huan,* July–Aug. 1970, JPRS 51,678, 48.

23. VN, no. 102, Feb. 1972, 34.

24. Truong-Chinh, *Selected Writings* (Hanoi, 1977), 585. See also Le Duan, WP, item 302, 23; Dec. 1963 Party resolution, VN, no. 96, July 1971, 19.

25. Le Duan, March 1966, PM, no. 1076, 24.

26. No author, *South Vietnam: Initial Failure of the U.S. "Limited War"* (Hanoi, 1967), 11.

27. Quynh Cu, *Nghien Cuu Lich Su,* Dec. 1968, JPRS 48,179, 55–62; State Dept. memo, Feb. 17, 1967, 8, DDRS 80:207A; Hinh and Tho, *South Vietnamese Society,* 86–87, 153; Nguyen Van Vinh speech, April 1966, WP, item 303, 5; Aug. 3, 1967 circular, VN, no. 20, March 1968, 4.

28. Truong-Chinh, *Selected Writings,* 607.

29. Le Duan, mid-1966 statement, VN, no. 102, Feb. 1972, 35. See also *Initial Failure of the U.S.,* 38–39; Aug. 3, 1967 circular, VN, 2.

30. Nguyen Van Vinh, April 1966, WP, 18. See also ibid., 13; Military Institute, *Vietnam: The Anti-U.S. Resistance War for National Salvation* (Hanoi, 1980), JPRS 80,968, 87–88.

31. Binh Dinh directive, Nov. 1, 1967, WP, nos. 28–29, April 1968, 13.

32. State Dept. memo, Feb. 17, 1967, 6, DDRS 80:207A. See also Nov. 20, 1967 document, WP, no. 24, April 1968, 4–5; Military Institute, *Anti-U.S. Resistance,* 87; Dec. 1, 1967 directive, VN, no. 18, Feb. 1968, 4; Sept. 1, 1967 document, VN, no. 20, March 1968, 8; Le Duan, mid-1966 statement, VN; Hoang Ngoc Lung, *The General Offensives of 1968–1969,* IM, 21–23.

Chapter 22: The Economic Impact of the War on the United States

1. Feb. 1959 memo, 12, Joseph M. Dodge Papers, Detroit Public Library, Budget Bureau, box 2. See also Charles A. Coombs, *The Arena of International Finance* (New York, 1976), chaps. 2–5; Stephen K. McNees, *New England Economic Review,* Jan.–Feb. 1982, 7–8; Stephen V. O. Clarke, *Federal Reserve Bank of New York Quarterly Review,* Summer 1980, 21; George W. Ball, *The Past Has Another Pattern* (New York, 1982), 204–7.

2. Lt. Gen. Frank Z. Mildren, June 1968–July 1970 debriefing, 24, DDRS R:228A.

3. Lawrence S. Ritter, ed., *Selected Papers of Allan Sproul* (New York, 1980), 20. For the general impact, see Leonard B. Taylor, *Financial Management of the Vietnam Conflict, 1962–1972* (U.S. Dept. of the Army, 1974), 22–25; Robert W. Stevens, *Vain Hopes, Grim Realities: The Economic Consequences of the Vietnam War* (New York, 1976), 75–99; First National City Bank *Monthly Economic Letter,* Jan. 1972, 11; McGeorge Bundy to Johnson, July 19, 1965, NSC; U.S. Congress, Joint Economic Comm., *Economic Effects of Vietnam Spending,* 90:1, July 7, 1967, 3; "Holding the Line on the 1967 Budget," n.d., Kermit Gordon Papers, Kennedy Library, box 11; Richard N. Gardner, *Sterling-Dollar Diplomacy* (New York, 1969), lxvii; *Wash. Post,* June 15, 1969; *Congressional Quarterly Weekly Report,* Feb. 13, 1982, 234; *Economic Report of the President, 1977,* 227, 231, 233, 246, 268, 302; OECD Economic Survey, *United States* (Paris, 1979), 22; Jacques S. Gansler, *The Defense Industry* (Cambridge, 1980), 19; Clarke, *Quarterly Review,* 30.

4. Robert Triffin, U.S. Congress, Joint Economic Comm., *Hearings: A Foreign Eco-*

nomic Policy for the 1970's, 91:2, Sept. 30, 1970, 1033; Clarke, *Quarterly Review,* 31; *Economic Report of the President,* 296, 302; memo of conversation, French Finance Ministry, Aug. 30–31, 1965; minutes, Advisory Comm. on International Monetary Arrangements, Oct. 20, 1965, Walter Heller Papers, Kennedy Library, box 45.

5. Coombs, *Arena of International Finance,* 165. See also ibid., 158–64; minutes, Advisory Comm. on International Monetary Arrangements, Oct. 13, 1966, Heller Papers, box 45; Lyndon B. Johnson, *The Vantage Point* (New York, 1971), 317; NSC, "The Gold Crisis: Nov. 1967–March 1968," DDRS 79:276A, 277A.

6. NSC, "Gold Crisis," 5, DDRS 79:277A.

Chapter 23: The Balance of Forces in the War at the End of 1967

1. Mid-1966, WP, item 65, 4. See also Le Duan, March 1966, WP, item 302, 12, 16; Van Tien Dung, *After Political Failure the U.S. Imperialists Are Facing Military Defeat in South Vietnam* (Hanoi, 1966), 10–35.

2. Le Duan, WP, item 302, 21.

3. Ibid. See also Military Institute, *Vietnam: The Anti-U.S. Resistance War for National Salvation* (Hanoi, 1980), JPRS 80,968, 93.

4. *Tuyen Huan,* April 1967, JPRS 41,673, 16–27.

5. Lyndon B. Johnson, *The Vantage Point* (New York, 1971), 378. See also George A. Carver, Jr., memo, Oct. 15, 1966, DDRS 80:229B; CIA estimate, Jan. 9, 1967, DDRS 78:37B; CIA estimate, Dec. 8, 1967, 3, V-3, DDRS 78:37C.

Chapter 24: The Tet Offensive

1. Military Institute, *Vietnam: The Anti-U.S. Resistance War for National Salvation* (Hanoi, 1980), JPRS 80,968, 93.

2. See also ibid., 101; Hoang Ngoc Lung, *The General Offensives of 1968–69,* IM, 22–25; for contingencies on the offensive, see *Quan Doi Nhan Dan,* Jan. 4, 6, 11, 1968, *Nhan Dan,* Jan. 27, 1968, JPRS 44,610, 3–16; Le Duan, *Thu Vao Nam* (Hanoi, 1985), 189–96, reveals most regarding the Party's premises.

3. *Quan Doi Nhan Dan,* Jan. 11, 1968, 4–5. See also Hoang Ngoc Lung, *General Offensives,* 32ff.; William M. Momyer, *Airpower in Three Wars* (U.S. Office of Air Force History, 1978), 311; Don Oberdorfer, *Tet!* (Garden City, 1971), 54; *Nhan Dan,* Jan. 13, 1968, JPRS 44,469, 17–21; Aug. 3, 1967, document, WP, no. 20, March 1968, 4.

4. W. W. Rostow, *The Diffusion of Power* (New York, 1972), 462.

5. Lyndon B. Johnson, *The Vantage Point* (New York, 1971), 384. See also Oberdorfer, *Tet,* 118–19; Westmoreland chronology, "Vietnam General-Tet 1968" file, Westmoreland Papers, Historical Records Branch, Dept. of the Army; Momyer, *Airpower,* 303, 320–21; Westmoreland to Wheeler and Sharp, Feb. 12, 1968, NSC; CIA memo, Feb. 15, 1968, DDRS 78:38A; Townsend Hoopes, *The Limits of Intervention* (New York, 1969), 144–45; Military Institute, *Anti-U.S. Resistance War,* 103; William C. Westmoreland, *A Soldier Reports* (Garden City, 1976), 339.

6. *PP,* IV, 539. See also ibid., 547; Rostow, *Diffusion of Power,* 464.

7. *PP,* IV, 533. See also ibid., 536; GP, 351.

8. Westmoreland, *Soldier Reports,* 234–35; GP, 352–54; Thomas Powers, *The Man Who Kept Secrets* (New York, 1981), 236–45; U.S. House, Select Comm. on Intelligence, *Hearings: U.S. Intelligence Agencies and Activities,* 94:1. Sept.–Dec. 1975, 683–717, 1684–89; *International Herald Tribune,* Aug. 26, 1983; SA, 787.

9. Feb. 26, 1968 report, DDRS 80:96D.

10. CIA report, n.d. (late Feb. 1968), 9, DDRS 78:38D.

11. George C. Herring, *America's Longest War* (New York, 1979), 189. See also Oberdorfer, *Tet,* 256, 262; Hoang Ngoc Lung, *General Offensives,* 28, 46–47; U. S. G. Sharp and William C. Westmoreland, *Report on the War in Vietnam* (Washington, 1968), 158; Momyer, *Airpower,* 312; Hoopes, *Limits,* 140–42; SA, 836; CIA memo, Feb. 10, 1968, NSC.

12. *Quan Doi Nhan Dan,* Feb. 4, 1968, JPRS 44,849, 50–51. See also CIA memo, Feb. 10, 1968; Habib memo, Feb. 26, 1968, 5, NSC; Party analysis, n.d., VN, no. 45, Oct. 1968, 8; Rostow to Johnson, Feb. 16, 1968, NSC; Sharp and Westmoreland, *Report on the War,* 161.

13. *PP,* IV, 547.

14. Sharp and Westmoreland, *Report on the War,* 235. See also CIA Feb. 26, 1968, outlook, 5; Habib Feb. 26, 1968, memo, 8; Wheeler to Johnson, Feb. 27, 1968; Rostow, draft memo, March 1, 1968, NSC; Hoopes, *Limits,* 156; *PP,* IV, 540; Dong Van Khuyen, *The RVNAF,* IM, 140.

15. CIA Feb. 26, 1968, memo, 5, NSC. See also Clifford Group, "Outline . . . ," March 4, 1968, 4, NSC.

Chapter 25: The Tet Offensive's Impact on Washington

1. Doris Kearns, *Lyndon Johnson and the American Dream* (New York, 1976), 347. See also Townsend Hoopes, *The Limits of Intervention* (New York, 1969), 134–35; W. W. Rostow, *The Diffusion of Power* (New York, 1972), 520; *Nhan Dan,* Jan. 13, 1968, JPRS 44,469, 17–21; notes of Johnson meeting with senior advisers, Feb. 9, 1968, 4, NSC.

2. Fowler to Johnson, March 4, 1968; Rostow to Johnson, March 14, 1968, DDRS 80:65A. See also Charles A. Coombs, *The Arena of International Finance* (New York, 1976), 167.

3. Johnson to Moro, March 15, 1968, DDRS 79:277A. The NSC's file, "The Gold Crisis: Nov. 1967–March 1968," DDRS 79:276A, 277A, fully documents this period.

4. For the economy, see Coombs, *Arena of International Finance,* 167–72; Lyndon B. Johnson, *The Vantage Point* (New York, 1971), 537; *Business Week,* March 23, 1968, 32. Wheeler's use of Westmoreland is documented in Westmoreland's "The Origins of the Post-Tet 1968 Plans . . . ," Nov. 9, 1970, Westmoreland Papers; *A Soldier Reports* (Garden City, 1976), 355–58; as well as Kearns, *American Dream,* 343; Herbert Y. Schandler, *The Unmaking of a President* (Princeton, 1977), 98ff.; John B. Henry, "February, 1968," *Foreign Policy,* Fall 1971, 18–20; notes of Johnson meeting, Feb. 9, 1968; Hoopes, *Limits,* 173.

5. Wheeler to Johnson, Feb. 27, 1968, NSC. See also Hoopes, *Limits,* 152–53, 162; *PP,* IV, 550ff., 583; Clark M. Clifford, "A Viet Nam Reappraisal . . . ," *Foreign Affairs,* 47 (1969), 610–13; Henry, "February, 1968," 27; Rostow, draft memo, March 1, 1968, 13;

Taylor, memo, March 2, 1968; Clifford Comm. draft memos, March 4, 1968, NSC; Systems Analysis, Defense Dept., memo, n.d. (ca. March 1–2, 1968), DDRS 80:101A; CIA questions, March 1, 1968, DDRS 78:38B.

6. Johnson, *Vantage Point,* 397.

7. Kearns, *American Dream,* 343. See also Johnson, *Vantage Point,* 400ff.

8. Harry McPherson, *A Political Education* (Boston, 1972), 433–34. See also Hoopes, *Limits,* 205; Ronnie Dugger, *The Politician* (New York, 1982), 155–63.

9. Clifford, "A Viet Nam Reappraisal," 612. See also Schandler, *Unmaking of a President,* 165.

10. Rostow, *Diffusion of Power,* 520–21. See also Hoopes, *Limits,* 204–5; Johnson, *Vantage Point,* 409.

11. Johnson, *Vantage Point,* 423. See also ibid., 415; Henry Owen to Ralph Clough, March 18, 1968, NSC; Clifford, "A Viet Nam Reappraisal," 612.

12. McPherson, *Political Education,* 436; George W. Ball, *The Past Has Another Pattern* (New York, 1982), 407–9; Hoopes, *Limits,* 214ff.; Schandler, *Unmaking of a President,* 260–61; Johnson, *Vantage Point,* 418.

13. State Dept. memo, n.d. (ca. March 1–2, 1968), 4, DDRS 80:101A. See also Kearns, *American Dream,* 346–47; Johnson, *Vantage Point,* 493–94; draft memo for Johnson, March 4, 1968, tab B; CIA briefing book, March 13, 1968, attachment "Increasing the Effectiveness . . ."; CIA memo, "Communist Reactions . . . ," March 13, 1968; memo on NSC meeting, March 27, 1968, NSC; Habib memo, Feb. 26, 1968, DDRS 80:96D.

14. *PP,* IV, 598. See also Hoopes, *Limits,* 312–13.

15. Lt. Gen. Julian J. Ewell, debriefing, Sept. 17, 1969, 12, DDRS R:221B. See also McPherson, *Political Education,* 364–69; CIA memo, March 30, 1968, DDRS 78:38C.

16. Ewell debriefing, 19. See also BDM VI (1), 3–75.

17. March 1, 1968 draft memo for Johnson, 10, NSC. See also AID, 130–31.

18. NSSM, 5033. See also ibid., 4991, 4994.

19. Ibid., 4979.

Chapter 26: Assessing the Tet Offensive

1. SA, 837. See also Tran Van Tra, *Concluding the 30-Years War* (Ho Chi Minh City, 1982), JPRS 82,783, 36; internal assessments, VN, nos. 30–32, April 1968, 4; VN, no. 45, Oct. 1968; *Tuyen Huan,* March 1968, JPRS 45,298, 1–8; Military Institute, *Vietnam: The Anti-U.S. Resistance War for National Salvation* (Hanoi, 1980), JPRS 80,968, 107–9; Hoang Ngoc Lung, *The General Offensives of 1968–69,* IM, 93–94, 104–5; GP, 362–64, 369–70.

2. 5th Special Forces report, Feb. 15, 1968, DDRS R:210C. See also Lt. Gen. Julian J. Ewell debriefing, Sept. 17, 1969, DDRS R:221B.

3. Military Institute, *Anti-U.S. Resistance War,* 110.

4. Memo for Johnson, March 1, 1968, draft, 2, NSC.

5. U. S. G. Sharp and William C. Westmoreland, *Report on the War in Vietnam* (Washington, 1968), 170. See also ibid., 160; NSSM, 4994; SA, 913.

6. "Southeast Asia Analysis Report," Dec. 1968, 55–56, DDRS 75:9B; 6th resolution COSVN, VN, no. 38, July 1968, 8; for residual support for NLF, see James W. Trullinger,

Jr., *Village at War* (New York, 1980), 142–44, 188; Tran Dinh Tho, *Pacification,* IM, 192.

7. Military Institute, *Anti-U.S. Resistance War,* 101, 107–10; SA, 914; [U.S.], "The Viet Cong Infrastructure: *Modus Operandi* of Selected Political Cadres," Dec. 1968, 54ff.; Nov. 27, 1968 directive, VN, no. 54, March 1969, 3; *Tuyen Huan,* 1–5; *Hoc Tap,* March 1968, JPRS 45,592, 15–16; Tran Le, *Doc Lap,* March 23, 1968, JPRS 45,905, 6–9; editorial, *Hoc Tap,* Oct. 1968, JPRS 47,040, 4–5; Commission for the Study of the History of the Party, *50 Years of Activities of the Communist Party of Vietnam* (Hanoi, 1980), 193; for one of many reports on overall U.S. position, see *Quan Doi Nhan Dan,* April 14–16, 1968, JPRS 45,464, 1–13.

8. Tran Van Tra, *30-Years War,* 36. See also SA, 907; assessment, VN, no. 45, Oct. 1968, 12. I have discussed this period in great detail with many people in Vietnam.

9. CIA estimate, Feb. 26, 1968, 4, NSC.

Chapter 27: The Nixon Administration's Confrontation with Vietnam and the World

1. H. R. Haldeman, *The Ends of Power* (New York, 1978), 83. See also Richard J. Whalen, *Catch the Falling Flag* (Boston, 1972), 25–29, 84–87, 130–40.

2. Henry Kissinger, *White House Years* (Boston, 1979), 26–28, 234–38; Seymour M. Hersh, *The Price of Power: Kissinger in the Nixon White House* (New York, 1983), 47–50; NSSM, 4977ff.

3. U.S. Senate, Comm. on Foreign Relations, *Hearings: Impact of the War in Southeast Asia on the U.S. Economy,* 91:2, April 15–16, 1970, 10, 17. See also BDM V, 6–20; Kissinger, *White House Years,* 274–75; Philip E. Converse and Howard Schuman, " 'Silent Majorities' and the Vietnam War," *Scientific American,* June 1970, 24; *Fortune,* Sept. 1969, 94.

4. *Business Week,* April 18, 1970, 32.

5. Kissinger, *White House Years,* 32. See also ibid., 212–22, 477; Robert W. Stevens, *Vain Hopes, Grim Realities* (New York, 1976), 99, 146–47; Lloyd Norman, *Army,* March 1970, 21–22; U.S. Senate, Comm. on Appropriations, *Hearings: Department of Defense Appropriations, 1974,* 93:1, March 1973, pt. 1, 323, 333–34, 411–12; DOD, 1973, pt. 3, 351–52; BDM V, 6–3.

6. Kissinger, *White House Years,* 35. See also ibid., 276–77, 477; Senate Comm. on Appropriations, *Hearings,* 381; Norman, *Army,* 22–23.

7. Kissinger, *White House Years,* 950.

8. Charles A. Coombs, *The Arena of International Finance* (New York, 1976), 219. See also ibid., 204–5, 210–11; Joyce Kolko, *America and the Crisis of World Capitalism* (Boston, 1974), 9–13; U.S. National Advisory Council on International Monetary and Financial Policies, *Annual Report, 1972–1973,* 119; Stephen V. O. Clarke, *Federal Reserve Bank of New York Quarterly Review,* Summer 1980, 29–31; *Economic Report of the President, 1977,* 296; *Wall Street Journal,* April 28, May 4, 1970; *Business Week,* May 2, 1970, 10, 18.

9. Kissinger, *White House Years,* 956. See also Coombs, *Arena of International Finance,* 214–18; Kolko, *Crisis of World Capitalism,* 12–19; *NYT,* July 7, Aug. 17, 1972.

10. U. Alexis Johnson, *DSB*, March 23, 1970, 387. See also Kissinger, *White House Years*, 224–28, 262–92, 476–77, 968, 1014; Roger Morris, *Uncertain Greatness: Henry Kissinger and the Nixon White House* (New York, 1977), 156–65; Bruce Palmer, *The 25-Year War* (Lexington, 1984), 100–104; Hersh, *Price of Power*, 186–96; Nixon Jan. 30, 1970, press conference, *DSB*, Feb. 16, 1970, 176; BDM V, 6–5; GP, 386; CIA report, April 17, 1970, DDRS 77:270C; Douglas Kinnard, *The War Managers* (Hanover, 1977), 140–43; Marshall Green, *DSB*, Feb. 8, 1971, 161–65.

Chapter 28: The Crisis of American Military Power

1. Lloyd Norman, *Army*, Feb. 1971, 21. See also BDM VI (1), 4–13ff.; NYT, April 19, 1970; Henry Kissinger, *White House Years* (Boston, 1979), 985–86, 994ff.; Seymour M. Hersh, *The Price of Power* (New York, 1983), 120, 128.

2. Maj. Gen. Richard A. Yudkin, *Air Force*, Feb. 1973, 34–35. See also Lt. Gen. Frank T. Mildren debriefing, June 1968–July 1970, 45, DDRS R:228A; U.S. Senate, Comm. on Appropriations, *Hearings: Department of Defense Appropriations, 1974*, 93:1, March 1973, pt. I, 143; SA, 825–28, 838, 848; J. L. Frisbee, *Air Force*, Sept. 1971, 45; DOD, 1972, 92:1, pt. I, 414, 917; BDM V, 6–20; VI (2), 11-65-69; 11th Armored Calvary Reg. report, Sept. 17, 1969, 11, DDRS R:217C; II Field Force report ending July 31, 1969, DDRS R:219A; Army Support Command, Danang, report ending April 30, 1970, DDRS R:227G; Maj. Gen. Arthur H. Sweeney debriefing, Nov. 1970–April 1972, 31, 46, DDRS R:237A; Nguyen Duy Hinh, *Lam Son 719*, IM, 135; *NYT*, June 21, 1972; Jack S. Ballard, *Development and Employment of Fixed-Wing Gunships, 1962–72* (U.S. Office of Air Force History, 1982), 149, 173.

3. BDM VII, chaps. 1, 3, 4; Richard A. Gabriel and Paul L. Savage, *Crisis in Command: Mismanagement in the Army* (New York, 1978), 13ff., 61–62, 67; Douglas Kinnard, *The War Managers* (Hanover, 1977), 71, 110–12; Edward L. King, *The Death of the Army* (New York, 1972), 71ff., 106; Ed Berger et al., *Foreign Policy*, Spring 1971, 146.

4. Col. R. D. Heinl, Jr., *Armed Forces Journal*, July 25, 1970, 10. See also BDM VII, chap. 1; Lt. Gen. Julian J. Ewell debriefing, Sept. 17, 1969, 5, DDRS R:221B; Robert Jay Lifton, *Home from the War* (New York, 1973), 65, 350–59; II Field Force report, Sept. 10, 1969, 53–54, DDRS R:215C.

5. Col. Robert D. Heinl, Jr., "The Collapse of the Armed Forces," *Armed Forces Journal*, June 7, 1971, 31.

6. BDM VII, 2-29, 4-4, 6-6-7; Alfred W. McCoy, *The Politics of Heroin in Southeast Asia* (New York, 1972), 185–210; *Army*, Feb. 1971, 9; *Wall Street Journal*, Dec. 18, 1970; Heinl, "Collapse," 30ff.; U.S. House, Comm. on Interstate and Foreign Commerce, *Report: Production and Abuse of Opiates in the Far East*, Oct. 1971, 8–10, 13–14; Ewell debriefing, 15.

7. Americal Div. report for period ending Oct. 31, 1968, 59, DDRS R:212B. See also Maj. Gen. Verne L. Bowers debriefing, March 1969–Sept. 1970, 4, DDRS R:230C; Maj. Gen. John J. Henessey, May 1970–Jan. 1971, debriefing, DDRS R:232C; Army Support Command, Saigon . . . , period ending April 30, 1971, 2, 33, DDRS R:234C; 23d Infantry Div., period ending Oct. 15, 1971, 94, DDRS R:235B; *Wash. Post*, April 24, 1973; Richard

A. Ratner, *University of Chicago Magazine,* May–June 1972, 18; *Wall Street Journal,* Sept. 1, 1970, Nov. 28, 1972; *NYT,* May 16, 1971; *Wash. Post,* Jan. 24, 1972; *San Francisco Chronicle,* July 1, 1970.

8. Maj. Gen. Arthur H. Sweeney, Nov. 1970–April 1972 debriefing, 3, 43, DDRS R:237A. See also Gabriel and Savage, *Crisis in Command,* 42–44, table 3; BDM VII, 4–23.

9. U.S. House, Comm. on Armed Services, *Report . . . Special Subcommittee on Disciplinary Problems in the U.S. Navy,* 92:2, Jan. 2, 1973, 17684. See also *NYT,* Nov. 6, 1972; *Wall Street Journal,* Nov. 15, 1972.

10. *Wash. Post,* Dec. 13, 1972.

11. BDM VI (2), 11–62. See also *Wash. Post,* Dec. 13, 1972; *NYT,* Dec. 30, 1972, Jan. 11, 1973.

12. Gen. Hamilton H. Howze, *Army,* Jan. 1971, 12, 14. See also DOD, 1972, pt. 1, 389–94; pt. 4, 814ff.; *NYT,* Nov. 10, 1972; U.S. Senate, Comm. on the Judiciary, *Hearings: Organized Subversion in the U.S. Armed Forces,* 94:1, Sept. 25, 1975, 3 parts.

13. *Wall Street Journal,* Nov. 11, 1971. See also Gabriel and Savage, *Crisis in Command,* table 4; *NYT,* Sept. 13, 1971, Nov. 15, 1972.

Chapter 29: The Revolution's Military Policy, 1969–1971

1. GP, 384.

2. Senior-level discussion, VN, no. 62, June 1969, 9. See also Vo Nguyen Giap, *People's War against U.S. Aero-Naval War* (Hanoi, 1975), 90, 132–34; Thanh Tin, *Hoc Tap,* Jan. 1971, JPRS 52,781, 91ff.; summary of COSVN resolution, VN, no. 67, Sept. 1969, 13–17.

3. GP, 384.

4. Military Institute, *Vietnam: The Anti-U.S. Resistance War for National Salvation* (Hanoi, 1980), JPRS 80,968, 115.

5. Gareth Porter, ed., *Vietnam: The Definitive Documentation of Human Decisions* (London, 1979), II, 535.

6. VN, no. 71, Jan. 1970, i. See also Military Institute, *Anti-U.S. Resistance,* 123–25; GP, 394–95; Resolution 14, Oct. 30, 1969, VN, no. 82, July 1970, 2.

7. Military Institute, *Anti-U.S. Resistance,* 116, 124, 133–34; Vo Nguyen Giap, *People's War,* 99, 158, 163; Giap, *Ecrits* (Hanoi, 1977), 297, 339, 350–53, 366; GP, 394–96; Phuong Hanh, *Quan Doi Nhan Dan,* Aug. 10, 1970, JPRS 51,795, 9–12; Le Duan, *The Vietnamese Revolution: Fundamental Problems, Essential Tasks* (Hanoi, 1973).

8. SA, 788, 837–39, 907; Military Institute, *Anti-U.S. Resistance,* 123–24; David W. P. Elliott, "NLF-DRV Strategy and the 1972 Spring Offensive" (Cornell Univ. East Asia Program, Jan. 1974), 17; CIA estimate, April 17, 1970, 13, 20–22, DDRS 77:270C; 5th Special Forces Group, Oct. 6, 1969, report, 3, 15, DDRS R:217B; II Field Force report period ending Oct. 31, 1969, 10–11, DDRS R:222E; Hoang Ngoc Lung, *The General Offensives of 1968–69,* IM, 131–33; Quyet Thang, *Hoc Tap,* Jan. 1971, JPRS 52,781, 70–72.

9. Hoang Ngoc Lung, *Strategy and Tactics,* IM, 100. See also Phuong Hanh, *Quan Doi Nhan Dan,* 9–12.

10. 25th Infantry Div. Sept. 13, 1969, report, 43, DDRS R:216C; 16th Aviation Group

report ending Jan. 31, 1970, 4, 23, DDRS R:224C; discussion of Resolution 10, ca. Feb. 1971, VN, no. 99, Oct. 1971; SA, 908.

11. Henry Kissinger, *White House Years* (Boston, 1979), 1010. See also ibid., 992, 1008-9; Nguyen Duy Hinh, *Lam Son 719*, IM, 127-29, 135, 155; Military Institute, *Anti-U.S. Resistance*, 135-37; Bruce Palmer, Jr., *The 25-Year War* (Lexington, 1984), 108-15.

12. Military Institute, *Anti-U.S. Resistance*, 136, 138. See also William W. Momyer, *Airpower in Three Wars* (U.S. Office of Air Force History, 1978), 321-24; Nguyen Duy Hinh, *Lam Son 719*.

13. *Thoi Su Pho Thong*, Jan. 1972, JPRS 55,546, 1,3. See also Elliott, "1972 Spring Offensive," 17-19; Military Institute, *Anti-U.S. Resistance*, 139-43.

Chapter 30: The United States and the RVN:
Vietnamization's Contradictions

1. James L. Collins, Jr., *The Development and the Training of the South Vietnamese Army, 1950-1972* (U.S. Dept. of the Army, 1975), 113. See also Kenneth Sams, *Air Force*, April 1971, 30.

2. CIA report, April 17, 1970, 14, DDRS 77:270C. See also ibid., 16; Collins, *Development and Training*, 102-14; Nguyen Duy Hinh, *Vietnamization and the Cease-Fire*, IM, 48, 74-77; DOD, 1972, pt. 5, 121; Thomas M. Rienzi, *Communications-Electronics, 1962-1970* (U.S. Dept. of the Army, 1972), 145; Dong Van Khuyen, *RVNAF Logistics*, IM, 184-85; David E. Ott, *Field Artillery, 1954-1973* (U.S. Dept. of the Army, 1975), 203; Lt. Gen. Frank T. Mildren June 1968-July 1970 debriefing, 55-65, DDRS R:228A.

3. Ott, *Field Artillery*, 230.

4. DOD, 1973, pt. 8, 403. See also Ott, *Field Artillery*, 215, 219; Collins, *Development and Training*, 109; Stephen T. Hosmer et al., *The Fall of South Vietnam* (New York, 1980), 73-74, 88-89; *NYT*, Nov. 21, 1969; *Wall Street Journal*, Jan. 20, 1970; Rienzi, *Communications*, 145-46; William Beecher, *Army*, Nov. 1970, 12-17.

5. *NYT*, April 19, 1970; Dong Van Khuyen, *The RVNAF*, IM, 75, 223; Collins, *Development and Training*, 93; Allan E. Goodman et al., *Asian Survey*, Jan. 1971, 14; CIA report, April 17, 1970, 15.

6. U.S. Senate, Comm. on Foreign Relations, *Report: Vietnam: December 1969*, 91:2, Feb. 2, 1970, 13.

7. Allan E. Goodman, "An Institutional Profile of the South Vietnamese Officer Corps," RM-6189, June 1970, RC, 74.

8. Goodman, *Asian Survey*, 10. See also ibid., 4-7; Nguyen Duy Hinh and Tran Dinh Tho, *The South Vietnamese Society*, IM, 146; Alfred W. McCoy, *The Politics of Heroin in Southeast Asia* (New York, 1972), 189, 201-2; *NYT*, June 28, 1972; *The Asian*, July 2-8, 1972; *Wash. Post*, Sept. 14, 1972.

9. U.S. Senate, Comm. on Foreign Relations, *Report: Vietnam: May 1972*, 92:2, June 29, 1972, 24. See also CIA report, April 17, 1970, 6; Hosmer, *Fall of South Vietnam*, 64.

10. Nguyen Duy Hinh, *Lam Son 719*, IM, 151. See also ibid., 158; Hinh, *Vietnamization*, 79; Senate Comm. on Foreign Relations, *Vietnam: May 1972*, 19.

Chapter 31: The Struggle for a Changing Rural South Vietnam

1. NSSM, 5023.

2. Ibid., 5051. See also Douglas S. Blaufarb, *The Counterinsurgency Era* (New York, 1977), 271–72; U.S. Senate, Comm. on Foreign Relations, *Report: Vietnam: December 1969,* 91:2, Feb. 2, 1970, 7; Tran Dinh Tho, *Pacification,* IM, 175–78; Komer in W. S. Thompson and D. D. Frizzell, eds., *The Lessons of Vietnam* (New York, 1977), 218–29; CIA report, April 17, 1970, 1–15, DDRS 77:270C.

3. Tran Dinh Tho, *Pacification,* 156.

4. Ibid., 72. See also Blaufarb, *Counterinsurgency,* 272; Stuart A. Herrington, *Silence Was a Weapon* (Novato, 1982), 12; SA, 913–14.

5. Cao Van Vien and Dong Van Khuyen, *Reflections on the Vietnam War,* IM, 62. See also Allan E. Goodman, *Politics in War* (Cambridge, 1973), 226–27; "Southeast Asia Analysis Report," Dec. 1968, 51, DDRS 75:9B; James W. Trullinger, Jr., *Village at War* (New York, 1980), 173; Herrington, *Silence Was a Weapon,* 196; NYT, Feb. 18, 1970.

6. Trullinger, *Village at War,* 173. See also William Colby, *Honorable Men* (New York, 1978), 272; *NYT,* Feb. 18, 1970; Senate Comm. on Foreign Relations, *Vietnam,* 6; Frank Snepp, *Decent Interval* (New York, 1977), 12; Hoang Ngoc Lung, *Strategy and Tactics,* IM, 44.

7. Goodman, *Politics in War,* 227. See also CIA April 17, 1970, report, 8; Trullinger, *Village at War,* 195–97; SA, 914; Blaufarb, *Counterinsurgency,* 274–75.

8. J. Millard Burr, "Land to the Tiller: Land Distribution in South Vietnam, 1970–1973" (Ph.D. thesis, Univ. of Oregon, 1976), 23. See also ibid., 175 and passim; Burr, "Land to the Tiller: Revolution and Land Reform in Viet Nam" (M.A. thesis, Univ. of Oregon, 1973), 217–19, 242–53; AID, 594–96; SA, 777, 929–30; Willard C. Muller, [AID], "The Land-to-the-Tiller Program," April 1973, 21–22, 39; Roy L. Prosterman, *Asian Survey,* Aug. 1970, 760.

9. SA, 931. See also Burr, Ph.D. thesis, 148; Muller, "Land-to-the-Tiller," 39; AID, 203, 596–98; Prosterman, *Asian Survey,* 760–61; for peasant opinion, see SA, 931; Control Data Corp., "The Impact of the Land to the Tiller Program in the Mekong Delta," Dec. 1972, 45; AID, memo, "Summary of CDC Study," March 13, 1973, 8.

10. AID, 163–64, 201–2; Charles Billo, AID, memo to John P. Vann, Sept. 5, 1969, 7, EC; V. L. Elliott, AID, "Development Problems in Viet-Nam," April 1973, 4; Clifton G. Barton, *A.I.D. Spring Review of Small Farmer Credit,* 11 (Feb. 1973), 34, passim; Ngo Vinh Long, "Agrarian Differentiation in the Southern Region of Vietnam," *Journal of Contemporary Asia,* 14 (1984), 283–305; Control Data Corp., "Impact," 67; Trullinger, *Village at War,* 151; *NYT,* Jan. 14, 1974.

11. 11th Armored Cavalry Reg., Sept. 17, 1969, report, 42, DDRS R:217C. See also Stanford Research Institute, *Land Reform in Vietnam* (Menlo Park, 1968), 174; James C. Scott, *The Moral Economy of the Peasant* (New Haven 1976), 166–67; Tran Van Giau in State Commission for Social Sciences, *Mot So Van De Khoa Hoc Xa Hoi Ve Don Bang Song Cuu Long* (Hanoi, 1982), 204.

12. CIA April 17, 1970, report, 7. See also Senate Comm. on Foreign Relations, *Vietnam,* 7.

13. Thompson and Frizzell, *Lessons of Vietnam,* 110–11. See also SA, 902.

14. Tran Dinh Tho, *Pacification,* 192.

15. Col. Charles E. Davis, Feb.–May 1971 debriefing, 3, 17, DDRS R:234A. See also SA, 918; *NYT,* Oct. 19, 1970; CIA April 17, 1970, report, 7–8.

16. Commission for the Study of the History of the Party, *50 Years of Activities of the Communist Party of Vietnam* (Hanoi, 1980), 196. See also, e.g., ca. Feb. 1971 document, VN, no. 99, Oct. 1971: summary in VN, no. 102, Feb. 1972, pt. 3.

17. Hoanh Son, *Hoc Tap,* Nov. 1971, JPRS 54, 731, 97–101; *Quan Doi Nhan Dan,* July 10, 1970, JPRS 51,212, 8–11; NSSM, 5051; *Tuyen Huan,* July–Aug. 1971, JPRS 54,356, 82–83; COSVN 02/73, VN, no. 113, June 1973, 68. Le Duan attempted to broaden the southern Party's urban class emphasis, but largely failed. See *Thu Vao Nam* (Hanoi, 1985), 273.

Chapter 32: The Communist Party's International Strategy

1. Daniel S. Papp, *Vietnam: The View from Moscow, Peking, Washington* (Jefferson, N.C., 1981), 20–21, 76–77; Gerald Segal, *The Great Power Triangle* (London, 1982), 15ff.; CIA memo, Feb. 11, 1965, 4–5, DDRS 77:28A; CIA review, Dec. 8, 1967, XIII-1-3, DDRS 78:37C.

2. Thomas M. Gottlieb, "Chinese Foreign Policy Factionalism and the Origins of the Strategic Triangle," R-1902, Nov. 1977, RC, xi–x; CIA Dec. 8, 1967, review; Eugene K. Lawson, *The Sino-Vietnamese Conflict* (New York, 1984).

3. William G. Hyland, "Soviet-American Relations: A New Cold War?" R-2763, May 1981, RC, 17; Roger Morris, *Uncertain Greatness* (New York, 1977), 24.

4. Hyland, "Soviet-American Relations," 12–13; for a sample of the many CIA analyses of the USSR and the war, see DDRS 77:27C; R:45E; 77:28B; 76:20E; 76:151E; 78:37C.

5. CIA memo, Oct. 7, 1965, 10, DDRS 77:86C. See also Ly Ban, *Nhan Dan,* Dec. 16–17, 1960, JPRS 8,046, 1–6.

6. Papp, *Vietnam,* 76–81; CIA Aug. 22, 1967, cable, DDRS 80:28C; cadre notebook, VN, no. 14, May 7, 1967, 4–5; NSSM, 4987–88; CIA report, Sept. 3, 1965, DDRS 76:20E; W. R. Smyser, *The Independent Vietnamese* (Athens, Ohio, 1980), 90–93, 104; János Radványi, *Delusion and Reality* (South Bend, 1978), 54–55.

7. Ibid.; CIA estimate, May 4, 1967, DDRS 76:151E; Arkady N. Shevchenko, *Breaking with Moscow* (New York, 1985), 199–200.

8. *Tuyen Huan,* July–Aug. 1970, JPRS 51,678, 49. See also Ho Chi Minh, *Selected Writings* (Hanoi, 1977), 362; Smyser, *Independent Vietnamese,* 120–22; Le Duan, *Ecrits* (Hanoi, 1976), 369; editorial, *Hoc Tap,* Aug. 1971, JPRS 54,260, 8.

9. *Tuyen Huan,* Aug. 1968, JPRS 46,594, 8; editorial, *Thoi Su Pho Thong,* Nov. 1968, JPRS 47,359, 10.

10. *Hoc Tap,* 9.

11. *Tuyen Huan,* Jan.–Feb. 1972, JPRS 56,123, 14–25; Seymour B. Hersh, *The Price of Power* (New York, 1983), 172, 300; Smyser, *Independent Vietnamese.*

12. Le Duan to Nguyen Chi Thanh, April 1966, VN, no. 8, Oct. 1967; April 1968 discussions, VN, no. 39, July 1968; Allan E. Goodman, *The Lost Peace* (Stanford, 1978), 24, 44–45, 68–69; Radványi, *Delusion and Reality,* 227–37; CIA May 4, 1967, estimate, 4.

Chapter 33: War on Two Fronts

1. Allan E. Goodman, *The Lost Peace* (Stanford, 1978), 69. See also GP, 348–49.

2. Roger Morris, *Uncertain Greatness* (New York, 1977), 203–5; Richard J. Whalen, *Catch the Falling Flag* (Boston, 1972), 133; Richard Nixon, *RN: The Memoirs of Richard Nixon* (New York, 1978), 345; Henry Kissinger, *White House Years* (Boston, 1979), 164–65; Marvin and Bernard Kalb, *Kissinger* (Boston, 1974), 122–31.

3. Charles W. Colson, *Born Again* (Old Tappan, N.J., 1976), 42. See also Richard Nixon, *No More Vietnams* (New York, 1985), 105, 141, 147.

4. Kissinger, *White House Years,* 31. See also NSSM, 4987–88; Thomas M. Gottlieb, "Chinese Foreign Policy Factionalism . . . ," R-1902, Nov. 1977, RC, 111–12.

5. Kissinger, *White House Years,* 160. See also ibid., 129, 141–44, 178–79; Morris, *Uncertain Greatness,* 96; Gottlieb, "Chinese Foreign Policy," 119.

6. Kissinger, *White House Years,* 191. See also ibid., 171, 178, 188–90; H. R. Haldeman, *The Ends of Power* (New York, 1978), 90–91; Morris, *Uncertain Greatness,* 97; Nixon, *Memoirs,* 413.

7. Nixon, *Memoirs,* 413. See also Kissinger, *White House Years,* 143–44, 329, 380–81, 554–56; William G. Hyland, "Soviet-American Relations: A New Cold War?" R-2763, May 1981, RC, 23; Marvin and Bernard Kalb, *Kissinger,* 112–13.

8. John W. Garver, "Sino-Soviet Conflict and the Sino-American Rapprochement," *Political Science Quarterly,* 96 (1981), 450–53; Gottlieb, "Chinese Foreign Policy," 132–34; Kissinger, *White House Years,* 554, 1052, 1073, 1086; Harry Gelman, "The Politburo's Management of Its America Problem," R-2707, April 1981, RC, 38; Kalb, *Kissinger,* 237; *Quan Doi Nhan Dan,* March 9, 1971, JPRS 52,949, 35–38.

9. Kissinger, *White House Years,* 757. See also ibid., 126, 711, chap. 18; W. R. Smyser, *The Independent Vietnamese* (Athens, Ohio, 1980); NSSM, 4988.

10. *NYT,* Nov. 1, 1970. See also Kissinger, *White House Years,* 261; *DSB,* Oct. 26, 1970, 465–70.

11. *NYT,* Nov. 1, 1970.

12. Truong-Chinh, *Selected Writings* (Hanoi, 1977), 723. See also Goodman, *Lost Peace,* 99; Nguoi Theo Doi Thoi, *Tien Phong,* Aug. 22, 26, 29, 1971, JPRS 55,165, 26–36, is a good example.

13. Military Institute, *Vietnam: The Anti-U.S. Resistance War for National Salvation* (Hanoi, 1980), JPRS 80,968, 142–43; Le Duan, *Thu Vao Nam* (Hanoi, 1985), 296–98.

14. Kissinger, *White House Years,* 1100. See also David W. P. Elliott, "NLF-DRV Strategy and the 1972 Spring Offensive" (Cornell Univ. East Asia Program, Jan. 1974), 18; *Thoi Su Pho Thong,* Jan. 1972, JPRS 55,546, 1–4; Hoanh Son, *Hoc Tap,* Nov. 1971, JPRS 54,731, 96–101; Ngo Quang Truong, *The Easter Offensive of 1972,* IM, 9ff.

15. David E. Ott, *Field Artillery, 1954–1973* (U.S. Dept. of the Army, 1975), 220. See also March 1972 Saigon Party resolution, VN, no. 108, Nov. 1972, 13.

16. Cao Van Vien, *The Final Collapse* (U.S. Army Center for Military History, 1983), 6. See also Kissinger, *White House Years,* 1104; Ngo Quang Truong, *Easter Offensive,* 10, 22–23; William W. Momyer, *Airpower in Three Wars* (U.S. Office of Air Force History, 1978), 326–32; *NYT,* July 2, 1972.

17. Ott, *Field Artillery,* 222.

18. Nixon, *Memoirs,* 594. See also Ngo Quang Truong, *Easter Offensive,* 22–23,

33–46; Cao Van Vien and Dong Van Khuyen, *Reflections on the Vietnam War,* IM, 107–8; *NYT,* June 24, 1972, Jan. 26, 1973.

19. *DSB,* May 22, 1972, 724–25. See also Kissinger, *White House Years,* 1113–18, 1180–81; U.S. Senate, Comm. on Foreign Relations, *Report: Vietnam: May 1972,* 92:2, June 29, 1972, 4ff.; Tran Van Tra, *Concluding the 30-Years War* (Ho Chi Minh City, 1982), JPRS 82,783, 66; Ngo Quang Truong, *Easter Offensive,* 158–60; Momyer, *Airpower,* 329; Cao Van Vien, *Final Collapse,* 6, 128; *NYT,* May 6, 1972; DOD, 1973, pt. 5, 16, 589, 867–70.

20. *NYT,* June 27, 29, July 2, 1972; *Wall Street Journal,* May 15, 1972; Ott, *Field Artillery,* 225–30; Senate Comm. on Foreign Relations, *Vietnam,* 31; Kissinger, *White House Years,* 1307.

21. Senate Comm. on Foreign Relations, *Vietnam,* 8. See also ibid., 14; SA, 800–805, 821, 907; *Quan Doi Nhan Dan,* May 18, 1972, JPRS 56,309, 16–18; Stuart A. Herrington, *Silence Was a Weapon* (Novato, 1982), 90, 114, 120–29; Dong Van Khuyen, *The RVNAF,* IM, 141; Elliott, "1972 Spring Offensive," 52.

22. Kissinger, *White House Years,* 1123, 1304. See also Senate Comm. on Foreign Relations, *Vietnam,* 17–23; Military Institute, *Anti-U.S. Resistance,* 146.

23. Kissinger, *White House Years,* 1123, 1161, 1201. See also Arkady N. Shevchenko, *Breaking with Moscow* (New York, 1985), 212–13; Nixon, *No More Vietnams,* 141, 147.

24. *DSB,* Sept. 11, 1972, 278.

25. Kissinger, *White House Years,* 1253.

Chapter 34: The Diplomatic Process: Illusions and Realities

1. GP, 409. See also Henry Kissinger, *White House Years* (Boston, 1979), 1195–96, 1304, 1317; P. J. Honey, "The History of the Vietnam Cease-fire," *China News Analysis,* March 21, 1975, 4; Richard Nixon, *No More Vietnams* (New York, 1985), 106.

2. Walter S. Dillard, *Sixty Days to Peace* (U.S. National Defense Univ., 1982), 62–63. See also Cao Van Vien, *The Final Collapse* (U.S. Army Center of Military History, 1983), 19; Kissinger, *White House Years,* 1363; *Wash. Post,* Sept. 14, Oct. 17, Nov. 15, Dec. 14, 19, 1972; *NYT,* Sept. 1, Nov. 25, Dec. 22, 1972; Nixon to Thieu, Dec. 31, 1971, EC.

3. Kissinger, *White House Years,* 1323. See also ibid., 1310–14; U.S. Senate, Comm. on Armed Services, *Hearings: Fiscal Year 1974 Authorization . . . ,* 93:1, March 1973, pt. 1, 430–34; Yves Lacoste, *Hérodote,* Jan.–March 1976, 86–117; *NYT,* Sept. 1, 1972.

4. Nixon to Thieu, Aug. 31, 1972, EC.

5. Kissinger, *White House Years,* 1315.

6. Ibid., 1334. See also ibid., 1329; GP, 409; Seymour M. Hersh, *The Price of Power* (New York, 1983), 574.

7. Richard Nixon, *RN: The Memoirs of Richard Nixon* (New York, 1978), 692. See also Kissinger, *White House Years,* 1339–40.

8. Kissinger, *White House Years,* 1348.

9. Nixon to Thieu, Oct. 16, 1972, EC. See also Kissinger, *White House Years,* 1368.

10. Dillard, *Sixty Days to Peace,* 60. See also Kissinger, *White House Years,* 1361–62, 1377, 1381, 1395; GP, 410–11; DOD, *Briefings on Bombings of North Vietnam,* 93:1, Jan.

9, 1973, 32; William E. LeGro, *Vietnam from Cease-Fire to Capitulation* (U.S. Army Center of Military History, 1981), 17.

11. Nixon to Thieu, Oct. 29, Nov. 8, 1972, EC.

12. Ibid., Oct. 29, Nov. 14, 1972, EC. See also ibid., Nov. 18, 23, 1972, Jan. 5, 17, 20, 1973, EC; *NYT,* Jan. 28, 1973.

13. Nixon to Thieu, Nov. 23, 1972, EC. See also ibid., Jan. 5, 1973.

14. Nixon to Thieu, Jan. 17, 1973, EC; Kissinger, *White House Years,* 1416, 1421; Nixon, *Memoirs,* 724, 749–50; *Wash. Post,* Dec. 22, 1972; *NYT,* Dec. 22, 1972; Nixon, *No More Vietnams,* 167ff.

15. Kissinger, *White House Years,* 1429. See also Gareth Porter, *A Peace Denied* (Bloomington, 1972), 144ff.; *Wash. Post,* Dec. 11, 1972.

16. *NYT,* Dec. 17, 1972. See also Kissinger, *White House Years,* 1434–35; *Congressional Quarterly Weekly Report,* Jan. 6, 1973, 3; Nixon, *Memoirs,* 724ff.; *Wall Street Journal,* Dec. 29, 1972.

17. Kissinger, *White House Years,* 1348.

18. *NYT,* Dec. 26, 1972. See also *Wash. Post,* Dec. 14, 30, 1972; *NYT,* Sept. 1, Dec. 18, 1972; *Aviation Week,* July 3, 1972, 12–15; William W. Momyer, *Airpower in Three Wars* (U.S. Office of Air Force History, 1978), 240–41; Hersh, *Price of Power,* 628–29; Military Institute, *Vietnam: The Anti-U.S. Resistance War for National Salvation* (Hanoi, 1980), JPRS 80,968, 150–51; William S. Turley, *Pacific Affairs,* 48 (1975), 385.

19. *NYT,* Dec. 22, 1972. See also *Wash. Post,* Dec. 28, 1972; *NYT,* Jan. 12, 1973; *Quan Doi Nhan Dan,* Dec. 31, 1972, JPRS 58,231, 3–4; Kissinger, *White House Years,* 1453.

20. Kissinger, *White House Years,* 1454. See also *Wash. Post,* Dec. 21, 1972; *NYT,* Dec. 23, 1972, Jan. 4, 1973; *Congressional Quarterly Weekly Report,* Jan. 6, 1973, 3.

21. *NYT,* Dec. 22, 1972.

22. Nixon, *Memoirs,* 724–25. See also ibid., 734–35; *NYT,* Dec. 29, 30, 1972; Allan E. Goodman, *The Lost Peace* (Stanford, 1978), 157.

23. *DSB,* Feb. 12, 1973, 153–54. See also ibid., 160; Kissinger, *White House Years,* 1462.

24. Kissinger, *White House Years,* 1467.

25. *DSB,* 170, 175. See also *NYT,* Jan. 28, 1973.

26. Tran Van Tra, *Concluding the 30-Years War* (Ho Chi Minh City, 1982), JPRS 82,783, 6, 33. See also ibid., 34; Le Duan, *Thu Vao Nam* (Hanoi, 1985), 359; LeGro, *Vietnam,* 28; SA, 788.

27. *Wall Street Journal,* Oct. 4, 1972. See also Pham Van Dong, *Ecrits* (Hanoi, 1977), 315; Nguyen Duy Hinh, *Vietnamization and the Cease-Fire,* IM, 126–28; *Wash. Post,* Nov. 22, 1972; Tran Van Tra, *30-Years War,* 33; *NYT,* Dec. 31, 1972.

28. *Wash. Post,* Jan. 18, 1973. See also ibid., Oct. 26, 1972, Jan. 23, 1973; *NYT,* Oct. 29, 1972.

29. GP, 426–27. See also Viet Hai, *Hoc Tap,* June 1971, JPRS 53,898, 58–70, compared to the novel by Nguyen Trung Thanh, *Dat Quang* (Hanoi, 1974), 32, 47–49, 96–99, which reveals the range of views on the RVN.

30. Nixon, *Memoirs,* 692. See also Nixon, *No More Vietnams,* 169; LeGro, *Vietnam,* 31–32; COSVN directive 03, late March 1973, VN, no. 115, Sept. 1973, 1–2; Tran Van Tra, *30-Years War,* 33; David W. P. Elliott, "NLF-DRV Strategy and the 1972 Spring Offensive" (Cornell Univ. East Asia Program, Jan. 1974), 58.

31. Deputy Secretary of Defense W. P. Clements, Jr., March 5, 1973, address, Defense Dept. release, 7. See also *Vietnam Courier*, June 1977, 2-3; *DSB*, March 19, 1973, 317-18; *NYT*, Feb. 1, 11, 15, March 6, 12, 1973; Henry Kissinger, *Years of Upheaval* (Boston, 1982), 23ff.

32. *NYT*, Oct. 21, 1972; *DSB*, April 2, 1973, 375; April 9, 1973, 429; *Wash. Post*, Jan. 26, 1973; Tran Van Tra, *30-Years War*, 11-12; Dillard, *Sixty Days to Peace*, 26, 36; DOD, 1974, April 1973, pt.1, 171; DOD, 1973, *Second Supplemental*, April 1973, 662-64; *NYT*, Oct. 25, Nov. 27, 1972, Jan. 26, 1973; Dong Van Khuyen, *The RVNAF*, IM, 281; *Wash. Post*, Oct. 28, 1973, Feb. 4, 1973; Comptroller General of the U.S., "Logistic Aspects of Vietnamization—1969-72," Jan. 31, 1973.

33. LeGro, *Vietnam*, 18-19. See also *NYT*, Nov. 27, 1972, March 30, 1973.

34. *NYT*, Jan. 9, 1973.

35. Nixon to Thieu, Jan. 17, 1973, EC. See also ibid., Jan. 5, 1973, EC.

36. *DSB*, Feb. 12, 1973, 169. See also ibid., 153-54; Nixon to Thieu, Jan. 20, 22, 1973, EC; *NYT*, Jan. 31, 1973.

37. Nixon, *Memoirs*, 724; Kissinger, *Years of Upheaval*, 43. See also Nixon, *No More Vietnams*, 165-69.

38. DOD, 1974, Sept. 1973, pt. 6, 1694. See also ibid., 1642-47; *NYT*, April 4, 1973.

39. Cao Van Vien, *The Final Collapse* (U.S. Army Center of Military History, 1983), 45-46; Stephen T. Hosmer et al., *The Fall of South Vietnam* (New York, 1980), 40-41, 81, 109; *NYT*, March 31, 1973.

40. *DSB*, April 2, 1973, 388. See also ibid., 388, 395, for Kissinger's public assumption regarding Sino-Soviet cooperation with the U.S.; Sullivan's views are in *DSB*, Feb. 19, 1973, 202, and esp. in an extemporaneous address found in *Rotary Balita* (Manila), Sept. 29, 1973, EC; Roger's confirmation is found in his Feb. 8, 1973, testimony to the House Foreign Affairs Comm., the Pentagon's in *NYT*, Jan. 20, 1973; *Wash. Post*, March 2, 1973; and DOD, 1974, May 1973, pt. 2, 319; see also *NYT*, Jan. 30, 1973.

41. *DSB*, April 2, 1973, 393.

Chapter 35: The Balance of Forces in South Vietnam, Early 1973

1. *Cong. Record*, Aug. 20, 1974, S 15496.

2. U.S. Senate, Comm. on Armed Services, *Hearings: Fiscal Year 1975 Authorization . . .* , 93:2, March 1974, pt. 4, 1891. See also Stephen T. Hosmer et al., *The Fall of South Vietnam* (New York, 1980), 72-73.

3. Henry Kissinger, *Years of Upheaval* (Boston, 1982), 32. See also Hosmer, *Fall of South Vietnam*, 72-73, 108-9; Allan E. Goodman, *Orbis*, Fall 1974, 812; U.S. Senate, Comm. on Foreign Relations, *Report: Vietnam: May 1974*, 93:2, Aug. 5, 1974, 14-15; *NYT*, Feb. 17, Nov. 8, 1973.

4. *Wash. Post*, Jan. 5, 1974. See also ibid., Sept. 30, 1973; *NYT*, Oct. 3, Nov. 25, 1973; Senate Comm. on Foreign Relations, *Vietnam*, 4; Arnold R. Isaacs, *Without Honor: Defeat in Vietnam and Cambodia* (Baltimore, 1983), 144.

5. U.S. House, Select Comm. on Intelligence, *Hearings: U.S. Intelligence Agencies and Activities*, 94:1, Nov.-Dec. 1975, 1658. See also Frank Snepp, *Decent Interval* (New York, 1977), 19; Hosmer, *Fall of South Vietnam*, 99.

6. Testimony of Edward L. Block to U.S. House Comm. on Foreign Affairs hearing, July 2, 1974, 2. See also Charles J. Timmes, "Military Operations after the Cease-Fire Agreement," *Military Review*, Aug. 1976, 69; Hosmer, *Fall of South Vietnam*, 98; Allan E. Goodman, *Asian Survey*, Jan. 1975, 816–19; U.S. Senate, Comm. on Armed Services, *Hearings: Military Procurement Supplemental . . . 1974*, 93:2, March 1974, 106; DOD, *Oversight of Fiscal Year 1975 Military Assistance to Vietnam*, 94:1, Jan. 1975, 77–79; *Wash. Post*, Jan. 23, 25, Sept. 30, 1973, Feb. 2, 1975; U.S. Senate, Comm. on Foreign Relations, *Report: Thailand, Laos, Cambodia, and Vietnam: April 1973*, 93:1, June 11, 1973, 33; U.S. Senate, Comm. on the Judiciary, *Report: Relief and Rehabilitation of War Victims . . .*, 93:2, Jan. 27, 1974, 6; *Cong. Record*, May 6, 1974, S7129; *NYT*, Aug. 1, 1973.

7. Senate Comm. on the Judiciary, *Relief and Rehabilitation*, 16.

8. *Wash. Post*, Nov. 23, 1973. See also ibid., Jan. 12, 1974; *NYT*, July 5, 1973; Block testimony, 7; Senate Comm. on Foreign Relations, *Vietnam: May 1974*, 1.

9. William E. LeGro, *Vietnam from Cease-Fire to Capitulation* (U.S. Army Center of Military History, 1981), 66–72; Goodman, *Orbis*, 816, 821; Jerry M. Silverman, "South Vietnam and the Return to Political Struggle," *Asian Survey*, Jan. 1974, 72–76; Senate Comm. on Foreign Relations, *Vietnam: May 1974*, 3; Stuart A. Herrington, *Peace with Honor?* (Novato, 1983), 22–23, 46–47, 110; Tran Dinh Tho, *Pacification*, IM, 175; Isaacs, *Without Honor*, 118–19; Tran Van Tra, *Concluding the 30-Years War* (Ho Chi Minh City, 1982), JPRS 82,783, 62, 72; *NYT*, July 31, Aug. 1, Sept. 8, 1973, Jan. 9, Aug. 11, 1974; *Wash. Post*, Nov. 23, Dec. 28, 1973, Sept. 3, 1974; *Wall Street Journal*, Feb. 28, 1973.

10. Senate Comm. on Foreign Relations, *Vietnam: May 1974*, 8. See also ibid., 21–22; Hoang Ngoc Lung, *Strategy and Tactics*, IM, 133–34; Hosmer, *Fall of South Vietnam*, 80, 103; Dong Van Khuyen, *RVNAF Logistics*, IM, 240, 335; Senate Comm. on Foreign Relations, *Vietnam: April 1973*, 33–34, 44–45; *Time*, Sept. 9, 1974, 29; DOD, 1974, May 30, 1973, pt. 2, 759.

11. Senate Comm. on the Judiciary, *Relief and Rehabilitation*, 187. See also Dong Van Khuyen, *The RVNAF*, 140–42, 346, 379; Nguyen Duy Hinh and Tran Dinh Tho, *The South Vietnamese Society*, IM, 114–15, 120; Herrington, *Peace with Honor*, 104–5; Isaacs, *Without Honor*, 300–301, 329; Cao Van Vien, *The Final Collapse* (U.S. Army Center of Military History, 1983), 44; Senate Comm. on Armed Services, *1975 Authorization*, pt. 4, 1910; Senate Comm. on Foreign Relations, *Vietnam: May 1974*, 8.

12. LeGro, *Vietnam*, 71–72; Snepp, *Decent Interval*, 118–19; *Time*, Sept. 9, 1974, 29; Senate Comm. on Foreign Relations, *Vietnam: May 1974*, 8.

Chapter 36: The Nixon Administration's Dilemmas of Power

1. Henry Kissinger, *Years of Upheaval* (Boston, 1982), 329. See also ibid., 152–53; *NYT*, July 15, 1973; U.S. Senate, Comm. on Appropriations, *Hearings: Department of Defense Appropriations, 1974*, 93:1, March 1973, pt. 1, 411–12; *International Herald Tribune*, Aug. 18–19, 1973.

2. Dec. 27, 1973, press conference, State Dept. release, 4.

3. Ibid., 7. See also Kissinger, *Years of Upheaval*, 169–70; *NYT*, May 2, Oct. 27, 1973; H. R. Haldeman, *The Ends of Power* (New York, 1977), 181; Thomas M. Franck and Edward Weisband, *Foreign Policy by Congress* (New York, 1979), 14ff.; *NYT*, May 2,

1973; DOD, 1974, July–Aug. 1973, pt. 4, 1184–86; pt. 5, 1691–1700; *International Herald Tribune,* June 5, 1973; *Congressional Quarterly Weekly Report,* April 21, 1973, 923–24.

4. *NYT,* Dec. 26, 1973. See also Kissinger, *Years of Upheaval,* 338–39, 359, 367; Richard Nixon, *RN: The Memoirs of Richard Nixon* (New York, 1978), 888.

5. Kissinger, *Years of Upheaval,* 328; *NYT,* Aug. 18, Dec. 14, 1973; *Wash. Post,* Jan. 17, 1974.

6. Kissinger, Dec. 27, 1973, press conference, 10. See also *Wash. Post,* Oct. 1, 1973; *NYT,* Oct. 10, 17, 1973; *Wall Street Journal,* Oct. 11, 1973.

7. *Wash. Post,* Feb. 9, 1974. See also ibid., Sept. 11, 1973; Harry Harding, *Problems of Communism,* March–April 1983, 7; Kissinger, *Years of Upheaval,* 46–47, 60–67, 678–79; Kenneth G. Lieberthal, "Sino-Soviet Conflict in the 1970s," R-2342, July 1978, RC, 77–79.

8. U.S. House, Comm. on Appropriations, *Hearings: Foreign Assistance . . . 1975,* 93:2, June 4, 1974, 103; *NYT,* Jan. 27, 1974; *DSB,* March 17, 1975, 329; Hoang Tung, *Hoc Tap,* March 1973, JPRS 59,055, 51; Daniel S. Papp, *Vietnam: The View from Moscow, Peking, Washington* (Jefferson, N.C., 1981), 192–93; *NYT,* July 29, 1973, Jan. 14, 1974; U.S. House, Comm. on International Relations, *Hearings: The Vietnam-Cambodian Emergency, 1975,* 94:1, March–May 1975, 511.

Chapter 37: Recovery and Response: The Communist Party's Strategy until Mid-1974

1. Tran Van Tra, *Concluding the 30-Years War* (Ho Chi Minh City, 1982), JPRS 82,783, 57. See also ibid., 38–65; William E. LeGro, *Vietnam from Cease-Fire to Capitulation* (U.S. Army Center of Military History, 1981), 30–31, 52; U.S. Senate, Comm. on Foreign Relations, *Report: Thailand, Laos, Cambodia and Vietnam: April 1973,* 93:1, June 11, 1973, 33, 36; Frank Snepp, *Decent Interval* (New York, 1977), 56.

2. Senate Comm. on Foreign Relations, *Vietnam: April 1973,* 46. See also Tran Van Tra, *30-Years War,* 45.

3. Military Institute, *Vietnam: The Anti-U.S. Resistance War for National Salvation* (Hanoi, 1980), JPRS 80,968, 162. See also Tran Van Tra, *30-Years War,* 70–74; *NYT,* Jan. 14, 1974; U.S. Senate, Comm. on Foreign Relations, *Report: Vietnam: May 1974,* 93:2, Aug. 5, 1974, 4.

4. Vu Duc, *Tap Chi Quan Doi Nhan Dan,* June 1973, JPRS 60,344, 5.

5. *Tap Chi Quan Doi Nhan Dan,* March 1975, JPRS 65,150, 2. See also Trung Dung, *Tap Chi Quan Doi Nhan Dan,* Sept. 1973, JPRS 60,710, 3–10; *Quan Doi Nhan Dan,* Nov. 21, 1973, JPRS 60,920, 17–19; and esp. Pham Hong Son, *Tap Chi Quan Doi Nhan Dan,* Oct. 1974, JPRS 63,785, 8–17.

6. Tran Sam, *Tap Chi Quan Doi Nhan Dan,* Oct. 1974, JPRS 63,785, 7.

7. Editorial, *Hoc Tap,* June 1973, JPRS 59,513, 6. See also Le Duan, *Some Present Tasks* (Hanoi, 1974), 8.

8. Commission for the Study of the History of the Party, *50 Years of Activities of the Communist Party of Vietnam* (Hanoi, 1980), 220–21; Pham Van Dong, *Ecrits* (Hanoi, 1977), 358; *Wash. Post,* Feb. 18, 1974.

9. Tran Van Tra, *30-Years War,* 87. See also LeGro, *Vietnam,* 65–71; DOD, *Over-*

sight of Fiscal Year 1975 Military Assistance to Vietnam, 94:1, Jan. 1975, 68; *Wash. Post,* Dec. 18, 1973; *NYT,* Jan. 9, 1974.

10. Hoang Nam, *Hoc Tap,* March 1974, JPRS 61,922, 82–83.

Chapter 38: The Deepening Crisis of the RVN Social System

1. *Years of Upheaval* (Boston, 1982), 85, 313.

2. Arnold R. Isaacs, *Without Honor* (Baltimore, 1983), 106–7. See also Nguyen Duy Hinh and Tran Dinh Tho, *The South Vietnamese Society,* IM, 146; *NYT,* July 28, 1974; *Le Monde,* May 17, 19, 1973.

3. Frank Snepp, *Decent Interval* (New York, 1977), 62; Walter S. Dillard, *Sixty Days to Peace* (U.S. National Defense Univ., 1983), 42, 73; Isaacs, *Without Honor,* 106–7; Communauté Vietnamienne, *Les Prisonniers politiques* (Paris, 1974), 83–84; *NYT,* Feb. 6, 1973, Aug. 19, 20, 1974; *Wash. Post,* Nov. 10, 1972, Jan. 8, 26, 1973.

4. Nguyen Duy Hinh and Tran Dinh Tho, *South Vietnamese Society,* 147; Isaacs, *Without Honor,* 105; U.S. Senate, Comm. on Foreign Relations, *Report: Vietnam: May 1974,* 93:2, Aug. 5, 1974, 10–12; AID, 310, 672; Jerry M. Silverman, *Asian Survey,* Jan. 1974, 69–75; Allan E. Goodman, *Asian Survey,* Jan. 1975, 80–81; *Wash. Post,* July 15, 1974; *International Herald Tribune,* July 22, 1974.

5. Cao Van Vien, *Leadership,* IM, 118–19; Dong Van Khuyen, *The RVNAF,* IM, 388; Nguyen Cao Ky, *Twenty Years and Twenty Days* (New York, 1976), 110 11; Stephen T. Hosmer et al., *The Fall of South Vietnam* (New York, 1980), 100–114; Senate Comm. on Foreign Relations, *Vietnam: May 1974,* 10–11; *NYT,* Jan. 10, July 28, 1974.

6. *Thoi-Bao Ga,* May–June 1974, 9. See also *NYT,* Sept. 14, 1973; *American Chamber of Commerce in Vietnam Bulletin,* Feb. 10, 1975, 11 (hereafter *Chamber Bulletin*).

7. Hosmer, *Fall of South Vietnam,* 55. See also ibid., 53–54; Nguyen Duy Hinh and Tran Dinh Tho, *South Vietnamese Society,* 148; *NYT,* Oct. 19, 1974.

8. Senate Comm. on Foreign Relations, *Vietnam: May 1974,* 13.

9. AID, 59–60, 104, 120, 187–99, 219, 240, 475; AID, *Vietnam Economic Data,* Oct.–Dec. 1974, 14, 17; Senate Comm. on Foreign Relations, *Vietnam: May 1974,* 28; World Bank, "Current Economic Position and Prospects of the Republic of Viet Nam," Jan. 18, 1974, 2–11; DOD, *Oversight of Fiscal Year 1975 . . . ,* 94:1, Jan. 1975, 88.

10. *Chamber Bulletin,* May 10, 1974, 3. See also AID, 207–9; AID, "Republic of Vietnam Economy," Nov. 1974, 48; *NYT,* Dec. 19, 1973; *Wash. Post,* March 6, June 3, 1974; Isaacs, *Without Honor,* 302–3; *Thoi-Bao Ga,* Sept.–Oct. 1974, 13.

11. AID, 197–202, 454; AID, "Republic of Vietnam Economy," 54, 58; Asian Development Bank, *Rural Asia* (New York, 1977), 77; Clifton G. Barton, *A.I.D. Spring Review of Small Farmer Credit,* 11 (Feb. 1973), 33; *NYT,* Jan. 14, 1974, Feb. 10, 1975.

12. AID, 235–36. See also ibid., 201, 471; AID, "Republic of Vietnam Economy," 6; *Vietnam Economic Data,* 16; Senate Comm. on Foreign Relations, *Vietnam: May 1974,* 37.

13. AID, 451; Nguyen Cao Ky, *Twenty Years,* 111; *International Herald Tribune,* July 1, 1974; *Thoi-Bao Ga,* May–June, 11–13; Sept.–Oct. 1974, 18–19; World Bank, "Current Economic Position," 68.

14. DOD, 1975, pt. 1, 503.

15. AID, 62. See also Arthur Smithies, "The Transition to Economic Development in Vietnam," Institute for Defense Analyses, Aug. 1974, F-22.

16. AID, 228–29. See also Smithies, "Development Strategy in Vietnam," Aug. 21, 1973, 2, Smithies Papers; Smithies in W. S. Thompson and D. D. Frizzell, eds., *The Lessons of Vietnam* (New York, 1977), 206–7; Smithies, "Transition," F-17–18; *Thoi-Bao Ga,* May–June 1974, 11–13; Senate Comm. on Foreign Relations, *Vietnam: May 1974,* 41.

17. World Bank, "Current Economic Position," 6.

18. Goodman, *Asian Survey,* 79. See also AID, 238; Senate Comm. on Foreign Relations, *Vietnam: May 1974,* 43; Gabriel Kolko, "The United States Effort to Mobilize World Bank Aid to Saigon," *Journal of Contemporary Asia,* 5 (1975), 42–52; Cao Van Vien, *The Final Collapse* (U.S. Army Center of Military History, 1983), 44, 47; U.S. Senate, Comm. on Foreign Relations, *Hearings: Foreign Assistance Authorization,* 93:2, June–July 1974, 108.

19. Hosmer, *Fall of South Vietnam,* 65. See also ibid., 51.

Chapter 39: Saigon and Washington, Mid-1974: The Conjunction of Two Crises

1. Kissinger Dec. 27, 1973, press conference, State Dept. release, 7. See also Kissinger, Jan. 10, 1977, State Dept. release, 3; *Business Week,* Nov. 10, 1973, 47; *NYT,* Aug. 15, 1973; *Wall Street Journal,* Nov. 14, 1973.

2. Kissinger PBS interview, Jan. 16, 1975, State Dept. release, 1; Kissinger Jan. 10, 1977, speech, 3.

3. *NYT,* Feb. 22, 1975.

4. Kissinger, *Years of Upheaval* (Boston, 1982), 125.

5. Nixon, *RN: The Memoirs of Richard Nixon* (New York, 1978), 969.

6. *President's Economic Report, 1977,* 246, 270; Kissinger, *Years of Upheaval,* 1000, 1011–12; *International Herald Tribune,* Oct. 2, 1974.

7. William E. LeGro, *Vietnam from Cease-Fire to Capitulation* (U.S. Army Center of Military History, 1981), 81. See also U.S. Senate, Comm. on Foreign Relations, *Hearings: Department of State Appropriations Authorization . . . 1974,* 93:1, April 1973, 357; U.S. Senate, Comm. on Armed Services, *Hearings: Fiscal Year 1974 Authorization . . . ,* 93:1, June–Aug. 1973, 5883, 5925–36; *NYT,* Jan. 20, 1974.

8. Comptroller General of the U.S., "Stronger Controls Needed over Major Types of U.S. Equipment Provided to the Republic of Vietnam Armed Forces," Dec. 18, 1974, 37. See also U.S. Senate, Comm. on Foreign Relations, *Report: Vietnam: May 1974,* 93:2, Aug. 5, 1974, 21ff.; *NYT,* Jan. 6, 1974; Arnold R. Isaacs, *Without Honor* (Baltimore, 1983), 313ff., 524.

9. Senate Comm. on Foreign Relations, *Vietnam,* 24; Isaacs, *Without Honor,* 314; Dong Van Khuyen, *The RVNAF,* IM, 373; LeGro, *Vietnam,* 80–86; Comptroller General, "Stronger Controls Needed," 50; U.S. Senate, Comm. on Armed Services, *Hearings: Fiscal Year 1975 Authorization . . . ,* 93:2, March 1974, pt. 4, 1897, 1901; U.S. Senate, Comm. on Appropriations, *Hearings: Department of Defense . . . 1975,* 93:2, March 1974, pt. 1, 88; Senate, Comm. on Appropriations, *Hearings: Department of Defense Appropria-*

tions, 1974, 93:1, March 1973, pt. 1, 211; *Business Week,* Nov. 9, 1974, 89; *NYT,* Jan. 6, May 18, July 7, 1974; *Wall Street Journal,* July 17, 1973, Aug. 14, 1974, Jan. 27, 1975.

10. *Congressional Quarterly Weekly Report,* Aug. 31, 1974, 2389. See also BDM III, 3-46; LeGro, *Vietnam,* 87; *Cong. Record,* Aug. 20, 1974, S 15497; transcript, Graham Martin interview, BBC, Nov. 27, 1977; Isaacs, *Without Honor,* 318-19; Dong Van Khuyen, *RVNAF,* 282-85; Frank Snepp, *Decent Interval* (New York, 1977), 108-9; U.S. House, Comm. on International Relations, *Hearings: The Vietnam-Cambodia Emergency, 1975,* 94:2, Jan. 27, 1976, 538.

11. *Congressional Quarterly Weekly Report,* Aug. 31, 1974, 2389; Sept. 14, 1974, 2507; *Wash. Post,* Aug. 23, 1974; House Comm. on International Relations, *Hearings: Vietnam . . . Emergency,* 538; Martin BBC interview; *Wall Street Journal,* Sept. 13, 1974; DOD, *Oversight of Fiscal Year 1975 Military Assistance to Vietnam,* 94:1, Jan. 1975, 5-7; DOD, 1975, June 1974, pt. 9, 10-11; Senate, Comm. on Armed Services, *Report: Authorizing Appropriations . . . 1975,* 93:2, May 29, 1974, 160-61; LeGro, *Vietnam,* 87.

12. *Wash. Post,* Aug. 23, 1974. See also *NYT,* Aug. 9, 1974; LeGro, *Vietnam,* 87; Isaacs, *Without Honor,* 315; Stuart A. Herrington, *Peace with Honor?* (Novato, 1983), 120-21.

13. Dong Van Khuyen, *RVNAF,* 286.

14. *American Chamber of Commerce in Vietnam Bulletin,* Oct. 25, 1974, 8. See also AID, 226-33.

15. AID, 186. See also ibid., 189; U.S. House, Comm. on Appropriations, *Hearings: Second Supplemental Appropriation Bill, 1974,* 93:2, March 1974, 834, 842, 886.

16. AID, "Republic of Vietnam Economy," Nov. 1974, 3.

17. AID, 232.

18. AID, "Republic of Vietnam Economy," 19; *NYT,* June 22, 1974; U.S. House, Comm. on Foreign Affairs, *Staff Report: United States Aid to Indochina,* 93:2, July 1974, 5; *NYT,* Sept. 30, 1974; U.S. Senate, Comm. on Appropriations, *Hearings: Foreign Assistance . . . 1975,* 93:2, June 1974, 1315; House Conference Report, *Foreign Assistance Act of 1974, S. 3394,* Dec. 17, 1974, 13-18, 35-45; *Wash. Post,* Dec. 28, 1974.

19. *NYT,* Oct. 3, 1974. See also *Thoa-Bao Ga,* April 1973, 1-8; Sept.–Oct. 1974, 8ff.; *NYT,* Oct. 2, 30, 1974; *Wash. Post,* Sept. 18, 1974, *Christian Science Monitor,* Sept. 10, 1974; Robert Shaplen, *New Yorker,* Jan. 6, 1975, 64ff.; Nguyen Cao Ky, *Twenty Years and Twenty Days* (New York, 1976), 205.

20. *DSB,* Nov. 11, 1974, 641. See also *NYT,* Oct. 26, 1974, Feb. 13, 1975; Dong Van Khuyen, *RVNAF,* 149-50; *Wash. Post,* Oct. 25, 1974; Senate Comm. on Foreign Relations, *Foreign Assistance Authorization,* 415; *International Herald Tribune,* June 12-13, 1976; *Cong. Record,* Oct. 1, 1974, 17961-62.

21. Shaplen, *New Yorker; Wash. Post,* Oct. 22, 25, Nov. 2, 1974; *Newsweek,* Nov. 4, 1974, 25.

Chapter 40: The Revolution's Perceptions and Plans, Late 1974

1. Captured documents in Allan E. Goodman, *The Lost Peace* (Stanford, 1978), 238-45, 251; Tran Minh, *Hoc Tap,* Feb. 1975, JPRS 64,572, 65-68; *Wash. Post,* Dec. 24,

1974; Tran Van Tra, *Concluding the 30-Years War* (Ho Chi Minh City, 1982), JPRS 82,783, 87.

2. Military Institute, *Vietnam: The Anti-U.S. Resistance War for National Salvation* (Hanoi, 1980), JPRS 80,698, 162–65; Tran Van Tra, *30-Years War,* 82; Le Duan, *Thu Vao Nam* (Hanoi, 1985), 361.

3. Pham Hong Son, *Tap Chi Quan Doi Nhan Dan,* Oct. 1974, JPRS 63,785, 8–17; William E. LeGro, *Vietnam from Cease-Fire to Capitulation* (U.S. Army Center of Military History, 1981), 146; Tran Van Tra, *30-Years War,* 83, 106; Military Institute, *Anti-U.S. Resistance,* 165–66; Le Duan, *Thu Vao Nam,* 355–69; Van Tien Dung, *Our Great Spring Victory: An Account of the Liberation of South Vietnam* (New York, 1977), 24–27.

4. Tran Van Tra, *30-Years War,* 93, 105–9, 123, 126, 132–33; Military Institute, *Anti-U.S. Resistance,* 170–71; Cao Van Vien, *The Final Collapse* (U.S. Army Center of Military History, 1983), 56–58, 67; LeGro, *Vietnam,* 136–37; Stephen T. Hosmer et al., *The Fall of South Vietnam* (New York, 1980), 160–63; Goodman, *Lost Peace,* 267; Frank Snepp, *Decent Interval* (New York, 1977), 132–35; *Wash. Post,* Dec. 24, 1974; Van Tien Dung, *Spring Victory,* 26–27.

Chapter 41: The End of the War

1. *NYT,* Feb. 13, 1975. See also Frank Snepp, *Decent Interval* (New York, 1977), 144; *NYT,* Oct. 6, 1974, Jan. 24, 1975; *Far Eastern Economic Review,* March 7, 1975, 13; *Baltimore Sun,* March 2, 1975.

2. P. Edward Haley, *Congress and the Fall of Vietnam and Cambodia* (Rutherford, N.J., 1982), 52–53; Snepp, *Decent Interval,* 146–49, 235; U.S. House, Comm. on International Relations, *Hearings: The Vietnam-Cambodia Emergency, 1975,* 94:2, Jan. 27, 1976, 561; Comptroller General of the U.S., "Stronger Controls Needed . . . ," Dec. 18, 1974; DOD, *Oversight of Fiscal Year 1975 Military Assistance to Vietnam,* 94:1, Jan. 1975, 11–17, 79, 97; DOD, 1976, Feb. 1975, pt. 1, 108; William E. LeGro, *Vietnam from Cease-Fire to Capitulation* (U.S. Army Center of Military History, 1981), 139; *NYT,* Jan. 11, 12, Feb. 22, 27, March 19, 1975; *Wash. Post,* Feb. 8, 1975; *Philadelphia Sunday Bulletin,* March 23, 1975.

3. Dong Van Khuyen, *RVNAF Logistics,* IM, 359. See also DOD, *Oversight,* 10–11, 77–78, 97; Nguyen Duy Hinh, *Vietnamization and the Cease-Fire,* IM, 171–73, 178, for somewhat different but less precise figures; Dong Van Khuyen, *The RVNAF,* IM, 288.

4. Stephen T. Hosmer et al., *The Fall of South Vietnam* (New York, 1980), 121. See also ibid., 111–12; House Comm. on International Relations, *Vietnam . . . Emergency, 1975,* 538–39, 604; Snepp, *Decent Interval,* 109–10, 155–57, 185–86; Cao Van Vien, *The Final Collapse* (U.S. Army Center of Military History, 1983), 56, 77; Gareth Porter, ed., *Vietnam: The Definitive Documentation of Human Decisions* (London, 1979), II, 660; *NYT,* March 18, 1975; *International Herald Tribune,* April 1, 1975.

5. *Final Collapse,* 76. See also House Comm. on International Relations, *Vietnam . . . Emergency, 1975,* 540–41; LeGro, *Vietnam,* 144; Denis Warner, *Not with Guns Alone* (Melbourne, 1977), 13.

6. Douglas B. Stuart, "The Fall of Vietnam: A Soldier's Perspective," *Parameters,* 11 (June 1981), 31. See also Cao Van Vien, *Final Collapse,* 69, 73, 79; *NYT,* Feb. 24, 1975; *International Herald Tribune,* Feb. 26, 1975; Van Tien Dung, *Our Great Spring Victory* (New York, 1977), 45–54.

7. *NYT,* March 20, 1975. See also Van Tien Dung, *Spring Victory,* 74, 102, 151; Cao Van Vien, *Final Collapse,* 72–86; Hosmer, *Fall of South Vietnam,* 170–74, 184; Snepp, *Decent Interval,* 185ff.; LeGro, *Vietnam,* 151; Military Institute, *Vietnam: The Anti-U.S. Resistance War for National Salvation* (Hanoi, 1980) JPRS 80,968, 173–75; Porter, *Vietnam,* 660; Stuart A. Herrington, *Peace with Honor?* (Novato, 1983), 147.

8. Hosmer, *Fall of South Vietnam,* 188. See also Snepp, *Decent Interval,* 195.

9. Hosmer, *Fall of South Vietnam,* 171–73, 178, 190–94, 202–17; Cao Van Vien, *Final Collapse,* 84, 95–105, and esp. 116; Snepp, *Decent Interval,* 187–88, 201–2; LeGro, *Vietnam,* 156–61; Porter, *Vietnam,* 661; *International Herald Tribune,* March 29–30, April 1, 1975; Defense Dept. Nov. 9, 1976, release.

10. Van Tien Dung speech, March 16, 1975, JPRS 64,624, 1–2; Le Hai Phong, *Tap Chi Quan Doi Nhan Dan,* April 1975, JPRS 65,090, 1–4; Dung, *Spring Victory,* 76, 87–114, 136, 142, 177; Military Institute, *Anti-U.S. Resistance War,* 172–74; Snepp, *Decent Interval,* 188–89; LeGro, *Vietnam,* 171; Tran Van Tra, *Concluding the 30-Years War* (Ho Chi Minh City, 1982), JPRS 82,783, 157.

11. Cao Van Vien, *Final Collapse,* 78, 84, 169–71; Hosmer, *Fall of South Vietnam,* 146, 178; Snepp, *Decent Interval,* 187–88.

12. Cao Van Vien, *Final Collapse,* 116, 141; Snepp, *Decent Interval,* 186–87; Hosmer, *Fall of South Vietnam,* 238–41; LeGro, *Vietnam,* 172; Tran Van Don, *Our Endless War* (San Rafael, 1978), 251; Nguyen Cao Ky, *Twenty Years and Twenty Days* (New York, 1976), 204ff.; *NYT,* March 28, 1975; *International Herald Tribune,* April 4, 5–6, 1975.

13. *NYT,* March 28, 1975; Snepp, *Decent Interval,* 234; LeGro, *Vietnam,* 170–71; Cao Van Vien, *Final Collapse,* 122–23; Haley, *Congress and the Fall of South Vietnam,* 92.

14. Cao Van Vien, *Final Collapse,* 117, 129, 138–40; Hosmer, *Fall of South Vietnam,* 200–201, 232; Military Institute, *Anti-U.S. Resistance War,* 177; *International Herald Tribune,* April 5–6, 1975.

15. Tran Van Tra, *30-Years War,* 139, 142, 196–209, 214; Van Tien Dung, *Spring Victory,* 114 15, 164 65, 180 81, 190 91, 247 48.

16. House Comm. on International Relations, *Vietnam . . . Emergency, 1975,* 133, 138, 602, 620; Snepp, *Decent Interval,* 288, 308, 319–30; Isaacs, *Without Honor,* 407–9; Cao Van Vien, *Final Collapse,* 145; *International Herald Tribune,* March 28, 1975.

17. *Wash. Post,* May 5, 1975. See also Snepp, *Decent Interval,* 392–97, 434–36, 446; Hosmer, *Fall of South Vietnam,* 246–47; Cao Van Vien, *Final Collapse,* 143; House Comm. on International Relations, *Vietnam . . . Emergency, 1975,* 545–47, 599; Tran Van Don, *Our Endless War,* 252.

18. Tran Van Tra, *30-Years War,* 200. Tiziano Terzani, who was in Saigon at the time, claims that Minh and his cabinet were in the hallway in order to meet the first soldiers but were then taken to a room to await senior officers and that it was not until 2:30 that afternoon that the radio station was put back into operation and Minh could read his surrender. Times also differ very slightly, but my own recollection supports those

given here. The identity of just who gave Minh the command to surrender unconditionally varies, and hence I use no names. See Tiziano Terzani, *Giai Phong: The Fall and Liberation of Saigon* (New York, 1976), 76–87; *Le Monde,* May 2, 1975; Vietnam News Agency, April 30, 1975, 3d transmission; Cao Van Vien, *Final Collapse,* 153.

Chronology

1858 *September.* French seize Danang.

1859 *February.* French occupy Saigon region.

1873 *November 19.* French attack Hanoi and take much of Tonkin Delta.

1874 *March 15.* French sovereignty over Cochin China recognized in Treaty of Saigon.

1883 *August 25.* Annam and Tonkin become French protectorates.

1890 *May 19.* Ho Chi Minh born.

1925 *June.* Ho Chi Minh creates Vietnam Revolutionary Youth Association in Canton.

1930 *February 3.* Ho Chi Minh merges three groups to form Vietnam Communist Party.

September 12 to mid-1931. Nghe Tinh Soviet movement.

1940 *June.* France capitulates to Germany, agrees to collaborate with Japan.

1941 *February 14.* Ho Chi Minh returns to Vietnam after thirty years' exile.

May 10. Viet Minh front created.

1945 *March 9.* Japanese disarm French and end French rule formally.

March–May. Famine in Tonkin reaches high point.

August 15. Japan surrenders.

August 17. Demonstration in Hanoi, spreads throughout country over following days and Viet Minh takes power.

September 2. Ho Chi Minh declares Vietnam independent and founds Democratic Republic of Vietnam.

September. British occupy Cochin China and French troops begin to return. Chinese occupy Vietnam north of sixteenth parallel.

1946 *February 28.* Franco-Chinese accord allows French to take northern half of Vietnam.

March 6. Franco-Vietnamese agreement recognizing DRV as a free state within the French Union.

November 22. After breakdown of March 6 accord and failure of negotiations, French bombard Haiphong, begin restoration of their authority.

December 19. Ho Chi Minh calls for resistance to France, and war begins.

1948 *June 5.* French create "State of Vietnam" with former emperor Bao Dai as chief of state.

1950 *February 7.* United States gives de jure recognition to Bao Dai's state.

May 8. United States begins direct economic and military aid grants to French in Indochina.

1951 *September 7.* United States begins direct economic assistance to Bao Dai.

November 19. Communists begin four-month offensive and take most of region north of Hanoi.

1954 *May 7.* Battle of Dien Bien Phu, begun March 13, ends in French defeat.

May 8–July 21. Geneva Conference on Indochina.

July 7. Ngo Dinh Diem appointed premier by Bao Dai.

1955 *January 1.* United States begins direct aid to Diem's government.

August 16. Last French high commissioner in Vietnam leaves.

October 23–26. Diem deposes Bao Dai and proclaims the "Republic of Vietnam."

1956 *January 11.* RVN issues Ordinance 6 permitting arrest and detention of anyone deemed dangerous to security.

1959 *January.* Communist Party Central Committee passes Resolution 15 sanctioning greater reliance on military activity.

May 6. Diem's Law 10/59 creating special tribunals for prison and execution of those endangering security.

1960 *December 20.* National Liberation Front of South Vietnam established.

December 31. 900 U.S. military personnel in Vietnam compared with 327 in May.

1961 *May 5.* President Kennedy declares United States is considering use of American forces in South Vietnam.

November 22. United States decides to expand military aid and advisers to RVN.

December 31. U.S. military personnel reaches 3,200.

1962 *February 8.* U.S. advisory group reorganized as "Military Assistance Command, Vietnam," under General Paul D. Harkins.

April. Strategic-hamlet program initiated.

December 31. U.S. military personnel reaches 11,300.

1963 *May 8.* Buddhist riots begin in Hué, spread, and continue sporadically the remainder of summer.

August 12. Henry Cabot Lodge replaces Frederick E. Nolting as U.S. ambassador to Saigon.

August 21. Martial law proclaimed throughout RVN. 1,400 Buddhists arrested.

August 24. United States encourages RVN generals to replace Diem.

September 2. Semiofficial Saigon paper charges United States with having planned abortive August 28 coup.

October 17. United States suspends assistance to Diem's elite guard.

November 1. Military coup kills Diem and his brother.

November 9. United States resumes commodity import aid suspended in August as gesture of disapproval of Diem.

November 22. President Kennedy assassinated.

December 31. U.S. military personnel reaches 16,300.

1964 *January 30.* Military coup led by Major General Nguyen Khanh replaces Minh government.

June 20. General William C. Westmoreland takes over MACV.

July 2. Maxwell D. Taylor replaces Lodge as ambassador.

July 30–31. RVNAF raids on DRV coastal islands.

August 2–4. Gulf of Tonkin incidents involving U.S. Navy.

August 4. First U.S. air strikes against DRV targets.

August 7. Congress approves Gulf of Tonkin Resolution sanctioning use of U.S. armed forces in Southeast Asia.

August 16. General Khanh ousts rivals from junta, installs new constitution.

August 27. New constitution withdrawn. Khanh pushed aside until September, when successive political crises follow throughout the month.

October 26–November 1. New government emerges under Tran Van Huong.

December 20. Khanh and allies purge junta partially.

December 31. 23,300 U.S. military personnel in South Vietnam.

1965 *January 27.* Huong ousted, General Khanh takes over government.

February 7. NLF attacks Pleiku base. U.S. planes bomb DRV next day.

February 18. Military units oust General Khanh in bloodless coup. Phan Huy Quat becomes new premier.

February 28. United States announces it will sustain bombing of DRV whenever it deems it essential.

June 8. State Department says U.S. troops will now go into combat routinely.

June 12. Premier Quat returns power to military. New regime led by Nguyen Cao Ky emerges on June 24.

July 8. Henry Cabot Lodge to replace Taylor as ambassador.

December 31. U.S. military personnel numbers 184,300.

1966 *January 31.* U.S. air attacks against DRV resumed.

February 6–8. Johnson meets Ky and Thieu in Honolulu; they issue proclamation of resolve to continue war.

March 10–16. Buddhist and student protests in Hué and Danang begin, continuing intermittently for weeks and spreading.

April 12. B-52s bomb DRV for the first time.

June 16. Saigon sends troops to Hué to put down protests.

December 31. U.S. military personnel reaches 385,300.

1967 *February 23–24.* Operation Junction City, the biggest land offensive of the war, begins along Cambodian border.

April 12. Ellsworth Bunker becomes new ambassador to Saigon.

May 11. Nguyen Cao Ky declares his candidacy for presidency in September 3 elections.

May 19. Nguyen Van Thieu declares candidacy for presidency.

June 30. Ruling Armed Forces Council agrees to run Thieu for presidency and Ky for vice-presidency.

December 31. U.S. military personnel rises to 485,300.

1968 *January 30–31.* Tet offensive begins.

March 31. Johnson withdraws from presidential race, calls for negotiations.

May 31. Paris Peace Conference begins.

July 2. General Creighton W. Abrams replaces Westmoreland as head of MACV.

November 1. United States halts bombing of DRV.

1969 *January 31.* 542,400 U.S. military personnel in South Vietnam, the wartime peak.

June 8. Nixon announces first U.S. troop withdrawal of 25,000.

June 10. Provisional Revolutionary Government (PRG) formed by NLF and others.

July 25. Nixon declares "Nixon Doctrine" regarding future American interventions.

September 3. Ho Chi Minh dies.

October 15. Massive antiwar demonstrations throughout United States.

November 15. About 250,000 in Washington protest war.

December 31. U.S. military personnel in South Vietnam at 474,000.

1970 *March 27–28.* ARVN attacks Communist forces in Cambodia.

April 30. U.S. troops enter Cambodia for first time.

May 3. United States resumes bombing of DRV.

May 4. Six students at Kent State University and Jackson State College killed by National Guard and police.

May 9. Hundreds of university antiwar protests throughout the United States, including over 75,000 in Washington.

December 31. 335,800 U.S. personnel remain in South Vietnam.

1971 *February 8.* ARVN attacks southern Laos to disrupt Ho Chi Minh Trail, in Lam Son 719 Campaign. Retreat begins in late February after heavy losses, ending in late March.

April 24. About half a million persons protest war in Washington.

June 13. Pentagon Papers begin to appear in *New York Times.*

July 15. Kissinger trip to China announced.

October 3. Thieu "reelected" as head of RVN without any rivals in race.

December 1. 184,000 U.S. personnel remain in South Vietnam.

1972 *January 25.* Nixon announces Kissinger has met with DRV representatives secretly thirteen times.

February 21. Nixon arrives in China for visit.

March 30. PAVN begins offensive along DMZ.

April 15. Nixon authorizes bombing of Hanoi-Haiphong area.

April 20. Kissinger visits Moscow to arrange summit.

May 8. Nixon announces mining of all DRV ports.

May 20. Nixon meets Brezhnev in Moscow.

September 11. PRG makes new peace proposal accepting Thieu's continuation in power.

October 8. DRV presents draft of peace agreement.

October 20. Nixon informs Pham Van Dong that the peace treaty is essentially complete.

October 23. United States asks for resumption of negotiations.

November 20. Kissinger and Le Duc Tho resume talks.

December 18. United States begins intensive bombing of Hanoi-Haiphong region.

December 30. United States halts bombing north of twentieth parallel and announces resumption of negotiations.

1973 *January 23.* Kissinger and Le Duc Tho initial peace agreement, which is signed four days later.

March 29. Last U.S. troops depart from South Vietnam.

April 30. Key Nixon aides resign as Watergate scandal mounts.

June 24. Graham Martin becomes new ambassador to Saigon.

June 29. House passes compromise bill imposing total ban on U.S. bombing in all of Indochina after August 15.

1974 *May 9.* House Judiciary Committee begins impeachment hearings against Nixon.

August 6. House cuts military aid to RVN to $700 million.

August 9. Nixon resigns.

December 18. Politburo begins to plan spring offensive.

1975 *January 6.* Phuoc Long Province falls to PAVN/PLAF attack.

March 8–10. PAVN begins probing attacks in MR I and cuts roads in MR II.

March 10. PAVN attacks Ban Me Thuot, which falls next day.

March 11. Thieu decides on major strategic withdrawals in MR I and II to save coastal cities and build strategic reserve.

March 12. Thieu orders Airborne Division in MR I to Saigon.

March 14. Thieu orders abandonment of most of Central Highlands, which leads to chaos.

March 25. Hué falls. Politburo decides to end war quickly.

March 29. Danang abandoned amid pandemonium; PAVN enters it the next day.

April 4. Prime Minister Tran Thien Khiem resigns, and Thieu changes cabinet.

April 21. Saigon surrounded by thirteen divisions; Thieu resigns in favor of Tran Van Huong.

April 25. Thieu leaves South Vietnam.

April 27. Duong Van Minh takes office of presidency as Communist army presses toward Saigon.

April 30. Last Americans leave during the early morning as Communist army begins entering city. Minh surrenders unconditionally.

Glossary

AID	U.S. Agency for International Development
ARVN	Army of the Republic of Vietnam
B2	Communist designation for the zone encompassing the southern half of South Vietnam
CIA	U.S. Central Intelligence Agency
CIDG	Civilian Irregular Defense Groups, RVN
CINCPAC	U.S. Commander in Chief, Pacific
CORDS	U.S. Civil Operations and Revolutionary Development Support
I Corps	Military region comprising the five northern provinces of South Vietnam. U.S. and RVN designation
II Corps	Military region comprising the Central Highlands and central coastal area. U.S. and RVN designation
III Corps	Military region comprising the eleven provinces around Saigon. U.S. and RVN designation
IV Corps	Military region comprising the Mekong Delta. U.S. and RVN designation
COSVN	Central Office for South Vietnam of the Communist Party
DAO	U.S. Defense Attaché Office
DMZ	Demilitarized zone along the seventeenth parallel dividing South Vietnam and the DRV
DRV	Democratic Republic of Vietnam
GVN	Government of Vietnam. Designation also used by United States and RVN to describe latter
HES	Hamlet Evaluation System
JCS	U.S. Joint Chiefs of Staff
JGS	Joint General Staff of the Republic of Vietnam Armed Forces
MAAG	U.S. Military Assistance Advisory Group
MACV	U.S. Military Assistance Command, Vietnam
MR	Military Region. Synonymous with the four corps and encompassing the same territorial divisions
NLF	National Liberation Front of South Vietnam
NSC	U.S. National Security Council

NV — North Vietnam

NVA — North Vietnam Army

PAVN — People's Army of Vietnam, the regular army of the DRV

PF — Popular Forces. RVN's military force recruited within a district and confined to it

PLAF — People's Liberation Armed Forces, the regular army of the NLF and then the PRG

PRG — Provisional Revolutionary Government of South Vietnam

PRU — Provincial Reconnaissance Unit. CIA-funded and -led group within Phoenix program

RD — Revolutionary Development. Pacification program of RVN; sometimes also called Rural Development

RF — Regional Forces. RVN military force recruited within a province and confined to it or the same Military Region

RVN — Republic of Vietnam

RVNAF — Republic of Vietnam Armed Forces

SEATO — Southeast Asia Treaty Organization

SV — South Vietnam

USIA — U.S. Information Agency

VC — Vietcong. Pejorative U.S. and RVN designation for the Communist Party in the south.

VCI — Vietcong infrastructure

VNAF — RVN Air Force

Index

Abrams, Gen. Creighton, 256, 322, 423, 426

Acheson, Dean, 318, 320

Agency for International Development (AID), 203, 220, 223–30, 246, 392, 495–8, 507–8

Agent Orange, 145

Agnew, Spiro, 450

agriculture: in the DRV, 265, 266; in South Vietnam, 224, 229, 245–6, 389–90, 393–4, 492–4. *See also* cooperativization plan; land reform; peasants

agroville program, 96, 103, 131

air defense system, DRV's, 191

air force, DRV, 191

air force, RVN (VNAF), 378, 424

Air Force, U.S., 144, 155–6, 181, 189, 358, 364–6, 441. *See also* air war against the DRV

air power, Nixon administration's reliance on, 357, 358

air war against the DRV, 123, 124, 165, 177, 181, 183, 190, 191, 358, 412; demoralization of the U.S. Air Force and, 365; 1964 decision on, 149–51; in 1968, 321, 324; Nixon administration and, 425, 426, 434–5, 439–42, 451; threats to resume (1973), 471

air war in South Vietnam, 189–92, 358, 424, 425

Alliance of National, Democratic, and Peace Forces, 331, 399

American armed forces in South Vietnam:

attacks on officers, 364; demoralization and resistance in, 363–7; generals, 176–7; officers, 359–60; organizational and command structure of, 143–4, 180–1; rivalries between services, 180–1; size of (1966–67), 166, 179; withdrawals of, 345, 348, 353, 354, 366, 436. *See also* Air Force, U.S.; Army, U.S.; Marines, U.S.; military strategy, U.S.; Navy, U.S.

Annam, 13, 14

antiaircraft system, the Revolution's, 372–4. *See also* air defense system, DRV's

antiwar movement in the U.S., 173–5, 319, 322, 345, 348, 353, 373; armed forces and, 365

Ap Bac, battle of (1963), 146, 147

armed forces of the Revolution: balance of forces and (1967), 293–6; cadres' role in, 253–4; civilian population and, 261–2; cooking in, 257; defectors from, 259; families of soldiers of, 260; leadership of, 253–5; morale of, 254–8; during negotiations (1972), 444–6; 1972 offensive by, 422–30; personal expression of soldiers in, 258; rank-and-file soldiers of, 255–60; self-criticism and criticism in, 256; size and composition of (1967–72), 186–7; size of (1973), 445; U.S. estimates of size and nature of (1967), 307. *See also*

615